Affective Disorders: Psychopathology and Treatment

Affective Disorders: Psychopathology and Treatment

EDUARDO R. VAL, M.D.
Associate Professor of Clinical Psychiatry

F. MOISES GAVIRIA, M.D.
Director, Affective Disorders Clinic
Associate Professor of Psychiatry and
Preventive Medicine

JOSEPH A. FLAHERTY, M.D.
Associate Professor of Psychiatry and Preventive
Medicine

Department of Psychiatry
Abraham Lincoln School of Medicine
University of Illinois Medical Center
Chicago, Illinois

YEAR BOOK MEDICAL PUBLISHERS, INC.
CHICAGO • LONDON

Library of Congress Cataloging in Publication Data
Main entry under title:

Affective disorders, psychopathology and treatment.

  Includes index.
  1. Affective disorders. I. Val, Eduardo R.
II. Gaviria, F. Moises. III. Flaherty, Joseph A.
[DNLM: 1. Affective disorders. 2. Affective
disorders—Therapy. WM 171 A256]
RC537.A32   616.85′27   81-19777
ISBN 0-8151-8952-4   AACR2

To our families

CONTRIBUTORS

SRINATH BELLUR, M.D. Assistant Professor of Neurology, Department of Neurology, Abraham Lincoln School of Medicine, University of Illinois Medical Center, Chicago, Illinois

NORMAN R. BERNSTEIN, M.D. Professor of Psychiatry, Department of Psychiatry, Abraham Lincoln School of Medicine, University of Illinois Medical Center, Chicago, Illinois

SARA C. CHARLES, M.D. Associate Professor of Clinical Psychiatry, Department of Psychiatry, Abraham Lincoln School of Medicine, University of Illinois Medical Center, Chicago, Illinois

FRANK A. DE LEON-JONES, M.D. Associate Chief of Staff for Research & Development, V.A. West Side Medical Center; Associate Professor of Psychiatry and Clinical Pharmacology, Abraham Lincoln School of Medicine, University of Illinois Medical Center, Chicago, Illinois

ELIZABETH DORUS, Ph.D. Research Associate and Assistant Professor, Department of Psychiatry, University of Chicago, The Pritzker School of Medicine, Chicago, Illinois

JAMES S. EATON, JR., M.D. Chief, Psychiatry Education Branch, National Institute of Mental Health, Bethesda, Maryland; Clinical Professor of Psychiatry, Georgetown University School of

Medicine, Washington, D.C.; Lecturer in Medicine and Psychiatry, Tulane University School of Medicine, New Orleans, Louisiana

JOSEPH A. FLAHERTY, M.D. Associate Professor of Psychiatry and Preventive Medicine; Director of Undergraduate Education in Psychiatry, Department of Psychiatry, Abraham Lincoln School of Medicine, University of Illinois Medical Center, Chicago, Illinois

F. MOISES GAVIRIA, M.D. Associate Professor of Psychiatry and Preventive Medicine; Director, Affective Disorders Clinic, Department of Psychiatry, Abraham Lincoln School of Medicine, University of Illinois Medical Center, Chicago, Illinois

CARL JACKSON, M.D. Assistant Professor of Psychiatry, Department of Psychiatry, Abraham Lincoln School of Medicine, University of Illinois Medical Center, Chicago, Illinois

HENRY LAHMEYER, M.D. Assistant Professor of Psychiatry, Department of Psychiatry, Abraham Lincoln School of Medicine, University of Illinois Medical Center, Chicago, Illinois

JONATHAN LEWIS, M.D. Assistant Professor of Psychiatry, Department of Psychiatry, Abraham Lincoln School of Medicine, University of Illinois Medical Center, Chicago, Illinois

HYMAN L. MUSLIN, M.D. Professor of Psychiatry, Department of Psychiatry, Abraham Lincoln School of Medicine, University of Illinois Medical Center, Chicago, Illinois

SUHAYL NASR, M.D. Assistant Professor of Psychiatry and Pharmacology, Abraham Lincoln School of Medicine, University of Illinois Medical Center, Chicago, Illinois

SANDRA G. NYE, J.D., M.S.W. Assistant Professor of Jurisprudence in Psychiatry, Department of Psychiatry; Former Director of Illinois Guardianship and Advisory Committee, Abraham Lincoln School of Medicine, University of Illinois Medical Center, Chicago, Illinois

ELVA O. POZNANSKI, M.D. Professor of Psychiatry, Department of Psychiatry, Abraham Lincoln School of Medicine, University of Illinois Medical Center, Chicago, Illinois

CHARLES H. RODGERS, Ph.D. Associate Professor of Psychiatry and Physiology, Abraham Lincoln School of Medicine, University of Illinois Medical Center, Chicago, Illinois

LINDA RYDMAN, B.A., B.S.N. Former Clinical Nursing Consultant, Affective Disorders Clinic, Abraham Lincoln School of Medicine, University of Illinois Medical Center, Chicago, Illinois

JOHN J. SCHWAB, M.D. Professor and Chairman of Psychiatry, Department of Psychiatry and Behavioral Sciences, University of Louisville School of Medicine, Louisville, Kentucky

ANNE SEIDEN, M.D. Associate Professor of Psychiatry, Department of Psychiatry, Abraham Lincoln School of Medicine, University of Illinois Medical Center, Chicago, Illinois; Chairperson, Department of Psychiatry, Cook County Hospital, Chicago, Illinois

RITA SHAUGHNESSY, Ph.D. Research Associate, Department of Psychiatry, University of Chicago, The Pritzker School of Medicine, Chicago, Illinois

EDUARDO R. VAL, M.D. Associate Professor of Clinical Psychiatry, Department of Psychiatry, Abraham Lincoln School of Medicine, University of Illinois Medical Center, Chicago, Illinois; Member of the Continuing Education Faculty, Chicago Institute for Psychoanalysis, Chicago, Illinois

CONTENTS

FOREWORD

THIS BOOK is essentially a product of the Department of Psychiatry of the University of Illinois School of Medicine and reflects this department's long-standing interest in affective states and their treatment. In the 1930s one member of the department, von Meduna, began research on convulsive therapy for depression using Metrazol. In the 1940s and 1950s, Franz Alexander and other analytic researchers displayed an interest in the depressive aspects of psychosomatic illness. Mel Sabshin became chairman of the department in 1961, after having conducted a major study and collaborated on a book on depression with Roy Grinker.

Shortly after my appointment as chairman in 1975, I became concerned about the lack of organization and modernization in our approach to the affective disorders. The establishment of the Affective Disorders Clinic suddenly transformed what had been a weakness into a strength by virtue of the dedication of a young and newly recruited faculty working in collaboration with other seasoned clinicians. The result was a sophisticated setting capable of offering a range of services, from detailed diagnostic assessments to group, family, and individual psychotherapy, pharmacologic maintenance, and inpatient treatment. This project, supported by the School of Medicine and the Illinois Department of Mental Health, developed into a referral center for the Chicago metropolitan area. As is often the case, because of the high standard of clinical care offered in this setting, research and educational endeavors soon followed. The clinic now serves as a training site for public health students, social workers, clinical psychologists, psychiatric residents, and medical students; for the latter the clinic is the most popular site for elective rotations in our system. Research activities have varied from studies of lithium flow in red blood cells, to psychoanalytic aspects of mourning reactions and characterologic issues, to social support networks and their role in buffering the negative sequelae of depressive illness.

Depression, as we all know, is probably the most prevalent of all mental disorders. We are also becoming aware of the affective component in another common disorder, the borderline personality. Current breakthroughs in treatment, coupled with epidemiologic data on suicide, reveal a distressing paradox: affective states, the most common disorders causing death through suicide, also constitute the most treatable group of psychiatric disorders. This simple fact highlights the necessity for all health professionals to be aware of the signs and symptoms of depression and to know how to treat these patients or where to refer them for treatment.

This book provides an integrated approach to the treatment of affective disorders, borrowing from the applied sciences of genetics, pharmacology, biochemistry, psychology, and sociology. It has achieved, I believe, an optimal balance between new findings and practical advice.

LESTER RUDY, M.D.
Professor and Head
Department of Psychiatry
Abraham Lincoln School of Medicine
University of Illinois Medical Center
Chicago, Illinois

PREFACE

OVER 300 YEARS AGO, Robert Burton, in his classic and in many ways still applicable masterpiece, *The Anatomy of Melancholy*, expressed the belief, based on his own arduous personal struggle with the illness, that anyone who could cure it "[would] have to be a Magician, a Chemist, a Philosopher, an Astrologer." Today, we may paraphrase Burton by stating that any investigator or clinician interested in the complex phenomena posed by this unique group of disorders is confronted with the same impossible task of assuming each of those personas.

Similarly, a book dealing with a subject of such magnitude cannot represent the effort of any one person or single point of view. The information, advances, and revisions taking place in the biologic, psychological, and social fields with respect to the normal and psychopathologic aspects of affective conditions have made it virtually impossible for anyone to have such renaissance expertise. An edited book should provide a forum in which contributors with special areas of interest in the overall subject may share their knowledge and wealth of experience and provide an organized approach to the subject so that the reader may gain a more in-depth and integrated perspective. This is the task that we have set ourselves in this project.

The book was designed primarily with the psychiatric resident's educational needs in mind, with the belief that the scope of the content presented not only offers basic and essential information but also provides what we think should be part of the core knowledge of any general psychiatrist. As such, we hope this book will also be of assistance to those practicing psychiatrists seeking board certification.

One of our editorial aims has been to emphasize as much as possible basic background knowledge in each of the areas covered by the different authors so that the reader not familiar with the subject can benefit from current revisions and advances. To that extent this book will be useful to medical students and mental health students from diverse disciplines.

The first section deals with diagnostic issues and includes the rationale for and descriptions of the new nosology introduced by the third edition of the *Diagnostic and Statistical Manual of Mental Disorders (DSM-III)* classification, which is a central focus of reference throughout the book. In addition, attention is given to the clinical considerations and course of affective disorders, in an attempt to bring data collated from different sources over the years into a *DSM-III* framework.

We felt that the interactions and interrelationships between physical illness and depression as well as the distinction among grief, mourning, and affective states were both subjects of much conceptual and diagnostic confusion, each deserving a special chapter to shed some light and clarification.

Part II deals with the psychopathology of the affective disturbances from different vantage points and gives a comprehensive, controversial, and up-to-date coverage of the blooming scientific contributions in this exciting field of psychiatry.

Treatment considerations constitute Part III, which begins with a much neglected area in the management of patients in general—the legal nature of the therapeutic contract. The content of this chapter has applicability not only to affective disorders but also to the treatment situation encountered in other psychiatric conditions. In the psychopharmacologic treatment chapter, the reader will find that the subject is approached in a unique manner—from the aspect of the pharmacologic agents as well as from the perspective of each diagnostic category, with stress on the pharmacokinetics and drug-to-drug interactions. The chapter on psychological management presents an integrated approach, drawing a clear distinction between the interventions to be used in the acute and maintenance phases and providing a treatment outline guide based on the current biopsychosocial understanding elaborated in the preceding sections. The material on management of affective illnesses in the context of the realities encountered in the clinical setting of primary practice offers a pragmatic set of guiding principles for practitioners to follow, including when to treat patients and when to refer them to the psychiatrist. The final chapter on treatment consists of the philosophy, the staff roles, and a description of the affective disorder clinic as a specialized tertiary center, as well as its indications and advantages as a systematic therapeutic approach.

Each life stage has specific issues and developmental conflicts that color and influence an individual's psychological makeup and behavior. In the last part of the book, affective disorders are viewed from the different life cycle perspectives, with emphasis on the biopsychosocial dynamics at play and the diagnostic and management implications unique to each phase.

We hope that the present volume comes close to fulfilling our objectives. In producing this book we were fortunate in having a gifted and diversified faculty group in our department from which to draw a large majority of our contributions. Such diversity of interest and ideological orientations in a single department are a direct reflection of the successful recruitment efforts and leadership of our department head, Dr. Lester Rudy, whose support and encouragement have made this book and its forerunner, the Midwest Symposium on Affective Disorders, a reality.

We are much indebted to our guest contributors, Drs. Eaton, Dorus, Shaughnessy, and Schwab, for their steadfast cooperation and participation in this venture.

Pat Kratochwill, the departmental business manager, has been a source of tireless support, a magic-worker in her own right, who helped us overcome what seemed at times insurmountable problems.

We also thank the secretarial staff: Cynthia Baines, Virginia Dwyer, Angela Surman, Mildred Sykes, Karen Watkins, and Onelia Zuniga. In particular, Virginia Dwyer had a central role in organizing, editing, and revising the entire manuscript, a task beyond and above her expected duties. To the Affective Disorders Clinic staff—Ed Altman, Marlene Grupp, Madeline Muecke, and Patricia Rodgers—our deepest personal thanks; their enthusiasm, dedication, and tireless commitment to patient care and research have contributed greatly to the realization of this project.

We would also like to acknowledge Linda Rydman's participation in organizing and implementing the Midwest Symposium, making possible the initial gathering of many of the contributions to this book.

Nancy Chorpenning, our publisher's medical editor, through her enthusiasm and support made our work an enjoyable experience.

EDUARDO R. VAL

F. MOISES GAVIRIA

JOSEPH A. FLAHERTY

PART I

DIAGNOSIS

1

DIAGNOSTIC CONSIDERATIONS

JOSEPH A. FLAHERTY, M.D.
F. MOISES GAVIRIA, M.D.
EDUARDO VAL, M.D.

THIS CHAPTER reviews the current diagnostic schema for classification of affective disorders, along with the nomenclature, descriptions, and criteria currently used in the third edition of the *Diagnostic and Statistical Manual of Mental Disorders (DSM-III)*.[5] First, however, it is essential to review the history and controversies of psychiatric nosology in general and affective disorders in particular.

It is probable that the first humans of this planet began to classify fellow humans into one or more groups using classificatory schemata based on a single principle (monothetic), such as sexual anatomy, or on multiple principles (polythetic), such as skin color and hair distribution. It is also likely that as the number of humankind grew, so did the number of criteria for classifying them. This desire to categorize people and things is so universal as to be considered part of human nature. In parallel with this drive to reduce the complexity of things by ordering them is a desire to find methods of classifying that tell us something about the likelihood of individuals in a category to do certain things, i.e., the predictive power of classification. In science, classification represents the attempt to reduce complexity by noting similarities at multiple levels in order to effectively communicate and to promote scientific investigation. In medicine these multiple levels of observation have traditionally focused on three areas: phenomenology, clinical course, and etiology and pathophysiology.

Phenomenology is the most basic level of classification and often the most reliable. In medicine, the assessment of phenomenologic data—the signs and symptoms of an illness—is the first stage in the diagnostic process. In psychiatry, however, the assessment of signs and symptoms has often been expressed in abstractions such as self-esteem or ego functioning; confusion and lack of reliability at this basic level creates and compounds the confusion in any diagnostic schema. Only when the basic signs and symptoms can be defined, agreed on, and similarly assessed by different observers will phenomenologic observation assume a scientific position in psychiatric classification. Aware of these problems, psychiatrists have begun to develop definitions, criteria, and instruments to quantitatively measure the basic phenomenologic data.

The next step in the diagnostic process is to group signs and symptoms in a logical manner. There are two basic approaches. One approach is to use statistical methods, such as factor or cluster analysis, whereby the basic data undergo computerized analysis of which signs or symptoms occur together most frequently and which groups or clusters of symptoms are commonly found together. Such a method does not identify certain symptoms as more important than others, nor does it incorporate clinical experiences that might offer insights into naturally occurring groupings.

For these reasons, clinicians have attempted to combine signs and symptoms into groupings referred to as syndromes. A syndrome is a combination of signs and symptoms that seem to occur together frequently, without particular regard to having a common clinical course and etiology. An example of a syndrome is catatonia, which consists of a marked motor and speech impairment, often to the degree of mutism and immobility; there is often an associated waxy flexibility—the tendency of limbs to remain for long periods in the same position as they are placed by the examiner. This syndrome may be based on a schizophrenic process, a tumor of the third ventricle, or other mental pathophysiology. The clinical course is similarly variable. Some patients show improvement with major tranquilizers, followed by repeated episodes; some have complete recovery; others have progressive deterioration in mental functioning. To refine a syndrome into a more specific diagnostic classification, clinical course and etiologic data must be considered.

Emil Kraepelin was one of the first psychiatrists to suggest that clinical course be a major consideration in the classification of psychiatric disorders.[15, 16] He differentiated manic-depressive illness from schizophrenia on the basis of the progressive downhill course of the latter. In this regard, he was in disagreement with Bleuler, who recommended diagnoses founded on basic observations and presumed basic pathophysiology.[6] It is now clear that clinical course is a useful but not sufficient consideration in the diagnostic process. It is useful because it provides a measure of validity by determining whether the arbitrary groupings clinicians have formed remain homogeneous in follow-up studies.

As with signs and symptoms, care must be taken to provide reliable methods of following clinical course. Methods used in medicine include response to different treatment, natural course without treatment, and objective ratings of changes in the basic signs and symptoms over time. Longitudinal studies also must differentiate levels of functioning, such as social, occupational, and familial, from the basic signs and symptoms. Even with improved data collection, clinical course data are never sufficient criteria for diagnosis, because patients with different etiologies and pathophysiologic processes may have a similar clinical course.

Patients having an acute psychotic episode in early adulthood but who are relatively asymptomatic thereafter could have had a drug-induced reaction, an acute adjustment reaction, or even, as Manfred Bleuler's recent work shows, a schizophrenia episode.[7] Similarly, patients with frequent (weekly) dramatic swings in mood may be a subgroup of bipolars called rapid cyclers, may have severe narcissistic personality disorders, or may be amphetamine addicts. The *DSM-III* emphasizes this point by recognizing the variation in etiologic factors (genetic, life events, illness) that may culminate in the phenomenology categorized as a major depressive episode.

Etiologic evidence is probably the most valid basis for classifying illness. Unfortunately, in psychiatry as well as medicine in general, such evidence is often lacking. For example, essential hypertension is a common medical syndrome that can be defined phenomenologically, has some variability in clinical course, but lacks basic etiologic evidence, despite many good hypotheses and certain pathophysiologic understanding. Etiologic considerations in psychiatry have generated considerable debate as to whether psychological, social, or biologic data are most relevant to causing mental disorders. Klein and Davis have commented on the antagonism between the biologic and psychological proponents: "The biophobes refuse to admit the usefulness of categorizations that imply discrete etiologies as anything more than a crude approximation to multifactorial interplay of variables which may be social, psychological, organic, etc. The psychophobes rely on discrete diagnostic categories in the hope that discovery will reveal the psychological and social factors to be ancillary epiphenomena."[14] Etiologic proof requires more than an association between the proposed etiologic agent and the phenomenon; the factors must be shown to be causally related. A finding of reduced catecholamine metabolites in depressed patients may be helpful in our understanding of these patients, but it fails to prove that this reduction causes depression. Reduced levels of 3-methoxy-4-hydroxyphenylglycol (MHPG) may be related to depression in many ways. First, this reduction may be the result of genetic (single or multiple) factors; the genetic loading may be necessary and sufficient to lower the MHPG, or necessary but not sufficient in the absence of other psychosocial and biologic factors. Likewise, reduced MHPG may be causally linked to the depression, may exist by itself or in combination with other factors, or may be only a byproduct of some other underlying pathophysiologic process that is causally related to depression. Although it is assumed that many psychiatric disorders are determined by multiple etiologic agents interacting with each other as well as on the symptoms themselves, certain single etiologic factors may account for much of the variance in symptom presentation and clinical course in certain disorders. For example, the spirochete clearly plays the critical role in the etiology of neurosyphilis, although host resistance factors do account for some of the variance in symptoms and clinical course. In a similar manner, identical twins with trisomy 21 (Down's syndrome) have variations in their intellectual capacities precisely to the extent that environmental factors differ. Lacking basic etiologic data, pathophysiologic data are useful to consider in the diagnostic process, because they do predict outcome. For example, the pathophysiology of phenylketonuria is currently more crucial in treatment of this illness than the basic genetic defect, except in the case of primary prevention.

Psychological and social variables have often been unfavorably regarded as possible causes of psychiatric disorders. This view does not stem merely from the fact that they are "soft" variables and, therefore, not important in "hard" medical science. Part of the credibility problem has been the lack of controlled longitudinal studies with reliable observation of psychological and social data. Psychodynamic formulations on etiology have focused on adult patients and used constructs difficult to apply in etiologic research. It will be necessary for both psychological and social research to translate etiologic theories into objective and reliable variables and to make observations at the time the variables have their presumed impact (usually from birth through childhood). Because of the complexity of etiologic research, diagnosticians have been cautious about including etiology in the diagnostic criteria unless the evidence is clear and irrefutable, as in the case of amphetamine delirium.

In summary, diagnostic groupings should be based on data derived from phenomena, clinical course, and etiology in a way that leads to reliable predictions and decisions on treatment. The process of grouping diagnostic factors requires a constant reassessment of the contributions of these factors. Groupings based on phenomenology are later refined by clinical course factors; these in turn may be refined by etiologic factors. When clinical syndromes become refined to the point of having a common etiology and similar clinical course and phenomenology, they are often referred to as an illness or disease. This process is illustrated by the syndrome formerly referred to as dropsy. The diagnosis of dropsy originally described generalized peripheral edema. From follow-up studies, autopsies, and pathophysiologic investigations, it became clear that dropsy was due to multiple factors such as a cardiac or renal failure. This finding led to further refinement in the phenomenology, distinguishing the patterns of cardiac versus renal edema. Further work on cardiac failure and edema led to the finding of multiple etiologic causes, such as myocardial infarction, cardiac infections, and genetic defects. These new groups were then followed and found to have different outcomes, which led to the discovery of additional phenomenologic and etiologic differences. The depressive syndrome is currently undergoing a similar refinement. This process illustrates the interactive nature of data in establishing precise diagnostic categories.

There is one pitfall in the process of continuous refinement. Ultimately, all patients have some differences in etiologic factors, in clinical course, or in phenomenology. Because of this, it is necessary to make an arbitrary decision when to quit "splitting" and start "lumping." These decisions must be based on the ultimate goal of diagnosis, treatment. For example, although it is possible to divide depressed patients into groups based on the presence of psychomotor agitation or retardation, such a distinction is useful only to the extent that it can predict treatment response.

There have always been people critical of any classification system. When Aristotle presented his original treatise, "Categories," separating things into genera and species, it triggered intense debate and divisiveness in his scholastic community as to whether any arbitrary classification system was useful. Critics of psychiatric classification schemes have focused on the notion that mental illness is a myth and does not qualify as an illness and that diagnoses are labels that serve society's needs for affirming the sanity of the majority. Although psychiatry must carefully examine and consider these criticisms, it also must further the study of mental phenomena in order to find some means of alleviating the pain and suffering of people who seek help. Psychiatrists can either throw up their hands or pursue the slow, methodological task of finding meaningful ways of classifying these patients.

CLASSIFICATION OF AFFECTIVE DISORDERS BEFORE *DSM-III*

The term "melancholia" was introduced into the literature by the Egyptians in 2600 B.C.[22] Around 400 B.C., Hippocrates described melancholia as a disorder resulting from the influence of black bile and phlegm on the brain, "darkening the spirit and making it melancholy."[17] In about 120 A.D., Aretareus noted the association between mania and melancholia.[13] He described the variety of forms seen in melancholic patients: "the patients are

dull or stern, dejected or unreasonably torpid, without any manifest cause
. . . they also become peevish, dispirited, sleepless . . . unreasonable
fear also seizes them." In the 19th century, Falret, a French physician,
coined the term *la folie circulaire*, which he described as a depressive
illness with remissions and attacks, sometimes alternating with mania,
sometimes associated with precipitating events, and common in women.[8]

In 1896, Kraepelin made a major contribution to psychiatry by dividing
the functional psychosis into dementia praecox and manic-depressive psychosis, based on the clinical course. Unlike his contemporary, Bleuler, he
expanded the notion of manic-depressive illness to include all varieties of
mood disturbance, while limiting the definition for dementia praecox.
Bleuler took a more expansive view of schizophrenia, and the result was a
controversy over the criteria for these two disorders. Kraepelin also believed that manic-depressive illness was of biologic origin and relatively
independent of social and psychological forces. This was in keeping with
contemporary German medicine since Griesinger pronounced that "mental
diseases are brain diseases" in the late 19th century.[12] This extreme position was somewhat in opposition to the new psychoanalytic community following the 1917 publication of Freud's *Mourning and Melancholia*, which
proposed a psychodynamic etiology for depression.[11] (It should be noted,
however, that Freud predicted that biologic [chemical] factors would eventually become crucial etiologically.)

The etiologic debate continued through the 20th century and was represented in diagnostic terms as a distinction between endogenous or biologic depression and reactive depression. This distinction seemed to resolve the controversy by allowing each etiologic school to have its own type
of depression. Besides being etiologically different, reactive depressions
were also regarded as less severe, or neurotic, and endogenous depressions
as more severe, or psychotic. Recent evidence does not justify such a distinction between endogenous and reactive; newer clinical observations also
imply that the severity of depression (psychotic-neurotic) may be a useful
measurement but is independent of diagnostic categories.[19]

In 1892 Adolf Meyer immigrated to the United States and made major
contributions to psychiatric nosology in the early 1900s.[18] His psychobiologic notion of psychiatry recognized the multiple influences of organic and
psychological factors and the impact of stress. His holistic orientation made
him favor the term "reactions" over "disease." This view was incorrectly
inferred to mean that biologic factors were less important. Meyer's holistic
approach and Freud's psychoanalytic approach weighed heavily in the formulation of the American Psychiatric Association's first *Diagnostic and Statistical Manual of Mental Disorders* (*DSM-I*, 1952).[3] In this manual, etiologic hypotheses were given undue consideration, as evidenced by the

frequent use of the term "reaction" (e.g., manic-depressive reaction) and the frequent reference to defense mechanism as an explanation for most psychiatric disorders.

In 1967 the second edition of the *Diagnostic and Statistical Manual of Mental Disorders (DSM-II)* was adopted by the American Psychiatric Association.[4] This manual referred to manic-depressive illness rather than to reaction, supposedly in recognition of the possible biologic etiologic factors and the clarity of this entity. At the same time the World Health Organization's *International Classification of Diseases (ICD)* referred to the same entity as manic-depressive psychosis, noting the severity and loss of reality sometimes associated with acute episodes.[28] The *DSM-II* also used "psychotic depression" to refer to depressions of psychotic proportion that were presumably related to clear environmental precipitants. This manual had another category for severe depression, involutional melancholia, referring to a depressive syndrome first occurring in the involutional period and having a distinct symptom picture of anorexia, insomnia, and preoccupation with guilt and somatic concerns. The term "depressive neurosis" was used to describe individuals with a sad affect; like other neuroses, depressive neurosis was presumed to have its basis in psychodynamic conflict stemming from the oedipal stage of development, and it was thought that current life experiences or situations reactivated these conflicts.

Since publication of the *DSM-II* in the late 1960s, there has been considerable discussion about the diagnostic categories for affective disorders. First, evidence on life events and depression fails to show a different symptomatology for those depressions preceded by life events and those occurring without any obvious precipitant.[19] This made the separate category of psychotic depression less valuable. Second, it became clear that not all individuals diagnosed as manic-depressive necessarily become psychotic, in terms of having hallucinations or delusions, but that the severity and presence of these symptoms seemed independent of diagnosis. Third, follow-up studies do not suggest that involutional melancholia is a distinct entity in terms of phenomena or clinical course.[26] Fourth, follow-up studies on the neurotic group show this to be a heterogeneous group composed of many different types of depression (e.g., unipolar, bipolar) and characterologic disorders. Fifth, research on an old personality classification, cyclothymia, found that this disorder was closely linked to the family of affective disorders. Sixth, it became clear that schizoaffective schizophrenia should not be considered an affective disorder until further studies established a clear connection with other affective disorders.

Most important, it became clear that diagnostic descriptions (as in *DSM-I* and *DSM-II*) were not sufficiently dependable to ensure reliability across raters. In this regard, some illuminating studies were performed by Cooper et al., showing the marked tendency for psychiatrists in the United States to diagnose schizophrenia in preference to manic-depressive illness, compared with psychiatrists in England.[9] An increased enthusiasm among psychiatrists to find new and reliable methods of classifying affective disorders began in the 1970s.

One diagnostic concept that gained wide acceptance in the 1970s was the primary versus secondary depression distinction. Primary referred to those depressions occurring without a preexisting psychiatric or medical condition; secondary referred to those occurring with a previous condition.[20] At this time there was also a clarification of the terms "unipolar" and "bipolar." Bipolar was reserved for those cyclic affective disorders with episodes of depression and mania or hypomania, whereas unipolar referred to recurrent episodes of depression only. Research studies employing the bipolar/unipolar division verified that these two groups are distinct phenomenologically, genetically, and in treatment response. Over the last ten years, George Winokur has further refined the unipolar condition into depressive spectrum disorder and pure depressive illness.[27]

There were additional attempts in the 1970s to categorize depression based on biochemical, genetic, or treatment response data. Typical of these efforts was the type A versus type B depression distinction. Type A referred to those depressions characterized by low MHPG metabolism, while type B depressions had normal to slightly high MHPG levels. This research was logically connected to tricyclic response, exploring whether these are amitriptyline-responsive depressions or desipramine-responsive depressions.

Perhaps the most significant development in the last decade has been the establishment of research criteria for depressive disorders. A group in St. Louis (Feighner and associates) established criteria that used operational definitions for each sign and symptom, as well as specific exclusion and inclusion criteria necessary to confirm the diagnosis for each of 15 conditions.[10] Spitzer et al. later expanded these criteria to include 23 functional disorders and demonstrated high inter-rater reliability; this second set of criteria is referred to as the Research Diagnostic Criteria (RDC).[24] Spitzer's group continued developing more specific diagnostic criteria, of which the Schedule for Affective Disorders and Schizophrenia (SADS) is a notable example. These research criteria made comparisons between research studies possible. Because of the need to guarantee reliable diagnosis in psychiatric research, the criteria allowed for few false positives in affective disorders, but a moderate percentage of false negatives. Spitzer continued his diagnostic work through the 1970s, culminating with the acceptance in July 1980 of *DSM-III* by the American Psychiatric Association.[5]

DSM-III CLASSIFICATION OF AFFECTIVE DISORDERS

There are some general differences between *DSM-III* and the previous editions. First, the individual patient is evaluated on several axes, each of which refers to a different class of information. The first axis is reserved for the specific clinical syndromes, such as bipolar disorder, manic. The second axis is reserved for personality or developmental disorders. Whereas patients have at least one disorder registered on axis I or II, they may have a diagnosis based on combined information from both these axes. In the case of two disorders being registered on axis I and/or II, the disorder responsible for the current health care visit is designated as the principal disorder. Axis III is reserved for any coexisting physical disorder (e.g., myocardial infarction) that the clinician feels is relevant to the patient's current condition. On axis IV, the clinician estimates the severity of psychosocial stressors (e.g., death of a parent or sibling) on a scale of 1 (none) to 7 (catastrophic). The fifth axis permits the clinician to indicate a judgment of the patient's highest level of sustained adaptive functioning over the last year, from 1 (superior) to 7 (grossly impaired). Although the coding of psychosocial stressors and adaptive functioning does not guarantee reliability between clinicians, it represents an excellent beginning to systematic collection of social data, affords a more holistic representation of each patient for communication purposes, and avoids hypothetical speculation in the diagnostic nomenclature.

Another difference in the *DSM-III* is the adoption of specific criteria for diagnosis rather than general descriptions. Also, a glossary of technical terms is added for clarification and greater reliability. In addition, psychotic level functioning is designated by the fifth digit of the first axis rather than being employed as a formal diagnostic criterion.

The general term "affective disorders" refers to a group of disorders characterized by a disturbance of mood that does not seem to be due to any other physical or mental disorder. Mood refers to a prolonged and pervasive emotional tone of a high or low nature. Disorders are further divided into major affective disorders, in which there is a full affective syndrome; other specific affective disorders, in which there is only a partial affective syndrome of at least two years' duration; and atypical affective disorders, or affective disorders that cannot be classified in the other two subclasses.

MAJOR AFFECTIVE DISORDERS

The group of major affective disorders consists of bipolar disorders and the major depressions. Affective disturbances clearly related to an organic mental disorder (e.g., amphetamine withdrawal) and schizophrenia are specifically excluded. As the definition of manic and depressive episodes are crucial to this class of disorders, they are described first.

A manic episode refers to a distinct period when the predominant mood is elevated, expansive, or irritable. This mood is often described as euphoric, high, overly cheerful, and infectious; it leads to a nondiscriminating need to interact and spread the mood to any friends or strangers encountered. At other times the high mood may be replaced by extreme irritability and belligerence.

The manic episodes usually have a degree of hyperactivity in behavior, thinking, and talking. The patient typically increases his social and sexual behavior. During these times the patient may design a variety of personal or occupational projects, spend whole nights working on them, often calling friends and colleagues at all hours. The increased expansiveness and optimism leads to buying sprees, poor financial investments, and impulsive decisions, and all too often results in job losses and disharmonious marital and social relationships. Manic speech is also hyperactive in that it is rapid, loud, and often impossible to interrupt; this is referred to as pressured speech. There is often an internal rhyming of words (clang associations), dramatic mannerisms, and even singing. Frequently, there is a flight of ideas, i.e., accelerated speech and jumping from topic to topic based on comprehensive but erratic associations or external distracting stimuli (another person, a sound outside). This effervescent speech usually continues until the listener shows fatigue or offers criticism, at which time there is often an outburst of hostile and aggressive speech. Both speech and behavior show a high degree of distractibility in response to any external cue. Along with hyperactivity there is often a marked decrease in the need for sleep, with no apparent loss of energy.

There is usually an inflated sense of self-esteem that varies from overconfidence to grandiose delusions. These individuals may feel able to perform physical and mental tasks for which they have no experience or talent. If delusions are present, they are consistent with the predominant mood (mood-congruent). Such delusions are usually an exaggeration of their already inflated self-esteem and newly perceived abilities. They commonly involve a special relationship with God or some popular or idealized public personality.

The term "hypomania" is used to describe a clinical syndrome with similar features but of less severity.

DIFFERENTIAL DIAGNOSIS.—The clinician should consider the possibility of an organic affective syndrome due to a substance such as amphetamine or to a neurologic illness such as multiple sclerosis.

A major consideration is schizophrenia, particularly paranoid type; schizoaffective psychosis should also be considered. Clinicians have traditionally relied on the schneiderian criteria for schizophrenia, such as thought insertion, delusions of being controlled, and persistent (longer than two weeks) auditory hallucinations, as exclusion criteria for a manic episode.[23] Recent data indicate that it is often extremely difficult to differentiate psychotic manic episodes from acute schizophrenic episodes.[20, 25] This is often due to excluding patients with any hallucination or paranoid ideation, equating bizarre behavior exclusively with schizophrenia, lack of familiarity with mixed affective states (described later), and a lack of agreement on the issues of mood-congruent delusions. Akiskal and Puzantian have provided an excellent summary of the common errors in the differential diagnosis of affective states and schizophrenia.[2]

The appendix at the end of this chapter lists the *DSM-III* diagnostic criteria for a manic episode, as well as criteria for all the affective disorders.

MAJOR DEPRESSIVE EPISODES

The major feature of these depressive episodes is a persistent (longer than two weeks) dysphoric mood in which the patient describes himself as sad, depressed, hopeless, down, or sometimes even as dead. The patient may not look particularly sad but may complain of "not caring anymore," or may admit to suicidal ideation and planning. There is often a withdrawal and lack of interest in social, occupational, and familial activities.

Frequently there is evidence of physiologic malfunction. The patient may have anorexia and resultant weight loss, or, less commonly, bulimia and weight gain. There is often insomnia during all or part of the night or hypersomnia during most of the day and night. The psychomotor sphere is commonly affected, manifested by psychomotor agitation (pacing, handwringing, shouting) or psychomotor retardation (slowed and impoverished speech, slowed body movements). The latter may be associated with a "pseudodementia" characterized by an apparent loss of recall and recent memory, which may be related to poor concentration and slowed thinking and disappears when the mood improves.

Feelings of worthlessness and hopelessness are often present and may be severe enough to form mood-congruent delusions; the typical themes in these delusions are related to sinfulness, poverty, inadequacy, or nihilism. Somatic preoccupation and somatic delusions, such as having cancer, are also common.

The term "melancholia" is added to major depressive episodes to designate depressions that are distinctly worse in the morning and are associated with early morning awakening, marked psychomotor agitation or retardation, significant anorexia or weight loss, and excessive or inappropriate guilt.

Although the essential features of major depressive illness are also seen in infants, children, and adolescents, each age group may differ in certain symptoms. These issues are discussed in chapter 18.

DIFFERENTIAL DIAGNOSIS.—As with mania, the first consideration should be of an organic affective syndrome, such as depression associated with reserpine or α-methyldopa use; infectious diseases, such as influenza; hypothyroidism; primary degenerative dementia; and tumors of the pancreas. Psychological reactions to physical illnesses that do not directly involve the central nervous system (e.g., myocardial infarction) and that meet the criteria for a major depressive episode should be diagnosed as a major depression on axis I, with the associated physical illness listed on axis II.

Schizophrenic disorders should also be considered. Affective disorders are often confused with schizophrenia, particularly when there are delusions and hallucinations. In addition, the mood of the depressed patient may often appear to be indifferent or the individual may be too depressed to register sadness, a state often confused with the flattened affect associated with schizophrenia.

Cyclothymic or dysthymic mood disorders bear the features of a major depressive episode but lack the severity or duration (two weeks or longer) needed for the diagnosis.

Major depressive episodes must also be distinguished from uncomplicated bereavement. The latter is not considered a major depressive episode unless it is unusually severe or prolonged. The length of normal bereavement is arbitrary and depends on social and cultural factors. Chapter 4 discusses these issues in greater detail.

BIPOLAR DISORDERS

Bipolar disorders are diagnosed if the patient currently meets the criteria for either mania or major depressive episode and has a clear history of the other condition. Patients who present with symptoms of both mania and depression, with at least one day of clear depressive symptoms are classified as having bipolar disorder, mixed. Patients who currently are experiencing a manic episode are referred to as bipolar, manic; those presenting with a major depressive episode are classified as bipolar, depressed. The frequency and order of manic and depressive episodes vary tremendously. Some patients, often referred to as rapid cyclers, may experience many complete mood cycles in a single month; other patients may have cycles occurring once every ten or more years. Some patients experience successive cycles of one mood over 20 years and then experience a cycle of the opposite mood.

MAJOR DEPRESSION

Individuals who have had one or more major depressive episodes but have never had a manic episode are classified as having a major depression. Sometimes these individuals are referred to as unipolars, or the disorder is referred to as unipolar depression. Besides the differential diagnostic issues discussed earlier, only the clinical course reveals which of these individuals will ultimately be reclassified as bipolar after experiencing a manic episode.

Further discussion of distinguishing features of the major affective disorders can be found in chapter 2.

OTHER SPECIFIC AFFECTIVE DISORDERS

This subclassification is reserved for long-standing mood disorders (at least two years' duration) that usually begin insidiously in early adult life and do not meet the criteria for a major affective disorder.

CYCLOTHYMIC DISORDER

A cyclothymic disorder is characterized by a chronic mood disturbance involving numerous episodes of depression and hypomania but lacking the severity and specificity of symptoms seen in either mania or a major depressive episode. The cycles may be separated by extended periods of normal mood, rapid and continuous changes in mood, or periods of mixed moods. The depressive periods are often characterized by insomnia or hypersomnia, decreased productivity, social withdrawal, and a lack of pleasure in sexual or social activities. The hypomanic episodes are often characterized by increased energy and decreased sleep needs, hypersexuality, increased productivity, optimism, overconfidence, and inappropriate laughing and joking. There is an absence of psychotic features such as delusions, hallucinations, and incoherence.

Cyclothymic disorders are probably more frequent than once considered, particularly among outpatients.[26] They seem to be more frequent in women and may occur more commonly in families with other affective disorders. However, prevalence rates cannot be accurately ascertained until careful epidemiologic studies are done.

DIFFERENTIAL DIAGNOSIS.—The major differential question is whether or not the individual meets the criteria for a major affective disorder. It should be noted that an individual with a major affective disorder may also have a concurrent cyclothymic disorder that persists between affective cycles. Similarly, a patient with a cyclothymic disorder may experience a full-bloom affective syndrome.

DYSTHYMIC DISORDER

A dysthymic disorder, sometimes referred to as depressive neurosis, is characterized by a chronic depressed mood or loss of interest and pleasure in most activities. The depressed mood may be associated with insomnia or hypersomnia, a low energy level, a pessimistic attitude, tearfulness, suicidal or morbid thoughts, and persistent feelings of inadequacy and reduced self-esteem; psychotic features are absent. The depressed mood is often persistent but may be intermittent; individuals with normal moods lasting several months are not considered to have the disorder. Individuals with a dysthymic disorder usually function at a constant level, although they may occasionally be hospitalized because of increased suicidal ideation or attempts. Like the cyclothymic disorders, dysthymic disorders can coexist with cycles of major affective episodes, in which case both diagnoses are given.

The dysthymic disorder usually begins in early adult life but may begin in adolescence or childhood. Predisposing factors include chronic physical disorders and chronic psychosocial stressors. It is apparently a common disorder, favoring women; evidence of familial patterns awaits further investigation. The differential diagnostic issues are similar to those cited for major depressive episodes.

ATYPICAL AFFECTIVE DISORDERS

A diagnosis of atypical bipolar disorder is given to individuals with some manic or hypomanic features, but without a clear manic episode, who have had episodes of major depression; these individuals have often been referred to as bipolar II. The term "atypical depression" is reserved for individuals with depressive symptoms who do not meet the other criteria for affective disorders; included are individuals who meet all criteria for dysthymic disorder except having had extended (longer than three months) periods of normal mood.

The appendix at the end of this chapter lists all the *DSM-III* criteria for affective disorders, along with the criteria for certain other disorders (e.g., amphetamine withdrawal) that must be distinguished from them. Further diagnostic considerations will be discussed in succeeding chapters.

THE FUTURE OF CLASSIFICATION OF AFFECTIVE DISORDERS

Although the *DSM-III* represents the latest consensus of the psychiatric community on the classification of affective disorders, efforts are already under way to refine these criteria and to provide additional methods of establishing diagnosis. These include biochemical and physiologic measurements such as sleep studies, dexamethasone suppression tests, and galvanic skin responses. In addition, attempts are being made to classify affective states by response to treatment interventions, such as response to lithium, specific tricyclics, monoamine oxidase inhibitors, and electroconvulsive therapy.

Several diagnostic areas will be redefined and developed in the near future in response to the following questions:

• How homogeneous is the unipolar depressive group? Is it a single entity, or should it be divided into early and late onset or depressive spectrum and pure depressive disease?

• How homogeneous are the dysthymic and cyclothymic disorders? If these groups prove to be heterogeneous, what criteria offer the most valid method of further subdivision?[1]

• What will be the fate of schizoaffective schizophrenia, which has gone from schizophrenia to affective disorder to its current *DSM-III* place as "other psychosis"? Is this a worthwhile diagnostic entity, or can each individual so diagnosed be more appropriately placed in another existing diagnostic group?

• What should be the relationship between severe character disorders, particularly the borderline personality, and bipolar disorder? Can an individual simply suffer from both disorders simultaneously, or is, in fact, the individual with diagnostic signs of both borderline personality and bipolar disorder suffering from a separate and distinct disorder?

• How will the newer biochemical, endocrinologic, and pharmacologic tests assist our classification of the affective disorders? Will laboratory assays of MHPG, 5-HIAA (5-hydroxyindoleacetic acid), lithium-red blood cell counterflow, and other measurements become practically useful in the diagnostic process?

• What impact will current cross-cultural research using common diagnostic criteria have on the nosology of affective disorders? Will the next accepted North American criteria for affective disorders represent a reconciliation of the *DSM-III* and the *ICD-9*?

Appendix*

Diagnostic criteria for a manic episode
A. One or more distinct periods with a predominantly elevated, expansive, or irritable mood. The elevated or irritable mood must be a prominent part of the illness and relatively persistent, although it may alternate or intermingle with depressive mood.

B. Duration of at least one week (or any duration if hospitalization is necessary), during which, for most of the time, at least three of the following symptoms have persisted (four if the mood is only irritable) and have been present to a significant degree:

1. increase in activity (either socially, at work, or sexually) or physical restlessness
2. more talkative than usual or pressure to keep talking
3. flight of ideas or subjective experience that thoughts are racing
4. inflated self-esteem (grandiosity, which may be delusional)
5. decreased need for sleep
6. distractibility, i.e., attention is too easily drawn to unimportant irrelevant external stimuli
7. excessive involvement in activities that have a high potential for painful consequences which is not recognized, e.g., buying sprees, sexual indiscretions, foolish business investments, reckless driving

C. Neither of the following dominates the clinical picture when an affective syndrome is absent (i.e., symptoms in criteria A and B above):

1. preoccupation with a mood-incongruent delusion or hallucination (see definition below)
2. bizarre behavior

D. Not superimposed on either Schizophrenia, Schizophreniform Disorder, or a Paranoid Disorder.

E. Not due to any Organic Mental Disorders, such as Substance Intoxication.

(*NOTE:* A hypomanic episode is a pathological disturbance similar to, but not as severe as, a manic episode.)

Fifth-digit code numbers and criteria for subclassification of manic episode
6- *In Remission.* This fifth-digit category should be used when in the past

---

*From *DSM-III.*[5] Reprinted with permission of the American Psychiatric Association.

the individual met the full criteria for a manic episode but now is essentially free of manic symptoms or has some signs of the disorder but does not meet the full criteria. The differentiation of this diagnosis from no mental disorder requires consideration of the period of time since the last episode, the number of previous episodes, and the need for continued evaluation or prophylactic treatment.

4- *With Psychotic Features*. This fifth-digit category should be used when there apparently is gross impairment in reality testing, as when there are delusions or hallucinations or grossly bizarre behavior. When possible, specify whether the psychotic features are mood-incongruent. (The non-ICD-9-CM fifth-digit 7 may be used to indicate that the psychotic features are mood-incongruent; otherwise, mood-congruence may be assumed.)

> *Mood-congruent Psychotic Features:* Delusions or hallucinations whose content is entirely consistent with the *themes of inflated worth, power, knowledge, identity, or special relationship to a deity or famous person; flight of ideas without apparent awareness* by the individual that the *speech is not understandable*.

> *Mood-incongruent Psychotic Features:* Either (*a*) or (*b*): (*a*) Delusions or hallucinations whose content does not involve themes of either inflated worth, power, knowledge, identity, or special relationship to a deity or famous person. Included are such symptoms as *persecutory delusions, thought insertion, and delusions of being controlled,* whose content has no apparent relationship to any of the themes noted above. (*b*) Any of the following catatonic symptoms: stupor, mutism, negativism, posturing.

2- *Without Psychotic Features*. Meets the criteria for manic episode, but no psychotic features are present.

0- *Unspecified*

Diagnostic criteria for major depressive episode
A. Dysphoric mood or loss of interest or pleasure in all or almost all usual activities and pastimes. The dysphoric mood is characterized by symptoms such as the following: depressed, sad, blue, hopeless, low, down in the dumps, irritable. The mood disturbance must be prominent and relatively persistent, but not necessarily the most dominant symptom, and does not include momentary shifts from one dysphoric mood to another dysphoric mood, e.g., anxiety to depression to anger, such as are seen in states of acute psychotic turmoil. (For children under six, dysphoric mood may have to be inferred from a persistently sad facial expression.)

B. At least four of the following symptoms have each been present nearly every day for a period of at least two weeks (in children under six, at least three of the first four).

1. poor appetite or significant weight loss (when not dieting) or increased appetite or significant weight gain (in children under six, consider failure to make expected weight gains)
2. insomnia or hypersomnia
3. psychomotor agitation or retardation (but not merely subjective feelings of restlessness or being slowed down) (in children under six, hypoactivity)
4. loss of interest or pleasure in usual activities, or decrease in sexual drive not limited to a period when delusional or hallucinating (in children under six, signs of apathy)
5. loss of energy; fatigue
6. feelings of worthlessness, self-reproach, or excessive or inappropriate guilt (either may be delusional)
7. complaints or evidence of diminished ability to think or concentrate, such as slowed thinking, or indecisiveness not associated with marked loosening of associations or incoherence
8. recurrent thoughts of death, suicidal ideation, wishes to be dead, or suicide attempt

C. Neither of the following dominate the clinical picture when an affective syndrome is absent (i.e., symptoms in criteria A and B above):

1. preoccupation with a mood-incongruent delusion or hallucination (see definition below)
2. bizarre behavior

D. Not superimposed on either Schizophrenia, Schizophreniform Disorder, or a Paranoid Disorder.

E. Not due to any Organic Mental Disorder or Uncomplicated Bereavement.

Fifth-digit code numbers and criteria for subclassification of major depressive episode (When psychotic features and Melancholia are present the coding system requires that the clinician record the single most clinically significant characteristic.)

6- In Remission.This fifth-digit category should be used when in the past the individual met the full criteria for a major depressive episode but now is essentially free of depressive symptoms or has some signs of the disorder but does not meet the full criteria.

4- *With Psychotic Features.* This fifth-digit category should be used when there apparently is gross impairment in reality testing, as when there are delusions or hallucinations, or depressive stupor (the individual is mute and unresponsive). When possible, specify whether the psychotic features are mood-congruent or mood-incongruent. (The non-ICD-9-CM fifth-digit 7 may be used instead to indicate that the psychotic features are mood-incongruent; otherwise, mood-congruence may be assumed.)

Mood-congruent Psychotic Features. Delusions or hallucinations whose content is entirely consistent with the themes of either personal inadequacy, guilt, disease, death, nihilism, or deserved punishment; depressive stupor (the individual is mute and unresponsive).

Mood-incongruent Psychotic Features. Delusions or hallucinations whose content does not involve themes of either personal inadequacy, guilt, disease, death, nihilism, or deserved punishment. Included here are such symptoms as persecutory delusions, thought insertion, thought broadcasting, and delusions of control, whose content has no apparent relationship to any of the themes noted above.

3- *With Melancholia.* Loss of pleasure in all or almost all activities, lack of reactivity to usually pleasurable stimuli (doesn't feel much better, even temporarily, when something good happens), and at least three of the following:

    a. distinct quality of depressed mood, i.e., the depressed mood is perceived as distinctly different from the kind of feeling experienced following the death of a loved one
    b. the depression is regularly worse in the morning
    c. early morning awakening (at least two hours before usual time of awakening)
    d. marked psychomotor retardation or agitation
    e. significant anorexia or weight loss
    f. excessive or inappropriate guilt

2- *Without Melancholia*

0- *Unspecified*

Diagnostic criteria for bipolar disorder, mixed
Use fifth-digit coding for manic episode.
A. Current (or most recent) episode involves the full symptomatic picture of both manic and major depressive episodes, intermixed or rapidly alternating every few days.

B. Depressive symptoms are prominent and last at least a full day.

Diagnostic criteria for bipolar disorder, manic
    Currently (or most recently) in a manic episode. (If there has been a previous manic episode, the current episode need not meet the full criteria for a manic episode.)

Diagnostic criteria for bipolar disorder, depressed
A. Has had one or more manic episodes.

B. Currently (or most recently) in a major depressive episode. (If there has been a previous major depressive episode, the current episode of depression need not meet the full criteria for a major depressive episode.)

Diagnostic criteria for major depression
A. One or more major depressive episodes.

B. Has never had a manic episode.

Diagnostic criteria for cyclothymic disorder
A. During the past two years, numerous periods during which some symptoms characteristic of both the depressive and the manic syndromes were present, but were not of sufficient severity and duration to meet the criteria for a major depressive or manic episode.

B. The depressive periods and hypomanic periods may be separated by periods of normal mood lasting as long as months at a time, they may be intermixed, or they may alternate.

C. During *depressive* periods there is depressed mood or loss of interest or pleasure in all or almost all usual activities and pastimes, and at least three of the following:

    1. insomnia or hypersomnia
    2. low energy or chronic fatigue
    3. feelings of inadequacy
    4. decreased effectiveness or productivity at school, work, or home

5. decreased attention, concentration, or ability to think clearly
6. social withdrawal
7. loss of interest in or enjoyment of sex
8. restriction of involvement in pleasurable activities; guilt over past activities
9. feeling slowed down
10. less talkative than usual
11. pessimistic attitude toward the future, or brooding about past events
12. tearfulness or crying

During *hypomanic* periods there is an elevated, expansive, or irritable mood and at least three of the following:

1. decreased need for sleep
2. more energy than usual
3. inflated self-esteem
4. increased productivity, often associated with unusual and self-imposed working hours
5. sharpened and unusually creative thinking
6. uninhibited people-seeking (extreme gregariousness)
7. hypersexuality without recognition of possibility of painful consequences
8. excessive involvement in pleasurable activities with lack of concern for the high potential for painful consequences, e.g., buying sprees, foolish business investments, reckless driving
9. physical restlessness
10. more talkative than usual
11. overoptimism or exaggeration of past achievements
12. inappropriate laughing, joking, punnjng

D. Absence of psychotic features such as delusions, hallucinations, incoherence, or loosening of associations.

E. Not due to any other mental disorder, such as partial remission of Bipolar Disorder. However, Cyclothymic Disorder may precede Bipolar Disorder.

Diagnostic criteria for dysthymic disorder
A. During the past two years (or one year for children and adolescents) the individual has been bothered most or all of the time by symptoms characteristic of the depressive syndrome but that are not of sufficient severity and duration to meet the criteria for a major depressive episode.

B. The manifestations of the depressive syndrome may be relatively persistent or separated by periods of normal mood lasting a few days to a few weeks, but no more than a few months at a time.

C. During the depressive periods there is either prominent depressed mood (e.g., sad, blue, down in the dumps, low) or marked loss of interest or pleasure in all, or almost all, usual activities and pastimes.

D. During the depressive periods at least three of the following symptoms are present:

1. insomnia or hypersomnia
2. low energy level or chronic tiredness
3. feelings of inadequacy, loss of self-esteem, or self-depreciation
4. decreased effectiveness or productivity at school, work, or home
5. decreased attention, concentration, or ability to think clearly
6. social withdrawal
7. loss of interest in or enjoyment of pleasurable activities
8. irritability or excessive anger (in children, expressed toward parents or caretakers)
9. inability to respond with apparent pleasure to praise or rewards
10. less active or talkative than usual, or feels slowed down or restless
11. pessimistic attitude toward the future, brooding about past events, or feeling sorry for self
12. tearfulness or crying
13. recurrent thoughts of death or suicide

E. Absence of psychotic features, such as delusions, hallucinations, or incoherence, or loosening of associations.

F. If the disturbance is superimposed on a preexisting mental disorder, such as Obsessive Compulsive Disorder or Alcohol Dependence, the depressed mood, by virtue of its intensity or effect on functioning, can be clearly distinguished from the individual's usual mood.

REFERENCES
1. Akiskal H.S., Khani M.K., Scott-Strauss A.: Cyclothymic temperamental disorders. *Psychiatr. Clin. North Am.* 2:527, 1979.
2. Akiskal H.S., Puzantian U.R.: Psychotic forms of depression and mania. *Psychiatr. Clin. North Am.* 2:419, 1979.
3. American Psychiatric Association: *Diagnostic and Statistical Manual of Mental Disorders*, ed. 1. Washington, D.C., APA, 1952.
4. American Psychiatric Association: *Diagnostic and Statistical Manual of Mental Disorders*, ed. 2. Washington, D.C., APA, 1968.

5. American Psychiatric Association: *Diagnostic and Statistical Manual of Mental Disorders,* ed. 3. Washington, D.C., APA, 1980.
6. Bleuler E.: *Dementia Praecox or the Group of Schizophrenias,* Zinkin J. (trans.). New York, International Universities Press, 1950.
7. Bleuler M.: On schizophrenic psychosis. *Am. J. Psychiatry* 136:1403–1409, 1979.
8. Cohen R.A.: Manic-depressive illness, in Freedman A.M., Kaplan H.I., Sadoch B.I. (eds.): *Comprehensive Textbook of Psychiatry,* ed. 2. Baltimore, Williams & Wilkins Co., 1975.
9. Cooper J.E., Kendell R.E., Gurland B.T., et al.: *Psychiatric Diagnosis in New York and London.* London, Oxford University Press, 1972.
10. Feighner J.P., Robbins E., Guze S.D., et al.: Diagnostic criteria for use in psychiatric research. *Arch. Gen. Psychiatry* 26:57–63, 1972.
11. Freud, S.: Mourning and melancholia (1917), in *The Complete Psychological Works of Sigmund Freud.* London, Hogarth Press, 1957, vol. 14.
12. Griesinger W.: *Mental Pathology and Therapeutics* (1895). New York, Gafner Press, 1965.
13. Kendell R.E.: The classification of depressive illness. *Maudsley Monographs,* No. 18, London, Oxford University Press, 1968.
14. Klein D.F., Davis J.: *Diagnosis and Drug Treatment of Psychiatric Disorders.* Baltimore, Williams & Wilkins Co., 1969.
15. Kraepelin E.: *Dementia Praecox and Paraphrenia.* Edinburgh, E. & S. Livingstone, 1919.
16. Kraepelin E.: *Manic Depressive Insanity and Paranoia.* Edinburgh, E. & S. Livingstone, 1921.
17. Lewis A.: Melancholia: A historical review, in *The State of Psychiatry: Essays and Addresses.* New York, Science House, 1967.
18. Meyer A.: *A Science of Man.* Springfield, Ill., Charles C Thomas, Publisher, 1957.
19. Paykel E.S., Myers J.K., Dienet M.N., et al.: Life events and depression: A controlled study. *Arch. Gen. Psychiatry* 21:753–760, 1969.
20. Pope H.G., Lipinski J.F.: Diagnoses in schizophrenia and manic-depressive illness. *Arch. Gen. Psychiatry* 35:811–828, 1978.
21. Robins E., Munoz R.A., Martin S. et al.: Primary and secondary affective disorders, in Zubin J., Freyhan F. (eds.): *Disorders of Mood.* Baltimore, John Hopkins University Press, 1972.
22. Roth M.: Psychiatric diagnosis in clinical and scientific settings, in Akiskal H.S., Webb W.L. (eds.): *Psychiatric Diagnosis: Exploration of Biological Predictors.* New York, Spectrum Publications, Inc., 1978.
23. Schneider K.: *Clinical Psychopathology,* Hamilton M.W. (trans.). New York, Grune & Stratton, 1959.
24. Spitzer R.L., Endicott I., Robbins E.: Clinical criteria for psychiatric diagnoses and DSM-III. *Am. J. Psychiatry* 132:1187–1192, 1976.
25. Taylor M.S., Abrams R.: The phenomenology of mania: A new look at some old patients. *Arch. Gen. Psychiatry* 29:520–522, 1973.
26. Weissman M.M., Myers J.K.: Affective disorders in a U.S. urban community. *Arch. Gen. Psychiatry* 35:1304–1310, 1978.
27. Winokur G.: Unipolar depression: Is it divisible into autonomous subtypes? *Arch. Gen. Psychiatry* 36:47, 1979.
28. World Health Organization: *Manual of the International Statistical Classification of Diseases, Injuries and Causes of Death,* Revision 8 (ICD-8), Geneva, World Health Organization, 1967.

2

MAJOR AFFECTIVE DISORDERS: CLINICAL CONSIDERATIONS

F. MOISES GAVIRIA, M.D.
JOSEPH A. FLAHERTY, M.D.
EDUARDO VAL, M.D.

SINCE THE STUDIES of Kraepelin,[49] numerous approaches have been used in an attempt to separate patients with depression as an outstanding component of their illness into meaningful diagnostic categories. In the third edition of *Diagnostic and Statistical Manual of Mental Disorders (DSM-III)*,[8] affective disorders are classified into major affective disorders, in which there is a full affective syndrome; other specific disorders, in which there is only a partial affective syndrome of at least two years' duration; and atypical affective disorders, a category for affective disorders that cannot be classified in either of the two specific subclasses. Major affective disorders are characterized by one or more episodes of major illness involving a prominent and persistent disturbance in mood, either manic or depressed, clearly distinguished from prior functioning. They include the bipolar disorder (the classic manic-depressive illness) and major depression, a term that corresponds to the unipolar affective disorder of Leonhard et al.[56] and Perris.[68]

In this chapter, we review these major affective disorders with emphasis on the onset, clinical presentation, and special forms of the disorder. The course and outcome of the major affective disorders will be given special attention, as will the differential diagnosis, since it has clinical and therapeutic implications. The widespread use of pharmacologic agents, such as lithium and antidepressants, and the ethical considerations underlying the decision to recommend a maintenance regimen for a given patient underscore the importance of the topic.[15, 23, 31, 79] Finally, we will approach the unresolved controversy surrounding the relationship between major affective disorders and underlying personality, a most important and difficult research topic.[34, 37, 38]

THE UNIPOLAR/BIPOLAR DISTINCTION

In 1957, Leonhard proposed differentiating patients with episodic affective disorders into a bipolar group (patients with both depressed and manic phases) and a unipolar group (patients with depressed phases only). For Leonhard, the polarity was a decisive factor in the differential diagnosis of these two clinical conditions.[55]

Perris,[68] in his classic study of 138 bipolar and unipolar patients, found that when affectively ill patients were divided by clinical variables, certain differences emerged, suggesting that these groupings have validity beyond their differences in the polarity of the affective episode. He found differences in past history, precipitant factors, age at onset, and course of the illness. Table 2–1 summarizes some of Perris' findings.

The work of Perris and Winokur provided evidence that bipolar illness begins early in life and involves more frequent episodes than unipolar illness. In addition, patients with bipolar illness have more extensive family histories of affective disorders, with an increased prevalence of affective disorders among parents or children.[97]

TABLE 2–1.—DIFFERENCES BETWEEN UNIPOLAR AND BIPOLAR PATIENTS[81]

	BIPOLARS	UNIPOLARS
Childhood environment	Higher incidence of unfavorable home conditions	. . .
Precipitating factors	. . .	Tendency to more frequent somatic factors
Personality traits	Significant predominance of "syntonic" personality pattern	Significant predominance of "asthenic" personality pattern
Median age at onset	About 30 years	About 45 years
Course of illness	Somewhat shorter episodes, more frequent relapses	Somewhat longer episodes, less frequent relapses
Mortality	Excess mortality	No excess mortality

*From Perris.[81]

Woodruff et al.,[104] in a study of 158 patients with the diagnosis of primary affective disorder,* reported that bipolars, when compared with unipolars, had a larger number of episodes, were hospitalized more frequently, attempted suicide with more frequency, and more often had a family history of primary affective disorders among first-degree relatives.

Beigel and Murphy[14] reported clinical characteristics of 25 age- and sex-matched pairs of unipolar and bipolar patients. The unipolar patients had more somatic complaints and were characterized by greater physical activity and overt expression of anger, as compared with bipolar patients, who had greater psychomotor withdrawal during the depressed phase. Kupfer and Foster[52] also reported that patients with bipolar depression had less psychomotor activity than patients with unipolar depression. Unlike Beigel and Murphy,[14] Dunner et al. could not demonstrate unipolar versus bipolar differences in either somatic complaints or hostility.[28]

Abrams and Taylor[1] studied a group of 28 unipolar and 15 bipolar patients for severity of illness, clinical psychopathology of the depressive syndrome, and response to electroconvulsive therapy (ECT). Bipolar patients had an earlier age at onset, were predominantly depressed females, and had a greater incidence of cyclothymia and mesomorphy and a greater genetic loading for affective illness. However, Abrams and Taylor concluded that despite the differentiation of unipolar and bipolar depressives by various biologic criteria, they exhibit a homogeneous syndrome of endogenous depression and a uniform response to ECT.[1]

Bech et al.[13] studied personality patterns in 13 unipolar and 23 bipolar patients using four questionnaires to evaluate personality traits: the Marke-Nyman Temperament Scale, the Zerssen Personality Scale, the Cesaree Mark Personality Scale, and the Eysenk Personality Inventory. They found a slight degree of substability of cyclothymia in both groups and much more pronounced similarities than differences in the personality patterns of unipolars and bipolars.

In summary, the bipolar/unipolar distinction has achieved considerable and rapid acceptance. The *DSM-III*[8] accepts the evidence pointing to the importance of the distinction between unipolar and bipolar forms of affective disorder; however, while the concept of bipolarity is well defined, in *DSM-III* the diagnosis of bipolar disorder is made when there is a manic episode, whether or not there has been a depressive episode. Unfortunately, the same clarity of criteria does not apply to the concept of unipolar depression or major depressive illness in *DSM-III*, as will be discussed later in this chapter.

---

*Primary affective disorder is an affective illness occurring in the absence of other preexisting psychiatric illness.

PHENOMENOLOGY OF THE MAJOR AFFECTIVE DISORDERS

BIPOLAR DISORDER (MANIC-DEPRESSIVE ILLNESS)

Current conceptions and classifications of manic-depressive reactions derive from the work of Kraepelin,[49] whose thinking in this area was influenced by Falret[30] and Baillarger.[10] In 1854 Falret published a description of the illness, calling it *la folie circulaire*. Working independently, Baillarger published a report on another series of patients, terming the illness *folie a double forme*. It was Kraepelin who saw that the different forms belonged to one nosologic entity. He included in the definition of manic-depressive insanity isolated attacks of mania and depression and, after some hesitation, the depressions of later life.

The term "manic-depressive illness" is applied to a group of mental diseases with a primary disturbance of affect from which all the other symptoms seem more or less directly derived. The affect is of a special kind, varying between the poles of cheerfulness and sadness. The illness has a second characteristic: periodically, elevation or depression of mood alternates with free intervals in which there is a complete return to normal. In fact, the capacity for recovery from the single attack without impairment of mental integrity is the third characteristic of the illness.

THE CLINICAL PICTURE.—The manic attack frequently begins with a slight mood of depression lasting only a few days and gradually changing to a mood of increasing elation accompanied by increased activity and restlessness. The following description of the manic episode by Slater et al.[81] portrays very accurately the changes in the manic patient.

After a short sleep, the patient rises early to a day of continuous and joyous activity. The housewife has most of her ordinary work done before breakfast and spends the rest of her day in an unnecessary spring cleaning or in dressing herself up in bright colors with a plentiful, but often inartistic, use of cosmetics and in running around to visit all her friends regardless of whether or not they want to see her. The businessman shows unusual enterprise, is full of plans which, inspired or not, he regards with uncritical optimism and takes considerable and unjustifiable risks in carrying out his ideas. The patient is self-assertive, boastful, and easily irritated when others fail to conform with his plans. Nothing is done quickly enough for him; no one can compare with him in efficiency and success. The past and present he regards with self-satisfaction and the future with radiant self-confidence. He is in an excellent humor with all the world and different trifles may tickle him to a loud hilarity. Sexual desire and enterprise are increased and, in women, may be the source of serious trouble and the main reason for seeking the doctor's advice.

Carlson and Goodwin,[22] in a longitudinal study of manic-depressive illness during an acute manic episode, divided the longitudinal course into three stages based mainly on the predominant mood: in stage 1, euphoria predominated; in stage 2, anger and irritability prevailed; in stage 3, severe panic predominated. In the initial phase of the manic episode, all 20 patients exhibited increased psychomotor activity, which included increased irritation and rate of speech and increased physical activity. The accompanying mood was labile but euphoria predominated, although irritability became obvious when the patient's many demands were not instantly satisfied.

During the initial stage, the cognitive state was characterized by expansiveness, grandiosity, and overconfidence. Thoughts were coherent, though sometimes tangential. Also frequently observed during this stage were increased sexuality or sexual preoccupations. Interest in religion, inappropriate spending of money, smoking, telephone use, and letter writing also increased. Some of the patients were aware of the mood change and described the feeling of "going high," having racing thoughts, and feeling as if they were in an airplane.

The second, or intermediate, stage was also observed in all patients. During this period, the pressure of speech and psychomotor activity increased. Mood, although euphoric at times, was now more prominently characterized by increasing dysphoria and depression. The irritability observed initially progressed to open hostility and anger, and the accompanying behavior was frequently explosive and assaultive. Racing thoughts progressed to a definitive flight of ideas, with increasing disorganization of the cognitive state. Preoccupations that were present earlier became more intense, with earlier paranoid and grandiose trends now apparent as frank delusions.

The final stage was seen in 14 of 20 patients and was characterized by a desperate, panic-stricken, hopeless state experienced by the patient as clearly dysphoric and accompanied by frenzied and frequently bizarre psychomotor activity. Thought processes that earlier had been only difficult to follow now became incoherent, and a definite loosening of associations was often described. Delusions were bizarre, and idiosyncratic hallucinations were present in 6 patients. Disorientation to time and place was observed in some patients, and 3 had ideas of reference.

Winokur and Tsuang[99] compared elation versus irritability in manic patients and found some clinical differences. They found that the irritable manics tended to be less grandiose and less frequently showed the symptoms of increased spending of money. Also, the irritable manics were less likely to show flight of ideas. Follow-up was not strikingly different.

Abrams and Taylor[1] studied 50 manic probands who had never suffered a depressive episode and compared this group of patients with the remaining bipolar manic-depressives for phenomenologic, demographic, genetic, and treatment response variables. They did not find any significant differences and concluded that unipolar mania is clinically homogeneous with bipolar manic-depressive illness.

Mixed States

While episodes of mania and depression, as opposite states, are frequently found, different authors have described mixed states in which depression and mania occur together. Himmelhoch,[42] in a comprehensive review of these mixed states, underscores the importance of further understanding them, because:

1. They have a major impact on the biologic theories of the affective disorders, manic-depressive illness in particular,
2. They reflect the influence of a host of neurologic, pharmacologic, medical, and social and interpersonal factors on the clinical manifestation of the major mood disorders, and,
3. They are, diagnostically speaking, chameleon-like in their presentation, appearing in some patients like schizophrenia, in others like psychotic depression and in still others like labile, hysteroid states, thereby creating a set of difficult diagnostic conundrums for the clinician.

Kotin and Goodwin[48] studied 20 manic-depressive patients throughout the course of hospitalization and found that significant depression occurred during manic periods in each of them. Depression during mania was frequently evidenced by expressed feelings of helplessness and hopelessness and thoughts of suicide. In this context, mania might be viewed as a process that can coexist with an ongoing depression.

Kraepelin[49] viewed mixed states as transitional states, occurring most often as the patient moved from a manic to a depressive phase or vice versa, but also occurring as interludes in more or less pure forms of mania or depression, and rarely occurring as independent attacks. The patient displays a mixture of the signs and symptoms usually present in only one phase of the illness. Kraepelin listed six types of mixed states: depressive or anxious mania, excited (agitated) depression, mania with poverty of thought, manic stupor, depression with flight of ideas, and inhibited mania.

The Switch Process

Since the classic description by Bunney et al. in 1977[16-18] of the switch process in manic-depressive illness, new documentation has been added to the understanding of this psychobiologic phenomenon. In a longitudinal systematic psychobiologic study, Bunney et al. reported the sequence of change in thought and mood during ten episodes of spontaneous behavioral switches from depression to mania and seven episodes of spontaneous switches out of mania into depression.

During the switch into mania and hypomania, the patients changed from a retarded depression to a period of normal behavior prior to the onset of mania or hypomania. During the depressed period, patients showed a high incidence of seclusiveness, nonverbalization, and dozing during the day-time. This was in contrast to their normal periods, which preceded the episodes of mania: the patients had a sudden appearance of spontaneous speech and motor activity, with normalization of mood, thoughtfulness, and concern for others. In addition, the patients joined group activities, were more friendly, pleasant, sociable, warm, smiling, and outgoing.

The switch into mania lasted one to ten days. Patients who switched rapidly into mania also tended to switch rapidly out of mania. In general, patients showed a sequence of behavior that included mania, hypomania, and a short, unstable transition period followed by depression.

Sitanam et al.,[80] in a study of circadian variations and sleep in patients who switch from depression into mania, classified the switches as "rapid" if they occurred within 24 hours or less and "slow" if they took more than 24 hours to occur. The authors did not find any patient who had both rapid and slow switches. The majority of rapid switches among the sample of patients studied occurred between 7:00 A.M. and 3:00 P.M., supporting the notion that both biologic and psychological factors may play a part. The data also emphasized that the switch process is more likely to occur rapidly than slowly, especially during the switch into mania as compared with the switch out of mania. Sitanam et al. concluded that the time of day is an important factor in the rapid switch process and is strongly related to the severity of the ensuing manic episode following a switch into mania.

Regarding the biochemical parameters, they found that catecholamines were functionally increased prior to the switch from depression into mania and that urinary norepinephrine levels were significantly elevated on the day prior to and during the manic episodes. Overall sleep and rapid eye movement were decreased prior to and during the switch into mania in a few patients. The authors hypothesized a dysfunction in the switch process into mania, with the possibility of a genetically transmitted defect. This defect must be activated and is reversible.

MAJOR DEPRESSION

The essential feature of major depression is either a dysphoric mood, usually depression, or loss of interest or pleasure in all or almost all usual activities and pastimes. This disturbance is prominent, relatively persis-tent, and associated with other symptoms of the depressive syndrome, including appetite disturbance, change in weight, sleep disturbance, psychomotor agitation or retardation, decreased energy, feelings of worth-lessness or guilt, difficulty concentrating or thinking, and thoughts of death or suicide or suicidal attempts.

The dysphoric mood experienced by patients is usually characterized as sadness or despondency, but some patients describe themselves as feeling hopeless, irritable, fearful, worried, or simply discouraged. Sometimes the mood disturbance is not expressed with synonyms for depressive mood but rather as a complaint of not "caring anymore" or as a painful inability to experience pleasure. The description of the depressive episode by Slater et al.[81] remains classic:

> An initial mood of indifference in a depressive state may last for a considerable time, but sooner or later is replaced by one of sadness, which may be of any degree from comparatively slight to a hopeless despair, overwhelming the whole of the mental life. Whatever is experienced seems to be painful. Even enjoyable experiences have this effect partly by making the patient more acutely aware of his incapacity for normal appreciation, partly because he is at once sensible of any unfortunate aspect they may have. Past, present and future are alike, seen through the same dark and gloomy veil, the whole life seems miserable and agonizing.

In some depressed patients, agitation is so overwhelming that other symptoms go almost unnoticed. These patients are brought to physicians when they are found by relatives or friends pacing, wringing their hands, bemoaning their fate, or clinging to everyone who will listen. They ask for reassurance, they beg for help, yet nothing satisfies them. In other patients, retardation is prominent, and marked slowing of both thought and motor behavior occurs. Tasks that once took minutes may require hours. These patients may be so slowed that it is painful to listen to their conversations. Psychomotor retardation can be so severe that a patient becomes mute or even stuporous.

Disturbance of sleep is the most important of the bodily symptoms. Insomnia sometimes precedes all other psychological symptoms, and restoration of sleep may be the first sign of approaching recovery. The patients may have difficulty in getting to sleep, but most typically wake early in the morning and are unable to fall asleep again.

Anorexia is a common symptom in this group of patients. Constipation is very common, sometimes fairly severe. Loss of weight may occur very early and may be out of proportion to normal weight loss.

Early- and Late-onset Major Depressive Illness: Winokur's Schema

Even though the *DSM-III* classification of major depression considers different clinical forms, such as the psychotic and melancholic form of the illness, there have been suggestions that important differences exist between patients with early and late onset of major depressive disorder. Although these findings have not been incorporated into the current classification of major depression, the important research conducted in this area merits a discussion of this classification attempt.

Winokur et al.[93, 94, 97, 98, 101, 102] have conducted systematic research on unipolar patients and advocate the heterogenicity of depressed patients based on age at onset and familial, clinical, phenomenologic, and follow-up studies. They identify two subgroups of unipolar depression: the depression spectrum disease and the pure depressive disease. Depression spectrum disease has an early onset, before age 40, and is more prevalent among female patients. More female relatives of the index patient are depressed, and male degree relatives have a high incidence of alcoholism and sociopathy. Male patients who suffer from the illness usually manifest symptoms of alcoholism or sociopathy but may appear as depressives, while a proportion of female patients may be alcoholics.[93] Pure depressive disease has a late onset, after age 40, and is more prevalent among male patients. The family studies showed equal amounts of depression in both male and female relatives and a negligible number of male relatives with alcoholism and sociopathy.[98] This difference between both subgroups is summarized in Table 2–2.

The most important biochemical finding has been the difference in response to the dexamethasone test. In a study of 86 unipolar depressed patients, Schlesser et al.[77] found that fully 82% of patients with familial pure depressive disease were resistant to dexamethasone suppression, while only 4% with depressive spectrum disease showed the failure of feedback inhibition. On this measure patients with depressive spectrum disease were very similar to nondepressed controls but significantly different from patients with familial and sporadic depression.

Clinically, there were also differences between the early- and late-onset subgroups. The early-onset group was more preoccupied with guilt, more fearful, more worrisome, and more irritable. The mental status examination was most frequently without evidence of agitation, psychomotor retardation, or formal thought disorder. They made suicidal plans and communicated their suicidal intent much more frequently than patients in the late-

TABLE 2–2.—DIFFERENCES IN THE COURSE OF ILLNESS AND OUTCOME BETWEEN DEPRESSIVE SPECTRUM AND PURE DEPRESSIVE ILLNESS

DEPRESSIVE SPECTRUM DISEASE	PURE DEPRESSIVE ILLNESS
Variable illness, less likely to have long periods of chronicity, less acute onset	More likely to have periods of chronicity; acute onset
Significantly higher incidence of real or threatened personal losses than later onset depressions	Lower incidence of real or threatened personal losses
More suicide attempts	More likelihood of rehospitalization for depression
Chronic cases begin in early life	Higher rate of episodes

onset group. Patients in the late-onset group showed less psychological response to their illness, tended to be more constipated, and had more significant weight loss and more mental status evidence of agitation.

Regarding the course of the illness, patients with depressive spectrum disease are less likely to have periods of chronicity, while patients with pure depressive illness are more likely to have periods of chronicity and more likely to have relapses. However, a later article by Valkenburg and Winokur[88] mentions that once patients were depressed, no clinically significant differences were found between the symptoms of patients with depressive spectrum disease and those of other depressive groups.

Regarding follow-up studies of early- and late-onset unipolars, early-onset patients are likely to have fewer episodes than late-onset patients. Male and female early-onset patients tend to have more suicide attempts and more family history of psychiatric hospitalizations, while male and female late-onset patients have a higher rate of episodes. In summary, depressed women with early onset (before age 40) and first-degree family members with a history of alcoholism and/or sociopathy as well as depression would most likely belong to the depressive spectrum disease group, while pure depression disease would be a rigorously diagnosed depression in a person who does not have such a family history.

While the previous systematic research regarding the validity of this subclassification of unipolar patients has been very consistent over the past ten years, many questions remain to be answered, such as (1) whether or not there are two subgroups different in their response to tricyclics, antidepressants, or monoaminooxidase inhibitors, (2) which one is more amenable to psychotherapy, (3) how consistent the biochemical findings are, and (4) what types of underlying personality these subgroups present.

Some researchers have shown skepticism regarding the possibility of clinically differentiating the depression of these subgroups. They state that once depressed, patients with depressive spectrum disease appear to suffer from the same symptoms as any other depressed patients, such as the bereaved, the widowed, bipolar depressives, or those with pure depressive illness, and they state that the small differences are compatible with random variations.[87, 88] This latter position is in line with the view of depression as a final common pathway by which several entities of different etiologies are expressed.[6]

Other Clinical Forms of Major Depression

MAJOR DEPRESSION WITH MELANCHOLIA.—The uncertainty as to whether or not involutional melancholia should be classified as a separate and distinct clinical entity is evident in the various nosologic groupings over the past three decades. In *DSM-I*,[6] involutional psychotic reaction was listed under the general heading of psychotic disorders and under the subheading of "Disorders Due to Disturbances of Metabolism, Growth, Nutrition or Endocrine Function." In *DSM-II*,[7] the psychotic depressive reaction of the middle years was recognized as a primary affective illness and was classified under major affective disorders. The disorder was described as:

> a disorder occurring in the involutional period and characterized by worry, anxiety, agitation, and severe insomnia. Feelings of guilt and somatic preoccupation are frequently present and may be of delusional proportions. Opinion is divided as to whether this psychosis can be distinguished from the other affective disorders. It is therefore recommended that involutional patients not be given this diagnosis unless all other affective disorders have been ruled out.

Epidemiologic studies support the concept that the factors that have generally been associated with involutional melancholia are not unique to that diagnosis; rather, they are characteristic of the psychiatric population in the involutional age range. Likewise, Ford[33] and Overall and Kleett[66] have found that the symptom profile patterns for the involutional melancholia diagnostic group closely resembled the general middle-aged group profile described without regard for clinical diagnosis. In Sweden, between 1968 and 1970, women between the ages of 38 and 68 were surveyed to determine possible changes in mental health status during the climacteric.[39] No statistically significant differences were observed in the rates of mental illness or depression in the various age strata as a function of menopause. Moreover, there was no evidence that character, personality, or emotional change occurred during the menopausal years. Weissman and Meyers[89] found similar results in the New Haven surveys of 1969 and 1976.

Several endocrinologic studies have explored the relationship of the climacteric process to the development of depression and have demonstrated that the symptoms and course of the illness are not influenced by hormonal treatment and that changes in the way of life do not precipitate or cause this particular form of depression.[76]

Winokur[96] studied 71 women who had an affective disorder either before or after the menopause to determine if they were at greater risk for depression during the menopause than at other times of the life span. The difference was not significant. There was a 7% risk of developing an affective disorder during the menopause and a 6% risk at other times. He concluded that menopause does not seem to be an important factor in precipitating an episode of affective disorder, and that such an episode may well be the result of the chance association of menopause, affective disorder, and age.

A third line of investigation has explored the relationship between certain types of premorbid personalities, such as obsessive-compulsive, schizoid, and hysterical, and their susceptibility to the impact of the involutional period. It was assumed that patients with premorbid obsessive-compulsive personalities had the greatest predisposition to develop involutional melancholia. However, systematic prospective studies comparing patients with affective disorders with control groups have failed to support this hypothesis.

The previous data led to the criticism of the concept of involutional melancholia as it was formulated in *DSM-II*, and it has been translated into the current concept of melancholia in *DSM-III*. In the *DSM-III* classification, the concept of involutional melancholia is abandoned, but the melancholic form of a major depression is retained with its own particular characteristics.

Sir Aubrey Lewis' description of melancholia remains a most comprehensive portrait of this form of depression:[57]

> The typical patient exhibits a facial expression of the utmost sadness and presents a dejected, distraught appearance. Unless the onset is acute, weight loss is pronounced so that the patient appears older than his age. Psychomotor agitation can extend to wringing of the hands, pacing the floor, repetitious pleas for help, and episodes of frenzied behavior. The mental content describes somatic delusions, nihilistic delusions, delusions of guilt about significant life occurrences and uncommonly projective paranoid delusions. Bizarre, somatic delusions involving all structures of the body and the earlier fixation of bowel function are the forerunners of absurd ideas about the alimentary tract. The stomach is filled with concrete, the bowels have not moved in years or a padlock is on the anus. Guilt is so prominent that patients berate themselves for unimportant transgressions of the past and believe that they have committed unpardonable sins. Predictions of some horrible but justified personal fate are accompanied by signs of extreme fearfulness. Self accusation and self condemnation progress to the point of desiring relief through death. Suicidal preoccupation with thoughts of just not waking up in the morning are common in the prodromal period and become more persistent as the illness progresses. Suicide is a threat at all times.

MAJOR DEPRESSION WITH PSYCHOTIC SYMPTOMATOLOGY. — Psychotic depressive reaction first appeared as a diagnosis in the *DSM-I* in 1952.[6] Listed as one of the affective reactions, psychotic depressive reaction was defined as a severe depression with manifest evidence of gross misinterpretation of reality, including, at times, delusions and hallucinations.

In the 1968 edition *(DSM-II)*,[7] psychiatric depressive reaction was removed from affective psychosis and placed in the group of other psychoses. The definition of psychotic reaction read:

> This psychosis is distinguished by a depressive mood, attributable to some experience. Ordinarily the individual has no history of repeated depressions or cyclothymic mood swings. The differentiation between the condition and depressive neurosis depends on whether the reaction impaired reality testing or functional adequacy enough to be considered as a psychosis.

The previous definition focused more sharply on exogenous factors. However, research conducted in the last ten years has moved away from a rigorous distinction between neurotic and psychotic. It has become clear that psychotic features can be present in any major depressive episode.[65]

This clinical form of major depression is relatively infrequent in current clinical practice. Only 10% of large samples of depressed patients show delusions, hallucinations, confusion, and other manifestations of impaired reality testing in sufficient proportions to be classified as psychotic forms of depression.[67] However, the identification of this form of depression has clinical usefulness, since a psychotic depression implies severe impairment, high suicidal risk, and possibly the need for hospitalization. Moreover, research indicates that patients with psychotic depressions do not respond to tricyclic antidepressants alone and may require combined tricyclic and phenothiazine treatments or ECT.

CLINICAL COURSE AND PROGNOSIS OF THE MAJOR AFFECTIVE DISORDERS

Research on the prognosis and course of manic-depressive illness over the last decade has been pursuing answers to the crucial questions already formulated by Lundquist[60] 40 years ago:

1. If a patient shows an endogenous emotional reaction of apparently manic-depressive nature, what are the prospects of his recovery, and what risk is there that the state may become chronic?

2. If he recovers, how long will this take, and what factors may tend to lengthen or shorten the duration of the disease?

3. If a patient has recovered from an attack of manic-depressive character, what are the risks of a recurrence of the attack? In the case of a recurrence, when will it happen and what will be the duration of the next attack?

4. How do the states of the disease which he has passed through affect the patient's capacity for work and the possibilities of his getting on in life?

According to Kraepelin,[49] manic-depressive psychosis, unlike dementia praecox, is usually characterized by a good prognosis; rarely does the disease become chronic. In Kraepelin's cases, as many as 60% to 70% had one attack only, and very few had more than four attacks. Mean duration of the separate episodes of illness was seven months, but the range varied considerably. In some cases, the attack lasted for several years.

Since Kraepelin's time, close to 20 well-conducted follow-up studies have taken place, representing a sample of 3,000 patients with major affective disorders, unipolar and bipolar, for different periods of time and with more or less strict diagnostic criteria and research methodology (Table 2–3). Following is an account of the systematic follow-up studies on patients with major affective disorders.

TABLE 2–3.—PROGNOSIS AND COURSE IN THE MAJOR AFFECTIVE DISORDERS

AUTHOR, YEAR	SAMPLE	FOLLOW-UP (YEARS)	FACTORS THAT AFFECT PROGNOSIS AND COURSE
Kraepelin, 1921[49]			60%–70% of manic depressives had 1 attack only; very few had more than 4 attacks; mean duration of separate episodes was 7 months
Pollock, 1931[71]	100 manic-depressives	11	Patients between ages 20 and 40 at time of first admission had fewer recurrences than patients younger or older
Rennie, 1942[75]	208 manic-depressives	20	21% of patients had single attack; recovery from first attack almost invariable; attacks tend to be prolonged after age 45; depression following elation is more common than vice versa
Poort, 1943[72]	39 bipolar affective disorders	10–15	22 patients (56%) become chronic, with different degrees of social impairment
Lundquist, 1945[60]	319 first admissions of manic depressives, 103 bipolar	10–20	Principal factor in prognosis seemed to be age; prognosis for recovery after first attack good; in older patients, the interval between 1st and 2d attack longer than between the following ones
Hastings, 1958[40]	68 bipolars	6–12	54% were well, 46% ill regarding social adjustment
Astrup et al., 1959[9]	270 patients; 96 manic-depressives	7–19	19 manic-depressives took a chronic course: 13 became atypical schizophrenics, 1 chronic mania, 5 senile dementia; 28 improved; 49 recovered.
Perris, 1966[68]	97 bipolars; 200 unipolar depressive psychotics	3 months; 2 years after discharge	Unipolar patients showed a tendency to require longer hospitalization; bipolars relapsed more frequently than unipolars over age 45 and had more admissions but shorter episodes
Bratfos and Haugh, 1968[15]	218	1–12; mean 6	Patients over 50 had incidence of chronicity; 1/4 were continuously ill over period of observation; 1/4 were free of symptoms
Winokur et al., 1969[97]	28 bipolars	18–36 months	60% had complete remission of symptoms with or without episodes; only 40% had complete social remission
Shobe and Brion, 1971[79]	111 manic-depressives, 15 bipolars	17.8	47% of manic-depressives recovered, 53% did not (unable to work or function socially most of the time)
Kern et al., 1972[44]	154	4 (conducted blind to diagnosis)	Significant correlation between poor outcome and history of neurotic traits, phobias during childhood, and hysterical personality

Study	Sample	Follow-up	Findings
Winokur, 1973[64]	225 unipolar depressed, 100 bipolars	Up to 20; diagnostic criteria for unipolars and bipolars used and diagnostic criteria for recovery, including social recovery	Length of recovery increased with length of the follow-up; unipolar group was heterogeneous
Carlson (NIMH study), 1974[23]	53 manic-depressives	38 months after discharge and 14.7 years after onset of illness	$1/3$ remained functionally impaired, with moderate to severe affective symptoms interfering with work, social, and family life
D'Elia et al., 1974[35]	83 with diagnosis of nonpsychotic depressive disorders	10	Diagnosis showed high stability over time; $2/3$ of population relapsed during follow-up; rate of attempted suicide and suicide during follow-up was high
Kolakowska, 1975[47]	70 female inpatients with primary recurrent depression	1–6; impact of pharmacologically treated affective illness	Brief and poor remissions over age 50; age at onset unrelated to frequency of episodes; course of illness showed common occurrence of brief, mild, or atypical depressive episodes
Fleiss et al., 1978[31]	140 bipolar manic-depressives	11.4; actuarial life tables used	No relation between episode frequency and age at onset of illness; most patients who relapsed did so with a manic episode; bipolars should have at least 2 episodes within a 5–8 year period to be considered for maintenance
Dunner et al., 1979[29]		Actuary life method used to derive estimate of a patient experiencing episode of affective illness within any interval of time to the start of follow-up	Odds close to 50-50 that bipolar patient will not experience an affective episode requiring additional treatment or hospitalization during first 3 years of maintenance on lithium

Pollock[71] observed 100 manic-depressives over a period of 11 years and found that patients who were between 20 and 40 years old at the time of their first admission had fewer recurrences of attacks than patients younger or older. Rennie's[75] follow-up of 208 manic-depressive psychotics for over 20 years revealed that patients having a first attack between ages 21 and 30 had the best prospect for recovery, but the prognosis was poor for those after age 40.

Poort[72] followed 39 patients with bipolar affective disorder for a period of 10 to 15 years. Of those 39 patients, 22 (56%) became chronic.

Lundquist[60] followed 103 patients with manic-depressive illness for 20 years and noted that some patients, even though they were clinically asymptomatic, had a degree of social impairment. He concluded that manic-depressive illness has a generally good prognosis.

Hastings[40] studied 68 patients with a diagnosis of affective disorder, with emphasis on their social adjustment. He graded each patient's social adjustment as excellent, good, fair, poor, and failing, and found that the manic-depressive diagnosis carried a 42% chance for reasonably satisfactory social and group adjustment. The finding was in contrast to the adjustment of schizophrenic patients, of whom only 29% achieved a satisfactory social adjustment.

Astrup et al.[9] followed 96 manic-depressives over a period of 7 to 19 years and found that 19 of them took a chronic course (13 became atypical schizophrenics, 1 suffered from mania, and 5 showed senile dementia), 28 improved, and 49 showed recovery from the illness.

Perris[68] followed 97 bipolar and 200 unipolar depressed patients for 38 months after discharge and found that bipolars relapsed more frequently than unipolars when over 45 years old. Female unipolars relapsed more frequently than males and bipolar patients had more admissions but shorter episodes than unipolars.

Bratfos and Haugh,[15] in a sample of 218 patients with mean time of follow-up of six years, found that patients over age 50 had an increase in incidence of chronicity. One fourth of the patients were continuously ill through the period of observation, while one fourth were free of symptoms.

Winokur et al.[97] carried out a prospective short-term follow-up on 28 hospitalized patients with a length of follow-up of 18 to 36 months. Only four patients were hospitalized for the first time; 60% had a complete remission of symptoms with or without episode, but only 40% had complete social remission.

Shobe and Brion[79] followed 111 manic-depressive patients from the onset of illness. The mean length of follow-up was 17.8 years and the range was 14 to 20 years. Forty-seven percent of the manic-depressive patients recovered while 53% did not, being unable to work or function socially most of the time.

Kern et al.[44] followed 154 patients over a four-year period in which the investigators were blind to the original diagnosis; the study emphasized the longitudinal function of the patient rather than the evaluation at follow-up. They found a significant correlation between poor outcome and history of neurotic traits, phobias during childhood, and hysterical personality. During the follow-up, 38% of the patients recovered, 22% improved, and 40% remained unimproved.

Several follow-up studies were reported by Winokur[95] and his associates as part of the Iowa 500 series. The sample included the study of 225 unipolar depressed patients for up to 20 years. They found that fewer than 5% of the patients ever showed mania in the follow-up period. Depressive males were most likely to have subsequent episodes, while depressive females were most likely to become chronic.

Carlson et al.[23] followed 53 manic-depressives who had an average of over five episodes of the illness. One third remained functionally impaired, with moderate to severe affective symptoms interfering with work, social activities, and family life.

D'Elia et al.[35] followed 83 patients with diagnoses of nonpsychotic depressive disorder for ten years. They found that the diagnoses showed a high stability over time. Two thirds of the population relapsed during follow-up, and the rate of suicide and attempted suicide was high.

Kolakowska[47] followed 70 female inpatients with recurrent depression over a period of one to six years. This study is a departure from the previous ones in the sense of the impact on the clinical course of pharmacologically treated affective illness. She found that age at onset did not significantly affect the frequency of episodes, that the psychopharmacologic treatment had an impact on the course of the illness, and that patients under pharmacologic treatment did not have the classic course of manic-depressive illness, but had instead brief, mild, and atypical depressive episodes separated by brief periods of remission.

With the initiation of lithium treatment in manic-depressive illness, the evaluation of the natural course of the illness among patients treated with lithium, as compared with those previously treated when lithium was not available, has become an important task. Fleiss et al.[31] obviated this problem by developing the actuary life method, an approach that allows for the possibility of estimating the probability of a patient experiencing an episode of affective illness within any interval of time from onset to the start of follow-up.

Dunner et al.,[29] using the actuary life method, found no relation between episode frequency and age at onset of illness. They recommend that bipolars should have at least two episodes to be considered for lithium maintenance.

Welner et al.,[91] in an excellent review article on the course and outcome of patients with affective disorders, discuss some of the methodological problems that make the comparison of follow-up studies difficult, such as the strict diagnostic criteria of the sample of patients, and the time span in the course of the illness that the follow-up will cover. They emphasize the need for studies that begin at the onset of the first episode, as well as the need for blind follow-up studies, plus the necessity of clearly defining remissions, episodes, intervals, and recidivism. They also emphasize not using classic symptoms exclusively as criteria for improvement but using, in addition, some other parameters, such as social functioning and social adjustment.

The following is a summary of the pertinent findings of the follow-up studies of patients with affective disorders.

1. Older patients have worse prognoses, as shown by recurrence of attacks, a chronic course, attacks recurring more frequently, and shorter intervals between episodes (Bratfos and Haugh,[15] Lundquist,[60] Kolakowska,[47] Pollock[71]).

2. Patients with only manic episodes have better prognoses than bipolars or unipolar depressed (Bratfos and Haugh,[15] Lundquist[60]).

3. The incidence of relapse is higher for women than for men (Bratfos and Haugh,[15] Perris,[68] Fleiss et al.[32]).

4. Bipolars relapse more frequently than unipolars (Perris[68]).

5. The prognosis for the first attack is good; 90% recover (Lundquist,[60] Rennie[75]).

6. Single attacks of manic-depressive illness are rare (Rennie[75]).

7. Rate of attempted suicide and suicide in follow-up is high among bipolar and unipolar patients (D'Elia et al.[35]).

8. Unipolar males have a greater propensity for relapses than females (Winokur et al.[97]).

9. Pharmacologic treatment changes the course of the illness, bringing about brief but more frequent episodes (Kolakowska[47]).

10. A percentage of patients remain functionally impaired during follow-up when they are evaluated regarding their social recovery (Winokur et al.[97]).

11. Age at onset does not seem to correlate significantly with the frequency of episodes (Kolakowska,[47] Fleiss et al.[31]).

12. The odds are close to 50-50 that a bipolar patient will not experience an affective episode during the first three years of maintenance on lithium (Dunner et al.[29]).

DIFFERENTIAL DIAGNOSIS OF THE MAJOR AFFECTIVE DISORDERS

BIPOLAR ILLNESS

The differentiation of bipolar illness from schizophrenia has not been entirely successful; that many bipolar manic-depressives have a prior misdiagnosis of schizophrenia confirms this fact. In a longitudinal study of 20 bipolar manic-depressives, Carlson and Goodwin[22] observed that phenomena suggestive of schizophrenia occurred frequently during the course and development of classic mania, despite the care initially taken to exclude patients with histories of first-rank symptoms of schizophrenia.

Taylor and Abrams,[84] in a study of 52 patients with an admitting diagnosis of schizophrenia or other nonaffective illness, noted that when those patients were assessed for affective disorders, the majority were rediagnosed as suffering from an affective disorder.

Pope and Lipinski[73] concluded that schizophrenic symptoms were nonspecific when the external validating criteria for affective disorders were met. They stated that clinical symptoms, especially those considered to be diagnostic for schizophrenia, were unreliable in determining the differential diagnosis of affective versus schizophrenic disorders.

Akiskal and Puzantian,[4] in a comprehensive review of differential diagnosis of psychotic forms of depression and mania, undertook a systematic analysis of an affectively ill sample in order to determine the origin of "schizophrenic" features that mislead clinicians into favoring a schizophrenic diagnosis in almost every other case of psychotic affective disorders. Some of the diagnostic pitfalls are mistaking paranoid ideation for schizophrenia, mistaking anhedonia and depressive depersonalization for schizophrenic emotional blunting, confusing formal thought disorder with flight of ideas, and heavy reliance on incidental schneiderian criteria in making differential diagnostic assignments of psychotic patients.

In cyclothymic disorders, there are hypomanic periods, but the full manic syndrome is not present. However, in some instances, a manic episode may be superimposed on a cyclothymic disorder. In such cases, both bipolar disorder and cyclothymic disorder should be diagnosed, since it is likely that when the individual recovers from the manic episode, the cyclothymic disorder will persist.[5]

Somatic disease, subclinical or clearly established, may be accompanied by severe depressive symptoms that override the manifestations of the primary process. Depressed mood and apathy or excitement and irritability may be found in hypertension, cardiovascular disease, uremia, various intracranial lesions such as general paralysis, cerebral arteriosclerosis, and

brain tumor, psychomotor epilepsy after infectious diseases, in toxic delir-
iums, in drug intoxications, and in drug withdrawal states.

The term "schizoaffective disorder" is retained in *DSM-III*[8] for those
instances in which the clinician is unable to make a differential diagnosis
between affective disorders and either schizophreniform disorder or schizophrenia. However, before using this term, the clinician should consider
particularly the diagnosis of major affective disorder with psychotic features.

Narcissistic personality disorder is one of the frequent differential diagnostic considerations in manic-depressive patients because patients with
that personality disorder frequently demonstrate transient periods of elation and depression, often with grandiosity and euphoria in one phase and
self-deprecation in a succeeding phase—manifestations similar to classic
manic-depressive disorder. To Kohut,[46] the distinction is made clear by the
longitudinal history of the patients' periods of euphoria on the one hand,
and depression on the other. Patients with the narcissistic character are
clearly responsive to a loss of the feeling of empathy with the therapist or
a significant other and are amenable to the therapist's interpretation. In
the manic-depressive, on the other hand, the psychic structure is poorly
integrated and disintegrates in the presence of stress; interpretation does
not relieve the clinical picture.

Krauthammer and Klerman[50] found that mania occurs secondary to drug
infections, neoplasms, epilepsy, and metabolic disturbances. That mania
can result from a variety of pharmacologic, structural, and metabolic disturbances suggests that mania, like depression, is a clinical syndrome with
multiple causes.

MAJOR DEPRESSIVE EPISODE

Making the distinction between grief and a major depressive disorder
can be difficult. However, grief usually does not last as long as an episode
of depression. Most bereaved persons experience fewer symptoms than patients with a major depressive episode.[24]

Obsessions occur commonly in major depressive disorders. The distinction between obsessional illness and major depressive disorder is also made
on the basis of chronology. If obsessions and compulsions antedate depressive symptoms, a diagnosis of major depressive disorder should not be
made.

In separation anxiety disorder, depressive symptoms are common, but if
the full depressive syndrome is not present, only separation anxiety disorder should be diagnosed.[8]

An organic affective syndrome with depression may be due to substances
such as reserpine, infectious disease (influenza, for example), or hypothy-

roidism. Only by excluding organic etiology can one make the diagnosis of a major depressive episode.

In schizophrenia, there is usually considerable depressive symptomatology; the schizophrenic may complain of shallowness of affect and of a depressive mood, but the setting is different. The schizophrenic lacks the warmth and natural expression of the depressive, and the single symptom is less important than the total picture.[4]

In dysthymic and cyclothymic disorders, there are features of the depressive syndrome, but these are not of sufficient severity and duration to meet the criteria for a major depressive episode. However, in some instances, a major depressive episode may be superimposed on one of these disorders. In such cases, both diagnoses apply.

PERSONALITY AND MAJOR AFFECTIVE DISORDERS

The existence of a relationship between temperament and "manic-depressive insanity" was clinically observed by Kraepelin.[49] He noticed that in at least half of his patient population, some of the personality features resembled the particular subtypes outlined by him: depressive, manic, irritable, and cyclothymic. Kraepelin also suspected that the association might be a subclinical expression of the disorder itself. Kretschmer,[51] using a classification of what he believed to be distinctive constitutional physical types, postulated a connection between temperament, disorders, and diverse body configurations. Manic-depressive illness and cyclothymic temperament were associated with a "pyknic" constitution, whereas schizoid personalities and schizophrenia were related to "leptosomatic" or "athletic" physical types. Sheldon et al.[78] modified Kretschmer's typology, but their findings were fundamentally in agreement.

Rennie,[75] in a study of 208 cases of manic-depressive reaction, mentioned that the characteristic personality was that of the outgoing syntropic type. This, however, was not invariable, since ergotropic personalities were observed in 46 patients of the group.

Astrup et al.[9] studied 96 manic-depressives in a follow-up of 7 to 19 years. They reported that manic-depressives, in contrast to the schizophrenics and patients with reactive psychoses, had predominantly syntropic and well-integrated personalities.

From the 1920s to the 1950s, much work was done in attempts to define the purely psychological precipitants of manic-depressive illness, on the assumption that finding those precipitants would reveal the "innate" changes about which Kraepelin had speculated.[49] The descriptive character of these patients during healthy intervals included "liveliness, talkativeness, social aggressiveness, carrying out a relatively stereotyped social performance's inner feeling . . . one of emptiness and need." The patient's strong dependency needs, covered by a superficial aura of well-being and social adjustment, was stressed.[12] The ideas expressed in this classic work have colored the management of manic-depressive patients to the present day, as the descriptions seem to have become a set of general guidelines on how to deal with these patients. The concept of the manic-depressive personality, although questioned, remains a powerful influence among those who work with this illness.

With the development of instruments for the diagnosis of major psychiatric illness, such as the Research Diagnostic Criteria, as well as a better understanding of the role that biologic factors play in the etiology of the major affective disorders, a departure from the emphasis on the manic-depressive personality took place. A phenomenologic approach (supported by the need to have homogeneous diagnostic groups that could be studied from a biochemical, genetic, or clinical perspective) shifted attention from the unresolved theme of the relationship between personality structure and the manic-depressive condition to the search for a homogeneous group of patients that could validate a pharmacogenetic diagnosis.

These developments translated into the concept that some personality disorders represent subclinical, subsyndromic, or subaffective manifestations of affective illness. According to this view, there exist affective personalities that represent gradual stages of transition to full-syndrome affective episodes. The habitual or lifelong affective traits are considered to be milder manifestations of the full-blown clinical affective states (Akiskal et al.,[5] Stone[82, 83]).

This hypothesis gave credence to the notion that cyclothymic personality and affective disorders were highly correlated traits. The work of Akiskal et al.[5] confirmed this previous hypothesis and explained why cyclothymic personality is now considered a subtype of affective disorder in *DSM-III*. Nevertheless, since only a reduced percentage of patients with bipolar illness have underlying cyclothymic personality, the relationship in those patients without underlying cyclothymic personality remains a matter of inquiry. Thus, at least in terms of understanding the components of affective disorders and the relative importance of the underlying personality, we seem to have come full circle back to Kraepelin, with one important difference: although manic-depressive illness is considered primarily a biologic disease, like hypertension, diabetes, or epilepsy, it can be imposed on any type of personality.[103]

We have stated the hypothesis that manic-depressive illness can be overimposed on any type of underlying personality organization. However, when the underlying personality is of a borderline nature,[34] special problems in the diagnostic course of the illness and treatment outcomes are present. Stone[82, 83] is of a similar opinion; he believes that between episodes, the personality of manic-depressives is restored to whichever level of organization was present originally. We have found that bipolar patients with a borderline organization differed significantly from bipolars without any personality disorder by having an earlier onset, a higher incidence of childhood and adolescent psychopathology, poorer functioning between episodes, and special problems during their follow-up and maintenance on lithium (Table 2–4).

The interaction between personality and clinical syndrome raised important questions about the relationship between psychotherapy and pharmacotherapy in the same patient. Even when only pharmacologic management was indicated, this was usually clouded by the expression of a psychological mechanism consistent with the personality structure. In this context, we emphasize the need for more prospective studies of bipolar patients, with special attention given to the various relationships among personality factors, clinical course, and treatment interventions.

The relationship between major depression or unipolar depressions and the underlying personality in each case is even more complex and controversial than with bipolarity. Earlier reports linked different types of depression to different personality traits; for example, a correlation was assumed to exist in patients suffering from involutional depression with premorbid obsessional personality characteristics.

Mendelson[63] referred to a depressive personality that occurs in those prone to neurotic depression characterized by a chronic pessimism, loneliness, dissatisfaction, guilt, or feelings of inadequacy.

TABLE 2–4. — BIPOLARS WITH AND WITHOUT A BORDERLINE
PERSONALITY DISORDER

TRAIT	WITH BORDERLINE PERSONALITY DISORDER (N = 13)	WITHOUT ANY PERSONALITY DISORDER (N = 75)	2-TAILED P
Age at onset	Early onset	Late onset	<0.0054
School performance	More often poor	Better	<0.0015
Childhood psychopathology	More evidence	Less evidence	< 0.021
Adolescent school performance	More often poor	Better	<0.0027
Adolescent psychopathology	More evidence	Less evidence	<0.0036
Function between episodes	Worse	Better	<0.0062
Symptomatology	More hallucinations and delusions	Fewer hallucinations and delusions	<0.0318
Recommended psychotherapy	More often	Less often	<0.0044
Termination	Clinic-initiated	Patient-initiated	<0.0081

Lazare and Klerman[54] reported a study in which hysterical personality features were found in 43% of 35 hospitalized depressed women. Hysterical patients were characterized by certain behavioral patterns during their depression which differentiated them from nonhysterical depressed patients; in addition, their hysterical features seemed to be less severe. However, Gershon et al.[36] found depressed hystericals more likely to display open hostility than depressed obsessionals.

Chodoff,[27] in an excellent review article, pointed out the methodological defects in the study of the relationship between personality and depression. He mentioned some of the following pitfalls:

1. Formulations about enduring personality characteristics are too often derived from behavior observed during periods of illness, or the state of illness or health of the patient when being observed is not specified.

2. The level of observation in many of the psychiatric contributions is often quite superficial.

3. Psychoanalytic observations are, by far, more intensive and searching, but the personality description emanating from these may fail to distinguish between observational and inferred data.

4. Not all of the psychiatric studies employ control groups, and of those that do, such groups are sometimes inadequately defined diagnostically or are not clearly differentiated from each other.

5. The use of controls is not compatible with psychoanalytic methods of observation, but that is no reason for the failure of psychoanalysts to include the appropriate demographic and clinical data in their reports.

Studies aimed at exploring this relationship have benefited from these criticisms and have incorporated some of the methodological suggestions previously discussed.

Hays,[38] in a study of the relationships between premorbid personality and unipolar depression, found that not only are certain types of personality more frequent among patients with unipolar depression (notably personalities marked by neurotic traits of anxiety, feelings of inadequacy, and the like), but that a general picture emerges when a complementary approach is adopted. That is, when the psychiatric illness attending certain personalities is examined, obsessional personalities develop more than the expected number of unipolar depressions, and so do patients with inferiority feelings. Hays concluded that, although there is no real consensus on the patterns associated with unipolar depressions, a connection between personality and depression possibly exists.

Hirschfield and Klerman[41] studied a sample of 119 depressed inpatients, 73 of whom had a major depressive disorder; 24, a manic or hypomanic episode; and the rest, other diagnoses. They administered to the patients a standardized structured interview (SADS) and a battery of personality tests: Maudsley Personality Interview, Marke Nyman Temperament Survey, Lazare Klerman, Armor Personality Inventory, and the Leyton Obsessional Interview. The depressive patients scored significantly higher on introversion neuroticism, obsessionality, solidity, and stability than published norms and significantly lower on validity. A factor analysis yielded three factors: (1) depressed patients were significantly lower than manics on "nonspecific neuroticism and emotional weakness," (2) they did not differ significantly on obsessionality factors, and (3) manics tended to be higher on the general sociability and suggestibility factor. The authors suggest that "there are abnormalities in the personalities of patients with affective disorders and that depressive patients, as compared with manics, are more likely to break under stress, have less energy, are more insecure and sensitive, tend to worry more, are less socially adroit, more needy and more obsessional than normal individuals."[41] However, Hirschfield and Klerman did not consider subtypes of unipolars, and since depressives are heterogeneous, one would expect that the personality profiles of various depressive disorders would differ. Postulating a characterologic tendency to dysphoria of a developmental origin in certain individuals, Yerevanian and Akiskal[105] studied 65 subjects with "characterologic depressions" (onset before age 25; depression symptoms present over five years almost on a daily basis, but not sufficient to fulfill the criteria for a major depressive episode, etc.). Based on the pharmacologic response, the existence of shortening of REM latency and other findings, they describe two distinct groups: a character spectrum group and a dysthymic or subaffective disorder group. Individuals in the latter group tend to have obsessive-introverted traits, may suffer from overimposed major depressions, display shortened REM latency, have relatives with primary affective disorder, and respond to tricyclics. Yerevanian and Akiskal are of the opinion that, with respect to the personality of the patient, this characterologic subaffective disorder is related at least to the unipolar group as cyclothymia is related to bipolar illness.

The investigations into and clinical observations on the relationship between major affective disorders and personality thus far reviewed suggest that:

1. Some personality structures may represent subaffective manifestations of affective disorder (Akiskal et al.,[5] Stone,[82, 83] Yerevanian and Akiskal[104]).

2. Unipolar and bipolar disorders are associated with different types of personality, with the bipolar group showing similar features as normal controls (Chodoff,[27] Cohen et al.,[25] Perris[68]).

3. An association between melancholic personality and unipolar depression seems to be empirically established (Hays,[38] Kraepelin,[49] Zerssen,[106] Tellenbach[86]).

4. The personality might represent a structural overcompensation for the inclination to develop an affective illness (Tellenbach[86]).

5. Certain personalities may repeatedly invite interpersonal conflict and thus create life events that precipitate a depressive episode (Akiskal[2]).

6. The personality structure favors the appearance of certain symptoms when an affective episode occurs and may independently provide the predisposition to both personality disorder and affective illness under the exposure to genetic and environmental influences (Akiskal and McKinney[3]).

7. Bipolar illness can be superimposed on any type of underlying personality organization, but when the underlying personality has a borderline organization, special problems in the diagnostic course of the illness and treatment outcomes are present (Gaviria et al.[34]).

From these general findings gleaned from previous research, it is clear that the relationship between personality and affective disorder remains a complex one and a subject of further inquiry.

REFERENCES

1. Abrams R., Taylor M.: Unipolar and bipolar depressive illness: Phenomenology and response to electroconvulsive therapy. *Arch. Gen. Psychiatry* 30:320–321, 1974.
2. Akiskal H.: A biobehavioral approach to depression, in Depue R.A. (ed.): *The Psychobiology of Depressive Disorders: Implications for the Effects of Stress.* New York, Academic Press, 1979, pp. 409–437.
3. Akiskal H., McKinney W.: Depressive disorders: Towards a unified hypothesis. *Science* 182:20–29, 1973.
4. Akiskal H., Puzantian U.: Psychotic forms of depression and mania. *Psychiatr. Clin. North Am.* 3:419–439, 1979.
5. Akiskal H., et al.: Cyclothymic disorders: Validating criteria for inclusion in the bipolar affective group. *Am. J. Psychiatry* 134:1227, 1977.
6. American Psychiatric Association: *Diagnostic and Statistical Manual of Mental Disorders*, ed. 1. Washington, D.C., APA, 1952.
7. American Psychiatric Association: *Diagnostic and Statistical Manual of Mental Disorders*, ed. 2. Washington, D.C., APA, 1968.
8. American Psychiatric Association: *Diagnostic and Statistical Manual of Mental Disorders*, ed. 3. Washington, D.C., APA, 1980.
9. Astrup C., Fossum A., Holmboe R.: A follow-up study of 270 patients with acute affective psychosis. *Acta Psychiatr. Scand.*, 34(suppl. 135):1–65, 1959.
10. Baillarger J.: Note on the type of insanity with attacks characterized by two regular periods, one of depression and one of excitation. *Bull. Acad. Natl. Med. Paris* 19:340, 188, 1853–1854.
11. Baker M., et al.: Depressive disease: Classification and clinical characteristics. *Compr. Psychiatry* 12:354–364, 1971.
12. Baker M., et al.: Depressive disease: The effect of the postpartum state. *Biol. Psychiatry* 3:357–365, 1971.
13. Bech P., et al.: Personality in unipolar and bipolar manic melancholic patients. *Acta Psychiatr. Scand.* 62:245–257, 1980.
14. Beigel A., Murphy D.: Unipolar and bipolar affective illness: Differences in

clinical characteristics accompanying depression. *Arch. Gen. Psychiatry* 24:215–220, 1971.

15. Bratfos C., Haugh J.: Course of manic depressive psychoses: A follow-up investigation of 215 patients. *Acta Psychiatr. Scand.* 44:89–112, 1968.
16. Bunney W., et al.: The switch process in manic depressive illness: I. A systematic study of sequential behavioral changes. *Arch. Gen. Psychiatry* 27:295–302, 1972.
17. Bunney W., et al.: The switch process in manic depressive illness: II. Relationships to catecholamines, REM sleep and drugs. *Arch. Gen. Psychiatry* 27:304–309, 1972.
18. Bunney W., Goodwin F., Murphy D.: The switch process in manic depressive illness. *Arch. Gen. Psychiatry* 27:312–317, 1972.
19. Cadoret R., Dorzab J., Baker M.: Depressive disease: A genetic study. *Arch. Gen. Psychiatry* 24:135, 1971.
20. Cadoret R., Winokur G., Clayton P.: Family history studies: Manic depressive disease versus depressive disease. *Br. J. Psychiatry* 116:625–635, 1970.
21. Cadoret R., et al.: Depressive disease: Life events and onset of illness. *Arch. Gen. Psychiatry* 26:133, 1972.
22. Carlson G., Goodwin F.: The stages of mania. *Arch. Gen. Psychiatry* 28:221–288, 1973.
23. Carlson G., et al.: Follow up of 53 bipolar manic depressive patients. *Br. J. Psychiatry* 124:134–139, 1974.
24. Clayton P., et al.: Mourning and depression: Their similarities and differences. *Can. Psychiatr. Assoc. J.* 19:309–312, 1974.
25. Cohen M., et al.: An intensive study of twelve cases of manic depressive psychosis. *Psychology* 17:103–138, 1954.
26. Conte H., et al.: A self-report borderline scale discriminative validity and preliminary norms. *J. Nerv. Ment. Dis.* 168:428–435, 1980.
27. Chodoff P.: The depressive personality. *Arch. Gen. Psychiatry* 27:666, 1972.
28. Dunner D., Dwyer T., Fieve R.: Depressive symptoms in patients with unipolar and bipolar affective disorders. *Compr. Psychiatry* 17:447–451, 1976.
29. Dunner D., Murphy D., Stallone F., et al.: Episode frequency prior to lithium treatment in bipolar manic depressive patients. *Compr. Psychiatry* 20:511–515, 1979.
30. Falret J.: *Clinical Lectures on Mental Medicine*. Paris, Baillieri, 1853–54, p. 188.
31. Fleiss J., Dunner D., Stallone F.: The life table: A method for analyzing long-term follow-up studies. *Arch. Gen. Psychiatry* 33:101–102, 1976.
32. Fleiss J., et al.: Actuarial studies of the course of manic depressive illness. *Compr. Psychiatry* 19:4, 1978.
33. Ford H.: Involutional melancholia, in Freedman A., et al. *Comprehensive Textbook of Psychiatry*, ed. 2. Baltimore, Williams & Wilkins Co., 1975.
34. Gaviria M., Flaherty J., Val E.: A comparison of bipolar patients with and without borderline personality organization, *Psychiatr. J. Univ. Ottawa*, in press.
35. D'Elia G., von Knorring L., Perris C.: Nonpsychotic depressive disorders: A 10-year follow-up. *Acta Psychiatr. Scand.*, suppl. 255:143–157, 1974.
36. Gershon E., Cramer M., Klerman G.: Hostility and depression. *Psychiatry* 31:224, 1968.
37. Gunderson J.: Characteristics of borderline, in Hartocollis P. (ed.): *Borderline*

Personality Disorders: The Concept, The Syndrome, The Patient. New York, International Universities Press, 1977.

38. Hays P.: Relationships between premorbid personalities and unipolar depressions. *Can. J. Psychiatry* 25:314–318, 1980.
39. Hallstrom J.: Mental disorders and sexuality in the climacteric, in Forsman H. (ed.): *Reports from the Psychiatric Research Center.* St Jorgen's Hospital, University of Goteborg, Stockholm, Sweden, 1973.
40. Hastings D.: Follow up results in psychiatric illness. *Am. J. Psychiatry* 114:1057–66, 1958.
41. Hirschfield R., Klerman G.: Personality attributes and affective disorders. *Am. J. Psychiatry* 136:67–70, 1979.
42. Himmelhoch J.: Mixed states, manic depressive illness and the nature of mood. *Psychiatr. Clin. North Am.* 2:1449–59, 1979.
43. Jacobson E.: Contributions to the metapsychology of cyclothymic depression, in *Depression.* New York, International Universities Press, 1971.
44. Kern T., et al.: The assessment and prediction of outcome in affective disorders. *Br. J. Psychiatry* 121:167–74, 1972.
45. Kernberg O.: Borderline personality organization. *J. Am. Psychiatr. Assoc.* 15:641–685, 1967.
46. Kohut H.: *The Analysis of the Self.* New York, International Universities Press, 1971.
47. Kolakowska T.: The clinical course of primary recurrent depression in pharmacologically treated female patients. *Br. J. Psychiatry* 126:336–45, 1975.
48. Kotin J., Goodwin F.: Depression during mania: Clinical observations and theoretical implications. *Am. J. Psychiatry* 129:55–62, 1972.
49. Kraepelin E.: *Manic-Depressive Insanity and Paranoia.* Edinburgh, E. & S. Livingstone, 1921.
50. Krauthammer C., Klerman G.L.: Secondary mania, manic syndromes associated with antecedent physical illness or drugs. *Arch. Gen. Psychiatry* 35:1333, 1978.
51. Kretschmer E.: *Psyche and Character,* ed. 2, rev. London, Routledge, 1936.
52. Kupfer D., Foster F.: Psychomotor activity in depression. Read before the new research annual meeting of the American Psychiatric Association, Detroit, Michigan, May, 1974.
53. Lange J.: The endogenous and reactive affective disorders and the manic-depressive constitution, in Bumke R. (ed.): *Handbook of Mental Diseases.* Berlin: Springer, 1928, vol. 6, pp. 191–194.
54. Lazare A., Klerman G.: Hysteria and depression: The frequency and significance of hysterical personality features in hospitalized depressed women. *Am. J. Psychiatry* 124:48, 1968.
55. Leonhard K.: *Auftrilung der Endogenen Psychosen.* Berlin, Academic Verlag, 1957.
56. Leonhard K., Korff I., Schulz H.: Temperaments in the families of monopolar and bipolar phasic psychosis. *Acta Psychiatr. Neurol.* 143:416, 1962.
57. Lewis A: Melancholia: A clinical survey of depressive states. *J. Ment. Sci.* 80:277–378, 1934.
58. Lonaugen A., Levine P.: Age at onset of bipolar affective illness. *Arch. Gen. Psychiatry* 35:1345–1348, 1978.
59. Lowry M., et al.: Baseline characteristics of pure depressive disease. *Neuropsychobiology* 4:333–343, 1978.

60. Lundquist G.: Prognoses and course in manic depressive psychoses. *Acta Psychiatr. Neurol. Scand.*, suppl. 35, pp. 1–96, 1945.
61. MacVane J., et al.: Psychological functioning of bipolar manic-depressives in remission. *Arch. Gen. Psychiatry* 35:1351–1354, 1978.
62. Mendlewicz J., Fieve R., Rainier J., et al.: Manic depressive illness: A comparison study of patients with and without a family history. *Br. J. Psychiatry* 120:523, 1972.
63. Mendelson M.: *Psychoanalytic Concepts of Depression.* Springfield, Ill., Charles C Thomas, Publisher, 1960.
64. Morrison J.: The Iowa 500 first follow-up. *Arch. Gen. Psychiatry* 29:678–682, 1973.
65. Nelson C., Bowers M.: Delusional, unipolar depression. *Arch. Gen. Psychiatry* 35:1321–1328, 1978.
66. Overall J., Klett C.: *Applied Multivariate Analysis.* New York, McGraw-Hill Book Co., 1972.
67. Pederson A.M., et al.: Epidemiological considerations of psychotic depression. *Arch. Gen. Psychiatry* 27:193–197, 1972.
68. Perris C.: A study of bipolar (manic-depressive) and unipolar recurrent depressive psychosis. *Acta Psychiatr. Scand.* 42:1, 1966.
69. Perris C.: Course of depressive psychosis. *Acta Psychiatr. Scand.* 44:238–248, 1968.
70. Perry J., Klerman G.: The borderline patient: A comparative analysis of four sets of diagnostic criteria. *Arch. Gen. Psychiatry* 35:141–150, 1978.
71. Pollock H.: Recurrence of attacks in manic depressive psychosis. *Am. J. Psychiatry* 11:562–573, 1931.
72. Poort R.: Catamnetic investigations on manic depressive psychosis with special reference to prognosis. *Acta Psychiatr. Neurol. Scand.* 20:59–74, 1945.
73. Pope H., Jr., Lipinski J., Jr.: Diagnosis in schizophrenia and manic depressive illness: A reassessment of the specificity of schizophrenic symptoms in the light of current research. *Arch. Gen. Psychiatry* 35:811–828, 1978.
74. Prien R.F., Caffey E., Klett C.: Factors associated with treatment success in lithium carbonate prophylaxis. *Arch. Gen. Psychiatry* 31:189–192, 1974.
75. Rennie A.: Prognosis in manic depressive psychosis. *Am. J. Psychiatry* 98:801–814, 1942.
76. Rosenthal S.: The involutional depressive syndrome. *Am. J. Psychiatry* 124:21–34, 1968.
77. Schlesser M., Winokur G., Sherman B.: Genetic subtypes of unipolar primary depressive illness distinguished by hypothalamic pituitary adrenal axis activity. *Lancet* 1:739–741, 1979.
78. Sheldon W., Stevens J., Tucker W.: *The Variety of Human Physique.* New York, Harper, 1940.
79. Shobe F., Brion P.: Long term prognosis in manic depressive illness: A follow up investigation of ill patients. *Arch. Gen. Psychiatry* 25:334–337, 1971.
80. Sitanam J., Gillin C., Bunney W.: The switch process in manic depressive illness: Circadian variations in time of switch and sleep and manic ratings before and after the switch. *Acta Psychiatr. Scand.* 58:267–278, 1978.
81. Slater E., Roth M., Mayer G. (eds.): *Clinical Psychiatry.* London, Williams & Wilkins Co., 1969.
82. Stone M.: Assessing vulnerability to schizophrenia or manic-depression in borderline states. *Schizophrenia Bull.* 5:105–110, 1979.

83. Stone M.: *The Borderline Syndrome: Constitution, Personality and Adaptation*. New York, McGraw-Hill Book Co., 1980.
84. Taylor M., Abrams R.: The phenomenology of mania: A new look at some old patients. *Arch. Gen. Psychiatry* 29:520–522, 1973.
85. Taylor M., Abrams R.: Manic states: A genetic study of early onset affective disorders. *Arch. Gen. Psychiatry* 28:656–658, 1973.
86. Tellenbach H.: *Melancholia*, ed. 3. Berlin, Springer, 1961.
87. Van Valkenburg C., Winokur G., et al.: Depression spectrum disease vs. pure depressive disease. Clinical, personality and course differences. *J. Nerv. Ment. Dis.* 165:341–346, 1977.
88. Van Valkenburg C., Winokur G.: Depression spectrum disease. *Psychiatr. Clin. North Am.* 2:469–482, 1979.
89. Weissman M., Meyers J.: Rates and risks of depressive symptoms in a United States urban community. *Acta Psychiatr. Scand.* 57:219–231, 1978.
90. Weissman M.: The myth of involutional melancholia. *J.A.M.A.* 242:8, 1979.
91. Welner A., Welner Z., Leonhard M.: Bipolar manic depressive disorder: A reassessment of course and outcome. *Compr. Psychiatry* 18:327–330, 1977.
92. Wetzel R., et al.: Personality as a subclinical expression of the affective disorders. *Compr. Psychiatry* 21:3, 1980.
93. Winokur G.: Depression spectrum disease: Description and family study. *Compr. Psychiatry* 13:1, 1972.
94. Winokur G.: Unipolar depression: Is it divisible into autonomous subtypes? *Arch. Gen. Psychiatry* 36:47–52, 1979.
95. Winokur G.: The Iowa 500 heterogenicity and course in manic depressive illness. *Compr. Psychiatry* 16:125–131, 1971.
96. Winokur G.: Depression in the menopause. *Am. J. Psychiatry* 130:92–93, 1973.
97. Winokur G., Clayton P., Reich T.: *Manic Depressive Illness*. St. Louis, C.V. Mosby Co., 1969.
98. Winokur G., et al.: Depressive disease: A genetic study. *Arch. Gen. Psychiatry* 25:135–44, 1972.
99. Winokur G., Tsuang M.: Elation versus irritability in mania. *Compr. Psychiatry* 16:435–436, 1975.
100. Winokur G., Morrison J.: The Iowa 500 follow up of 225 depressives. *Br. J. Psychiatry* 123:543–8, 1973.
101. Winokur G., et al.: Alcoholism: III. Diagnosis and familial psychiatric illness in 259 alcoholic probands. *Arch. Gen. Psychiatry* 23:104, 1970.
102. Winokur G., et al.: Is a familial definition of depression both feasible and valid? *J. Nerv. Ment. Dis.* 166:764–748, 1978.
103. Wolpert E.: A holistic approach to bipolar depressive illness, in Wolpert E.: *Manic Depressive Illness: History of a Syndrome*. New York, International Universities Press, 1977.
104. Woodruff R.A., Jr., Guze W.B., Clayton P.J.: Unipolar and bipolar primary affective disorder. *Br. J. Psychiatry* 119, 33–38, 1971.
105. Yerevanian B., Akiskal H.: "Neurotic," characterological and dysthymic depressions. *Psychiatr. Clin. North Am.* 2:595, 1979.
106. Zerssen V.: Premorbid personality and affective psychoses, in Burrow G. (ed.): *Handbook of Studies of Depression*. Amsterdam, Exerpta Medica, 1977.

3

DEPRESSION AND PHYSICAL ILLNESS

SARA C. CHARLES, M.D.

IT HAS BEEN OBSERVED that the incidence of depression is on the increase.[55] This statement comes as no surprise to the average physician, who has noted not only the ubiquity of depressive symptomatology but also the increased complexity in the clarification of its diagnosis, despite enormous advances in this area. Nowhere does the problem of diagnosis present more difficulties for the clinician than in the frequent but ill-defined spectrum of depressive symptomatology and its association with somatic illness.

The presenting symptoms of depression may be attributable to primary affective disease such as unipolar or bipolar illness and may or may not include physical complaints. Of particular concern, however, are symptoms that present as depression, various somatic complaints, or a combination of both that is actually of more elusive etiology. Establishing the diagnosis is often extremely difficult. Even when clearly identified, the depressive symptoms may be the initial manifestation of an undiagnosed medical condition rather than a pure depressive illness. Depressive symptoms may also become evident secondary to the development, diagnosis, and/or treatment of a known physical condition. Physicians have become increasingly aware of depressive symptoms that arise secondary to the use of a wide range of drugs prescribed for specific medical illnesses. Finally, one of the most difficult diagnostic dilemmas confronting clinicians is the depression that may be hidden or masked by somatic symptoms, so that what initially appears to be a physical illness is, in fact, a clinical depression.

Throughout this discussion, a distinction between depression as a symptomatic complaint and depression as a well-described clinical diagnosis, as defined in the *Diagnostic and Statistical Manual of Mental Disorders,* ed. 3 *(DSM-III)* and described in chapter 1, will be maintained. In patients with somatic symptoms, depressive symptomatic complaints are far more common than the full-blown clinical syndrome of depression.

DEPRESSION AS A FIRST SIGN OF PHYSICAL ILLNESS

A patient who comes to the attention of the general physician with complaints of apathy, depressed mood, insomnia, or generalized feelings of weakness and lassitude must be evaluated for the presence of primary affective illness by eliciting a good history. The precise inclusion and exclusion criteria of *DSM-III* facilitate this process. Most often, however, the clinical picture and history are not commensurate and the physician must carefully evaluate the patient's physical status by performing a general physical examination and routine laboratory and radiologic tests. A complete evaluation can save the physician and patient considerable time and energy, since the common symptoms of depression may well be the first evidence of an organic illness that may become readily apparent with the aid of laboratory or physical data.

Endocrine disorders are among the most common of the illnesses in which affective changes can be an initial manifestation. The early signs of hypothyroidism include lethargy, constipation, menstrual disturbance, decreased appetite, and slowing of motor activity, all of which may be confused with depression. Not associated with depression, however, are the dry skin, cold intolerance, dry hair, and aching muscles so characteristic of this disorder. Laboratory studies should show a decrease in T_4 and in the T_4/T_3 index. Variations in other thyroid functions depend on the etiology of the specific condition. Serum cholesterol, SGOT, and lactic dehydrogenase (LDH) levels may all be increased. The electrocardiogram may reflect bradycardia, low amplitude, and flattened or inverted T waves.

Increased anxiety and irritability, rather than depression, are associated with hyperthyroidism, except in rare cases of the so-called apathetic thyrotoxicosis.[63] The patient is usually elderly and has substantial muscular wasting, a small goiter, depression, absence of ocular manifestations, excessive weight loss, and cardiovascular dysfunction with atrial fibrillation. When the syndrome is wholly or partially present, the condition is often thought to be old age depression. Nonactivation of the CNS, as demonstrated by depressed and apathetic affect, absence of hyperkinetic motor activity, and slowed mentation, is the most significant presenting symptom. Laboratory findings show elevated values on thyroid function tests but lower values than those seen in the usual form of hyperkinetic hyperthyroidism.

Depression, as well as organic brain syndrome, has been reported as an initial manifestation of hyperparathyroidism,[51] although it is usually accompanied by other evidences of the disorder. A patient with hyperparathyroidism may have only subtle symptoms for many years prior to diagnosis. As a result, multiple and vague somatic complaints, especially related to the gastrointestinal tract, with easy fatigability and muscle weakness, may be mistaken as depressive equivalents until specific laboratory testing confirms the diagnosis of organic illness. Gatewood et al.[23] have suggested that routine measuring of serum calcium levels with the 12-channel autoanalyzer (SMA-12) has helped dramatically in identifying hyperparathyroidism, since hypercalcemia is a consistent finding in this disorder. Serum phosphate levels are usually low but may be normal. Serum magnesium levels have been reported to be low, and serum chloride levels may be elevated.

Hypoparathyroidism is not usually associated with depression. However, since hypoparathyroidism is most commonly a result of an operative procedure, a depression secondary to the primary disease process may be present.

Severe clinical depression may be a facet of Cushing's syndrome (hyperfunction of the adrenal gland), but other clinical signs are invariably present, such as increased body weight, hypertension, hirsutism, fatigability, and weakness. Laboratory tests, such as the dexamethasone suppression test, that demonstrate increased cortisol production in the absence of stress confirm the diagnosis. It is noteworthy that drug-induced Cushing's syndrome is usually accompanied by euphoria rather than depression.[7]

The hypokalemia associated with primary aldosteronism (hypersecretion of aldosterone) may also contribute to depressive complaints, but the diastolic hypertension, muscular weakness, polyuria, polydipsia, and prominent U waves on the electrocardiogram point to the basic diagnosis.

Hypofunction of the adrenal cortex (Addison's disease) has many symptoms that are easily confused with depression. Initially, the patient may notice a gradual development of weakness, lassitude, weight loss with anorexia, and constipation. The progression of the illness may be exceedingly slow, and in its milder forms, there may be no demonstrable abnormalities of any of the parameters measured on routine laboratory testing. However, definitive studies of adrenal stimulation with adrenocorticotropic hormone show abnormalities even in this stage of the disease.[30] Fortunately, primary adrenocortical insufficiency is rare, but in the presence of undiagnosed asthenia, this disorder must be considered.

A number of neurologic disorders have depression as an initial manifestation. Many patients with brain tumors develop nonspecific changes in mental functioning that may be confused with depression. Irritability, apathy, lack of attention to daily tasks, lack of initiative, drowsiness, and depressed mood may be the first signs of increased intracranial pressure, and considerable time may pass before more focal signs appear. In elderly patients especially this syndrome may be the harbinger of metastatic disease to the brain; in such cases the depression is often of marked severity.

The early stages of Parkinson's disease may suggest depression by the immobilized facial expression, monotonous voice, and slowness of movement. The resting tremor, stooped posture, and festinating gait that develop as the disease progresses, however, are unmistakable. In one series, depressive symptoms were present or had been present in the year preceding the initial evaluation in 57 (37%) of 153 patients.[10] Five of these patients had had one or more depressive episodes prior to the onset of the parkinsonism. It is not known if there is a specific relationship between these two disorders or if the development of depression is a separate phenomenon.

A wide range of other medical diseases may manifest themselves as depression, especially in the early stages. Lassitude, fatigue, and dysphoric mood may precede the diagnoses of such chronic infections as brucellosis, hepatitis, infectious mononucleosis, and tuberculosis—diseases whose identities may not be evident at onset. Many patients with carcinoma of the pancreas report depressed mood, insomnia, anorexia, and weight loss early in the disease, before the pain and jaundice more characteristic of the disorder become apparent. The urine, blood, and feces of these patients are often normal in the early stages, as is the radiologic examination. The serum amylase level is abnormal in only about 10% of cases.[30] Establishing the diagnosis, therefore, is often very difficult. Fras et al., in a study of 46 consecutive patients with a diagnosis of carcinoma of the pancreas, found that 76% of the patients had psychiatric symptoms. In 22 of these patients, mental symptoms characterized by depressive feelings, loss of ambition, anxiety, and a premonition of serious illness were the first symptoms noted.[21] Fras et al. suggest that the presence of these symptoms should aid the physician in suspecting this particular disease.

Acute intermittent porphyria is an uncommon mendelian dominant metabolic disorder characterized by periodic attacks of severe abdominal colic accompanied by vomiting or peripheral neuropathies and bulbar palsies. In a review of the literature, Markowitz found that 14% of cases presented initially with various psychiatric manifestations, including depression.[41] The Watson-Schwartz test is a valuable screening device for symptomatic patients but is unreliable in asymptomatic patients.

The fatigue and weight loss of early diabetes may suggest a depression, but a history of polydipsia, polyuria, and polyphagia is prominent. An elevated fasting blood sugar or two-hour postprandial sugar level above 120 mg/100 ml is highly suggestive of diabetes.

Psychiatric symptoms may precede the better-known manifestations of systemic lupus erythematosus by several years. Clinical manifestations are diverse, but depression has been reported as the most common manifestation.[5]

Other disorders associated with depression in their early stages are vitamin deficiencies such as pellegra, thiamine deficiency, and pernicious anemia. Urinary tract disease, especially uremia, is accompanied by depression. Electrolyte disorders[1] involving sodium, potassium, and magnesium and acid-base balance have been associated with depressive feelings in conjunction with lethargy, generalized weakness, and anorexia. Routine laboratory tests usually clarify the origin of the disorder.

CASE 1.—A 41-year-old married black domestic worker, mother of one child, was referred to the university hospital because of low WBC count (2,300/cu mm). The patient had been taking Librium, 30 mg/day, for six years for anxiety caused by her local medical doctor. She was taking no other medications and had no previous psychiatric or medical illnesses. She complained of difficulty falling asleep, periodic dizziness, low self-esteem, and a number of situational problems. The question of depression was raised, but criteria for a clinical diagnosis of depression were lacking. She was gradually weaned from Librium, a medical consultation was unremarkable, and the WBC count stabilized at about 4,500/cu mm. She began weekly supportive psychotherapy sessions.

Six months later, the patient underwent a total abdominal hysterectomy for myomata. Following this, she complained of hallucinatory experiences of "seeing people in caskets" and hearing voices that said "you're going to die," and she became very preoccupied with fears of dying and had feelings of "impending disaster." Her dream life reflected dysphoric content. It was unclear whether the patient was experiencing a psychotic decompensation or psychotic depressive reaction. She returned to work, however, and continued in her weekly supportive psychotherapy. No psychotropic medications were given. The hallucinatory experiences diminished and the episode resolved gradually over the next year.

Two and one-half years after her initial visit, the patient withdrew from psychotherapy because she felt too weak to come to her appointments. She complained of fatigue, dizziness, anorexia, and a 20-lb weight loss over a four-month period. When she was finally admitted to the hospital, she was found to have nephritis, vasculitis, pleuritis, myositis, and pancytopenia. Positive lupus erythematosus preparation was noted and she was given the diagnosis of systemic lupus erythematosus.

The patient was stabilized medically and resumed psychotherapy. She did well psychologically and terminated therapy in a short time. It is our assessment that her psychological disequilibrium, expressed both as depression and as psychotic disorganization, was most likely an early manifestation of systemic lupus erythematosus. This coincides with the findings of Bennett et al., who noted that while most neuropsychiatric symptoms of systemic lupus erythematosus occur during an exacerbation of the disease, occasionally they occur as isolated events and may antedate the better-known features of the disease by several years.[5] In the five years of follow-up, the patient has done well, has had no psychiatric symptomatology, and continues her medical treatment.

DEPRESSION SECONDARY TO PHYSICAL ILLNESS

Every physician has had to treat patients with medical illnesses and concomitant depressive symptoms, even full-blown depressive illness. Adams, writing in Harrison et al.'s *Textbook of Medicine,* suggests that depression is one of the most commonly overlooked diagnoses in clinical medicine.[30] Murphy[44] and Fawcett[17] have warned of the danger of this familiar situation. If a physician can identify a psychological explanation for the patient's dysphoria, he may not diagnose or treat the depression. For example, if a patient has just received a diagnosis of a life-threatening illness, the physician may rationalize that the patient has good reason for developing a depression and simply wait for the patient to "pull out of it" or "get through it." This is a gross disservice to the patient and his family, not only because of the disability that accompanies depression but also because of the associated danger of suicide. Dorpat et al., in a study of 80 completed suicides, found that 70% of the patients had one or more active illnesses, and in 51% of the cases the illnesses were considered to have contributed to the suicide.[15]

Depression is one of the most common ways in which a patient reacts to the development of a physical illness. Other frequent psychological reactions are anxiety and denial. In depression, the patient acknowledges the loss of function or body part or whatever other psychological meaning the illness may represent and manifests many of the expected reactions to loss—insomnia, loss of interest and appetite, apathy, crying spells, dysphoric mood, and, in some cases, suicidal preoccupation. The patient who reacts with anxiety fends off the depressive feelings, but considerable energy is expended in worry, fear, and apprehension, which may be of such severity that they interfere with proper treatment. A patient with symptoms of breast tumor, for example, may worry about disfigurement, malignancy, her marital situation, and the dangers of anesthesia to such a degree that she refuses to have the recommended surgery. Denial is a psychological mechanism of defense whereby the illness is not acknowledged and the patient's thinking and activity reflect the belief that that part of reality does not exist. A certain degree of denial can be useful, for it enables the patient to cope more effectively with the demands of the illness. Excessive denial, however, may interfere with treatment and contribute to shorter survival time.[12]

A number of factors contribute to a patient's reaction to the onset of illness and its diagnosis. The psychological significance of each variable is unique for each patient, and the treating physician must weigh these factors as best he can. The age of a patient always plays a role. The development of diabetes in adolescence, for example, has far different implications than the onset of diabetes in midlife.[62] Mode of onset is another factor. A patient who has sufficient time to adjust to a slowly developing peptic ulcer is in marked contrast to the patient who suffers the traumatic loss of an eye in an auto accident. The degree of disability imposed by the illness and its impact on the patient's work, family relationships, and socioeconomic status are considerations. The nature of the disease itself plays a major role. A patient confronted with breast surgery has a very different response to the diagnosis of carcinoma than to the diagnosis of fibroadenoma. The patient's perception of his or her body image and the changes imposed by a specific illness have far-reaching consequences. The nature and length of the treatment for a given illness may also play a role in the development of depression. It has been noted, for example, that patients with severe burns are initially shocked, frequently emotionally labile, and suffer from insomnia, but are not particularly depressed or realistically concerned about their future. If hospitalization exceeds one month, however, most patients develop depressive symptoms, often to a degree of severe impairment.[3] An additional factor that pertains to all patients is their relationship with significant others and the support they derive from these persons.

A vast body of literature has developed around three main areas pertaining to the nature of a disease and its associated degree of disability. One area is the impact of surgery on a patient: whether the surgery is for a curable or an uncurable disease, the emotional significance of the involved organ, and the complications accompanying such surgery.[6, 9, 69] The second area involves the diagnosis of such chronic diseases as diabetes, hypertension, and arthritis.[8, 62] The third area is related to life-threatening disorders such as cancer and heart disease, especially myocardial infarction.[19, 49, 68]

An individual response to illness may include not only depression, anxiety, and denial, but also a variety of coping behaviors unique to the patient. Common mechanisms are (1) seeking intellectual information about the illness and its treatment, (2) requesting support from family, friends, and health personnel, (3) learning specific skills related to the illness, such as changing dressings or injecting insulin, (4) setting concrete goals, such as regaining the use of a limb or speaking again, (5) reevaluating the meaning of one's life, and (6) rehearsing possible outcomes of the illness and treatment.

Depression that develops with the entire spectrum of defined symptomatology must be treated as such. Antidepressant medication, electroconvulsive therapy, and supportive psychotherapy may all be of value. Awareness of the psychological significance of a specific illness to a specific patient, as well as sensitivity to the patient's use of coping and defensive mechanisms, can aid the physician in strengthening the patient and alleviating a prolonged, crippling, depressive response to illness.

CASE 2.—A 50-year-old black married woman, mother of two, was referred by her cardiologist for evaluation prior to proposed coronary bypass surgery. The patient had functioned well and worked regularly until three years prior to admission. At that time, she experienced the sudden onset of a leaking cerebral aneurysm that required repair with the insertion of a metal clip. Postoperatively she had mild neurologic damage, but regained full use of her left side and full memory and returned to work. She had no personal or family history of psychiatric illness.

Approximately one year prior to admission, the patient began to have chest pain on exertion, which culminated in a myocardial infarction. She made a good recovery and after six months returned to work. Shortly thereafter she developed angina, bilateral arm paresthesias, and shortness of breath. She was placed on propranolol (Inderal) and, because of the results of angiography and lack of resolution of symptoms, surgery was recommended. At the time of admission, she seemed withdrawn, cried easily, and was especially bothered by insomnia and nightmares. She had a morbid fear of the "clip slipping off" while she was under anesthesia. It was unclear whether the Inderal or her reaction to her incapacitating illness and the projected surgery was the initiating mechanism of her depressive symptomatology. The Inderal, therefore, was discontinued, but her symptoms persisted. The patient finally agreed to surgical intervention and underwent a triple coronary bypass successfully. Postoperatively she continued to experience insomnia, dysphoria, crying spells, anorexia, and considerable incisional pain. She had suicidal ideation but no plan. Psychotherapeutic sessions while she was still in the hospital focused on the disability precipitated by her heart disease, her consequent major financial concerns, and the fear that she would be unable to return to work and support herself as she had in the past. On discharge she was given the diagnosis of depression secondary to physical illness, and follow-up treatment was recommended. The patient, however, was negativistic, refused active psychiatric intervention, and was quite withdrawn socially. Her depressed mood continued for approximately six months postoperatively, at which time at a follow-up medical clinic visit she described feeling well physically, more settled financially, and more sociable with her friends and family, with no complaints of depression.

During the sessions with the patient in the hospital, it became clear that she had never dealt with the "insult" of the first illness, the leaking cerebral aneurysm. The onset of the second illness necessitated a complete reevaluation of her image of herself and her physical limitations. Six months after surgery, her symptoms of depression had resolved and she was making appropriate plans to readjust her life to these limitations.

DEPRESSION AND DRUG THERAPY

For the clinician to assess the etiology of a depression in a patient he is currently treating pharmacologically for a diagnosed medical or psychiatric illness, he must be cognizant of a number of factors. McClelland has noted that there is almost always multifactorial causation of psychiatric reactions to drug use.[42]

One factor always to be considered is the patient's reaction to having the diagnosed illness. Depression is a natural response to the loss of function imposed by illness. Another factor noted with increasing frequency is that patients who have had a previous episode of depression are more likely to develop a depressive illness while taking certain drugs. Oral contraceptives[46] and reserpine[26] have been especially implicated. A history of previous affective illness, therefore, should be considered in planning drug therapy and assessing drug response.

The age of a patient has some impact on the clinical picture. Elderly patients frequently develop depressive complaints. Not only are they more likely to be suffering from psychological losses and debilitating diseases, but they also may be taking a large number of drugs for these illnesses, which may result in depressive or sedative side effects.[54] In a survey of 1,042 patients on medication, Hurwitz noted that 118 developed adverse reactions. Of these 118, 18.6% were taking five or fewer drugs per day, while 81.4% were taking six or more drugs per day.[31]

Often a patient may complain of drowsiness, lack of energy, and social withdrawal and may show evidence of apathy with motor and speech retardation while on drug therapy. These are symptoms commonly attributed to depression, but they may also be associated with the use of drugs that cause CNS sedation. Symptoms may be due to overmedication, the side effect of a therapeutic dosage of a drug, or drug interaction. Although drug interactions are not notable causes of depression,[54] drugs with the property of CNS sedation may interact with other drugs having that same property, resulting in markedly increased sedation. Since such drugs (e.g., bedtime hypnotics, antianxiety agents, antidepressants, narcotics, alcohol, antihistamines, antihypertensives, and a rash of over-the-counter drugs) are widely used, the likelihood of sedation occurring secondary to drug use is considerable. A concise drug history, including daily dosage, is essential in order to distinguish sedation from depressive symptomatic complaints.

Salzman and Shader point out that depressive symptoms in a patient taking multiple drugs may be the early harbinger of a toxic delirium.[54] The rapid development of an acute confusional state differentiates this condition from an actual affective disorder.

A host of other nondrug variables, including metabolic differences, personality structure, socioeconomic class, and various environmental factors, may contribute to adverse drug reaction.

Although approximately 200 specific drugs have been implicated as possible causes of depression,[67] only a few groups of drugs have been associated with any frequency. These are (1) oral contraceptives, (2) antihypertensive agents, and (3) psychotropic drugs.

There is no specific mechanism to explain the development of depression secondary to the use of these drugs, but a review of the biochemical aspects of affective disorders raises some plausible hypotheses. Whitloch and Evans[67] have suggested that any drug depleting levels of dopamine, norepinephrine, and 5-hydroxytryptamine (5-HT),[57] drugs that augment the levels and availability of acetylcholine in the brain,[32] or drugs that potentiate the activity of monoamine oxidase may, in certain circumstances, cause depression.

ORAL CONTRACEPTIVES

It has been estimated that 5% to 7% of women taking oral contraceptives develop symptoms of depression.[36] There are a few reported cases of psychosis associated with use of these drugs,[33] and in one study psychiatric symptoms occurred with sufficient severity in 10% of patients to warrant changing to another form of contraception.[40] It has long been suggested that drug factors alone may engender depressive symptomatology. On the other hand, some recent studies have suggested that the incidence of depression among users of oral contraceptives is no higher than among matched controls not taking such medication.[18] The literature on this topic is replete with contradictory studies, not only because of problems associated with research design and assessment of data, but also because of the complexity and psychological significance of nondrug factors that are inherent to the controversial and emotionally laden area of birth control.

Parry and Rush reviewed the literature on biologic mechanisms of oral contraceptives and noted that oral contraceptives affect the metabolism of tryptophan, a precursor of serotonin, by several mechanisms, with the end result that less tryptophan is available for conversion to serotonin and tryptamine in the brain.[48] This depletion of brain serotonin supports the catecholamine theory. Norepinephrine, vitamin, and endocrine metabolism are also altered by oral contraceptives, which may explain additional biochemical mechanisms contributing to the reduced level of neurotransmitters in the brain.

Clinicians continue to observe the onset of depressive symptoms in a significant number of patients taking oral contraceptives. Whether the predominant factor involved is biochemical or psychological has not been elucidated. More than likely, the multifactorial theory of causation is more significant here than with most drugs. Nonetheless, the evidence strongly suggests that oral contraceptives do affect the level of neurotransmitter amines in the brain, which may play a significant role in the development of depression in these patients.

ANTIHYPERTENSIVE DRUGS

Reserpine was introduced into Western medicine in the early 1950s. From the onset of its use as an antihypertensive agent, a greater than expected incidence of depression was observed in patients taking this drug. Goodwin et al.[26] reviewed the literature on the association of reserpine and depression and noted, first, that most depressions occurred when the dose of reserpine was greater than 0.5 mg/day, and, second, that most patients had been taking the drug for a year or more when the depression developed. The single most reliable predictor of the development of depressive symptomatology was a past history of affective illness.[26] The biochemical mechanism of reserpine's action on the CNS is its ability to deplete brain amines. It has been strongly suggested that this central action of the drug accounts for the tranquilizing properties and depression, although this is not well established. Its antihypertensive action has been shown to be related to the depletion of norepinephrine stores in peripheral adrenergic nerve endings.

The work with reserpine has provided the model not only for the catecholamine theory of depression but for subsequent understanding of the relationship between antihypertensive drugs and depression. It continues to be commonly noted that many patients on antihypertensive medication develop not only complaints of drowsiness and sedation but full-blown depressions.

Table 3–1 presents an overview of the commonly used antihypertensive agents and their association with depressive symptomatology. A few considerations in the use of these drugs are of major importance. The tricyclic antidepressants are believed to antagonize the hypotensive properties of the adrenergic neuron-blocking agents such as guanethidine, and the result is antagonism of the antihypertensive effects of these agents. Sympathomimetic amines and phenothiazines may act as antagonists in a similar manner.[43] The effects of clonidine (Catapres) may also be inhibited by tricyclic antidepressants.[43] Methyldopa (Aldomet) has been noted to increase the toxicity of haloperidol and lithium.[43] In choosing antihypertensive drugs for the elderly, O'Malley and O'Brien[47] suggest that since this group seems more prone than others to the unwanted CNS effects of these drugs, either a thiazide diuretic or a beta-adrenergic blocking agent is the drug of first choice.

This overview of antihypertensive drugs is particularly important because of the frequent occurrence of both hypertension and depression in a large percentage of patients. The clinician must decide whether either or both conditions are sufficiently debilitating to merit pharmacologic treatment. Some authors suggest that a combination of thiazide and antidepressant drugs be tried prior to using other antihypertensive agents that may

TABLE 3–1.—ANTIHYPERTENSIVE DRUGS PRODUCING DEPRESSIVE SYMPTOMS

CHARACTERISTIC	GROUP I PREDOMINANTLY ALPHA-RECEPTOR AGONISTS	GROUP II GANGLIONIC BLOCKING AGENTS	GROUP III ADRENERGIC NEURON-BLOCKING AGENTS	GROUP IV RECEPTOR-BLOCKING AGENTS
Site of action	CNS	Autonomic nervous system	Peripheral sympathetic nervous system (postganglionic nerve ending)	Peripheral sympathetic nervous system
Physiologic response	Decreases sympathetic tone	Vasodilates the arterioles	Depletes norepinephrine in the adrenergic nerve ending	Decreases sympathetic response
Clinical effect	Decreases arterial pressure	Decreases systolic and diastolic pressure (limited clinical use)	Decreases systolic more than diastolic pressure	Alpha blockers: used in diagnostic testing Beta blockers: balanced reduction in elevated diastolic pressure
Representative drugs	Methyldopa (Aldomet), clonidine (Catapres)	Hydralazine (Apresoline), prazapin (Minipress)	Reserpine (Serapsil), guanethidine (Ismelin)	Alpha blocker: phentolamine (Regitine) Beta blocker: propranolol (Inderal) metoprolal
Association with depression	Common: cross blood-brain barrier	Minimal or none	Reserpine (common), crosses blood-brain barrier; guanethidine (uncommon), does not cross blood-brain barrier	Propranolol (Inderal), beta blocker; common

exacerbate the depressive syndrome. Greenblatt and Shader suggest that doxepin may be useful in patients receiving guanethidine-like drugs, since it does not appear to antagonize the antihypertensive effects of guanethidine.[27] Consultation and cooperation between generalists and specialists are often necessary to effectively treat patients with both conditions.

PSYCHOTROPIC DRUGS

Many patients with diagnosed schizophrenic illness who are being treated with antipsychotic drugs develop symptoms of depression.[4] This may be due to a superimposed affective illness, which should be treated with concomitant antidepressant drugs. Antipsychotic drugs of the aliphatic derivatives (chlorpromazine) and piperidine derivatives (thioridazine) are especially likely to have prominent sedative effects that resemble depression. Reduction of dosage frequently clears the symptomatology. The development of parkinsonian side effects secondary to antipsychotics may also initially resemble depression; anti-Parkinson medication added to the patient's regime may clarify the condition. The "postpsychotic depression" that occurs during the reintegration process following psychotic decompensation must also be considered as a possible etiology of depression in a patient on major tranquilizers.[52] McClelland suggests that more studies are needed to clarify the etiology of depression in this group of patients because of the multiple factors involved.[42]

Some studies have noted the worsening of depression in patients on antidepressant drugs.[54] Many of the common sedative drugs, including alcohol, have been implicated in precipitating or exacerbating depressive symptomatology. An increasing body of literature associates the development of depression with the benzodiazapines.[53] The data are particularly relevant, as formerly it was common practice to treat mild anxiety/depressive symptoms with the common minor tranquilizers. Again, more data are needed to ascertain the source of the depression in the entire group of patients on psychotropic medication.

CASE 3.—A 34-year-old married white housewife, mother of three, developed hypertension after her last pregnancy. She began having episodes of increased blood pressure (up to 220/120) associated with severe headaches. She was placed on Regroton (50 mg of chlorthalidone and 0.25 mg of reserpine) and Aldactone (spironolactone), 25 mg, per day. She was well stabilized on this regime, and her blood pressure was usually around 135/80. She had no previous or family history of depression.

After three years on this drug regimen, the patient noted the gradual onset of dysphoric feelings, mild withdrawal, social isolation, decreased initiative, decreased sexual interest, and hypersomnia. The symptoms worsened and she became increasingly irritable, with frequent crying spells. She denied suicidal ideation. Upon reading an article in the newspaper about the side effects of hypertensive drugs, she discontinued the Regroton on her own initiative. She then informed her physician of her action. She remained off hypertensive medication for several weeks, during which time her blood pressure increased and the headaches returned, but the depression lifted. She was placed on propranolol (Inderal) and a diuretic and has remained normotensive without any symptoms of depression for four years.

The patient and her doctor clearly associated the onset of her depression with her drug therapy. With a change in medication, her symptoms abated.

DEPRESSION MASKED BY COMPLAINTS OF PHYSICAL ILLNESS

Many patients, after physical and laboratory evaluation, are found to have no organic basis for their complaint, but persist in describing their distress in terms of physical illness. In such patients further evaluation is imperative, and the final diagnosis is frequently one of depression—one that is masked but too often missed.

A masked depression (or a depression masked by physical complaints) is one in which the patient has symptoms of a somatic disturbance but denies a lowering of mood.[28] Some authors distinguish further between masked depression and a somatic or depressive equivalent. In masked depression, the physical symptoms are predominant, but careful clinical assessment reveals other parameters of depression, such as mood, appetite, or sleep disturbances. The depression is present and observable but often not recognized because the physical symptoms are much in the foreground and the diagnostician tends either to disregard other symptoms or to be unappreciative of their significance. Authors who use the term "depressive equivalent" describe a patient who has physical complaints but no depressive symptoms and no evidence of a depressive mood. These are not always clearly distinguishable categories, but an awareness of these terms and characteristics can contribute to more precise diagnosis and treatment.

The importance of masked depression in the spectrum of depressive illness is underlined by the observation that only one of every four or five depressed persons consults a psychiatrist.[39] It has been suggested that the ways in which depression is revealed are myriad, physical complaints being only one expression. Yet in this era, it is probably more socially acceptable to have a physical illness than an emotional one, and patients tend to bring their depression to the general physician rather than to the psychiatrist.

To diagnose a masked depression, the physician must be aware of its possibility, take a careful history (mindful of the usual parameters associated with depression), and observe the patient for supporting evidence.

A patient with masked depression usually visits a nonpsychiatric physician with somatic complaints that most often affect the CNS, gastrointestinal system, cardiovascular system, and musculoskeletal system. The chief complaints include lethargy, palpitations, abdominal pains or spasms, headache, backache, chest pains, and many vague and poorly defined somatic disturbances. Often patients give a history of multiple workups by other physicians and specialists. The patient persists with his complaints and is generally unconvinced that the physician has done sufficient tests or procedures merited by the illness.

In the initial interview, the physician must take some time and listen carefully to the somatic complaints and theories of illness that are of concern to the patient. This can help establish rapport, communicate interest, and enable the physician to obtain significant information more directly and less defensively.

Open-ended questions are most helpful. "Can you tell me about your sleep patterns?" is preferable to "Do you have insomnia?" If the patient gives insufficient information, it can be obtained later by direct questioning. The physician should explore the patient's sleep patterns, eating habits and appetite, interest in usual daily activities, variations in mood, alertness, and concentration, as well as recent significant losses. The patient may inadvertently acknowledge a loss of interest in his professional or social sphere, decreased sexual interest, or underlying feelings of pessimism. The feeling on the part of the patient that no doctor will find the source of his difficulty or that he will never be cured is also significant. Such phenomena strongly suggest dysphoric mood and depression.

The patient's medical and drug history should be carefully noted, as should the characterologic traits exhibited by the patient. Lesse has suggested that masked depression is often found in the obsessive personality—those who are precise, self-exacting, rigid, and demanding—because these patients are much more likely to allow themselves somatic symptoms than emotional ones.[37] A previous history of depression or a similar episode in the past, a family history of depressive illness, and some evidence of diurnal variation, especially the gradual alleviation of symptoms as the day progresses, all support the possibility of an underlying depression.

The diagnosis is made by establishing (1) the lack of an organic disorder to explain the physical complaint, and (2) the presence of the usual vegetative signs of depression, even though the patient denies feeling "depressed." Strengthening the diagnosis is evidence of a positive family history of depressive illness and diurnal fluctuations of the complaint. Positive response to therapeutic doses of antidepressant medication is confirmatory.

The differential diagnosis of a masked depression is often very complex, and the definitive diagnosis may take some time to establish. The presence of somatic symptoms not directly attributable to a specific organic disease is not an automatic indication of a masked depression. A masked depression is *not a specific diagnosis* but a clinical phenomenon. The clinical manifestations may be masking primary depressive illness, such as unipolar or bipolar disease, or may be an expression of a secondary affective disturbance. Since the symptoms peculiar to this phenomenon bridge both psychological and physical illness, the differential diagnosis includes a large number of possibilities.

The absence of organic disease must first be established. Next to be considered is the newly named group of illnesses in *DSM-III*, the "psychological factors affecting physical condition" category. These illnesses are the classic psychophysiologic or psychosomatic disorders of the past that are distinguished by the presence of demonstrable organic dysfunction or organic pathology, even though psychological factors are clearly evident. Factitious disorders (e.g., Munchausen's syndrome), in which the patient, because of severe intrapsychic conflicts, complains of a disorder but does not actually experience it, must be ruled out. The possibility of voluntarily contrived symptoms due to malingering must also be assessed. A most difficult group of disorders to distinguish from masked depression are the somatoform disorders. These disorders are characterized by physical complaints but no organic disease, and positive evidence that psychological factors play a significant role in their development. Somatization disorder (*DSM-III*), formerly Briquet's disease, has clear diagnostic criteria that distinguish it from masked depression.

Conversion disorder also has clear criteria that are readily distinguishable. These illnesses present some difficulties in assessment, however, and in a significant proportion of cases that occur in the absence of hysteria, a diagnosed medical or neurologic illness related to the symptom may eventually become manifest.[24] Psychogenic pain disorder (*DSM-III*) may often blur a somatic complaint of pain that is masking depression. Again, most helpful in distinguishing these two conditions is the finding of data supportive of a depressive condition.[22, 64] Hypochondriasis (*DSM-III*) must also be ruled out, although many clinicians feel it may be a mask for a variety of conditions, including depression. The last disorder that must be considered is the generalized anxiety disorder, the symptoms of which are far more discrete than the usual autonomic symptoms associated with masked depressive complaints.

Note should be made of dementia as a mask for depression in the elderly. It has been estimated that approximately 7% to 10% of patients who present with symptoms of early organic brain disease are in fact suffering from pseudodementia, a true depressive illness.[50]

Case 4. A 46-year-old man complained of having back pain for the past two years. He had been evaluated by specialists in orthopedics, physical medicine, and neurosurgery, none of whom could discern a physical basis for his complaint. His medical history revealed three prior episodes of severe depression with suicidal ideation, each of which culminated in hospitalization and treatment with electro-convulsive therapy. Additional interviewing revealed that with each illness resulting in hospitalization, his employment was terminated.

His recent complaint consisted essentially of pain in the lower back. He denied feelings of depression or recent significant loss. He acknowledged periodic insomnia and feeling better as the day went on. He had a family history of depressive illness. He was also aware that the threat of becoming seriously depressed was associated in his mind with a threat to his present employment status. The diagnosis of recurrent unipolar depression was given, antidepressant medication was initiated, and the patient improved.

This patient had a physical complaint for which no etiologic factor could be found. His history of depressive episodes in the past and positive family history raised the possibility of a masked depression. In addition, this patient had insomnia, diurnal variation in his symptomatology, mild loss of appetite, and increased irritability. These factors played a significant role in the current expression of his depression. It was seemingly acceptable to this man and his former employers that he have a physical illness, but his previous experience had taught him that a psychiatric illness could threaten his job status.

Treatment on an outpatient basis was successful, but the definitive diagnosis had been delayed for years because of the masking of the depression by his somatic complaint.

Symptoms of depression are frequently observed in the general patient population. Symptoms may be clear-cut expressions of a unipolar or bipolar affective illness that is readily diagnosed, or they may be a manifestation of another group of disorders. Depression may be the first evidence of an undiagnosed physical illness, a secondary reaction to a medical, surgical, or psychiatric illness, or a side effect of drug therapy for a medical or psychiatric illness. On occasion, the depression may not be readily apparent but masked by a somatic complaint. An approach to the clarification and definition of these varied manifestations of depression has been presented.

REFERENCES

1. Altshule M.D.: Nonpsychological causes of depression. *Med. Sci.* 16:36–40, 1965.
2. American Psychiatric Association: *Diagnostic and Statistical Manual of Mental Disorders*, ed. 3. Washington, D.C., APA, 1980.
3. Andreasen N.J., Noyes R., Hartford C.E., et al.: Management of emotional reactions in seriously burned adults. *N. Engl. J. Med.* 286:65–69, 1972.
4. Ayd F.J.: Drug induced depression: fact or fallacy? *N.Y. State J. Med.* 58:354, 1958.
5. Bennett R.L., et al.: Neuropsychiatric problems in systematic lupus erythematosus. *Br. Med. J.* 4:342–345, 1972.

6. Blazer D.G., Petrie W.M., Wilson W.P.: Affective psychoses following renal transplant. *Dis. Nerv. Syst.* 37:663–667, 1976.
7. Brown G.M.: Psychiatric and neurologic aspects of endocrine disease. *Hosp. Pract.* August 1975, pp. 71–79.
8. Carter F.S.: Treatment of depression associated with chronic gastrointestinal and cardiovascular disorders. *Psychosomatics* 9:314–318, 1968.
9. Castelnuovo-Tedesco P.: Organ transplant, body image, psychosis. *Psychoanal. Q.* 42:349–363, 1973.
10. Celesia G.G., Wanamaker W.M.: Psychiatric disturbances in Parkinson's disease. *Dis. Nerv. Syst.* 33:577–583, 1972.
11. Cleghorn R.A., Curtis G.C.: Psychosomatic accompaniments of latent and manifest depressive affect. *Can. Psych. Assoc. J.* 4:13–23, 1959.
12. Derogatis L.R., Abeloff M.D., Melisaratos N.: Psychological coping mechanisms and survival time in metastatic breast cancer. *J.A.M.A.* 242:1504–1508, 1979.
13. Dorfman W.: The relative effectiveness of different antidepressants in masked depression. *Psychosomatics* 3:101, 1962.
14. Dorfman W.: Depression and psychosomatic illness. *Psychother. Psychosom.* 23:87–93, 1974.
15. Dorpat T.L., et al.: The relationship of physical illness to suicide, in Resnick H.L.P. (ed.): *Suicidal Behaviors.* Boston, Little, Brown & Co., 1968.
16. Dowling R.H., Knox S.J.: Somatic symptoms in depressive illness. *Br. J. Psychiatry* 110:720–722, 1964.
17. Fawcett J.: Suicidal depression and physical illness. *J.A.M.A.* 219:1303–1306, 1972.
18. Fleming O., Seage C.P.: Incidence of depressive symptoms in users of the oral contraceptive. *Br. J. Psychiatry* 132:431–440, 1978.
19. Forester B.M., Kornfield D.S., Fleiss J.: Psychiatric aspects of radiotherapy. *Am. J. Psychiatry* 135:960–963, 1978.
20. Forrest A.J., Wolkind S.N.: Masked depression in men with low back pain. *Rheumatol. Rehabil.* 13:148–152, 1974.
21. Fras I., Litin E.M., Pearson S.S.: Comparison of psychiatric symptoms in carcinoma of the pancreas with those in some other intra-abdominal neoplasms. *Am. J. Psychiatry* 123:1553–1562, 1967.
22. Gade G.N., Hofeldt F.D., Treece G.L.: Diabetic neuropathic cachexia. *J.A.M.A.* 243:1160–1162, 1980.
23. Gatewood J.W., Organ L.H., Mead B.T.: Mental changes associated with hyperparathyroidism. *Am. J. Psychiatry* 132:129–132, 1975.
24. Gatfield P.D., Guze S.B.: Prognosis and differential diagnoses of conversion reactions. *Dis. Nerv. Syst.* 23:623–631, 1962.
25. Goldberg S., Smith C., Connell A.: Emotion-related gastritis. *Am. J. Gastroenterol.* 65:41–45, 1976.
26. Goodwin F.K., Ebert M.H., Bunney W.E.: Mental effects of reserpine in man: A review, in Shader R.I. (ed.): *Psychiatric Complications of Medical Drugs.* New York, Raven Press, 1972.
27. Greenblatt D.J., Shader R.I.: Psychotropic drugs in the general hospital, in Shader R.I. (ed.): *Manual of Medical Therapeutics.* Boston, Little, Brown & Co., 1975.
28. Harari E., Fail L.: Masked depression or missed depression? *Med. J. Aust.* 1:92–93, 1976.

29. Hare E.H.: The changing content of psychiatric illness. *J. Psychosom. Res.* 18:283–289, 1974.
30. Harrison T.R., et al.: *Principles of Internal Medicine*, ed. 9. Isselbacher K., et al. (eds.). New York, McGraw-Hill Book Co., 1980, p. 153.
31. Hurwitz N.: Predisposing factors in adverse reactions to drugs. *Br. Med. J.* 1:536–539, 1969.
32. Janowsky D.S., Davis J.M., El-Yousef M., et al.: A cholinergic-adrenergic hypothesis of mania and depression. *Lancet* 2:632–635, 1972.
33. Kane F.J.: Psychiatric reactions to oral contraceptives. *Am. J. Obstet. Gynecol.* 102:1053–1063, 1968.
34. Kielholz P. (ed.): *Masked Depression*. Bern, Hans Huber, Publishers, 1973.
35. Kral V.A.: Masked depression in middle aged men. *Can. Med. Assoc. J.* 79:1–5, 1958.
36. Depression and oral contraception, editorial. *Br. Med. J.* 4:127–128, 1970.
37. Lesse S.: Masked depression: A diagnostic and therapeutic problem. *Dis. Nerv. Syst.* 29:169–173, 1968.
38. Ling W., et al.: Depressive illness in childhood presenting as severe headache. *Am. J. Dis. Child.* 120:122–124, 1970.
39. Lopez-Ibor J.J.: Masked depression. *Br. J. Psychiatry* 120:245–258, 1972.
40. Malek-Ahmadi P., Behrmann P.J.: Depressive syndrome induced by oral contraceptives. *Dis. Nerv. Syst.* 37:406–408, 1976.
41. Markowitz M.: Acute intermittent porphyria. *Ann. Intern. Med.* 41:1170–1188, 1954.
42. McClelland H.A.: Psychiatric disorders, in Davis D.M. (ed.): *Textbook of Adverse Drug Reactions*. Oxford, England, Oxford University Press, 1977.
43. Drugs that cause psychiatric symptoms. *Med. Lett.* 19:21–24, 1977.
44. Murphy G.E.: The physician's responsibility for suicide. *Ann. Intern. Med.* 82:305–309, 1975.
45. Nakcagawa T., et al.: A clinical and psychophysiological study of depression in internal medicine. *Psychosomatics* 17:173–179, 1976.
46. Nilsson A., Almgren P.E.: Psychiatric symptoms of the post-partum period as related to use of oral contraceptives. *Br. Med. J.* 2:453–455, 1968.
47. O'Malley K., O'Brien E.: Management of hypertension in the elderly. *N. Engl. J. Med.* 302:1397–1401, 1980.
48. Parry B.L., Rush A.J.: Oral contraceptives and depressive symptomatology: Biologic mechanisms. *Compr. Psychiatry* 20:347–358, 1979.
49. Peteet J.R.: Depression in cancer patients. *J.A.M.A.* 241:1487–1489, 1979.
50. Raskin A., Shader R.I., Salzman C.: Pseudodementia of depression. *Psychopharmacol. Bull.* 14:64–66, 1978.
51. Reinfrank R.F.: Primary hyperparathyroidism with depression. *Arch. Intern. Med.* 108:606–610, 1961.
52. Roth S.S.: The seemingly ubiquitous depression following acute schizophrenic episodes: A neglected area of clinical discussion. *Am. J. Psychiatry* 127:51–58, 1970.
53. Ryan H.F., Merrill F.B., Scott G.E., et al.: Increase in suicidal thoughts and tendencies: Association with diazepam therapy. *J.A.M.A.* 203:1137–1139, 1968.
54. Salzman C., Shader R.I.: Depression in the elderly. *J. Am. Geriatr. Soc.* 26:303–308, 1968.
55. Sartorius N.: Depressive illness as a worldwide problem, in Kielholz P. (ed.):

(ed.): *Depression in Everyday Practice*. Bern, Hans Huber, Publishers, 1974.

56. Schapira K.: Deceptive presentations of depression. *Br. J. Clin. Pract.* 29:501–504, 1972.

57. Schildkraut J.J.: *Neuropsychopharmacology and the Affective Disorders*. Boston, Little, Brown & Co., 1970.

58. Shader R.I. (ed.): *Manual of Medical Therapeutics*. Boston, Little, Brown & Co., 1975.

59. Simpson F., Waal-Manning H.: Hypertension and depression: Interrelated problems in therapy. *J. R. Coll. Physicians Lond.* 6:14–24, 1971.

60. Snaith R., McCoubrie M.: Antihypertensive drugs and depression. *Psychol. Med.* 4:393–398, 1974.

61. Stoeckle J.D., Davidson G.E.: Bodily complaints and other symptoms of depressive reaction. *J.A.M.A.* 180:134–139, 1962.

62. Sullivan B.J.: Adjustment in diabetic adolescent girls. *Psychosom. Med.* 41:127–138, 1979.

63. Thomas F.B., Mazzaferri E.L., Skillman T.G.: Apathetic thyrotoxicosis: A distinctive clinical and laboratory entity. *Ann. Intern. Med.* 72:679–685, 1970.

64. Turkington R.W.: Depression masquerading as diabetic neuropathy. *J.A.M.A.* 243:1147–1150, 1980.

65. Udell B., Hornstra R.K.: Presenting problems and diagnosis. *Compr. Psychiatry* 17:437–445, 1976.

66. Walters A.: Psychogenic regional headache. *Headache* 13:107–116, 1973.

67. Whitlock F.A., Evans L.E.: Drugs and depression. *Drugs* 15:53–71, 1978.

68. Wishnie H.A., Hackett T.P., Cassem N.H.: Psychological hazards of convalescence following myocardial infarction. *J.A.M.A.* 215:1292–1296, 1971.

69. Wolf S.R.: Emotional reactions to hysterectomy. *Postgrad. Med.* 47:165–169, 1970.

70. Woodruff R.A., Clayton P.J., Guze S.B.: Hysteria: Studies of diagnosis, outcome and prevalence. *J.A.M.A.* 215:425–428, 1971.

4

GRIEF, MOURNING, AND
AFFECTIVE STATES

JONATHAN LEWIS, M.D.

THE NEWLY BEREAVED WIDOW is easily identified. She sits at home among her friends and with a tense smile acknowledges their attempts to console her. A handkerchief is clutched tightly in her hands. She sighs deeply and relaxes momentarily until another friend enters the room. Then her composure evaporates as a flood of memories and emotions overwhelm her, and she sobs as she grasps the newcomer in a grief-filled embrace. The comment is overheard: the death is unbelievable and so unexpected. The widow nods, responding that she still feels numb and cannot quite believe it herself though she knows it to be so.

The days that follow are difficult for the widow. Her mind is filled with thoughts of her dead husband. She paces, seemingly aimlessly, thinking that life now has little meaning if it no longer includes her lifelong partner. She goes over every detail of their past in her mind. Roaming through the house, she catches sight of a favorite photograph of him and dissolves in tears. But as days pass, the tears come less frequently, sleep is welcomed again, and her appetite returns. The widow resumes some of her previous activities, returns to work, and begins socializing. In time she may even remarry, but she will probably never forget her first husband. She will keep some treasured items of his in a special place. She may experience accesses of grief on certain occasions, such as anniversaries. She will never be completely free of his memory.

This is the familiar face of grief. Bereavement, after all, is part of the human condition, and anyone who lives long enough will eventually experience it. But what is grief? And what is its relation to depressive conditions? Is the woman portrayed above related in any way to the patient who, severely depressed, sits ruminating, wringing his hands, crying for no apparent reason, and crucifying himself on a cross of uncommitted crimes? Or is she, as some believe, the model of a mildly depressed person reacting to an identifiable event? These questions have usually been answered in two ways. One view is that grief is in many ways very similar to a mild form of depression. The alternate view holds that grief, while superficially resembling depression, is a unique entity with a clearly identifiable cause and typical course and outcome. Let us briefly consider these positions and the history of their development.

HISTORICAL BACKGROUND

Perhaps the best-known work comparing grief and depression is Freud's 1917 classic paper, "Mourning and Melancholia."[16] Freud considered grief and mourning to be a natural response to the loss of a loved person and justified the comparison of mourning to melancholia on the basis of their clinical similarities. Indeed, they appeared to Freud to be identical except for one characteristic. Here it is worth quoting Freud, as the clarity of his statement cannot be surpassed:

> The distinguishing mental features of melancholia are a profoundly painful dejection, cessation of interest in the outside world, loss of the capacity to love, inhibition of all activity, and a lowering of the self-regarding feelings to a degree that finds utterance in self-reproaches and self-revilings, and culminates in a delusional expectation of punishment. This picture becomes a little more intelligible when we consider that, with one exception, the same traits are met with in mourning. The disturbance of self-regard is absent in mourning; but otherwise the features are the same.[16 (p. 244)]

Freud then described other ways in which grief and depression differ at a deep psychological level. For example, he concurred with an observation first made by Karl Abraham that grief is evoked by an external loss, while depression is associated with a loss within.[1] This differentiation between internal and external is reflected in the mourner's view that the world outside himself is diminished, while the melancholic feels that it is himself who has become worthless, or as Freud put it, "In mourning it is the world which has become poor and empty; in melancholia it is the ego itself."[16 (p. 246)]

Freud stated further that a successful outcome in mourning consisted of a great diminution in the strength of the emotional bond to the deceased which exists in the mind of the bereaved. In contrast to this, the melancholic tenaciously clings to the lost love object through a psychological incorporation, ensuring that although the loved person is lost, "the love-relation need not be given up."[16 (p. 249)]

Our first attempt to determine if grief is in any way related to depression has resulted in a certain degree of ambiguity. Freud essentially stated that while grief and depression are alike in appearance, their deeper psychological processes differ greatly. Some forbearance is required of the reader as we pursue in some detail the development of the psychoanalytic arguments. For what happened next was that Karl Abraham, always deferring to the genius of his mentor, nonetheless stood Freud on his head.

Whereas Freud viewed the goal of the "work" of mourning as being emotional disengagement—the decathexis—of the bereaved from the loved person, Abraham described the opposite. Successful mourning, he stated, resulted in the introjection of the loved object, just as Freud had described for melancholia.[2] In this way the mourner was consoled by the fact that the lost love-object was now inside the self, preserving the previous relationship and protecting it from being lost again. Abraham thus postulated that the psychological processes in mourning and melancholia were identical and that the differences between the two entities resided more in the content, or nature, of the object relationship between the bereaved and the lost person. When this relationship was intensely ambivalent—that is, when hateful feelings existed in a degree approaching or perhaps even surpassing the loving emotions directed at the object—the result was melancholia. When the ambivalently regarded object was introjected, the hostility originally experienced for the other was now turned upon part of the self. In normal mourning, love outweighs feelings of hatred and the process of introjection proceeds without the development of melancholia. Abraham thus took the position that not only do grief and depression possess clinical similarities, but they share a single psychological process.

The early psychoanalytic studies of mourning provided the first model of what today might be called the normal grief reaction. Fifty years passed before anyone tried to demonstrate Freud's assertion that grief was similar to depression in its clinical appearance. In 1968, Clayton et al. stated that the findings of their prospective study of an unselected population of bereaved subjects "corroborate[d] some of Freud's statements," e.g., that the characteristics of mourning include painful dejection, loss of interest in the outside world, loss of the capacity to form new relationships, a turning away from activities not associated with the deceased, and the absence of disturbances in self-esteem.[10 (p. 176)] Clayton and her colleagues discovered that only three symptoms—depressed mood, sleep disturbance, and crying—occurred in more than half the bereaved subjects studied. They concluded that normal grief could be classified as a reactive depression but that it could be distinguished from a major affective illness. They maintained that there was a normal depression of bereavement which was the model of a mild, agitated depressive reaction to a clear-cut loss.[7, 9–11]

This position was incorporated into the third edition of the American Psychiatric Association's *Diagnostic and Statistical Manual of Mental Disorders (DSM-III)*, a volume to which Clayton contributed.[5] "Uncomplicated bereavement" is categorized in *DSM-III* as one of the conditions that can be a "focus of attention or treatment" without an emotional disorder being present. It is noted that a normal grief reaction frequently has the same characteristics as a "full-depressive syndrome," typified by feelings of sadness, anorexia, weight loss, and insomnia. Yet this syndrome is sharply differentiated from the category of affective disorders, especially major depression. Thus the position taken in *DSM-III* on the relation of grief to depression is quite consistent with that of Clayton's group.

Earlier editions of the manual had no provision for classifying normal bereavement reactions. In terms of the diagnostic criteria set forth in the *DSM-I* and *DSM-II*, only pathologic grief reactions could be categorized, and these were subsumed under the heading of "adjustment reaction."[3, 4] This diagnostic rubric, carried over in *DSM-III* as "adjustment disorder," is conceptualized as a maladaptation to an identifiable stressor that impairs functioning for a period of time, limited by the extent and duration of the stress. Except for disturbed reactions that become chronic or that precipitate some other psychiatric disorder, pathologic grief reactions could be placed in this category.

We have briefly touched on the development of the idea that grief and depression share many clinical features and that grief may be classified as a mild form of depression. This idea can be traced from Freud, by way of Clayton and colleagues, to the official pronouncements of the American Psychiatric Association. We now turn to the alternate approach, which views grief as a unique entity.

The description of the natural history of grief originated with Lindemann's now classic article, "Symptomatology and Management of Acute Grief."[18] Lindemann studied 101 bereaved patients, using a series of psychiatric interviews for each patient. The content of the interviews was recorded and analyzed for the presence of symptoms and for changes in mental status over time. The patients were drawn from four populations: (1) patients in psychiatric treatment at the time they were bereaved, (2) relatives of medically ill patients who died in the hospital, (3) relatives of servicemen who died in World War II, and (4) relatives of victims of a disastrous fire in a Boston nightclub (the Coconut Grove fire). Many of the subjects of the study had a grief reaction severe enough to require hospitalization, although the percentage of hospitalized subjects in the study is not specified by Lindemann. Nonetheless, he noted that the presentation of acute grief was "remarkably uniform" among all types of patients. Lindemann identified a pathognomonic somatic complex in grief consisting of "sensations of somatic distress occurring in waves lasting from twenty minutes to an hour at a time, a feeling of tightness in the throat, choking with shortness of breath, need for sighing, an empty feeling in the abdomen, lack of muscular power, and an intense subjective distress described as tension or mental pain."[18 (p. 141)] In addition to these symptoms, Lindemann found that there consistently appeared in the mourner (1) a preoccupation with the image of the deceased, (2) feelings of guilt and hostility, and (3) loss of typical patterns of conduct. A less prevalent finding, and one which Lindemann believed to be associated with more pathologic grief reactions, was the "appearance of traits of the deceased in the behavior of the bereaved, especially symptoms shown during the last illness."[18 (p. 142)] This last is a manifestation of introjection or identification, while the preoccupation with the image of the deceased is comparable to what Freud termed a "hypercathexis" of the love-object. Lindemann's work, however, was in the tradition of descriptive psychiatry rather than psychoanalysis. His contribution consisted of a highly accurate description of typical phenomena of grief and set the stage for a consideration of grief as a natural human reaction deserving study in its own right. From this work came the conception of normal grief as a reaction to loss that proceeds in a typical and predictable manner over time.

NORMAL GRIEF

The normal grief reaction was conceptualized as an adaptational process involving specific stages by John Bowlby and George Pollock. Bowlby[8] identified these stages as (1) protest, (2) despair, and (3) detachment, while Pollock[26] described phases of the mourning process which he identified as (1) shock, (2) grief reaction, and (3) separation reaction. Despite the differences in terminology, the description of the process by both authors is similar and can be summarized as follows. The initial reaction to the news of a bereavement is shock, numbness, or disbelief; the fact of death is disavowed. This is followed by an agitated protest of the death and a yearning for the lost object. The intense psychic and somatic pain described by Lindemann is experienced during this stage. There follows a stage of despair, sorrow, and disorganization, and finally, if the process is successfully completed, there results a phase of reorganization in which the bereaved regains the capacity to develop new attachments.

Basing his work on Bowlby's formulations, C. Murray Parkes, in a series of studies, further elaborated the concept of grief as a process.[23, 24] The process as described by Parkes usually begins with a period of numbness and disbelief that lasts from several hours to a few weeks. Forty-five percent of Parkes's subjects reported a feeling of numbness upon learning the news of a death, and 75% stated that they had difficulty accepting the death. The process then becomes dominated by agitation and waves of psychic distress. In a passage that confirms Lindemann's description, Parkes stated, "The most characteristic feature of grief is not prolonged depression but acute and episodic 'pangs'. . . . Pangs of grief begin within a few hours or days of bereavement and usually reach a peak of severity within five to fourteen days."[23] (p. 39) Parkes differentiates clearly between feelings of grief and depression, in contrast to the position of Clayton and the *DSM-III*.

Parkes emphasized the episodic nature of the psychic pain in grief and referred to it as a "restless pining for the lost object."[24] He attributed this behavior to a biologically based impulse to search for the missing person. This phase is characterized by the symptoms of restlessness, crying, and irritability, as if the bereaved were crying out in alarm and protest in response to separation, as animals and children do when deserted. Insomnia, anorexia, and social withdrawal are also found predominantly in this period, and the bereaved is preoccupied by an image of the deceased in his yearning and searching behavior. The process continues into a phase of disorganization and despair as the bereaved gives up the hope of recovering the dead person, and achieves resolution in the phase of reorganization. These phases are not distinct but shade into one another, with various symptoms predominating at different times. Parkes found that in most people, even a year after their bereavement, the "process of grieving was still going on, and, although the principal features were all past their peak, there was no sense in which grief could be said to have finished."[22] (p. 464)

Parkes and Bowlby contend that the grief process is phylogenetically based and has adaptive significance. In the context of separation, the agitated crying out and searching behavior serves the purpose of reuniting the organism with the lost object. In the special case of separation through death, reunion is impossible, but the process nonetheless persists and becomes elaborated in a set of culturally determined mourning rites and rituals. Pollock sees the mourning process as a form of psychological adaptation in which the internal psychic milieu is brought into conformity with external reality. This view is consistent with that of the early analysts, who also felt that an alteration in the internal world must take place in mourning.

PATHOLOGIC GRIEF

The normal process of grief and mourning may be distributed in a multitude of ways, but these disturbances fall into two basic categories.[21] Grief can act as a general, nonspecific life stress and, as such, may affect an individual much as would any other stressor. The resulting psychic disequilibrium may, if severe enough, precipitate a psychiatric illness, a psychosomatic reaction, or social maladjustment. Alternatively, a disturbed response in bereavement may be specifically related to the grief reaction itself. In this instance, any of the separate components or stages of the grief reaction may be altered, intensified, or prolonged. Thus, a psychiatric or physical illness that occurs soon after bereavement may be dynamically and specifically linked to the grief reaction, or the stress of bereavement may simply be one contributor among a number of factors that result in mental or physical impairment.

An unusual variant of pathologic grief is described by Helene Deutsch in "Absence of Grief."[12] Deutsch reported the lack of any discernible reaction to death in both children and adults, but it was her conviction that "unmanifested grief will be found expressed to the full in some way or another."[12 (p. 13)]

The normal grief reaction as described above consists of somatic, psychological, and social components, any of which can be disturbed in a pathologic grief reaction. In the somatic realm, the death of a loved person has been linked, both specifically and generally, to the precipitation of the whole gamut of psychosomatic disorders, as well as to illnesses not generally considered psychogenic in origin. For example, Fedders[14] reported a case of acute intermittent porphyria, the two most severe episodes of which closely followed upon the deaths of the patient's niece and maternal grandfather. Lindemann,[19] in a study of patients with ulcerative colitis, found that the onset of the colitis in 26 of 45 subjects had been preceded closely in time by the death of a person significant for the patient. Stamm and Drapkin[30] described a case of severe and complicated asthma in a man whose son died of a crushing injury to the chest incurred in an automobile accident in which the father had been driving. They believed that the asthmatic wheezing represented an identification with the dead son and his injury and, additionally, served as a symbolic punishment for the father. This last example is an illustration of a specific reaction to bereavement that is dynamically related to the death.

In a study of 28 cases of pathologic grief, Wretmark[33] found 4 cases in which the symptom complex was dominated by somatic disturbances, including peptic ulcer, asthma, eczema, and diarrhea. Volkan[31] described boils as a reaction to bereavement. Cases of urticaria, hematemesis, and gross tremors in response to the stress of bereavement have been seen by this author, the first of which is described here.

CASE 1.—A 30-year-old woman came to the emergency department with a generalized pruritic urticaria. She had no previous history of allergy, hives, or other skin disorder. Her father had died two weeks earlier, and the day after his death she developed a rash, which subsequently worsened. She was unable to cry after her father's death and felt herself to be "crying through my skin." In the course of the evaluation, it became apparent that her inability to cry was associated with the mechanism of denial. Reasoning backward, if she did not cry, then her father was not really dead. However, her skin betrayed the underlying conflict between denial and the acceptance of reality. The inhibition of weeping was associated with the appearance of "weeping" lesions of the skin as a manifestation of this conflict.

Many other illnesses have been linked to the period of bereavement, including cancer, thyrotoxicosis, leukemia, coronary thrombosis, lupus erythematosus, congestive heart failure, and diabetes.[13, 21, 27, 29] Occasionally, habit patterns change, resulting in alcoholism or obesity in a bereaved person.

CASE 2.—A 32-year-old woman gained 20 lb in excess of her usual weight after the death of her father. The father had suffered from cancer, and during his illness his weight fell from 220 to 140 lb. The daughter, after her weight gain, weighed 140 lb. Thus, she symbolically kept her father alive in herself by partial identification with him, duplicating his weight at the time of his death.

In the sphere of social behavior, the most notable alteration following the death of a significant person is the development of delinquency in adolescents as a manifestation of unexpressed grief.[13] Shoor and Speed identified 12 such cases and reported that the delinquent actions ceased in those adolescents in whom the mourning processes could be initiated and carried to completion in therapy.[28] This finding, as well as the resolution of other types of symptoms with successful treatment of the underlying grief reaction, confirms Deutsch's contention that all unresolved grief is given expression in some form and that the process of mourning must be initiated and worked through if symptoms are to be alleviated.[12]

In the psychological sphere, grief reactions have precipitated or exacerbated every possible psychiatric syndrome. These are considered in the next section, with special attention given to affective disorders.

GRIEF AND PSYCHIATRIC DISTURBANCE

Freud stated that "although mourning involves grave departures from the normal attitudes to life, it never occurs to us to regard it as a pathological condition and to refer it to medical treatment. We rely on its being overcome after a certain lapse of time, and we look upon any interference with it as useless or even harmful."[16 (p. 244)] Indeed, disturbances in the reaction to bereavement serious enough to require treatment are relatively rare. Clayton et al.,[10, 11] in their studies of normal grief, found that fewer than 1% of their subjects sought psychiatric care as a direct result of their response to bereavement. Similar studies consistently confirm the finding that the incidence of pathologic grief reaction is 1% or less.

The problem can be viewed from another perspective. In surveying patients admitted to a psychiatric clinic, Parkes found that six times as many patients as expected had been bereaved in the six months preceding their admission.[20] These bereaved patients constituted approximately 3% of the total. The implication of Parkes's study is that the stress of bereavement may contribute, in a nonspecific way, to the precipitation of a psychiatric illness. In a study of the relation between significant life events and the onset of depressive illness, Paykel et al.[25] found that separations of all types, including death, divorce, and children leaving home, were significantly more frequent in the six months prior to the onset of a depressive illness when depressed patients were compared with a control group. Although this study confounds grief with other types of separation, it tends to confirm Parkes's findings.

These studies refer to the nonspecific, stressful quality of bereavement, which tends to precipitate psychiatric illness in predisposed persons. Additionally, a psychiatric illness may result during the period of bereavement, consisting of a specific distortion of the grief reaction itself and producing chronic grief, inhibited or delayed grief, or exaggerated grief reactions. These categories are not mutually exclusive. Thus, a nonspecific psychiatric syndrome may occur in the place of a grief reaction so that an inhibited or delayed grief reaction is coincident with the onset of the disturbance.

CASE 3.—The mother of the patient described in Case 1 died seven years before the father. The patient was unable to cry after her mother's death and became agitated and anxious, requiring treatment with ataraxics. Several months later, while walking home from work, she suddenly thought, "My mother is really dead," and broke into a torrent of tears. Soon afterward her anxiety abated. In this instance a delayed and inhibited grief reaction was in some way replaced or manifested by a psychoneurotic condition.

Parkes states that the normal preoccupation of the bereaved with thoughts of death and disease appears to predispose susceptible persons to neurotic symptoms such as phobias concerning death and sickness, obsessional rituals, hypochondriasis, and panic attacks. Although the neurotic symptoms are stimulated by reminders of the dead person, the symptoms themselves in no way differ from neurotic symptoms arising for other reasons.

CASE 4.—A 23-year-old woman took to her bed one week before her father's death. He had been ill for many years with a crippling neurologic condition which had rendered him helpless and bedridden. During his last hospitalization, his respirations were mechanically assisted and he expressed great anxiety about not being able to catch his breath. His daughter developed many physical symptoms, all of which could be traced to an identification with the father's symptoms during his long illness and final hospitalization. For example, she experienced muscular weakness, paresthesias, and dizziness, mimicking his neurologic condition. She had panic attacks during which she felt she would suffocate. During episodes of derealization, she felt as if the room was tilting and that she was separated from the immediate reality, in her "space world." Her symptoms were often precipitated by reminders of her father, and any emerging feelings of grief were almost immediately replaced by one of the neurotic symptoms or by erotic or aggressive fantasies. In this case, a panoply of neurotic symptoms developed, while overt signs of grief were both repressed and suppressed by the patient.

Even schizophrenic symptoms may appear in the absence of grief. Volkan described a case of pathologic grief in the guise of a paranoid reaction.[32] The patient's symptoms consisted of suspiciousness, paranoid delusions, and somatic complaints. When it was discovered that the onset of these symptoms coincided with the death of his younger half brother, the treatment was focused on this issue. During the course of treatment, it was discovered that the paranoid delusions were specifically related to fantasies about the half brother's death. As therapy progressed, the patient was able to renew an arrested grief reaction, and with the initiation of mourning, the paranoid symptoms resolved.

Turning to the relationship between grief and affective illness, an interesting finding emerges from the literature. Contrary to what might be expected, the precipitation of a serious depressive episode during bereavement is a relatively unusual occurrence. Parkes noted this in his study, "Bereavement and Mental Illness."[21] Of 21 patients with pathologic grief reactions, none had a major depression. He states, "It is worth noting that the so-called 'endogenous' (anergic or retarded) form of depression has rarely been described following bereavement."[21 (p. 21)] Although no statistics were provided, Lindemann found it remarkable that agitated depressions also represented only a "small fraction" of the grief reactions in his study.[18] In another early study, Anderson categorized 100 patients hospitalized with pathologic grief reactions.[6] Of these, 15 were diagnosed as having manic-depressive responses, further distinguished as agitated depression (8), anergic depression (4), and hypomania (3). The majority, 85 patients, had neurotic symptoms, including anxiety states (59), hysteria (19), and obsessional tension states (7). It was Anderson's contention that these diagnoses were neither clear-cut nor static but were liable to change as the work of mourning proceeded. He also believed that the neurotic symptoms often represented defensive adaptations, serving to ward off depression. Nonetheless, actual depressive illness in response to bereavement occurred in only a minority of the manifest cases. Considering that only 1% of bereaved persons have a pathologic reaction to bereavement and that only a small percentage of this 1% develop a major affective disorder, the relative rarity of an association between severe depression and grief can be appreciated.

For an explanation of a finding so contrary to the popularly held belief of correspondence between grief and depression, we must have recourse once again to the intensive investigatory powers of psychoanalysis. It will be remembered that both Abraham and Freud emphasized that grief was a response to an external, consciously realized loss, whereas depression was founded largely upon unconscious mechanisms. Although Abraham showed that the psychological process of introjection occurs both in mourning and in melancholia, I believe the fact that bereavement always entails an external, objective loss in some way protects most mourners from becoming seriously depressed. Even though it is typical for a mourner to feel guilty and to blame himself irrationally for the death of a loved person, in much the same way that some depressed patients are obsessed with their guilt, there always remains the objective reality with which the mourner can compare the workings of his mind. This repetitious comparison of inner and outer realities is the very thing Freud described as the grief-work, which eventually leads to healing and recovery. Perhaps it is the objective reality of the death which in some way protects the mourner from developing a psychotic depression.

No less curious is the finding that hypomania, and even frank mania, can occur in bereavement. Parkes discovered 13 cases in the literature and added one of his own.[21] Anderson, in the article cited above, had 3 cases of hypomania in a total of 100 instances of morbid grief. Lindemann also noted hypomania to be a variation of morbid grief.[18] He described disturbed behavior consisting of *"overactivity without a sense of loss,* rather with a sense of well being and zest, the activities being of an expansive and adventurous nature and bearing semblance to the activities formerly carried out by the deceased."[18 (p. 144)] By way of illustration, a patient seen by the author is described here.

CASE 5.—A 28-year-old woman with no history of cyclothymia presented with symptoms typical of mania, including flight of ideas, pressured speech, confusion, disorganization, and distractability. Her stream of speech was characterized by repeated references to electric light bulbs, the meaning of which was completely incomprehensible at the outset. Because the patient had an excellent support system, it was possible to treat her as an outpatient, using supportive psychotherapy along with adjunctive psychotropics (perphenazine). Collateral informants reported that the patient's disturbance originated immediately after the death of an older woman who had been a friend of the patient's grandmother. In the previous two years, both her grandmother and mother had died. She had responded to these deaths without disturbance and with very little grief. Now, in response to the death of a relatively less significant figure, this disturbed reaction appeared. Within two weeks, the patient reintegrated well enough to be able to explain her references to light bulbs. The grandmother's friend was named Mrs. Edison. The associated thoughts in her mind were: death—mother—grandmother—Mrs. Edison—Commonwealth Edison Company—electric light bulb. In essence, she was now manifesting, in a distorted way, her previously unexpressed grief for both her grandmother and her mother.

Psychotherapy continued for approximately nine months, during which time the psychotropic medication was gradually decreased in strength and eventually discontinued entirely. The result of the combined therapy was complete remission of all symptoms and resumption of the premorbid level of functioning. Approximately one year after termination of treatment, the patient's younger sister and her original psychotherapist died within a short time of each other. Interestingly enough, she experienced an appropriate grief reaction to both these deaths. However, a second episode of mania occurred some time later in response to a multitude of stresses that occurred around the anniversary of the mother's death. This second episode was similarly treated with supportive psychotherapy and medication and resolved in less than one month.

It is quite clear that the initial manic episode was directly related to the bereavement, but the dynamics of this relationship remain obscure. Also obscure is the reason for the lack of occurrence of mania following the subsequent bereavements. It seems probable that mania in some way acts as a defense against the painful feelings of grief, just as it may defend against depression. Furthermore, it seems likely that the development of hypomania or mania is related to the process of introjection, as if there were a sudden and complete introjection of the image of the lost object. There is then a merger of the introject with the self-representation associated with an unleashing of manic energy. The whole of this process serves as a denial of death. In general, all forms of morbid grief appear to have this aim.

TREATMENT CONSIDERATIONS

If the purpose of pathologic symptoms in disturbed grief reactions is the denial of death, then the treatment of these conditions must be directed toward an acceptance of external reality. This is a delicate and often painful task. Lindemann felt that it could be done, in uncomplicated instances, in approximately six weeks with 8 to 10 psychiatric interviews.[18] Volkan, who devised a specific form of "re-grief" therapy, found that the process generally takes two months.[32] My experience has been that the nature, duration, and outcome of treatment depend very much on the individual, his premorbid disposition, the specific symptoms, and the therapist. Because morbid grief reactions assume such diverse forms, flexibility of treatment techniques is essential, even though the supraordinate goal remains the promotion of grief and mourning.

In especially difficult instances, the activation of an arrested mourning process may require years of intensive psychoanalytic treatment. Several reports of analytic treatment[15, 17] indicate that the death of a parent during a patient's adolescence may result in a pathologic grief reaction which takes the form of a disavowal of the loss, prolonged mourning, and an interference with psychological maturation.

When bereavement precipitates a physical illness or exacerbates a preexisting condition, the initiation of medical, along with psychological, treatment is essential.

CASE 6.—An 18-year-old woman was admitted to the hospital when, following the death of her great-grandmother, she developed intractable vomiting of such severity that dehydration and an associated electrolyte imbalance ensued. The symptoms appeared to be determined by both physical and psychological factors. In the psychological realm, the patient had felt "disgusted," sick, and nauseated at the sight of her relatives eating and drinking with great gusto after the funeral. Not only did she proclaim her alienation from these "hypocritical" relatives by her inability to ingest food, but she also identified with her great-grandmother, who was anorexic during the latter stages of her illness. On physical examination the patient was discovered to be pregnant, and she had a small duodenal polypoid lesion with an associated duodenitis, all of which provided the biologic substrate for the primary symptom. Treatment consisted of nasogastric suctioning, intravenous therapy, antiemetics, and antacids. Additionally, the patient was seen several times in psychiatric consultation during her 11-day hospitalization. Psychological treatment consisted of support during a period of severe regression; the patient became almost entirely mute except for tearful requests that she be allowed to go home to be cared for by her mother. She emerged from this regression shortly and began to grieve openly for an older woman in the bed next to her who died of cancer, as her great-grandmother had. When the patient was seen for a follow-up visit one week after discharge, she was vibrant and without symptoms of any kind. She felt no further anger, sadness, or grief, and her memories of her great-grandmother were all pleasant ones. With combined medical and psychological treatment, this complex reaction resolved within three weeks.

Treatment must fit the presentation of the illness. Thus, the psychotic, manic reaction described above was treated with a combination of antipsychotic medication and supportive psychotherapy. Neurotic manifestations may be treated successfully with psychotherapy alone. In these instances, transference becomes the vehicle by which the mourning process may be initiated and worked through, the therapist often being placed in the role of the deceased. The termination of the therapy then becomes the focus for reliving and resolution of the original bereavement.

Although no particular formula for the mangement of pathologic grief reactions can be put forth, it is helpful to keep in mind the diverse manifestations of the various stages of the mourning process. It is also useful to know that symptoms unilaterally represent a denial of death and that this denial is necessary to preserve emotional equilibrium. Not even the healthiest of minds is capable of accepting, comprehending, and integrating the death of a loved person without the intervention of the defensive capacity for denial. Only in this way is the overwhelming impact of this reality managed. Thus, the therapist's task is to respect and even accept the denial, in whatever form it may take, as much as it is to encourage the patient to accept external reality. Failure to respect that patient's need for denial may produce an untoward outcome.

CASE 7.—A young married woman sought evaluation because of marital difficulties, including a tendency on her part to lose control of her aggressive impulses toward her husband. During the course of three diagnostic sessions, the patient spontaneously brought to light the fact that her father had died two years before. In her associations, the patient spoke of her father in the present tense as if he were still alive. She had taken his suits and hung them in her bedroom closet. She recalled that she had not cried or grieved in any way at the time of his death. It was quite clear that a pathologic grief reaction was established, and it seemed likely that the symptoms of hostility toward the husband were related to the arrested grief. At the conclusion of the evaluation period, the patient was apprised of the therapist's understanding and was told that he believed some investigation of the patient's feelings about her father would be necessary if her symptoms were to be fully understood. The patient left this session, never to return.

In this case, the patient's need to defend against the emergence of grief was threatened by the therapist's formulation. Whether or not the formulation was accurate was immaterial, as the early intrusion into the patient's defensive system precluded any possibility of her deriving benefit from treatment. A failure such as this is often more instructive than our successes, and this particular failure indicates how exquisitely delicate is the process of treatment of pathologic grief reactions. It also reveals how great a necessity is the capacity for denial of death.

In light of the commonplace identification of grief and depression, it is most interesting to find how few bereaved persons actually develop a major affective disorder. This is an impression based on incidental findings of studies not designed to investigate this specific correlation. Needed are good epidemiologic surveys designed to determine the incidence of various affective disorders in the first year of bereavement, which could then be compared with the incidence of affective disorders in the general population. The family history and previous history of those who develop affective disorders during bereavement might be studied for evidence of a predisposition for the condition. Especially interesting would be a history of prior bereavements, particularly during childhood, and the nature of the grief reaction at that time.

Again, it is merely an impression that the incidence of affective disorder is actually lower in a bereaved population than among the general population. But if this were true, it might indicate that grief protects against the development of depression. The implications for an understanding of psychic processes are fascinating.

REFERENCES

1. Abraham K.: Notes on the psycho-analytical investigation and treatment of manic-depressive insanity and allied conditions, in *Selected Papers of Karl Abraham*. New York, Basic Books, 1954.
2. Abraham K.: A short study of the development of the libido, viewed in the

light of mental disorders, in *Selected Papers of Karl Abraham*. New York, Basic Books, 1954.

3. American Psychiatric Association: *Diagnostic and Statistical Manual of Mental Disorders*, ed. 1. Washington, D.C., APA, 1952.
4. American Psychiatric Association: *Diagnostic and Statistical Manual of Mental Disorders*, ed. 2. Washington, D.C., APA, 1968.
5. American Psychiatric Association: *Diagnostic and Stastistical Manual of Mental Disorders*, ed. 3. Washington, D.C., APA, 1980.
6. Anderson C.: Aspects of pathological grief and mourning. *Int. J. Psychoanal.* 30:48, 1949.
7. Bornstein P.E., et al.: The depression of widowhood after thirteen months. *Br. J. Psychiatry.* 122:561, 1973.
8. Bowlby J.: Processes of mourning. *Int. J. Psychoanal.* 42:317, 1961.
9. Clayton P.: Mortality and morbidity in the first year of widowhood. *Arch. Gen. Psychiatry* 30:747,1974.
10. Clayton P., Desmarais L., Winokur G.: A study of normal bereavement. *Am. J. Psychiatry* 125:64, 1968.
11. Clayton P.J., Halikes J.A., Maurice W.L.: The bereavement of the widowed. *Dis. Nerv. Syst.* 32:597, 1971.
12. Deutsch H.: Absence of grief. *Psychoanal. Q.* 6:12, 1937.
13. Epstein G., et al.: Research on bereavement: A selective and critical review. *Compr. Psychiatry* 16:537, 1975.
14. Fedders D.: Mourning precipitates porphyria. *Med. Ann. District Columbia* 41:508, 1972.
15. Fleming J., Altschul S.: Activation of mourning and growth by psycho-analysis. *Int. J. Psychoanal.* 44:419, 1963.
16. Freud S.: Mourning and melancholia, in *The Standard Edition*. London, Hogarth Press, 1963, vol. 14.
17. Giovacchini P.: The frozen introject. *Int. J. Psychoanal.* 48:61, 1967.
18. Lindemann E.: Symptomatology and management of acute grief. *Am. J. Psychiatry* 101:141, 1944.
19. Lindemann E.: Psychiatric problems in conservative treatment of ulcerative colitis. *Arch. Neurol. Psychiatry* 53:322, 1945.
20. Parkes C.: Effects of bereavement on physical and mental health: A study of the medical records of widows. *Br. Med. J.* 2:274, 1964.
21. Parkes C.: Bereavement and mental illness. *Br. J. Med. Psychol.* 38:198, 1965.
22. Parkes C.: The first year of bereavement. *Psychiatry* 33:444, 1970.
23. Parkes C.: *Bereavement*. New York, International Universities Press, 1972.
24. Parkes C.: 'Seeking' and 'finding' a lost object: Evidence from recent studies of the reaction to bereavement, in *Normal and Pathological Responses to Bereavement*. New York, MSS Information Corp., 1974.
25. Paykel E., Myers J., Dienelt M.N.: Life events and depression. *Arch. Gen. Psychiatry* 21:753, 1969.
26. Pollock G.: Mourning and adaptation. *Int. J. Psychoanal.* 42:341, 1961.
27. Schamle A.: Relationship of separation and depression to disease. *Psychosom. Med.* 20:259, 1958.
28. Shoor M., Speed M.: Delinquency as a manifestation of the mourning process. *Psychiatr. Q.* 37:540, 1963.
29. Siggins L.: Mourning: A critical survey of the literature. *Int. J. Psychoanal.* 47:14, 1966.

30. Stamm J., Drapkin A.: The successful treatment of a severe case of bronchial asthma: A manifestation of an abnormal mourning reaction and traumatic neurosis. *J. Nerv. Ment. Dis.* 142:180, 1966.
31. Volkan V.: The recognition and prevention of pathological grief, in *Normal and Pathological Responses to Bereavement.* New York, MSS Information Corp., 1974.
32. Volkan V.: "Re-grief" therapy. in Schoenberg B., et al. (eds.): *Bereavement.* New York, Columbia University Press, 1975.
33. Wretmark G.: A study in grief reactions. *Acta Psychiatr. Neurol.* 34:292, 1959.

PART II

PSYCHOPATHOLOGY OF AFFECTIVE DISORDERS

5

SOCIAL AND EPIDEMIOLOGIC ASPECTS OF AFFECTIVE DISORDERS

JOSEPH A. FLAHERTY, M.D.
F. MOISES GAVIRIA, M.D.
EDUARDO VAL, M.D.

THE DIAGNOSIS and treatment of any psychiatric disorder must be considered in the context of the environment in which symptoms occur. Environmental factors may have either a protective or a deleterious influence on the clinical course of an affective disorder. The presentation and persistence of specific affective symptoms are also influenced by social and cultural factors. It is essential that clinicians understand each patient's specific social milieu in order to formulate an accurate diagnostic assessment and to be of continuing help in the treatment process. This chapter reviews the epidemiologic and sociocultural factors involved in affective disorders.

EPIDEMIOLOGY OF AFFECTIVE DISORDERS

An epidemiologic perspective on affective disorders can be useful in two ways. First, it enlarges the clinician's index of suspicion on the possibility of mood disorders in a given patient. Second, it induces hypotheses as to the etiology of these disorders. It is no longer sufficient to note that depression is higher in the elderly or in women; why these differences occur is now the salient question.

Epidemiologic studies of affective disorders have measured the preva-

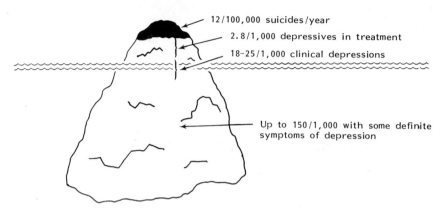

12/100,000 suicides/year

2.8/1,000 depressives in treatment

18-25/1,000 clinical depressions

Up to 150/1,000 with some definite symptoms of depression

Fig 5–1.—The tip of the iceberg: suicides and depressives in treatment compared with the depressive population. Adapted from Watts.[73]

lence, incidence, duration, and severity of specific symptoms as well as of specific affective disorders. All these measurements, particularly those related to diagnostic assessment, have undergone continued change throughout this century. These changes make comparisons between studies done at different times with different measurements extremely difficult, although certain trends can be seen. The new *Diagnostic and Statistical Manual of Mental Disorders (DSM-III)*[1] and its precursor, the Research Diagnostic Criteria (RDC),[65] have gained wide acceptance by researchers in affective disorders, which should allow more reliable comparisons in the future. These criteria have sometimes been used in conjunction with the Schedule for Affective Disorders and Schizophrenia (SADS), a structured interview format which increases inter-rater reliability.[21] A variety of symptom rating scales are also being used in epidemiologic studies, including those by Beck[7] and Zung.[84, 86]

Depression now rivals schizophrenia as the nation's number one mental health problem, The National Institute for Mental Health estimates that at least 8 million Americans are clinically depressed and that each year 125,000 individuals are hospitalized for this condition.[55] As Watts has noted, hospitalized patients and others who seek treatment constitute the tip of the iceberg, while individuals with mild to severe depression go unnoticed, despite symptoms that produce personal and social discomfort (Fig 5–1).[73]

DEPRESSIVE SYMPTOMS IN COMMUNITY SURVEYS

Estimates of depressive symptoms in the community vary from less than 5% to 44%. This wide range reflects sample and survey instrument differences. The results from three recent surveys will be used throughout this chapter. In 1975 Levitt and Lubin conducted a National Depression Survey (NDS) of depression proneness in a community sample of over 3,000 randomly selected adults and adolescents.[38] They used a rating scale of 171 adjectives describing depressive symptoms. Weissman and Myers conducted a community survey using their own depression index modified from other scales.[78] Most recently, Blumenthal utilized the Zung Self-Rating Depression Scale (SRS) in estimating depressive symptoms in a community sample of 106 married couples.[9]

DEPRESSION SYNDROME RATES IN COMMUNITY SURVEYS

Community-wide prevalence rates of both treated and untreated populations of any specific psychiatric disorder are generally unavailable in the United States.[77] However, Weissman and Myers surveyed over 1,000 households using the SRS-RDC; this survey provides the most recent statistics on certain categories of depression.[77]

Weissman and Myers found a rate of 4.3% for major affective disorders. This figure is higher than earlier reports of 1% to 3%.[22] The 4.3% figure is close to the previously reported rates of 3.8% for combined psychotic and neurotic depression *(DSM-II)* found by Helgason in Iceland.[62] Bipolar illness constituted 28% of all major affective disorders, or 1.2% of the entire sample, which compares favorably with the only previous estimate of 1%.[35] The survey's finding of a relatively low rate of bipolar illness, as compared to unipolar illness, is consistent with general clinical experience.

Weissman and Myers also found that only 14% of major depressions were secondary to another preexisting illness. Alcoholism accounted for 44% of the primary diagnoses in all cases of secondary depression.

Minor affective disorders were diagnosed in 2.5% of the population. Although this group is not exactly equivalent to any *DSM-II* category, the 2.5% figure is close to earlier estimates of 3% for depressive neurosis.

We will now consider the rates of depressive symptoms and illness by reviewing the sociodemographic variables.

AGE

When considering overall depression rates (i.e., all diagnostic types), traditional psychiatric epidemiology holds that depression increases with age.[36, 85] However, as Klerman noted, there is a post-World War II trend of depression in younger people.[33]

The incidence of bipolar illness peaks in the mid-20s. However, primary affective disorders are clearly recognizable in adolescence, and investigators have reported that between 33% and 40% of bipolar patients have their first episode prior to age 20.[24, 83] The incidence of unipolar illness (major recurrent depression) is traditionally reported to be more common in midlife. Therefore, the prevalence rates of all major depressive illness can be expected to rise after the mid-20s due to the accumulation of incidence rates. The age at onset for major affective disorders shows a greater range and an older mean when compared with schizophrenia: schizophrenia is most commonly diagnosed between ages 15 and 25, with the majority of cases diagnosed before age 30.

The prevalence rates for milder types of depression and for depressive symptomatology have yielded inconsistent findings when correlated with age. Weissman and Myers report a high rate of moderate depression in younger women and a decrease with age; the opposite pattern was found in men.[78] Blumenthal found no significant variation by age in depressive symptomatology.[9] Craig and Van Nalta found that younger patients reported more depression for all but one of 16 symptoms.[16] The inconsistent findings may be due to different rating measures and the willingness to report symptoms. Kales and Kales found that younger patients with insomnia secondary to depression are more willing to admit to depression, anxiety, and self-doubt.[31]

The elderly patient poses particular problems in the diagnosis of affective disorders. Blazer and Williams note that the elderly are more likely to have masked depression and that clinicians are likely to overlook milder depressions that are associated with somatic symptoms and cognitive impairment (pseudodementia).[8] In their survey of 997 elderly patients (aged 65 or older), they found a rate of 14.7% for dysphoric symptoms in general, and a 3.7% rate for symptoms consistent with a major affective disorder.

Recently, more attention has been paid to depression in childhood. There are two basic views on the manifestations of childhood depression.[34] One holds that depression in childhood resembles adult depression in essential characteristics (e.g., dysphoric mood, low self-esteem, diminished psychomotor behavior), with some development-specific modifications in symptoms (e.g., enuresis), and that depression in childhood can be identified using adult research criteria.[13] The alternative view holds that depression in childhood is often masked and must be inferred from certain behaviors or "depressive equivalents," such as delinquency, somatic complaints, and school problems. It is predictable that new rating scales for depression in childhood will lead to more reliable data on the epidemiology of these disorders.[51]

Like depression itself, the suicide rate increases with age, with peak periods from 17 to 22 and after 45.[61] Adolescent suicide in this country has risen in recent years to the point of being second only to accidents as a leading cause of death in adolescents and young adults.[56] After age 55, suicide rates level off for women but continue to increase for men (Fig 5–2).

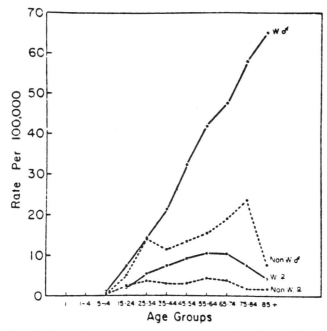

Fig 5–2.—Suicide rate by age, color, and sex in the United States in 1959. (From *Vital Statistics of the United States.* U.S. Dept. of Health, Education and Welfare, Washington, D.C., 1959, vol. 1.

SEX

Women have outnumbered men in depression of all types. The female:male ratio has varied from 1.5 to 2.1 for primary affective disorders in most countries.[74] However, in certain countries, such as Iraq, these differences are reduced,[6] while in other countries, such as India, the sex ratios may be reversed.[68] In the NDS, females consistently scored higher than males on depression proneness in all age groups. On a majority of symptoms measured, Craig and Van Nalta's community survey also showed that women had significantly higher prevalence rates for depression symptoms than men.[16] In an excellent literature review on sex differences in depression, Weissman and Klerman concluded that even considering the methodological problems (e.g., women are noted to report symptoms more readily than men; women go to the doctor more often), women have a greater tendency toward depression.[74] Speculation as to why this is so includes the following:

1. *An X-linkage for depression.* Although there are considerable data available indicating a genetic factor involved in affective states, the specific genetics are not known.[63] Some data favor the X-linkage hypothesis with

bipolar patients. Another explanation for different depression rates between the sexes reflects a differential interaction between genotype and environment.

2. *Female endocrinology as a predisposition to depression.* Research in this area has focused on hormonal fluctuations and the frequency of premenstrual tension as factors predisposing women to depression.[69] Work is also being done on changes in catecholamine metabolites during the menstrual cycle.[17] Winokur reports that women are not necessarily at greater risk for unipolar depression during the menopausal period,[82] and Weissman reports that there is no rise in depressive symptoms at that time. None of the reports so far have shown causative evidence.

3. *A relationship between depression and birth control pills.* Although there are tentative data linking birth control preparations to depression, there is no causative evidence to date.[81] The influence of methodology in such research is difficult to assess; the effect of the woman's decision not to become pregnant as well as her selection of a contraceptive method are important factors.

4. *Birth, the postpartum period, and predisposition of women to depression.* Women are at greater risk for psychiatric disorders, particularly depression, in the postpartum period, although the mechanisms are not understood.[12] Although the dramatic fall in estrogen, progesterone, and thyroid levels in the immediate postpartum period may account for transient psychological changes, they do not explain the increased incidence of affective states.

5. *Females are taught by society to value being helpless, powerless, and nonassertive; these roles may predispose to depression when under stress.* This hypothesis proposes that women are socially conditioned to a cognitive set against assertion.[74] Young girls may value the "feminine" trait of being helpless; this learning becomes internalized in childhood. As a result of this posture, women may develop a limited set of responses to stressful life events, which could result in a depressive state when these events accumulate. In this regard, more grief reactions (major depressive symptoms occurring after a death) have been reported in women (16.2%) than in men (2.7%).[77]

6. *A link between marriage and depression for women.* There is conflicting evidence on both rates of depression and depressive symptoms in men and women in the various marital status categories. While some evidence suggests that marriage may provide a buffer against depression in men but not in women, this hypothesis remains to be validated.[25] Proponents of this hypothesis point out that women more commonly have roles limited only to family (mother, wife); men usually have these roles as well as an occupational role. Even if a woman works, her position is often more restricted

and less esteemed than a man's. Suicide rates are clearly higher in divorced people of both sexes, followed by widows, never-marrieds, and married persons, in that order. It should also be noted that male suicide rates are three times higher than for females, but that women attempt suicide more often.

How the impact of the women's movement—the advent of more working women, fewer children, and greater independence—affects sex differences in depression is yet to be seen.

EDUCATIONAL ATTAINMENT

Faris and Dunham found a positive correlation between manic-depressive illness and education and a negative correlation between schizophrenia and education;[23] this conclusion has not been supported, particularly in reference to depression. The NDS did not find any significant relationship between educational level alone and depression proneness; however, black Americans with less than five years of education showed considerably more depression.

RACE

This area of epidemiology has been confusing and often misleading. Typical pre-1960s reports held that blacks were markedly less depressed than whites by a ratio of 1:4. Issues arising from these findings were whether differences were cultural or genetic, and whether diagnostic methods were racially biased. In explaining the seemingly low incidence of depression in Southern blacks, Prange and Vitols suggested that stoicism, the extended family, and Fundamentalist religious beliefs help mitigate depression in blacks generally.[52] Another explanation for low depression rates among black Americans was that blacks have been conditioned over centuries to expect that depressive symptoms will be misinterpreted as laziness and malingering. Studies in Ghana and Nigeria that found high incident rates of depression (20% and 17%, respectively) argue against any racial-genetic explanation.

Newer research has shown that the racial differences reported are compounded by socioeconomic differences, and that within each socioeconomic group the incidence of depression for blacks and whites is similar. Weissman and Myers report that whites are more likely than nonwhites to experience a major depression, while the reverse is true for minor depressive disorders.[77] The latter finding is consistent with other reports of a general increase in depressive symptoms in nonwhites.[72, 78] Suicide rates have historically been low for black Americans, a difference that is rapidly evaporating. Whether current studies, which show at least equal rates for blacks and whites in depression, have to do with integration and the civil rights movement of the 1960s or with better diagnostic criteria is not readily provable.

CULTURE AND ETHNICITY

The particular influence of culture and ethnicity on affective states is often confounded by related variables such as migration, race, and economic status. There are, however, two specific issues worth addressing here: the cultural influence on the symptomatology and the etiology of affective disorders.

The most noteworthy finding in cultural and ethnic differences in symptomatology is the greater tendency for certain cultural groups to present with somatic symptoms as a central manifestation of depression. It is not certain, however, whether these differences are due to culture per se, to lower-class status, or to membership in a minority group. This tendency for somatic presentations has often been associated with patients from Hispanic cultures[66] and, more recently, with Chinese-Americans. It has also been shown that depressed Italian-Americans tend to have more hypochondriacal symptoms than either Irish- or Jewish-Americans.[46] Perhaps the stigma associated with mental illness in different cultures leads to a presentation of physical symptoms because of their "legitimacy" value.

The effect of the cultural and ethnic milieu on the etiology of psychiatric disorders such as alcoholism, suicide, schizophrenia, and depression has also been researched. Specific variables studied have been family types, child-rearing habits, degrees of repression and tolerance for self-expression and hostility, self-concept, and body image.[41] One hypothesis holds that certain societies are relatively free of depression simply through the absence of Judeo-Christian ethics. This view has been largely discredited by studies showing a higher incidence of depression among certain African nations without this ethical system. For example, studies on the Yoruba (Africa) have shown that depression there is manifested by dysphoric mood and certain neurovegatative symptoms (e.g., anorexia), but is relatively free of guilt feelings and self-castigation.[37] Another cultural theory of depression holds that very tightly linked and regimented societies favor the development of depression over schizophrenia. The Hutterite population in the United States has been cited as an example of this theory by Eaton and Weil.[19] Research on the relative degrees of homogeneity of genetic pools within ethnic groups may eventually provide further data on the role these variables play in the etiology of depression.

SOCIAL CLASS

Original work by Hollingshead and Redlich shows that a diagnosis of depressive neurosis is positively correlated with social class.[28] However, their population included only patients in treatment, rendering the findings difficult to extrapolate to whole populations. Weissman and Myers report that the rates of major affective disorders are associated with upper-class status.[77] The bulk of recent studies on both treated and untreated populations shows a greater overall rate of depression in the lower classes. To illustrate the complexity of these matters, Schwab et al. report that in research on medical patients, social class and depression depend on the measurements used: upper-class patients are more often diagnosed as depressed when an interview is used, whereas lower-class patients are more often diagnosed as depressed on the basis of a symptom checklist.[59]

There may also be a social class difference in the way depressive symptoms present. Some clinicians have noted that upper-class patients tend to present with a loss of interest in life or with so-called existential questions, middle-class patients present with loneliness and guilt, and lower-class patients present with futility, hopelessness, and self-hatred.

INCOME

Most investigators have not measured income independent of social class. However, when income is measured, studies have shown a greater tendency in lower income groups toward all mental illness. The NDS shows a curvilinear relationship between depression proneness and income, with peaks of depression seen at poverty level income and again at incomes over \$25,000 (1970). Schwab et al. reported some interesting findings on the relationship of depression to income. They found a significant and marked increase in almost all depressive symptoms in the lowest income group as compared with the highest income group (Table 5–1). The only depressive symptoms more associated with high income levels were "thoughts of suicide" and "blame-self."[58] Periods of national economic depression have not correlated with an increase in clinical depression, although there have been increases in the male suicide rate during these times.

RELIGION

Although most textbooks state that manic-depressive illness is higher in Jews, the data are questionable, as some of the findings come out of research on treated populations in New York City, where there is a disproportionately high number of Jews.[39] Newer studies have shown low rates for Jews living in Israel and a higher rate for Eastern European Jews.[40] The NDS did not find any significant differences in depression proneness by religion, although suicide rates have been reported as significantly lower in Catholics and Jews.

TABLE 5–1.—PERCENTAGE OF INCOME GROUPS REPORTING ITEMS "OFTEN" OR "ALL THE TIME" (N = 1,200)*†

| | ANNUAL INCOME | | | | | |
	<$3,000 %	$3,000–5,999 %	$6,000–9,999 %	$10,000–14,999 %	$15,000+ %	Tau
Powerlessness	61.0	43.0	24.0	19.0	10.0	−0.30+
Future gloomy	20.0	7.0	7.0	4.0	2.0	−0.25+
Bodily ailments	7.0	4.0	2.0	0.4	0.5	−0.19+
Could not take care of things	9.0	3.0	1.0	0.4	1.0	−0.19+
Alone and helpless	17.0	6.0	6.0	3.0	2.0	−0.18+
Could not enjoy things	22.0	7.0	5.0	4.0	2.0	−0.17+
Crying	14.0	11.0	6.0	3.0	3.0	−0.16+
Trouble sleeping	26.0	18.0	12.0	6.0	14.0	−0.15+
Trouble getting to sleep	27.0	18.0	13.0	6.0	13.0	−0.14+
People not caring	18.0	6.0	5.0	8.0	2.0	−0.14+
Low spirits	9.0	3.0	1.0	0.4	0.9	−0.13+
Loss of appetite	9.0	4.0	4.0	0.0	1.4	−0.13+
Hopelessness	9.0	6.0	3.0	2.0	1.4	−0.13+
Things turning out wrong	26.0	17.0	13.0	6.0	8.0	−0.11+
Worthwhile?	15.0	6.0	7.0	4.0	4.0	−0.08+
Tired in the morning	18.0	16.0	13.0	8.0	14.0	n.s.
Thoughts of suicide	3.0	1.2	3.0	4.0	3.0	0.03++
Blame self	26.0	21.0	23.0	23.0	24.0	0.06+

*From Schwab J.J., et al.: Human ecology and depressive symptomatology, in Masserman J. (ed.): *Social Psychiatry*. New York, Grune & Stratton, 1976, vol. 2. Reproduced by permission.
†Total N of 1,367 varies slightly from item to item because of a few "don't know" responses. The 278 students were excluded from this income analysis. Single plus, $P < 0.001$; double plus, $P < 0.05$.

OCCUPATION

The NDS suggests that depression proneness has a curvilinear relationship with occupation: it is highest at the top and bottom levels of occupational status. Among whites there were more depressive symptoms at the bottom and top of a prestige of occupation scale; this was not true for blacks. Physicians, dentists, insurance salesmen, and police have the highest suicide rates. Among physicians, the overall rate of depression is especially high for psychiatrists and women. The high rate for physicians and dentists diminishes somewhat when the statistics are age-corrected for comparison with other occupations, as the mean age for members of these groups is higher than that of many other occupations. A recent study of depression during medical internship found that 30% of a group of first-year residents in all specialties experienced significant depression.[70] Over 7% had strong suicidal ideation at some time. Depression among interns correlated with a personal or family history of depression.[70]

MIGRATION

The issue of migration and depression accentuates the central controversy over nurture versus nature in mental health studies. Although mentally ill and depressed migrants can clearly be identified, this is only an initial step toward resolving the etiologic questions about why migrants become mentally ill. To what extent is selection significant? Are certain types of mentally ill or depression-prone individuals more or less likely to migrate? To what extent does the host country aggravate or alleviate the stresses of migration? How does the migrant's desire and capacity to assimilate the host country's culture influence the future development of depression?

Odegard showed that Norwegian immigrants to the United States had a lower incidence of depression than native Norwegians.[45] Although Odegard believed these differences were due to the selection process, Murphy has noted that this is not necessarily true. Regarding mental illness in general, Murphy reports that the relatively large size of the immigrant population in Canada favors the immigrant to that country, while the dominance of the majority culture in the United States puts greater pressure on the immigrant here.[43]

Certain migrants neither assimilate the majority culture nor maintain an attachment with their own culture. Brody, in a study of rural to urban migration within Brazil, has shown that many migrants, "the lost ones," need psychiatric help because of feelings of rootlessness, inadequacy, and alienation associated with the loss of cultural supports.[10]

Research into the relationship of migration and depression needs to be carefully examined, not just for sociodemographic factors and incident rates; it must also be placed in the context of the entire migration process. More critical research may be done on the increasing numbers of international migrants (e.g., Cubans, Vietnamese, Haitians) and some of these interesting questions will be answered.

TIME OF YEAR

Although some reports suggest an increase in suicide and depression in late December, most international studies predict springtime. In the United States, April is the peak for both.

GENERAL MEDICAL POPULATION

In a 1969 community survey, only 18% of the patients reporting serious symptoms of depression had sought any mental health treatment; only 10% had seen a psychiatrist in the previous year. However, in this same group of depressed individuals, 87% had sought medical care in the preceding year.[78] The implication is clear: any effort to increase the detection and treatment of depression must rely heavily on primary care practitioners.

Schwab, studying hospitalized medical patients, has shown that 25% of females and 16% of males were significantly depressed based on rating scales, research protocols, and diagnoses by medical staffs. In the 41- to 55-year-old and over-71-year-old age groups, depression was higher in males. Schwab also found that 50% of depressed patients in both the 10- to 25-year-old and 26- to 40-year-old age groups had suicidal thoughts.[60]

Depression, however, is generally an ambulatory disorder, so it is expected that a majority of depressives will be seen in the primary practitioner's office. Watts has shown that 30% of the patients attending a private practice had clinically significant emotional illness.[73] In all emotional disorders seen by a practitioner, estimates of the percentage of depression range from 35% to 40%.[42] This could be a conservative estimate, considering that many psychophysiologic disorders are now being rediagnosed as depression. Extrapolating from the previous two studies, we estimate that in an average-sized medical practice a physician will see up to 20 new cases of depression each year. These figures attest to the importance of the primary practitioner in the early identification of affective disorders. Since the incidence of depressive disorders is higher than that of many other illnesses physicians routinely screen for, it is advisable for physicians to learn screening methods for affective disorders.

The epidemiologic data presented here should broaden the clinician's index of suspicion in certain populations (e.g., women, elderly) as well as raise questions about the multiple etiologies of depressive disorders. However, one must be extremely cautious in directly applying epidemiologic data to differential diagnostic thinking. Any patient, regardless of age, sex, income, or race, is a candidate for depression. The challenge of future epidemiologic research on affective states will be to focus on why certain populations are at higher risk for depression.

SOCIOLOGY OF AFFECTIVE DISORDERS

In this section we examine the work on life events, help-seeking behavior, social adjustment and disability, role theory, social networks, and social support systems to gain a comprehensive picture of the sociology of affective disorders.

Over the last 25 years there has been considerable work relating life events, stress, and emotional status to the individual's susceptibility to physical illness.[18, 26, 27, 53] On a separate but related track has been the controversial attempt to link life events to the onset of affective states. Some writers argue that most depressions are reactions to the stress from specific life events; others argue that life events are only coincidentally related to, or are consequences of, depression.

Efforts have been made to quantify research in this area with a scale developed by Holmes and Rahe (Table 5–2).[29] These two investigators assigned a numerical figure to many stressful life events (such as the death of a spouse, specific financial difficulties, birth of a child) based on the normal population's estimate of the stress potential inherent in these events. Then correlations were made between an individual's total stress points and the later occurrence of physical and emotional problems. Using 33 common life events, Paykel et al. found that depressed patients reported three times as many stressful life events as their matched controls.[47, 48] This work was continued by separating life events into entrances (marriage, childbirth, new person in the home) and exits (death of a friend or family member, separation, divorce, dismissal from work). Arguments and interpersonal difficulties were specifically omitted because it was felt that patient groups might retrospectively skew the reporting of these events, based on their current mood. Results revealed the obvious: depressives had significantly more exits (25% vs. 5%) than the normal population, but few differences in the number of entrances. Paykel et al. also found that recovered depressives had a significantly higher number of entrances and other desirable events than they had prior to depression. This, of course, could be more a consequence than a cause of recovery from depression. Paykel et al. also found that depressives who relapsed after treatment had significantly more stressful life events than those who did not relapse.

TABLE 5–2.—SOCIAL READJUSTMENT
RATING SCALE*

EVENTS	SCALE OF IMPACT
Death of spouse	100
Divorce	73
Marital separation	65
Jail term	63
Death of close family member	63
Personal injury or illness	53
Marriage	50
Fired at work	47
Marital reconciliation	45
Change in health of family member	44
Pregnancy	40
Sex difficulties	39
Gain of new family member	39
Business readjustment	39
Change in financial state	38
Death of a close friend	37
Change to different line of work	36
Change in number of arguments with spouse	35
Mortgage over $10,000	31
Foreclosure of mortgage or loan	30
Change in responsibilities at work/school	29
Live away from parents for first time	29
Trouble with in-laws	29
Outstanding personal achievement	28
Wife begins or stops work	26
Begin or end school	26
Change in living conditions	25
Revision of personal habits	24
Trouble with boss	23
Change in work hours or conditions	20
Change in residence	20
Change in schools	20
Change in recreation	19
Change in church activities	19
Change in social activities	18
Mortgage or loan less than $10,000	17
Change in sleeping habits	16
Change in number of family get-togethers	15
Change in eating habits	15
Vacation	13
Christmas	12
Minor violations of the law	11

*Reprinted with permission from Holmes T.H., Rahe
R.H.: The social readjustment rating scale. *J. Psychosom.
Res.* 11:213–218, 1967. Copyright 1967, Pergamon Press,
Ltd.

These researchers also tried to differentiate the symptom pattern in depressions preceded by a significant stress. They found that there is neither a symptom differential nor a difference in frequency of life events to distinguish the so-called reactive depressions from the so-called endogenous depressions.[49] Other writers have indicated that the absence of specific and significant stresses prior to the depressive symptoms is an indicator of positive response to tricyclic treatment.

Related to the issue of life events is the concept of "stressors," ongoing stressful situations that can be associated with depressive illness. Ilfeld found that depression is most clearly associated with the social stressors of marriage and parenting, with financial and job-related stressors also significant.[30] Although he does not deny the multifactorial etiologies in depression, Ilfeld makes a strong case for these stressors as being causally related to depressive symptoms. This concept of stressors raises the question as to whether, in the development of depression, specific life events are more important than the relative intensity of difficult life situations.

SOCIAL ADJUSTMENT AND DISABILITY

A further consideration in the sociology of affective disorders is the relationship between depression and social adjustment. Since the early work on treatment outcomes, many writers and teachers have emphasized that certain treatments primarily affect the overt symptoms, while others have a more profound influence on social functioning. This has been more clearly shown in schizophrenia: major tranquilizers act primarily to diminish and prevent hallucinations and delusions; group or individual psychotherapy has a more marked effect on resocialization and interpersonal relationships.

Weissman and co-workers have observed that symptom reduction can be achieved with pharmacotherapy in three to six weeks but that social functioning may take months longer to return to normal. They also found that patients who relapsed had, at the time of relapse, more impairment in work functioning than a matched group who did not relapse. Neither the social functioning nor the symptom picture during the acute illness predicted which group would relapse.[67, 76, 80] Further studies with depressed women found that work performance and anxious rumination were the most sensitive variables; they improved the most rapidly during recovery and deteriorated the fastest during relapse. Furthermore, social adaptation at work and in the community is likely to be influenced by the patient's previous personal, cultural, and familial expectations.

When working with depressed patients, the clinician needs to separate out the symptom picture (sadness, immobility, pessimism, insomnia, weight loss) from the social disability (deterioriated relationships with family and friends, loss of a job) and devise a comprehensive treatment plan covering both. Treatment of a social disability could include group, family, and individual therapy, environmental manipulation, occupational counseling, referral to community agencies, and encouraging the patient to reconnect with supportive individuals and agencies (e.g., church, social clubs, friends, professional affiliations).

The degree of importance American psychiatry now gives to social functioning is reflected in the *DSM-III*.[1] The new coding used in this manual has a specific axis for indicating the patient's highest level of adaptive functioning during the last year, ranging from superior to grossly impaired. Adaptive functioning is conceptualized as a composite of functioning in three areas: social relations, occupational functioning, and use of leisure time.

ROLE THEORY AND DEPRESSION

The relationship of roles and depression stems from the notion that roles are directly related to well-being and self-esteem. When people are given the "Who are you?" test, they characteristically respond in terms of their various roles, such as wife, husband, teacher, mother, and son. Poor performance or disappointment in a role, as well as real or threatened loss of a role, can have negative consequences on one's self-esteem, resulting in depression.

Bart has tried to explain depression in women through role theory.[2-4] She finds the following factors to be associated with depression in mothers: maternal loss after overprotective or overinvolved relationships with children and maternal loss following no significant interest in any other role. She has also related depression to the concept of the stereotypic "Jewish mother," where the maternal role is particularly valued. She found that Jewish women have a higher incidence of depression than other ethnic groups, except when compared with women also having overinvolved and overprotective relationships with their children.

Brown et al. related role restriction and social status to depression, using data from a community survey in London.[11] They found that working-class women with young children living at home had the highest rates of depression. The amount of support that a boyfriend or husband provided these mothers was an important factor in preventing depression. Also, employment outside the home seemed to offer some protection by alleviating boredom, increasing self-esteem, and increasing social contacts.

Weissman and Paykel have found supporting data for the relationship between role performance and depressive symptoms.[79] Their work showed that acutely depressed women experienced definite social maladjustment in their various roles, compared with a control group.

NETWORKS AND SOCIAL SUPPORT SYSTEMS

Social networks are usually defined by an individual's multiple relationships and the interrelationship between these various individuals. "Social support system" usually refers to the people and institutions surrounding an individual that may help him through transitions, losses, and crises. Much is known about how these resources help people in their day-to-day living. It is also useful to examine the relationship between these social resources and mental illness.

It has been shown that posthospitalized mental patients are at high risk for rehospitalization if they have a small, poorly connected social network.[64] There is also evidence indicating that social networks and support systems influence whether or not one is recognized as ill,[32] has the resources to deal with being ill or under stress,[50] seeks help for illness, is hospitalized, or adapts to community life.[44]

With particular emphasis on depressive illness, Walker et al. analyzed the social support networks and the crisis of bereavement.[71] Their findings support the argument that a close-knit network drawn from family, neighborhood, and friends reduces or eliminates loneliness in widows.[71] Clayton et al. examined the differences in social supports between two groups of recently widowed women, those with reactive depressions and those with few depressive symptoms. They found that the depressed group had significantly fewer relatives in their immediate geographic area.[15] Brown et al. have identified the absence of a close confiding relationship as one of four vulnerability factors associated with the onset of depression in the face of adverse experiences.[11] These and other data have led Cassel to hypothesize that an individual's support networks provide the buffer between stressful life events and psychiatric illness or depression.[14]

There is evidence, however, to suggest that a cohesive and demanding social network might favor the development of depression. The Hutterites have been found to have significantly more depression than the general population.[5] This group, as described by Eaton and Weil, has strong social cohesion and clear-cut social expectations.[19] Although these factors protect the Hutterites from the uncertainties of life, they are also a source of psychological stress. Strong guilt feelings were found in the Hutterites, who feared they could not live up to their group's expectations. These and similar data have led Bart to suggest that if people who follow traditional societal expectations are more likely to become depressed, then "it is possible that society is not only schizophrenic for those left out, but depressogenic for those left in."[5]

Newer research on the social variables will be directed toward the relative influence of the social variables in preventing depression and in symptom exacerbation in depressed populations. Previous work suggests that social support variables may emerge as the most predictive social variable in depression. If this is true, there will be a need for simple, reliable, and valid means of assessing social support systems in a manner that will lend itself to treatment planning. Only when this is achieved will social treatment planning achieve par with the psychological and pharmacologic treatments.

Inherent in this discussion of the social variables is the issue of causation. To prove causation it would be necessary to perform a long prospective study, following individuals through childhood and adulthood; psychological, biologic, genetic, and social data would need to be collected on each individual. Such a study has not been done. Most researchers on depression hold that for the major affective disorders, a biologic vulnerability is required; within that context social and psychological factors may determine which individuals have symptoms that have significant effects on the ongoing clinical course. It is generally assumed that psychosocial factors may play a more marked role in the development of the other affective disorders, although this is not proved. In fact, some investigators are raising the possibility of genetic influence in these disorders as well.

This chapter has presented an overview of epidemiologic findings and social aspects of affective disorders. Although some statistics are not useful in assessing an individual patient, they should add a new level to the understanding of these patients. Further, they should convey the message that in any patient with an affective disorder, even when a biologic lesion is most probable, social factors are involved in the presentation of symptoms, response to therapy, the prevention of relapse, and the successful integration of the individual into society. Awareness of these factors provides the clinician with a comprehensive view of affective illness and will better enable him to be of help to these patients.

REFERENCES

1. American Psychiatric Association: *Diagnostic and Statistical Manual of Mental Disorders*, ed. 3. Washington, D.C., APA, 1980.
2. Bart P.: Are you a housewife or do you work?, in *Transactions of Women: Resource for a Changing World*. Cambridge, Mass., Radcliffe Institute for Women, 1972.
3. Bart P.: *Depression in Middle Aged Women: Some Sociocultural Factors*, thesis. UCLA, 1967.
4. Bart P.: Portnoy's mother's complaint. *Transaction* 7:13, 1970.
5. Bart P.: The sociology of depression, in Roman P.M., Harrison T. (eds.): *Explorations in Psychiatric Sociology*. Philadelphia, F.A. Davis Co., 1974, chap. 7.

6. Bazzoni W.: Affective disorders in Iraq. *Br. J. Psychiatry* 117:195–203, 1970.
7. Beck A.T., et al.: An inventory for measuring depression. *Arch. Gen. Psychiatry* 4:461–471, 1961.
8. Blazer D., Williams C.D.: Epidemiology of dysphoria and depression in an elderly population. *Am. J. Psychiatry* 137:439–443, 1980.
9. Blumenthal M.D.: Measuring depressive symptomatology in a general population. *Arch. Gen. Psychiatry* 32:971–978, 1975.
10. Brody E.B.: *The Lost Ones: Social Forces and Mental Illness in Rio de Janeiro.* New York, International Universities Press, 1973.
11. Brown G., Bhrolchain M., Harris T.: Social class and psychiatric disturbance among women in an urban population. *Sociology* 9:225–254, 1975.
12. Butts H.F.: Postpartum psychiatric problems. *J. Natl. Med. Assoc.* 65:136–139, 1973.
13. Carlson G.A., Cantwell D.P.: Unmasking masked depression in children and adolescents. *Am. J. Psychiatry* 137:4, 1980.
14. Cassel J.: The contribution of the social environment to most resistance. *Am. J. Public Health* 64:1040–1043, 1974.
15. Clayton P., Halikes J., Maurice W.: The depression of widowhood. *Br. J. Psychiatry* 120:71–77, 1972.
16. Craig T.J., Van Nalta D.A.: Influence of demographic characteristics on two measures of depressive symptoms. *Arch. Gen. Psychiatry* 36:149–159, 1979.
17. DeLeon-Jones F., Lahmeyer H., Miller M.O.: 3-Methoxy, 4-hydroxy methylglycol (MHPG) and the menstrual cycle. Unpublished manuscript.
18. Dohrenmend B.S., Dohrenmend B.P.: *Stressful Life Events: Their Nature and Effects.* New York, John Wiley & Sons, 1974.
19. Eaton J.W., Weil R.J.: *Culture and Mental Disorders.* Glencoe, Ill., The Free Press, 1955.
20. Eliot T.S.: *The Wasteland.* New York, Harcourt, Brace, and Jankovitch, 1955.
21. Endicott J., Spitzer R.L.: A diagnostic interview: The schedule for affective disorders and schizophrenia. *Arch. Gen. Psychiatry* 37:837–844, 1978.
22. Essen-Moller E., et al.: Individual traits and morbidity in a Swedish rural population. *Acta Psychiatr. Neurol. Scand.,* suppl. 100, pp. 1–160, 1956.
23. Faris R.E., Dunham H.W.: *Mental Disorders in Urban Areas.* Chicago, University of Chicago Press, 1939.
24. Ferris C.: A study of bipolar (manic-depressive) and unipolar depressive psychosis. *Acta Psychiatr. Scand.,* vol. 42, suppl. 194, 1966.
25. Gove W.R.: The relationship between sex roles, marital status, and mental illness. *Soc. Forces* 51:33–44, 1972.
26. Hinkle L.E., Christenson W., Kane F., et al.: An investigation of the relationship between life experience, personality characteristics and general susceptibility to illness. *Psychosom. Med.* 20:278–295, 1958.
27. Hinkle L.E., Wolf H.G.: The nature of man's adaptation to his total environment and the relation of this to illness. *Arch. Intern. Med.* 99:442–460, 1957.
28. Hollingshead A.B., Redlich F.C.: *Social Class and Mental Illness: A Community Study.* New York, John Wiley & Sons, 1958.
29. Holmes T.H., Rahe R.H.: The social readjustment rating scale. *J. Psychosom. Res.* 11:213–218, 1967.
30. Ilfeld F.W.: Current social stressors and symptoms of depression. *Am. J. Psychiatry* 134:161–166, 1977.
31. Kales A., Kales J.D.: Sleep disorders. *N. Engl. J. Med.* 200:487–499, 1974.

32. Kaplan B.H., et al.: Social support and health. *Med. Care* 15:47–57, 1977.
33. Klerman G.L.: Clinical research in depression. *Arch. Gen. Psychiatry* 24:305–319, 1971.
34. Kovacs M., Beck A.T.: An empirical-clinical approach towards a definition of childhood depression, in Schulterhaudt J.G., Baskin A. (eds.): *Depression in Childhood: Diagnosis, Treatment and Conceptual Models*. New York, Raven Press, 1977.
35. Krauthammer C., Klerman G.C.: The epidemiology of mania, in Shopsin B. (ed.): *Mania*. New York, Plenum Publishing Corp., 1978.
36. Leighton D.C., et al.: *The Character of Change*. New York, Basic Books, 1963.
37. Leighton A., Lambo T.A., Hughes C.C., et al.: *Psychiatric Disorder Among the Yoruba*. Ithaca, New York, Cornell University Press, 1963.
38. Levitt E.E., Lubin B.: *Depression: Concepts, Controversies and Some New Facts*. New York, Springer Publishing Co., 1975.
39. Malzberg G.: The distribution of mental disease according to religious affiliation in New York State, 1949–1951. *Ment. Hygiene* 46:510–522, 1962.
40. Maoz M.D., Levy S., Brand N., et al.: An epidemiologic survey of mental disorders in a community of newcomers to Israel. *J. Coll. Gen. Practitioners* 11:1267–1284, 1966.
41. Marsella A.I.: Depressive experience and disorder versus cultures, in Triandis H.C., Draguns J.G. (eds.): *Handbook of Cross-Cultural Psychology: Psychopathology*. Boston, Allyn & Bacon, Inc., vol. 6, 1980.
42. Mitchell A.R.: *Psychological Medicine in Family Practice*. Baltimore, Williams & Wilkins Co., 1971.
43. Murphy H.B.M.: The low rate of mental hospitalization shown by immigrants to Canada, in Zwingmann C., Pfister-Ammende H. (eds): *Uprooting and After*. New York, Springer-Verlag, 1973.
44. McKinlay J.: Social networks, lay consultation and helpseeking behavior. *Soc. Forces* 51:275–292, 1973.
45. Odegard O.: Emigration and insanity. *Acta Psychiatr. Neurol.*, suppl. 4, 1932.
46. Opler M.K., Singer J.L.: Ethnic differences in behavior and psychopathology. *Int. J. Soc. Psychiatry* 2:11, 1956.
47. Paykel E.S.: Life stress and psychiatric disorder, in Dohrenmend B.S., Dohrenmend B.P. (eds.): *Stressful Life Events: Their Nature and Effects*. New York, John Wiley & Sons, 1973, chap. 8.
48. Paykel E.S., Meyers J.K., Dienelt M.N., et al.: Life events and depression: A controlled study. *Arch. Gen. Psychiatry* 21:753, 1969.
49. Paykel E.S., Prusoff B.A., Klerman G.C.: The endogenous-neurotic continuum: Rater independence and factor distribution. *J. Psychiatr. Res.* 8:73–90, 1971.
50. Pilisuk M., Froland C.: Social networks, kinships, social support and health. *Soc. Sci. Med.*, to be published.
51. Poznanski E.D., Cook S.C., Carroll B.J.: A depression rating scale for children. *Pediatrics* 64:442–450, 1979.
52. Prange W.A., Vitols M.M.: Cultural aspects of the relatively low incidence of depression in Southern Negroes. *Int. J. Soc. Psychiatry* 3:104–112, 1962.
53. Rahe R.H., et al.: A model for life changes and illness research. *Arch. Gen. Psychiatry* 31:162–177, 1974.
54. Rawnsley K.: Epidemiology of affective disorders, in *Recent Developments in*

Affective Disorders. Br. J. Psychiatry, Special Publication No. 2, 1968, pp. 26–27.

55. Report to the President by the President's Mental Health Commission. Washington, D.C., 1978.

56. Ripley H.S.: Depression and the life span-epidemiology, in Usdin G. (ed.): *Depression.* New York, Brunner/Mazel, Inc., 1977.

57. Robins E., et al.: A contrast of the three more common illnesses with the ten less common in a study and 18-month follow-up of 314 psychiatric emergency room patients: II. Characteristics of patients with three more common illnesses. *Arch. Gen. Psychiatry* 34:269–281, 1977.

58. Schwab J.J., et al.: Human ecology and depressive symptomatology, in Masserman J.D. (ed.): *Social Psychiatry.* New York, Grune & Stratton, vol. 2, 1976.

59. Schwab J.J., Bialow M.R., Brown J.M., et al.: Sociocultural aspects of depression in medical inpatients: II. Symptomatology and class. *Arch. Gen. Psychiatry* 17:539–543, 1967.

60. Schwab J.J., Biaelow M., Brown J., et al.: Diagnosing depression in medical inpatients. *Ann. Intern. Med.* 67:695–707, 1967.

61. Schneidman E.S.: Psychiatric emergencies, in Freedman A.M., Kaplan H.I., Sadock B.J. (eds.): *Comprehensive Textbook of Psychiatry.* Baltimore, Williams & Wilkins Co., 1975.

62. Silverman C.: *The Epidemiology of Depression.* Baltimore, Johns Hopkins University Press, 1968.

63. Slater E., Cowie V.: *The Genetics of Mental Disorders.* Oxford Monographs on Medical Genetics, London, Oxford University Press, 1971.

64. Sokolowsky J., Coltne C., Berger D., et al.: Personal networks of ex-mental patients in a Manhattan SRO hotel. *Hum. Organiz.* 37:5–15, 1969.

65. Spitzer R.L., Endicott J., Robins E.: *The Research Diagnostic Criteria.* Biometrics Research Division, New York State Dept. of Mental Health, New York, 1975.

66. Stoker D., et al.: Women in psychotherapy: A cross-cultural comparison. *Int. J. Soc. Psychiatry* 14:5–22, 1968.

67. Tanner J., Weissman M.M., Prusott B.: Social adjustment and clinical relapse in depressed outpatients. *Compr. Psychiatry* 16:541–555, 1975.

68. Teja J., Aggawal A.K., Nararg R.L.: Depression versus cultures. *Br. J. Psychiatry* 119:253–260, 1971.

69. Toncs C.: Premenstrual tension. *Br. J. Hosp. Med.* 7:383–387, 1968.

70. Valko R.J., Clayton P.J.: Depression in the internship. *Dis. Nerv. Syst.* 36(1):26–29, 1975.

71. Walker K., MacBride A., Vaehon M.: Social support networks and the crisis of bereavement. *Soc. Sci. Med.* 11:35–41, 1977.

72. Warheit G.J., et al.: An analysis of social class and racial differences in depressive symptomatology in the community: A community study. *J. Health Soc. Behav.* 14:291–299, 1973.

73. Watts C.H.: *Depressive Disorders in the Community.* Bristol, England, John Wright & Sons, 1966.

74. Weissman M.M., Klerman G.L.: Sex differences and the epidemiology of depression. *Arch. Gen. Psychiatry* 34:98–111, 1977.

75. Weissman M.M., Klerman G.L.: The epidemiology of mental disorders: Emerging trends. *Arch. Gen. Psychiatry* 35:705–712, 1978.

76. Weissman M.M., Klerman G.L., Paykel E.S., et al.: Treatment effects on the social adjustment of depressed women. *Arch. Gen. Psychiatry* 30:771–778, 1976.
77. Weissman M.M., Myers J.K.: Affective disorders in a U.S. urban community. *Arch. Gen. Psychiatry* 35:1304–1310, 1978.
78. Weissman M.M., Myers J.K.: Rates and risks of depressive symptoms in a United States urban community. *Acta Psychiatry Scand.* 57:219–231, 1978.
79. Weissman M., Paykel E.S.: *The Depressed Woman.* Chicago, University of Chicago Press, 1974.
80. Weissman M.M., Paykel E.S., Seigal R., et al.: The social role performance of depressed women: Comparisons with a normal group. *Am. J. Orthopsychiatry* 41:390–405, 1971.
81. Weissman M.M., Slaby A.E.: Oral contraceptives and psychiatric disturbance: Evidence from research. *Br. J. Psychiatry* 123:513–518, 1973.
82. Winokur G.: Unipolar depression. *Arch. Gen. Psychiatry* 36:47–52, 1979.
83. Winokur G., Clayton P.T., Reich T.: *Manic Depressive Illness.* St. Louis, C.V. Mosby Co., 1969.
84. Zung W.W.K.: A self-rating depression scale. *Arch. Gen. Psychiatry* 12:63–70, 1964.
85. Zung W.W.K.: From art to science: The diagnosis and treatment of depression. *Arch. Gen. Psychiatry* 29:238, 1973.
86. Zung W.W.K.: The status inventory: An adjunct to the self-rating scale. *J. Clin. Psychol.* 28:539–543, 1972.
87. Zung W.W.K., Green R.L.: Detection of affective disorders in the aged, in Eisdorfer C., Faun W.E. (eds.): *Psychopharmacology in Aging.* New York, Plenum Publishing Corp., 1973.

6

BIOCHEMICAL ASPECTS OF AFFECTIVE DISORDERS

FRANK A. DeLEON-JONES, M.D.

THE LAST 20 years of research into causes of the affective disorders have persuaded investigators of the clinical and biologic heterogeneity of these disorders. The results of different lines of biochemical investigation, based on direct clinical observation of these disorders, and the effect of antidepressant treatments have led to a number of hypotheses on the pathogenesis of the affective disorders, some of which are reviewed herein. Before these hypotheses are examined, a brief review of the catecholamine biosynthetic pathway is in order.

Catecholamines are formed in brain chromaffin cells, sympathetic nerves, and sympathetic ganglia from the amino acid precursor tyrosine by a sequence of enzymatic steps, as shown in Figure 6–1. Tyrosine is normally present in the circulation in a concentration of about 5×10^{-5}M. It is taken up from the bloodstream and concentrated within the brain and, perhaps, also in other sympathetic tissue, by an active transport mechanism. The conversion of tyrosine to norepinephrine (NE) and epinephrine was first demonstrated in the adrenal medulla and later confirmed in sympathetic nerves, ganglia, heart, arterial and venous tissue, and brain. Among the various enzymes of the biosynthetic pathway, tyrosine hydroxylase appears to be a unique constituent of catecholamine-containing neurons and chromaffin cells and is considered to be the rate-limiting step in the formation of NE and dopamine. Therefore, synthesis of these compounds in brain and other tissues can be markedly reduced with inhibitors of tyrosine hydroxylase.

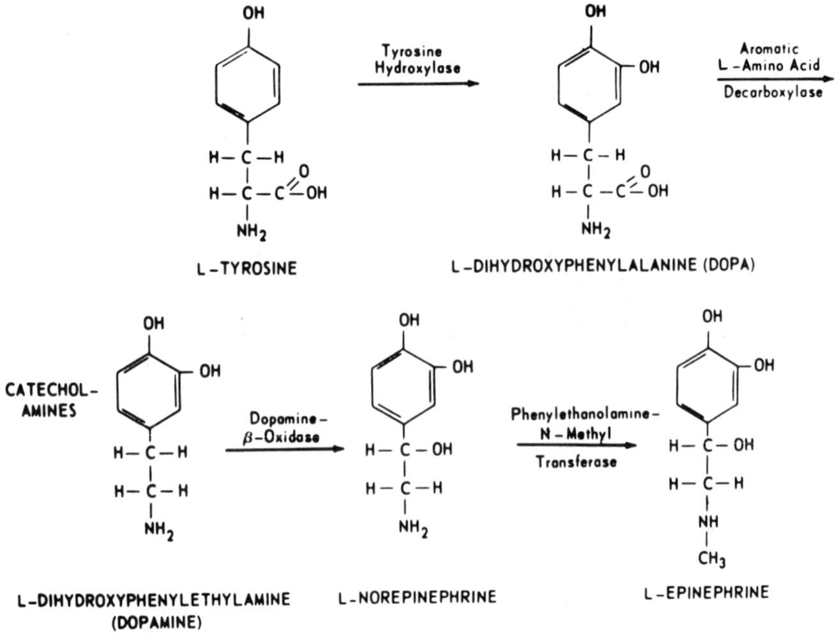

Fig 6–1.—Enzymatic processes in the formation of catecholamines from tyrosine.

Once synthesized, a large percentage of intraneuronal NE is stored within highly specialized subcellular particles, or granules, in sympathetic nerve endings and chromaffin cells, and presumably also in the CNS. It is currently believed that catecholamines are released from the chromaffin cell by a process of exocytosis, along with chromogranin, adenosine triphosphate (ATP), and some dopamine β-hydroxylase. Whether or not these cellular phenomena are applicable to the sympathetic nerve endings in general remains to be determined.

Catecholamines are inactivated by two main mechanisms: an intracellular and extracellular process. Figure 6–2 illustrates the catabolism of NE. It should be noted that in the peripheral nervous system, the aldehyde intermediate produced by the action of monoamine oxidase (MAO) on NE and normetanephrine (NM) can oxidize to the corresponding acid or be reduced to the corresponding glycol. Oxidation usually exceeds reduction and thus vanillylmandelic acid (VMA) is predominant. In the CNS the reductive pathway predominates and the dominant metabolite is the resulting glycol derivative, 3-methoxy-4-hydroxyphenylglycol (MHPG), which is the major metabolite of NE found in the brain. Very little, if any, VMA is found in the brain. Some NM is also found in the brain and spinal cord.

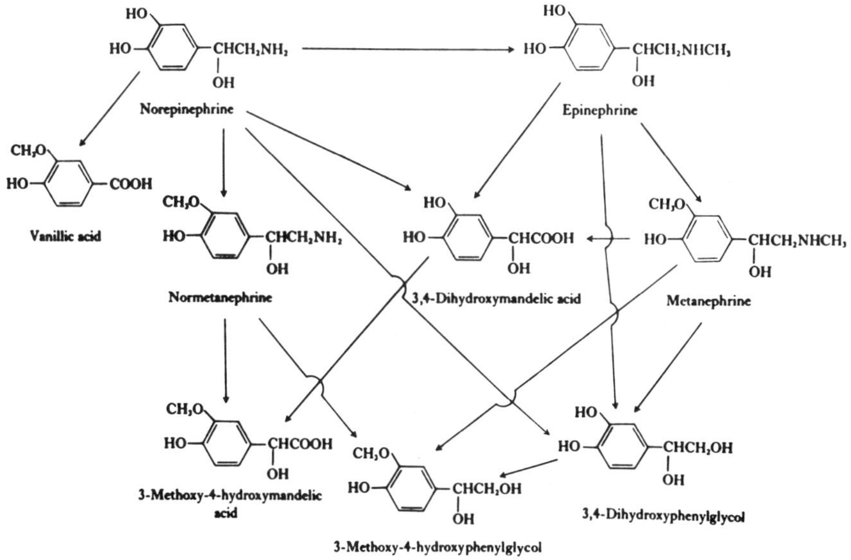

Fig 6-2.—Catabolism of norepinephrine.

Destruction of noradrenergic neurons in the brain or spinal cord causes a marked reduction of these metabolites. In many species a large fraction of MHPG formed in the brain is sulfate-conjugated. Since MHPG sulfate readily diffuses from the brain into the CSF or general circulation, an estimate of its concentration in the CSF or urine is thought to provide a possible reflection of activity of noradrenergic neurons in the brain. It should be kept in mind, however, that the contribution of peripheral noradrenergic tissue to urinary content of MHPG is large and that it is quite probable that relatively large changes in the formation of MHPG by the brain are necessary to produce detectable changes in urinary MHPG. Nevertheless, measurement of this metabolite in urine is still a reasonable strategy for obtaining information on possible alterations of central NE metabolism in some psychiatric disorders.

CATECHOLAMINE HYPOTHESIS OF AFFECTIVE DISORDERS

Two observations at about the same time led to the formulation of the catecholamine hypothesis of affective disorders. The first was the result of a decision by the Geigy Pharmaceutical Company, in 1951, to investigate antipsychotic properties of tricyclic drugs in clinical trials because of their resemblance to chlorpromazine. Although schizophrenic psychoses showed little response to imipramine, Kuhn noted that the depressive features of these patients showed marked improvement.[65] Subsequent clinical trials confirmed the antidepressant property of the drug, and imipramine was introduced to the European market in 1958 and in North America the following year. Like many other advances in pharmacology, the antidepressant action of the tricyclics was a serendipitous finding. Imipramine was investigated as a consequence of the success of chlorpromazine in schizophrenia. However, it proved to be more effective in the treatment of depression than of schizophrenia.

The second observation, which proved to be seminal in the investigation of the role of biogenic amines and tricylic drugs in the affective disorders, was that reserpine tended to cause depression, especially among hypertensives taking it in large doses. Reserpine-induced depression was thought to be clinically indistinguishable from naturally occurring depressions in man, although several observers have questioned whether reserpine-induced sedation in animals is a proper model for studying depression in man.[81] This sedation was found to be associated with decreased levels of NE, dopamine, and serotonin (5-HT). It is believed that reserpine depletes intraneuronal stores of catecholamines and 5-HT by interfering with their bindings, thereby leading to increased metabolic inactivation.[61] The central role of NE among neurotransmitters was suggested by giving dihydroxyphenylalanine, an NE precursor that crosses the blood-brain barrier. It was found that dihydroxyphenylalanine reverses reserpine-induced sedation. It appeared that drugs causing depletion or inactivation of NE centrally produce sedation or depression, whereas drugs raising or potentiating brain NE frequently are antidepressants.[102] This set the stage for elucidating the mode of action of imipramine.

Imipramine does not inhibit MAO or catechol-o-methyltransferase (COMT), the two enzymes involved in NE metabolism. The mechanism by which these drugs exert their antidepressant properties is thought to be the inhibition of re-uptake and release of NE and 5-HT. The experimental observations that led to these conclusions may be summarized as follows: Tricyclics (1) potentiate the peripheral actions of catecholamines, (2) reverse the reserpine syndrome in animals, and (3) block the uptake of exogenous NE and 5-HT into brain tissue.

The observations that these drugs altered affective states in humans and that they had profound effects on catecholamine disposition and metabolism in the brain prompted the formulation of a hypothesis about the pathophysiology of the affective disorders. The catecholamine hypothesis of affective disorders first appeared in 1965.[20, 102] It proposed that depression is related to a functional deficiency of neurotransmitters at important central adrenergic receptor sites, whereas mania is associated with a functional excess. It was clearly recognized, however, that abnormalities in catecholamine metabolism alone could not conceivably account for all the diverse clinical and biologic phenomena in the affective disorders. Thus Schildkraut, as early as 1965, noted that the hypothesized absolute or relative functional deficiency of NE at receptors could occur as a result of a number of different biochemical mechanisms, including a decrease in NE biosynthesis, impairment of NE binding and storage, increased intracellular release and deamination of NE, or a decrease in receptor sensitivity to NE, and that these biochemical differences might be related to differences in the clinical phenomenology or subtypes of depressive disorders.[102]

For obvious reasons, studies of catecholamines in humans have been done in bodily fluids such as urine, CSF, and plasma. Urinary NE and NM, which are derived from pools of NE outside the CNS, have been reported to be altered in patients with manic-depressive illness.[46, 69, 124] Strom-Olsen and Weil-Malherbe found that urinary excretion of NE and epinephrine was greater during the manic phase in patients with manic-depressive disorders.[115] Bjorum et al. reported elevated excretion of NE and epinephrine in a series of manic patients,[8] whereas no significant changes in the excretion of either amine were observed in patients with endogenous depressions. (Retarded depressions were not separately characterized.) Shinfuku et al. reported increases in the urinary excretion of NE during mania in a single patient with regular manic-depressive mood changes.[107] Greenspan et al. found that excretion of NE and NM was greater during hypomania than during normothymic periods or during periods of retarded depression.[50] In a longitudinal study of depressed patients, Schildkraut et al. observed a gradual rise in NM excretion during the period of definitive clinical improvement in depressed patients treated with imipramine.[101] Bunney et al. measured urinary catecholamines daily in a group of patients. Norepinephrine and dopamine were elevated before and during the manic episode. In particular, NE was significantly increased one day before the shift from depression to mania.[20]

MHPG, a naturally occurring catecholamine metabolite, was initially discovered by Axelrod and associates in 1959.[5] A number of subsequent reports have shown that MHPG is the major metabolite of brain NE.[46, 70, 78, 98–100, 105] In addition, it has been shown that either stress or direct stimulation of the locus coeruleus produces an increased turnover of NE and an increase in the sulfate conjugate of MHPG in the rat cerebrum, and that these effects are abolished by ablation of the locus coeruleus, suggesting that MHPG in the brain may reflect functional activity of central noradrenergic neurons.[1, 62, 63] There is also evidence suggesting that a significant fraction of urinary MHPG has its origins in the metabolism of NE within the brain, whereas urinary NE, NM, metanephrine (M), and perhaps VMA originate in pools of catecholamines outside the CNS.[46, 68, 70, 73, 75, 77]

It should be noted, however, that although there is general agreement that MHPG is the major metabolite of brain NE, definitive information is not available as to the exact amount of MHPG excreted in urine that is derived from the brain. For this reason, assaying urinary MHPG along with other catecholamine metabolites that have their origins outside the CNS might be a reasonable strategy for clinical studies of the catecholamine hypothesis of affective disorders.

Using this approach, Maas and associates found, in an initial pilot study, that a diagnostically heterogeneous group of hospitalized depressed patients excreted significantly less MHPG than healthy subjects, although urinary NM and M levels for the two groups were the same.[71] Subsequently, Greenspan and associates,[51] Bond and associates,[10] and DeLeon-Jones and associates[34] published data indicating that bipolar patients excreted significantly less MHPG during periods of euthymia or mania. Moreover, Schildkraut and associates recently showed that patients with a bipolar depressive disorder represent a clinically identifiable subgroup of depressed patients who excrete less than normal quantities of MHPG.[104] Thus there seems to be agreement among separate groups of researchers that some depressed patients excrete less than normal quantities of MHPG.

Inspection of the data presented in the initial report by Maas and associates,[71] as well as in other reports,[33, 95, 104] indicates that not every depressed patient excretes less than normal quantities of urinary MHPG. There are also disparate findings as to the levels of MHPG present in the CSF of depressed patients.[49, 84, 108, 126] It has been found that patients who excrete less MHPG can be identified by their behavioral responses to desimipramine or imipramine; that is, a low pretreatment urinary MHPG predicts a favorable response to desimipramine or imipramine, but pretreatment values of NM, M, or VMA are not significantly related to treatment response.[74]

Fawcett et al. have shown that patients who excrete less than normal quantities of MHPG respond with an elevation of mood when given *d*-amphetamine, whereas patients who excrete normal or greater than normal quantities of MHPG either do not respond or respond with a worsening of mood when given *d*-amphetamine.[41] Schildkraut found that patients who excrete normal or greater than normal quantities of MHPG responded best to amitriptyline.[103] The findings of Maas et al.,[74] Fawcett et al.,[41] and Schildkraut[103] have been confirmed by a recent report of Beckmann and Goodwin.[7] They measured the urinary excretion of MHPG in a group of unipolar depressed patients who met the criteria of Feighner and associates for a primary affective disorder. They measured MHPG excretion before and during the fourth week of treatment with either imipramine hydrochloride or amitriptyline hydrochloride. In the group given imipramine, the mean pretreatment MHPG level was significantly lower in the nine responders than in the seven nonresponders; the converse was found with the group given amitriptyline.[6]

Maas and associates also showed that patients who respond to amphetamine, desimipramine, or imipramine with an elevation of mood have modest increments or no change in MHPG excretion during treatment, whereas patients who do not respond to these drugs have decreased MHPG excretion during treatment.[41, 74] However, the Beckmann and Goodwin study showed that although responders to imipramine appeared to have a smaller decrease in MHPG excretion than nonresponders, there was no increase in MHPG excretion during response to imipramine.[7] Therefore this study did not confirm the findings of Maas and associates.

In a recent report, DeLeon-Jones et al. presented data indicating that a subgroup of depressed patients who excrete less than normal quantities of MHPG could be identified by the application of explicit clinical criteria.[35] They found no significant difference in the excretion of NM, M, and VMA among any of the diagnostic subgroups or between each patient group and a healthy comparison group. However, depressed patients diagnosed as having primary affective disorder and bipolar illness excreted significantly less MHPG than the healthy comparison group. This study suggests that the classification system of primary affective disorder and bipolar depressive disorder may be the most helpful in identifying those patients who excrete low amounts of MHPG. The agitated-retarded and the psychotic-nonpsychotic distinctions were not found to be helpful in identifying depressed subjects who excrete less than normal amounts of MHPG.

A review of the studies cited above indicates that at least two groups of depressives can be identified, as follows:

Group A:
1. Low pretreatment 24-hour urinary MHPG
2. Favorable clinical response to imipramine or desimipramine
3. Respond to a test dose of *d*-amphetamine with brightened mood (as reflected in the Clyde Scale "unhappy" factor)
4. Poor response to amitriptyline

Group B:
1. High or normal 24-hour urinary MHPG
2. No response to imipramine or desimipramine
3. No response to a test dose of *d*-amphetamine
4. Positive response to amitriptyline

It is speculated that the pathophysiology of group A primarily involves a disorder of NE metabolism or disposition, whereas that of group B reflects a disorder involving 5-HT metabolism or disposition.[77] This particular hypothesis is currently being investigated by a number of centers. Numerous investigations suggest that NE, as reflected by changes in MHPG excretion, may be implicated in the pathogenesis of the affective disorders.

The role of dopamine as it might relate to the affective disorders is also under study. Homovanillic acid (HVA), a deaminated o-methylated metabolite of dopamine, can be determined in lumbar CSF and may provide information about the cerebral metabolism of dopamine. Interpretation of such findings is complicated by the fact that the concentration of HVA in lumbar CSF is considerably lower than in ventricular CSF, suggesting that there may be a transport system for the removal of HVA in the region of the fourth ventricle.[83] Moreover, as noted above, the rate of efflux of one or another metabolite from the CSF may vary. Therefore, measurements of baseline levels of metabolites in lumbar CSF, at an instant in time, do not necessarily reflect the rates of production of the metabolites during a given time interval.

Baseline levels of HVA in the CSF have been found to be lower in depressed patients than in control subjects in a number of studies,[2, 7, 92, 93, 97, 126] but not in all.[112, 116, 117, 121] The accumulation of HVA following probenecid administration has been found to be decreased in at least certain subgroups of depressed patients when compared with controls.[47, 97, 111, 112, 121, 122] Levels of HVA following probenecid administration, however, were higher in a diagnostically heterogeneous group of depressed patients than in a control population in one study.[13] In two of these studies, differences were observed in CSF HVA accumulation after probenecid administration when depressed and hypomanic patients were compared,[47,112] but one study has recently reported that CSF HVA accumulation was significantly higher in manic patients than in patients with bipolar depressions.[14]

Homovanillic acid in CSF of patients with subtypes of depressive disorders has also been explored by a few investigators. Van Praag and associates[121, 122] have reported that subnormal accumulation of HVA occurs in depressed patients with motor retardation. Other investigators observed no difference in CSF levels of HVA after probenecid administration when patients with unipolar and bipolar depressions were compared.[123] Although Goodwin et al. initially found that patients diagnosed as bipolar I had significantly higher CSF levels of HVA following probenecid administration than patients diagnosed as bipolar II or unipolar,[47] this finding was not confirmed in a larger series of patients.[48] This line of inquiry requires further investigation, however. In summary a number of studies, although not all, have found that baseline levels of HVA in the CSF, and the accumulation of HVA in the CSF after probenecid administration, are reduced in at least some patients with depressive disorders.

THE SWITCH PROCESS IN AFFECTIVE DISORDERS

A significant amount of evidence has accumulated which suggests that pharmacologic agents may precipitate manic or depressive episodes in individuals with affective disorders. Some studies further suggest that the switch into depression is preceded by changes in brain catecholamine metabolism.[10, 20, 34] One of these studies showed that changes in MHPG excretion into urine preceded the switch from depression into mania and from mania into depression in a patient with repeated episodes of manic-depressive illness.[34] Both tricyclic compounds and MAO inhibitors precipitate mania and hypomania in approximately 10% of depressed patients. The action mode of these two classes of drugs supports the hypothesis that increases in functional monoamines in the CNS may be associated with the onset of manic symptoms. A number of drugs have also been associated with the onset of depression; reserpine, imipramine plus parachlorophenylalanine (PCPA), MAO inhibitors plus PCPA, physotigmine, cortisol, and amphetamine withdrawal. These compounds generally tend to decrease levels of monoamines in the CNS. In conclusion, study of the action mode of pharmacologic agents that precipitate switches into mania or depression will provide important information on the pathogenesis of the manic-depressive process.

STUDIES OF ENZYMES INVOLVED IN THE METABOLISM OF MONOAMINES

Enzymes of monoamine metabolism have been repeatedly studied in affective illness. Erythrocyte-soluble COMT activity has been reported reduced, elevated, and unchanged in different studies of patients with affective disorders.[38, 39, 44, 79] Unipolar/bipolar differences have been reported in some research,[38] but other studies have not found any.[44, 79]

In an initial series of studies on patients with primary affective disorders, the activity of COMT in red blood cells was significantly reduced in depressed women but not men, and more marked reductions were observed in women with unipolar depressions than in women with bipolar depressions.[28, 38] A similar reduction in red blood cell COMT activity in depressed women was confirmed by other investigators.[15] Davidson and associates reported a correlation between red blood cell COMT activity and clinical response to imipramine in a series of women with unipolar depressive disorders. The most favorable responses were observed in patients with relatively low COMT activity. Additional research will be needed to confirm these intriguing findings.[32]

Reduced platelet MAO activity in bipolar patients was initially reported by Murphy and Weiss[84] and later replicated in two other studies.[66, 67] Other studies, however, found higher activity in bipolar patients.[38, 90, 91]

INDOLEAMINE (SEROTONIN) HYPOTHESIS

Researchers have reported reduced functional levels of brain serotonin in patients with affective disorders, which may directly contribute or predispose to symptoms of depression and possibly mania. The strongest support for this hypothesis comes from repeated demonstrations in different laboratories that CSF levels of 5-hydroxyindoleacetic acid (5-HIAA), the major serotonin metabolite, are reduced approximately 30% in depressed patients[4, 30, 36, 120] or at least in a subgroup of depressed patients,[3] compared with controls. However, the single largest study of this type, involving 85 depressed patients and 27 controls, found essentially identical levels in both groups.[97]

Additional support for the serotonin hypothesis is derived from the fact that some studies found lower values of both serotonin[93, 106] and 5-HIAA[11, 93] in the brains of suicides, relative to controls. However, a reduction in brain serotonin cannot be said to have been proved in suicides, given the methodological problems inherent in postmortem investigations; furthermore, not all studies are in agreement with these findings. Nevertheless, it is encouraging that a recent comprehensive study of depressed subjects showed that the patient subgroup with low 5-HIAA levels had a higher incidence of suicide attempts.[3] It should be noted that a serotonin-deficient state has been postulated to function together with changes in catecholamines (so-called permissive hypothesis) to increase the susceptibility of bipolar individuals to manic and depressive episodes.[58, 82, 96] The evidence that serotonin depletion, as induced by PCPA administration, leads to irritability and enhanced responsiveness to stimuli in human beings and animals,[101] and that elevating brain serotonin, as by tryptophan treatment, leads to sedative effects,[52, 85, 96] is compatible with this interpretation.

Studies of tryptophan levels in plasma and CSF, blood serotonin and serotonin uptake measurements, and the urinary excretion of 5-HIAA, tryptamine, and other indoleamine metabolites can only be considered as equivocal, with as many negative studies as those showing a difference. There is substantial evidence for the efficacy of tricyclic drugs and some MAO inhibitors in depressed patients; given the small increment for possible improvement of their effects, the limited data suggesting enhancement by tryptophan cannot be disregarded. More persuasive is the apparent reversal of the therapeutic effects of imipramine and tranylcypromine by the serotonin synthesis inhibitor PCPA.[109, 110] If these results prove to be replicable and represent interference with serotonin synthesis, they would implicate the serotonin system in the mode of action of these drugs more clearly than any evidence previously available. Whether other drug effects in affective disorder patients, such as those of lithium carbonate, are also mediated in part by the serotonergic neurotransmitter system[60] and are also reversible by PCPA is not yet known.

CHOLINERGIC HYPOTHESIS OF MANIA AND DEPRESSION

Central cholinergic factors may play a role in the etiology of affective disorders; specifically, a given affective state may represent a balance between a central cholinergic and adrenergic neurotransmitter activity in those areas of the brain which regulate affect, with depression being a disease of cholinergic dominance and mania being the converse. Support for this hypothesis comes from animal experiments demonstrating antagonistic cholinergic and adrenergic central behavioral effects. Furthermore, reserpine, a drug which causes depression, has central cholinomimetic properties. Conversely, tricyclic antidepressants have central anticholinergic properties. In man, physostigmine and other centrally acting cholinomimetic agents that increase central choline levels counteract mania and may cause depression in some individuals. The evidence for a cholinergic-adrenergic hypothesis of mania and depression has been postulated by Janowsky et al.[56]

ENDORPHINS

Two lines of evidence led a number of investigators to search for an endogenous opiate-like substance. The characterization of a highly specific opiate receptor suggested the possibility of an endogenous ligand.[64] The demonstration that analgesia produced by electrical stimulation of the periaqueductal gray matter could be blocked by the opiate antagonist naloxone also suggested the existence of an endogenous morphine-like factor.[1] Several endogenous peptides with opiate-like activity have now been isolated from the brain and chemically characterized. Hughes and associates[54] recently reported the existence of a substance in the brain with morphine-like biologic activity. Simultaneously, Terenius and Whalstrom[118] extracted a morphine-like factor that had agonistic activity in opiate-binding studies with brain homogenates. Hughes and co-workers[54] then identified the structure of two endogenous opiate-like pentapeptides, now called leucine-enkephalin and methionine-enkephalin. Methionine-enkephalin proved to be sequence 61–65 of the pituitary hormone β-lipotropin (β-LPH). Several larger fragments of β-LPH have also been reported to be endogenous morphine-like factors.[64] The most important may be β-endorphin, which is identical to β-LPH 61–91. The term endorphin is now commonly used for the entire class of opiate-like peptides.[64]

These discoveries initiated a search for a physiologic role of these opioid compounds (endorphins). Since morphine and its congeners affect mood, pain appreciation, sleep, respiration, and release of pituitary hormones, these physiologic functions are currently under investigation.

A number of strategies are being used to study possible functions of endorphins in man. These involve the direct administration of endorphins and attempts to measure endogenous opioid substances in urine, plasma, and CSF by radioimmune and radioreceptor assays. One strategy attempts to increase the release of endorphins through a variety of techniques such as experimental induction of pain and stress, the implantation of electrodes in the brain, and the use of narcotic antagonists to study the effects of blocking the endorphin systems. If endorphins act to regulate aspects of neurophysiologic function, a pure narcotic antagonist administered to man should alter such function. Naloxone and Naltrexone, which reverse the effects of endorphins, are two relatively pure narcotic antagonists in current use.

There are a number of theoretical reasons for suggesting that endorphins may play a role in mania. Opioids produce euphoria that is similar to the euphoria associated with mania. It has been suggested that the behavior of cats given morphine may provide a model for mania.[27, 37] Furthermore, some manic patients experience markedly less pain in response to experimental stimuli than do normal individuals, which is compatible with a theory of altered endorphins in mania.[18] It has been reported that naloxone produces a decrease in some of the symptoms of mania in a small percentage of patients. Another study, however, found no antimanic effects with naloxone.[40] No therapeutic effects of naloxone in depression have been reported to date.

It has also been reported in a preliminary study that β-endorphin given to a small number of schizophrenic patients produced euphoria in some. In addition, β-endorphin had a rapid, albeit transient, antidepressant effect in two depressed subjects.[59]

ELECTROLYTES AND AFFECTIVE DISORDERS

Changes in the intracellular-extracellular sodium-potassium ratio across specific membranes within the brain could have effects on cellular excitability that could be associated with the mood variations observed in the affective disorders. Much attention has therefore been given to the possible roles of sodium, potassium, and related cations, such as calcium and magnesium, in the etiopathogenesis of the affective disorders.

Several hypotheses have been suggested in the past two decades as to the role of electrolytes in affective disorders, based on measurements of electrolyte imbalances in patients. Coppen and Shaw postulated that affective disorders might result from changes in the distribution of sodium across cell membranes.[29] It has also been reported that in depressed patients, sodium moves intracellularly as a homeostatic mechanism to replace potassium lost from the cell.[31] This results in a rise in residual sodium. These findings have not been replicated by others.[6] Nevertheless, several reports continue to associate depression with sodium retention.[55, 86–88] Changes in sodium concentration in depressed subjects have also been reported for CSF[119] and saliva.[46] A series of studies suggests that sodium levels of erythrocytes in subjects with neurotic depression are lower than in psychotic depressives and controls, and that these levels are not altered by recovery.[55, 86–88] Potassium levels do not appear to be altered during disease or recovery.

Both magnesium and calcium stabilize nerve membranes; however, these cations have effects on each other's properties in that magnesium may inhibit the release of neurotransmitters that depend on the presence of calcium. Most reports have failed to show any consistent changes in magnesium levels in subjects with affective disorders.[9, 43, 89] An elevation in plasma magnesium in depressed but not manic patients has been reported,[21] and an increase in urinary levels of magnesium has been noted.[8]

Transient but significant increases in serum total calcium and inorganic phosphorus have been observed to coincide with periodically recurrent, abrupt, spontaneous exacerbations of psychotic agitation and mania.[24, 25, 42, 114, 119] In a patient with periodic psychosis, reduction in duration and severity of episodes correlated with reduction of observed periodic serum calcium increases following progressive reduction of dietary calcium.[114] Conversely, in a patient with paranoid psychosis secondary to pseudohypothyroidism, increase in serum calcium following intravenous calcium lactate infusion repeatedly provoked exacerbations of the psychosis.[113] In periodically agitated patients increases in serum calcium appear to be associated with decreases in CSF calcium.[23, 24, 57, 119] By contrast, it has been reported that normal and depressed subjects have minimal rises in CSF calcium in the presence of marked increases in serum calcium.

It has been suggested that small but significant increases in total serum calcium may precede or coincide with the switch into mania or an excited psychosis.[22] In fact, as a recent report indicates, the experimental perturbation of serum calcium may alter the frequency and severity of psychotic episodes in patients with periodic illnesses. In a double-blind study dihydrotachysterol (DHT) was given orally to eight psychotic patients; in each case marked increases in psychosis and agitation accompanied increases in serum calcium and phosphorous within two weeks after the active drug was substituted for a placebo.[26]

This review of the role of electrolytes in affective disorders suggests that it is premature to reach any conclusions as to their true role, although some intriguing leads exist; more work is needed here. One important area of investigation is the relationship between electrolytes and hormones in the production of affective illness. Unfortunately, a review of this topic transcends the scope of this chapter. Still another area beyond this chapter is the effect of lithium on electrolytes in affective illness.[55]

REFERENCES

1. Akil H.: Enkephalin: Physiological implications, in Usdin E., Hamburg D., Barchas J. (eds.): *Neuroregulators and Psychiatric Disorders*. New York, Oxford University Press, 1977.

2. Arbuthnott G.W., et al.: The effect of unilateral and bilateral lesions in the locus coeruleus on the levels of 3-methoxy-4-hydroxyphenylglycol (MHPG) in neocortex. *Experientia* 29:52, 1973.

3. Asberg M., Thoren P., Traskman L.: Serotonin depression: A biochemical sub-group within the affective disorders? *Science* 191:478, 1976.

4. Ashcroft G.W., et al.: 5-Hydroxindole compounds in the cerebrospinal fluid of patients with psychiatric or neurological diseases. *Lancet* 2:1049, 1966.

5. Axelrod J., Kopin I.J., Mann J.D.: 3-Methoxy-4-hydroxyphenylglycol sulfate: A new metabolite of epinephrine and norepinephrine. *Biochem. Biophys. Acta* 36:576, 1959.

6. Baer L., et al.: Sodium balance and distribution in lithium carbonate therapy. *Arch. Gen. Psychiatry* 22:40, 1970.

7. Beckmann H., Goodwin F.K.: Antidepressant response to tricyclics and urinary MHPG in unipolar patients: Clinical response to imipramine or amitriptyline. *Arch. Gen. Psychiatry* 32:17, 1975.

8. Bjorum N., Mellerup E.T., Rafaelsen O.J.: Electrolytes in urine in endogenous depression. *Acta Psychiatr. Scand.* 48:337, 1972.

9. Bjorum N.: Electrolytes in blood in endogenous depression. *Acta Psychiatr. Scand.* 48:59, 1972.

10. Bond P.A., Jenner F.A., Sampson G.A.: Daily variations of the urine content of 3-methoxy-4-hydroxyphenyglycol in two manic-depressive patients. *Psychol. Med.* 2:81, 1972.

11. Bourne H.R., et al.: Noradrenaline, 5-hydroxytryptamine, and 5-hydroxyindoleacetic acid in hindbrains of suicidal patients. *Lancet* 2:805, 1968.

12. Bowers M.B. Jr.: Cerebrospinal fluid 5-hydroxyindoleacetic acid (5-HIAA) and homovanillic acid (HVA) following probenecid in unipolar depressives treated with amitriptyline. *Psychopharmacologia* 23:26, 1972.

13. Bowers M.B.: CSF acid monoamine metabolites as a possible reflection of central MAO activities in chronic schizophrenia. *Biol. Psychiatry* 11:245, 1976.

14. Bowers M.B. Jr., Heninger G.R., Gerbode F.: Cerebrospinal fluid, 5-hydroxy-indoleacetic acid and homovanillic acid in psychiatric patients. *Int. J. Neuropharmacol.* 8:255, 1969.
15. Breese G.R., et al.: 3-Methoxy-4-hydroxyphenylglycol excretion and behavioural changes in rat and monkey after central sympathectomy with 6-hydroxydopamine. *Nature New Biol.* 240:287, 1972.
16. Briggs M.H., Briggs M.: Hormonal influences on erythrocyte catechol-O-methyl transferase activity in humans. *Experientia* 29:278, 1973.
17. Brodie H.K.H., Sack R., Siever L.: Clinical studies on L-5-hydroxytryptophan in depression, in Barchas J., Usdin E.: *Serotonin and Behavior.* New York, Academic Press, 1973, p. 549.
18. Buchsbaum M.S., Davis G.C., Bunney W.E. Jr.: Naloxone alters pain and somatosensory evoked potentials in normal subjects. *Nature* 270:620, 1977.
19. Bunney W.E. Jr., Davis J.M.: Norepinephrine in depressive reactions: A review. *Arch. Gen. Psychiatry* 13:483, 1965.
20. Bunney W.E. Jr., et al.: The "switch process" in manic-depressive illness: II. Relationships to catecholamines, REM sleep, and drugs. *Arch. Gen. Psychiatry* 27:304, 1972.
21. Cade J.F.J.: A significant elevation of plasma magnesium levels in schizophrenia and depressive states. *Med. J. Aust.* 1:195, 1964.
22. Carman J.S., et al.: Increased serum calcium and phosphorous with the switch into manic or excited psychotic states. *Br. J. Psychiatry* 135:55, 1967.
23. Carman J.S., et al.: Calcium, ECT, lithium and mood. Read before the 127th annual meeting of the American Psychiatric Association, Detroit, Michigan, May 4–8, 1974.
24. Carman J.S., Wyatt R.J.: Alterations in CSF and serum total calcium with changes in psychiatric state, in Usdin E., Hamburg D.A., Barchas J.D. (eds.): *Neuroregulators and Psychiatric Disorders.* New York, Oxford University Press, 1977.
25. Carman J.S., Wyatt R.J.: Calcium: Bivalent cation in the bivalent psychoses. *Biol. Psychiatry* 14:295, 1979.
26. Carman J.S., Wyatt R.J.: Calcium: Pacesetting the periodic psychoses. *Am. J. Psychiatry* 136:1035, 1979.
27. Carroll B.J., Sharp P.T.: An animal model of mania. *Psychopharmacologia* 26:10, 1972.
28. Cohn C.K., Dunner D.L., Axelrod J.: Reduced catechol-O-methyltransferase activity in red blood cells of women with primary affective disorders. *Science* 170:1323, 1970.
29. Coppen A., Shaw D.M.: Mineral metabolism in melancholia. *Br. Med. J.* 2:1439, 1963.
30. Coppen A., et al.: Abnormalities of indoleamines in affective disorders. *Arch. Gen. Psychiatry* 26:474, 1972.
31. Cox J.R., Pearson R.E., Speight C.J.: Changes in sodium, potassium and body fluid spaces in repression and dementia. *Gerontol. Clinica* 13:233, 1971.
32. Davidson J.R.T., et al.: Red blood cell catechol-O-methyltransferase and response to imipramine in unipolar depressive women. *Am. J. Psychiatry* 133:952, 1976.
33. Dekirmenjian H., Maas J., Fawcett J.A.: Urinary excretion of NE and its metabolites in human control subjects. Read before the 126th annual meeting of the American Psychiatric Association, Honolulu, Hawaii, May 7–11, 1971.

34. DeLeon-Jones F., et al.: Urinary catecholamine metabolites during behavioral changes in a patient with manic-depressive cycles. *Science* 179:300, 1973.
35. DeLeon-Jones F., et al.: Diagnostic subgroups of affective disorders and their urinary excretion of catecholamine metabolites. *Am. J. Psychiatry* 132:1141, 1975.
36. Dencker S.J., et al.: Acid monoamine metabolites of cerebrospinal fluid in mental depression and mania. *Neurochem. J.* 13:1545, 1966.
37. Dhasmana K.M., et al.: Role of central dopaminergic receptors in manic responses of cats to morphine. *Psychopharmacologia* 24:380, 1972.
38. Dunner D.L., et al.: Differential catechol-O-methyltransferase activity in unipolar affective illness. *Arch. Gen. Psychiatry* 25:348, 1971.
39. Epstein R., et al.: Electrophoretic pattern of red blood cell catechol-O-methyltransferase in schizophrenia and manic depressive illness. *Biol. Psychiatry* 11:613, 1976.
40. Emrich H., et al.: A possible antipsychotic action of naloxone, in Usdin E., Bunney W.E. Jr., Kline N.S. (eds.): *Endorphins in Mental Health Research.* New York, Macmillan Publishing Co., to be published.
41. Fawcett J., Maas J.W., Dekirmenjian H.: Depression and MHPG excretion: Response to dextroamphetamine and tricyclic antidepressants. *Arch. Gen. Psychiatry* 26:246, 1972.
42. Fischback R.: Changes in calcium metabolism in depression and during medication with thymoleptics. *Arzneimittelforsch.* 21:27, 1971.
43. Frizel D., Coppen A., Marks V.: Plasma magnesium and calcium in depression. *Br. J. Psychiatry* 115:1375, 1969.
44. Gershon E., Jonas W.: Affective erythrocyte soluble catechol-O-methyltransferase activity in primary disorder. *Arch. Gen. Psychiatry* 32:1351, 1975.
45. Glen A.I.M., Ongley G.C., Robinson K.: Diminished membrane transport in manic-depressive psychosis and recurrent depression. *Lancet* 2:241, 1968.
46. Glowinski J., Kopin I.J., Axelrod J.: Metabolism of (H^3) norepinephrine in the rat brain. *J. Neurochem.* 12:35, 1965.
47. Goodwin F.K., et al.: Cerebrospinal fluid amine metabolites in affective illness: The probenacid. *Am. J. Psychiatry* 130:73, 1973.
48. Goodwin F.K., Post R.M., Freedman D.X. (eds.): *Biology of the Major Psychoses.* New York, Raven Press, 1975, vol. 54.
49. Gordon E.K., Oliver J.: 3-Methoxy-4-hydroxyphenylethylene glycol in human cerebrospinal fluid. *Clin. Chem. Acta* 35:145, 1971.
50. Greenspan K., et al.: Catecholamine metabolism in affective disorders. *Arch. Gen. Psychiatry* 21:710, 1969.
51. Greenspan J., et al.: Catecholamine metabolism in affective disorders: 3. MHPG and other catecholamine metabolites in patients treated with lithium carbonate. *J. Psychiatr. Res.* 7:171, 1970.
52. Harvey J.A., Scholsberg A.J., Yunger L.M.: Behavioral correlates of serotonin depletion. *Fed. Proc.* 34:1976, 1975.
53. Hughes J., et al.: The antidepressant drugs. *N. Engl. J. Med.* 272:1159, 1965.
54. Hughes S., et al.: Identification of two related pentapeptides from the brain with potent opiate agonist activity. *Nature* 258:577, 1975.
55. Hullin R.P., et al.: Metabolic balance studies on the effect of lithium salts in manic-depressive psychosis. *Br. J. Psychiatry* 114:1561, 1968.
56. Janowsky D., et al.: A cholinergic-adrenergic hypothesis of mania and depression. *Lancet* 23:632, 1972.

57. Jimerson D.C., et al.: CSF calcium: Clinical correlates in affective illness and schizophrenia. *Biol. Psychiatry* 14:37, 1979.
58. Kety S.: Brain amines and affective disorders: Overall review, in Ho B., McIsaac W. (eds.): *Brain Chemistry and Mental Disease.* New York, Plenum Press, 1971.
59. Kline N.S., et al.: Beta-endorphin-induced changes in schizophrenic and depressed patients. *Arch. Gen. Psychiatry* 34:1111, 1977.
60. Knapp S., Mandell A.J.: Effects of lithium chloride on parameters of biosynthetic capacity for 5-hydroxytryptamine in rat brain. *J. Pharmacol. Exp. Ther.* 193:812, 1975.
61. Kopin I.J.: Storage and metabolism of catecholamines: The role of monoamine oxidase. *Pharmacol. Rev.* 16:179, 1964.
62. Korf J., Aghajanian G.K., Roth R.H.: Stimulation and destruction of the locus coeruleus: Opposite effects on 3-methoxy-4-hydroxy-phenylglycol sulfate levels in the rat cerebral cortex. *Eur. J. Pharmacol.* 21:305, 1973.
63. Korf J., Roth R.H., Aghajanian G.K.: Alterations in turnover and endogenous levels of norepinephrine in cerebral cortex following electrical stimulation and acute axotomy of cerebral noradrenergic pathways. *Eur. J. Pharmacol.* 23:276, 1973.
64. Kosterlitz H.W. (ed.): *Opiates and Endogenous Opioid Peptides.* Amsterdam, Elsevier North-Holland, Inc., 1976.
65. Kuhn R.: Über die Behandlung depressive Zustande mit einem Iminodibenzylderivat (G22355). *Schweiz. Med. Wochenschr.* 87:1135, 1957.
66. Leckman J.F., et al.: Reduced MAO activity in first-degree relatives of individuals with bipolar affective disorders: A preliminary report. *Sci. Proc. Am. Psychiatr. Assoc.* 129:128, 1977.
67. Landowski J., Lysiak W., Angielski S.: Monoamine oxidase activity in blood platelets from patients with cyclophenic depressive syndromes. *Biochem. Med.* 14:347, 1975.
68. Maas J.W., Landis D.H.: Brain norepinephrine and behavior: A behavioral and kinetic study. *Psychosom. Med.* 27:399, 1965.
69. Maas J.W., Landis D.H.: A technique for assaying the kinetics of norepinephrine metabolism in the central nervous system in vivo. *Psychosom. Med.* 28:247, 1966.
70. Maas J.W., Landis D.H.: In vivo studies of the metabolism of norepinephrine in the central nervous system. *J. Pharmacol. Exp. Ther.* 163:147, 1968.
71. Maas J.W., Fawcett J., Dekirmenjian H.: 3-Methoxy-4-hydroxyphenylglycol (MHPG) excretion in depressive states: A pilot study. *Arch. Gen. Psychiatry* 19:129, 1968.
72. Maas J.W., Landis D.H.: The metabolism of circulating norepinephrine by human subjects. *J. Pharmacol. Exp. Ther.* 177:600, 1971.
73. Maas J.W., et al.: Catecholamine metabolite excretion following intraventricular injection of 6-OH-dopamine. *Brain Res.* 41:507, 1972.
74. Maas J.W., Fawcett J.A., Dekirmenjian H.: Catecholamine metabolism, depressive illness, and drug response. *Arch. Gen. Psychiatry* 26:252, 1972.
75. Maas J.W., et al.: Excretion of catecholamine metabolites following intraventricular injection of 6-hydroxy-dopamine in the *Macaca speciosa. Eur. J. Pharmacol.* 23:121, 1973.
76. Maas J.W.: Biogenic amines and depression. *Arch. Gen. Psychiatry* 32:1357, 1975.

77. Maas J.W., et al.: 3-Methoxy-4-hyroxyphenyl-glycol production by human brain in vivo. *Science* 205:1025, 1979.

78. Mannarino E., Kirshner N., Nashold B.S. Jr.: The metabolism of (c) noradrenaline by cat brain in vivo. *J. Neurochem.* 10:373, 1963.

79. Mattson B., et al.: Catechol-O-methyltransferase and plasma monoamine oxidase in patients with affective disorders. *Acta Psychiatr. Scand.* 255:187, 1974.

80. Meister A.: *Biochemistry of the Amino Acids*, ed. 2. New York, Academic Press, 1965, vol. 2.

81. Mendels J., Frazer A.: Brain biogenic amine depletion and mood. *Arch. Gen. Psychiatry* 30:447, 1974.

82. Mendels J., Frazer A.: Reduced central serotonergic activity in mania: Implication for the relationship between depression and mania. *Br. J. Psychiatry* 126:241, 1975.

83. Moir A.T.B., et al.: Cerebral metabolites in cerebrospinal fluid as a biochemical approach to the brain. *Brain* 93:357, 1970.

84. Murphy D.L., Weiss R.: Reduced monoamine oxidase activity in blood platelets from bipolar depressed patients. *Am. J. Psychiatry* 128:1351, 1972.

85. Murphy D.L., et al.: Tryptophan in affective disorders: Indoleamine changes and differential clinical effects. *Psychopharmacologia* 34:11, 1974.

86. Naylor G.J., NcNamee H.B., Moody J.P.: Erythrocyte sodium and potassium in depressive illness. *J. Psychosom. Res.* 11:173, 1970.

87. Naylor G.J., McNamee H.B., Moody J.P.: The plasma control of erythrocyte sodium and potassium metabolism in depressive illness. *J. Psychosom. Res.* 14:179, 1970.

88. Naylor G.J., McNamee H.B., Moody J.P.: Changes in erythrocyte sodium and potassium on recovery from a depressive illness. *Br. J. Psychiatry* 118:219, 1971.

89. Naylor G.J., Fleming L.W., Stewart W.K.: Plasma magnesium and calcium fluid in depressive psychosis. *Br. J. Psychiatry* 120:63, 1972.

90. Nies A., et al.: Amines and monoamine oxidase in relation to aging and depression in man. *Psychosom. Med.* 33:(5)470, 1971.

91. Nies A., et al.: Comparison of monoamine oxidase substrate activities in twins, schizophrenics and controls. *Adv. Biochem. Psychopharmacol.* 12:59, 1974.

92. Papeschi R., McClure D.J.: Homovanillic and 5-hydroxyindoleacetic acid in cerebrospinal fluid of depressed patients. *Arch. Gen. Psychiatry* 25:354, 1971.

93. Pare C.M.B., et al.: 5-Hydroxytryptamine, noradrenaline, and dopamine in brainstem, hypothalamus, and caudate nucleus of controls and of patients committing suicide by coal gas poisoning. *Lancet* 2:133, 1969.

94. Post R.M., et al.: Central norepinephrine metabolism in affective illness: MHPG in the cerebrospinal fluid. *Science* 179:1002, 1973.

95. Ho B.T., McIsaac W.M.: *Brain Chemistry and Mental Disease*. New York, Plenum Press, 1971.

96. Prange A.J. Jr., et al.: Tryptophan in mania: Contribution to a permissive hypothesis of affective disorders. *Arch. Gen. Psychiatry* 30:56, 1974.

97. Roos B.E., Sjostrom R.: 5-Hydroxyindoleacetic acid and homovanillic acid levels in the cerebrospinal fluid after probenecid application in patients with manic-depressive psychosis. *Clin. Pharmacol.* 1:153, 1969.

98. Rutledge C.O., Weiner N.: The effect of reserpine upon the synthesis of norepinephrine in the isolated rabbit heart. *J. Pharmacol. Exp. Ther.* 157:290, 1967.

99. Schanberg S.M., et al.: 3-Methoxy-4-hydroxyphenylglycol sulfate in brain and cerebrospinal fluid. *Biochem. Pharmacol.* 17:2006, 1968.
100. Schanberg S.M., et al.: Effects of psychoactive drugs on the metabolism of intracisternally administered serotonin in rat brain. *Biochem. Pharmacol.* 18:1971, 1969.
101. Schildkraut J.J., Gordon E.K., Durell J.: Catecholamine metabolism in affective disorders: I. Normetanephrine and VMA excretion in depressed patients treated with imipramine. *J. Psychiatr. Res.* 3:213, 1965.
102. Schildkraut J.J.: The catecholamine hypothesis of affective disorders: A review of supporting evidence. *Am. J. Psychiatry* 122:509, 1965.
103. Schildkraut J.J.: Norepinephrine metabolites as biochemical criteria for classifying depressive disorders and predicting responses to treatment preliminary findings. *Am. J. Psychiatry* 130:695, 1973.
104. Schildkraut J.J., et al.: MHPG excretion in depressive disorders: Relation to clinical subtypes and desynchronized sleep. *Science* 181:762, 1973.
105. Sharman D.F.: Glycol metabolites of noradrenaline in brain tissue. *Br. J. Pharmacol.* 36:523, 1969.
106. Shaw D.M., Camps F.E., Eccleston E.G.: 5-Hydroxytryptamine in the hindbrain of depressive suicides. *Br. J. Psychiatry* 113:1407, 1967.
107. Shinfuku N., Omura M., Kayano M.: Catecholamine excretion in manic depressive patients. *Yonago Acta Med.* 5:109, 1961.
108. Shopsin B., et al.: Cerebrospinal fluid MHPG: An assessment of norepinephrine metabolism in affective disorders. *Arch. Gen. Psychiatry* 28:230, 1973.
109. Shopsin B., et al.: Use of synthesis inhibitors in defining a role for biogenic amines during imipramine treatment in depressive patients. *Psychopharmacol. Commun.* 1:239, 1975.
110. Shopsin B., Friedman E., Gershon S.: Parachlorophenylamine reversal of tranylcypramine effects in depressed patients. *Arch. Gen. Psychiatry* 33:811, 1975.
111. Sjöström R.: 5-Hydroxyindole acetic and homovanillic acid in cerebrospinal fluid in manic depressive psychosis and the effect of probenacid treatment. *Eur. J. Clin. Pharmacol.* 6:75, 1973.
112. Sjöström R., Roos B.E.: 5-Hydroxyindolacetic acid and homovanillic acid in cerebrospinal fluid in manic-depressive psychosis. *Eur. J. Clin. Pharmacol.* 4:170, 1972.
113. Snowdon J.A., Macfie A.C., Pearce J.B.: Hypocalcemic myopathy with paranoid psychosis. *J. Neurol. Neurosurg. Psychiatry* 39:48, 1976.
114. Speijer N.: Treatment of a periodical psychosis (degenerative psychosis) based upon hematological and biochemical deviations from the normal. *Folia Psychiatr. Neurol. Neurochirurg. Neerlandica* 53:718, 1950.
115. Strom-Olsen R., Weil-Malherbe H.: Humoral changes in manic depressives with particular reference to catecholamines in urine. *J. Ment. Sci.* 104:696, 1958.
116. Subrahmanyam S.: Role of biogenic amines in certain pathological conditions. *Brain Res.* 87:355, 1975.
117. Takahashi S.: CSF monoamine metabolites in alcoholism: A comparative study with depression. *Folia Psychiatr. Neurol. Jpn.* 28:347, 1974.
118. Terenius L., Whalstrom A.: Search for an endogenous ligand for the opiate receptor. *Acta Physiol. Scand.* 94:74, 1975.
119. Ueno Y.: Electrolyte metabolism in blood and cerebrospinal fluid in psychosis. *Folia Psychiatr. Neurol. Jpn.* 15:304, 1961.

120. Van Praag H.M., Korf J.: Endogenous depressions with and without disturbances in the 5-hydroxytryptamine metabolism: A biochemical classification. *Psychopharmacologia* 9:148, 1971.
121. Van Praag H.M., Korf J., Schut D.: Cerebral monoamines and depression: An investigation with the probenacid technique. *Arch. Gen. Psychiatry* 28:827, 1973.
122. Van Praag H.M.: Therapy-resistant depressions: Biochemical and pharmacological considerations. *Pharmakopsychiatr. Neuropsychopharmakol.* 7:281, 1974.
123. Watson K., Hartmann E., Schildkraut J.J.: Amphetamine withdrawal, affective sleep patterns, and MHPG excretion. *Am. J. Psychiatry* 129:263, 1972.
124. Weil-Malherbe H., Witby L., Axelrod J.: The uptake of circulating (^{3}H) norepinephrine by the pituitary gland and various areas of the brain. *J. Neurochem.* 8:55, 1961.
125. White A.: *Principles of Biochemistry*, ed. 4. New York, McGraw-Hill Book Co., 1968.
126. Wilk S., et al.: Cerebrospinal fluid levels of MHPG in affective disorders. *Nature* 235:440, 1972.

7

NEUROENDOCRINE ASPECTS: AN OVERVIEW

CHARLES H. RODGERS, Ph.D.

THE PYTHAGOREAN DOCTRINE proposed that mind and intellect resided in the brain, but the manner in which the brain in turn regulates body state and behavior has been described only recently. It is now appreciated that the brain regulates body chemistry and behavior partly through the endocrine system, thereby providing a physiologic basis for the observation that endocrinal and behavioral dysfunctions are somehow related.[32] Psychiatric research during the past 10 years has demonstrated with increasing frequency the coexistence of behavioral and physiologic pathology, yet the causes and nature of the relationship remain unknown. In view of the complex nature of the subject matter, this chapter is organized as follows: first, the physiology of two endocrine glands, the adrenals and gonads, implicated in affective states are reviewed, followed by a brief review of hormone-behavior relationships in normal states. Finally, there is a discussion of endocrine changes concomitant with depressive illness. Evidence for and against biogenic amine regulation of endocrine function will not be discussed; interested readers may consult Carroll,[15] Ettigi and Brown,[31] Imura et al.,[48] and Schwartz and McCormack[93] for details.

PHYSIOLOGY OF THE ADRENALS AND GONADS

Several levels within the organism interact in controlling adrenal and gonadal function (Fig 7-1). The adrenal cortex secretes several steroid hormones in response to adrenocorticotropic hormone (ACTH), although only

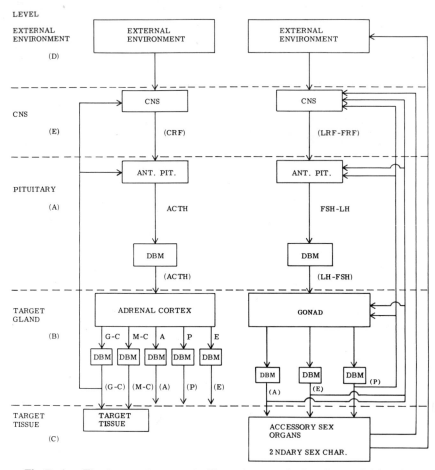

Fig 7–1.—The two systems controlling adrenocortical and gonadal functions. DBM = compartment(s) for distribution, metabolism, and binding of hormone; G-C = glucocorticoid; M-C = mineralocorticoid; A = androgens; P = progestins; E = estrogens.

cortisol and the sex hormones are discussed herein. Current evidence suggests that ACTH is ubiquitous throughout the body. It is found in chromophobe cells of the adenohypophysis, possibly in several limbic system areas,[51, 107] and in a type of gonadotrope cell of the adenohypophysis containing both follicle-stimulating hormone (FSH) and ACTH.[63] Because the limbic system contains both cholinergic and adrenergic fibers, it is not clear whether ACTH is associated exclusively with one type of neuron. The presence of ACTH in nervous and endocrine system tissues indicates that it might be released from multiple sites and subject to multiple feedback control, as will be elaborated subsequently; however, some of the control resides at the anterior pituitary and the CNS (see Fig 7–1). Feedback sites for glucocorticoid at the adenohypophysis may make ACTH-secreting cells less sensitive to CNS corticotropin-releasing factor (CRF), thus reducing ACTH release. Alternatively, glucocorticoid is taken up and bound within the limbic system.[16, 38]

The phylogenetically older brain (limbic lobe) is postulated as mediating emotional behavior, and because of extensive neuroanatomical connections with more recently evolved brain regions, the limbic system is viewed as an integrator of "internal and external perception."[58] The mediobasal hypothalamus, considered the final common pathway for brain regulation of pituitary function, is the critical CNS site for interfacing regions thought to mediate affective behavior[105] and those believed to modulate release of pituitary hormones. On the neuronal level, afferents of fibers involved in behavioral and endocrine mediation modulate mediobasal hypothalamic neurohumoral control of adenohypophyseal function. Numerous fiber systems have been shown to mediate increased ACTH release after stress in several species. Circadian rhythms of cortisol as well as different stresses appear to be conveyed by different groups of fibers.[36, 83] Suppression of ACTH may occur through inhibition of CRF activity (directly or indirectly), as has been shown in the cat,[59] or by direct action on the adenohypophysis, as has been shown in the rat.[109] It should be noted, however, that stress can be additive in the lower mammal such that high levels of glucocorticoid may sensitize the system, causing more ACTH to be released.[25] Additional cortisol release on an already elevated level of cortisol may be similar to observations made in certain unipolar depressed patients.

The release of ACTH in the human is entrained with the external environment (see Fig 7–1), whereas gonadal hormone secretion is not. Light acts as a zeitgeber (synchronizer) of diurnal variation of serum cortisol; in the blind, cortisol rhythms peak at times they are usually decreasing in the sighted.[9] Activation of the pituitary-adrenal axis denoting physiologic stress occurs in response to a number of events (e.g., hospitalization[8, 74]) and in association with pathologic behaviors.[13, 15, 24, 39, 72, 73, 90, 100] Adenohypophyseal hormones in addition to ACTH may be *increased* (prolactin, growth hormone (GH), antidiuretic hormone (ADH) or *decreased* (luteinizing hormone (LH), thyroid-stimulating hormone (TSH), oxytocin) in response to stress or trauma; however, extreme stress may inhibit GH release via GH inhibitory factor (somatostatin). Both prolactin and ADH may in turn cause more ACTH to be released. Antidiuretic hormone has CRF-like activity,[28] and prolactin decreases the adrenal enzyme 5 α-reductase, which in turn increases glucocorticoid levels.[68, 108] Thus, activation of the pituitary-adrenal axis may result from several events, including increased secretion of other anterior and/or posterior pituitary regulatory hormones.

The decreased release of LH caused by stressful stimuli is reflected in reduced gonadal secretion. Psychological stress,[60] fear-provoking stimuli,[26] massive obesity,[41] and Cushing's syndrome (hypercortisolemia) decrease plasma testosterone levels;[55, 96] a subsequent reduction in fear is related to a return to higher testosterone levels.[26] In healthy female volunteers ovulation is blocked by environmental stress,[74] also observed after prison internment.[81] Stress can thus be seen to have ubiquitous effects on various hormone levels and organ systems owing to the primary and secondary physiologic activity of increased cortisol secretion. The neurophysiologic and psychological consequences of high glucocorticoid levels (as in Cushing's syndrome) have been elaborately studied;[44] such excesses have been related to an inability to integrate sensory information[44] and to the development of mental disorders ranging from euphoria to schizophrenia.[69]

Adrenocortical and gonadal functions also interface via estrogen. The sex steroids are bound throughout limbic system regions translocating to the cell nuclei and may increase or decrease CNS activity. A small amount of testosterone is aromatized to estrogen in CNS cells. Estrogen may act at the anterior pituitary, adrenal, and brain to increase glucocorticoid secretion or decrease biologic availability of cortisol by increasing corticosteroid-binding globulin (CBG) in sera.[110] Increased binding of glucocorticoid causes reduced central inhibition of ACTH secretion, allowing more ACTH to be released. Approximately 2% of cortisol circulates unbound (free), with about 90% bound to CBG in normal,[22] in contrast to depressed, patients;[17] decreases in the level of free cortisol can cause its release from CBG.[69] Alternatively, after cortisol saturates CBG (about 20 µg/100 ml), free cortisol increases in the plasma. Thus, the synthesis of CBG in the liver, which can be stimulated by estrogen, determines the ratio of free to bound cortisol. Liver dysfunction may thus have direct consequences on serum levels of cortisol.

The synthesis of the sex hormones occurs primarily in the gonads in response to FSH and LH (gonadotropins) secreted by the adenohypophysis. As shown in Figure 7–1, accessory sex organs and secondary sex characteristics are noteworthy in their feedback relationships to the external environment and the CNS and depend on receptors to take up and bind sex hormone. Sex hormones, like other hormones, exert physiologic activity by binding to receptors, and the presence of excess hormone may decrease the number of active receptor sites.[35]

Because estradiol, progesterone, and testosterone bind to regions throughout most of the limbic system, they have great potential to influence behavior and pituitary functions. In addition, estradiol induces lactogenic hormone receptors (prolactin, GH, placental hormone) in the liver.[75] Importantly, estrogen and progesterone have been shown to increase and decrease, respectively, hypothalamic tyrosine hydroxylase activity in the lower mammalian female,[4] and estrogen has been shown to decrease monoamine oxidase levels in female depressed patients;[50] thus, estrogen can alter both the synthesis and the metabolism of catecholamines.

In summary, gonadal hormones influence the metabolic clearance of hormones,[60] the level of biologically available hormones in plasma (cortisol, estradiol, testosterone), specific liver receptor systems, the rate-limiting step in the synthesis of central catecholamines, and the re-uptake of norepinephrine. Each of the estrogen functions may have direct consequences for hormone-behavior relationships.

HORMONE-BEHAVIOR RELATIONSHIPS IN NORMAL STATES

Hormone-behavior relationships in the human have been of continuing interest and the source of much debate. Some of the difficulty may arise from misconceptions about the relationship of hormones to behavior, even in lower mammals, and some may be due to the source(s) of information. Complex patterns of behavior in lower mammals requiring hormones, such as sexual behavior, still depend on experience for full and efficient expression; the hormone in such instances does not guarantee by its presence effective behavioral expression. Observations in the human based on clinical situations after removal of one or more endocrine glands, or following exogenous hormone administration, have limited value and can be misleading in understanding behavioral dynamics. Brain regulation of endocrine function is complex, and the resulting changes on circulating levels of hormone may influence behavior in a variety of ways. It is becoming increasingly clear, for example, that in the animal[84, 85] and human psychotic,[67] the CNS may induce changes in liver functioning that may be important in altered states of behavior. Thus, prior to reviewing pathologic states wherein both behavioral and endocrinal changes have been reported, it might be useful to review instances in which hormones may be related to normal human behavior.

The discussion in this section will focus on sexual functions for several reasons. First, sexual behavior in the human may be a form of behavior most likely to depend on circulating hormones. Second, sexual behavior is commonly disturbed, or altered, during affective disorder states. Third, historically, sex hormones have been viewed as providing some basis for mood or affect.

Libido and sexual behavior in the human male depend on a threshold amount of plasma testosterone, which varies between and within individuals. Sexual impotence in otherwise healthy men does not appear to be based on endocrine dysfunction,[6, 27, 53] nor does penile tumescence during REM sleep relate directly to variations in plasma testosterone.[91] This is in contrast to the nonhuman primate, which shows increased aggressiveness, dominance, and sexual behavior with increased levels of plasma testosterone.[54, 80, 86, 87] Libido and the expression of sexuality in the human have been controlled clinically by the administration of estrogen, progestins, an antiandrogen, or tranquilizers, which decrease plasma testosterone levels below threshold amounts for behavior.[29, 52, 60, 62, 66] A similar reduction in plasma testosterone levels in heroin addicts or during high levels of methadone maintenance is thought to account for decreased libido.[2, 61] Even though a variety of hormones and treatments decrease plasma testosterone levels below amounts required for behavior, penile tumescence still occurs.[66] Similarly, long after castration and the cessation of sexual behavior in the male rat, penile tumescence continues for long periods.[82] Although the spinal component remains (penile tumescence), the integrated behavioral pattern essential for effective behavioral expression is disrupted by significant reduction of testosterone in the lower mammal, nonhuman primate, and the human male.

The object of sexual expression is not provided by testosterone or estradiol in the human, as homosexuals have not shown consistent and significant differences from heterosexual men in plasma levels of these hormones.[3, 33] These findings are consistent with a 1943 report by Hoskins[46] that sex hormone treatment was not effective in treating male or female homosexuals.

The extent to which hormones (possibly androgen) facilitate libido in the human female remains unclear, although the female appears to be able to function normally in the absence of hormones.[56] In contrast, the female nonhuman primate undergoes definite menstrual cycle variations in a number of social and nonsocial behaviors.[42] Data also are unclear on the extent that changes in mood may be related to the menstrual cycle, although there has been a suggestion that deaths from suicide and accidents occur with greater frequency during the midluteal phase of the cycle.[57] Extensive reviews on the incidence of psychological effects of steroid contraception have failed to find hormone-induced changes; rather, depression and irritability appear related to previous psychiatric disorders or premenstrual disposition.[23, 71] Estrogen and progesterone thus appear able to facilitate the occurrence of an existing tendency for certain behavior without providing or initiating the direction for its expression. The effects of therapeutic doses of cortisol on personality may be similarly viewed as intensifying an existing mood or personality disposition.

Interest in recent years has centered on the extent to which behavior may induce changes in serum levels of hormone: Can behavior in the human cause a "reflex" release of hormone, as observed in certain lower mammalian species? Assessments of serum hormone levels have been made following coitus in males and females. Neither coitus nor orgasm increased circulating plasma levels of LH, FSH, GH, progesterone, or estradiol in women,[64, 98] nor did coitus or ejaculation in males increase circulating levels of LH, FSH, or testosterone.[95, 98] Other forms of behavior have been found to influence levels of serum hormone. A well-documented case of pseudocyesis of 38 weeks showed elevated levels of serum prolactin and LH returning to normal along with menstruation after the patient understood her condition.[111] Prolactin release in response to infant suckling resulting in milk-letdown has been documented in the human female,[1] and the frequent observation of milk-letdown in lactating mothers in response to emotional stimuli, the infant's cry, or at expected times of nursing are commonplace.

There is no simple answer to the question of whether human behavior depends on an absolute level of circulating hormones. A minimal level of testosterone is essential for libido and full sexual expression in the human male, but it is unclear to what extent female sexuality depends on circulating levels or absolute amount of hormones. Particular responses in the human may in turn induce changes in hormone secretions, but sexual responses do not induce changes in sex hormone level or several other adenohypophyseal hormones. Alternatively, hormones appear to have the capacity to facilitate dormant behavior by lowering behavioral thresholds, enabling the behaviors to be elicited more easily; however, such hormones do not seem able to initiate the direction behavior might take. Physiologically, hormones may influence human behavior by initiating changes at the neurophysiologic, neurochemical, and biochemical levels. The changes may be expected to occur at central and peripheral levels, especially if initiated by changes in circulating levels of hormones. The increased complexity of the human CNS not only enables behavior to be less dependent on hormones, but may serve to obscure instances where hormones influence behavior. Thus, hormone-behavior relationships must be assessed and compared across species for a better understanding of the physiologic contribution to the relationships.

DEPRESSIVE ILLNESS CONCOMITANT WITH ENDOCRINE CHANGES

Endocrine changes concomitant with affective disorders are not necessarily unique to such disorders but may apply to other psychopathologic states. Thus, changes in adrenocortical and gonadal hormone levels have been reported for various schizophrenias, periodic psychoses, depression, mania, manic-depression, and anorexia nervosa. Such observations illustrate several problems pertinent to a discussion of endocrinal and behavioral dysfunction. Some of these problems, not necessarily mutually exclusive, are (1) arriving at a differential diagnosis within the class of affective disorders, (2) behaviors congruent with more than one diagnostic classification, (3) changes in endocrinal and other physiologic function associated with life span, and the possible relationship to the onset of psychopathology, (4) the potential for involving similar changes of endocrine function in different states of psychopathology, and (5) the attendant physiologic effects on other organic functions brought about by dysfunction in one or more of the endocrine glands. Knowledge concerning some of the problem areas is accumulating rapidly, while advancement in others is relatively limited.

From the 1950s through the present, numerous studies have shown pituitary-adrenal activation during episodes of affective disturbance. These findings have been fairly consistent, even though methods of assessing activation and arriving at a diagnosis differed. Indeed, hyperadrenocortical activity has been associated with psychoses,[8, 10, 47, 49, 73, 100] anxiety,[72] mania,[88] and protein deficiency (anorexia nervosa).[21, 37, 97, 106] The extent that thyroid function also may be altered in depressive states or involved in the treatment of depression has been controversial,[5, 20, 30, 45, 65, 76, 77, 103] although it should be mentioned again that activation of the pituitary-adrenal axis may decrease TSH release from the adenohypophysis. Increased pituitary-adrenal activity also was associated with decreased gonadotropin levels in the male and female as shown by reduced estradiol and testosterone levels. Importantly, amenorrhea has been noted to precede and attend frank psychological symptoms of endogenous depression.[70] However, schizophrenia also is associated with disrupted gonadotropin release in females and males.[10, 40, 78, 79, 101] The finding that several psychiatric disorders are associated with similar changes in endocrine function without apparent specificity for the type of behavioral dysfunction is interesting. Some researchers have speculated that such multiple changes are evidence for CNS dysfunction, as similar disturbances have been noted after damage to the brain.[102] Others view certain of the changes (pituitary-adrenal) as evidence for decreased levels of CNS norepinephrine.[31, 88] Each view has some support by data and is consistent with certain effects hormones may have on behavior; other physiologic data are relevant, however, and do not exclusively support one or the other view.

The effects of activation of the pituitary-adrenal axis on other physiologic activity would be expected to result in decreased gonadal and possibly thyroidal function; such change was noted previously to further increase the activation of the pituitary-adrenal axis. Associated increases from such activation in prolactin and ADH along with the noted decreased estradiol level all can exert further increases in cortisol levels. Because each of these hormones possesses both primary and secondary physiologic effects, numerous body systems will be influenced rather than certain levels exclusively.

Recent studies using more elaborate designs and sophisticated methodology to assess both endocrinal and psychological variables have been more specific in relating adrenocortical activation to specific affective states. In depressed patients plasma cortisol has been reported to be elevated throughout the 24-hour period and to normalize following recovery from depression.[14, 90] Urinary free cortisol, plasma cortisol, plasma free cortisol, and free cortisol in the cerebrospinal fluid (CSF) have been reported to be elevated during depression.[14, 17, 104] Of increasing interest are findings showing that patients diagnosed as having primary affective disorder, depressed type, show an early escape from dexamethasone (DEX) on the dexamethasone suppression test (DST) when DEX is administered in quantities between 1 and 8 mg.[12, 18, 19, 92, 99] The DST is used for the clinical diagnosis of Cushing's syndrome: 1 mg of DEX is administered between 11 and 12 P.M. and the level of plasma cortisol is measured the following morning at 8 A.M.[22] Normal patients have suppressed plasma cortisol levels for 24 hours following the DST,[31] whereas unipolar depressed patients fail to show decreased levels for 24 hours following DEX administration. The more severe the depressed state, the sooner cortisol may return to high levels following DEX administration.[15, 18] The reported percentage of unipolar patients showing early escape from DST has varied from 48% to 80%, depending on the study. Further, patients with bipolar disorders wherein normal plasma cortisol suppression in response to DEX occurs during the manic phase fail to show suppression while in a depressed phase.[17, 92] The reasons for only a percentage of patients meeting the criteria of primary affective disorder of the unipolar type escape early after DST, and for bipolar patients showing early escape only during the depressed phase, are not clear, but may argue against a unifying biologic cause of primary affective disorders. Interestingly, various psychiatric disorders have been associated with elevated cortisol levels, but unipolar and bipolar patients in a depressed state had the highest levels. Even in the same patient with a bipolar disturbance, plasma cortisol was higher during the depressed than during the manic phase.[18, 19, 92]

The data on hypercortisolemia in patients with unipolar depression suggest there may be a critical point for high levels of plasma cortisol. Once that point is passed, the setpoint for negative feedback control increases, so that suppression occurs for only brief periods of time. If areas of the limbic system are more highly activated during a primary affective disorder of depression, and if ACTH is present in a number of limbic system regions, as has been suggested,[51, 107] then both brain and pituitary sources of ACTH might be responsible for the observed hypercortisolemia. It is reasonable to expect a reduction in the amount of active cortisol receptor material in both pituitary and brain tissues as a result of prolonged elevation of cortisol levels. The reduction in receptor material together with the highly activated limbic system could account for the relatively free running secretion of cortisol, subject to only brief periods of negative feedback regulation. A recent finding that high levels of estrogen reduce prolonged and persistent depression in women, owing possibly to a reduction in monoamine oxidase levels,[50] suggests an additional factor contributing to the elevated cortisol level in women. It will be recalled that exogenous estrogen can increase the binding of cortisol in plasma by increasing CBG; thus, an additional effect of estrogen administration would be to lower free cortisol levels below the hypothetical critical point.

It is clear that hypercortisolemia, as in Cushing's syndrome, has definite effects on psychological function in nonpsychiatric patients.[44, 69] It is not clear, however, that elevated plasma cortisol induces primary depression; it may be a product of the disturbed mental state.[77] Elevated cortisol levels might contribute to or intensify the subjective feeling states of the patient, which in turn might induce ACTH release via CNS mechanisms. That cortisol levels might be associated with a patient's subjective feeling states is consistent with hormone-behavior relationships and thus provide a means by which emotional stimuli may contribute to the "reflex" release of hormones.

Future contributions of research on disruptions of neuroendocrine regulatory systems concomitant with affective disorders promise to be interesting. Current efforts involve increasing the accuracy of diagnosing primary affective disorders, enabling more effective and beneficial therapies to be initiated sooner, and assessing possible genetic contributions to the class of affective disorders. It is hoped that studies might be initiated to attempt to delineate the extent to which disruptions in neuroendocrine regulatory systems contribute to the persistence of psychopathology, and whether normalization of such systems might facilitate recovery of more effective behavioral patterns. It is anticipated that future studies on endocrine concomitants of psychopathology will be enlightening and provocative.

REFERENCES

1. Aono T., et al.: The initiation of human lactation and prolactin response to suckling. *J. Clin. Endocrinol. Metab.* 44:1101, 1977.
2. Azizi F., et al.: Decreased serum testosterone concentration in male heroin and methadone addicts. *Steroids* 22:467, 1973.
3. Barlow D.H., et al.: Plasma testosterone levels and male homosexuality: A failure to replicate. *Arch. Sex. Behav.* 3:571, 1974.

4. Beattie C.W., Rodgers C.H., Soyka L.F.: Influence of ovariectomy and ovarian steroids on hypothalamic tyrosine hydroxylase activity in the rat. *Endocrinology* 91:276, 1972.
5. Benkert O., Gordon A., Martschke D.: The comparison of thyrotropin releasing hormone, luteinising hormone-releasing hormone and placebo in depressive patients using a double-blind cross-over technique. *Psychopharmacologia* 40:191, 1974.
6. Benkert O., et al.: Sexual impotence: Studies of the hypothalamic-pituitary-thyroid axis and the effect of oral thyrotropin-releasing factor. *Arch. Sex. Behav.* 5:275, 1976.
7. Bern H.A., Knowles F.G.W.: Neurosecretion, in Martini L., Ganong W.F. (eds.): *Neuroendocrinology*. New York, Academic Press, 1966, vol. 1.
8. Board F., Persky H., Hamburg D.A.: Psychological stress and endocrine functions. *Psychosom. Med.* 18:324, 1956.
9. Bodenheimer S., Winter J.S.D., Faiman C.: Diurnal rhythms of serum gonadotropins, testosterone, estradiol and cortisol in blind men. *J. Clin. Endocrinol. Metab.* 37:472, 1973.
10. Brambilla F., et al.: Psychoendocrine investigation in schizophrenia: Relationship between pituitary-gonadal function and behavior. *Dis. Nerv. Syst.*, suppl. 362, 1974.
11. Bransome E.D. Jr.: Adrenal cortex. *Ann. Rev. Physiol.* 30:171, 1968.
12. Brown W.A., Shuey I.: Response to dexamethasone and subtype of depression. *Arch. Gen. Psychiatry* 37:747, 1980.
13. Bunney W.E., Mason J.W., Hamburg D.A.: Correlations between behavioral variables and urinary 17-hydroxycorticoids in depressed patients. *Psychosom. Med.* 27:299, 1965.
14. Carroll B.J.: Limbic system-adrenal cortex regulation in depression and schizophrenia. *Psychosom. Med.* 38:106, 1976.
15. Carroll B.J.: Neuroendocrine function in psychiatric disorders, in Lipton M.A., DiMascio A., Killam K.F. (eds.): *Psychopharmacology: A Generation of Progress*. New York, Raven Press, 1978.
16. Carroll B.J., Heath B., Jarrett D.B.: Corticosteroids in brain tissue. *Endocrinology* 97:290, 1975.
17. Carroll B.J., Curtis G.C., Mendels J.: Cerebrospinal fluid and plasma free cortisol concentrations in depression. *Psychol. Med.* 6:235, 1976.
18. Carroll B.J., Curtis G.C., Mendels J.: Neuroendocrine regulation in depression: I. Limbic system-adrenocortical dysfunction. *Arch. Gen. Psychiatry* 33:1039, 1976.
19. Carroll B.J., Curtis G.C., Mendels J.: Neuroendocrine regulation in depression: II. Discrimination of depressed from nondepressed patients. *Arch. Gen. Psychiatry* 33:1051, 1976.
20. Coppen A., et al.: Thyrotrophin-releasing hormone in the treatment of depression. *Lancet* 2:433, 1974.
21. Crisp A.H.: Primary anorexia nervosa. *Gut* 9:370, 1968.
22. Cryer P.E.: *Diagnostic Endocrinology*. New York, Oxford University Press, 1976.
23. Cullberg J.: Mood changes and menstrual symptoms with different gestagen/estrogen combinations: A double-blind comparison with a placebo. *Acta Psychiatr. Scand.*, suppl. 236:1–86, 1972.
24. Curtis G.C., et al.: The effect of sustained affect on the diurnal rhythm of adrenal cortical activity. *Psychosom. Med.* 28:696, 1966.

25. Dallman M.F., Jones M.T.: Corticosteroid feedback control of ACTH secretion: Effect of stress-induced corticosterone secretion on subsequent stress responses in the rat. *Endocrinology* 92:1367, 1973.
26. Davidson J.M., Smith E.R., Levine S.: Testosterone, in Ursin H., Baade E., Levine S. (eds.): *Psychobiology of Stress*. New York, Academic Press, 1978.
27. Delitala G., et al.: Luteinizing hormone, follicle-stimulating hormone and testosterone in normal and impotent men following LHRH and HCG stimulation. *Clin. Endocrinol.* 6:11, 1977.
28. DeWied D., et al.: Release of ACTH by substances of central nervous system origin. *Endocrinology* 85:561, 1969.
29. Dotti A., Reda M.: Major tranquilizers and sexual function, in Sandler M., Gessa G.L. (eds.): *Sexual Behavior: Pharmacology and Biochemistry*. New York, Raven Press, 1975.
30. Ehrensing R.H., et al.: Affective state and thyrotropin and prolactin responses after repeated injections of thyrotropin-releasing hormone in depressed patients. *Am. J. Psychiatry* 131:714, 1974.
31. Ettigi P.G., Brown G.M.: Psychoneuroendocrinology of affective disorder: An overview. *Am. J. Psychiatry* 134:493, 1977.
32. Fenichel O.: Organ neuroses, in *The Psychoanalytic Theory of Neurosis*. New York, W.W. Norton & Co., 1945.
33. Friedman R.C., et al.: Hormones and sexual orientation in men. *Am. J. Psychiatry* 134:571, 1977.
34. Ganong W.F.: Neuroendocrine integrating mechanisms, in Martini L., Ganong W.F. (eds.): *Neuroendocrinology*. New York, Academic Press, 1966, vol. 1.
35. Ganong W.F.: Physiologic principles, in *The Nervous System*, ed. 2. Los Altos, Calif., Lange Publishers, 1979.
36. Ganong W.F., Forsham P.H.: Adenohypophysis and adrenal cortex. *Ann. Rev. Physiol.* 22:579, 1960.
37. Garfinkel P.F., et al.: Hypothalamic-pituitary function in anorexia nervosa. *Arch. Gen. Psychiatry* 32:739, 1975.
38. Gerlach J.L., McEwen B.S.: Rat brain binds adrenal steroid hormone: Radioautography of hippocampus with corticosterone. *Science* 175:1133, 1972.
39. Gibbons J.L.: The secretion rate of corticosterone in depressive illness. *J. Psychosom. Res.* 10:263, 1966.
40. Gimes R., Toth F., Fornadi F.: Colpocytology, a prognostic aid in the treatment of schizophrenia. *Acta Cytol.* 13:133, 1969.
41. Glass A.R., et al.: Low serum testosterone and sex-hormone binding-globulin in massively obese men. *J. Clin. Endocrinol. Metab.* 45:1211, 1977.
42. Goy R.W., Resko J.A.: Gonadal hormones and behavior of normal and pseudohermaphroditic nonhuman female primates, in Astwood E.B. (ed):*Recent Progress in Hormone Research*. New York, Academic Press, 1972, vol. 28.
43. Harris G.W.: Sex hormones, brain development and brain function. *Endocrinology* 75:627, 1964.
44. Henkin, R.I.: The neuroendocrine control of perception. *Nerv. Ment. Dis.*, vol. 54, 1970.
45. Hollister L.E., et al.: Protirelin (TRH) in depression. *Arch. Gen. Psychiatry* 31:468, 1974.
46. Hoskins R.G.: Psychosexuality in schizophrenia: Some endocrine considerations. *Psychosom. Med.* 5:3, 1943.

47. Hoskins R.G., Pincus G.: Sex-hormone relationships in schizophrenic men. *Psychosom. Med.* 11:102, 1949.
48. Imura H., et al.: The role of biogenic amines in the regulation of pituitary hormone release in man, with special reference to circadian rhythmicity, in Kawakami M. (ed.): *Biological Rhythms in Neuroendocrine Activity*. Tokyo, Igaku-Shoin, Ltd., 1974.
49. Jenner F.A.: The physiology and biochemistry of periodic psychoses including periodic catatonia, in Himwich H.E. (ed.): *Biochemistry, Schizophrenias, and Affective Illnesses*. Baltimore, Williams & Wilkins Co., 1970.
50. Klaiber E.L., et al.: Estrogen therapy for severe persistent depressions in women. *Arch. Gen. Psychiatry* 36:550, 1979.
51. Krieger D.T., Liotta A.S.: Pituitary hormones in brain: Where, how, and why? *Science* 205:366, 1979.
52. Laschet U., Laschet L.: Antiandrogens in the treatment of sexual deviations of men. *J. Steroid Biochem.* 6:821, 1975.
53. Legros J.J., et al.: FSH, LH and testosterone blood levels in patients with psychogenic impotence. *Endocrinol. Exp.* 7:59, 1973.
54. Leshner A.I., Candland D.K.: Endocrine effects of grouping and dominance rank in squirrel monkeys. *Physiol. Behav.* 8:441, 1972.
55. Luton J-P., et al.: Reversible gonadotropin deficiency in male Cushing's disease. *J. Clin. Endocrinol. Metab.* 45:488, 1977.
56. Luttge W.G.: The role of gonadal hormones in the sexual behavior of the rhesus monkey and human: A literature survey. *Arch. Sex. Behav.* 1:61, 1971.
57. MacKinnon P.C.B., MacKinnon I.L.: Hazards of the menstrual cycle. *Br. Med. J.* 1:555, 1956.
58. MacLean P.D.: Psychosomatic disease and the "visceral brain": Recent developments bearing on the Papez theory of emotion. *Psychosom. Med.* 11:338, 1949.
59. Maran J.W., et al.: Organization of the medial hypothalamus for control of adrenocorticotropin in the cat. *Endocrinology* 103:957, 1978.
60. Marcus R., Korenman S.G.: Estrogens and the human male. *Ann. Rev. Med.* 27:357, 1976.
61. Mendelson J.H., Mendelson J.E., Patch V.D.: Plasma testosterone levels in heroin addiction and during methadone maintenance. *J. Pharmacol. Exp. Ther.* 192:211, 1975.
62. Money J.: Use of an androgen-depleting hormone in the treatment of male sex offenders. *J. Sex. Res.* 6:165, 1970.
63. Moriarty G.C., Garner L.L.: Immunocytochemical studies of cells in the rat adenohypophysis containing both ACTH and FSH. *Nature* 265:356, 1977.
64. Morris N.M., Udry J.R., Underwood L.E.: A study of the relationship between coitus and the luteinizing hormone surge. *Fertil. Steril.* 28:440, 1977.
65. Mountjoy C.Q., et al.: A double-blind crossover sequential trial of oral thyrotropin-releasing hormone in depression. *Lancet* 1:958, 1974.
66. Murray M.A.F., et al.: Endocrine changes in male sexual deviants after treatment with anti-androgens, estrogens or tranquillizers. *J. Endocrinol.* 67:179, 1975.
67. Nomura J., et al.: Role of the central nervous system in hepatic steroid and ammonia metabolism. *Psychoneuroendocrinology* 4:47, 1979.
68. Ogle T.F., Kitay J.I.: Interactions of prolactin and adrenocorticotropin in the

regulation of adrenocortical secretions in female rats. *Endocrinology* 104:40, 1979.

69. Orth D.N.: Function of the adrenal glands, in Brobeck J.R. (ed.): *Best and Taylor's Physiological Basis of Medical Practice*, ed. 9. Baltimore, Williams & Wilkins Co, 1973.

70. Ossofsky H.J.: Amenorrhea in endogenous depression. *Int. Pharmacopsychiatry* 9:100, 1974.

71. Pascetto G.: Estroprogesterone treatment and neuropsychiatric problems. *Sist. Nerv. (Milan)* 11:348, 1969.

72. Persky H., et al.: Adrenal cortical function in anxious human subjects. *Arch. Neurol. Psychiatry* 76:549, 1965.

73. Persky H., Zuckerman M., Curtis G.C.: Endocrine function in emotionally disturbed and normal men. *J. Nerv. Ment. Dis.* 146:488, 1968.

74. Peyser M.R., et al.: Stress-induced delay of ovulation. *Obstet. Gynecol.* 42:667, 1973.

75. Posner B.I., Kelly P.A., Friesen H.G.: Prolactin receptors in rat liver: Possible induction by prolactin. *Science* 188:57, 1975.

76. Prange A.J. Jr., et al.: Thyroid-imipramine clinical and chemical interaction: Evidence for a receptor deficit in depression. *J. Psychiatr. Res.* 9:187, 1972.

77. Prange A.J. Jr., et al.: The role of hormones in depression. *Life Sci.* 20:1305, 1977.

78. Rey J.H., Nicholson-Bailey U., Trappl A.: Endocrine activity in psychiatric patients with menstrual disorders. *Br. Med. J.* 2:843, 1957.

79. Ripley H.S., Papanicolaou G.N.: The menstrual cycle with vaginal smear studies in schizophrenia, depression and elation. *Am. J. Psychiatry* 98:567, 1942.

80. Robinson J.A., et al.: Effects of age and season on sexual behavior and plasma testosterone and dihydrotestosterone concentrations of laboratory-housed male rhesus monkeys (macaca mulatta). *Biol. Reprod.* 13:203, 1975.

81. Rodgers C.H.: Neuroendocrine mechanisms responsible for gonadotropin release. *J. Reprod. Med.* 14:1, 1975.

82. Rodgers C.H., Alheid G.: Relationship of sexual behavior and castration to tumescence in the male rat. *Physiol. Behav.* 9:581, 1972.

83. Rodgers C.H., Schwartz N.B., Nequin L.G.: Interaction between the ovarian and adrenocortical regulating systems: Occurrence of ovulation, in Kawakami M. (ed.): *Biological Rhythms in Neuroendocrine Activity*. Tokyo, Igaku-Shoin, Ltd., 1974.

84. Rodgers C.H., Chatterton R.T. Jr.: In vitro liver clearance of tritiated estradiol-17β in the female rat after retrochiasmatic transection and ovariectomy. *Steroids* 31:151, 1978.

85. Rodgers C.H., Chatterton R.T. Jr.: The effects of lesions of the lateral septum on the concentrations and binding of estradiol-17β in serum and on the clearance of ^{3}H-estradiol-17β by the liver in vitro. Unpublished data.

86. Rose R.M., Holaday J.W., Bernstein I.S.: Plasma testosterone, dominance rank and aggressive behaviour in male rhesus monkeys. *Nature* 231:366, 1971.

87. Rose R.M., Gordon T.P., Bernstein I.S.: Plasma testosterone levels in the male rhesus: Influences of sexual and social stimuli. *Science* 178:643, 1972.

88. Sachar E.J.: Twenty-four-hour cortisol secretory patterns in depressed and manic patients. *Prog. Brain Res.* 42:81, 1975.

89. Sachar E.J., et al.: Recent studies of episodic secretion of cortisol and testosterone: Implications for psychoendocrine research. *Psychosom. Med.* 34:474, 1972.

90. Sachar E.J., et al.: Disrupted 24-hour patterns of cortisol secretion in psychotic depression. *Arch. Gen. Psychiatry* 28:19, 1973.

91. Schiavi R.C., et al.: Luteinizing hormone and testosterone during nocturnal sleep: Relation to penile tumescent cycles. *Arch. Sex. Behav.* 6:97, 1977.

92. Schlesser M.A., Winokur G., Sherman B.M.: Hypothalamic-pituitary-adrenal axis activity in depressive illness. *Arch. Gen. Psychiatry* 37:737, 1980.

93. Schwartz N.B., McCormack C.E.: Reproduction: Gonadal function and its regulation. *Ann. Rev. Physiol.* 34:425, 1972.

94. Selkurt E.E. (ed.): *Physiology*, ed. 4. Boston, Little, Brown & Co., 1976.

95. Shirai M., et al.: Effects of ejaculation induced by manual stimulation on plasma gonadotropin and testosterone levels in infertile man. *Tohoku J. Exp. Med.* 114:91, 1974.

96. Smals A.G.H., Kloppenborg P.W.C., Benraad Th. J.: Plasma testosterone profiles in Cushing's syndrome. *J. Clin. Endocrinol. Metab.* 45:240, 1977.

97. Smith S.R., Bledsoe T., Chhetri M.K.: Cortisol metabolism and the pituitary-adrenal axis in adults with protein-calorie malnutrition. *J. Clin. Endocrinol. Metab.* 40:43, 1975.

98. Stearns E.L., Winter J.S.D., Faiman C.: Effects of coitus on gonadotropin, prolactin and sex steroid levels in man. *J. Clin. Endocrinol. Metab.* 37:687, 1973.

99. Stokes P.E., et al.: Pituitary-adrenal function in depressed patients: Resistance to dexamethasone suppression. *J. Psychiatr. Res.* 12:271, 1975.

100. Suwa N., et al.: Psychic state and adrenocortical function: A psychophysiologic study of emotion. *J. Nerv. Ment. Dis.* 134:268, 1962.

101. Suwa N., et al.: Psychic state and gonadal function: Psychophysiologic study of emotion. *J. Nerv. Ment. Dis.* 143:36, 1966.

102. Suwa N., Yamashita I.: *Psychophysiological Studies of Emotion and Mental Disorders*. Sapporo, Japan, Hokkaido University Medical School Press, 1972.

103. Takahashi S., et al.: Thyrotropin responses to TRH in depressive illness: Relation to clinical subtypes and prolonged duration of depressive episode. *Fol. Psychiatr. Neurol. Japon.* 28:355, 1974.

104. Traskman L., et al.: Cortisol in the CSF of depressed and suicidal patients. *Arch. Gen. Psychiatry* 37:761, 1980.

105. Valenstein E.S.: *Brain Control: A Critical Examination of Brain Stimulation and Psychosurgery*. New York, John Wiley & Sons, 1973.

106. Warren M.P., Vande Wiele R.L.: Clinical and metabolic features of anorexia nervosa. *Am. J. Obstet. Gynecol.* 117:435, 1973.

107. Watson S.J., Richard C.W. III, Barchas J.D.: Adrenocorticotropin in rat brain: Immunocytochemical localization in cells and axons. *Science* 200:1180, 1978.

108. Witorsch R.J., Kitay J.I.: Pituitary hormones affecting adrenal 5α-reductase activity: ACTH, growth hormone and prolactin. *Endocrinology* 91:764, 1972.

109. Yasuda N., et al.: Studies on the site of action of vasopressin in inducing adrenocorticotropin secretion. *Endocrinology* 103:906, 1978.

110. Yates F.E.: The liver and the adrenal cortex. *Gastroenterology* 53:477, 1967.

111. Yen S.S.C., Rebar R.W., Quesenberry W.: Pituitary function in pseudocyesis. *J. Clin. Endocrinol. Metab.* 43:132, 1976.

8

NEUROPHYSIOLOGIC ASPECTS

SRINATH BELLUR, M.D.

THE NEUROPHYSIOLOGIC VIEW of affect has developed in parallel with but separate from clinical psychiatry. Although the terminology used in the two disciplines is somewhat different, there is considerable common ground. As the clinical study of affective disorders continues, it is essential that neurophysiologic data and theories be incorporated.

NEUROPHYSIOLOGY AND AFFECT

AFFECT AND EMOTION

The neurophysiologic perspective on affect makes a necessary but somewhat artificial distinction between the subjective experience of emotion and the expression of emotion through behavioral patterns.[31] Although only the subjective experience is referred to as "affect," both components are used in the assessment and understanding of affective disorders.

Affects are classified on two separate dimensions. First, they can be differentiated along a continuum from disagreeable to agreeable. Second, they are divided into categories referred to as basic, specific, and general.[26]

Basic affects are those that are immediately dependent on interoceptive sensory inputs. They originate from different internal states associated with basic bodily needs—for air, food, water, sexual outlet, and excretory activities.

Specific affects, on the other hand, originate from exteroceptive sensory inputs; they represent the affective responses to the perceptual inputs of all the senses. These affects may be innate (unlearned) or conditioned (learned). An example of a learned specific affect is the agreeable or disagreeable feeling aroused on hearing different kinds of music or seeing different art forms. Unlearned specific affects include those associated with repugnant odors, startling sounds, and intense light. Although it is likely that these latter examples are somewhat conditioned, they are basically generated by an innate (unlearned) response.

General affects are second-order affects; they are derived from basic and specific affects. Once derived, they have a tendency to persist or recur "after the fact," in McLean's terminology.[26] General affects have one common link: they are all useful in preserving the self or the species. Those which provide information on threats to the self or species are disagreeable; those which signal the removal of threats are agreeable.[26]

The second component of emotion is its expression. Excluding verbal behavior, there are six general categories of the behavioral expression of emotion: searching (desire), aggressive (anger), protective (fear), dejected (sorrow), gratulant (joy), and caressive (affectionate). When these major categories are combined with one another and with language and introspection, they lead to more complex variations such as obsessive-compulsive, ritualistic, superstitious, schizoid, and depressive thoughts or behaviors.[26]

NEURAL SYSTEMS AND AFFECTIVE BEHAVIOR

It is not possible to trace precisely the neural circuitry that generates affect. However, one can begin to understand this complex process by reviewing the evolution of the forebrain. During evolution, the forebrain expands along three basic patterns, characterized as reptilian, paleomammalian, and neomammalian. The human counterpart of the reptilian forebrain includes the globus pallidus, putamen caudate, and peripallidal structures. The paleomammalian brain is represented by the limbic system and the neomammalian brain is represented by the neocortex.

The basal ganglia (reptilian brain) apparently control the basic affects, i.e., those dependent on internal states derived from basic desires. McLean regards these affects as being species-typical behavior.[26] This consists of genetically determined actions such as selecting a home site, establishing and defending territory, hunting, homing, and forming social hierarchies. Destruction of the dopamine-containing neurons in the substantia nigra, as well as those spanning the interpeduncular fossa (groups A9 and A10 of Dahlstrom and Fuxe[5]) profoundly retards spontaneous behavior of this type in animals and causes affective blunting. This is in marked contrast to the mobilizing and hyperactive effects of apomorphine, a dopaminergic agonist. The main avenues of the basic expression of affective responses are through the ventral diencephalon, with the lateral and medial forebrain bundles. These bundles are the main pathways leading to and from the striatal (reptilian) and limbic (paleomammalian) systems. The lateral forebrain bundle includes the ansa and the fasciculus lenticularis as well as the nigrostriatal and strionigral pathways.[26]

The role played by the limbic system in affective functions has been well studied from clinical observations. Neuronal discharges in or near the limbic cortex of the temporal lobe (as in epilepsy) may trigger a broad spectrum of vivid affective feelings. Case histories of limbic epilepsy indicate (1) that the limbic system is basic for affective feelings of reality of the self and the environment, and (2) that ictal phenomena may result in changes of mood (affect), distortions of perceptions, and distortions of sensations, giving rise to basic, specific, and general affects.

All affects (basic, specific, and general) modulated by the limbic system are associated with threat to self-preservation. The basic affects include those associated with hunger and thirst. Specific affects include those associated with unpleasant tastes, odors (smoke), and somatic sensations (pain). General affects are associated with fear, terror, sadness, unfamiliarity, and anger. These general affects are free-floating and are not readily indentified with a particular person or situation.

Visual, auditory, somatic, and visceral information reaches the limbic system extensively through subcortical pathways. The hippocampus projects to the basal forebrain, the preoptic region, and the hypothalamus. This explains the prolonged behavioral and autonomic changes seen after hippocampal discharges, including agitated states on one hand and enhanced pleasure and sexual reaction on the other. Neuroanatomical studies have shown that in primates the fornix projects to the medial preoptic area and perifornicial areas. The intermediate zones of Hess (perifornicial region) are implicated in the expression of anger. The medial preoptic area is responsible for gonadotrophic function and sexual differentiation. The fornix also projects to the tuberal area, which modulates adrenocorticotrophic hormone release, cardiovascular reflexes, and visceral responsiveness. The hippocampus is also implicated in rapid eye movement (REM) sleep regulation.

In summary, information from exteroceptive and interoceptive systems interacts in the hippocampal formation and influences hypothalamic and other brain stem structures involved in affective behavior.

The neocortex is responsible for somatic, auditory, and visual functions. The neocortex has evolved so that it is primarily oriented toward the external environment and therefore to specific affects.[26] However, the precise mechanism by which neocortically mediated specific affects are executed is not known. The exception to this is the role played by pain. Head and Holmes[16] have outlined the function of the thalamus in the thalamic pain syndromes, in which there is an exaggerated, specific affective response to pain.

PLEASURE AND NONPLEASURE PATHWAYS

Heath[17] has collected a body of data on humans indicating that pathways for pleasurable emotional expression include the septal region, medial forebrain bundle, and the interpeduncular nuclei in the mesencephalon. Sites for adversive emotional expression are located in the hippocampus, parts of the amygdalae, the periaqueductal sites of the mesencephalon, and sites in the medial hypothalamus near the third ventricle. These conclusions are based on extensive studies of depth recording after electrical and chemical stimulation of these specific brain structures.

HEMISPHERIC SPECIALIZATION

Intracarotid short-acting barbiturate injection into the internal carotid artery (Wada test) suggests a lateralized hemispheric modulation of affect. Terzian and Cecotto[38] have reported that patients display certain characteristic responses as this anesthetic wears off. Amytal injection on the left side induces a sense of guilt, despair, and anxiety about the future, whereas right carotid injection induces euphoria, a sense of grandiosity, and often manic behavior. Similar results are noted after hemispheric injury.

Galin,[11] in an extensive review of the psychiatric literature on unilateral electroconvulsive therapy for relief of depression, concluded that the therapeutic effect may depend on which hemisphere gets the treatment. He has suggested that the therapeutic effect can be understood in terms of changing the balance between the specialized hemispheres.

THE ROLE OF DRIVE AND REINFORCEMENT

The role of drive and reinforcement have been summarized by Olds.[28] He believes that two sets of catecholamine fibers are reward neurons. Stimulation of these cause reward behavior. One set, a norepinephrine group, is involved in rewards that come at the end of a consummatory process and that carry the notion of satiety and demise of the drive. The other set of neurons, a dopaminergic system, might be involved in rewards that come near the beginning of the consummatory process and are involved in a positive response to the initial event.

Brain pathways mediating the experience and expression of affect influence neural activities such as arousal, autonomic reactivity, intracortical processing of event-related potentials, and circadian rhythms. The evaluation of these neuronal activities as reflected in the EEG, cortical-evoked potentials, polygraph sleep studies, and electrodermal activity are discussed below.

ELECTROENCEPHALOGRAPHY

The EEG records repetitive waves from the surface of the brain that are believed to be summated action potentials generated by the pyramidal neurons in the cortex. These synaptic potentials are the responses of cortical cells to rhythmic volleys of the thalamic afferent impulses. The frequency and size of the thalamic discharges and, thus, of the cortical potentials are determined by the underlying circuitry among the thalamic cells. During behavioral arousal, reticular inputs abolish the rhythmic thalamic nuclear discharges and cause cortical desynchronization.[20]

Electroencephalograph rhythms have been assigned functional roles in maintaining various levels of consciousness, modulation of evoked cortical potentials, memory functions, and inhibitory descending pyramidal influences.[20] Thus, it is evident that the EEG can be used to evaluate certain aspects of emotional behavior. Currently the value of EEG in psychiatry is limited from a diagnostic and prognostic perspective. Nevertheless, interesting observations have been made in this field, and although their significance is often unclear, they represent a challenge to investigators and may prove to be important. Many EEG studies of mania, endogenous depression, and involutional depression suffer from (1) a lack of adequate methods of quantification that can be applied to psychiatric symptoms, (2) a heterogeneity in sample selection, with patients differing widely in age, diagnosis, and duration of illness, and (3) the lack of control populations.[20]

Most EEG studies of affective disorders have been carried out with bipolar patients. There has been little work done in characterologic forms of affective disorders (e.g., dysthmic and cyclothymic disorders).

Despite the apparent normality of EEG records in many bipolar patients, a 20% to 40% incidence of abnormalities and the scatter of normal EEG attributes in these disorders is greater than normal. Ten of Dalen's[6] 35 cases of manic patients had EEG abnormalities. A significant proportion of bipolar patients show fast dominant records, but it has been argued that this may be sedative-hypnotic induced.[7] The mean alpha frequency tends to be high in manic patients and relatively low in depressed patients, although the alpha frequency does not shift between phases of illness.[8] Hurst et al.[19] claim that the mean frequency, amplitude, and the percent time of alpha frequencies are lower than normal in bipolar patients. On photic stimulation, these patients show a response of higher amplitude in the 4 to

20 flashes per second range and of lower amplitude in the 21 to 26 flashes per second range than controls. Compared with depressives, manic patients have a significantly greater incidence of second- and third-order harmonics and of responses to flash frequencies in the 14 to 26 flashes per second range during photic stimulation. Perris[29] has shown that patients with reactive depression may have a higher alpha index than patients with endogenous depression.

The association of temporal lobe epilepsy with depression is well known. It may be an aural or prodromal phenomenon or may occur episodically after temporal lobectomy. Weil[40] has described cases of periodic depression associated with an increased incidence of temporal lobe spikes.

Shagass[33] has evaluated a method for establishing a "sedation threshold" that has useful applications. An intravenous injection of 0.5 mg/kg of sodium amylobarbitone is repeated every 40 seconds until well past the point where speech becomes slurred. The amount of 15- to 30-Hz activity in the frontal area is noted. A dose-response curve is plotted between the integrated dose of sodium amytal and integrated amount of frontal fast activity. The resulting curve is S-shaped and shows an inflection point corresponding to the onset of slurred speech. Beyond this inflection point the amount of fast activity falls sharply. Sedation threshold is defined as the amount of amylobarbitone sodium in mg/kg of body weight required to reach this inflection point. The sedation threshold has no correlation with sex or age.

Shagass and Jones[34] found the sedation threshold in non-patient controls to be 3.09 mg/kg, compared with 4.42 in obsessive-compulsive states, 4.78 in neurotic-depressions, and 5.27 in anxiety states. In the organic psychoses the mean threshold was 1.94 mg/kg; in endogenous depression, it was 2.81 mg/kg; and in mania it was 3.45 mg/kg. The most interesting applicability of this test is in distinguishing the so-called neurotic from endogenous depressions; regardless of the degree of agitation, patients with endogenous depression have a lower sedation threshold than those with neurotic depression. Perris[29] has observed that patients with unipolar depression have sedation thresholds essentially in the same range of neurotic depressives.

CORTICAL EVOKED RESPONSES

Average evoked responses (AER) are recordings obtained from the brain surface. In this technique a sensory stimulus (light flash or auditory tone) is presented repeatedly and its cortical responses are summated. The process of summating tends to cancel random noise, and the time-locked, stimulus-evoked cortical responses are brought forth clearly as a series of positive and negative responses, depending on the underlying cortical events.

In AER to light stimuli there are two wave components that have been of interest: a positive event (P100) occurring at around 100 msec and a negative event (N140) occurring at around 140 msec after visual stimulation. There are individuals whose AER components P100 and N140 increase in amplitude with increasing stimulus intensity; in others, the response decreases with increasing stimulus intensity. These two response groups are termed "augmenters" and "reducers," respectively.[4] The tendency to augment or reduce is partly genetic.[3] There are studies that suggest that "reducers" have higher thresholds of tolerance for pain and noise. Hemphill et al.[18] and Hall and Stride[13] have found that depressives have high pain thresholds compared with controls.

Buchsbaum[4] has found that unipolar depressive patients are AER reducers for peak P100 and N140 in comparison with normal controls, whereas bipolar patients are clear augmenters. It was also found that schizophrenic patients are reducers, like unipolar reducers. In studies of platelet monoamineoxidase (MAO) in chronic schizophrenics, Murphy and Wyatt[27] have shown that they tend to have low levels, like bipolar patients, whereas unipolars have normal or high levels. Thus, AERs are useful in distinguishing schizophrenics from bipolar patients, and MAO levels are useful in distinguishing unipolar patients from schizophrenics. Used together, these could provide a useful diagnostic tool.

Shagass[35] has further enumerated a list of probable evoked potential differences between schizophrenics and patients with affective psychoses. According to him the auditory AER in schizophrenics have a lower amplitude with shorter latency and the visual AER have less of an after-rhythm. Schizophrenics are reducers of visual AER, whereas bipolar affective disorder patients are augmenters. Wave shape variability before 100 msec is less than normal in schizophrenics but greater than normal in manics. However, wave shape variability after 100 msec is greater in schizophrenics.

Following is a brief summary of evoked potential findings in affective disorders:[35]

> Manic states tend to have a greater than normal somatic evoked response variability before 100 msec, they also show low contingent negative variation and prolonged slow potential negativity. In depressive states bipolar are visual "augmenters" with male unipolar being "reducers." Unipolar depressive have shorter visual AER latencies than controls. The amplitude of the right visual AER is greater than the left visual AER in depressive before therapy. Depressed patients have reduced somatic evoked potential amplitude recovery but a faster latency recovery, they also have low contingent negative variation with prolonged slow potential negativity.

SLEEP STUDIES

That the depressed patient has changes in sleep patterns is well known. Normal sleep is usually characterized by the early onset of slow wave or delta sleep (stages III and IV) and, after about 90 minutes, a period of REM sleep. These cycles of REM sleep continue to occur every 90 to 100 minutes until awakening. The duration of individual REM bouts also increases progressively through the night.[10] In depression these patterns are disrupted,[14, 24] and REM sleep often precedes delta sleep, with a diminution of delta sleep.[15] Kupfer and Gordon[23] have noted that nonpsychotic unipolar patients spend less time in sleep during illness than in remission. During illness they have a marked sleep continuity disturbance, with intermittent wakefulness and early morning wakefulness. In addition they have less delta sleep time, with a clear preponderance of stages I and II. However, most characteristically they have reduced REM latencies.[21]

Sleep time in the bipolar depressive during depression is markedly different from that in the unipolar depressive. Sleep time in bipolar depressives, rather than being discontinuous or decreased, tends to be unchanged or even increased.[9, 22] However, both delta sleep and REM latency are reduced in this group also. Kupfer and Gordon[23] also noted that in depression, decreased sleep time with frequent awakenings is not an obligatory feature. However, the loss of delta sleep with early REM is common.

Vogel[39] has suggested that depressive sleep abnormalities represent a "damaged," weakened sleep cycle "oscillator" and its correlate, a circadian rhythm disturbance. Rapid eye movement sleep deprivation improves depression to the extent that it stimulates the oscillator and corrects one manifestation of the circadian rhythm disturbance.

Sitaram et al.,[36] in a study of patients with primary affective illness in remission, found that these patients demonstrate a supersensitive cholinergic REM induction. This cholinergic supersensitivity is reportedly present both during illness and during clinical remissions.

Early REM onset or shortened REM latency in depression has been used to delineate a subclass of depression called "subaffective dysthymia" (in *DSM-III*, dysthymic disorder), which seems to be nosologically distinct in terms of its course, response to therapy, and outcome.[41]

In summary, there have been many speculations about the significance of REM sleep alterations in clinical depression; the exact significance is not known. Recent work has suggested that REM deprivation may improve depression. One possibility is that shortened REM latency may simply mirror a significant alteration in the circadian rhythm. There has been much speculation and some evidence from endocrine studies that such an alteration exists.[32]

ELECTRODERMAL ACTIVITY

The sudorific activity of the sweat glands, along with some nonsudorific activities, results in certain measurable electrical changes of the skin. These activities are said to be modulated by a hierarchy of suprasegmental CNS control mechanisms. Also involved are certain hormonal and peripheral factors. Various techniques and the parameters measured have been outlined in detail in a published monograph.[30] The main areas studied have been tonic electrodermal measures and measures of electrodermal responsivity, habituation, and conditioning. There have been efforts to relate these psychophysiologic factors to depression. Unfortunately, the results of such studies lack comparability because different diagnostic schemes were employed.[37]

Lader and Wing,[25] in a study of electrodermal activity in depression, have shown that skin conductance level in a group of agitated depressives was higher than in normals, and higher in normals than in retarded depressives. They also demonstrated that within the dimension of tonic electrodermal activity, depression is not a unitary phenomenon. The more relevant variable appears to be the degree of agitation within the depression category.

Electrodermal responsivity (phasic responses) in the depressed patient may be reduced. The relationship between scores on depression scales and electrodermal responsivity has received some attention. Greenfield et al.[12] have shown that patients with a lower MMPI depression score have a greater response than those with less depression. In studies of habituation of skin conductance to auditory tones, skin conductance levels for normal subjects, uncomplicated depressives, and retarded depressives tended to be lower, compared with levels in agitated depressives. Normal subjects habituate faster to auditory tones than agitated depressives.[25] In this context it is interesting to note that Bassett and Ashby[2] evaluated palmar sweating in depressed women patients and concluded that there is an increase in palmar sweating prior to improvement in clinical status. It has also been suggested that changes in skin resistance activity might be useful in predicting recovery in depressed patients.[37] Alexander,[1] in a study comparing differential conditioning of depressed patients with that of controls, showed that conditioning responses were greatly reduced among depressive patients. Conditioned responses for depressed patients were frequently delayed, while responses to unconditioned stimuli were normal.

REFERENCES

1. Alexander L.: Objective approach to psychiatric diagnosis and evaluation of drug effects by means of conditional reflex technique, in Masserman J. (ed.): *Biological Psychiatry*. New York, Grune & Stratton, 1958.

2. Bassett M., Ashby W.R.: The effect of electro-convulsive therapy on the psychogalvanic response. *J. Ment. Sci.* 100:632, 1954.

3. Buchsbaum M.: Average evoked response and stimulus intensity in identical and fraternal twins. *Physiol. Psychol.* 2:365-370, 1974.

4. Buchsbaum M.: Average evoked response augmenting/reducing in schizophrenia and affective disorders. *Res. Publ. Assoc. Res. Nerv. Ment. Dis.* 54:129–142, 1975.

5. Dahlstrom A., Fuxe K.: Evidence for the existence of monoamine-containing neurons in the central nervous system. *Acta Physiol. Scand.* 62:5, 1964.

6. Dalen P.: Family history, the electroencephalogram and perinatal factors in manic conditions. *Acta Psychiatr. Scand.* 41:527, 1965.

7. Davis P.A.: Evaluation of the electroencephalogram of schizophrenic patients. *Am. J. Psychiatry* 96:851, 1939–40.

8. Davis P.A.: The electroencephalograms of manic-depressive patients. *Am. J. Psychiatry* 98:430, 1941.

9. Detre T.P., et al.: Hypersomnia and manic-depressive disease. *Am. J. Psychiatry* 128:1303, 1972.

10. Feinberg I.: Functional implications of changes in sleep physiology with age, in Gershon S., Terry R. (ed.): *Neurobiology of Aging.* New York, Raven Press, 1975.

11. Galin D.: Hemispheric specialization: Implications for psychiatry, in Grenell R.G., Gabay S. (eds.): *Biological Foundations of Psychiatry.* New York, Raven Press, 1976, vol. l.

12. Greenfield N., et al.: The relationship between physiological and psychological responsivity: Depression and galvanic skin response. *J. Nerv. Ment. Dis.* 136:535, 1963.

13. Hall K.R.L., Stride E.: The varying response to pain in various psychiatric disorders: A study in abnormal psychology. *Br. J. Med. Psychol.* 27:48, 1954.

14. Hartmann E.: Longitudinal studies of sleep and dream patterns in manic-depressive patients. *Arch. Gen. Psychiatry* 19:312, 1968.

15. Hawkins D.R., Mendels J.: Sleep disturbances in depressive syndromes. *Am. J. Psychiatry* 123:682, 1966.

16. Head H., Holmes G.: Sensory disturbances associated with certain lesions of the optic thalamus, in *The Brain. Studies in Neurology.* London, Oxford University Press, 1920, vol. 2, pt. 4, chap. 2.

17. Heath R.G.: Emotion and sensory perception: Human and animal studies, in Grenell R.G., Gabay S. (eds.): *Biological Foundations of Psychiatry.* New York, Raven Press, 1976, vol. l.

18. Hemphill R.E., et al.: A preliminary report on fatigue and pain tolerance in depressive psychoneurotic patients. *Br. J. Psychiatry* 98:433, 1952.

19. Hurst L.A., et al.: The electroencephalogram in manic-depressive psychosis. *J. Ment. Sci.* 100:220–240, 1954.

20. Kiloh L.G., McComas A.J., Osselton J.W.: *Clinical Electroencephalography,* ed. 3. London, Butterworth, 1974.

21. Kupfer D.J., Foster F.G.: Interval between onset of sleep and rapid eye movements sleep as an indicator of depression. *Lancet,* 2:684, 1972.

22. Kupfer D.J., et al.: Classification of depressions: A guide for the clinician. Read before a symposium on advances in the treatment of affective disturbances. Rutgers Univ., Nov. 14–15, 1973.

23. Kupfer D.J., Gordon F.F.: The sleep of psychotic patients: Does it all look alike? *Res. Publ. Assoc. Res. Nerv. Ment. Dis.* 54:143–164, 1975.

24. Kupfer D.J., et al.: EEG sleep changes as predictors in depression. *Am. J. Psychiatry* 133:622, 1976.
25. Lader M.H., Wing L.: RS Physiological measures in agitated and retarded depressed patients. *J. Psychiatr. Res.* 7:89, 1969.
26. McLean P.D.: Sensory and perceptive factors in emotional functions of the triune brain, in Grenell R.G., Gabay S. (eds.): *Biological Foundations of Psychiatry*. New York, Raven Press, 1976, vol. 1.
27. Murphy D.L., Wyatt R.J.: Reduced MAO activity in blood platelets from schizophrenic patients. *Nature* 238:225, 1972.
28. Olds J.: Behavioral studies of hypothalamic functions: Drives and reinforcement, in Grenell R.G., Gabay S. (eds.): *Biological Foundations of Psychiatry*. New York, Raven Press, 1976, vol. 1.
29. Perris C.: A study of bipolar and unipolar recurrent depressive psychoses. *Acta Psychiatr. Scand.* 42(suppl. 194):118, 1966.
30. Prokasy W.F., Raskin D.C.: Electrodermal activity in psychological research. New York, Academic Press, 1973.
31. Ruch T.C.: Neurophysiology of emotion, in Ruch T.C., Patton H.D., Woodbury W.J., et al. (eds.): *Neurophysiology*, ed. 2. Philadelphia, W.B. Saunders Co., 1965, chap. 26.
32. Sachar E.J., et at.: Disrupted 24-hour patterns of cortisol secretion in psychotic depression. *Arch. Gen. Psychiatry* 28:19, 1973.
33. Shagass C.: The sedation threshold: A method for estimating tension in psychiatric patients. *Electroencephalogr. Clin. Neurophysiol.* 6:221, 1954.
34. Shagass C., Jones A.L.: A neurophysiological test for psychiatric diagnosis: Results in 750 patients. *Am. J. Psychiatry* 114:1002, 1958.
35. Shagass C.: EEG and evoked potentials and psychoses. *Res. Publ. Assoc. Res. Nerv. Ment. Dis.* 54:101–127, 1975.
36. Sitaram N., et al.: Faster cholinergic REM sleep induction in euthymic patients with primary affective illness. *Science* 208:200, 1980.
37. Stern J.A., Jones C.L.: Personality and psychopathology, in Prokasy W.F., Raskin D.C. (eds.): *Electrodermal Activity in Psychological Research*. New York, Academic Press, 1973.
38. Terzian H., Cecotto C.: Determinazione e studio della dominanza emisferica mediante iniezione intra carotide di amytal sodico nett'uano: Part I. *Boll. Soc. Ital. Biol. Sper.* 35:623, 1959.
39. Vogel G.W.: Improvement of depression by REM sleep deprivation. *Arch. Gen. Psychiatry* 37:247, 1980.
40. Weil A.A.: EEG findings in a certain type of psychosomatic headache: Dysrhythmic migraine. *Electroencephalogr. Clin. Neurophysiol.* 4:181, 1952.
41. Yerevanian B.I., Akiskal H.S.: Neurotic, characterological and dysthymic depression. *Psychiatr. Clin. North Am.* 2:595, 1979.

9

GENETIC ASPECTS

ELIZABETH DORUS, Ph.D.
RITA SHAUGHNESSY, Ph.D.

COMPELLING EVIDENCE exists that genetic factors contribute to the etiology of some forms of affective disorders. Concordance rates for affective disorders in members of monozygotic twin pairs (68%) and dizygotic twin pairs (23%), based on seven studies, suggest a genetic effect.[54] The prevalence of affective disorders in the families of bipolar patients (patients having both manic and depressive episodes) and unipolar patients (patients having recurrent depression) is considerably higher than the incidence in the general population.[1] More telling, however, is the evidence from adoption studies and from the study of members of twin pairs reared apart. Mendlewicz and Rainer[45] found a higher prevalence of affective disorders in the biologic parents than in the adopting parents of bipolar patients who had been adopted before age 1. Similarly, the concordance rates for members of monozygotic twin pairs reared apart are compatible with a genetic explanation for the etiology of affective disorders.[54]

The task, then, is to specify what genetic factors result in vulnerability to affective disorders and how they interact with nongenetic factors. Broadly speaking, there are three kinds of genetic abnormalities: (1) structural abnormalities of chromosomes, (2) chromosome aneuploidy (i.e., an abnormal number of chromosomes), and (3) a gene or genes which code for products that effect the disorder. In this chapter, we review the studies in which these kinds of abnormalities have been evaluated. Although no answer is available to the question of etiology from a genetic point of view, we can rule out some factors and point to interesting leads.

165

STRUCTURAL ABNORMALITIES OF CHROMOSOMES

Technical developments in cytogenetics over the past several decades have made possible the study of human chromosomes. These advances led, in 1956,[68] to the first accurate count of 46 chromosomes in human cells: 22 pairs of autosomal chromosomes in males and females, with sex chromosomes X and Y in males (the chromosomal complement or karyotype for males is denoted 46,XY) and two X chromosomes in females (the karyotype for females is denoted 46,XX). Caspersson et al.[13] first described the use of quinacrine derivatives for staining human chromosomes to reveal banding patterns. Quinacrine banding and Giemsa banding, among other techniques, made it possible to identify each chromosome on the basis of its unique banding pattern and to specify regions of chromosomes involved in duplications, deletions, and rearrangements.

Prior to the development of banding techniques, the autosomal chromosomes were arranged in the order of decreasing length and were assigned to groups on the basis of similar length and position of the centromere. Most chromosome abnormalities could thus be defined only in terms of the group assignments of the chromosomes involved. Although the X chromosome could not be distinguished from other chromosomes of similar morphology, studies of sex chromatin or Barr bodies in interphase nuclei of various tissues, such as the oral mucosa, could reveal the number of X chromosomes in the complement.

During the prebanding period, Ebaugh et al.[21] conducted chromosome studies on 23 bipolar patients and found one female with 45,X/46,XX mosaicism (the presence of two cell lines). It is not known whether the association between the chromosome abnormality and the disorder was fortuitous or whether the chromosome abnormality contributed to vulnerability to the disorder. Nielsen et al.[49] examined the chromosomes of 22 monozygotic and 27 dizygotic twin pairs, of whom one or both members had a unipolar or bipolar disorder, by using routine staining techniques and banding techniques in cases of presumed abnormalities. They found no relationship between chromosome variation and affective illness.

Chromosomes during the late prophase–early metaphase stage of mitosis are elongated compared with those in the mid-metaphase stage, and more refined banding can be seen.[76] Using banding techniques on mid-metaphase chromosomes, Escobar[23] found no abnormalities in nine bipolar patients. An X-linked factor in the etiology of some forms of bipolar illness has been hypothesized on the basis of the higher prevalence of affective disorders in women than in men and on the basis of some X-linkage studies. Escobar, therefore, also examined the X chromosome in five bipolar patients for whom approximately 20 bands could be visualized during late prophase–early metaphase, but he detected no structural abnormalities.

Chromosome studies based on present technology, although conducted on a limited number of bipolar patients, suggest that it is unlikely that an abnormality of chromosome structure is involved in the etiology of this disorder. To our knowledge, no chromosome studies on unipolar patients have been published.

CHROMOSOME ANEUPLOIDY

An abnormal number of a particular chromosome in an individual is associated with an excess or deficiency of the gene products coded for by genes on that chromosome. It is therefore of interest to ask whether individuals with aneuploidy of a particular chromosome are at greater risk of developing an affective disorder than individuals having a normal chromosome complement. Most aneuploidies result in nonviable fetuses. The common exceptions are trisomy 21 (Down's syndrome), in which an individual has an additional chromosome 21, and the sex chromosome aneuploidies, including 45,X (Turner's syndrome), 47,XXY (Klinefelter's syndrome), and 47,XYY (in which a male has an additional Y chromosome).

In the case of trisomy 21 and 47,XYY, we can be fairly confident that no increased risk for affective disorders exists. We have no evidence that females having a 45,X chromosome complement are at increased risk for mood disturbances; on the contrary, they have been described as being notably placid. Males with a 47,XXY chromosome complement appear to have an increased risk for various kinds of psychiatric disturbance; in particular, the prevalence of such males is elevated in samples of schizophrenic patients.[25] Cases of 47,XXY males with bipolar illness have been reported[12]; this led to speculation whether an excess of an X-linked gene product could be involved in the etiology of these disorders. Epidemiologic studies of the relationship between the 47,XXY karyotype and affective disorders would be informative.

In summary, it appears that aneuploidy, by itself, has no general effect on the regulation of mood. The X-chromosome aneuploidies, although rare, deserve attention in view of the hypothesis that an X-linked factor plays a role in the etiology of some affective disorders.

GENES INVOLVED IN AFFECTIVE DISORDERS

PEDIGREE STUDIES

Prevalence of Affective Disorders in Relatives of Index Patients

Pedigree studies have provided the most extensive evidence that affective disorders run in families and may be heritable. Angst and Perris assessed the frequency and type of affective disorders among first-degree relatives of bipolar and unipolar patients; their results were in substantial agreement.[1] They found a significantly higher prevalence of affective disorders in relatives of bipolar patients (20%) than in relatives of unipolar patients (13%), suggesting that bipolar illness may have a more potent genetic component. Relatives of bipolar patients tended to have bipolar or cyclic disorders rather than recurrent depression, whereas the converse was true for relatives of unipolar patients.

With respect to the heterogeneity of unipolar illness, Winokur[74] used the pedigree study method to distinguish between depressive spectrum and pure depressive disease. The former is characterized by a family history of alcoholism or sociopathy, especially in male relatives, and an early onset (before age 40) of the disorder in the index patient; the latter is characterized by a family history of depression in both male and female relatives and a late onset (after age 40) in the index patient.

Since schizoaffective illness has a component of mood disturbance as well as disordered thought processes, and since it responds to lithium treatment in some cases, its relationship to affective disorders has been questioned. Apparently, this illness does not result from a combination of genes involved in the transmission of schizophrenia and of those involved in the transmission of bipolar illness; matings between schizophrenics and bipolar patients rarely produce schizoaffective offspring.[55] Tsuang et al.[69] found an elevated prevalence of affective disorders, but not of schizophrenia, in first-degree relatives of schizoaffective patients; Mendlewicz[41] reported an elevated prevalence of affective disorders and a slightly elevated prevalence of schizophrenia.

These various pedigree studies strongly support the contention that relatives of patients with affective disorders are at greater risk for affective disorders themselves than are members of the general population. No simple mode of transmission of affective disorders has been discovered in such studies. The results have been instructive, however, in showing the complexity of the problem of specifying the mode of transmission and in indicating the variety of phenotypes, with respect to mood disorders, that can exist within a pedigree.

Mathematical Models for the Study of Modes of Transmission

In recent years, mathematically sophisticated methods for the analysis of pedigree data have been developed. One of these methods is segregation analysis, designed to assess hypotheses concerning the mode of transmission of a trait or disorder.[22] The aim is to determine how closely the observed patterns of transmission match those which would be expected if a specified mode of transmission were operating. Among the hypotheses that can be tested are those of dominance, co-dominance, recessivity, and additivity. Factors that might obscure mendelian modes of transmission, such as variable age at onset or variable penetrance of the gene or genes in question, can be taken into account. Assumptions concerning threshold effects can be varied. Advances in computer technology have made possible the iterative procedures required for computation of maximum likelihood estimates, that is, estimates of the likelihood of the observed data, given the assumed model.

Segregation analyses have been conducted on pedigrees in which the index patients had an affective disorder. The results are conflicting in two ways: more than one hypothetical mode of transmission has provided an acceptable fit to a set of data,[26] and differences among sets of data exist in the hypothetical models that provide a fit.[27] Apart from these particular inconsistencies, a general limitation of segregation analysis is that it can never prove a mode of transmission; it can only rule out models from which the data deviate significantly. As described below, segregation analysis has also been used for evaluation of the genetic control of biochemical traits that may be relevant to affective disorders.

Linkage Studies

The ultimate goal in genetic studies is to map the gene or genes involved in the etiology of affective disorders on chromosomes. At present, only about one fiftieth of the structural genes in man have been mapped.[40] The X chromosome has been mapped most extensively, and some genes have been assigned to all chromosomes in man. During meiosis, crossing over, or the exchange of genetic material, occurs between homologous chromosomes. The greater the proximity or linkage between two gene loci, the less the likelihood of crossing over between them and the greater the deviation from an independent assortment of genes within pedigrees. A marker gene is a gene that has been mapped on a particular chromosome. Linkage studies allow one to determine whether a gene locus involved in the determination of a disorder is in close proximity to a marker gene on a chromosome.

Winokur et al.[75] first reported evidence for an association between X-linked markers (protan and deutan color-blindness and the Xg blood system) and manic-depressive illness within pedigrees. The results of subsequent X-linkage studies have been both stimulating and conflicting. Mendlewicz et al.[43] reported linkage between the locus for the Xg blood group and a dominant gene on the X chromosome for bipolar illness; similarly, some studies suggested linkage with the gene loci for protan and deutan color-blindness.[42] These studies prompted reports of affected father-son pairs from pedigrees having no history of psychiatric illness in the maternal line. Since a male offspring inherits a Y, not an X chromosome from his father, these pairs would be inconsistent with X linkage. All one can conclude from such pairs, however, is that X linkage is not the mode of transmission in all pedigrees. Nonlinkage established in linkage studies would, on the other hand, constitute evidence for the absence of an X-chromosome effect. Gershon et al.,[31] in fact, failed to find linkage between a gene locus for bipolar illness and the loci for color-blindness, whereas Leckman et al.[38] failed to find linkage with the locus controlling the Xg blood system.

Problems with the X-linkage hypothesis exist, apart from the conflicting results of linkage studies. The gene loci for protan and deutan color-blindness and for the Xg blood system may be sufficiently far apart that a gene locus between them could not be linked simultaneously to both.[28] Estimates of linkage depend on determining which members of a pedigree have affective disorders with a common genetic basis and which do not. Given the variability in the history and symptoms of affective disturbance from one member of a pedigree to another, and given the possibility of nongenetic causes of mood disorders in some members or of unique gene-environment interactions, this task is difficult.

BIOLOGIC STUDIES

The lack of clarity in the results of pedigree studies and a growing interest in the biologic bases of behavior have led investigators to search for genetically controlled biologic traits that distinguish between individuals vulnerable to affective disorders and those not vulnerable. We will review (1) studies of cell membrane characteristics reflected in lithium transport, and will note some issues involved in many biologic studies of affective disorders, (2) studies of the enzymes involved in catecholamine metabolism, (3) electrophysiologic studies, and (4) studies of the major histocompatibility complex.

Lithium Transport Studies

The specific effectiveness of lithium in the treatment of affective disorders, particularly bipolar illness, suggested that an abnormality in electrolyte distribution may be present in such patients. In the past ten years, research in this area has focused, in part, on cation transport across the red cell membrane.

Genetic factors contribute to the interindividual variability in the red cell lithium concentration–plasma lithium concentration ratio (lithium ratio). Dorus et al.[15] found that the mean within-pair differences in the lithium ratio in vitro and in vivo for monozygotic twin pairs were significantly smaller than those for dizygotic twin pairs. On the basis of this preliminary evidence for genetic control, Dorus et al.[18] assessed the lithium ratio in vitro in members of psychiatrically normal families. Evidence for a considerable degree of genetic control was obtained; parent-offspring and sibling-sibling correlations did not differ significantly from 0.50, the correlation expected if a quantitative trait is under complete polygenic control. The possibility that such correlations were inflated due to common nongenetic influences could not be ruled out. There were no statistically significant differences in the magnitude of the sibling-sibling correlations (brother-brother, brother-sister, and sister-sister) or of the parent-offspring correlations, suggesting the absence of X-chromosome effects. Results of analyses to determine whether dominance effects (the disproportionate effects of one or more genes) or additive effects (the cumulative effects of a large number of genes with equal effects) are involved were equivocal.

When patients take lithium carbonate, typically their extracellular concentrations of lithium are greater than their intracellular concentrations. Several operationally distinct pathways of red cell lithium transport have recently been elucidated. The pathway primarily responsible for the observed distribution of lithium is a lithium-sodium counterflow mechanism.[19, 51] Lithium is driven from the red cell against its electrochemical gradient by an oppositely directed sodium gradient. Lithium-sodium counterflow is significantly negatively correlated with the lithium ratio; individuals having low lithium-sodium counterflow have a high lithium ratio, and vice versa. Under physiologic conditions, when lithium is absent, this exchange mechanism is one of sodium-sodium exchange.

Given that the considerable interindividual variability in the lithium ratio (or lithium-sodium counterflow) is under genetic control, it is important to determine whether this variability is associated with affective disorders.[14] Most, although not all, investigators report that, on the average, the lithium ratios are significantly higher in bipolar patients than in normal individuals. Unipolar depressed patients, on the other hand, appear not to differ from normal individuals. Genetic heterogeneity in groups of patients with unipolar depression may obscure significant differences that exist among subgroups of patients and normal individuals.

Evidence that bipolar patients differ from normal individuals with respect to lithium transport characteristics is not sufficient to implicate this variable in the *etiology* of bipolar illness. Such an implication would require demonstrating that, within pedigrees, the genes controlling the biologic trait and the genes contributing to the development of a psychiatric illness are assorted nonindependently; that is, within a family, psychiatrically ill relatives should differ from psychiatrically well relatives with respect to the biologic trait. Dorus et al.[16] found that, among the relatives of bipolar patients, those with a history of a major or a minor affective disorder had a significantly higher mean lithium ratio than those with no such history or than normal individuals with no family history of major psychoses. Relatives with no history of affective illness did not differ from normal individuals with regard to the lithium ratio. Prospective studies would be necessary for an answer to the question of the etiologic significance of this within-pedigree association.

Substantial overlap exists in the distribution of lithium transport values in patients and normal individuals. Bipolar illness undoubtedly is heterogeneous with respect to the significance of cell membrane factors. Rybakowski[56] found that bipolar patients with affected first-degree relatives had a higher mean lithium ratio than patients having no affected first-degree relatives. Similarly, monozygotic twin pairs concordant for affective disorders and identified on the basis of a bipolar member have a higher mean lithium ratio in vivo than monozygotic twin pairs discordant for affective disorders.[44] A study by Shaughnessy et al.[59] contributes to an understanding of the significance of high lithium ratios in ostensibly normal individuals. In an assessment of various personality characteristics, normal women with a high lithium ratio had less regard for accepted moral codes and less concern about their social image than normal women whose lithium ratio was low.

An important question in this regard concerns the fundamental function of a sodium-sodium exchange system. Canessa et al.[11] reported greater red cell lithium-sodium counterflow in 36 patients with essential hypertension than in 26 normal individuals. Duhm and Becker[20] have documented a substantial interindividual variability in lithium-sodium exchange in the red cells of several species of mammals. Thus, in preliminary findings on man, low lithium-sodium counterflow is associated with affective disorders and high counterflow is associated with essential hypertension; a wide range of values, however, appears to be typical in various mammalian species.

Whether sodium-sodium exchange is present in the brain is relevant to an understanding of the pathophysiology of affective disorders and the mode of action of lithium in their treatment. Szentistvany et al.[64] found evidence for a phloretin-sensitive component of lithium transport in nerve cell cultures from chick embryo brains. In contrast, Saneto et al.,[57] in the first report of its kind, found no evidence of such a system in human clonal neuroblastoma cells. In general, the question of what can be inferred about CNS function from findings in peripheral tissues, such as red cells, is common to many studies of the relationship between biologic traits and affective disorders.

Studies of Enzymes Involved in Catecholamine Metabolism

The catecholamines, dopamine, epinephrine, and norepinephrine, are neurotransmitters, that is, biochemical agents that are released at synapses and produce changes in neuronal activity. Since behavior results, in part, from transmission of nerve impulses, it is important to understand the factors that regulate the function of the neurotransmitters. Early reports suggested that a deficit or excess of neurotransmitters might be responsible for depression and mania, respectively.[24] For example, reserpine, which is frequently prescribed for hypertension, caused depression in a number of patients;[2] it was later discovered that reserpine depletes central stores of dopamine, norepinephrine, and serotonin. The relationship between levels of catecholamines and psychiatric disorders is not as simple as was once postulated. Nevertheless, the assumption of a relationship has led to fruitful studies of the enzymes that regulate the metabolism of the catecholamine neurotransmitters.

Monoamine oxidase (MAO) is the enzyme that converts the catecholamines to their corresponding aldehydes. Two forms of MAO (types A and B), defined in terms of substrate specificities, have been identified in brain and other tissues in man.[35] Both types are present in some tissues such as liver; in other tissues, one form predominates. Monoamine oxidase in the brain is primarily type A, whereas MAO in platelets is type B.[46]

Twin[50] and pedigree[52] studies have provided evidence that genetic factors contribute to interindividual variability in platelet MAO activity. No evidence of X-linked gene effects exists. Whether dominance or additive gene effects are involved in platelet MAO activity is unresolved. The suggestion of non-normality in distributions of platelet MAO activities provides limited support for the presence of dominance effects.[48, 52] Bimodality has been clearly demonstrated in the distribution of MAO activity in skin fibroblasts, which is primarily of type A (our calculation).[4]

Although reports to the contrary exist, lower than average platelet MAO activity seems to be associated with bipolar illness[47, 37] and alcoholism.[60, 61] Monoamine oxidase activity in unipolar depressed patients has not been studied in detail; results thus far have been equivocal.[36, 39]

As was the case with lithium transport, nonindependent assorting of the biologic variable and the psychiatric disorder must be shown within pedigrees before the variable can be implicated in the genetic etiology of the disorder. Pandey et al.[53] found that among first-degree relatives of bipolar patients, those relatives with a history of bipolar illness or alcoholism had a significantly lower mean MAO activity than relatives with no such history or normal individuals from families with no history of major psychoses. In two other studies, relatives of bipolar patients had a significantly lower mean MAO activity than normal controls. In neither study were within-pedigree relationships demonstrated.[32, 37] Finally, Sullivan et al.[62] reported that, among first-degree relatives of alcoholics with low MAO activity, those relatives with a history of a psychiatric illness had a significantly lower mean MAO activity than relatives with no such history.

Buchsbaum et al.[9] used an elegant research strategy to determine the significance of low MAO activity in normal individuals. They found that college students with low MAO activity had more psychological counseling contacts themselves and had a higher prevalence of suicides and suicide attempts in their families than students having high MAO activity.

Although some promising results have been reported, it is difficult to elucidate the relationship between variability in MAO activity and psychiatric illness. Substantial evidence exists that platelet MAO activity is reduced, on the average, in chronic schizophrenics.[10] An adequate explanation of the significance of platelet MAO would have to account for its reduction in psychiatric disorders that are genetically disparate.

Catechol-o-methyltransferase (COMT) is the enzyme which acts on the catecholamines or their aldehydes to produce the corresponding o-methylated derivative. Red cell COMT activity is under a substantial degree of genetic control. In the case of COMT activity, in contrast to MAO activity, progress has been made in determining the mode of transmission. A study of a large number of unrelated individuals has shown that the distribution of COMT activity values is bimodal; segregation analyses indicated that low red cell COMT activity is controlled by an autosomal recessive gene.[72]

It is still unclear whether or not extreme levels of COMT activity are associated with the presence of affective disorders. Some investigators report elevated COMT activity in patients with affective disorders; others report no difference between such patients and normal individuals; still others report lower than average levels of COMT activity in patients with affective disorders.[29] Either variability in COMT activity is not relevant to the pathophysiology of affective disorders or the heterogeneity of affective disorders has led to conflicting results.

Dopamine-β-hydroxylase (DBH), the enzyme which converts dopamine to norepinephrine, is also under substantial genetic control.[71] Pedigree analyses indicate that, as in the case of COMT, a low level of DBH activity is inherited by means of an autosomal recessive gene.[70] As is the case with COMT activity, studies in which patients with affective disorders are compared with normal individuals have yielded conflicting results.[29]

In summary, it appears that at least one enzyme involved in catecholamine metabolism, MAO, may play a role in some affective disorders. The lack of specificity of the relationship between low levels of MAO activity and any one psychiatric disorder makes drawing inferences from the results difficult. Another question pertains to the importance of these findings for an understanding of the function of MAO in the brain. These problems notwithstanding, investigations on the role of neurotransmitters in affective disorders will continue. For example, numerous peptides have recently been identified which have a neurotransmitter function in the brain and which may be related to behavior.[58]

Electrophysiologic Studies: Average Evoked Response

Electrophysiologic techniques provide a noninvasive means of monitoring CNS activity in man. These techniques allow the monitoring of cortical responses to specific sensory events. They are limited by our deficient understanding of the neurophysiology that underlies these responses.

The amplitude of the average evoked response (AER) to sensory stimulation is related to the modulation by the CNS of the intensity of incoming stimuli. In man, the amplitude of response to a stimulus does not always increase directly with an increase in stimulus intensity.[67] In some individuals, the amplitude of the response becomes greater as the intensity of the stimulus increases (augmenters); in others, the amplitude decreases (reducers).[5]

Variability in the AER appears to be under at least partial genetic control, although heritability may not be a large factor.[30] A high correlation was found for augmentation or reduction in monozygotic twin pairs, but the correlation for dizygotic pairs was nearly zero. Results from pedigree studies provide evidence that dominance effects or interactive dominance effects among several gene loci may be involved in the transmission of the trait.

It appeared reasonable to investigate whether augmenting is related to mania and reducing to depression. Most results indicate that, in fact, relative to normal individuals, bipolar patients tend to be augmenters and unipolar patients tend to be reducers, regardless of the mood state.[6, 7] Buchsbaum et al.[6] found that college students who were augmenters had pronounced thrill- and adventure-seeking characteristics; students who were reducers were less thrill- and adventure-seeking and had elevated Minnesota Multiphasic Personality Inventory (MMPI) depression scale scores. In the only family study that has been conducted on this problem,[30] the investigators failed to find a within-pedigree difference between ill and well relatives of 31 bipolar and 10 unipolar patients with respect to AER. The results of this study are difficult to interpret, since in the data analysis neither the patients nor their relatives with bipolar and unipolar disorders were considered separately.

Major Histocompatibility Complex

The major histocompatibility complex (MHC) is a group of interrelated loci in the same chromosomal region in mammals. The alleles or genes at these loci produce cell surface antigens that are related to immune response. In man, the MHC, called the HLA complex, is mapped on chromosome 6. Four loci (A, B, C, and D) having a total of at least 50 genes have been identified.[73] Some HLA alleles could produce surface antigens that interfere with the binding of neurotransmitters to receptor sites, thus contributing to the development of presumably nonimmunologic disorders such as affective illness.[63]

A number of studies, reviewed by Temple et al.,[66] have been conducted on the frequency of HLA alleles in patients with affective disorders relative to that in normal individuals. Apart from Shapiro's confirmation of his own finding of an elevated prevalence of an allele at the B locus (BW16) in a Danish population, no consistent data were obtained.

This area of research poses statistical problems. Because of the large number of alleles that must be evaluated, a number of significant differences between patients having affective disorders and normal individuals would be expected by chance. Furthermore, correlations exist among the frequencies of particular alleles; the frequency of alleles at a locus totals 1, and since the loci are linked, the segregation of alleles at different loci does not occur independently. James et al.[34] have developed a conservative method for applying analysis of covariance to such results. It is clear, however, that large numbers of subjects are needed for adequate evaluation of hypotheses.

A strategy that obviates these statistical problems involves studying the segregation of HLA alleles and affective disorders within pedigrees. Targum et al.[65] found no relationship between HLA alleles at loci A and B and the presence or absence of affective disorders in nine families. At present, research on the HLA system in relation to affective disorders does not appear promising, but the complexity of this system has yet to be appreciated.

MULTIPLE FACTORS IN VULNERABILITY TO AFFECTIVE DISORDERS

Although variables such as the lithium ratio, platelet MAO activity, and AER may be involved in the pathophysiology, and perhaps the genetic etiology, of some affective disorders, no one variable is sufficient to account for the presence or absence of a disorder. Vulnerability may not be controlled by the functioning of one biochemical or neurophysiologic system or, from a genetic perspective, by the action of a single gene. It may be fruitful to study the combined effects of a number of genetic and nongenetic factors.

Several investigators have used multivariate approaches, with promising results. Buchsbaum[8] found that the accuracy of discrimination among bipolar patients, unipolar patients, schizophrenic patients, and normal individuals improved when platelet MAO activity and AER were considered simultaneously. College students who had either a combination of low

MAO activity and augmenting of the AER or high MAO activity and reducing of the AER had a greater degree of psychopathology, particularly affective disorders, than other students.[33] Dorus et al.[17] classified first-degree relatives of bipolar patients on the basis of both their lithium ratio and their platelet MAO activity. All 13 relatives who had *both* a high lithium ratio and a low MAO activity had a history of an affective disorder, whereas the number of relatives with and without such a history was approximately equal in the three other lithium ratio-MAO activity groups. Shaughnessy et al.[59] assessed personality characteristics and psychopathology in women with extreme values of both the lithium ratio and MAO activity. Women having both a high lithium ratio and low MAO activity were found to differ significantly from the other three groups of women on a larger number of personality scales than any of the other groups.

Such findings, although preliminary, suggest that vulnerability to affective disorders may best be conceived of as arising from the additive or interactive effects of a number of contributing genetic factors. Undoubtedly, nongenetic factors also contribute to vulnerability to some affective disorders. Individuals who experience the early loss of a parent, for example, are more likely to experience depression than individuals who do not.[3] In contrast to the investigation of the causes of schizophrenia, there had been a notable paucity of studies on affective disorders that address the issue of gene-environment interactions. Eventually, major gene effects may be identified in some forms of affective disorders; the challenge with respect to other forms will be to identify both genetic and nongenetic factors and to understand their interactions.

SUMMARY

Studies of related individuals reared apart support the contention from twin and pedigree studies that genetic factors play a role in the etiology of affective disorders. No evidence exists for consistent structural abnormalities of chromosomes in patients who have affective disorders; with the development of more refined methods, structural variants may be detected, however. Chromosome aneuploidy, in general, is not related to mood disturbance. The X-chromosome aneuploidies are of particular interest in relation to the hypothesis of the involvement of an X-linked gene in the etiology of some forms of affective disorders.

The prevalence of various affective disorders is increased in the relatives of bipolar, unipolar, and schizoaffective patients. The use of mathematical models to determine the mode of transmission of affective disorders has yielded equivocal results. X-linkage studies in which protan and deutan color-blindness and the Xg blood system are used as markers have provided preliminary evidence of a gene locus on the X chromosome in some pedigree studies. X-linkage is inconsistent with data from other pedigree studies, however. Linkage of a hypothetical gene locus with the color-blindness and the Xg blood system loci simultaneously may be unlikely, given our present knowledge of the map of the X chromosome.

The fact that pedigrees do not exhibit mendelian modes of genetic transmission has led investigators to study genetically controlled biologic traits which might discriminate between individuals vulnerable to and those not vulnerable to affective disorders. The distribution of cations has been of interest, since cations are integrally involved in neuronal function and since lithium is effective in the treatment of some forms of affective disorders. Most investigations of red cell lithium transport indicate that bipolar patients have higher lithium ratios or lower lithium-sodium counterflow than normal individuals. Furthermore, in one study, first-degree relatives of bipolar patients who themselves had a history of affective disorders had a higher lithium ratio than unaffected relatives or individuals from families free of psychiatric illness. The hypothesis that a cell membrane abnormality, reflected in lithium transport, is involved in some forms of bipolar illness is viable. Prospective studies are needed. In this research, however, as in other kinds of research on peripheral tissues, the implications for brain function are unclear.

Catecholamine metabolism may be altered in some affective disorders. Among the enzymes involved in catecholamine metabolism which have been studied, platelet MAO and its activity appear to be of interest. Preliminary evidence suggests that platelet MAO activity is lower, on the average, in bipolar patients and alcoholics than in normal individuals. It is difficult to reconcile the results of various studies of the activity of this enzyme in relatives of patients having affective disorders. Even if reduced MAO activity is implicated in the etiology of some affective disorders, such reductions are not specific to affective disorders; strong evidence exists for reductions in chronic schizophrenics as well.

With respect to average evoked response, bipolar patients tend to be augmenters and unipolar patients tend to be reducers. While an argument can be made for the involvement of the major histocompatibility complex in presumably nonimmunologic disorders, such as affective disorders, the results obtained thus far are preliminary and not promising.

Affective disorders are undoubtedly genetically heterogeneous. Such heterogeneity may obscure important differences between patients and normal individuals in biologic studies and may confound the results of linkage studies and the segregation analysis of pedigree data. Major gene effects may eventually be identified; interesting findings may also result from the assumption that multiple genetic and environmental factors have complex interactions in the development of affective disorders.

ACKNOWLEDGMENTS

This work was supported by NIMH Research Scientist Development Award MH00111 (Dorus). E. Lanzl provided editorial assistance and J. Harris provided research assistance.

REFERENCES

1. Angst J., Perris C.: The nosology of endogenous depression: Comparison of the results of two studies. *Int. J. Ment. Health* 1:145, 1972.
2. Berger P.A., Barchas J.D.: Biochemical hypotheses of affective disorders, in Barchas J.D., et al. (eds.): *Psychopharmacology: From Theory to Practice.* New York, Oxford University Press, 1977.
3. Birtchnell J.: Depression in relation to early and recent parent death. *Br. J. Psychiatry* 116:299, 1970.
4. Breakefield X.O., Giller E.L.: Human skin fibroblasts in neuropsychiatric disorders. *Psychopharmacol. Bull.* 16:63, 1980.
5. Buchsbaum M., Silverman J.: Stimulus intensity control and the corticol evoked response. *Psychosom. Med.* 30:12, 1968.
6. Buchsbaum M.S., et al.: AER in affective disorders. *Am. J. Psychiatry* 128:51, 1971.
7. Buchsbaum M., et al.: Average evoked response in bipolar and unipolar affective disorders: Relationship to sex, age of onset and monoamine oxidase. *Biol. Psychiatry* 7:199, 1973.
8. Buchsbaum M.: Average evoked response augmenting/reducing in schizophrenia and affective disorders, in Freedman D.X. (ed.): *Biology of the Major Psychoses: A Comparative Analysis.* New York, Raven Press, 1975.
9. Buchsbaum M.S., Coursey R.D., Murphy D.L.: The biochemical high-risk paradigm: Behavioral and familial correlates of low platelet monoamine oxidase activity. *Science* 194:339, 1976.
10. Buchsbaum M.S., Rieder R.O.: Biologic heterogeneity and psychiatric research. *Arch. Gen. Psychiatry* 36:1163, 1979.
11. Canessa M., et al.: Increased sodium-lithium countertransport in red cells of patients with essential hypertension. *N. Engl. J. Med.* 302:772, 1980.
12. Caroff S.N.: Klinefelter's syndrome and bipolar affective illness: A case report. *Am. J. Psychiatry* 135:748, 1978.
13. Caspersson T., Zech L., Johansson C.: Differential binding of alkylating fluorochromes in human chromosomes. *Exp. Cell Res.* 60:315, 1970.
14. Dorus E.: Membranes and electrolytes in the biology of depression, in Friedman E., Mann J., Gershon S. (eds.): *Depression and Antidepressants.* New York, Raven Press, to be published.
15. Dorus E., Pandey G.N., Davis J.M.: Genetic determinant of lithium ion distribution: An in vitro and in vivo monozygotic-dizygotic twin study. *Arch. Gen. Psychiatry* 32:1097, 1975.
16. Dorus E., et al.: Lithium transport across red-cell membrane: A cell membrane abnormality in manic-depressive illness. *Science* 205:932, 1979.
17. Dorus E., et al.: Low platelet monoamine oxidase activity, high red blood cell lithium ratio and affective disorders: A multivariate assessment of genetic vulnerability to affective disorders. *Biol. Psychiatry* 14:989, 1979.

18. Dorus E., et al.: Lithium transport across the RBC membrane: A study of genetic factors. *Arch. Gen. Psychiatry* 37:80, 1980.
19. Duhm J., et al.: Studies on the lithium transport across the red cell membrane: I. Li$^+$ uphill transport by the Na$^+$-dependent Li$^+$ countertransport system of human erythrocytes. *Pflugers Arch.* 364:147, 1976.
20. Duhm J., Becker B.F.: Studies on lithium transport across the red cell membrane: V. On the nature of the Na$^+$-dependent Li$^+$ countertransport system of mammalian erythrocytes. *J. Membrane Biol.* 51:263, 1979.
21. Ebaugh I.A., et al.: Chromosome studies in patients with affective disorder (manic-depressive illness). *Arch. Gen. Psychiatry* 19:751, 1968.
22. Elston R.C.: Segregation analysis, in Mielke J.H., Crawford M.H. (eds.): *Current Developments in Anthropological Genetics*. New York, Plenum Publishing Corp., 1980.
23. Escobar J.I.: A cytogenetic study of bipolar affective illness. *Compr. Psychiatry* 19:331, 1978.
24. Everett G.M., Toman J.E.P.: Mode of action of Rauwolfia alkaloids and motor activity, in Masserman J. (ed.): *Biological Psychiatry*. New York, Grune & Stratton, 1959.
25. Forssman H.: The mental implications of sex chromosome aberrations. *Br. J. Psychiatry* 117:353, 1970.
26. Gershon E.S., Dunner D.L., Goodwin F.K.: Toward a biology of affective disorders: Genetic contributions. *Arch. Gen. Psychiatry* 25:1, 1971.
27. Gershon E.S., et al.: The inheritance of affective disorders: A review of data and of hypotheses. *Behav. Genet.* 6:227, 1976.
28. Gershon E.S., Bunney W.E. Jr.: The question of X-linkage in bipolar manic depressive illness. *J. Psychiatr. Res.* 13:99, 1977.
29. Gershon E.S., et al.: Genetic studies and biologic strategies in the affective disorders. *Prog. Med. Genet.* 2:101, 1977.
30. Gershon E.S., Buchsbaum M.S.: A genetic study of average evoked response augmentation/reduction in affective disorders, in Shagass C., Gershon S., Friedhoff A.J. (eds.): *Psychopathology and Brain Dysfunction*. New York, Raven Press, 1977.
31. Gershon E.S., et al.: Color blindness not closely linked to bipolar illness: Report of a new pedigree series. *Arch. Gen. Psychiatry* 36:1423, 1979.
32. Gershon E.S., et al.: Platelet monoamine oxidase (MAO) activity and genetic vulnerability to bipolar (BP) affective illness. *Psychopharmacol. Bull.* 15:27, 1979.
33. Haier R.J., Buchsbaum M.S., Murphy D.L.: Screening young adults for psychiatric vulnerability: A preliminary comparison of biological and clinical measures. *Psychopharmacol. Bull.* 15:7, 1979.
34. James N., et al.: Genetic markers in affective disorders: ABO and HLA, in Mendlewicz J., Shopsin B. (eds.): *Genetic Aspects of Affective Illness*. New York, Spectrum Publications, 1979.
35. Johnston J.P.: Some observations upon a new inhibitor of monoamine oxidase in brain-tissue. *Biochem. Pharmacol.* 17:1285, 1968.
36. Landowski J., Wieslawa L., Angielski S.: Monoamine oxidase activity in blood platelets from patients with cyclophrenic depressive symptoms. *Biochem. Med.* 14:347, 1975.
37. Leckman J.F., et al.: Reduced MAO activity in first-degree relatives of individuals with bipolar affective disorders. *Arch. Gen. Psychiatry* 34:601, 1977.

38. Leckman J.F., et al.: New data do not suggest linkage between the Xg blood group and bipolar illness. *Arch. Gen. Psychiatry* 36:1435, 1979.
39. Mann J.: Altered platelet monoamine oxidase activity in affective disorders. *Psychol. Med.* 9:729, 1979.
40. McKusick V.A., Ruddle F.H.: The status of the gene map of the human chromosomes. *Science* 196:390, 1977.
41. Mendlewicz J.: Genetic studies in schizoaffective illness, in Gershon E.S., et al. (eds.): *The Impact of Biology on Modern Psychiatry*. New York, Plenum Press, 1977.
42. Mendlewicz J., Fleiss J.L.: Linkage studies with X-chromosome markers in bipolar (manic-depressive) and unipolar (depressive) illnesses. *Biol. Psychiatry* 9:261, 1974.
43. Mendlewicz J., Fleiss J.L., Fieve R.R.: Linkage studies in affective disorders: The Xg blood group and manic-depressive illness, in Fieve R.R., Rosenthal D., Brill H. (eds.): *Genetic Research in Psychiatry*. Baltimore, Md., The Johns Hopkins University Press, 1975.
44. Mendlewicz J., et al.: Lithium accumulation in erythrocytes of manic-depressive patients: An in vivo twin study. *Br. J. Psychiatry* 133:436, 1978.
45. Mendlewicz J., Rainer J.D.: Adoption study supporting genetic transmission in manic-depressive illness. *Nature* 268:327, 1977.
46. Murphy D.L.: Clinical, genetic, hormonal and drug influences on the activity of human platelet monoamine oxidase, in *Monoamine Oxidase and Its Inhibition*. Ciba Foundation Symposium No. 39, Elsevier, Excerpta Medica, 1976.
47. Murphy D.L., Wyatt R.J.: Reduced monoamine oxidase activity in blood platelets from schizophrenic patients. *Nature* 238:225, 1972.
48. Murphy D.L., et al.: Platelet and plasma amine oxidase activity in 680 normals: Sex and age differences and stability over time. *Biochem. Med.* 16:254, 1976.
49. Nielsen J., Homma A., Bertelsen A.: Cytogenic investigation in twins with manic-depressive disorders (22 monozygotic and 27 dizygotic twin pairs). *Br. J. Psychiatry* 130:352, 1977.
50. Nies A., et al.: Genetic control of platelet and plasma monoamine oxidase activity. *Arch. Gen. Psychiatry* 28:834, 1973.
51. Pandey G.N., et al.: Lithium transport pathways in human red cells. *J. Genet. Physiol.* 72:233, 1978.
52. Pandey G.N., et al.: Genetic control of platelet monoamine oxidase activity: Studies on normal families. *Life Sci.* 25:1173, 1979.
53. Pandey G.N., et al.: Reduced platelet MAO activity and vulnerability to psychiatric disorders. *Psychiatry Res.* 2:315, 1980.
54. Price J.: The genetics of depressive behavior, in Coppen A., Walk A. (eds.): *Recent Developments in Affective Disorders. Br. J. Psychiatry* Special Publication No. 2, 1968, p. 37.
55. Rosenthal D.: *Genetic Theory and Abnormal Behavior*. New York, McGraw-Hill Book Co., 1970.
56. Rybakowski J.: Pharmacogenetic aspect of red blood cell lithium index in manic-depressive psychosis. *Biol. Psychiatry* 12:425, 1977.
57. Saneto R.P., et al.: Lithium uptake at physiological ion concentrations in a human clonal neuroblastoma cell line. *J. Neurochem.*, to be published.
58. Snyder S.H.: Brain peptides as neurotransmitters. *Science* 209:976, 1980.
59. Shaughnessy R., et al.: Personality correlates of platelet monoamine oxidase activity and red cell lithium transport. *Psychiatry Res.* 2:63, 1980.

60. Sullivan J., Stanfield C.N., Dackis C.: Platelet MAO activity in schizophrenia and other psychiatric illnesses. *Am. J. Psychiatry* 134:1098, 1977.
61. Sullivan J.L., et al.: Stability of low blood platelet monoamine oxidase acitivity in human alcoholics. *Biol. Psychiatry* 13:391, 1978.
62. Sullivan J.L., et al.: Familial, biochemical and clinical correlates of alcoholics with low platelet monoamine oxidase activity. *Biol. Psychiatry* 14:385, 1979.
63. Svejgaard A., Ryder L.P.: Interaction of HLA molecules with nonimmunological ligands as an explanation of HLA and disease associations. *Lancet* 2:547, 1976.
64. Szentistvanyi I., et al.: Na-dependent Li-transport in primary nerve cell cultures. *Neurosci. Letters* 13:157, 1979.
65. Targum S.D., et al.: Human leukocyte antigen system not closely linked to or associated with bipolar manic-depressive illness. *Biol. Psychiatry* 14:615, 1979.
66. Temple H., Dupont B., Shopsin B.: Histocompatibility studies in an affectively ill Jewish population, in Mendlewicz J., Shopsin B. (eds.): *Genetic Aspects of Affective Illness*. New York, SP Medical and Scientific Books, 1979.
67. Tepas D.O., Armington J.C.: Properties of evoked potentials. *Vision Res.* 2:449, 1962.
68. Tjio J.H., Levan A.: The chromosome number of man. *Hereditas* 42:1, 1956.
69. Tsuang M.T., et al.: A family history study of schizo-affective disorder. *Biol. Psychiatry* 12:331, 1977.
70. Weinshilboum R.M., et al.: Inheritance of very low serum dopamine-beta-hydroxylase activity. *Am. J. Hum. Genet.* 27:573, 1975.
71. Weinshilboum R.M., et al.: Genetic control of human serum-dopamine-β-hydroxylase, in Usdin E., Kvetnansky R., Kopin I.J. (eds.): *Catecholamines and Stress*. Oxford, Pergamon Press, 1976.
72. Weinshilboum R.M., Raymond F.A.: Inheritance of low erythrocyte catechol-O-methyltransferase activity in man. *Am. J. Hum. Genet.* 29:125, 1977.
73. WHO-IUIS Terminology Committee: Nomenclature for factors of the HLA system. *J. Immunogenetics* 3:435, 1976.
74. Winokur G.: Depression spectrum disease: Description and family study. *Compr. Psychiatry* 13:3, 1972.
75. Winokur G., Clayton P.J., Reich T.: *Manic-depressive illness*. St. Louis, C.V. Mosby Co., 1969.
76. Yunis J.J.: High resolution of human chromosomes. *Science* 191:1268, 1976.

10

PSYCHOLOGICAL ASPECTS

EDUARDO VAL, M.D.
JOSEPH A. FLAHERTY, M.D.
F. MOISES GAVIRIA, M.D.

THE PRECEDING CHAPTERS have adumbrated the changing views, supported by clinical research, on the nosologic and sociobiologic aspects of affective disorders. The new orientations and contributions pose challenges to some of the long-standing psychological theories. There is a need for a major assimilation and integration of modern psychological theories with the clinical and research findings, particularly in relationship to some of the past and current concepts of psychoanalytic psychology.

A satisfactory discussion of the psychology of affective disorders must consider the entire spectrum of affective disturbances, address areas of agreement among different psychological theories, and attempt to resolve or discard any contradictory observations. Within the framework of these guiding principles, we review and discuss (1) the evolution of the psychoanalytic concepts of affective disorders, (2) the contributions of the cognitive and learned helplessness models, and (3) the relationship between personality and affective disorders.

PSYCHOANALYTIC STUDY OF AFFECTIVE DISORDERS

Psychoanalysis as a scientific discipline has provided a theoretical model of behavior, a method for observing behavior, and therapeutic techniques derived from its theoretical tenets. The basic formulations and principles on which psychoanalytic theory was constructed continued to influence theoreticians after Freud. Some of these basic assumptions have undergone major revisions reflecting new work on energy and drives, the search for a stimulus-free state, thought formation, nosologic and therapeutic classifications, and self and object relationships. Unfortunately, to a great extent these contributions have not been assimilated into the general psychiatric literature on affective disturbances, which, by and large, is still limited to a drive-conflict model or to the notion of hostility turned against the self. Correction of the discrepancy is attempted in this section.

OVERVIEW

Psychoanalysis evolved in the late 1800s with observations that hysterical individuals suffered from unacceptable or traumatic ideas that were dissociated from consciousness.[20] From this initial concept came formulations on the unconscious as a descriptive and dynamic phenomenon, the role of infantile wishes in governing dreams, and the operation of the repression mechanism.[34, 35] Symptoms were viewed as the result of unconscious wishes attempting to reach consciousness and discharge, battling with the opposing forces of repression. Repression was seen as creating an increase in libidinal tension thus causing anxiety; anxiety appeared either as an anxiety state when the repressive barrier had been overcome or through symbolic symptom formation. Behaviors and symptoms, then, could be invested with meaning and interpreted as expressions of conflict resolutions. Thus psychoanalysis, from its inception, has been theoretically based on a conflict model. The topographic model was the essential construct used to understand behavior during this first phase of psychoanalytic ideas. Treatment emphasized making the unconscious conscious and overcoming resistances. Distinctive psychosexual stages were recognized during this period, and the existence of diverse psychic mechanisms responsible for symptom formation and choice were discovered. The works of Abraham and Freud's early ideas on depression were part of the early conceptual scaffolding.

A reciprocal influence between theory and clinical observation has been the pillar of psychoanalytic formulations. Whenever new clinical observations could not be satisfactorily explained by available theory, Freud reviewed the theory to assimilate the new observations and, if necessary, introduced major revisions. The conceptualization of the ego as a psychic agency to explain the resistance encountered when attempting to make the subject aware of his unconscious material was among such major revisions. The ego was viewed as a structural entity, a coherent organization of functions that mediated between the external and internal world and was responsible for the operation of unconscious defenses. Resistances—clinically observable phenomena—were the expression of defensive mechanisms, an abstracted and operationally defined set of functions. A corollary to this formulation was that defenses were activated by anxiety rather than the obverse, anxiety as result of defenses (repression), as had been earlier postulated.[36, 37] This fundamental step permitted the recognition of anxiety not only as an important factor in developmental growth and maturation, but also as a signal for defensive and adaptational aims. Within the id-ego-superego model, Freud added new views to his original ideas on depression.

The last phase of theory formation in Freud's writings focused on the ego; it established the foundation for the concept of a relationship between defenses and character and the biologic roots of the ego, which culminated in Hartmann's concept of apparatuses of primary autonomy.[40, 50] These apparatuses are present at birth and need to be developed. They involve activities such as memory, perception, language, thinking, and mobility. Under ideal developmental circumstances, inborn ego apparatuses develop into functions that are conflict-free. The major proposition introduced by this assumption was that mental development is the result of the interactions between an inborn set of potential functions and the environment, not simply the outcome of conflict over drives or with love objects. Rather, these primary apparatuses (memory, perception, etc.) have a biologically determined evolution. Moreover, these biologic apparatuses of the ego could themselves be subjects of primary alterations, thus participating in shaping the development of conflicts in the interaction with the environment. This view allows for the role of constitution and inheritance in determining pathology in a more specific manner than previously postulated. The reciprocal interaction between the primary autonomous apparatuses and the environment is a process defined as adaptation by Hartmann.[50] He and his associates further distinguished between maturation (the unfolding of biologic processes) and development (the unfolding that combines both biologic and psychological processes).

These contributions, referred to in general terms as "psychoanalytic ego psychology," brought into sharper focus interest in the formation of psychological structures (that is, functions that are consistent, enduring, and predictable) and in the role that mothering objects played in relation to the acquisition of these structures, via the process called "progressive internalization." The shift toward object relationships and structure formation culminated in an elaboration of the concept of object constancy. This refers to a critical period when the child is able to maintain a representation of the object in its absence, regardless of the state of need. Once object constancy is achieved, the child has acquired sufficient internalized functions and needs progressively less assistance from the environment. Although the concept of object constancy acquired diverse functional qualities with later writers, it nevertheless paved the way for a better comprehension of the role of preoedipal and oedipal regulatory mechanisms.

Many ego psychology contributions anticipated, paralleled, or were points of departure for investigations and theory formation, some intricately related to the recognition of normal and pathologic affective phenomena. Two examples are the observational research and theories of Spitz[109-112] Bowlby,[17-19] and Mahler[81, 82] on the mother-child dyad, and the work of Jacobson,[56, 58] Sandler et al.,[101-103] and Kernberg[63, 64] on the ego as a system of functions and internalized object relationships (endopsychic representation).

The progressive theoretical shift toward object relationships resulted in the exploration of more primitive pathologic states. Two contemporary authors, Kernberg and Kohut, although endorsing opposing and controversial views, are representative. Kernberg[63, 64] focused on the different levels of ego organization, based on the development of internalized object relations. His formulations include the borderline personality organization concept. This diagnostic category is applied to individuals who display a specific and stable form of pathologic ego organization consisting of problems of identity integration and typical defensive operations. Within that psychostructural diagnostic frame, Kernberg assumes that all patients can be classified as having a neurotic, borderline, or psychotic personality organization. Although Kernberg's contributions are not directly concerned with the psychopathology of affective disturbances, they have some bearing on the complex issues of the interrelationship between affective disorders and personality.

From extensive studies of individuals with narcissistic disturbances, Kohut offered a redefinition of narcissism in functional terms and postulated the existence of two parallel developmental paths of self-organization whose vicissitudes determine the regulation of self-esteem and the attainment of a stable sense of self. His contributions to the theory of vulnerability of the self as it relates to mood changes have a direct bearing on the psychopathology of affective disorders and their differential diagnoses.[72-74]

PSYCHOANALYSIS AND DEPRESSION

A major obstacle in assessing the psychoanalytic view of depression is that authors generally avoid defining what is meant by depression. Freud, Abraham, Fenichel, and Jacobson are among the few whose clinical data indicate they were referring to manic-depressive patients. With other authors it is not evident whether they were referring to depression as a clinical syndrome, as a transient adaptational reaction encountered in the course of psychotherapy, or as a characterologic phenomenon. Nevertheless, we can approach the psychoanalytic concepts of depression from a historical and theoretical viewpoint.

Grief and Melancholia: Abraham and Freud

Gaylin[41] has pointed out that depression was the first clinical entity for which the basic psychoanalytic theory was conceived not by Freud but by Abraham. His contributions preceded and followed Freud's *"Mourning and Melancholia."* The theoretical cornerstone at the time was Abraham's observation on the similarities and differences between grief and melancholy. Both were seen as a mourning process, but melancholia was characterized by an intense ambivalence over the loss due to unconscious hostility. In accordance with the evolving theoretical views of that period, Abraham's first explanation was in terms of a formula based on projection of unconscious hostility[1]:

The pronounced feelings of inadequacy from which such patients suffer arise from this discomforting internal perception. If the content of the perception is repressed and projected externally, the patient gets the idea that he is not loved by his environment but hated by it (again first of all by his parents, etc., and then by a wider circle of people). This idea is detached from its primary causal connection with his own attitude of hate, and is brought into association with other—psychical and physical—deficiencies. It seems as though a great quantity of such feelings of inferiority favored the formation of depressive states. . . . People do not love me, they hate me . . . because of my inborn defects. Therefore I am unhappy and depressed.

This formula already contains the presence of the depressed person's negative view of himself postulated by modern cognitive theory. Abraham's later work is within the frame of his ideas on the stages of psychosexual development.[2] From his observation of the similarities between manic-depressive and obsessional patients in terms of their possessiveness, cleanliness, and orderly traits, he extrapolated that both were fixated at an anal stage, with the melancholic showing further regressive tendencies to an oral sadistic phase resulting in the destructive incorporation of the lost object. This regression was the mechanism responsible for the self-punishment and guilty ideation found in depressive conditions. In addition, Abraham stressed several factors that he believed to be important in the psychogenesis of depression:

1. A constitutional and inherited tendency to experience oral pleasure (but not the disorder per se).

2. Fixation at the oral sadistic phase, which, in connection with the above, is responsible for the excessive needs and tendency for experiencing excessive frustration (thus the pathogenesis, by implication, could be the result of the inherited factor, regardless of optimal mothering).

3. Disappointment at a preoedipal level.

4. Repetition of the original disappointment later in adult life, which reactivates the primary condition.

In summary, Abraham postulated that a vulnerability to depression stems from a fixation in a depression-prone personality. Furthermore, he established a dynamic connection between loss, mourning, and depression. His work influenced the explorations into the association between personality and depression and into the correlations between psychopathology and psychosexual developmental fixations. In recent years the universality of a personality constellation in affective conditions has been questioned. Yet, at least for a subgroup of depressives, his observations seem to have been sustained.

Elaborating Abraham's ideas, Freud further delineated the similarities and distinction between mourning and melancholia.[39] Both were observed to have in common (1) a profound painful dejection, (2) cessation of interest in the outside world, (3) loss of capacity to love, and (4) inhibition of all activities.

The distinctive feature of melancholia was the presence of a disturbance in self-regard (self-esteem). In addition, the mechanisms of mourning and melancholia were also different. Mourning was always related to a consciously perceived and real loss, whereas melancholia was related either to an unconsciously perceived and imagined loss or to the loss of an ambivalently held object. Mourning was seen by Freud as a normal reaction in which there was a temporary detachment from the world and investment in the self, at times even accompanied by a transient identification with the lost object and, occasionally, by an expression of hostility. Yet in mourning there was an eventual reinvestment in the object and finally the lost object was replaced, with the world impoverished only temporarily. In contrast, according to Freud, in melancholia the self itself was impoverished. This pathologic state, he maintained, was the result of a regression to a primitive level of identification (via introjection) in which the object was part of the self or an extension of the self—what he referred to as a narcissistic identification. The self-reproaches and self-punishment, including suicide, were explained as reproaches against the lost object, now experienced as part of oneself. Freud pointed out that "the loss of a love object is an excellent opportunity for the ambivalence in love relationship to make itself effective and come into the open."[39] What distinguished melancholia from "obsessional states of depression" for him was regression to a more primitive level in melancholia. Freud believed that the ambivalence was, at least in certain cases, constitutional and was a predisposing factor to depression. He believed further that some forms of melancholia were due to somatic factors ("toxins"). In the midst of the beginning formulations of the structural theory, Freud reconsidered, in passing, the problem of melancholia from the point of view of a conflict between the ego and superego,[36] observing that in melancholia, unlike the obsessional neurosis, "the ego does not rebel" but admits its guilt and submits to the punishment. Thus, Freud outlined two explanatory mechanisms of depression, one with narcissistic dynamics and another in terms of a conflictual model. Regarding etiology, he proposed the existence of psychogenetic as well as toxin-induced (somatic) depressions.[39] This view of causation was consistent with his nosologic classification of neuroses into "actual neuroses" and "psychoneuroses."[38] The former were thought to be the direct effect of somatic toxins ("sexual noxae"). In actual neurosis the source of excitation and the precipitating cause of the disturbance were thought to lie in the somatic field instead of the psychic one.[78] The psychoneuroses, on the other hand, were the consequences of infantile conflicts. Recently Wolpert, in a series of publications, elaborated the relationship between the actual neuroses concept and affective disorders.[94, 123, 124] Wolpert conceptualizes bipolar illness as a genetically determined actual neurosis.

That symptoms can be either the direct expression of a physiologic state or "the symbolic expression of infantile conflicts" is a vital distinction in the understanding of the psychology of affective conditions, a point to which we will return in discussing the management of such conditions (see chap. 14).

Toward Depression as a Basic Ego State: Rado, Fenichel, Bibring, and Jacobson

A series of progressive theoretical steps taken by Rado and Fenichel paved the way for Bibring's contributions. Rado focused attention on the fact that those predisposed to depression display an intensive craving to be admired and loved[95]; he pointed to the importance of self-esteem as a central factor. However, it was up to Fenichel to explicate the relationship between depression and self-esteem by giving primary importance to the loss of self-esteem over the loss of the object.[31] He pointed out that anything invested with self-esteem (love object, job, ideals), when lost, produces depression. As Fenichel stated, "Patients who react to disappointment in love with severe depressions are always persons to whom the love experience meant not only sexual gratification but narcissistic gratification as well. With their love they lose their very existence." Thus, Fenichel made the fall in self-esteem the key factor in depression.

Within the framework provided by Rado, Fenichel, and the work of Hartmann in ego psychology, Bibring took the next logical theoretical step. His essential contribution was the discovery that depression is the emotional correlate of a particular state of the ego.[14] In this sense depression, like anxiety, is a basic ego state. Like anxiety, depression is no longer the consequence of repressed libido, but an ego reaction. Depression is an emotional indication of "the state of helplessness and powerlessness of the ego" brought about by a breakdown of self-esteem.[14] Freud and Fenichel emphasized the role of self-esteem, whereas for Bibring the lowering of self-esteem in itself was not sufficient; only when a state of helplessness and hopelessness ensued could one speak of depression.

The sense of well-being and confidence that constitutes self-esteem depends on the maintenance of certain goals that he called narcissistic aspirations. Bibring distinguished three groups of narcissistic aspirations that correlate with specific psychosexual stages: (1) the wish to be worthy, to be loved, to be appreciated (oral); (2) the wish to be good, to be loving (anal); and (3) the wish to be strong, superior, great, secure (phallic). Bibring believed that "it is exactly from the tension between these highly charged narcissistic aspirations on the one hand, and the ego's acute awareness of its (real and imaginary) helplessness and incapacity to live up to them on the other hand, that depression results."[14] In this approach, vulnerability to depression goes beyond oral fixation and may be encountered at any level of psychosexual development. Anthony has further elaborated the correlation among the psychosexual stages, their narcissistic aspirations, the core conflicts with their respective defensive positions, and corresponding precipitant threats (Table 10–1).[5]

The real or imaginary helplessness can have multiple causes. Somatic disturbances, by exhausting the person and rendering him unable to fulfill his aspirations, may cause depression. Psychological factors, by threatening the balance of aspiration, may bring the same outcome; that is, a promotion may threaten the defensive sense of superiority by provoking the loss of the much needed admiration necessary for the maintenance of self-esteem equilibrium. This theoretical approach explains why depression occurs not only in the face of losses but in the face of achievements and success. Moreover, it clearly distinguishes between lowered self-esteem and the affective state of sadness, neither of which are synonymous with depression. In addition, it permits a unique perspective on the mechanisms implicated in mourning and depression. In normal mourning, as pointed out by Basch, "there is frustration due to missing an object through which and with which to reach one's goals, and when a new object has been found mourning terminates. What is mourned in normal grief is not inability but lack of opportunity to achieve one's goals when deprived of a suitable object. Only if a state of hopelessness about this situation supervenes does depression replace mourning."[8] Thus, it is the helplessness experienced by the unavailability of the object that characterizes depression.

The clinical and theoretical interest of Jacobson[54, 55, 57, 59] in the subject of affective disorders covers a span of over 40 years. Following Abraham, she takes as a basic premise that an early and premature disappointment in and

TABLE 10–1.—AN EPIGENETIC THEORY OF DEPRESSION, FOLLOWING BIBRING*

PSYCHOSEXUAL LEVEL	NARCISSISTIC ASPIRATION	DEFENSIVE NEED	DEPRESSION FOLLOWS DISCOVERY OF:	CENTRAL, CONFLICT IS OVER:
Oral	To be loved To get supplies To be cared for	To be independent To be self-supporting	Not being loved Not being independent	Dependency needs
Anal	To be good To be loving To be clean	Not to be bad and defiant Not to be hostile Not to be dirty	Lack of control over impulses and objects Feeling of helplessness Guilt	Controls
Phallic	To be admired To be center of attention To be strong and triumphant	To be modest To be inconspicuous To be submissive	Fear of being defeated Fear of being ridiculed Fear of retaliation	Competition

*From Anthony.[5] Reproduced by permission of Little, Brown & Co., copyright 1975.

disillusionment with the parental objects predisposes the individual to depression. Influenced in her theoretical approach by Hartmann's progressive internalization, structure formation, and endopsychic representation, Jacobson postulates her own sequence of infant psychic development in terms of the relationship between the self and the object world.[56, 58] Her theory suggests that psychological functions develop out of an undifferentiated psychophysiologic matrix by the gradual formation of internalized images of oneself and other significant persons, the so-called self and object representations.

According to her, the fundamental aim of development is the integration, organization, and unification of these representations into a stable self. To achieve this, the child must go through different developmental stages of managing and neutralizing his aggressive impulses and fantasies. During the early stages these impulses and fantasies are affected by the child's magical and omnipotent view of the world and his parents. Through progressive and optimal frustrations and disappointments, the child is gradually able to modify those perceptions and to accept and establish more realistic parental images. Simultaneously, the child is able to form a more stable and differentiated image of himself. However, if very early or traumatic disappointment occurs, the child's omnipotence is not gradually neutralized, and instead a devalued view of the parents and himself sets in. As a result, omnipotent retaliatory fantasies are retained. The suddenly devalued parent is not only worthless but the source of badness and punishment. Due to the lack of developmental self-differentiation, the child ascribes to himself the same self-deflation and self-destruction in parallel with the parent. As a consequence, the child develops a precocious and archaic punitive superego invested with primitive and omnipotent aggression. This phenomenon is seen as the source of the pessimism so prevalent in depression. This developmental "primal depression" is the one reactivated by disillusionment in adulthood.

The preponderance of aggression and the archaic and punitive superego are responsible for the alteration in self-esteem. Jacobson defines self-esteem as an affective-cognitive state, the expression of the discrepancy or harmony between the self-representations (the way one perceives oneself) and the wishful concept of the self (the ideal self). For her, as for Bibring, loss of self-esteem represents the central psychopathologic problem of depression. In discussing psychotic and neurotic forms of depression, she points out that self-esteem is implicated in both. The difference between the two is that in psychotic depressions the level of regression is more intense and on a more primitive level, due to more defective preexisting ego and superego formations.

Developmental Observations and Theories of Depression: Spitz, Bowlby, Klein, and Sandler

Each of the authors so far mentioned gives evidence that depression is rooted in early life experiences, yet their conclusions were founded on reconstructions from their work with adults suffering from depression. In contrast, the theoretical contributions of Spitz, Bowlby, Klein, and Sandler are based on the direct observation of children.

Based on studies of infants born to imprisoned mothers who were separated from them after several months, Spitz made a series of observations leading to the description of the anaclitic depression and hospitalism syndromes.[109–112] From these and later observations he concluded that the infant's affective states influence its perception and relationship with the mothering object. The reciprocal interaction between infant and mother influences both mother and child and is the basis of a communication system long before the acquisition of verbal language. The mother functions as an external auxiliary ego vital to the infant's development.

Initially, the communication is primarily by means of tension states, posture, skin and body contact. Later, the biologic aspects become less dominant and are replaced by progressively more complex communication interaction with the mother. Certain modal points in the infant's development, which are crucial both in that interaction and in further ego integration, are called "psychic organizers." Spitz identifies three sequential psychic organizers: the smiling response, the separation anxiety, and the ability to communicate a semantic "no." These developmental cornerstones call for phase-appropriate interventions by the mother as an external auxiliary ego through the provision of optimal frustration. According to Spitz:[113]

The first of the organizers of the psyche (the smiling response) structures perception and establishes the beginning of the ego. The second (separation anxiety) integrates object relations with the drives and establishes the ego as an organized psychic structure with a variety of systems, apparatuses, and functions. The third organizer (the ability to communicate "no") finally opens the road for the development of object relations on the human pattern, that is, the pattern of semantic communication. This makes possible both the emergence of the self and the beginning of social relations on the human level.

The importance of the object's assistance in psychic development is demonstrated in the anaclitic depression Spitz recognized in 6- to 8-month-old infants after prolonged separation from their mothers. This condition, which follows the loss of a good mother-infant relationship, consists of progressive symptoms ranging from a tendency to cry or to be demanding, to insomnia, to weight loss and motor retardation. For the anaclitic depression to occur, a good infant-mother relationship was essential. Indeed, in cases with previously bad mother-child interaction, no anaclitic depression was found. These findings prompted Spitz to state that "it would seem that any substitute was at least as good as the unsatisfactory biological mother."

Recovery from anaclitic depression was achieved when the child was returned to the mother. When the deprivation of the mother persisted, as in the Foundling Home setting, the condition worsened, with the infant becoming passive, withdrawn, displaying lack of coordination and motor retardation, and in some cases eventually dying. This syndrome of hospitalism, or marasmus, Spitz concluded, was due to the affective (emotional) deprivation, since the child was otherwise well physically attended. What was absent was the individual and optimal affective care. Thus, Spitz's investigation demonstrated the presence of a phenomenon similar to that in adult depression taking place before verbal language had been acquired. In addition, his theory of affects as influencing the perceptions of object relations and as signals of communication between mother and infant predicted some of the contemporary views of psychoanalysis in general and depression in particular.

Influenced by Fairbairn's "object seeking"[30] concept as basis for object relations and by the work of Klein[69] and Winnicott,[120] Bowlby has, in a series of articles and books, advanced an "attachment theory" to explain infant and child behavior as well as childhood and adulthood psychopathology.[17-19] He hypothesized that when the mothering object is temporarily unavailable, the attachment process is interrupted, and as a result, a predictable set of distinctive and sequential behaviors unfold that he labeled protest, despair, and detachment. These sequential events are part of normal mourning. Bowlby believes that mourning not only takes place in childhood, but that abnormalities in normal developmental mourning are the basis later in life for many psychopathologic disorders, including adult depression. Many authors, among them Robertson and Robertson[98] and Anna Freud,[33] have questioned the presence of mourning in children, since they argue that mourning depends on the level of object constancy and ego maturity. There is also some evidence questioning the relationship of loss to depression.[25] Klerman, in reviewing the literature and on the basis of his own findings, concludes that: "(1) loss and separation are not universal in all depressions, (2) not all individuals who experience losses and separations will develop depressions, and (3) loss and depression are not specific to clinical depressions."[71] Recently the role of parental death in childhood and the risk for adult depression have been reviewed extensively by Tennant et al., applying rigorous methodology to minimize the effect of interrelated variables associated with the death occurrence. They believe that the current stage of evidence indicates that parental death in childhood has little impact on the risk of depression in adulthood.[118]

The main problem faced in evaluating the role of loss is that the mere absence of the parent may not produce an abnormal state, since a parental substitute may provide the needed psychological assistance without any primary disturbance occurring. On the other hand, the presence of a parent does not rule out the experience of a loss by lack of affective (emotional) availability, as Spitz has shown.

From direct work with disturbed children and the construction of a complex internalized object relations system, Klein postulates the existence of two basic developmental "positions."[69] In order of sequence, they are the schizoid-paranoid and depressive positions. Before acquiring the ability to relate to whole objects, the infant uses "splitting" of the mothering object into part-objects that are invested separately with "good" and "bad" qualities. One of the developmental tasks is the internalization of these good and bad part-objects and their integration into whole objects, with the infant's feeling minimal and manageable ambivalence toward them. According to Klein, the infant, in order to defend himself against the danger posed by the internalized bad part-object, projects the bad inner object into the environment. In this way the child can then experience the anxiety as coming from without, the so-called persecutory anxiety, which is the hallmark of the schizoparanoid position. The depressive position takes place when the infant is 4 to 5 months old, when maturation allows him to begin to perceive and form whole objects. Due to this maturational step the infant can now realize that the good and bad part-objects (the good breast-mother) both belong to the same mother. However, during this stage the infant must deal with his own ambivalence, since he can no longer externalize the bad part-object. Now that the aggression is recognized as his own, a new anxiety ensues. He fears that his own destructive impulses have destroyed or will destroy the very same object he loves and depends on. This different type of dread is called by Klein "depressive anxiety," the central anxiety of the depressive position. For Klein, the role of aggression in the infant is innate and determines the fate of the object relations. Her followers, however, have emphasized that the quality of the mothering also has a positive or negative bearing on the effects of the innate aggression and on the object internalization outcome. At any rate, a healthy resolution of these vicissitudes is the achievement of tolerance to ambivalence without feelings of primitive retaliation or internal destruction. A deviant outcome of the depressive position is to become inhibited, depressed, or avoidant in order to protect the preservation of the good object. Another defensive organization outcome is to disavow the importance of the good object. In this situation, the individual relies precociously and defensively on himself, maintaining a sense of self-sufficiency and no need for others, which Klein sees as a "manic" defense against the experience of depression.[70] Klein's work has received much criticism on the grounds that she ascribes a fantasy life and perception of dependency to the infant long before symbolic thinking is possible. In this regard Klein, more than any of the previous workers, epitomizes what Goldberg has aptly referred to as "adultmorphization" of the infant.[44]

Leaving aside the problem of timing and validity of the mental processes postulated, Klein's contributions on the existence of a universal depressive phase in childhood share some similarities with Benedek's depressive constellation,[13] Zetzell's capacity to bear depression,[126] Mahler's depressive response as part of the individuation-separation process,[81, 82] and Winnicott's achievement of "concern for the object."[120, 121] Sandler and Joffe also offered the opinion that a "depressive reaction" occurs in childhood.[60, 103] Approaching depression from the self-esteem perspective, they postulate the presence of a basic ideal state of well-being, a state they believe to be more fundamental than self-esteem, and on which self-esteem is built. Essentially, they note that a psychobiologic state of well-being exists in the infant dyadic relationship with the mothering object. When this balance is altered, it brings about a change in the state which they refer as a "depressive reaction." Sandler and Joffe consider this response to be, developmentally, as basic and fundamental as anxiety. This depressive reaction is not viewed as synonymous with depression; only if the experience of helplessness and resignation follows can one speak of depression. Again, in line with Spitz, Sandler and Joffe note that what is lost (whether or not the loss is actual) is the state of well-being, the integration of the psychobiologic self-organization in relationship to the object. Thus, the object acts as a vehicle for the maintenance of the child's feelings of security and well-being. Its loss results in the loss of narcissistic (self) integration.

In summary, the developmental views on depression indicate that depression as an affective state plays a crucial role in psychic formation. Moreover, losses can occur and be experienced long before verbal language is present and are part and parcel of human growth. Only when a steady state of helplessness, hopelessness, and paralysis is present does depression, as a clinical state, exist. From these lines of thinking one can conclude that depression is an adaptive phenomenon. The depressive reaction or response is a signal, like anxiety, for the organism to overcome the transient helplessness; when it fails, clinical depression ensues. As Klerman stated, "depressions are maladaptive outcomes of partially successful attempts at adaptation."[77]

The Interpersonal School: Cohen, Arieti and Bemporad, and Bonime

Based on the observations obtained from intensive psychoanalytic psychotherapy of 12 manic-depressive patients, using a Sullivanian approach, Cohen and her co-workers investigated the patterns of interaction between the parents and the manic-depressive patient as a child and the way these patterns influenced the manic-depressive character structure.[26] Instead of focusing solely on the intrapsychic events or taking the oral traits as being the result of constitutional overintensity of oral drives (overindulgence or frustration during the oral stage), they concentrated on discovering the possible experiences with "significant others" that might be responsible for the development of particular patterns of interaction conducive to the formation of a specific personality and eventual manic-depressive illness. A consistent finding in the family background was observed. Families of manic-depressives perceived themselves to be in a usually low-prestige position in the community or as being socially isolated. Their chief interest in the future manic-depressive child was as a potential vehicle in overcoming the family's position or resolving the parents' needs for recognition and prestige, creating in the child an inflated sense of importance. The marital subsystem was characterized by one parent (usually the father) as weak, devalued, and failing in the family's perception, with the other parent aggressively striving, by means of the child, to resolve the family's plight. Due to the special role they held in the family group, these children in their adulthood show a liability to rejection and feelings of loneliness when their sense of importance to others is not as forthcoming as it was before, making them extremely sensitive to envy and competition. These investigators believed that out of that typical family constellation the child learns special interpersonal maneuvers. The crucial disturbance in interpersonal relations centers around closeness (identification) to and separation from his mother. The principal source of anxiety is the fear of abandonment. Since the child has been used as an extension of his mother, he is unable to behave autonomously. He is, as Cohen et al. put it, "unable to recognize others as whole, separate persons." This accounts for the perception and experience of others as "pieces of property" that belong to him and from whom he demands constant support. Clinical decompensation occurs when these demands are not fulfilled. Depression, in the view of these authors, is an interpersonal attempt to win back the needed support. Manic behavior, on the other hand is a response whose aim is to deny the need for others. Cohen and her co-workers hold that the manic-depressive does not experience genuine guilt but that self-reproaches and guilt are an interpersonal ploy to elicit intervention by significant others in order to regain the needed support. The contributions of Cohen et al. are also of historical value. They were the first to delineate and link family dynamics to manic-depressive disorders and were among the first to stress the presence of chronic, persistent, reinforcing patterns of parental involvement beyond early childhood. These family dynamics findings are by no means specific to manic-depressives, as is clearly observable in the family theory and research literature of the last two decades.[52] Furthermore, what they seem to be describing is more consistent with the pathogenesis of narcissistic configurations in general.

The culturalist, interpersonal viewpoint explains behavior as a reaction and adaptation to demands occurring in the interpersonal social matrix. Bonime is one of the extreme proponents of such a position on depression.[16] He stresses that the depressive's outward behavior is disguised hostility, a way of affecting others by his suffering. For him, depression is more than an episodic illness; it is a way of life, an everyday mode of relating, characterized by manipulativeness, hostility, and exploitation of others. As a child the depression-prone individual lacked nurturance, recognition, and respect from his parents. He pursues in adulthood the fulfillment of those unrealized childhood needs of which he feels he has been cheated.

Arieti and Bemporad conceptualize depression as "a complex emotion that arises when an individual is deprived (or deprives himself) of an element of life that is necessary for a satisfactory state of self."[6] They believe that individuals predisposed to depression are organized interpersonally around a dominant goal or dominant person ("dominant other"). Dynamically the person depends on the dominant other for self-esteem, acceptance, and approval. Depression results from the deprivation (emotional and cognitive) of those gratifications. The dominant goal serves the same purpose, except that the fulfillment is derived from values and achievements, viewed by Arieti and Bemporad as cognitive manifestation of what and how others evaluate and think of the depressive person. They distinguish between mild and severe depression. In the latter, the dominant other or goal is used to absolve a sense of inner badness, whereas in the former, the dominant dynamics are used to obtain pleasure and meaning. That is, mild depressions do not reach the more primitive defensive purposes with underlying negative and paranoid blaming attitudes that characterize the more severe type.

Psychology of the Self: Kohut

Psychoanalytic investigations of patients with predominant disturbances in their self-esteem regulation and their corresponding transferential vicissitudes brought about the introduction of metapsychological and treatment reconceptualizations by Heinz Kohut.[72, 73] These revisions and new ideas were necessitated by the limitations encountered in trying to explain the disturbances within the framework of classic drive-and-defense psychology. His work is of central importance not only for the diagnostic differentiation between narcissistic disorders and subclinical forms of manic-depressive phenomena, but also for the new perspective it offers on the regulation of self-esteem and affective states and on the pathogenesis of affective disorders.

According to Kohut's postulates, the self develops from separate nuclei into a cohesive and enduring psychological construct. For the self to become cohesive, firm, and stable, it needs the assistance of objects performing phase-appropriate and timely functions for the child, psychic activity that the child is unable to carry out independently due to his psychic immaturity. During this self-formation, the object is experienced as part of the self and as vital to the organization of the self. The caretaking object, by providing the organization and structure out of which the self develops, performs what Kohut evocatively designates as "selfobject" functions.

As Wolf puts it metaphorically: "The selfobjects are like the glue that holds the self cohesively together."[122] It should be kept in mind that not only are selfobjects vital for the self, they are also experienced as part of the self. They are not experienced as independent. If the infant experiences hunger and is fed and satiated, he does not experience the event as coming from an external source but from within. Thus, if he is assisted properly, a sense of order and prediction about himself emerges, the basis for the development of a sense of confidence. Kohut formulates two kinds of selfobjects: a mirroring selfobject, whose function involves responding to and confirming the child's innate sense of vigor, greatness, and perfection, and an idealized parent imago selfobject, the source of calmness, security, and guidance. These sets of functions are only separated for didactic purposes, since they can be performed by the same object at the same or different times. Moreover, the selfobject performs multiple functions for the nascent self, from basic neurophysiologic reactions to more mature, complex ones during later developmental phases.

At birth the neonate is without self, but through interactions with the selfobjects a nuclear self crystalizes. According to Kohut and Wolf this occurs (1) when the idealizing and mirroring has been properly attended to, (2) as a consequence of minor, nontraumatic failure in the response of the mirroring and the idealized selfobjects, and (3) when these unavoidable and nontraumatic failures lead to the gradual replacement of selfobjects and their functions by a self and its functions.[74]

The counterparts of the selfobjects in the emergent self are two separate but parallel formations, "the grandiose self" and "the idealized parental imago," which under optimal rearing conditions are gradually tamed and ultimately integrated into the adult personality, providing the "fuel" for ambitions and purposes (grandiose self) and guiding the ideals and values (the idealized parental image). Kohut's psychoanalytic psychology of the self postulates that the functions performed by the selfobject are essential to the formation of an endurable and firm sense of self. Lack of self-cohesiveness results from the failing responses and interventions on the side of the selfobject interacting with inherited biologic factors. When insufficient cohesion or integration of the self is present, there is a tendency toward regressive fragmentation, expressed behaviorally in terms of either fear of disintegration, hypochondriacal concerns, depression, or self-esteem oscillations. Kohut classifies the self disorders into primary or secondary disturbances according to the lack or presence of self-cohesion. The secondary disturbances of the self are experiential and behavioral manifestations of a strong and well-integrated self. The self is able to tolerate wide swings of self-esteem without fragmentation. There is no need for the availability of the selfobjects to maintain self-integration. The classic psychoneuroses are examples of secondary disturbances of the self. The primary disturbances of the self are divided into four subgroups in order of severity, according to the degree of lack of self-integration: (1) narcissistic personality disorders, (2) narcissistic behavior disorders, (3) borderline states, and (4) psychoses.[73, 74]

In psychoses, there is a severe lack of cohesion with *serious* distortion of the self and secondary attempts at self-organization via delusional formation. In borderline states, the self is enfeebled and in functional chaos (constant state of fragmentation), but, unlike the case in psychoses, is well covered by effective defensive structures. The self in narcissistic behavior disorders is more resilient and not subjected to the constant chaotic disorganization experienced in the prior groups. The decompensations are manifested through temporary symptomatic behavior like perversive activities, delinquency, and addictive behavior. The group of narcissistic personality disorders is closely related to the narcissistic behavior disorders in that fragmentation is also temporary, but the symptoms (hypochondria, depression, self-esteem oscillations) are more psychological than behavioral.

The pathogenesis of affective disorders is seen by Kohut as resulting from the experience of the nascent self with the selfobject's depressive or overstimulating responses. He believes that a model of affective disturbances can be better formulated through understanding the vicissitudes of the developing self and the omnipotent selfobject than through the dynamics of drive-defense conflict—as in aggression turned onto the self or sadistic superego dynamics, as proposed by some of the authors previously reviewed.

The pathogenesis of depression varies according to which type of self-pathology is involved. Some depressions of the psychotic type are due to inherited biologic factors interacting with the almost total deprivation, at crucial phases of self-development, of joyful and stimulating responses by the selfobject. This situation creates a self with a tendency toward depletion of assertiveness and self-esteem, resulting in self-rejection and self-blame, postulated by Kohut to be the central mechanisms of psychotic depressions. In the same manner, the lack of calming and integrating responses by the selfobjects produces a tendency toward defensive, uncontrollable, and unrealistic heightened self-acceptance found in mania.

In narcissistic personality disorders, the loss of anything invested with selfobject functions essential to the maintenance of self-cohesion could result in depression. Furthermore, within the framework of the psychology of the self, psychoneurotic depression occurs as the result of structural conflicts in a well-established and firm self.

To summarize, depression can be a primary or secondary disturbance of the self, and its pathogenesis is of a narcissistic (selfobject) or conflictual nature.

Recent Additions and Revisions

We have already mentioned that early in his writing, Freud distinguished between actual neuroses and psychoneuroses. Later, during the year of publication of "Mourning and Melancholia," (in which he spoke of a possible toxic etiology for some cases of depression), a paper on the general theory of the neuroses was published.[38] In this work, Freud divided the neurotic states into (1) traumatic neuroses, in which the ego attempts, through repetition of symptoms, to overcome the overwhelming danger experienced; (2) psychoneuroses, in which symptoms are compromised formations over conflicts, having symbolic meaning; and (3) actual neuroses, in which symptoms are a direct consequence of "entirely somatic" processes, therefore having "no 'sense,' no psychical meaning."[38] Moreover, the symptoms of actual neuroses were viewed as being, in many cases, the nucleus for overimposed psychoneurotic symptoms. As Wolpert has recently pointed out, Freud's "actual neuroses" theory took a clear physiologic character, falling just short of establishing the presence or absence of physiologic factors affecting the psyche and linking actual neuroses with specific mental disorders. Such a conceptual step was taken by Wolpert.[123, 124] He introduced the hypothesis that in accordance with psychophysiologic, psychopharmacologic, and clinical evidence, depression and mania in manic-depressive illness are genetically determined actual neuroses. Wolpert states, "the psychological symptoms are the outcome of an alteration of periodic excess and lack of physiological energy."[123] He considers this condition to be a basic vulnerability that can be triggered by "spontaneous" shifts in the physiologic state or by psychogenetic factors. Recurrent depressive disorders (unipolars) are conceived of in similar terms as manic-depressive illness. Single depressive episodes, on the other hand, are viewed as strictly psychological in origin.

Drawing from the work of other scientific disciplines, such as philosophy of science,[100] neuropsychology,[106, 119] and cognitive psychology[24, 92] Basch has advanced major modifications and revisions of some of the fundamental constructs of psychoanalytic metapsychology that have profound implications, particularly for the conceptualization of depression.[7-9] Basch argues that in order to understand the basis for cognition, affects, perception, and motivation, one must turn to disciplines outside of psychoanalysis. He also asserts that psychoanalytic theory must be compatible with those findings.

The findings of cognitive psychology and of research on the neurophysiology of affects are of fundamental importance in this respect, since they challenge some of the long-held psychoanalytic postulations of energy discharge governing brain activity and the presence of primitive thinking in infants.

In the view of cognitive psychology theory, the child, during the entire developmental period, is involved in building "schemata" (basic organizations of behavior relevant to each other) through a process of assimilation and accommodation in interaction with the environment. Piaget has outlined a series of stages with characteristic cognitive transactions, beginning with what he calls a sensorimotor period, progressively unfolding through preoperational thinking and a stage of concrete operations to a final period of formal operations.[92] Piaget has demonstrated that in the first developmental phase (sensorimotor), occurring roughly from birth to about 16 to 18 months of age, learning is imageless, involving nonreflective activity and having an absence of recall through symbolic representation. At the beginning of the sensorimotor period the infant is a reflexive organism that responds to the environment in an undifferentiated manner. Through a pattern-matching process, schemata are formed (relatively coherent organizations developing vis-à-vis the environment), which enable the child to recognize progressively previous experiences. Since, during this period, the child is capable only of schemata matching, not categorization (abstraction), this is a stage of presymbolic cognition.

Only in the preoperational period is the child able to understand and use symbols, albeit in a very basic way. For example, he can understand that a given person can be another child's mother (thus showing the ability to abstract rudimentarily the concept of mother), but he cannot further abstract and classify the same person in another category, for instance, as a teacher of another child.

Although the neural substrate is responsible for the readiness for cognitive development, it is the environmental interaction that promotes actual development. In this relationship to the environment the child is not a passive but an active guide. Contrary to previous beliefs, the infant does not avoid stimuli or seek discharge but actively searches for optimal stimulation; e.g., in the mother-child relationship, a communication feedback loop for both parties is established from the beginning. According to modern neurobiologic evidence, the nervous system not only does not seek constant release of accumulated energy, it has its own source of metabolic energy, its own inhibitory mechanisms; and it needs, not avoids, environmental stimulation.[84] Research on sensory deprivation has demonstrated the same. The human brain in development recapitulates the phylogenetic evolution of the brain, from the primitive reptilian brain to the mammalian neocortex. Therefore the human brain comprises at birth a hierarchical organization of early brains as well as newer complex structures capable of more sophisticated analysis of the same basic functions. Higher level structures control the lower ones by inhibiting their actions when necessary.

The neocortex has traditionally been regarded as the site for higher cognitive functions, having many connections with subcortical areas and separate specialized functional areas. At the beginning of his extrauterine existence the newborn is a "noncortical being." Soon, however, the cerebral cortex starts to function, its activities increasing until a reciprocal functional correlation is established with the rest of the brain.[28] Despite the lack of neocortical dominance, the child's brain is equipped from the beginning with communication systems under subcortical control. The research findings of Tomkins and associates have demonstrated the presence of inborn, involuntary, neuromuscular facial systems under subcortical control that correspond to the facial expression of the more complex emotional states of adults, among them sadness, anger, joy, and surprise.[53, 119] These inborn patterns of signal communication serve the function of eliciting the parent's responses. In the interaction with the caretakers, these affective systems form the foundation for an orderly and progressively complex communication through the association of reward and avoidance, pleasure and unpleasure, and similar groupings.

These affective reactions are part and parcel of the pattern-matching, of sensorimotor cognition. The sensorimotor period is basically a neurobiologic organizational stage for ordering and communicating that provides the engrams or schemata for progressive and more complex matchings, which in turn constitute the basis for the beginning of predictive behavior.[8] According to Basch, during this presymbolic stage "the mother does not exist for the infant as a concept but as a part of these sensorimotor recognition patterns associated with order."[8] He relies fundamentally on her to obtain that order. In contrast, at the beginning of symbolic operation, by virtue of having the ability for rudimentary abstraction, the infant starts to separate the world into self and others and to form concepts. Whereas in the sensorimotor phase the presence of mother reactivated the pattern-matching of feeling secure, in this phase an image of mother becomes attached to a sense of safety. A concept of well-being, security, and being cared for is formed that stands for the "object," a symbolic representation.[8] The progression toward more complex symbolic representation eventually makes the child take over the functions of his own self-regulation and become more independent of external assistance. (This phenomenon correlates with the development of object constancy.)

In Basch's view the brain's main goal is to create order through constant and progressive abstraction, from presymbolic to more complex symbolic operations, from subcortical control to cortical regulation. For Basch, depression is a particular type of disturbance in the ordering process. According to him, the central aspects of depression, helplessness and hopelessness, are manifestations of the lack of ability to predict and create meaningful order. Depression, then, is a failure in procuring help for the restoration of order. It is either an initial failure to bring the appropriate assistance of the mother, in the case of the sensorimotor infant, or it is failure to obtain the necessary functional symbolic representation in later developmental stages (e.g., the inability to perceive oneself as a worthy person by the internalized parental object). Thus, depression can be viewed as a disturbance in the presymbolic or symbolic communication process.

Since both presymbolic and symbolic communication takes place through the brain as a message center, any disturbance in these signal-processing functions may also result in the failure of the ordering activity. Such disturbances are characteristic of the so-called organic or somatic depressions (e.g., the neurophysiologic shifts in bipolar disorders and reserpine-induced depression). The alteration in presymbolic and symbolic communication involves the so-called functional or psychological depression. Thus, depression is a syndrome but not necessarily a biologic or a psychological illness.

Further, Basch points out that a significant difference exists between presymbolic and symbolic models of depression. Presymbolic depressions are encountered in early infancy. They are the result of the lack of optimal and consistent response by the caretaker, affecting the pattern-matching ordering functions.[8] According to Basch, the loss experienced in infancy is the loss of the pattern-matching ordering functions and not the loss of the mother per se. In his view, the loss of ordering function can be due to either the lack of the mother's real availability or the mother's emotional unavailability by unempathic responses, either overstimulation or understimulation, each of which causes a sense of inconsistency and unpredictability. The restoration of the response appropriate to the signals transmitted by the infant reestablishes order and reverses the condition. The anaclitic depressions described by Spitz belong to this group. In contrast, in depression at the symbolic level, restoration of environmental support is of no avail. The symbolic distortions, needs, conflicts, or deficits require resolution through psychotherapy.

This approach to depression emphasizes that the failure responsible for the disorder can occur at different levels in the ordering and message-processing functions and that depression is a general system dysfunction.

PSYCHOANALYSIS AND MANIA

In 1953 Katan stated that there was little knowledge about the dynamics of mania. Thirty years later, we could say the same. By and large, mania has been considered a cognitive-affective state, the opposite of depression but sharing the same dynamics. Mania, for Abraham, was a state in which the impulses had not succumbed to repression.[1] He later viewed it also as a regression to the oral cannibalistic state.[2] Bibring interpreted mania as a defensive reaction formation against depression, one usually combined with denial of the causes provoking depression.[14] In mania, according to Freud, the differences between ego and superego disappear. The ego is powerless and the superego omnipotent in melancholia, whereas in mania the ego regains omnipotence, fusing with the superego. For Fenichel the increase of self-esteem is the center of manic phenomena, with a concomitant decrease of conscience.[31] Mania and depression are viewed as opposite states. What the depressive is striving for seems to be what the manic achieves. Furthermore, for Fenichel, mania is the expression of the loving elements of the ambivalence present in depression.

A totally different perspective is taken by Katan.[61] Instead of viewing mania as the result of impulsive expression or as a defensive reaction, Katan regards it as an attempt at restoring a normal relationship and at resolving conflicts with reality. However, he admits his inability to explain what is responsible for the sudden change from depression to mania other than the ego displaying an excess of power. He points out that the role of denial, so prevalent in mania, is in the service of maintaining optimism. Mania is essentially governed by the pleasure principle. Lewin also stresses the role of the drive to obtain pleasure and the existence of denial resulting from the intensification of oral wishes.[79] For Jacobson also, mania is a conflict solution whereby the individual escapes into an illusion of power with the purpose of discharging his aggression freely and diffusely. She assumes that in the manic state there is a fusion of the self with the imagined omnipotence of the love object. During mania there is a denial of the existence of any unpleasure or destruction. The entire world becomes an endless and indestructible pleasure.[59]

Though there are frequent observations in the literature on the distinction between depression as a normal developmental effect and as a pathologic condition, similar comparisons between manic elation and the normal state of elation are absent. Pao corrected this omission, drawing on Mahler's separation individuation theories.[88] Mahler et al. observed that during the practicing subphase proper (10 to 18 months of age), the child, through recently acquired locomotion skills, behaves as if "intoxicated with his own faculties."[82] It is during this elation aspect of the practicing phase that the child is in need of the mother's emotional refueling. Mood oscillations are of great importance at this stage; periods of elation are replaced by a state of "low-keyedness" when the child becomes aware that mother is absent. Thus, elation and depression are developmental affective states. On the basis of these observations, Pao proposes that elation should be limited to the "normal" pleasurable world associated with mastery and joy, while mania and hypomania should be confined to the affective conditions.[88]

Kohut, as we have seen, paid particular attention to the vicissitudes of elation in the development of the self.[72-74] Some of the selfobject functions are to mirror the child's exhibitionism and omnipotence, to provide calmness, and to curb any overstimulation. In his conception, a failure on the side of the selfobject, by an unempathic, excessive, or phase-inappropriate response of the mirroring activities, increases the grandiosity. On the other hand, a lack of optimal and sufficient calming and soothing intervention leaves the child alone to cope with his grandiosity and exhibitionism. In either case the seeds are planted for future disturbances in the regulation of elation and stimulation. Indeed, Kohut believes that in manic-depressive patients the grandiose self and the idealized parent imago configurations are poorly integrated due to those selfobject failures in combination with inherited biologic factors. Decompensation into mania or depression occurs in reaction to diverse stresses. When the individual becomes unable to contain the archaic cathexes, in Kohut's words, "the exhibitionism and grandiosity of the grandiose self thus begin to flood the ego (mania) and the omnipotent aggressivity of the idealized parent image destroys the patient's realistic self-esteem (depression)."[72]

We have already alluded to Wolpert's concept of mania as a genetically determined actual neurosis. In his theoretical considerations Basch has not specifically addressed himself to the phenomenon of mania. However, on the basis of his conceptualization of depression as a system dysfunction of the ordering process, one can extrapolate that the manic state is an attempt at overcoming the helplessness and powerlessness by way of overactivity—

an attempt, in short, at restoration. In manic behavior, then, as in depression, the failure in the ordering process might occur at the level of the signal-processing function or at the level of presymbolic or symbolic communication.

COGNITIVE AND LEARNED HELPLESSNESS MODELS

COGNITIVE MODEL

Since Abraham, distortions in the self-view have been described as part of the symptomatology of depression. However, they were generally considered to be secondary elaborations of the disorder. Beck, the main proponent of the cognitive model of depression (in a way reminiscent of Abraham's first contribution), considers the cognitive distortion as a primary disturbance.[11, 12, 75] Clinically, changes in self-esteem and vegetative signs are seen as secondarily induced by the primary cognitive disturbances. Cognition is broadly defined and encompasses the ways in which facts are perceived and processed, the mechanisms and content of memory recall, and the problem-solving attitudes and strategies. A central postulate of this approach is the concept of "cognitive structure" or "schemata" (a set of previous, organized experiences which become special lenses through which subsequent life events are perceived, experienced and organized).[75] These cognitive structures are laid down early developmentally. In the case of depression, the schemata are dominated by what Beck considers to be a basic "cognitive trial" composed of (1) negative expectations of the environment, (2) a negative view of oneself, and (3) a negative expectation of the future. Beck believes that this typical cognitive distortion occurs in all categories of depression. These basic distortions appear in the individual's dreams, free associations, and daily general adaptation to stress. The content of this depressive cognition is reinforced and maintained by a series of characteristic thinking mechanisms.

Depressive patients show a distorted construction of temporal experience, particularly in reference to the future. The depressed individual selectively recalls experiences with negative content or negative implications; the recall is biased toward negative material. In assessing situations there is also a tendency to assign global and personalized meaning to events, with a bias toward negatively toned interpretation. These particular thinking processes also involve a tendency to disqualify previous positive experiences and overemphasize prior failures. According to Kovacs and Beck, if the depressed individual fails, he believes it's because he lacks ability, whereas if he succeeds, he attributes it to external factors. The combination of the negative content themes and certain systematic errors of the thinking are responsible for the stereotyped conclusions and evaluations of the depressed patient. One error of thinking involves arbitrary inference, by which the individual draws certain conclusions in the absence of any evidence or contrary to existing evidence. Overgeneralization and lack of discrimination are other errors in the thinking processes. The combination of these errors and negative content form the premises by which the "depressogenic schemata [are] constructed which function like a 'template,' actively screening, coding and categorizing the information."[75] Developmentally, these depressogenic schemata are laid down early and are likely to be activated by conditions that resemble the original circumstances under which they were developed. Beck believes that loss of a parent during childhood, interpretation of losses as irreversible and traumatic, and contact with parents whose own belief systems are of a negative nature are some factors and situations responsible for the development of depressogenic schemata. However, as Kovacs and Beck remark, "what makes these schemata remarkable is probably not their uniqueness in the depression-prone person's development, but the individual's lack of opportunity or lack of experience in submitting them to examination."[75] Certainly the existence of a negative cognitive set per se does not necessarily signify that depression is present or that it might eventually happen. Many personalities display the cognitive triad without ever suffering depression. Furthermore, depression may occur without concomitant negative cognition, as in some of the masked depressions. In some instances the cognitive set disappears when depression lifts, indicating that negative cognition could be secondarily induced and not be a primary phenomenon, as Beck believes.

LEARNED HELPLESSNESS MODEL

The development of the learned helplessness model was achieved through animal experiments. In the classic experiment, dogs were placed in a two-compartment shuttle box divided by a barrier. When a traumatic electrical shock was administered the dogs ran frantically, defecated, and urinated until they accidentally crossed the barrier, escaping the shock in a random fashion. By the second trial, the dogs had "learned" that by crossing the barrier quickly they could avoid the shock. This behavior was reinforced in consecutive trials. In this manner the dogs eventually "learned" to avoid the shock completely. However, when a second group of experimental dogs were placed in a restraining hammock and subjected to a pretrial shock, they failed to master the escape avoidance behavior and instead became passive.[104]

From the conclusions drawn from this classic experiment and its variations, Seligman and his colleagues arrived at the concept of "learned helplessness," which involves two aspects: an interference with adaptive responding produced by inescapable shock and a process that they believe underlines the behavior. Thus, the term "learned helplessness" describes both the behavior itself, in the context of the experiment, and the process that causes it.[105]

The lack of ability to control the shock in the pretrial dogs has two behavioral consequences: (1) the dogs fail to initiate responses to escape shock, or they are slower at initiating them than the control dogs; and (2) if the dogs do turn off the shock, they have more trouble learning that they themselves are responsible for it.

In summary, the experience with a trauma in which the dog has no control produces the learning of helplessness when confronted with the same conditions again.

Seligman believes that the phenomenon of learned helplessness in animals may provide a model for understanding reactive depression in human beings.[105] Four lines of evidence are given that seem to indicate that the two phenomena are similar: (1) the behavioral and physiologic symptomatology, (2) etiological factors, (3) curative conditions, and (4) prevention.

Experimentally induced, uncontrollable trauma produces effects on the animal closely related to depression, such as passivity, retardation, anorexia, weight loss, and norepinephrine depletion. Etiologically it is not the trauma per se that produces the interference with the later response, but rather not having control over the trauma.

Maier has also provided evidence that it is the learned expectation of lack of control that is responsible for interference with adaptive response rather than a motor passive response reinforced by the shock, as proposed by some critics.[83] To quote Seligman,[105]

One cause of laboratory produced helplessness seems to be learning that one can not control important events. Learning that responding and reinforcement are independent results in a cognitive set which has two basic effects: few responses to control reinforcement are initiated and associating successful responding with reinforcement becomes more difficult.

Seligman believes that the concept of helplessness and the cognitive negative set (put forward by Bibring and Beck, respectively) are similar in that the "patient has learned or believes that he can not control those elements of his life that relieve suffering or bring him gratification.[105]

In other words, learning that the trauma is uncontrollable not only reduces initiative to escape, but also makes it difficult to learn that responding produces relief.

In summary, the sense of uncontrollability and trauma are present in the learned helplessness experiment, but neither factor is the essential cause of depression. What seems to be the important determinant is the *expectation* of a lack of control over the stress.

PERSONALITY AND AFFECTIVE DISORDERS

Personality refers to the totality of an individual's objective and observable behavior and his subjectively reportable inner experience. This concept of personality implies predictable and consistent patterns of reactions to stimuli and stresses. These consistent patterns of perceiving, relating to, and thinking about the environment and oneself that are exhibited in a wide range of important social and personal contexts are referred to as personality traits. They are as much a part of "personality styles"[106] as of personality disorders. Only when personality traits become inflexible and maladaptive, causing social, interpersonal, occupational, or subjective distress, do they signify a personality disorder. These enduring maladaptive manifestations are long-standing, often observable by adolescence or childhood, and persist throughout adult life.

The clinical and research studies on personality are beset with fundamental questions regarding the relationship between nature and nurture, or, more precisely, between temperament (the inherited and constitutional factors) and character (the psychosocially determined aspects).

TEMPERAMENT

Investigations into the biologic aspects of normal personality have failed to provide evidence of direct biologic correlates to personality characteristics, while some correlation between certain pathologic disorders and psychophysiologic measurements have been more promising. The existence of a relationship between temperament and "manic-depressive insanity" was clinically observed by Kraepelin.[76] He noticed that in at least half of his patient population, some of the personality features resembled the particular subtypes outlined by him: depressive, manic, irritable, and cyclothymic. Kraepelin also suspected that the association might be a subclinical expression of the disorder itself. Kretschmer, based on a classification of what he believed to be distinctive constitutional physical types, postulated some correlation between the temperament, the disorder, and the body configuration.[77] Manic-depressive illness and cyclothymic temperament were associated with a "pyknic" constitution, whereas schizoid personalities and schizophrenia were related to "leptosomatic" or "athletic" physical types. Sheldon et al.[107] modified Kretschmer's typology, but their findings were fundamentally in agreement. Recently Zerssen,[128] applying modern statistical analysis and self-rating personality scales, obtained results not compatible with the assumptions of Kretschmer and Sheldon et al. In any event, the increasing evidence favoring the role of heredity in affective illness has brought about the reemergence of interest in the role of genetics in determining whether or not certain personality types are more vulnerable to affective disorders than others. Stone has recently formulated a hypothesis and provided evidence that within the borderline personality disturbances group (see Kernberg,[63] Gunderson and Singer,[46] Spitzer et al.,[113] and Grinker et al.[45]), some cases may be closely tied genotypically to affective disorders and could prove to be, phenotypically, subclinical expressions of affective conditions.[114–116] In a series of 34 outpatients who met the criteria for Kernberg's borderline personality organization, Stone found statistically significant correlation between the presence of affective "temperament-positive" features (a scale measurement constructed from Kraeplin's temperamental variables) and a family history of affective disorders. This relationship was not observed within the neurotic group. Recently Akiskal et al. have shown that cyclothymic personalities are at high risk of being borderline personalities due to the unstable sense of identity that results from the short and irregular cycles of depression and hypomania.[4] They imply that all borderline personalities may indeed be afflicted with affective disorders. Despite their overgeneralization, Akiskal and his associates nevertheless convincingly demonstrate that cyclothymic disorders may, at least in their sample, be related to bipolar conditions in terms of family distribution, follow-up outcome, pharmacologic hypomania, and lithium response. Thus, these authors have shown that the cyclothymic personality may be related to a bipolar disorder, confirming Kraepelin's description of a subaffective form of the disorder.

TABLE 10–2.—CLINICAL, TREATMENT RESPONSE, OUTCOME, AND SLEEP EEG FINDINGS SUPPORTING A DYSTHYMIC–CHARACTER SPECTRUM DIVISION OF CHARACTEROLOGIC DEPRESSIONS*

	SUBAFFECTIVE DYSTHYMIA	CHARACTER SPECTRUM
Sex ratio	About even	Female preponderance
Onset	Less vague	"Depressed all my life"
Course	Intermittent	Continuous
Sleep	More hypersomnic	More insomniac
Superimposed depressive episode	Common	Rare
Personality	"Stable"	"Unstable"
Family history	Affective disorder	Alcoholism
Developmental object loss	Less common	More common
Response to tricyclics	Fair	Poor
Pharmacologic hypomania	Yes	No
Alcohol and drug abuse	Less common	More common
Social prognosis	Less unfavorable	Unfavorable
REM latency	Short	Normal

*From Yerevanian and Akiskal.[125] Reproduced by permission.

Postulating a characterologic tendency to dysphoria in certain individuals that is of developmental origin, Yerevanian and Akiskal studied 65 subjects with characterologic depressions (onset before age 25; depression symptoms present over five years almost on a daily basis, but not sufficient to fulfill the criteria for major depressive episodes, etc.).[125] Based on the pharmacologic response, the shortening of rapid eye movement (REM) latency, and other findings, they describe two distinct groups: a character spectrum and a dysthymic subaffective disorder (Table 10–2). In the latter, the individuals tend to have obsessive-introverted traits, may suffer from overimposed major depressions, display shortened REM latency, have relatives with primary affective disorders, and respond to tricyclics. Yerevanian and Akiskal are of the opinion that this characterologic subaffective group is related to the unipolar group as cyclothymia is to bipolar illness.

Evidence seems to exist, then, supporting Kraepelin's assertion that affective temperaments influence certain types of personality pathology, types that are related to the respective affective disorders.

CHARACTER

Evidence on the character aspects of the personality equation has been gathered through psychoanalytic observation and psychometric measurement. Psychoanalytic theory has taken into consideration the constitutional factors in personality formation through the formulation of the "complementary series" and the endowment of the ego with biologic dispositions and trends. Yet the focus has remained exclusively on the character aspects of personality, to the degree that character and personality are used almost interchangeably.

From the psychoanalytic viewpoint, traits are the expression of defensive and adaptive mechanisms, which are themselves the reflection of the different types of psychosexual organization. Character is the "crystallization"[32] of defensive mechanisms that provide the individual with an "armor"[96] by which he reacts to internal and external stimuli and conflicts in a consistent and predictable manner. Following the psychosexual line of development, character types were traditionally classified as oral, anal, phallic, and genital, depending on the level of psychosexual organization achieved. As previously pointed out, Abraham gave primary consideration to orality in affective disorders, but also observed that anal (obsessive-compulsive) traits were present as well in some cases during intermorbid periods. After Abraham, psychoanalytic authors of diverse theoretical persuasions, such as Fenichel, Rado, Bonime, Bemporad, and Arieti, increasingly emphasized the oral aspects of depression-prone personalities. Chodoff, in reviewing the psychoanalytic literature, observes that the concept of oral character has lost "its mooring in psychosexual and constitutional orality"[23] and has come to imply the presence of exaggerated affectional and supportive needs and of excessive dependency traits. A composite description of the "oral character" given by Chodoff includes the following features: (1) dependency on narcissistic supplies from others, directly or indirectly, in order to maintain self-esteem; (2) low tolerance of frustration; and (3) use of submissive, manipulative coercive, demanding, and placating interpersonal maneuvers to maintain an ambivalent relationship with an external or internalized object needed to provide the supplies.

A major drawback to psychoanalytic observations of affective disorders and premorbid personality is that diagnostic categorizations of the former are not considered explicitly or dealt with at all. Thus, correlation between the different personalities and affective disorder types is difficult to establish. Among the exceptions are the work of Jacobson[59] and Cohen et al.[26] These authors are concerned with outlining the personality of manic-depressive individuals, whom they find to be apparently well adjusted during the intermorbid phase—an observation that is in agreement with the recent psychometric findings. Jacobson's clinical observations underline the intense and vested emotional object relationship and good level of functioning found in the personality background of manic-depressives. Nevertheless, she believes that they show a specific ego weakness in their remarkable vulnerability to frustration, intolerance, hurt, and disappointment. Dynamically they display an oscillating mixture of pseudoindependence and dependency, differing in this way from the compulsives who maintain the pseudoindependence as a steady defensive position. In contrast, Cohen et al. found overconscientiousness and overscrupulousness (compulsive traits) in their sample but the same tendency to overpossessiveness that Jacobson had observed earlier. Between episodes these patients were found to be superficially well adjusted, hard workers, conventional, and socially shallow.

Some contemporary psychoanalytic theories offer a new dimensional understanding of personality that deserves attention, since they have a bearing on the etiologic considerations of affective disturbances as well as on symptom expression and illness adaptation. Over the last decade Kernberg has advocated the establishment of psychoanalytic criteria for the differential diagnosis of different types and degrees of severity of character pathology.[63, 64] Taking into consideration the vicissitudes of internalized representation of self and others, ego integration, and the types of defensive mechanism in operation, he offered a classification of character pathology according to the different levels of organization achieved: low, intermediate, and high. This nosology offers a new dimension in that each traditional descriptive personality diagnosis (e.g., obsessive-compulsive, hysterical, etc.) can be placed at any point on the ego organization continuum. Kernberg's psychostructural diagnosis allows one to estimate whether the individual's level of organization is at neurotic, borderline, or psychotic level.

This assessment of the actual psychological function (beyond trait or descriptive considerations and beyond self-reporting attitudes, as in the case of psychometric measurements) brings into question the value of findings that are only concerned with traits in the relationship between personality and affective disorders, since different levels of ego organization may be in operation. Likewise the description of either external appearances in the interpersonal relationships or of the presenting symptoms may not reflect the existing internal psychostructural organization (as is the case with some of the narcissistic personalities whose surface appearance is of a socially well-adjusted person). Blacker and Levitt[15] and Cornfield and Malen[27] have made similar observations in a different nosologic context. A systematic psychostructural diagnostic approach to research on affective disorders and personality has not yet been reported, although work is being carried on at different medical centers.

Based on our own clinical work and some preliminary research data, we are of the opinion that affective disorders, certainly bipolar disorders, and a narrow group of recurrent depressions could coexist with the entire spectrum of premorbid personality organizations, from normality to archaic borderline or psychotic integration. Stone is of a similar opinion.[116] He believes that between episodes, the personality of manic-depressives is restored to whichever preexisting level of organization it originally had. Kernberg has cautiously voiced the opinion that he could not reach definitive conclusions about the evaluation of the structural personality characteristic of patients with bipolar illness.[65, 66*]

The coexistence of diverse personality organization and bipolar illness raises doubts about the long-held causal assumptions between the diagnostic categories of manic-depression (or "psychotic" depression) and the developmental level of self and object differentiation or ego fixation attained as primary etiologic factors, as accorded by Giovacchini,[43] Kohut,[73, 74] Rinsley,[97] and others. All these authors, despite their diverse theoretical persuasions, stress that manic-depressive states and some depressions are conditions that arise from early disturbance in self and object relationships, resulting in more primitive self or ego organization. Their view is limited by the assumption of a continuum model of psychopathology, ranging from normality to psychosis, that corresponds to different developmental stages. Thus, the affective disorder's developmental disturbances occur earlier

---

*More recently, Kernberg has stated his belief that bipolar illness coexists with all types of personality organizations (personal communication to the authors).

than borderline disorder but later than psychoses. The evidence gathered seems to indicate, at least for bipolars and certain unipolars, that a mixed model of psychopathology is more cogent. A discrete entity like the bipolar state can exist on any personality level of function or fixation. This reconceptualization has theoretical, research, and clinical implications in terms of the role of predisposition, vulnerability, the reciprocal interactions between levels of personality organization and bipolar disorder—implications affecting outcome, severity, and symptom expression.

We have already discussed Kohut's views and classifications of the psychopathology of the self and referred to the placement of bipolar patients within the archaic form of self pathology. However, narcissistic personality disorder deserves some attention since some of the objective and subjective symptoms raise differential diagnostic considerations which Kohut himself refers to as "minor and fluttering replicas of manic-depressive psychosis."[72] The narcissistic personality may involve the following areas in his complaints and pathologic features: "(1) in the sexual sphere: perverse fantasies, lack of interest in sex; (2) in the social sphere: work inhibitions, inability to form and maintain significant relationships, delinquent activities; (3) in his manifest personality features: lack of humor, lack of empathy for other people's needs and feelings, lack of a sense of proportion, tendency toward attacks of uncontrolled rage, pathologic lying; and (4) in the psychosomatic sphere: hypochondriacal preoccupations with physical and mental health, vegetative disturbances in various organ systems."[72] Any of the above features, coupled with self-esteem vulnerability, rapid mood oscillations, and tendency toward hypomanic stimulation, calls for distinguishing this group not only from bipolar disorders in general, but in particular from the bipolar rapid cyclers and from cyclothymia. Preodor and Wolpert have made the same claim regarding adolescents.[94] On the other hand, narcissistic personalities are at high risk of developing major depressive disorders when they lose the sustaining selfobject, particularly during the middle-age life cycle, when some of their narcissistic invested functions are lost, or in a period of reorganization.[67] Thus narcissistic personalities may predispose to a major depressive occurrence and need to be differentiated diagnostically from those with bipolar disorders. On the other hand, narcissistic personalities may independently coexist and interact with a primary affective disturbance.

Regardless of which theoretical approach is taken in assessing personality psychopathology, Kernberg's psychostructural levels or Kohut's self disorders classification, what is important to keep in mind is that the symptom expression and severity of primary affective disturbances may vary according to the degree of personality pathology present.

PSYCHOMETRIC FINDINGS

In the last three decades a series of inventories, mainly self-report instruments, have been introduced in the evaluation of personality and affective disorders. Some were primarily constructed for general purposes and applied to the studies of affective disturbances (e.g., Eysenck's Maudsley Personality Inventory[29] and Cattell's 16-factor personality instrument[22]), while others were specifically designed for testing some of the prevailing hypotheses on affective pathology (Zerssen[128]).

As with other research efforts, part of the difficulty in drawing conclusions stems from the different diagnostic criteria used. Nevertheless, since these investigations are more recent, the unipolar-bipolar distinction is more frequently applied. Murray and Blackburn, using Cattell's 16 Personality Factor Questionnaire, compared the personality profile of individuals diagnosed as having chronic anxiety neurosis, bipolar illness, and unipolar disorders, during the illness phase and after recovery.[87] Their findings were consistent with those of Roth et al.[99] and Kerr et al.[68] in that the anxious group proved to be more anxiety-prone and neurotic. However, during the active phase of illness, these differences disappeared. During the recovery period, unipolars were closer to the chronic anxious group and quite different from the bipolar group. Pilowsky,[93] also applying Cattell's scale, compared neurotic depression and psychotic depression and found that a relationship seems to exist between submissiveness and psychotic depression. However, the major drawback to this conclusion, one acknowledged by the author, is that the assessment took place during the illness episode, when personality measurements may show more dependency, as demonstrated by Liebowitz.[80] A selected number of Cattell's inventory items were administered by Cardoret to unipolar depressive probands and their relatives.[21] Their late-onset group, associated with less alcoholism and affective illness in the relatives, showed more "strength" in the superego subscale, perhaps indicating a more severe superego regulation and less flexibility, which in turn could account for the frequent obsessive and guilt-ridden symptoms encountered in this age group.

The relationship between obsessional personality structure and involutional depression has long been reported. Zerssen[128] reports that Tellenbach[117] described a "melancholic type" of personality consisting of orderliness, conscientiousness, meticulousness, high value achievement, conventional thinking, and dependency, a type which was associated with unipolar depressions but not limited to the involutional type of unipolar disorder. These premorbid characteristics have been independently recognized in different worldwide cultures. Zerssen objectified Tellenbach's "melancholic type" description by constructing a retrospective inventory that was administered to unipolar, bipolar, and obsessive-compulsive patients, as well as to healthy controls. He found that unipolars scored higher in melancholic features than obsessive-compulsive neurotics, whereas bipolar healthy controls showed no differences.[128]

In 1966, Carlo Perris, employing a shortened version of the Marke and Nyman inventory comparing bipolars with unipolars during remission, reported evidence that the two groups clearly differed.[90] Later he found further evidence that bipolars had a personality profile similar to that of the general population.[91]

To determine the personality characteristics reported in the literature, Hirschfeld and Klerman[51] administered an extensive battery of available tests used by some of the European authors, as well as their own battery (Lazare-Klerman-Armor Personality Inventory), to recurrent depressive and manic patients diagnosed according to Research Diagnostic Criteria and Schedule for Affective Disorders and Schizophrenia guidelines. According to them, "the results suggest that depressive patients are more likely to break down under stress, have less energy, are more insecure and sensitive, tend to worry more, are less socially adroit, are more needy, and are more obsessional than normal individuals. Manic patients, on the other hand, have much more normal personality profiles, at least as far as the assessed dimensions indicate" (Table 10–3).[51]

In summary, the investigations and clinical observations thus far reviewed suggest that (1) some personality structures may represent subaffective manifestation of affective disorders, (2) unipolar and bipolar disorders are associated with different types of personality, with the bipolar group showing features similar to normal controls, (3) an association between the melancholic personality and unipolar depression seems to be empirically established, and (4) depression-prone individuals appear to depend on others for self-esteem maintenance. Except for these general findings, the relationship between personality and affective disorders remains a complex and obscure one.

The unipolars seem to be a very heterogeneous group. On the other hand, their premorbid personalities seem also to be of different types and degrees of severity. In some cases, as postulated by Tellenbach, the melancholic features may be a structural compensation for the inclination to depression. In others, the need for narcissistic supplies and dependency on others makes them vulnerable to depression. In still other circumstances the premorbid features may only color the depressive symptoms or determine certain specific symptoms in addition to the universal depressive ones, without having any direct effect on the affective episode or providing any vulnerability to it.

A hindrance in the investigations on this subject, as pointed out by Cho-

TABLE 10–3.—PERSONALITY AND AFFECTIVE DISORDER STUDIES

STUDY, YEAR	DIAGNOSTIC SAMPLE	METHODOLOGY	FINDINGS
Kraepelin, 1913	Manic-depressive psychosis	Clinical observations	50% of manic-depressive patients show depressive, manic, irritable, or cyclothymic temperaments, corresponding to manic-depressive illness subtypes
Perris, 1966	Bipolars, unipolars	Instrument: Marke and Nyman inventory	Bipolars higher in substability Unipolars higher in subvalidity
Perris, 1971	Bipolars, unipolars, normal controls	Instrument: Marke and Nyman inventory	Bipolars and normals show same profiles
Cardoret et al., 1971	Unipolar: early and late onset groups	Instrument: selected items from Cattell's 16 personality factors	Late onset: more rigid superego
Chodoff, 1972	Involutional depression Neurotic depression Unipolar and bipolar	Review of literature	Correlation between obsessional personality and involutional depression; bipolar seems to fall within "normal" range during episodes; unipolar shows greater degree of premorbid neuroticism
Murray and Blackburn, 1974	Chronic anxiety vs. bipolars vs. unipolars	Instrument: Cattell's 16 personality factors	During episode both bipolar and unipolar show as much anxiety as chronic anxiety group; on recovery, unipolar more similar to chronic anxiety population

Donelly et al., 1976	Bipolar, Unipolar (Feighner's criteria)	Instrument: MMPI	*On admission* Bipolar, low profiles (less psychopathology) Unipolar, high profiles *On remission* No significant differences
Pilowsky, 1979	Nonendogenous vs. endogenous vs. nondepressed	Instrument: Cattell's 16 personality factors	"Endogenous" show more submissive, dependent personality
Hirschfeld and Klerman, 1979	Mania group Depression group using RDC and SADS	Instruments: Self reports Maudsley Personality Inventory Lazare-Klerman-Armor Personality Inventory Leyton Obsessionality Inventory Marke and Nyman temperament survey	*Depressive patients* Higher on introversion, neuroticism, obsessionality, solidity and stability; mania patients, except for obsessional traits, like normals; depressed patients more labile under stress, more insecure, more sensitive, worry more, more needy and obsessional
Akiskal et al., 1979	Cyclothymic personalities	Follow-up clinical observations, family history, drug response	Cyclothymia is subsyndromic form of bipolar illness
Yerevanian and Akiskal, 1979	"Characterologic depression" defined by their own criteria	Follow-up clinical observations, family history, drug response, sleep studies	Two types of "characterologic depressions": (a) character spectrum, (b) dysthymic disorder; dysthymic disorders are subaffective forms of unipolar depressions

doff, has been the relative superficiality of some of the studies and the lack of more in-depth observations.[23] Certainly the description of personality features or defensive operations, obtained either by paper and pencil test or through clinical interviews, are insufficient, since the same cluster of personality traits can be found in personalities with various degrees of ego organization. A psychostructural assessment as a new dimensional diagnostic axis needs to be taken into consideration in future research as well as in clinical evaluations. This new dimensional assessment may shed some light on the role of personality in the prediction of the clinical course and long-term outcome and on the specific psychological management needed, all of which have received little attention.

CONCLUSIONS: IMPLICATIONS FOR RESEARCH AND CLINICAL WORK

After assessing the literature of the psychology of affective disturbances, we conclude that despite many theoretical disagreements and contradictory positions, some areas of agreement emerge.

Perhaps the crucial area of agreement, from Bibring on, is that of the role of helplessness as a central phenomenon of depression, a theory which appears to be a common denominator in the work of Seligman, Beck, Spitz, and Basch. The presence of a developmental affective state of depression that plays a similar role to that of anxiety in the maturation process seems likewise universally accepted. This affective state is clearly distinguished from the symptom or feeling of sadness on the one hand, and from the state of clinical depression on the other (a condition which occurs when the adaptive efforts of the helplessness as a signal have failed). A hint is given in the literature, namely by Mahler and Kohut, that elation and stimulation could reach a similar level of signal organization, but elaboration on the subject is lacking.

The distinction between presymbolic and symbolic depression has resolved the need to rely on the fallacy of adultomorphization. A corollary to Basch's fundamental contribution to this distinction is that certain behaviors, determined by presymbolic events, are not amenable to psychological recall, thus being unreachable by introspection and beyond the means of interpretation, as pointed out by Gedo.[42] The hypothesis of the mechanism of depression offered by the sensorimotor presymbolic model receives support, at least from an objective behavioral point of view, from the experiments of loss and separation in animals conducted by Harlow and Harlow,[48] McKinney et al.,[85, 86] Kaufman and Rosenblum,[62] and Seligman.[105]

The role of loss is not universal to depression, yet the distinction between loss of the object and loss of the functions provided by the object (selfobject's functions) needs to be taken into consideration in future research, since parental substitution may correct the psychological need without any dysfunction occurring; conversely, the presence of a parent does not rule out the loss of the crucial emotional availability. The importance of early losses is not only as a causation factor but as influencing the onset, manifestation, and outcome of affective disorders. Perris found that childhood losses tend to correlate with earlier onset.[89] Beck et al. also noted a positive association between severity of depression and childhood losses.[10] The presence of certain characterologic features in a heterogeneous depressive population studied by Akiskal was predicted by the history of childhood losses.[3] These characterologic traits in turn were predictive of chronicity and poor social outcome. Our own retrospective study of a series of bipolar patients showed that childhood losses were not significantly correlated with either early illness onset or characterologically severe features.

However, childhood disturbances and poor school performance were associated with more character pathology, more severe symptoms, a chronic course, and poorer therapeutic outcome. These findings clearly point to the need for conducting prospective studies into risk factors involved, beyond just retrospective correlation of childhood losses. Such studies will need to consider (1) the evaluation of object loss, as well as of the loss of the object's functional aspects, and (2) the inherited neurophysiologic factors, together with their effects on both sides of the mother-child dyad and their eventual effects on character formation. Certainly the personality characteristics of bipolar disorders between episodes emerge, on the whole, as similar to those of the general population. This is compatible with the hypothesis that bipolar disorders are "actual neuroses." Statistically the actual neuroses are associated at random with diverse personalities in the general population. In some cases the premorbid personality is of a severe nature, raising intriguing questions as to whether the character pathology is related to (1) an early expression of a genetic neurophysiologic factor in the temperamental sphere of the personality, (2) a subaffective clinical form (as proposed by Akiskal), or (3) difficulties in the parent-child relationship, independent of any neurophysiologic determinant, whose influences, in the expression of manic-depression, are felt only later in adulthood. Recurrent depressive disorders constitute a heterogeneous group of conditions with multiple etiologic variables at play. Some may be "actual neuroses," whereas in others the pathogenesis may be primarily psychogenic in origin.

Depression has been viewed as a general system phenomenon indicating a dysfunction that can be caused by any of the following determinants: genetic neurobiologic (depressive phase of bipolar illness, some of the unipolar depressions), chemical (reserpine-induced), toxic or metabolic (organic brain syndromes, thyroid disturbances), or psychological factors (presymbolic or symbolic losses or failures). Mania has largely been discussed as the opposite state to depression. As depression is distinct from sadness, so is mania from elation. Mania and depression are polarized clinical states, and either one can exist without its related affective subset—sadness or elation. In this sense the term "affective disorder" is a misnomer, since these disturbances do not necessarily involve the affect of sadness or elation.

Also like depression, mania is not limited to bipolar disorders. The phenomenon of hypomania is part of borderline and narcissistic personality disorders. Manic behavior is infrequently encountered but nevertheless present in certain "organic" conditions (tertiary lues, delirium). Thus, affective disorders can also be viewed as general system dysfunctions.

The learned helplessness model (characterized by an expected lack of control over outcome) assumes a pivotal role in the mechanism of depression at any level. In the genetically determined depression that affects the signal-processing and ordering functions of the brain, the individual indeed does not have control and thus "learns" to expect lack of control. During childhood, a failure in ordering and predictability creates the expectation of a lack of control either at the presymbolic or symbolic level. This sensitizes the individual to the model of learned helplessness when faced with similar conditions in the future. Sudden changes in familiar environmental conditions by the alteration of expected clues and feedback could create the possibility of the acceptance of lack of control. Even depressogenic schemata are not sufficient to account for depression. For depression to occur the schemata must be accompanied by the subject's belief that the negative perceptions and conditions are not changeable and, therefore, are beyond his control.

In summary, what makes the psychological aspects of affective disorders unique is that psychological phenomena can be regarded as secondarily induced processes, the filtration of the neurophysiologic genetic determinants through the psychological organization of the individual, as in the case of primary affective disturbances, whereas in other types of affective disorders the psychological phenomena can be regarded as primarily involved in their causation. In either case the affective symptomatology has meaning within the historical psychic reality of the individual. From the clinical point of view, then, a comprehensive approach is warranted in which etiologic and dynamic factors as well as mixed psychopathologic models need to be considered, all of which highlights the central importance of evaluating the patient as a total individual. We believe that the psychological approaches not only do not run counter to the phenomenologic assumptions, but actually enhance them, allowing for more integral and more promising treatment management and future research designs.

REFERENCES

1. Abraham K.: Notes on the psycho-analytical investigation and treatment of manic depression, insanity and allied conditions (1911), in *Selected Papers of Karl Abraham*. New York, Basic Books, 1953.
2. Abraham K.: A short study of the development of the libido, viewed in the light of mental disorders (1924), in *Selected Papers of Karl Abraham*. New York, Basic Books, 1953.
3. Akiskal H.S.: A biobehavioral approach to depression, in Depue R.A. (ed.): *The Psychobiology of the Depressive Disorders: Implication for the Effects of Stress*. New York, Academic Press, 1979.
4. Akiskal H.S., Khani M.K., Scott-Strauss A.: Cyclothymic temperamental disorders. *Psychiatr. Clin. North Am.* 2:527, 1979.
5. Anthony J.E.: Childhood depression, in Anthony J.E., Benedek T. (eds.): *Depression and Human Existence*. Boston, Little, Brown & Co., 1975.
6. Arieti S., Bemporad J.: *Severe and Mild Depression: The Psychotherapeutic Approach*. New York, Basic Books, 1978.
7. Basch M.: Psychoanalysis and theory formation. *Ann. Psychoanal.* 1:39, 1973.
8. Basch M.: Toward a theory that encompasses depression: A revision of existing causal hypotheses in psychoanalysis, in Anthony E., Benedek T. (eds.): *Depression and Human Existence*. Boston, Little, Brown & Co., 1975.
9. Basch M.: Psychoanalysis and communication science. *Ann. Psychoanal.* 4:385, 1975.
10. Beck A.T., Sethi B., Tuthill R.: Child bereavement and adult depression. *Arch. Gen. Psychiatry* 9:295, 1963.
11. Beck A.T.: *Depression: Clinical, Experimental and Theoretical Aspects*. New York, Harper & Row, 1967.
12. Beck A.T.: The development of depression: A cognitive model, in Friedman R.J., Katz M.M. (eds.): *The Psychology of Depression: Contemporary Theory and Research*. Washington, D.C., U.S. Government Printing Office, 1974.
13. Benedek T.: Toward the biology of the depression constellation. *J. Am. Psychoanal. Assoc.* 4:389, 1956.
14. Bibring E.: The mechanism of depression, in Greenacre P. (ed.): *Affective Disorders*. New York, International Universities Press, 1953.
15. Blacker K.H., Levitt M.: The differential diagnosis of obsessive-compulsive symptoms. *Compr. Psychiatry* 20:532, 1979.
16. Bonime W.: The psychodynamics of neurotic depression. *J. Am. Acad. Psychoanal.* 4:301, 1976.
17. Bowlby J.: Pathological mourning and childhood mourning. *J. Am. Psychoanal. Assoc.* 11:500, 1963.
18. Bowlby J.: *Attachment and Loss*. New York, Basic Books, 1969, vol. 1.
19. Bowlby J.: *Attachment and Loss*. New York, Basic Books, 1973, vol. 2.
20. Brever J., Freud S.: Studies on hysteria (1893–1895), in *Standard Edition*. London, Hogarth Press, 1973, vol. 2.
21. Cardoret R.J.: Depressive disease: Personality factors in patients with their relatives. *Biol. Psychiatry* 3:85, 1971.
22. Cattell R.: *The Scientific Analysis of Personality*. Chicago, Aldine Press, 1966.
23. Chodoff P.: The depressive personality. *Arch. Gen. Psychiatry* 27:666, 1972.

24. Church J.: *Language and the Discovery of Reality*. New York, Random House, 1961.
25. Clayton P.J., Desmarais L., Winokour G.A.: A study of normal bereavement. *Am. J. Psychiatry* 125:168, 1968.
26. Cohen M.B., et al.: An intensive study of twelve cases of manic-depressive psychosis. *Psychiatry* 17:103, 1954.
27. Cornfield R., Malen R.: A multidimensional view of the obsessive character. *Compr. Psychiatry* 19:73, 1978.
28. Delgado J.: *Physical Control of the Mind*. New York, Harper & Row, 1969.
29. Eysenck H.: *Manual of the Maudsley Personality Inventory*. London, University of London Press, 1959.
30. Fairbairn W.R.D.: *Psychoanalytic Studies of the Personality*. London, Tavistock, 1966.
31. Fenichel O.: Depression and mania, in Fenichel O. (ed.): *The Psychoanalytic Theory of Neurosis*. New York, W.W. Norton & Co., 1945.
32. Freud A.: *The Ego and the Mechanisms of Defense*. New York, International Universities Press, 1946.
33. Freud A.: Discussion, in Bowlby J.: Grief and mourning in infancy and early childhood. *Psychoanal. Study Child* 13:255, 1960.
34. Freud S.: The interpretation of dreams (1900), in *Standard Edition*. London, Hogarth Press, 1973, vol. 4.
35. Freud S.: Papers on metapsychology (1915), in *Standard Edition*. London, Hogarth Press, 1973, vol. 14.
36. Freud S.: The ego and the id (1923), in *Standard Edition*. London, Hogarth Press, 1973, vol. 19.
37. Freud S.: Inhibitions, symptoms and anxiety (1926), in *Standard Edition*. London, Hogarth Press, 1973, vol. 20.
38. Freud S.: The common neurotic state: Part III. General theory of the neurosis (1917), in *Standard Edition*. London, Hogarth Press, 1973, vol. 16.
39. Freud S.: Mourning and melancholia (1917), in *Standard Edition*. London, Hogarth Press, 1973, vol. 17.
40. Freud S.: Analysis terminable and interminable (1937), in *Standard Edition*. London, Hogarth Press, 1973, vol. 23.
41. Gaylin W.: *The Meaning of Despair*. New York, Science House, 1968.
42. Gedo J.: *Beyond Interpretation: Toward a Revised Theory for Psychoanalysis*. New York, International Universities Press, 1979.
43. Giovacchini P.: *Treatment of Primitive Mental States*. New York, Jason Aronson, 1979.
44. Goldberg A.: The evolution of psychoanalytic concepts of depression, in Anthony E., Benedek T. (eds.): *Depression and Human Existence*. Boston, Little, Brown & Co., 1975.
45. Grinker R., Weible B., Drye R.: *The Borderline Syndrome*. New York, Basic Books, 1969.
46. Gunderson J., Singer M.: Defining borderline patients: An overview, *Am. J. Psychiatry* 132:1, 1975.
47. Gunderson J.: Characteristics of borderlines, in Hartocollis P. (ed.): *Borderline Personality Disorders: The Concept, The Syndrome, The Patient*. New York, International Universities Press, 1977.
48. Harlow H. F., Harlow M.K.: Learning to love. *Am. Science* 56:244, 1966.

49. Harlow H.F., Harlow M.K., Suomi S.J.: From thought to therapy: Lessons from a private laboratory. *Am. Scientist* 59:538, 1971.
50. Hartmann H.: *Ego Psychology and the Problem of Adaptation*. New York, International Universities Press, 1958.
51. Hirschfeld R.M.A., Klerman G.L.: Personality attributes and affective disorders. *Am. J. Psychiatry* 136:67, 1979.
52. Howells J.G.: *Principles of Family Psychiatry*. New York, Brunner/Mazel, 1975.
53. Izard C.: *Human Emotions*. New York, Plenum Publishing Corp., 1977.
54. Jacobson, E.: Depression: Oedipus conflict in the development of depressive mechanism. *Psychoanal. Q.* 9:541, 1943.
55. Jacobson E.: Effect of disappointment of the ego and superego formation in normal and depressive development. *Psychoanal. Rev.* 33:129–147, 1946.
56. Jacobson E.: The self and the object world: Vicissitudes of their infantile cathexes and their influences or ideational and affective development. *Psychoanal. Study Child* 9:75, 1954.
57. Jacobson E.: Contribution to the metapsychology of cyclothymic depressions, in Greenacre P. (ed.): *Affective Disorders*. New York, International Universities Press, 1961.
58. Jacobson E.: *The Self and the Object World*. New York, International Universities Press, 1964.
59. Jacobson E.: *Depression: Comparative Studies of Normal, Neurotic, and Psychotic Conditions*. New York, International Universities Press, 1971.
60. Joffe W.G., Sandler J.: Notes on pain, depression and individuation. *Psychoanal. Study Child* 20:394, 1965.
61. Katan M.: Mania and the pleasure principle, in Greenacre P.(ed.): *Affective Disorders*. New York, International Universities Press, 1953.
62. Kaufman I.C., Rosenblum L.A.: Depression in infant monkeys separated from their mothers. *Science* 155:1030, 1967.
63. Kernberg O.F.: *Borderline Conditions and Pathological Narcissism*. New York, Jason Aronson, 1975.
64. Kernberg O.F.: *Object Relations Theories and Clinical Psychoanalysis*. New York, Jason Aronson, 1976.
65. Kernberg O.F.: The structural diagnosis of borderline personality organization, in Hartocollis P. (ed.): *Borderline Personality Disorders: The Concepts, The Syndrome, The Patient*. New York, International Universities Press, 1978.
66. Kernberg O.F.: Two reviews of the literature on borderlines: An assessment. *Schizophr. Bull.* 5:53, 1979.
67. Kernberg O.F.: *Internal World and External Reality: Object Relations Theory Applied*. New York, Jason Aronson, 1980.
68. Kerr T.A., et al.: The relationship between the Maudsley Personality Inventory and the course of affective disorders. *Br. J. Psychiatry* 116:11, 1970.
69. Klein M.: *Love, Guilt, and Reparation*. New York, Delacorte Press, 1975.
70. Klein M.: Mourning and its relation to manic-depressive states, in Klein M. (ed.): *Love, Guilt, and Reparation*. New York, Delacorte Press, 1975.
71. Klerman G.L.: Depression and adaptation, in Friedman R.J., Katz M.M. (eds.): *The Psychology of Depression: Contemporary Theory and Research*. Washington, D.C., U.S. Government Printing Office, 1974.

72. Kohut H.: *The Analysis of the Self*. New York, International Universities Press, 1971.
73. Kohut H.: *The Restoration of the Self*. New York, International Universities Press, 1977.
74. Kohut H., Wolf E.: The disorders of the self and their treatment: An outline. *Int. J. Psychoanal*. 59:413, 1978.
75. Kovacs M., Beck A.T.: Maladaptive cognitive structures in depression. *Am. J. Psychiatry* 135:525, 1978.
76. Kraepelin E.: *Manic-Depressive Insanity and Paranoia*. Edinburgh, Livingstone, 1921.
77. Kretschmer E.: *Physique and Character*. London, Kegan Paul, 1925.
78. LaPlanche J., Pontalis J.B.: *The Language for Psychoanalysis*. New Haven, Yale University Press, 1976.
79. Lewin B.D.: *The Psychoanalysis of Elation*. New York, W.W. Norton Co., 1950.
80. Liebowitz M.R.: Personality features of patients with primary affective disorders. *Acta Psychiatr. Scand*. 60:214, 1979.
81. Mahler M.: On the first of three subphases of the separation-individuation process. *Int. J. Psychoanal*. 53:333, 1972.
82. Mahler M., Pine F., Bergman A.: *The Psychological Birth of the Human Infant*. New York, Basic Books, 1975.
83. Maier S.F.: Failure to escape traumatic shock: Incompatible skeletal motor responses or learned helplessness? *Learning Motivation* 1:157, 1970.
84. McCanley R., Hobson J.: The neurobiological origins of psychoanalytic dream theory. *Am. J. Psychiatry* 134:1211, 1977.
85. McKinney W.T., Bunney W.E.: Animal model of depression: Review of evidence: Implications for research. *Arch. Gen. Psychiatry* 21:240, 1969.
86. McKinney W.T., Suomi S.J., Harlow H.F.: Depression in primates. *Am. J. Psychiatry* 127:10, 1971.
87. Murray L.G., Blackburn I.M.: Personality differences in patients with depressive illness and anxiety neurosis. *Acta Psychiatr. Scand*. 50:183, 1974.
88. Pao P.: Elation, hypomania and mania. *J. Am. Psychoanal. Assoc*. 19:787, 1971.
89. Perris C.: A study of bipolar (manic-depressive) and unipolar recurrent depressive psychoses. *Acta Psychiatr. Scand. Suppl*. 194:7, 1966.
90. Perris C.: A study of bipolar (manic-depressive) and unipolar recurrent depressive psychoses. *Acta Psychiatr. Scand. Suppl*. 194:68, 1966.
91. Perris C.: A study of bipolar (manic-depressive) and unipolar recurrent depressive psychoses. *Acta Psychiatr. Scand. Suppl*. 221:43, 1971.
92. Piaget J., Inhelder B.: *The Psychology of the Child*. New York, Basic Books, 1969.
93. Pilowsky I.: Personality and depressive illness. *Acta Psychiatr. Scand*. 60:170, 1979.
94. Preodor D., Wolpert E.A.: Manic-depressive illness in adolescence. *J. Youth Adolesc*. 8:111, 1979.
95. Rado S.: The problem of melancholia. *Int. J. Psychoanal*. 9:420, 1951.
96. Reich W.: On character analysis, in Fliess R. (ed.): *The Psychoanalytic Reader*. New York, International Universities Press, 1973.
97. Rinsley D.: Borderline psychopathology: A review of etiology, dynamics and treatment. *Int. Rev. Psychoanal*. 5:45, 1978.

98. Robertson J., Robertson J.: Young children in brief separation: A fresh look. *Psychoanal. Study Child* 26:264, 1971.
99. Roth M., et al.: Studies in the classification of affective disorders: The relationship between anxiety states and depressive illness. *Br. J. Psychiatry* 121:147, 1972.
100. Ryle G.: *The Concept of Mind*. New York, Barnes and Noble, 1949.
101. Sandler J.: The background of safety. *Int. J. Psychoanal.* 41:352, 1960.
102. Sandler J., Rosenblatt B.: The concept of the representational world. *Psychoanal. Study Child* 17:128, 1962.
103. Sandler J., Joffe W.G.: Notes on childhood depression. *Int. J. Psychoanal.* 46:68, 1965.
104. Seligman M.E.P., Maier S.F.: Failure to escape traumatic shock. *J. Exp. Psychology* 74:1, 1967.
105. Seligman M.E.P.: Depression and learned helplessness, in Friedman R.J., Katz M.M. (eds.): *The Psychology of Depression: Contemporary Theory and Research*. Washington, D.C., U.S. Government Printing Office, 1974.
106. Shapiro D.: *Neurotic Styles*. New York, Basic Books, 1965.
107. Sheldon W.A., Stevens J.S., Tucker W.B.: *The Variety of Human Physique*. New York, Harper, 1940.
108. Simeons A.T.W.: *Man's Presumptuous Brain*. New York, Dutton, 1962.
109. Spitz R.: Hospitalism: An inquiry into the genesis of psychiatric conditions in early childhood. *Psychoanal. Study Child* 1:53, 1945.
110. Spitz R.: Anaclitic depression: An inquiry into the genesis of psychiatric conditions in early childhood: II. *Psychoanal. Study Child* 2:313, 1946.
111. Spitz R.: Hospitalism: A follow-up report. *Psychoanal. Study Child* 2:113, 1946.
112. Spitz R.: *The First Year of Life*. New York, International Universities Press, 1965.
113. Spitzer R., Endicott J., Gibbon M.: Crossing the border into borderline personality and borderline schizophrenia. *Arch. Gen. Psychiatry* 36:17, 1979.
114. Stone M.: Assessing vulnerability to schizophrenia on manic-depression in borderline states. *Schizophr. Bull.* 5:105, 1979.
115. Stone M.: Contemporary shift of the borderline concept from a subschizophrenic disorder to a subaffective disorder. *Psychiatr. Clin. North Am.* 3:577, 1979.
116. Stone M.: *The Borderline Syndromes: Constitution, Personality and Adaptation*. New York, McGraw-Hill Book Co., 1980.
117. Tellenbach H.: *Melancholia*, cited by von Zerssen D.: Premorbid personality and affective psychoses, in Burrows G. (ed.) *Handbook of Studies on Depression*. Amsterdam, Excerpta Medica, 1977.
118. Tennant C., Bebbington P., Hurry J.: Parental death in childhood and risk of adult depressive disorders: A review. *Psychol. Med.* 10:289, 1980.
119. Tomkins S.S.: *Affect, Imagery, Consciousness*. New York, Springer, 1962, vol. 1; 1963, vol. 2.
120. Winnicott D.W.: *Collected Papers*. London, Tavistock, 1958.
121. Winnicott D.W.: *The Maturational Processes and the Facilitating Environment: Studies in the Theory of Emotional Development*. New York, International Universities Press, 1965.
122. Wolf E.: Developmental line of selfobject relations, in Goldberg A. (ed.): *Advances in Self Psychology*. New York, International Universities Press, 1980.

123. Wolpert E.A.: Manic depressive illness as an actual neurosis, in Anthony E., Benedek T. (eds.): *Depression and Human Existence*. Boston, Little, Brown & Co., 1975.

124. Wolpert E.A.: A holistic approach to bipolar depressive illness, in Wolpert E.A. (ed.): *Manic-Depressive Illness*. New York, International Universities Press, 1977.

125. Yerevanian B.I., Akiskal H.S.: "Neurotic," characterological and dysthymic depressions. *Psychiatr. Clin. North Am.* 2:595, 1979.

126. Zetzell E.R.: The depressive position, in Greenacre P. (ed.): *Affective Disorders*. New York, International Universities Press, 1961.

127. Zetzell E.R.: On the incapacity to bear depression, in Schur M. (ed.): *Drives, Affects, Behavior*. New York, International Universities Press, 1965, vol. 2.

128. Zerssen D. von: Premorbid personality and affective psychoses, in Burrows G. (ed.): *Handbook of Studies on Depression*. Amsterdam, Excerpta Medica, 1977.

11

SUICIDE

SUHAYL NASR, M.D.

SUICIDE is the human act of self-annihilation. The word suicide first came into use in the middle of the 17th century, although the act has been known for millennia. (Socrates was one of its most famous victims.[36]) Society has taken various positions toward suicide, ranging from complete condemnation (excommunication and no burial rites for Catholics) to acceptance (hara-kiri in Japan). The predominant attitude of civilized society is one of condemnation. As Kant says, it is an insult to humanity and oneself. This most individualistic of all actions disturbs society profoundly. Seeing a man who appears not to care for the things which it prizes, society is compelled to question all that it has thought desirable. Society is troubled and its natural and nervous reaction is to condemn suicide.[34] In this way it bolsters its own values.

More directly, one can reflect on the emotions experienced when a relative, friend, colleague, or patient suicides. Together with the shock, disbelief, and grief, there is also the uneasy and uncomfortable feeling, difficult to express even to oneself, of anger toward the victim. Why did he or she do it, why now, why here, and why to us? This chapter addresses these questions, starting with Durkheim's theory, then discusses the methodological difficulties in suicide research. In later sections the epidemiology of suicide is discussed, several profiles of individuals who completed suicide are described, and some approaches to the treatment of a suicidal patient are offered.

Durkheim's study of suicide[16] ushered in the era of scientific inquiry into suicide. He was interested in the forces of society that affect the individual. Durkheim described three types of suicide: (1) *egoistic suicide*, which re-

229

sults from lack of integration of the individual into society (lack of marriage and family ties, lack of affiliation with religious, political, or national communities); (2) *altruistic suicide,* which occurs when the individual takes his own life because of higher commandments (religious, political or military orders); and (3) *anomic suicide,* which occurs when the individual becomes alienated from his usual social fabric (by sudden wealth or bankruptcy or recent divorce). Durkheim's predominantly sociological theory has been confirmed by, among other factors, the observed decrease in suicide rate during World Wars I and II, and increased suicide rate during the Great Depression of the early 1930s.[10] Durkheim, however, was not interested in the individual aspect of suicide. His theory needs revision in view of the highly frequent psychopathology, particularly depression, recently reported in retrospective assessment of individuals who completed suicide. A theory that considers suicide as a separate illness or as a complication of depressive illness in some individuals is likely to be more productive and to induce active prevention and treatment: to combat a specific illness in a specific individual is more realistic than to combat social forces through one individual.

Progress in the study of suicide has been hampered by the difficult methodological problems. The nature and finality of the suicidal act precludes any prospective studies on both practical and ethical grounds. Research has thus been confined mainly to retrospective analysis of reported and completed suicides. The findings of these studies have been generally consistent. They all suffer from a serious shortcoming, namely, underreporting of suicide.

Analysis of certified suicides reveals a rate of 11.7 suicides per 100,000 individuals per year for 1979 in the United States.[28] This is equivalent to 26,500 suicides in 1979 (the ninth overall leading cause of death in the country). The true figure is probably two to three times larger. Minor variations in this rate have occurred over the years, but the rate has been relatively stable for the past 30 years.[3] Different countries report different suicide rates. The rate for the United States is about the eighth highest in the world. Burvill[10] showed that despite a change in the instruments used for suicide, the rate remained stable in Australia between 1910 and 1977. A pleasant and unexplained decline in suicide rate has been occurring in Britain, from a peak of 12.1 per 100,000 population per year in 1967 to 7.8 in 1977.[8]

Coroners are usually reluctant to certify a death as suicide unless the evidence is very clear. Several factors affect this crucial decision-making process: legal-financial (some insurance companies do not reimburse survivors of suicide victims), religious (Catholics are denied burial rites unless mental illness is invoked), protection of survivors from guilt or shame, and protection of the individual who committed suicide (this is particularly true for physician suicides).

PROFILES OF SUICIDAL PATIENTS

Assuming that individuals who are likely to commit suicide come from the same population as those who have already completed suicide, analysis of completed certified suicides has been used to develop a profile of the individual who is most at risk. Suicide, however, is as protean as any other human experience or act. It defies simple categorization. The following sociodemographic, illness, and personality profiles are not sufficient to predict suicide but may facilitate the identification of persons who are closer to suicide than most other people. A similar example in general medicine would be the use of risk factors to identify persons at risk for coronary artery disease, with the attendant usefulness and limitations of such a method.

SOCIODEMOGRAPHIC PROFILE

AGE.—The risk for suicide increases with age.[13] For men the rate increases sharply after age 45 and remains elevated; for women the rate increases between ages 55 and 65 and then decreases. The elderly attempt suicide less often than younger people but they are more frequently successful, accounting for 25% of the suicides although they make up only 10% of the total population. In recent years there has been an increase in the suicide rate among adolescents and young adults between the ages of 15 and 25. Solomon and Hellon in Alberta, Canada,[39] and Murphy and Wetzel in the United States[30] applied the method of cohort analysis to the study of suicide rates. This method examines the rate of suicide for each age group (five-year cohorts) and follows the same group of individuals as they enter the subsequent age group. Both studies reported an increase in the suicide rate of adolescents. Both studies also found that once a cohort attained a higher suicide rate, it was likely to remain at a higher suicide rate than the preceding cohort, for the rest of life. These findings imply that suicide rates in the United States and in Alberta are likely to increase as adolescents enter the higher suicide rate age.

SEX.—Traditionally, men commit suicide two to four times more frequently than women; women attempt suicide three to four times more often than men. The ratio of male to female suicide has been gradually approaching 1.[10] Burvill studied suicide rates in Australia between 1910 and

1977 and found a male:female ratio of 1:1.6 for 1977. A decrease in male suicide rates rather than an increase in female suicide rates accounted for the trend toward equal suicide rates.[10]

RACE.—Whites are reported to commit suicide more often than blacks with the exception of the young age groups, in which blacks commit suicide twice as often as whites.[3] This difference tends to disappear when other sociodemographic factors are considered (sex, religion, occupation, employment). The suicide rate among native American and Alaskan Indians greatly exceeds the national rate.[32]

MARITAL STATUS.—The risk for suicide increases for persons who are divorced, widowed, or separated. It is higher for single persons than for married ones and higher for childless married individuals than for married ones with children.[32]

OCCUPATIONAL STATUS.—The suicide rate is higher among unemployed than employed persons.[37] Certain professions are associated with higher suicide rates, notably physicians, dentists, pharmacists, and lawyers.[32] Most suicides by physicians occur before age 50. Female physicians and psychiatrists have the highest suicide rates among physicians.[12] A recent study reports that medical students have a suicide rate that is similar to the general population of the same age.[33] Several factors have been implicated in the increased suicide rate for physicians. Among these are difficulty in accepting the patient role when indicated, easy access to and knowledge of lethal drugs and dosages, difficulty in recognizing and identifying a troubled colleague who is abusing drugs or alcohol, and familiarity with death.

RELIGION.—Some data indicate that suicide occurs less frequently among Catholics than Jews or Protestants. However, the difference between the three groups loses its significance when other demographic factors, such as age, race, and sex, are controlled for. The more active and involved the person is in his religion, the less likely he is to commit suicide, regardless of specific faith.[32]

IMMIGRATION.—Suicide occurs more frequently in urban than rural areas. First-generation immigrants to the United States have suicide rates that are similar to those of their countries of origin. Later generations have rates similar to the general population.[32] A similar finding is reported for immigrants to Australia, with the exception of a higher suicide rate among older first-generation immigrant men.[10]

PARENTAL HISTORY OF VIOLENCE.—History of suicide, attempted suicide, or murder in the family increases the probability of suicide among the offspring.[25] Lloyd recently reported that early parental loss by death increases the risk for depression and attempted suicide.[25]

HISTORY OF SUICIDE ATTEMPT.—Follow-up of individuals who attempted suicide reveals that 30% to 60% will repeat the attempt and that 5% to 10% will eventually succeed. This is most likely to occur in the 90 days following the attempt.[31] This finding has led to several investigations into the relationship between attempted suicide and completed suicide. There is general agreement among researchers at present that these are two different populations and that inferences from one to the other are limited. The major demographic differences are in age (attempters are younger), sex (reverse of completed suicides), and race (more blacks attempt suicide). The personality types are also reportedly different. Suicide attempters are generally described as sociopathic or hysterical or suffering from organic brain syndromes. However, Goldney[19] recently studied 110 women who attempted suicide and compared them with 25 matched outpatient psychiatric patients. He found that women who attempted suicide were not more hysterical than the controls. It may well be that individuals who attempt suicide have a milder form of whatever pathology leads to completed suicide.

ILLNESS PROFILE

CHRONIC PHYSICAL OR MENTAL ILLNESS.—Patients who are suffering from chronic illness (e.g., Huntington's disease or chronic renal failure) or terminal illness (e.g., cancer) have an increased risk of suicide. Dorpat et al. reported that 50% to 70% of individuals who completed suicide had a physical illness.[15] Andreason et al.[1] found that patients with secondary depression (including depression secondary to physical illness) tended to have more suicidal behavior than patients with primary depressive disease. Loss of mobility among persons for whom physical activity was occupationally or recreationally important, disfigurement (particularly among women), and chronic intractable pain are other factors contributing to suicides and attempted suicides.[32]

Using the data of the Psychiatric Case Register of Monroe County, New York, Babigian and Odoroff[4] found that among patients with psychiatric illness white males had 8 times more risk of committing suicide, and white females 11.3 times more risk, than the general population. In a study of suicide among patients with mental illness, Tsuang and Woolson[41] found an increased suicide rate for male schizophrenics and an increased accident rate for female schizophrenics over a four-decade follow-up period. The control group for this study consisted of acute surgical patients matched for time of admission, age, sex, and private or public payment at the time of admission.

Patients with a history of substance or alcohol abuse are also more prone to suicide than the general population (see Solomon and Arnon[38] for a recent review).

DEPRESSION.—Suicide is to depression what death is to cancer. An individual may die of causes other than cancer, and the presence of cancer does not necessarily result in death. Likewise, a person may commit suicide without having a diagnosable depression, and depression is neither necessary nor sufficient for suicide. The two are nevertheless intricately linked. Fifteen percent of patients who have affective disorders eventually commit suicide.[26] On the other hand, Kraft and Babigian[23] reported that 50% of suicides in Monroe County, New York had had previous contact with the Psychiatric Case Register. In a series of 100 consecutive suicides, Barraclough et al.[5] found that 64 had uncomplicated clinical depression, 6 had depression with other serious illness, and 10 had depression with alcoholism. Seven other victims had significantly depressed mood associated with phobia (3), addiction (3), and acute schizoaffective exacerbation (1). Thus in this study, 87% of the suicide victims had evidence of depression or depressive mood. This study used the "psychological autopsy" method, in which the data are obtained from clinical records, physicians, family members, or any other person familiar with the suicide victim.

Tsuang[40] examined the suicide rate in a group of 225 depressed patients followed for up to 40 years and the surgical controls mentioned earlier. He found a higher suicide rate among depressed patients than among controls. Most suicides occurred in the first decade of follow-up. Avery and Winokur[2] further refined these data by studying the rate of suicide and attempted suicide in 519 depressed patients and comparing the effects of different treatments. They confirmed an earlier finding by Pofkorny that the period of greatest suicidal risk for the depressed hospitalized patient is the first year following discharge from the hospital. They also confirmed earlier findings of significantly reduced suicide risk for patients treated with electroconvulsive therapy (ECT), compared with those treated with tricyclic antidepressants. This relationship held true after controlling for history of suicide attempt.

Biochemical and physiologic studies of suicide generally consist of retrospective review of data on patients who commit suicide. To date, there are no definitive findings in this area (see Hankoff[20] for recent review). Three areas may be helpful in understanding suicide as it relates to depression:

1. Elevated urinary 17 OHCS in patients who committed suicide. There is evidence[11] for the usefulness of the dexamethasone suppression test in the diagnosis of endogenous depression and its potential for predicting response to antidepressants.

2. Reduced levels of 5-hydroxyindoleacetic acid in the cerebrospinal fluid of patients who commit suicide. This may imply that serotonin-deficiency depressions may be particularly associated with increased suicide risk.

3. Reduced activity of the enzyme monoamine oxidase (MAO) in the

platelets of randomly selected college students who reported psychopathology or history of suicide attempts.[9] This reduced level of platelet MAO activity has also been reported in patients with chronic mental illness.[7]

Thus, there is evidence that depression, mainly as an illness, but also as a predominant mood, is closely associated with increased suicide risk.

PSYCHOLOGICAL PROFILE

Leonard[24] describes three psychological characteristics that are associated with an increased risk for suicide:

1. The *controlling* person may become suicidal when he or she loses control over events or forces in his or her life (e.g., a business executive who loses in a corporate game).

2. The *dependent-dissatisfied* person may work his way to isolation, despondency, and suicide when the sources of his dependency have been used up by repetitive, angry, unappreciative, and demanding behavior.

3. The *symbiotic* person becomes suicidal when he loses the strong member of the relationship. The increased suicide rate among schizophrenics following the death of a parent supports this hypothesis.

Fawcett and Susman[18] describe five psychological characteristics that are associated with increased suicide risk:

1. Persons with *poor interpersonal relationships* are at high risk for suicide whenever their narcissistic needs are threatened or stressful life events require their dependence on other people with whom they had failed to nurture a warm and mutually interdependent relationship. Patients with borderline or narcissistic personality have a high rate of impulsive suicide attempts. This characteristic is similar to the dependent-dissatisfied described by Leonard.

2. Persons with *paranoid symptomatology*. Some patients with paranoid delusions may commit suicide because of fear of punishment or persecution. On the other hand, when paranoid patients gain insight into their projected feelings, they feel guilty and depressed and are more likely to commit suicide.

3. History of *suicide attempts during* a previous *regression*. Patients who attempted suicide during a previous psychotic episode are more likely to repeat the attempt in their relapse than those who had not attempted suicide.

4. *Pathologic perfectionism*. Patients with obsessive-compulsive personality disorder are prone to depression. Their rigidity increases their suicidal risk during a depression because of their inability to modify their self-expectations or to cope with the feeling of depression. This concept is similar to the controlling characteristic described by Leonard.

5. The sudden emptiness created by a depression may increase the sui-

cidal risk of individuals with *stimulus-hungry life patterns,* particularly if they have a history of *impulsive* behavior.

The three psychological characteristics described by Leonard and the five described by Fawcett and Susman may be associated with an increased risk for suicide when either a clinical depression or an excess of stressful events occurs. These characteristics are not to be confounded with personality disorders or traits. Attempts at describing a suicidal personality have not been fruitful.

ASSESSMENT OF THE ACUTELY SUICIDAL PATIENT

Thus far we have described a matrix of sociologic, demographic, physical, and psychological characteristics of individuals who are at risk for suicide. The next task is to identify those individuals who are currently at risk for suicide. Barraclough et al.[5] reported that among 100 consecutive suicides, 48% had visited a physician in the week prior to their suicide, 70% in the month prior to their suicide. The clinical setting of a doctor-patient relationship is an important one to focus on in identifying patients at risk for suicide. Following is a list of factors that can increase the index of suspicion about current suicide potential.

HISTORY

In addition to the history obtained for the presenting complaint, a probe into several other areas may prove useful:

1. *Symptoms of depression:* disturbance of appetite for pleasure, food, or sex; disturbance in sleep or increased use of hypnotics; unusual recent statements such as "I won't bother you for too long any more."

2. *Unusual recent behavior:* giving away valued possessions, discontinuance of close relationships, buying additional insurance, increased risk-taking such as driving while intoxicated or taking aircraft pilot lessons, deteriorating work record, increased alcohol or drug abuse, and extreme social withdrawal.

3. *Recent increase in stressful life events:* loss of work or promotion, additional debt, new child, death in immediate family, recently diagnosed physical illness.

MENTAL STATUS EXAMINATION

In addition to the customary mental status examination, including assessments of mood and affect, special attention to the following areas may increase the rate of identification of patients at high risk for suicide:

1. *Abrupt behavioral or clinical change.* The classic description is that of

a depressed and agitated patient who suddenly becomes calm and peaceful, only to commit suicide shortly thereafter. Sudden increase in agitation and anxiety may also indicate the presence of disturbing suicidal thoughts or plans. Sudden changes in therapists initiated by the patient may indicate a negation of the need for help and increased isolation, leading to higher suicidal risk.

2. Beck et al.[6] reported that *hopelessness* is an important independent factor associated with increased acute suicidal risk. Wetzel et al.[43] recently replicated this finding.

3. *Suicidal ideas, ideation, and plans.* The distinction between these three levels of suicidal potential is somewhat arbitrary. Suicidal ideas are

TABLE 11-1.—ASSESSMENT OF SUICIDAL POTENTIAL*

COGNITIVE AND AFFECTIVE		
Despair with any affect	Yes	No
Intention to die	Yes	No
Self-hate	Yes	No
Recurrent ideas of suicide	Yes	No
Affective ambivalence about dying or receiving help	Yes	No
Repudiate help	Yes	No
Concealing a recent suicide attempt	Yes	No
Perceiving oneself as being in a crisis situation	Yes	No
Specific plan	Yes	No
Lethal method	Yes	No
Moderate or high degree of distress		
(especially in the context of lethality of method)	Yes	No
INTERPERSONAL AND SOCIAL		
A shift toward interpersonal or social isolation	Yes	No
Intention or thoughts of getting even with or getting back at others by		
harming oneself	Yes	No
Living alone	Yes	No
PERSONAL AND FAMILY HISTORY		
Previous suicide attempt or gesture (especially within last three months)	Yes	No
History of recurrent thoughts of suicide or self-hate	Yes	No
Suicidal behavior in a family member	Yes	No
LIFE STRESSES		
Recent loss (personal, job, etc.) or anniversary of loss	Yes	No
Recent failure or acclaim	Yes	No
ASSOCIATED CONDITIONS		
Any acute psychosis	Yes	No
Alcoholism and drug abuse	Yes	No
Physical illness that is in reality or that is perceived as disabling or life-		
threatening	Yes	No
Depression or despair in chronic psychiatric conditions such as schizophrenia	Yes	No
OTHER		
Access to or previous experience with contemplated means	Yes	No
Presence of strong reality factors	Yes	No
Suicidal warnings or communication (e.g., making wills, giving away		
possessions)	Yes	No

*This list was compiled by Dr. James Newman from various sources.

said to exist when the patient has an occasional passive wish to be dead. Suicidal ideation describes a more frequent preoccupation with death wishes and a feeling that "things will be better off if I were dead." Suicidal plans include various levels of detailed plans on how, where, and when to carry out the suicide. Suicidal plans are certainly more serious than suicidal ideas. The myth of stimulating suicidal thoughts by inquiring about them is unfounded.

Table 11–1 is a checklist of factors that should be considered—but not relied on exclusively—in the assessment of patients for suicide potential. The decision of high suicide risk is a clinical judgment usually based on sociodemographic and psychological factors, the presence of clinical depression, recent history of disturbed social network, and, more important, the presence of suicidal ideation or plans.

TREATMENT

Once the patient is identified as being at high risk of suicide, it is imperative to consider the situation as an emergency and to treat the patient accordingly. Reports in the literature and clinical experience concur that the only goal of treatment of a suicidal patient is the preservation of life until the patient is no longer suicidal. A highly suicidal stage is transient in nature. However, individuals who reach this stage are more likely to reach it again within the following year. Because of the multifactorial etiology of suicide, treatment of the suicidal patient should include several resources. The interventions available range from chemotherapy to hospitalization to psychosocial therapy. It is best always to involve a psychiatrist in the evaluation and treatment of a suicidal patient if the primary care person is not a psychiatrist. It is important for the primary care person to remain actively involved in the treatment in order to make use of the special trust relationship that already exists.

CHEMOTHERAPY

Tricyclic antidepressants are the treatment of choice if a clinical depression is the basis for the suicidal state. When tricyclics are given on an outpatient basis, the physician should prescribe only a nonlethal total dose and request that the medicine be dispensed by a family member or significant other. It is also advisable to ask the significant other to clear the house of all other medications, alcohol, and firearms, and to remind the patient and his family of the two weeks' time lag until an antidepressant effect is felt.

An occasional patient may be severely depressed and actively suicidal (e.g., banging head against walls) and may need immediate ECT because of the earlier onset of remission.

HOSPITALIZATION

The decision to hospitalize a suicidal patient must rest on several factors weighed together, as summarized by Mintz:[29]

The degree of suicidal risk or lethality, the quantity and quality of supervision available at the patient's home, the skill and experience of the treating physician, the anticipated duration of the current crisis, the effect of hospitalization on the continuation of treatment (e.g., psychologist or psychiatrist without hospital admitting privileges), the degree of increased feelings of dependency expected in the patient in response to hospitalization, the desirability of ECT, and the therapist's willingness and capacity to tolerate his own anxiety and uncertainty should he decide against hospitalization.

Once the patient is hospitalized, plans for discharge should always include family members or significant others. The therapist should clearly and openly discuss the current suicidal state of the patient and preview the details of home visits or passes.

The clinician should examine the effect of hospitalization on the relationship between the patient and his immediate family or environment. Family members should be actively involved in treatment so that the patient may return to an improved home or work environment. Hospitalization should be viewed as a step in the direction of preserving life and not as an end to itself (some patients commit suicide in hospitals). Familiarity between clinician and the ward staff and a constructive ward atmosphere contribute to the successful management of a suicidal patient.

PSYCHOSOCIAL THERAPY

Schneidman[36] divides the suicidal state of mind into lethality and perturbation. The latter refers to how upset the individual is (subdivided into high, medium, or low). The former refers to the likelihood of suicide (also subdivided into high, medium, or low). The psychotherapeutic approach to high suicide risk is to decrease lethality through a reduction in perturbation. Several avenues are available to reduce the perturbation of the suicidal individual.

It is best to make certain decisions for the suicidal patient, particularly decisions on hospitalization. This relieves the patient of the burden of decision making in a time of crisis and avoids unnecessary risk-taking on the part of the clinician. It also reassures the patient that the clinician is aware of the suicidal potential of the patient and is experienced in handling such crises.

If the patient is being treated on an outpatient basis, the clinician should obtain a verbal commitment from the patient that he will call the clinician before acting on his suicidal thoughts or impulses. This commitment should be renewed every 24 hours until the suicidal perturbation is decreased by other means. The clinician should, of course, be available 24 hours a day for these patients.

The clinician should monitor the lethality of the patient on at least a daily basis. This reassures the patient that his suffering is taken seriously and that he is not expected to "just snap out of it." Kiev and Berber[22] report that they give their patients the message, "you are not responsible for the way you feel," to relieve the patient from the burden of depression and suicidal thinking. Furthermore, the clinician should make use of the trust in the relationship to transfuse the patient with realistic hope about the outcome of his illness.

The clinician should actively involve significant others in the treatment of the suicidal patient. This involvement serves several purposes. First, it is important to assess whether the significant others in the suicidal patient's life are aware of the suicidal potential of the patient and their responses to it. Some family members may feel guilty and angry over the patient's suicidal potential and so further exacerbate his suicidal state. Other family members may overestimate the suicidal risk of the individual and further alienate him. Second, the clinician may offer a chance to other family members to reduce their own level of anxiety and unhappiness, thus turning them into better support systems for the patient. Third, the clinician may facilitate the direct communication of feelings and thoughts between patients and their significant others, thus strengthening the home environment of the patient.

Patients and their families can benefit from education about depression, suicide, and management of stressful life events. Kiev and Berber[22] offer their patients "life strategy workshops" geared toward the development of life-styles that minimize depressive episodes. They also report educating patients about biochemical factors in depression and their influence on the presence of suicidal ideas. The Affective Disorders Clinic of the University of Illinois uses a group medication model for the maintenance therapy of unipolar and bipolar patients. This model offers education about depression and its treatment and also provides patients with an additional social support system that is useful in times of crises. The successful prevention of suicide in this high-risk population may lie in the long-term maintenance therapy offered these patients even in the absence of acute symptoms. This is in contrast to the usual episodic care and individual treatment offered to depressed patients.

Every effort should be made to use community resources to support the patient (e.g., housing, finances, work). The clinician should actively explore the patient's needs and possible solutions to these needs.

Managing a suicidal patient is an emotionally draining and time-consuming effort. It is highly recommended that clinicians limit their practice to two or three such patients at a time, that clinicians seek consultation with other colleagues on the management of these patients, and that clinicians seek the assistance of other mental health professionals in the management of the suicidal patient (e.g., psychiatric social worker meeting with family and exploring community resources, internist reexamining the management of a chronic illness). Should there be any concern about the breach of confidentiality, several mental health codes (e.g., State of Illinois, 1979) allow such consultations and reaching out in times of imminent danger to the life of the individual in order to enlist significant others in the treatment process.

Once a patient commits suicide, it is recommended that the clinician who was involved with the patient seek a trusted colleague to talk with him about the patient, the circumstances of the last contact with the patient and of the suicide, the nature of the relationship between the clinician and the patient, and the feelings generated by the suicide. This conversation helps the clinician develop a perspective on that suicide and enables him to treat the next suicidal patient with more confidence.

Attention should also be directed to the survivors of the suicide victim. Time should be spent with them to examine and alleviate the feelings of guilt, anger, and depression that a suicide generates. Occasionally, this hostility may be directed at the treating clinician (sometimes deservedly so) and may result in malpractice lawsuits if not handled adequately.

The recent advances in the identification, classification, and treatment of depression usher in a new hope for the identification and prevention of suicide. Complete prevention of suicide may be tantamount to prevention of death. For the currently suicidal individual, every physician and clinician should utilize his knowledge and skills to prevent a suicide, for "when there's life, there's hope."

REFERENCES

1. Andreason N.C., Winokur G.: Secondary depression: Familial, clinical, and research perspectives. *Am. J. Psychiatry* 136:62, 1979.
2. Avery D., Winokur G.: Suicide, attempted suicide, and relapse rates in depression: Occurrence after ECT and antidepressant therapy. *Arch. Gen. Psychiatry* 35:749, 1978.

3. Babigian H.M.: Multiple aspects of suicide. *J. Forensic Sci.* 19:267, 1974.
4. Babigian H.M., Odoroff C.L.: The mortality experience of a population with psychiatric illness. *Am. J. Psychiatry* 126:470, 1969.
5. Barraclough B., Bunch J., Nelson B.: A hundred cases of suicide: Clinical aspects. *Br. J. Psychiatry* 125:355, 1974.
6. Beck A.R., Kovacs M., Weissman A.: Hopelessness and suicidal intent: An overview. *J.A.M.A.* 234:1146, 1975.
7. Brockington I.: Reduced platelet MAO activity in chronic mental illness. Read before the research meeting of the Laboratory of Biological Psychiatry, Illinois State Psychiatric Institute, Chicago, November 1980.
8. Brown J.H.: Suicide in Britain: More attempts, fewer deaths, lessons for public policy. *Arch. Gen. Psychiatry* 36:1119, 1979.
9. Buchsbaum M.S., Coursey R.D., Murphy D.L.: The biochemical high-risk paradigm: Behavioral and familial correlates of low platelet monoamine oxidase activity. *Science* 194:339, 1976.
10. Burvill P.W.: Changing patterns of suicide in Australia, 1910–1977. *Acta Psychiatr. Scand.* 62:258, 1980.
11. Carroll B.J., Feinberg M., Greden J.F., et al.: A specific laboratory test for the diagnosis of melancholia. *Arch. Gen. Psychiatry* 38:15, 1981.
12. Craig A.G., Pitts F.N.: Suicide by physicians. *Dis. Nerv. Syst.* 29:763, 1968.
13. Diertz Jean: Suicide statistics. *Psychiatr. News* 16:30, 1981.
14. Dorpat T.L., Ripley H.S.: A study of suicide in the Seattle area. *Compr. Psychiatry* 1:349, 1960.
15. Dorpat T.L., Anderson W.F., Ripley H.S.: The relationship of physical illness to suicide, in Resnik H.L. (ed.): *Suicidal Behaviors: Diagnosis and Management.* Boston, Little, Brown & Co., 1968.
16. Durkheim E.: *Suicide, A Study in Sociology,* Spaulding J.A., Simpson G. (trans.). Glencoe, Ill., Free Press, 1951.
17. Fawcett J.: Saving the suicidal patient: The state of the art, in Ayd F. (ed.): *Mood Disorders: The World's Major Public Health Problem.* Baltimore, Ayd Communications Publication, 1978.
18. Fawcett J., Susman P.: The clinical assessment of acute suicidal potential: A review. *Rush Presbyterian-St. Luke's Med. Bull.* 14:86, 1975.
19. Goldney R.D.: Are young women who attempt suicide hysterical? *Br. J. Psychiatry* 138:141, 1981.
20. Hankoff L.D.: Physiochemical correlates of suicide, in Hankoff L.D. (ed.): *Suicide Theory and Clinical Aspects.* Littleton, Mass., PSG Publishing Co., Inc., 1979.
21. Jennings C., Barraclough B.: Legal and administrative influences on the English suicide rate since 1900. *Psychol. Med.* 10:407, 1980.
22. Kiev A., Berber W.S.: *The Suicidal Patient,* monograph. Cincinnati, Merrell-National Laboratories, May 1980.
23. Kraft D.P., Babigian H.M.: Suicide by persons with and without psychiatric contacts. *Arch. Gen. Psychiatry* 33:209, 1976.
24. Leonard C.V.: *Understanding and Preventing Suicide.* Springfield, Ill., Charles C Thomas, Publisher, 1967.
25. Lloyd C.: Life events and depressive disorder reviewed. *Arch. Gen. Psychiatry* 37:529, 1980.
26. Lundquist G.: Prognosis and course in manic-depressive psychosis: A followup study of 319 first admissions. *Acta Psychiatr. Neurol.* 35(suppl.):1, 1945.

27. Metropolitan Life Insurance Co.: *Statistical Bull*. 60:10, 1979.
28. Metropolitan Life Insurance Co.: *Statistical Bull*. 61:15, 1980.
29. Mintz R.S.: Basic considerations in the psychotherapy of the depressed suicidal patient. *Am. J. Psychotherapy* 25:56, 1971.
30. Murphy G.E., Wetzel R.D.: Suicide risk by birth cohort in U.S., 1949 to 1974. *Arch. Gen. Psychiatry* 37:519, 1980.
31. Pederson A.M., Tefft B.M., Babigian H.M.: Risk of mortality of suicide attempters compared with psychiatric and general populations. *Suicide* 5:145, 1975.
32. Resnik H.L.P.: Psychiatric emergencies: Suicide, in Kaplan H.I., Freedman A.M., Sadock B.J. (eds.): *Comprehensive Textbook of Psychiatry*, ed. 3. Baltimore, Williams & Wilkins, 1980.
33. Rockwell F., Rockwell D., Cove N.: Fifty-two medical student suicides. *Am. J. Psychiatry* 138:198, 1981.
34. Romano J.: Personal communication, 1964.
35. Rose D., Rosow I.: Physicians who kill themselves. *Arch. Gen. Psychiatry* 29:800, 1973.
36. Schneidman E.S.: Psychotherapy with suicidal patients, in Karasu T.B., Bella K.L. (eds.): *Specialized Techniques in Individual Psychotherapy*. New York, Brunner/Mazel, Inc., 1980.
37. Shepherd D.M., Barraclough B.M.: Work and suicide, an empirical investigation. *Br. J. Psychiatry* 136:469, 1980.
38. Solomon J., Arnon D.: Alcohol and other substance abusers, in Hankoff L.D. (ed.): *Suicide Theory and Clinical Aspects*. Littleton, Mass., PSG Publishing Co., Inc., 1979.
39. Solomon M.I., Hellon C.P.: Suicide and age in Alberta, Canada, 1951–1977. *Arch. Gen. Psychiatry* 37:511, 1980.
40. Tsuang M.T.: Suicide in schizophrenics, manics, depressives, and surgical controls: Comparison with general population suicide mortality. *Arch. Gen. Psychiatry* 35:153, 1978.
41. Tsuang M.T., Woolson R.F.: Excess mortality in schizophrenia and affective disorders: Do suicides and accidental deaths solely account for this excess? *Arch. Gen. Psychiatry* 35:1181, 1978.
42. Weltzer H.: Physicians, in Hankoff L.D. (ed.): *Suicide Theory and Clinical Aspects*. Littleton, Mass., PSG Publishing Co., Inc., 1979.
43. Wetzel R.D., Margulies T., Davis R., et al.: Hopelessness, depression and suicide intent. *J. Clin. Psychiatry* 41:159, 1980.

PART III

TREATMENT

12

THE LEGAL NATURE OF THE THERAPEUTIC CONTRACT: RAMIFICATIONS FOR TREATMENT OF AFFECTIVE DISORDERS

SANDRA G. NYE, J.D., M.S.W.

IN EVERY ASPECT of societal living, it is the social institution of the law that regulates relationships of all sorts—between society and the individual, between individuals as they relate to each other, and certainly between the care provider and the individual with whom he has a professional relationship. To an extent greater than that considered comfortable by many psychiatrists, the law thus regulates the practice of psychiatry and has an impact on the nature of the relationship between psychiatrist and patient. In recent years, the medical profession has been at great risk for legal involvement. It is ironic that psychiatrists are statistically at the bottom of the risk list for lawsuits,[1] inasmuch as mental health care delivery, as an aspect of the development of individual civil rights law, has probably been the arena for more legal activity than any other aspect of medicine.

An understanding of several basic legal concepts is necessary in any discussion of the law of psychiatric practice because the psychiatrist-patient relationship is both a legal and a clinical one. From time to time, treatment decisions are influenced by factors other than clinical exigencies. Economic factors become the determiner at times; so may legal mandates or restrictions.

This chapter addresses issues confronting psychiatrists in the legal context of their relationships with their patients, especially issues that arise in the treatment of patients suffering from affective disorders and whose depressive self-destructive or assaultive and impulsive behaviors frequently broach questions of legal intervention.

THE PSYCHIATRIST-PATIENT RELATIONSHIP
AS A LEGAL ENTITY

The legal nature of the therapist-patient relationship is that of a contract.[8] This is so whether or not the word "contract" is ever spoken, whether or not anything has been put in writing, and whether or not the patient is paying a fee for services. The contract commences either when actual service delivery commences or when therapist and patient arrange to enter into the relationship.

The concept of a "meeting of the minds" as the essence of the contract is commonly known. In simplest terms, it refers to a mutuality of expectations: the parties to the contract each understand what is to be done by whom. The relevance of this concept to the psychiatrist-patient contract is apparent. The freedom of the individual to choose whether or not and with whom to enter into a contractual relationship cannot, ipso facto, be presumed when one of the contracting parties is suffering from a mental or emotional disorder such that his cognitive capacity or his judgment, or both, are impaired.[12, 18]

The "meeting of the minds" or mutuality of expectations requirement has been directly adapted for medical practice in the concept of informed consent, without which the physician may not, in a voluntary treatment situation, treat a patient. A question must always arise as to the *clinical* capacity of the patient to give an informed consent. An uninformed consent is a legal nullity; it is no consent at all. For a consent to be valid, three major requirements must be met. The consentor (the patient and/or guardian or parent) must be informed as to the following:

1. *The nature of the condition being treated.* There is some concern about the effect on patients and their families who are exposed to psychiatric diagnoses. Under some circumstances, it might suffice to inform the consentor descriptively of the condition being treated. It is to be noted, however, that if a diagnosis is to be recorded and disseminated (for instance, to a third party payor or a state mental health department), the consentor has an absolute right to know what that diagnosis is so that he or she can make an informed decision as to whether or not to permit this to occur.

2. *Treatment alternatives* possible for the condition being treated and the *probable success of the treatment.* The consentor should be informed of the particular advantages of the various treatment alternatives, including availability and cost.

3. *Foreseeable risks of the several alternatives,* including side effects, and *benefits.* The consentor must be helped to consider the risk/benefit ratio in determining a course of action. It is entirely appropriate to "sell" the treatment modality preferred by the psychiatrist so long as the patient has been properly informed of risks and alternatives.[5, 6, 9, 13]

The old common law rule (that which developed over centuries of case law in Great Britain, from which our United States law generally derives), handled very neatly the issue of legal competence to enter into a contract: an incompetent person could void or cancel his contracts. To protect the commercial world, therefore, a person was presumed to be legally competent unless he had been adjudicated (by a judge in a court hearing) to be incompetent.[17] The medical world has been aware of this concept for years and has used it to obtain a signature on a consent form, even when the patient's hand needed to be guided. The point has always been, of course, to treat the patient's ills as promptly and effectively as possible and to avoid legal (or other) obstacles in the way of that goal. What has not been as well known to the medical world is the second half of the "presumption of competency" rule. Even in the commercial arena, if the condition of the individual was obviously such that he did not know what he was doing (or his behavior was so bizarre as to put the other party on notice), evidence of incompetence could be adduced to overcome the presumption of competence in a legal proceeding to set aside the contract. In essence, a psychiatrist, like any other physician, is required to have the informed consent of his patient in order to treat. When the patient's clinical condition is such that he or she cannot give informed consent or informed refusal, some form of substituted consent is required.*

TERMINATION AND ABANDONMENT

A concomitant of the right of the patient to give an informed consent is the right to refuse treatment, or the right to refuse to enter into a treatment contract. A competent patient (one who has not been adjudicated incompetent by a court proceeding) has that right.[15] A patient also has a right to withdraw from treatment, even when treatment is still required (Miles v. Harris, 194 S.W. 839 [Tex. 1917]).[8] When a psychiatric patient interrupts treatment, careful assessment must be made of the patient's condition and any element of risk involved. The assessment and determination as to the action to be taken *must* be thoroughly documented as a protection to the clinician, should adverse consequences to the patient result.

If the patient is assessed to be at risk, a determination must be made of the possible involvement of significant others and hospitalization (voluntary

---

*Grannum v. Berard, 70 Wash. 2d 304,422 P.2d 812 (1967); Demers v. Gerety, 85 N.M. 641 515 P.2d 645 (Cf. App. 1973). See also Foster[3] and Slovenko.[16]

or involuntary). If the patient is precipitous in terminating treatment but is not at risk, clinically appropriate steps should be taken and documented, followed up with a letter reiterating the clinician's opinion as to the inadvisability of the termination and the importance of continuing. A copy of the letter should be placed in the patient's record.

The other side of the coin is precipitous termination by the clinician. Although a private practitioner has a right to refuse to treat a patient (with the possible exception of rendering emergency services) and may withdraw for any reason (including the patient's recalcitrance or failure to pay the bill), the clinician must withdraw in a clinically appropriate manner, by offering a referral, if indicated. Precipitous withdrawal by the clinician, withdrawal in an inappropriate manner, or leaving a patient stranded when no other services are available exposes the clinician to a lawsuit for abandonment.[8]

COMMITMENT AND CONSENT

Until relatively recently, a commitment proceeding took care of the problem: the commitment was considered to be in the nature of a judicial order on the patient to accept treatment and/or a judicial fiat to the mental health care provider to treat. Court decisions in the past two years indicate that this is no longer the case. Even after commitment, unless there is specific statutory authority to treat over the patient's objection, some form of substituted consent must be obtained. Most commitment statutes today provide for involuntary treatment only if a patient is found to be "dangerous to self or others" or, by reason of his mental condition, is unable to care for his or her basic physical needs. Thus commitment, or a judicial order for involuntary treatment, is not a viable vehicle for imposing treatment on a patient who does not meet either of these criteria and whose refusal is a product of the disease rather than of a rational and informed decision.

For example, the severely depressed patient who refuses desperately needed treatment but who has not expressed any suicidal ideation, the manic or hypomanic who is driving his family to distraction but has not yet reached a stage of sufficient agitation or belligerence to be deemed "dangerous," are not subject to commitment under today's standards.

Even when commitment is possible, several recent court decisions indicate that, while a committed patient may be required to submit to hospitalization, he may still refuse forms of treatment that are not to his liking.*

---

*Davis v. Hubbard, 49 LW 2215, Sept. 30 1980 (U.S.D.C. N. Ohio); Rennie v. Klein, 462 F. Supp. 1131 (N.J. 1978) and 476 F. Supp. 1294 (N.J. 1979); Rogers v. Orkin, 49 LW 2406, Dec. 23, 1980).

Decisions of this nature appear on their face to be absurd; the process by which the court has declared the patient to be mentally ill and in need of involuntary treatment for his own protection and for that of the community deprives the patient of his freedom of choice of locale and places him in the treatment setting, but does not remove from the patient, or confer upon another, the power of decision as to treatment or modality. Medication and electroconvulsive therapy have been the particular targets of these decisions, which generally hold that a legal proceeding in addition to commitment may be necessary to force the recalcitrant patient to accept a prescribed treatment.[17] It is suggested by these decisions that the issue of the patient's actual capacity to make or communicate responsible decisions as to the care of his person must be determined in a competency hearing. If in such hearing the patient is adjudicated incompetent, in whole or in part, a guardian (or conservator, or trustee, or committee—the nomenclature varies from one jurisdiction to another) may be appointed with power to substitute his judgment for that of the patient and to give or decline informed consent on the patient's behalf.

If the patient is not committable, is clearly in need of treatment, but is refusing treatment because his illness has impaired his judgment, the use of a guardian with power to consent to treatment can be an effective method for management of the situation. Local counsel should be retained for advice as to the availability of this mechanism in a given jurisdiction. In Illinois, for example, a "guardian of the person" can be appointed in any case in which a patient lacks sufficient understanding or capacity to make or communicate responsible decisions concerning the care of his person and/or estate (Ill. Rev. Stat., Ch. 110–1/2, §11a, Probate Act of 1975 [1979]). Since a major mental health law revision in 1978, a form of limited guardianship is available: if a person is adjudged to be "disabled" and to lack some but not all of the capacity as specified above, the court may appoint a limited guardian of the person or estate, or both. The court enters a written order stating the factual basis for its findings, the limits of the duties and powers of the guardian, and the legal disabilities to which the disabled person is subject.

The substituted consent concept aroused public interest in the dramatic case of Karen Ann Quinlan (*In the Matter of Karen Ann Quinlan*, 355 A.2d 647 [N.J. 1976]). Since that time, several other cases have been decided around the country, further delineating the parameters of substituted consent. In Illinois, it was clearly the intent of the legislature to use this mechanism as an adjunct to the commitment process. While constitutional lawyers have been in general agreement that the *state* may intervene in an individual's constitutionally protected rights to privacy and liberty only where there is a danger to society (invoking the police power of the State) or helplessness and a need for care (invoking the *parens patriae* power), the notion of guardianship or conservationship in cases in which the individual in question suffers from impairment of judgment is a time-honored concept. If a patient *cannot*, by reason of illness, give an informed consent or refusal for treatment, the guardianship mechanism should be explored.

CONFIDENTIALITY, PRIVACY, AND THE PATIENT AT RISK

The law recognizes that trust is the very essence of the therapeutic relationship. Courts have become aware, too, of the unique power of the pyschotherapist vis-à-vis the patient and the corollary dependency of the patient on the therapist. This recognition has been, in a sense, formalized by defining the duty of the therapist to the patient as that of a *fiduciary*.* Fiduciary means trust. One who owes a fiduciary duty to another owes the very highest duty to protect that person's interests, even above and beyond one's own self-interest. Thus, in any instance in which the therapist's interests may be adverse to that of the patient, the choice must be to place the patient's interests first.

CONFIDENTIALITY

The notion of confidentiality as a sine qua non of psychiatric treatment is so well known and documented as to require no general explanation here. Suffice it to say that the legal rules of confidentiality exceed the parameters of medical ethics and clinical appropriateness; court decisions tell us that inherent in every contract for psychotherapy is an *implied warranty* of confidentiality.† The patient is entitled to assume that, absent some rule of law requiring disclosure (such as a child abuse reporting statute), a therapist will not disclose confidential information without the patient's informed consent.

A patient who is aggrieved by a therapist's breach of confidentiality has several legal remedies by which to seek redress, including a lawsuit for breach of contract based on a breach of the implied warranty. The mental health professional treating a mood-disordered patient may find himself in a serious double-bind. Absent the patient's informed consent to disclose, the therapist might be at risk for a lawsuit if, over the patient's objection, he invokes the aid of the patient's family or others as protection for the patient or warns them of his volatility. At the same time, there are cases which indicate that a therapist does have a duty to protect the patient, and

---

*Alexander v. Knight, 197 Pa. Super. 79, 177 A.2d 142 (1962); Hammonds v. Aetna Casualty and Surety Company, 243 F. Supp. 793 (N.D. Ohio 1965). See also Foster.[3]

†Due v. Rue, 345 N.Y.S. 2d 560, aff'd 33 N.Y.2d 902, 352 N.Y.S.2d 626, 307 N.E.2d 823, 20 A.L.R.3d 1109.

particularly to protect him or others from his own suicidality or homicidality, if either is an issue.

The best advice I can offer with respect to this aspect is the following: When there is a choice between risk to the clinician of a lawsuit and risk to the patient's or someone else's life or safety, the clinician, by reason of the fiduciary relationship with the patient, must consider the welfare of the patient first. Failure to invoke the aid of the family or other resources in the community, including the police, when the patient is at risk for suicide or homicide places the clinician at far greater risk of lawsuit than a breach of confidentiality which the therapist deems necessary to prevent the patient from harming himself.

PRIVACY

The legal concept of privacy is multifaceted, each aspect having relevance to the therapeutic situation:

1. *The right to control one's own body.** This is a basis upon which the right to refuse treatment is predicated. The patient has the right to determine what is to be done to his body, including what substances, if any, are to be introduced into it.

2. *The right to have personal facts kept private.†* This is a corollary to the patient's confidentiality rights. The patient may decide who, if anyone, can have access to personal, private information about him or her.

3. *The right to control the use of one's likeness and identity.‡* A patient may determine how, if at all, his or her name and/or pictures may be used.

4. *The right to the privacy of one's treatment sessions.§* The patient has the right to determine who, if anyone, in addition to treatment personnel or participants may be present at or observe or have knowledge of his or her treatment.

These rights may be relinquished or waived by the patient who gives informed consent to the waiver or relinquishment.[11] This must be done as part of the contract between therapist and patient. It may be agreed upon prior to or on commencement of the treatment, or it may be added later. In any of the above examples, this writer recommends that waiver be in the form of a written informed consent by the patient (or parent or guard-

---

*Winters v. Miller, 446 F.2d 65 (2d Cir. 1970), cert. den. 404 V.S. 985 (1971) (etc. from p. 47 of brief-bracketed citations; Grisewold v. Connecticut, 381 V.S. 479, 484 (1965).

†Roe v. Wade, 410 U.S. 113, 153 (1973); In re Lifschutz, 467 P.2d 557, 567 (1970); Caesar v. Mountanos, 542 F.2d 1064, 1066 (1976). See also Parr[14] and Waltz and Scheuneman.[19]

‡Griffin v. Medical Society of the State of New York, 11 N.Y.S. 2d 109 (N.Y. 1939); Feeney v. Young, 181, N.Y.S. (N.Y. 1920). See also Holder[8] and Waltz and Scheuneman.[19]

§Hagne v. Williams, 37 N.H. 328, 181 A.2d 345, 349, Sup. Ct. N.H. (1962); DeMay v. Roberts, 9 N.W. 146 (Mich, 1881).

ian), outlining with great specificity who will be privy to the private facts and for what purpose.

In some research or teaching settings, a condition of acceptance for treatment might be the patient's willingness to relinquish some aspect(s) of his privacy rights.[8] In any agency or institutional practice setting in which there is no decline option, such conditions for treatment would be violative either of the patient's rights or the agency's funding or other service mandates.

The following generalizations may be inferred (taking into account the reader's own setting, which may permit other policies):

1. Medication or other treatment may not be imposed on an unwilling patient except *(a)* in an emergency wherein it is necessary to prevent the patient from harming himself or another, or *(b)* as a result of legal due process.

2. Even in the absence of a treatment contract or other legal sanctions, identified information about a person, including the fact of "patienthood" or "nonpatienthood," should not be disclosed without the person's written, informed consent. For example, patient material, including charts and tapes, may not be used for teaching purposes without consent.

3. Names and pictures of patients and patient treatment vignettes, including videotapes, may not be used without informed consent, even for such worthy purposes as good will, teaching, fund raising, board of directors orientation, or volunteer recruitment.

4. Treatment sessions may not be observed or listened in on by trainees or others without specific consent. This precludes (unless the patient has given informed consent) the use of audiocassettes or videotapes, classroom use of clinical records by students, or use of a two-way mirror or live interviews of patients for demonstration, grand rounds, or presentation at professional meetings.

THE POTENTIALLY HARMFUL OR SELF-DESTRUCTIVE PATIENT

Much has been written about the right or duty of a therapist to prevent a patient from suicide or from committing a crime, including an act of violence upon another. The notorious *Tarasoff* (Tarasoff v. Board of Regents of the Univ. of Calif., 551 P.2d 334 [Col. 1976]) and *Milano* (McIntosh v. Milano, 168 N.J. Super. 466 [1979]) cases have caused considerable consternation to therapists, who are justifiably concerned over their ability to predict violence, much less control the behavior of a patient. Particularly in light of the high duty of confidentiality and the risk of legal retribution from the patient, therapists overwhelmingly resist any notion of a duty to warn or otherwise be responsible for a potential victim.

The issue of whether or not a therapist has a legal duty to protect the public or a specific intended victim from a dangerous patient is as yet unsettled. The California court in *Tarasoff* held that a therapist has a duty to act to prevent the patient from harming another. This may include hospitalization or other alternatives, including a warning to a known potential victim. In New Jersey, the *Milano* court adopted the *Tarasoff* view. Maryland, however, has rejected the concept in Shaw v. Glickman, 415 A.2d 625 (med. Cf. Spec. App. 1980), based on that state's confidentiality statute. In Illinois, a slightly different situation obtains: in the case of Schneider v. Vine, 15344, App. Ct. of Ill., 4th Dist. appeal dismissed on technicality, the patient murdered several members of a family. In that case, no potential victim had been named by the patient, who had not appeared to the therapist to be dangerous. The plaintiffs (surviving members of the family and the estate of the victims) contended that the therapist had a duty to the general public to act to prevent a patient from committing violence.

The trial court rejected this theory and dismissed the case. The plaintiffs appealed, but the appellate court declined, on the basis of a technicality, to consider the appeal. Thus, while there was no precedent set in the case, at least one trial court has expressed itself as declining to impose on a therapist liability for the behavior of a patient when there was no expressed threat of violence and no potential victim named.

Should or *may* a therapist breach the confidentiality of a patient when the therapist has reason to believe a patient to be dangerous to himself or others? It is suggested that, if the situation is so clear that the therapist is convinced that action should be taken, the primary effort should be in the nature of a clinical intervention, probably hospitalization. If the patient declines hospitalization, the aid of the patient's family should be invoked, if feasible. The next step would be an effort to involuntarily hospitalize. If none of these options are available or efficacious, or if there simply is not the time for these interventions, there is legal precedent to protect the therapist from liability for disclosure to the police or to others (including an intended victim). This precedent derives from two sources: a common law rule that every citizen has a duty to prevent the commission of a felony,[4] and cases in which courts have declined to impose liability on physicians for breach of confidentiality when a physician warned others that the patients suffered from contagious diseases.[*]

Attempts to impose a statutory *duty* on therapists to warn or disclose should be resisted for all the obvious reasons: the uncertainty of predictions of dangerousness, the adverse impact on the therapeutic relationship (prob-

---

*Horne v. Patton, 287 So.2d 824 (Ala. 1974); Simonsen v. Swenson, 177 N.W. 831 (Neb. 1920).

ably the best protection against the potential violent behavior), and the doubtful efficacy of warning an intended victim. Illinois has met the issue by *permitting* (not mandating) the therapist to disclose confidential information when, at the sole discretion of the therapist, it appears necessary to do so to protect the patient or others from imminent risk of serious harm or disease (Ill. Rev. Stat., Ch. 91-1/2, §811, *Mental Health and Developmental Disabilities Confidentiality Act* [1979]). Further, the Illinois statute includes a clause immunizing the therapist against civil or criminal liability by reason of disclosure under the section. This approach seems optional in that the therapist is free to exercise his or her clinical judgment with minimal legal risk.

The position of the therapist treating a suicidal patient is by far more clear: if the patient is at risk for suicide, the therapist has a duty to take steps to prevent the event.[8] From a legal point of view, the issue will be "foreseeability": would the "reasonably prudent psychiatrist" under the circumstances have anticipated a suicide attempt, and if so, what would the appropriate intervention have been? In cases in which suicidality is the presenting problem, failure to guard the patient has been interpreted by the courts as "obvious" negligence. The only question, in such cases, has been the amount of damages to be awarded.* An abortive suicide attempt that results in injury to the patient or others is also a basis for a lawsuit.

The clinical approaches to suicidality are possibly as many and varied as there are numbers of clinicians. I will not presume to argue, from a clinical perspective, the philosophy, efficacy, or correctness of any of these approaches. A view of this matter from the perspective of the *legal* consequences to the clinician, however, suggests the following guidelines:

1. The use of paradox is risky. While some modalities accept or advocate telling a patient that you agree with him that his life is not worth living and that killing himself seems the only thing to do, a judge or jury is not familiar with the technique of paradox and might be expected to react with outrage if the patient follows through.

2. An "understanding" with a patient that you will not take responsibility for his behavior, or a stance that you refuse to be manipulated by suicide threats or gestures and will thus not intervene if he behaves in this manner, is perfectly good practice in some modalities. Again, nonclinician surviving families, judges, and juries will be hard put to understand or accept this position, particularly if the persons suing for malpractice, or even wrongful death, are not the patient with whom you had the "understanding," but the heirs of the deceased patient, who are not party to the "agreement" you had with the patient.

---

*Meir v. Ross General Hospital, 67 Cal. Rptr. 471 (Cal., 1968); U.S. v. Gray, 199 I.2d 239 (CCA10, 1952).

DOCUMENTATION

Malpractice is a major bugaboo for clinicians. Although mental health professionals are least likely of all health care providers to be sued for malpractice, there is a certain incidence of these cases, and precautions should be taken to minimize lawsuit exposure. To win a malpractice case, a patient must establish *all* of the following:

1. He or she was a patient of the clinician being sued; that is to say, the clinician owed a duty of due care to the individual.

2. The clinician was negligent and breached the duty. Another way to state this is that the clinician failed to do that which a duly careful member of his profession would have done under the same circumstances.

3. The negligence of the clinician was the direct cause of an injury to the patient that would not have occurred had the clinician not been negligent.

4. The patient did not contribute to his own injury.[8] The law does not impose upon a therapist any duty to cure, nor is there an implied warranty in the patient-therapist contract of results.[7] Unless the therapist (most unwisely) expressly promises or guarantees a result, so long as one acts "in the manner of a duly careful member of the profession" and is not negligent in service delivery, even if the treatment is not successful or a good-faith error was made in diagnosis or treatment, there is no malpractice.

Often the only instrument available to the clinician as evidence of the quality of care delivered is the clinical record. Aside from the other uses of the record (e.g., communication among staff treating the patient, assuring continuity of care, accountability for audit and payment purposes, supervision), the record is also a means for the clinician to establish what was done for the patient and why. Recording, therefore, should be done with an eye toward establishing that the care provided was appropriate and that it was provided nonnegligently. In a lawsuit, it may be the only protection the clinician has. The rule is, record to reflect the high quality of your service. Unfortunately, courts have taken the view that an incomplete or negligently made record is evidence of negligence in patient care.*

Questions frequently arise as to how much to record and how long records should be kept. As to what and how much recording, several aspects must be considered. The right of a patient to see his record is fairly well established in most jurisdictions, and the trend in this direction continues. Too, others may have access to the record for other than medical purposes and sometimes against the patient's interest. Sufficient data should be recorded to validate the appropriateness of the service delivered. The therapist may decline to record certain highly sensitive material and should

---

*Foley v. Bishop Clarkson Memorial Hospital, 173 N.W.2d 881 (Neb. 1970). See also Holder and *J.A.M.A.*[8,10]

avoid speculations, hunches, judgmental statements, and impressionistic remarks. In fact, inclusion of the *content* of a psychotherapy session in the clinical record may well be inappropriate, depending on the setting and the accessibility of psychiatric records in the jurisdiction in which the care is delivered. Process records kept for reminders, supervision, or consultation should be kept as the *therapist's* record, not the patient's, and should be shredded when no longer needed for the purpose for which they were made.*

Records should be kept for as long as they may be needed (1) to assure continuity of clinical care and (2) to establish the appropriateness of care. There is in every jurisdiction a statute of limitations: a law limiting the time during which a lawsuit may be brought. As the statutes vary from one jurisdiction to another, it is important to ascertain the statute of limitations for malpractice and breach of contract suits in the jurisdiction of the practice. It is suggested that records be kept for at least the period of the longest applicable statute of limitations after the case has been closed. Records may be updated and abstracted from time to time and unnecessary, out-of-date, or irrelevant material removed and destroyed. However, under no circumstances should a record be altered or destroyed in an effort to suppress evidence of wrongdoing on the part of the care provider or after a subpoena has been received demanding it.

REFERENCES

1. Cohen R.J.: *Malpractice.* New York, The Free Press, 1979.
2. Dawidoff D.J.: *The Malpractice of Psychiatrists.* Springfield, Ill., Charles C Thomas, Publisher, 1973, p. 43.
3. Foster H.H.: Informed consent of mental patients, in Barton W.E., Sanborn C.J. (eds.): *Law and the Mental Health Professions.* New York, International Universities Press, 1978.
4. Foster H.: The conflict and reconciliation of the ethical interests of therapist and patient. *J. Psychiatry Law* 3:39, 1975.
5. Fraser G.H., Chadsey P.D.: Informed consent in malpractice cases. *Willamette Law J.* 6:183, 1970.
6. Friedman R.: Informed consent revisited. *Curr. Med.* 19:30, 1972.
7. Guarantee of medical results, editorial comments. *J.A.M.A.* 219:431, 1972.
8. Holder A.R.: *Medical Malpractice Law,* ed. 2. New York, John Wiley & Sons, 1978.
9. Halmstrom J.: Informed consent: Alternatives. *Law Forum* 739, 1973.
10. The importance of medical records, editorial comments. *J.A.M.A.* 228:1, 1974.
11. Legal implications of photographing surgical operations, editorial comments. *J.A.M.A.* 198:221, 1966.
12. Meisel A.: The exception to the informed consent doctrine: Striking a balance between competing values in decision making. *Wisc. L. Rev.* 413, 1979.

---

*Carr v. St. Paul Fire and Marine Insurance Co., 384 F. Supp. (D.C. Ark; 1974); Thor v. Boska, 113 Cal. Rptr. 296 (Cal., 1974); James v. Spear, 338 P.2d 22 (Cal., 1959). See also Cohen[1] and Holder.[8]

13. Noll J.O.: The psychotherapist and informed consent. *Am. J. Psychiatry* 133:1451, 1976.
14. Parr I.: Problems of confidentiality and privileged communications in psychiatry. *Legal Med. Ann.* 327, 1971.
15. Right to refuse necessary treatment, editorial comments. *J.A.M.A.* 221:335, 1972.
16. Slovenko R.: Psychotherapy and informed consent: A search in judicial regulations, in Barton W.E., Sanborn C.J. (eds.): *Law and the Mental Health Professions.* New York, International Universities Press, 1978.
17. Stone A.: *Mental Health and Law.* Boston, Little, Brown & Co., 1972.
18. Slovenko R.: *Psychiatry and Law.* Boston, Little, Brown & Co., 1972.
19. Waltz J.R., Scheuneman T.W.: Informed consent to therapy. *Northwestern Univ. L. Rev.* 64:628, 1970.
20. Warren S., Brandeis L.: The right to privacy. *Harvard L. Rev.* 195:63, 1890.

13

PSYCHOPHARMACOLOGIC
TREATMENT APPROACHES

HENRY LAHMEYER, M.D.

SOMATIC TREATMENT of affective disorders has advanced markedly in the past 20 years. Increased nosologic precision has been a direct result of the new somatic options available. Clinical subgroups have been described that correspond to differential pharmacologic responses, although a one-to-one correspondence has not yet been achieved. As the number of treatable conditions has increased, so has interest in treatment failures. Patient personality issues bearing on medication compliance and the doctor-patient dyad have become essential areas of knowledge for the practicing psychiatrist. In the discussion that follows, it should be kept in mind that somatic therapies are usually necessary for the major affective disorders but that psychotherapy and environmental alterations have roles as important as the somatic treatment itself. Treatment of affective disorders is impossible without a good therapeutic alliance and an understanding of the dynamics involved in patient compliance or noncompliance.

Effective treatment of patients with affective disorders requires that the physician consider several matters simultaneously: (1) diagnosis and severity of the illness, (2) predicted course of the illness, and (3) therapeutic options available. The combined weight of these three parameters will lead to a unique treatment course for each individual. Because these variables change continuously in any individual, corresponding adjustments in treatment must be made.

DIAGNOSIS AND SEVERITY OF THE ILLNESS

The third edition of the *Diagnostic and Statistical Manual of Mental Disorders (DSM-III)* categorizes affective disorders as major affective disorders, other specific affective disorders, and atypical affective disorders. Major affective disorders are further classified according to severity and presence of psychosis. Strauss stated that in addition to severity of illness, the diagnosis of depression should also reflect the symptom course, precipitants, personality, and level of functioning.[130] These represent the axes now used in *DSM-III*, with the exception of axis III, which is physical disorder.

The *DSM-III* offers clear definitions of bipolar and major depressive disorders, validated by consensus of members of the psychiatric profession. The major depressive disorders with so-called endogenous features respond best to treatment.[18] These endogenous symptoms of sleep disturbance, loss of appetite and weight, constipation, psychomotor alterations, loss of interest, pleasure, or sexual drive, diurnal mood variation, excessive guilt, lack of environmental reactivity, and depressed mood that is perceived as alien are important symptoms to monitor, since they may respond early in treatment before the patient feels subjectively better. This means they must also be differentiated from possible side effects of antidepressants.

A few comments regarding the biologic classification of affective disorders should be made. Even though this classification has little current clinical usefulness, it might become more relevant in the near future. Bertilsson, cited by Goodwin et al.,[65] has described Type A and B depressions. Type A depression reponds to amphetamines with euphoria, is associated with low urinary levels of 3-methoxy-4-hydroxyphenylglycol (MHPG), and responds to imipramine or other tricyclics with primary norepinephrine re-uptake blockade. Type B or serotonin-deficient depression has no euphoric response to amphetamines, is associated with high urinary MHPG levels, and responds to amitriptyline, which has more serotonin re-uptake blocking effect. This grouping remains to be validated in further research.

Schatzberg has pointed out that conflicting results have been obtained when MHPG levels are used as a treatment predictor.[119] In an effort to clarify this, he found that patients with low MHPG levels prior to treatment responded best to maprotiline, a new tetracyclic antidepressant. The high MHPG group, however, responded when maprotiline dosage was increased and blood levels raised. Blood level measurements thus may increase the practical value of MHPG. The pharmacologic challenge with amphetamines as a predictor of response to imipramine or desipramine has some clinical support.[50] Goodwin et al. have reviewed other potentially useful biologic hypotheses, such as platelet monoamine oxidase

(MAO) activity, erythrocyte catechol-o-methyltransference (COMT) activity, 5-hydroxyindoleacetic acid (5-HIAA) excretion, and autonomic responsiveness.[65]

High levels and lack of diurnal variation in cortisol levels have been documented in depression.[118] Carroll et al. have demonstrated that many endogenous depressions do not respond to dexamethasone suppression.[31] This test may prove useful in separating antidepressant responders from nonresponders.[23] All these tests have shown some promise as predictors of response, but only the dexamethasone test is easily exploited clinically.

Sleep parameters may be more useful clinically if the work of Kupfer can be replicated.[91] Rapid eye movement (REM) sleep generally occurs much earlier in the sleep of primary depressives (shortened REM latency). Amitriptyline normalizes REM latency in two to three days in those patients who eventually respond to amitriptyline. This technique is noninvasive and could require only one to two hours of sleep monitoring. Home recordings are becoming available so that costs for such a test might become reasonable. Sensory modality-specific brain evoked potentials have also been used to differentiate treatment responders from nonresponders. Baron and associates report that lithium responders show greater augmentation on auditory evoked response (AER).[16] Conversely, imipramine responders show more reduction on AER than nonresponders.[65] Average evoked response studies currently require very expensive technology and are available to fewer psychiatric institutions than sleep technology.

PREDICTED COURSE OF THE ILLNESS

Course is impossible to predict on the basis of clinical presentation alone. However, one can increase the probability of predicting course if the following areas are considered: (1) age at onset, (2) bipolarity, (3) past frequency of illness, (4) family history, and (5) sex.

Affective disorders tend to recur frequently. Age at onset for bipolars is earlier (mean age, 31) than for unipolars (mean age, 41). The older the patient is at onset, the more likely he is to have a recurrence in a relatively short period of time. Cycle length tends to decrease with each additional episode, which suggests a gradual acceleration of the cycling process. Lithium maintenance is probably indicated after three to four recurrences or if the patient is older.[39]

Among bipolar depressives, men show more mania and women more depression. Family history is stronger in bipolar than in unipolar illness. Unipolars have little mania in the family history; bipolars have more mania in the family history and frequently have a family history of depression or suicide. A patient presenting initially with depression but with a family history of bipolar illness may actually be a bipolar type I or type II. Fieve and associates have defined type II as unipolar depressives with a family history of bipolar illness or unipolars who develop spontaneous hypomania or who develop hypomania in response to antidepressants.[53]

THERAPEUTIC OPTIONS AVAILABLE

PATIENT VARIABLES

Patient and clinic variables must be considered in making therapeutic choices. Weissman has pointed out that major affective disorders require psychotherapy for social rehabilitation, but that psychotherapy alone does not prevent relapse.[138] On the other hand, somatic therapies are often useful in treatment and maintenance, but in some resistant cases psychotherapy is the only effective intervention. Supportive psychotherapy is needed for drug compliance and patient education, while psychological aspects of somatic therapies must be considered when weighing various therapeutic options. A thorough review of the subject has recently been made by Weissman.[138] Several issues are particularly germane to the present discussion.

Individuals who experience a clear-cut deviation in mood from a previously perceived normality are easiest to treat. They can clearly describe their symptoms, they are highly motivated, and, generally, underlying personality defenses complicate treatment less. An identified underlying character disorder will usually alter the otherwise straightforward treatment. Characterologically depressed individuals give up their depression only reluctantly, since it provides secondary gain and is familiar, and strong passivity may persist even though depression improves. They may experience considerable social pressure as they improve and will resist the "push" from the environment because they are afraid of the change. Characterologically hypomanic patients resist the loss of their "highs" when lithium is advised; some patients will skip lithium therapy if they feel extra energy is needed. This may be for creativity, life stress, or as a more nonspecific "releasor," used much as alcohol is used, to behave in ways that would normally produce shame.

Families and physicians alike have difficulty with the concept of illness. Unacceptable behavior can be written off as illness by patient or family and lead to infantilization of patient and dependency on or rebellion toward the physician. Behavior that is defensive and characterologic must be distinguished from more extreme fluctuations in mood and be examined in psychotherapy. Extreme fluctuations in mood, when they occur, require somatic therapies and often a more structured psychotherapeutic stance. Family therapy is sometimes needed for patients who play the "manic game"—using the diagnosis of mania to rationalize the affected member's behavior or to make him a scapegoat.[40, 69]

The symbolic meaning of the medication to the patient is an oft-neglected consideration in this era of the remedicalization of psychiatry. A firm therapeutic alliance must be established before medication can be considered. Patients should understand the role of medication and take an active part in this aspect of treatment, just as would be expected in any other aspect of psychotherapy. In general, minor fluctuations in mood do not require pharmacologic adjustments, and a patient's focusing on pharmacology in those instances must be seen as defensive. Medication can be perceived as rejection of the patient's psychological being, so the physician must be careful not to prescribe medication when therapy is going poorly. Medication should be given only when firm indications are present.

Much has been said of the "magic" patients expect from pills.[84] Depressed patients especially expect that passive character traits will also vanish—that the power of the physician will be infused with the pills. Obsessional patients fear loss of control and complain that not enough is being done; when self-punitive feelings coexist, some of these patients will try to induce a similar helpless feeling in the physician who, if unwary, will find himself prescribing very high dosages, switching medications frequently, or using unlikely combinations.

These examples illustrate the importance of the dynamics of medication-giving when considering therapeutic options. Drugs have effects on physiochemical processes but not directly on personality or behavior (see Docherty and associates[45] for further discussion).

Early investigators feared that pharmacotherapy would have a negative effect on psychotherapy, but several recent well-controlled studies have shown the opposite. Antidepressants heighten the patient's perception of the therapist as an empathic person.[69, 95] There is also evidence that psychological and somatic antidepressant treatments affect some of the same psychological mechanisms.[1] DiMascio and associates found that a combination of psychotherapy and antidepressants is superior to either alone.[44] However, it has been shown that only those affectively ill patients who are symptom-free while being maintained on antidepressants make progress in psychotherapy.[138] Drug therapy alone relieves symptoms but does not lead to improved social functioning.

Klein and associates point out the importance of timing in the initiation of psychotherapy.[81] Insight-oriented therapy during the acute phase of illness is often harmful, while a supportive approach that helps keep the patient's activities structured is useful. Support can be given in the form of meeting with the family, explaining the illness, and giving them guidelines for helping the patient and physician.

Shakir and associates note that group therapy is helpful for lithium maintenance and helps patients with chronic concerns about threat of recurrence and the chronicity of the illness.[123] In one group, patients helped each other identify recurrences and encouraged many patients who had previously dropped out of treatment to remain on lithium therapy. Previous studies have shown that discontinuing lithium is the most important factor in treatment failure.[134]

At the most basic level, patients will not improve when suffering from a major affective disorder if they don't have adequate pharmacologic treatment. For this, a strong therapeutic alliance is needed. Most personality traits are altered little by medication; for this they need psychotherapy. Social rehabilitation can be aided by group, family, and individual therapy; sometimes several treatment modalities must be combined. Effective treatment, therefore, requires a bimodal approach that pays attention to levels of biologic and psychological organization simultaneously.

PHARMACOLOGIC OPTIONS

All drugs used in the treatment of affective disorders are potentially very toxic and lethal. Patient reliability, therefore, is essential. The treatment team must know how each patient comprehends the complex issues of lithium and antidepressant treatment. Physical disability can limit or dictate somatic therapy. For example, tricyclics and MAO inhibitors have major side effects at therapeutic levels which may be prohibitive in patients with closed-angle glaucoma, prostatic hypertrophy, or organic brain syndrome.[100]

These patient variables may prove important when considering maintenance therapy for recurrent unipolar depression. Side effect profile and patient compliance variables are therefore the important considerations.

SOCIAL VARIABLES

The previous course of the illness and the patient's response to treatment must be taken into account in deciding whether to hospitalize a patient or not. Serious suicidal thoughts, hopelessness, or social deterioration to the point of exhausting social and family supports are good indicators of the need for hospitalization. Hospitalization will often relieve the patient and social system of a stress that can promote the severity of an illness. Psychosis is an indication for hospitalization.

The more severely ill patients require more complex, extended interventions. The major affective disorders require somatic therapy, whether one chooses pharmacologic agents, electroconvulsive therapy (ECT), or a combination of the two. During the episode of major affective disorder and, more importantly, after the episode, individual, group, family, and appropriate combinations of psychological therapies are needed.[33] The other specific affective disorders may not require somatic therapies; they do require consistent efforts in their psychological management.

The remainder of this discussion addresses only the somatic therapies, with particular emphasis on the practical management, logical decision making, drug side effects, drug-drug interactions, and some general principles of pharmacotherapy. Before the management of the affective disorders is considered, several pharmacologic points should be made about the specific agents.

TRICYCLIC ANTIDEPRESSANTS

PHARMACOLOGY

Tricyclic antidepressants are similar to phenothiazines in structure and were first used in treating schizophrenics. In 1957–1958, Kuhn found that these compounds had little antipsychotic efficacy but were mood elevating and behaviorally activating.[83, 90] Tricyclic compounds have two benzene rings joined by a central seven-membered ring. The central ring is connected to an aliphatic chain with a terminal nitrogen which has either one methyl (secondary amines) or two methyl groups attached (tertiary amines) (Fig 13–1).[70] The relationship of the tricyclics to the phenothiazines and to each other is shown in Figure 13–2.

TABLE 13–1.—TRICYCLIC ANTIDEPRESSANT PROFILE

	SEDATION	ANTICHOLINERGIC	STRUCTURE	DOSAGE AND PLASMA LEVEL RESPONSE CURVE
Amitriptyline (Elavil)	+ + + +	+ + + +	Tertiary amine	150–300 mg; linear
Doxepin (Sinequan)	+ + +	+ +	Tertiary amine	150–300 mg; linear
Imipramine (Tofranil)	+ +	+ + +	Tertiary amine	150–300 mg; linear
Nortriptyline (Aventyl, Pamelor)	+ +	+ +	Secondary amine	Therapeutic window, approx. 75–150 mg/day
Desipramine (Norpramine	+	±	Secondary amine	100–200 mg/day; unknown
Protriptyline (Vivactil)	–	+	Secondary amine	Therapeutic window, 40–70 mg/day

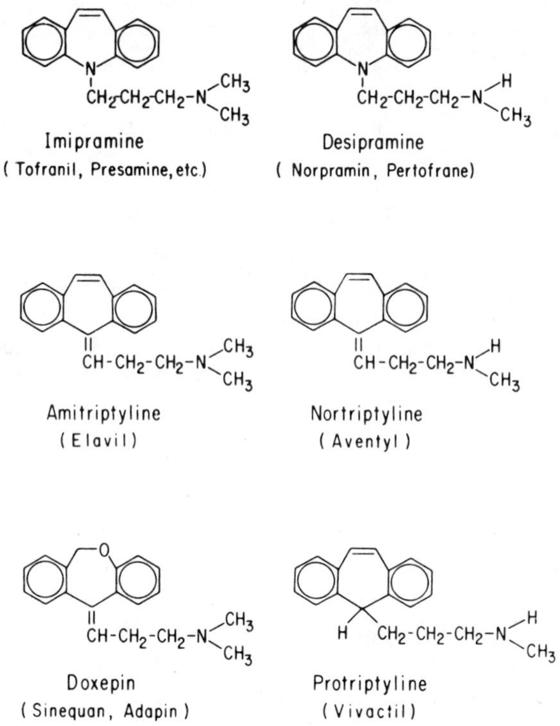

Fig 13-1.—Tricyclic antidepressants. (From Baldessarini R.J.: Chemotherapy, in Armand M., Nicholi J.V. (eds.): *Harvard Guide to Modern Psychiatry.* Cambridge, Mass., Belknap Press of Harvard University Press, 1978. Used with permission.)

Table 13-1 lists some of the secondary and tertiary amines, their relative effects on neurotransmitter systems, and a summary of the plasma level–therapeutic response relationship. Tertiary amines are first metabolized to several active metabolites, although the parent compound may also be active. Secondary amines have only one active metabolite. Because of the more complex metabolism of the tertiary amines, plasma level determinations may have less relationship to clinical response.[61] Wide variations in plasma levels exist between individuals taking the same dosage of tricyclics. Genetic factors play a role in absorption metabolism and clinical response.[87]

Tricyclics are primarily metabolized by the liver; they are partially protein-bound and partially free in plasma. This equilibrium and the rate of liver metabolism is genetically determined, which partially accounts for individual dosage requirements.[2] Tricyclic half-life is approximately 24 hours but increases markedly with age because liver metabolism slows and

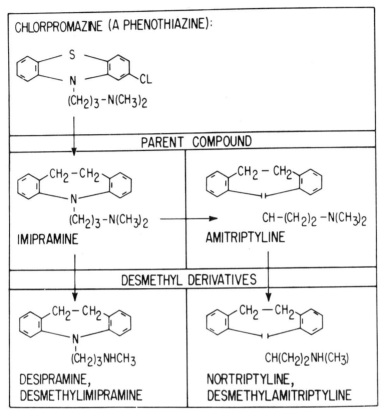

Fig 13–2.—Structures of major tricyclic antidepressants and their relationship to the phenothiazines. (From Klein D.F., et al.: *Diagnosis and Drug Treatment of Psychiatric Disorders: Adults and Children,* Baltimore, the Williams & Wilkins Co., copyright 1981. Used with permission.)

plasma protein binding decreases. The elderly thus require smaller dosages, since the drug amount delivered to the CNS is increased while CNS tolerance is reduced.[42] Exogenous factors also play a role in altering plasma blood levels. Table 13–2 lists drugs that raise or lower tricyclic levels. These drugs apparently act by affecting liver enzymes and either compete with or induce the enzymes. Polypharmacy should therefore generally be avoided.[26, 141]

The relationship of plasma levels to clinical response is complex and the value of routine plasma levels in the clinical setting is controversial. Several investigators have demonstrated that the plasma level–dose response curve for a secondary amine, nortriptyline, is an inverted U, so that low and high

TABLE 13–2.—DRUGS AFFECTING
TRICYCLIC BLOOD LEVELS

RAISE TCA LEVELS
Methylphenidate (Ritalin)
Disulfiram
Phenothiazines
Estrogens
Morphine
Meperidine
Antacids
LOWER TCA LEVELS
Barbiturates
Smoking
Ethanol
Glutethimide
Anticonvulsants
Meprobamate
Chloral hydrate

blood levels correlate with poor results.[81] This leaves a narrow range of effective blood levels, the "therapeutic window." In reviewing the literature on the tertiary amines, Shaw indicates that in general, blood levels positively correlate with clinical response.[124] Higher dosages may produce side effects but do not inhibit clinical response.

Tricyclics have a cocaine-like action, blocking the re-uptake of biogenic amines. Doxepin may have additional mechanisms since it seems to block the antihypertensive effect of guanethidine less than the other tricyclics. These agents also have differential effects on serotonin, norepinephrine, and acetylcholine.[117] The precise combination of effects in a given individual is not predictable unless family or previous personal history of tricyclic response is available. The anticholinergic effects are especially relevant, since they cause most of the side effects. Table 13–1 lists the tricyclics in order of decreasing anticholinergic activity.[126]

SIDE EFFECTS

Side effects of tricyclics are summarized in Table 13–3. The anticholinergic effects are dose-related and are more bothersome to the elderly.

Cardiovascular effects are the most important side effects. Tricyclics have quinidine-like effects and therefore slow conduction time. Doxepin, unlike the other tricyclics, has little effect on cardiac conduction. Apparently it is a less potent blocker of amine re-uptake, although cardiac toxicity can occur with overdose,[122] an effect that may increase heart block[71] but can improve premature atrial or ventricular contractions.[19] The negative ionotropic effect may aggravate heart failure.[24] Palpitations can result from the anticholinergic action.[37] Orthostatic hypotension can be marked and dangerous in patients at risk for stroke but can be useful in monitoring pharmacologic activity.[63] Tricyclics produce negative ionotropic effects, so congestive heart failure and postmyocardial infarction are relative contraindications.[100]

Davidson studied sudden death in men experiencing cold or exercise stress at the time of the first snowfall at the beginning of the Canadian winter and found that for every death in an individual not on tricyclics, there were eight in persons who had been taking tricyclics.[41] The combination of cardiac disease, stress, and tricyclic antidepressants may be particularly lethal.

TOXICITY

Tricyclic overdoses are particularly difficult to manage and are usually treated by the internist[120]; patients can present with coma, hypotension, and severe cardiac arrhythmias.[21, 37] Supportive measures, including intravenous fluids and cardiac monitoring, are often necessary and frequently must continue for days, since the plasma and tissue half-life of tricyclics is very long. Physostigmine will alleviate the comatose state but the effect is transient, and some risk of seizure exists with this treatment.[100] The psychiatrist must remember that consciousness may fluctuate, so apparent recovery must last 24 hours before transfer or discharge is considered.

Drug-drug interactions can lead to toxicity[97] (Table 13–4): (1) Anticholinergic drugs such as phenothiazines, proprietary sleeping pills, and antihistamines increase the possibility of toxic psychosis. (2) Some drugs are degraded more slowly because of blockade of the amine pump. Levodopa can thus produce more cardiovascular and cerebrotoxic effects, while reserpine, which releases catecholamine levels, can cause paradoxic hypertension, since degradation of catecholamines is blocked by tricyclics.

MONOAMINE OXIDASE INHIBITORS

PHARMACOLOGY

Monoamine oxidase inhibitor use began in the late 1950s and introduced the modern era of mood-altering psychopharmacology. Structurally, MAO inhibitors are similar to amphetamines.[70] Some have hydrazine structures and others are the result of cyclization of amphetamine-nonhydrazines. Monoamine oxidase inhibitors suppress not only MAO, but also COMT, both of which are important in the regulation of norepinephrine, serotonin, and dopamine metabolism. As enzyme inhibition occurs, over one to two

TABLE 13–3.—TRICYCLIC SIDE EFFECTS*

SYMPTOM	RELATIVE FREQUENCY	MECHANISM	THERAPY
ANTICHOLINERGICS			
Dry mouth	15.4%. Very common: amitriptyline most, imipramine less, desipramine least	Binds receptor side of acetylcholine	Neostigmine Pilocarpine 1%–2%
Blurred vision		Anticholinergic	
Constipation	4.6%		
Toxic psychosis	35% over age 40	Same, aggravated by prostatic hypertrophy	Physostigmine, 1–2 mg intramuscularly as needed
Delayed micturition and ejaculation	Fairly common		Reversed by dihydroergotamine, 10–20 drops 3 times a day
Acute glaucoma	Rare, more common with amitriptyline	Same	Pilocarpine drops
CARDIOVASCULAR			
Postural hypotension	Uncommon in normals; common in patients with cardiovascular disease	Central adrenergic neurons or peripheral	May be useful in hypertensives; tell patients about reaction; steroids
Hypertension	Uncommon	Can potentiate pressor effects of epinephrine or norepinephrine	Discontinue
Arrhythmias Prolonged PR interval and T wave inversion	Common, not present with doxepin	Anticholinergic and adrenergic	Avoid in patients with preexisting defects, PAT, CHF angina
Heart block	May occur in preexisting right or left bundle-branch block or occasionally in normals	Quinidine-like effect	Cardiac consultation indicated
Premature atrial and ventricular contractions	May be improved	Quinidine-like action prolongs intraventricular depolarization and repolarization	May be able to discontinue quinidine and procainamide

Cardiomyopathy	Uncommon	Negative ionotropic action; depletes amines	May aggravate heart failure
Left bundle-branch block	Rarely in normals	Quinidine-like effect	Usually benign
NEUROLOGIC			
Tremor	Common		
Sedation	Common, 10%	Anticholinergic except with doxepin	Bedtime dosage
Mania	Common in bipolars	Increase in biogenic amines	Cover with lithium or avoid in bipolars
Seizures	Rare	Central anticholinergic	Discontinue
ALLERGIC			
Eosinophilia	4%–7%	Unknown	Benign
Jaundice	Rare	Probably obstructive as with phenothiazines	Discontinue
Agranulocytosis	Rare	Idiosyncratic	Discontinue
Rashes–edema	Rare	Allergic	Usually transient
MISCELLANEOUS			
Weight gain	Common	Alterations in glucose metabolism	Diet and exercise; avoid caloric fluids
Hyperpigmentation	Protriptyline		Discontinue
Perspiration	Common	Adrenergic	Benign
Nausea and vomiting	Common in early treatment		Increase dose gradually

*Data from Kantor et al.,[76] 1978, and Mielke,[100] 1975. PAT = paroxysmal atrial tachycardia; CHF = congestive heart failure.

TABLE 13–4.—SOME SIGNIFICANT DRUG-DRUG INTERACTIONS

AGENT	ANTIPSYCHOTICS	MAOs	TRICYCLICS
Meperidine		Resembles narcotic overdose or excitement seizures and fever	
Oral hypoglycemics		Potentiation	
Insulin		Potentiation	
Diuretics		Hypotension	
Eutonyl Nitrofuran Funzolidane Procarbazine			Have MAO inhibiting properties and therefore dangerous when combined with tricyclics or sympathomimetics
Amphetamines Methylphenidate (Ritalin) Neosynephrine		Hypertension; intracranial hemorrhage possible	
Anesthetics	Potentiate hypotension	Potentiation	Cardiac arrhythmias
Levodopa	Antagonism	Hypertension	Decreased absorption
Reserpine	Potentiation	Hypertension; CNS excitement	Hypertension arrhythmias
Aldomet	Potentiation	Paradoxic hypertension	Antagonism
Guanethidine	Some antagonism with withdrawal hypotension	Potentiation of severe hypertension	Antagonism, severe withdrawal hypotension
Hypotensive diuretics	Potentiation	Potentiation	Potentiation
Clonidine	Potentiation (?)	Potentiation (?)	Antagonism
Anticholinergics (antiparkinsonian atropine drugs)	Potentiation	Potentiation of dry mouth and CNS delirium	Same as for MAO but more so

weeks, intracellular amine concentrations rise, but amine levels also rise immediately after administration so that direct action on catecholamine storage sites must also occur. This results in some psychic stimulation within a matter of days, especially for tranylcypromine, but full antidepressant effects may take two to four weeks.

Phenelzine has a higher incidence of anticholinergic side effects but has less potential for hypertensive crisis. Phenelzine is metabolized by acetylation. The rate of acetylation varies widely from individual to individual, so that flexibility in dosage is needed with phenelzine.[73] Slow acetylators and patients who achieve over 85% MAO inhibition are most likely to respond to these agents.[94]

SIDE EFFECTS

Loss of appetite, dry mouth, headache, and orthostatic hypotension and mental confusion are common complaints. Insomnia and overactivity can also occur.

TOXICITY

Liver damage has been reported, although it is very rare. Hypertensive reactions to certain foods containing tyramine and sympathomimetic drugs can occur, so cardiovascular instability is a relative contraindication for these drugs.[20] Table 13–5 lists foods and drugs to be avoided.

The half-life of MAO inhibitors in not long, but MAO inhibition is. This must be remembered because monoamine depleters such as amphetamines and tyramine will produce toxic effects for up to ten days after MAO inhibitors are discontinued. Because of the long-lasting MAO inhibition, a washout of at least ten days is required before tricyclic antidepressants or tyramine-containing foods can be ingested. Paradoxic hypertension can occur with reserpine or guanethidine. Hypertensive crises can be treated with the α-blocker phentolamine in doses of 5 mg as needed, until the crisis passes. If phentolamine is unavailable, the α-blocking properties of chlorpromazine can be exploited. Patients with preexisting cardiovascular disease and those judged unable or unwilling to follow the diet should be excluded from this type of therapy.

TABLE 13–5.—FOODS AND DRUGS THAT CAN LEAD
TO HYPERTENSIVE CRISIS

FOOD OR DRUG	POTENTIAL
Red wine	+ +
Beer	+ +
Vanilla	
Aged cheese (camembert, liederkranz, edam, cheddar)	+ + + +
Fava beans	
Pickled herring	+ + + +
Coffee	+
Canned figs	
Chocolate	
Yeasts and yeast products	+ +
Yogurt	
Chicken livers	
Amphetamines	+ + + +
Cold remedies with sympathomimetics (neosynephrine)	+ +
Levodopa, Aldomet	+ + +
Bee venom	
Aged meats	+ + + +

LITHIUM

PHARMACOLOGY

Lithium carbonate is the most commonly used lithium salt for the treatment and prophylaxis of affective disorders. Lithium is a member of the alkaline metal group of elements and physiologically shares properties with sodium and potassium. The mechanism of action is unknown, but lithium may act to increase serotonin turnover and decrease norepinephrine availability in such a way that receptor activation potential is modulated.[58] Many other mechanisms have been postulated, but none convincingly explains the action of lithium as prophylactic for both mania and depression.[12]

Lithium is excreted, unmetabolized, by the kidney. In the kidney it competes with sodium for reabsorption; low serum sodium levels can produce higher blood lithium levels and sodium loading can lead to lithium depletion. Natriuretic diuretics can produce lithium toxicity, as can excessive sweating. Lithium readily passes through cell membranes and the blood-brain barrier. The half-life is approximately 24 hours but may be much longer in the aged.[42] The distribution across the cell membrane is probably genetically determined.[46] These genetic differences lead to different intracellular lithium concentrations and might account for lack of clinical response in some individuals. Red blood cell levels may more closely correspond to CNS lithium levels than plasma levels. This monitoring can be useful in nonresponders and in cases of toxicity when normal plasma levels exist.[98]

SIDE EFFECTS

Early in treatment lithium produces nausea, which is probably a direct effect of the salt on the gastric mucosa. This can be partially alleviated by administering the drug with meals.

Table 13–6 lists other negative side effects of lithium in order of importance. Vomiting, diarrhea, and muscle twitching are early signs of toxicity in young adults, while mental confusion more commonly occurs in the elderly.

Hand tremor can occur without other signs of toxicity and can be treated, if desired, with propranolol.[79] Some patients maintained on lithium for prophylaxis develop diabetes insipidis, while others develop an inability to acidify their urine; both might be indicators of irreversible renal damage.[17, 72] Ostrow has found that patients maintained on lithium develop hyperchloremic metabolic acidosis, and some develop mild hypercal-

TABLE 13–6.—SIDE EFFECTS OF LITHIUM TREATMENT

	INITIAL HARMLESS EFFECT	PERSISTENT, USUALLY HARMLESS	PRODOME OF INTOXICATION	PERSISTENT, POSSIBLY HARMFUL
Nausea	+	+	−	
Loose stools	+	+	−	
Vomiting, diarrhea	−	−	+	
Fine tremor of hands	+	+	−	
Coarse tremor of hands	−	−	+	
Weight gain	−	+	−	
Acne	−	+	−	
Sluggishness	−	±	+	
Vertigo	−	−	+	
Dysarthria	−	−	+	
Polyuria, polydypsia	+	+	−	+
Edema	−	+	−	
Leukocytosis	−	+	−	+
Increased reflexes	−	−	+	
Goiter, hyperthyroidism	−	+	−	+
Cardiac AV blockade	−	−	−	+

cemia.[106] This finding implies possible long-term renal effects of lithium and may bear on the etiology of manic-depressive psychosis, since shifts in blood and CSF calcium levels correlate with changes in affective states.[30] Cardiac effects are generally limited to nonspecific T wave changes similar to those produced by hypokalemia, but an increased incidence of sudden death in susceptible individuals is noted in a review by Reisberg and Gershon.[113] Intracardiac conduction is slowed, particularly at the AV node. Heart block should be carefully assessed by a cardiologist prior to initiation of lithium therapy.[139, 143]

Hypothyroidism and goiter can develop and should be watched for.[7] Weight gain and acne are common complaints and can be somewhat avoided by drinking noncaloric fluids, since lithium often induces increased fluid intake.

TOXICITY

Toxicity is associated with high intracellular lithium levels, but suicide by overdose of lithium is rare because vomiting usually ensues.[120] West and Meltzer have also reported toxicities in acute mania when blood levels were below toxic range, but they did not measure red blood cell levels.[140] Toxicity that develops gradually over days because of hot weather, diuretics, or salt ingestion can produce severe neurologic signs, oliguria, and mental confusion; some of these effects may be irreversible.[93] Sodium loading and dialysis have been recommended as treatment for severe toxicity.[113] Toxicities have also been known to occur within the normal serum lithium range of 0.6 to 1.5 mEq/L. Elizur and associates point out the usefulness of the red blood cell-plasma ratio in these situations.[47]

PHARMACOLOGIC MANAGEMENT OF THE MAJOR AFFECTIVE DISORDERS

MANAGEMENT OF THE DEPRESSIVE PHASE

As previously mentioned, antidepressants have considerable toxic potential. Because these drugs are not without risks, we should question whether their risk-benefit ratio warrants their use. Girdwood compared the relative risk of antidepressants versus the morbid risk of depression.[59] He calculated that with a risk of suicide in the range of 1 in 40 untreated depressive episodes, the relative risk of death was 10,000 per million untreated illnesses, compared with only 2.3 deaths per million prescriptions of amitriptyline or 17.2 deaths per million prescriptions of phenelzine. It appears that the risk of death for untreated cases of depression is approximately 100 to 1,000 times greater than if treated with antidepressants. These figures are particularly applicable to the major affective disorders, in which the risk-benefit ratio is clearly favorable.

Severely depressed individuals are more likely to be suicidal, although this is less true if marked retardation has set in. Agitated, suicidal patients are at particular risk even in an inpatient setting, and suicides there are often rationalized by the notion that strong intent is impossible to prevent.

Tricyclic Antidepressants

Patients at low risk of suicide should be treated with adequate doses of one chosen tricyclic for at least four weeks before switching to another tricyclic. If no response occurs in this period, MAO inhibitor or another tricyclic can be tried. Predictors of a positive response to tricyclics are upper socioeconomic class, insidious onset, anorexia, weight loss, middle and late insomnia, and psychomotor disturbance.[104, 18] Previous positive response to a particular tricyclic or a family history of a specific drug response is also helpful in predicting response.[107] Symptoms of depression must be assessed and differentiated from tricyclic side effects. Drug choice should be based on side effects, since all tricyclic antidepressants are equally efficacious (see Table 13–3).[103]

An agitated patient with insomnia should ideally be given amitriptyline or doxepin, since these are the most sedating. Dosage should be increased until mild side effects occur, such as postural hypotension and blurred vision. For amitriptyline, 75 mg is generally given the first week, 150 mg the second, 225 mg the third, and 300 mg the fourth week.[78] If side effects are not tolerated well with amitriptyline, one should reconsider the severity of the depression, since severely depressed individuals usually tolerate side effects, whereas nonendogenously depressed or anxious patients are often exquisitely sensitive to side effects.

Nortriptyline and doxepin have fewer anticholinergic effects and are generally sedating enough to improve sleep. The secondary amine nortriptyline should be given for four weeks in sufficient doses to produce mild side effects. If no or only minimal response is achieved, the dosage should be reduced somewhat for seven days. Plasma determinations of nortriptyline are useful if clinical response is delayed or toxicity appears.

Table 13–7 summarizes studies that have shown a relationship between tricyclic blood levels and clinical response. Tricyclic blood level determinations are not as useful clinically as anticonvulsant blood levels in the management of seizure disorders, but these determinations can be useful in cases of poor response to medication or to monitor toxicity in a vulnerable patient (e.g., the elderly depressed person).

Amitriptyline, doxepin, and nortriptyline are sedating, and a bedtime dosage is most rational. The half-life of all the tricyclics is sufficiently long (greater than 24 hours) that once-daily administration is adequate.

MAO Inhibitors

Patients who can reliably follow a diet and patients who are hospitalized and are either refractory to tricyclics or cannot tolerate their side effects should be given a trial of MAO inhibitors. Some atypical depressives with immature personality features or nonspecific panic attacks or neurotics with agoraphobia may respond better to these agents than to tricyclics.[80, 116.]

Because these drugs have stimulant properties they should be given during the day. Tranylcypromine is usually given in dosages of 30 mg/day for three weeks. If no signs of improvement occur, the dosage can be increased in 10-mg increments every ten days until postural hypotension occurs. Three additional weeks at this dosage without results represents a clinical failure.[124] Phenelzine, a hydrazine derivative, is usually given in doses of 50–75 mg/day. Phenelzine is metabolized by the liver through a process called acetylation. If side effects are not experienced, "fast acetylation" can be assumed and dosage increased. Phenelzine produces less stimulation and has less toxic risk of food reaction, so it is more appropriate for agitated patients. Isocarboxazid in doses of 20–30 mg/day is even safer than phenelzine and therefore is ideal for older patients.[124] Doses in the range of 20–30 mg/day should be adequate.

TABLE 13–7.—TRICYCLIC PLASMA LEVELS AND OUTCOME

AUTHOR, NO. OF SUBJECTS, POPULATION STUDIED	DOSE, DURATION OF STUDY	PLASMA LEVELS, ng/ml (unless stated otherwise)	MAJOR FINDINGS	COMMENTS
NORTRIPTYLINE				
Asberg et al. N = 19 Endogenous	75–225 mg/day; 2 wk	Range, 32–164; mean, 90.1 (± 40.1)	Curvilinear relationship; therapeutic range, 50–140 ng/ml	2-wk treatment period and concomitant use of barbiturates were drawbacks, corrected in future studies
Burrows et al. N = 80 Mixed depressives, including "personality problems" and bereaved	75–250 mg/day; most patients (n = 65) given 150 mg/day for 4 wk	Range not given; mean at 4 dose levels: 75 mg, 65.9 (± 34.2); 150 mg, 170.9 (± 108.2); 200 mg, 227.0 (± 108.1); 250 mg, 378 (± 92)	No significant relationships found for sample as a whole	Sample included patients with depressive character disorders and bereaved, diagnostic groups unlikely to benefit from antidepressants
Kragh-Sorenson et al. N = 30 Endogenous	150 mg/day; 4 wk	Range, 48–238; mean at 4 wk, 141 (± 48.2)	Negative correlation of plasma level and effect	Supports possibility of curvilinear relationship because 18/21 with 175 ng/ml but 1/8 with 175 ng/ml recovered; bottom of therapeutic window not defined, since only 1 patient had 50 ng/ml
Burrows et al. N = 40 Mixed depressives	Dose adjusted to keep half of patients at 49 ng/ml, half at 140 ng/ml	Specific data not given; half of patients at 140 ng/ml, half at 49 ng/ml	Neither blood level superior	See comments on sample of other Burrows study; design of this study would not detect curvilinear relationship
Kragh-Sorenson et al. N = 24 Endogenous	Dose adjusted to achieve two groups: 180 ng/ml and 150 ng/ml	Range in 150 group, 82–168 ng/ml; in 180 group, 170–296 ng/ml	Clinical response better in group with plasma level = 150 ng/ml	Well-done study; after 4 wk 2 patients at 180 and 3 patients at 168–178 ng/ml had level lowered to 150; all recovered by 6th wk; 5 patients continuing at 180 did not recover by 6th wk (this was prospectively planned)

Burrows et al. N = 32 Mixed depressives	150 mg/day; 4 wk	Range, 24–592; mean at 4 wk, 171 (±19)	No correlations	Lack of correlation obtained by this group may be due to exclusion of all severely depressed patients; thus, sample studied contains preponderance of patients least likely to respond to the drug
Ziegler et al. N = 18 Feighner criteria depressives	Dose increased, if no side effects, up to 150 mg/day by end of 8 days; length of study, 6 wk	Mean plasma level, 138 ng/ml; mean dose by 6 wk, 127 mg/day (by pill count); range of plasma level, 53–252 ng/ml	9 patients in therapeutic window all rated recovered, but only 3/6 above window improved	This is 4th study in which best clinical response was found when plasma levels of nortriptyline were kept below upper level of therapeutic window (139 ng/ml)
PROTRIPTYLINE Whyte et al. N = 28 Mixed depressives	10 mg q.i.d. for 3½ wk	Mean, 808 nmol/L (±47)	Negative correlation of plasma level and effect; post hoc division into low, median, and high plasma level group suggests curvilinear relationship; median plasma levels associated with best response	Should be interpreted cautiously; only 50% of sample improved, including 5/15 depressive psychotics; therefore, 40 mg/day protriptyline may be too low, and good responders may contain high percent of placebo responders
IMIPRAMINE Walter N = 16 Endogenous depression	In 8 patients, 150–225 mg/day; in 8 patients, weight-multiplied	Imipramine range, 2.5–71.0 ng/L; mean at 4 wk, 33.8 ng/L	Responders have significantly higher levels	Desipramine levels not measured; unclear how this relates to outcome
Ballinger et al. N = 31 Neurotic depression and unipolar depressives	150 mg/day; 13 patients also received amylobarbital and 6 nitrazepam; 3 wk	Range of desipramine, 20–600 mg/ml; range with imipramine and desipramine, 100–1,400 mg/ml.	No correlations	Study lasted 3 wk, probably too short for complete therapeutic effect; pure imipramine group did best; since assignment to barbiturate depended on presence of symptoms, these patients may have had insufficient imipramine dose, and the barbiturate served to lower it further

(Continued)

TABLE 13–7.—*Continued.*

AUTHOR, NO. OF SUBJECTS, POPULATION STUDIED	DOSE, DURATION OF STUDY	PLASMA LEVELS, ng/ml (unless stated otherwise)	MAJOR FINDINGS	COMMENTS
Perel et al. N = 18 Endogenous	150 mg/day; 4 wk	Not given; sum of imipramine and desipramine determined	Positive correlation between plasma level and effect	Delusional depressives removed post hoc
Gram et al. N = 24 Endogenous	75 mg t.i.d.; 5 wk	Range of imipramine, 22–232 ng/L; range of desipramine, 19–585 ng/L	No correlation between plasma level of imipramine, desipramine, or both and clinical effect	Post hoc, 11/12 recovered patients had 45 ng/L of imipramine and 75 ng/L of desipramine; this requires testing in prospective studies; high concentration of imipramine or desipramine did not have deleterious effect
Glassman et al. N = 60 Endogenous depressives	1 wk of observation followed by 1 wk of placebo and 28 days of imipramine, 3.5 mg/kg	Total tricyclic (imipramine, desipramine) mean levels, 200 ng/ml ± 137; range, 50–1,050 ng/ml	Patients above median plasma level (180 ng/ml) had superior response; data clearly suggest linear rather than curvilinear relationship	Delusional unipolar females did poorly even if plasma level was above median
Oliver-Martin et al. N = 24 Endogenous and neurotic depression	75 mg at noon and 75 mg at 7 A.M. for 3 wk	Imipramine, 108–118 ng/ml; desmethy imipramine, 130–160 ng/ml	Improvement correlates with plasma levels of imipramine plus desmethy imipramine alone but not imipramine levels alone; no neurotic depressions improved	Patients also received lithium, benzodiazepines, methaqualone, levopromazine; short treatment period; 54% of original sample eliminated for analysis because taking phenothiazines
AMITRIPTYLINE Braithwaite et al. N = 15 Mixed depressive illness	150 mg/day; 6 wk	Nortriptyline range, 20–278 ng/ml; amitriptyline range, 20–228 ng/ml	Positive correlation of plasma level and effect	Braithwaite concludes plasma concentrations of total tricyclic <120 ng/ml are ineffective; Kane analysis of data indicates this is not true, that patients below did improve

Ziegler et al. N = 18 Feighner criteria	Amitriptyline, if tolerated, to 150 mg h.s.; mean dose (131 mg/day) by 6 wk	Total tricyclic mean, approx. 120 ng/ml; nortriptyline mean, approx. 60 ng/ml at 6 wk	Positive correlation between plasma level of total tricyclic and between amitriptyline alone and improvement	One patient who had total tricyclic level >250 was excluded post hoc (she had done poorly), although 2 of Braithwaite's patients >250 did well; arbitrary exclusion makes analyses less definitive
Kupfer et al. N = 16 Diagnoses, based on Research Diagnostic Criteria, included 11 unipolar (2 psychotic), 4 bipolar (2 psychotic), 1 schizoaffective	Active medication for 26 days; a 7-day placebo period followed by a fixed dose schedule with a final dose of 200 mg of amitriptyline on days 14–26	Total tricyclic varied, 538–69 ng/ml	Significant correlation was found for plasma level of combined tricyclic, amitriptyline alone, nortriptyline alone, and clinical outcome; 77% of patients who achieved level of 200 ng/ml responded; no responders <200 ng/ml	Low response rate (7/16) and 200-mg dose require caution in interpretation; authors suggest some patients improved after the study when dose was raised; not clear what portion of variance is accounted for by plasma level or dose
Coppen N = 54 Unipolar primary depressives, Criteria of Research Council, Hamilton score of 16 or more	75 mg/day for 3 days; thereafter, 150 mg for 39 days; 7 to 12-day placebo period preceded active drug	Amitriptyline range, 46–391 ng/ml; nortriptyline, 39–366 ng/ml	Negative correlation of Hamilton score and nortriptyline level was only significant correlation	Improvement rate of 1/3 recovered, 1/3 unimproved, 1/3 intermediate (final Hamilton, 7–15) is low; 150-mg dose of amitriptyline is low; plasma concentration of combined tricyclic antidepressants is not reported; how a more optimal dose (300 mg) would have affected total plasma level and percent improvement unclear
DOXEPIN Kline et al. N = 12 Mild to moderate primary depression	39–150 mg/day	Desmethy doxepin, less or greater than 20 ng/ml	Levels >20 ng/ml produced good results	

(Continued)

TABLE 13–7. — *Continued.*

AUTHOR, NO. OF SUBJECTS, POPULATION STUDIED	DOSE, DURATION OF STUDY	PLASMA LEVELS, ng/ml (unless stated otherwise)	MAJOR FINDINGS	COMMENTS
Friedel and Raskind Primary or secondary affective disorders, RDC criteria	50–300 mg/day, single bedtime dose	Desmethy doxepin plus doxepin combined, >110 ng/ml, resulted in good response; little or no improvement if level ≤60 ng/ml	Correlation of blood level and clinical response	Patients treated for unreported period of time
CLORIMIPRAMINE Broadherst et al. N = 14 Endogenous depression	50 mg t.i.d.	251–700 ng/ml of desmethy clorimipramine	Responders within range of 251–700 ng/ ml; nonresponders <250 ng/ml	Drug-free washout of 3 days; plasma levels obtained only 2 hr after 1st A.M. dose; study lasted only 3 wk
BUTRIPTYLINE Burrows et al. N = 10 Primary depressive illness	50 mg t.i.d. for 3 wk	35–295 ng/ml butriptyline; desmethy butriptyline not obtained	No relationship between clinical response and plasma level	Treated for only 3 wk; small sample size; fluctuating plasma levels
MAPROTILINE Angst and Rothweiler N = 20 "Depressive psychosis"	10 patients, 150 mg/ day, 107–1,277 ng/ ml; 10 patients, 225 mg/day		No significant correlation when all 20 cases analyzed; 1 patient with highest level did not improve; patient with 2d highest level had marked improvement; if these two are removed, there are significant correlations of level and several measures of improvement	Decision to exclude 2 cases from analysis is post hoc manipulation of data; results should be considered interesting leads requiring validation

Modified from Klein.[81] All authors cited in the first column appear in references at the end of the chapter.

Several investigators have studied the correlation of MAO inhibition and clinical effect (see Klein and associates for review[81]). The results seem to indicate a correlation between platelet MAO inhibition and clinical effect. Recently new MAO inhibitors have been developed that specifically inhibit MAO A and B. These agents may prove useful in furthering our understanding of the biochemistry of depression and in identifying subtypes of depression that respond selectively to these agents. Lipper points out important differences in clorgyline, which primarily inhibits MAO A, versus paragyline, which primarily inhibits MAO B.[96] Clorgyline, in his study, was effective for both endogenous and atypical depression. This work will require further replication but, like the other new antidepressants discussed below, may lead to more specific pharmacotherapy in the future.

Maintenance Therapy

Tricyclics or MAO inhibitors can be maintained for six months or longer after an acute episode and recovery. Table 13–8 lists studies which have found that maintenance tricyclics are useful in preventing relapse. Maintenance dosages of tricyclics are generally one half to two thirds of treatment dosages.[81] Frequent recurrences of depression may warrant a trial of lithium. Lithium is the drug of choice for frequent recurrent bipolar illness (mania and depression) and is prophylactic for recurrent unipolar depression. Davis has concluded that lithium is equally effective as prophylaxis for bipolar and unipolar disorders.[43]

Despite the use of maintenance lithium or tricyclics, patients can relapse. If relapse seems imminent, the tricyclic dosage can be increased again to approach previously effective dosage. Blood levels, if available, are

TABLE 13–8.—Studies Showing That Maintenance
Tricyclics Prevent Relapse*

STUDY	DRUG	LENGTH OF STUDY	P†
Prien et al.,[112] 1973	Imipramine	Over 6 months	<.01
Seager and Bird,[121] 1962	Imipramine	6 Months	<.008
Klerman et al.,[84] 1974, and Paykel et al.,[108] 1975	Amitriptyline	8 Months	
Mindham et al.,[101, 102] 1972, 1973	Imipramine	6 Months	<.005
Coppen et al.,[38] 1978			
Stein et al.,[128] 1980	Amitriptyline	6 Months	<.05

*Table from Davis,[43] 1976. Copyright 1976, the American Psychiatric Association. Reprinted by permission.
†Level of significance in difference between tricyclic and placebo groups.

useful for determining patient compliance and changes in metabolic state. Patients maintained on lithium may benefit from the addition of tricyclics if relapse is imminent. An occasional patient benefits from this combination indefinitely. Antidepressants have been shown to be present in breast milk in the same concentrations as the mother's serum, but infant blood levels are undetectable, so this does not present a contraindication.[6, 135]

MANAGEMENT OF THE MANIC PHASE

Manic episodes usually require hospitalization, but even in the hospital these patients can be unmanageable, requiring an inordinate amount of staff time and patience. It is therefore essential to recognize mania in its early states and to institute somatic therapies.

Antipsychotics are the drugs of choice for acute mania. Less severely ill, cooperative patients can be started on lithium carbonate without antipsychotics. Because lithium requires two to three weeks to become effective, antipsychotics can be added to the regimen if sleep disturbance or other symptoms of mania escalate during this period. Chlorpromazine and haloperidol have been shown to be equally effective in treating acute mania, although haloperidol produces less sedation and hypotension.[81] Dosages usually must be high but could be titrated to the clinical situation. Once it is determined that idiosyncratic reactions to the chosen antipsychotic are not occurring, the dosage should be increased rapidly. A loading dose can be given until some sedation is achieved. Dosage should then be reduced by 30% to 50% or the long half-life of these drugs will lead to accumulation and excessive sedation.

As the mania comes under enough control that antipsychotic dosage can be reduced by 50%, lithium can usually be started concurrently. Lithium started prior to this is risky because excessive sweating and agitation will obscure possible toxic reactions.[133] Cases of haloperidol-lithium toxicity have been reported by Cohen and Cohen,[34] but Baastrup has noted how infrequently this happens.[10] We have reported one case of irreversible renal and neurologic toxicity with combined haloperidol-lithium therapy.[93] The author has also observed several cases of reversible toxicity with the haloperidol-lithium combination in patients with questionable organic brain syndrome presenting as mania and agrees with Ayd that this is a risk factor to be avoided.[8] Many case reports also attest to the possibility of acute delirium due to antipsychotics.[67, 98] Combination therapy, therefore, runs the risks of several toxicities, yet etiology in these cases would be unclear.

Before lithium is instituted, baseline electrolytes, urinalysis, complete blood count, and thyroid functions must be determined (Table 13–9). Creatinine clearance should also be determined. There is no absolute contrain-

TABLE 13–9.—PROCEDURE FOR LITHIUM THERAPY

TIME	ACTION	COMMENT
Pretreatment	Measure: Thyroid functions ECG Creatinine clearance Electrolytes CBC	Relative contraindications: renal disease, AV node cardiac conduction abnormality, planned pregnancy
Day 1	Administer 300 mg lithium carbonate with evening meal	
Day 2	Administer 300 mg lithium 4 times a day	Small or elderly, 2 to 3 doses per day.
Day 3–4	Measure lithium blood level before morning dose, 12 hr after last dose	If level <0.5 mEq/L, increase dosage by 300 mg/day; if >1.2 mEq/L, reduce by 300 mg/day
Day 8	Measure lithium level	If blood level 0.8 to 1.5 mEq/L, do not adjust; if levels are erratic, consider sodium loading or loss
Days 14, 21, 28	Measure lithium level	Adjust if needed
Thereafter, 4- to 6-wk intervals	Measure lithium level	If patient is in therapeutic range but confusion, hand tremors, polyuria, or other troublesome side effects occur, reduce dosage until lower end of therapeutic range achieved
Yearly	Measure: Thyroid function Creatinine clearance ECG if at critical age or preexisting problems	

dication to lithium use except AV node conduction pathology. However, several conditions require close supervision. Patients with renal failure should be monitored more closely, since the kidney is the organ of excretion, and lowered creatinine clearance rates will mean that less lithium is required to maintain therapeutic blood levels. Patients taking thiazide diuretics will accumulate lithium also.[100] The first trimester of pregnancy is a relative contraindication, since flaccidity, cyanosis, and heart murmurs may be present in neonates born to mothers taking lithium.[137] Although it is difficult to say that the incidence of neonatal defects is higher than in the general population, lithium should be administered during pregnancy only if there are very strong indications. The presence of lithium in breast milk is a contraindication to breast-feeding.[64]

Lithium should be started slowly in the elderly. In other adult patients a test dose of 300 mg with the evening meal can be given, followed by a 300-mg tablet three times a day, with the clinical picture carefully monitored. The first lithium blood level can be obtained in three or four days. Lithium has a half-life of approximately 24 hours in patients with normal creatinine clearance, and steady-state blood levels will not be achieved for six to seven days after initiation of a fixed dosage. Lithium blood levels are measured 12 hours after the last dose, usually the morning after an evening dose. If the first blood level is less than 0.5 mEq/L, another 300-mg tablet should be added, but if it is 0.8 to 0.9 mEq/L, the dosage is probably sufficient to achieve the steady-state blood level of 0.8 to 1.2 mEq/L that is desired. If the blood level is higher than 1.2 mEq/L four to five days after initiation of therapy, the daily dose should be reduced by one tablet. Accurate blood levels can be obtained one week after dosage is adjusted. In the geriatric group or in patients with poor creatinine clearance, a steady state will not be achieved for a proportionately longer time. A clearance of 60 rather than 120 ml/minute requires 14 days for steady-state lithium levels to be achieved. Lithium starts to produce therapeutic effects in about two weeks. Thereafter antipsychotics can be reduced as the patient progresses. As mania subsides, lithium tolerance is decreased, blood levels rise, and less oral lithium is required. Once control with lithium is established the drug can be maintained for six months, then tapered and discontinued.

LITHIUM MAINTENANCE

If recurrences of mania or depression occur at the rate of two or more episodes in four years, maintenance lithium should be attempted. Klerman advocates maintenance lithium for all patients under age 40 who present with mania, since the probability of recurrence in this group is 80%.[82] Ban postulates further that onset of bipolar illness prior to age 30 usually occurs in patients with positive family history, who are more likely to be lithium-responsive.[15] Further research is needed to clarify this issue of heterogeneity. Until more data become available, Klerman's position seems extreme. The severity and frequency of life disruption with manic episodes must be considered before lithium maintenance therapy, with its attendent possible risks, is instituted. For example, Kadrmas and associates have observed that postpartum mania tends to recur in subsequent postpartum periods and not at other times; the advisability of committing this group of women to lithium maintenance is therefore questionable.[74] Maintenance requires a firm therapeutic alliance and sufficient cognitive ability in the patient to understand the maintenance concept and side effects. Unstable alcoholics or unstable suicidal patients are poor risks. Some patients prefer to be manic and will not take any medication. Psychosis during a manic episode seems to predict an especially low relapse rate during the maintenance phase, whether patients are schizoaffective or bipolar I.[52]

Maintenance therapy with lithium requires the following monitoring:

1. Monthly assays of lithium blood levels to maintain a level of 0.6 to 1.2 mEq/L
2. Yearly thyroxine level measurements
3. Yearly creatinine clearance determinations
4. Yearly ECGs in men over age 40 and women past menopause who have preexisting heart disease

OTHER SOMATIC APPROACHES

New Antidepressant Drugs

A number of new compounds are being developed. Some have tetracyclic structure, but many belong to other compound classes. Several of the new antidepressants have been extensively used in Europe but are not available here. Because recent Food and Drug Administration guidelines have made it possible to speed acceptance of new drugs, amoxapine (Asendin) and triimipramine (Surmontil) and maprotiline (Ludiomil) have become available in the United States.

Table 13–10 lists many of these new compounds. Most carry European brand names. The table gives only rough estimates of biogenic amine re-uptake blockade potency as well as anticholinergic potency; dosages are also approximations for most of the drugs. Gaps in the table exist because data on these compounds are less well established. Several new compounds that are more specific inhibitors of the re-uptake of serotonin, norepinephrine, and dopamine than tricyclics are currently undergoing clinical trials and may become available for general use in the next few years.[51] These compounds could be useful for some resistant depressions. In general, these compounds appear to have fewer side effects and therefore will be useful in treating geriatric patients and chronically depressed patients, who are more troubled by side effects. The serotonin re-uptake inhibitors include zimelidine, fluoxetine, fluroxamine, and trazadone. The norepinephrine blocker maprotiline and analogues of maprotiline seem to be as effective as imipramine and amitriptyline. Trazadone is the most widely tested of the new group of serotonin blockers. It is generally effective and has few side effects but is very sedating, probably because of its serotonin re-up-

TABLE 13-10.—NEW ANTIDEPRESSANTS*

ANTIDEPRESSANT	SEDATION	ANTICHOLINERGIC	BLOCKADE			DOSAGE (mg/day)	STRUCTURE
			NOREPINEPHRINE	SEROTONIN	DOPAMINE		
Iprindole (Tertran)	+ + +	0	0	0	+ +	50–150	
Mianserin			+ +	0	+ +	180–210	Tetracyclic
Fluoxetine			0	+ +	0	40–80	
Nisoxetine			+ + + +	0	+		
Nomifensine	0	+	+ + + +	+	+ + + +	100–200	Tetrahydroisoquinoline
Maprotiline (Ludiomil)	+ + + +	+ +	+ + + +	0	0	50–300	Tetracyclic
Trazodone (Trihico)		0	0	+ + + +	0	50–800	Triazolopyridine
Zimelidine		0	0	+ + + +	0	50–150	
Fluroxamine	±	0	±	+ + + +	0	50–300	(2-Amino-ethyl) oxame ether
Bupropion		0	0	+	+ + +	200–600	
Alprazolam	+	0				0.5–4.0	Benzodiazepam
Butriptyline (Evadyne)			0	0			
Amoxapine (Asendin)	+ + +	+ +	+	+	+ +	200–400	Tricyclic
Chlorimipramine (Anafranil)	+ + +	+ +	+ +	+ + + +	+		Tricyclic
Triimipramine (Surmontil)	+ + +	+ +					
Viloxazine (Viralan)			+ + +	0			

*Information obtained from Susler,[131] 1980; Feighner,[51] 1980; Ayd,[9] 1980; and Zis and Goodwin,[147] 1979.

take blockade. The tricyclic chlorimipramine (Anafranil) has been used widely in Europe and England for primary depression as well as obsessive-compulsive states, phobic disorders, and sleep-related disorders, particularly cataplexy.[3]

ANTIPSYCHOTICS

Psychotic depressed patients who are delusional or hallucinating respond poorly to tricyclics alone. Stern and associates have noted that some of these patients respond to a combination of tricyclics and antipsychotics.[129] Baldessarini recommends antipsychotics for involutional-agitated depressives when delusions are present.[11] They are best treated with antipsychotics such as haloperidol or the phenothiazines in antipsychotic dosages or until sedation is extreme. Failure to respond in three to four weeks usually indicates the need for ECT although tricyclics added to antipsychotics will help some patients.

ELECTROCONVULSIVE THERAPY

Glassman et al. recommend ECT for psychotic depression.[60] Electroconvulsive therapy should be the treatment of choice for major depressive disorders not responsive to tricyclics, where suicidal risk is high. Response is generally more rapid and reliable with ECT than with tricyclics, although a two- to three-week time lag in response to ECT is common.[55] Relapse will occur if prophylactic tricyclics or lithium are not used after a course of ECT. Controversy exists as to the CNS damage caused by ECT,[56] but no well-controlled studies have been done to show that ECT causes organic brain damage.[54] Unilateral ECT seems to cause less confusion,[127] and ECT monitored by EEG may require fewer treatments and lower anesthetic dosage, making the procedure safer overall.[144]

Electroconvulsive therapy is also the safest therapy for middle-aged men with compromised cardiovascular status. Brain tumor is a relative contraindication to this form of treatment. Spinal deossification may require more profound muscle relaxation. Kalinowsky and Hippius[75] feel there are no absolute medical contraindications to ECT.

PSYCHOMOTOR STIMULANTS

Dextroamphetamine and methylphenidate (Ritalin) are useful in the early stages of treatment to improve activity and may help raise plasma tricyclic levels to therapeutic levels.[36] Ritalin has also proved useful in treating elderly patients unable to tolerate tricyclic side effects[77] and anergically depressed, medically ill patients.

COMBINATION THERAPY

Shopsin and Kline advocate the combined use of MAO and tricyclics in patients who are unresponsive to either alone.[125] The drugs should be started simultaneously, for example, phenelzine, 15 mg three times a day, and amitriptyline, 75 mg at bedtime. Side effects have not been reported to be worse than either drug alone, but close monitoring is indicated. Moderately severe depressions that were first treated with tricyclics and MAO inhibitors and proved refractory should be treated with ECT before combination therapy is used. Tryptophan and thyroxin have also been advocated as adjuncts in the treatment of refractory depressions. Tryptophan has been reported to potentiate the action of MAO inhibitors in depressed patients, particularly those with bipolar affective disorders.[49] Cole and associates, summarizing their review of the effects of tryptophan in affective disorders, state that tryptophan may be as useful as tricyclics in primary depression but the effects may surface after a few weeks of treatment.[35] Dosages for primary depression are reported to be 6 gm/day or less. Studies using tryptophan in combination with MAO inhibitions have used 6 to 9 gm/day of tryptophan. Tryptophan is not approved by the FDA for treatment of depression and can only be obtained over the counter. Triiodothyronine (T_3) or thyroid-stimulating hormone (TSH) may potentiate or hasten the onset of tricyclic antidepressant action, especially in women, even though they are euthyroid.[110, 111]

TREATMENT OF SPECIAL AFFECTIVE DISORDERS CONDITIONS

RESISTANT MANIA

Most manic episodes can be controlled if sufficient antipsychotic medication is used. Occasionally a change to a different class of antipsychotic is useful. Some very psychotic patients seem particularly prone to neurologic toxicity and therefore must be carefully monitored when either lithium or lithium and antipsychotics are used. Usually ECT is rapidly effective in calming the acute manic and is the safest treatment in these instances. Chouinard and associates have described the use of tryptophan, 6 to 9 gm/ day, alone or in combination with lithium to treat resistant mania or as prophylaxis for bipolar disease.[32]

RAPID CYCLERS

Some rapid cycling bipolar patients do not respond to lithium, although some may be better controlled with a combination of lithium and antipsychotics. These patients are the subject of intensive biologic research. An especially interesting finding is that some of these patients have fast biologic clocks, and although lithium slows the clocks,[48] it may not slow them enough to permit physiologic processes to become resynchronized.[89] New pharmacologic agents that can accomplish this may be developed for this group, or some nonpharmacologic means of pacing may be found. Carbamazepine is being tried as pharmacologic treatment for these lithium-resistant patients.[14, 132] Some patients benefit from prolixin deconoate or enanthate. This should not be given unless cycles are frequent.

In conclusion, several principles of the pharmacologic drug treatment of affective disorders should be reviewed in each case:

1. Treatment is complex; a flexible approach is needed.

2. Bipolar and major depressive disorders almost always require psychotropics and usually require maintenance therapy.

3. Single drug use is preferable to multiple drug approaches. Combination therapy should only be attempted after adequate dosages of psychotropics have been tried for an adequate length of time.

4. Tricyclic drug choice should be based on side effects and history of patient or family member drug response, since in equivalent dosages they are all equally efficacious.

5. Clear-cut, classic presentations of affective illness respond best to treatment. The most severe forms of these illnesses—rapid cycles—are often difficult to treat. Atypical forms of depression are also difficult to treat.

6. The most common reasons for drug failure are (a) failure of the patient to take the drug or take it properly, and (b) inadequate dosages for inadequate lengths of time.

REFERENCES

1. Akiskal H.S., McKinney W.T.: Overview of recent research in depression. *Arch. Gen. Psychiatry* 32:285, 1975.
2. Alexander B., Price-Evans P.A., Sjoquist F.: Steady state plasma levels of nortriptyline in twins: Influence of genetic factors and drug therapy. *Br. Med. J.* 4:764, 1969.
3. Anath J., et al.: Chlorimipramine therapy for obsessive-compulsive neurosis. *Am. J. Psychiatry* 136:700, 1979.
4. Angst J., Rothweiler R.: Blood levels and clinical effects of maprotiline, in *Classification and Prediction of Outcome of Depression.* Symposium Schlob Reinharshausen/Rhein, September 23–26, 1973, pp. 237–244. Stuttgart, F.K. Schattauer Verlag, 1973.
5. Asberg M., et al.: Relationship between plasma level and therapeutic effect of nortriptyline. *Br. Med. J.* 3:331, 1971.
6. Ayd F.: *Int. Drug Ther. Newsletter* 8:33, 1973.
7. Ayd F.J. Jr.: Effects of lithium on thyroid function in man. *Int. Drug Ther. Newsletter,* vol. 9, 1974.
8. Ayd F.: Lithium-haloperidol for mania: Is it safe or hazardous? *Int. Drug Ther. Newsletter* 10:29, 1975.

9. Ayd F.: Amoxapine: A new tricyclic antidepressant. *Int. Drug Ther. Newsletter* 15:33, 1980.

10. Baastrup P.C., et al.: Adverse reactions in treatment with lithium carbonate and haloperidol. *J.A.M.A.* 236:2645, 1976.

11. Baldessarini R.J.: Chemotherapy, in Armand M., Nicholi J.V. (eds.): *Harvard Guide to Modern Psychiatry.* Cambridge, Mass., Harvard University Press, 1978.

12. Baldessarini R.J., Lipinski J.F.: Lithium salts: 1970–1975. *Ann. Intern. Med.* 83:527, 1975.

13. Ballanger J.C., Post R.M.: Carbamazine in manic-depressive illness: A new treatment. *Am. J. Psychiatry* 137:782, 1980.

14. Ballinger B.R., et al.: The effects of hypnotics on imipramine treatment. *Psychopharmacologia* 39:267, 1974.

15. Ban T.A.: Perspectives in biological psychiatry: Part 2. Affective disorders. *Psychosomatics* 18:59, 1977.

16. Baron M., et al.: Lithium carbonate response in depression. *Arch. Gen. Psychiatry* 32:1107, 1975.

17. Batlle D., et al.: Distal nephron function in patients receiving chronic lithium therapy. *Kidney Int.,* in press.

18. Beilski R.J., Friedel R.O.: Prediction of tricyclic antidepressant response. *Arch. Gen. Psychiatry* 33:1479, 1976.

19. Bigger J.T., et al.: Cardiac antiarrhythmic effect of imipramine. *N. Engl. J. Med.* 296:206, 1977.

20. Boakes A.J.: Monoamine oxidase inhibitors: Interactions with other drugs and foodstuffs. *Prescribers J.* 11:109, 1971.

21. Boston Collaborative Drug Surveillance Program: Adverse reaction to the tricyclic-antidepressant drugs. *Lancet* 1:529, 1972.

22. Braithwaite R.A., et al.: Plasma concentrations of amitriptyline and clinical response. *Lancet* 1:1297, 1972.

23. Brown W.A., Shuey I.: Response to dexamethasone and subtype of depression. *Arch. Gen. Psychiatry* 37:747, 1980.

24. Burckhardt D., et al.: Cardiovascular effects of tricyclic and tetracyclic antidepressants. *J.A.M.A.* 239:213, 1978.

25. Burrows G.D., et al.: A new antidepressant butriptyline: Plasma levels and clinical response. *Med. J. Aust.* 2:604, 1977.

26. Burrows G.D., Mowbray R.M., Davies D.: A sequential comparison of doxepin and placebo in depressed patients. *Med. J. Aust.* 1:364, 1972.

27. Burrows G., Davies G., Scoggins B.: Plasma concentration of nortriptyline and clinical response in depressive illness. *Lancet* 2:619, 1972.

28. Burrows G., et al.: Plasma nortriptyline and clinical response. *Clin. Pharmacol. Ther.* 16:639, 1974.

29. Burrows G., et al.: A sequential trial comparing two plasma levels and nortriptyline. *Aust. N.Z. J. Psychiatry* 8:21, 1974.

30. Carmen J.S., et al.: Calcium and calcium-regulating hormones in the biphasic periodic psychoses. *J. Operational Psychiatry* 11:5, 1980.

31. Carroll B.J., Martin F.R., Davies B.: Resistance to suppression by dexamethasone of plasma 11-OHCS levels in severe depressive illness. *Br. Med. J.* 3:285, 1968.

32. Chouinard G., et al.: Potentiation of lithium by tryptophan in a patient with bipolar illness. *Am. J. Psychiatry* 136:719, 1980.

33. Cohen R.A.: Manic-depressive illness, in Freedman A.M., Kaplan H.I., Sadock B.J. (eds.): *Comprehensive Textbook of Psychiatry*. Baltimore, Williams & Wilkins Co., 1975.

34. Cohen W.J., Cohen N.H.: Lithium carbonate, haloperidol, and irreversible brain damage. *J.A.M.A.* 230:1283, 1974.

35. Cole J.O., Hartmann E., Brigham P.: L-Tryptophan: Clinical studies. *McLean Hosp. J.* 5:37, 1980.

36. Cooper T.B., Simpson G.M.: Concomitant imipramine and methylphenidate administration: A case report. *Am. J. Psychiatry* 130:721, 1973.

37. Copeland D.S.: Tricyclic antidepressant and cardiac death. *Drug Ther. Bull.* 10:55, 1972.

38. Coppen A., et al.: Amitriptyline plasma concentration and clinical effect: A World Health Organization Collaborative study. *Lancet* 1:63, 1978.

39. Corfman E.: Depression, manic-depressive illness, and biological rhythms. DHEW Publication No. (ADM) 79, 1979.

40. Davenport Y.B., et al.: Couples group therapy as an adjunct to lithium maintenance of the manic patient. *Am. J. Orthopsychiatry* 47:495, 1977.

41. Davidson S.J.: Psychotropic drugs, stress, and cardiomyopathies. *Br. Assoc. Pharmacol.* April 1976.

42. Davis J.M.: Psychopharmacology in the aged: Use of psychotropic drugs in geriatric patients. *J. Geriatr. Psychiatry* 7:145, 1974.

43. Davis J.M.: Overview: Maintenance therapy in psychiatry: II. Affective disorders. *Am. J. Psychiatry* 133:1, 1976.

44. DiMascio A., et al.: Differential symptom reduction by drugs and psychotherapy in acute depression. *Arch. Gen. Psychiatry* 36:1450, 1979.

45. Docherty J.P., et al.: Psychotherapy and pharmacotherapy: Conceptual issues. *Am. J. Psychiatry* 134:529, 1977.

46. Dorus E., et al.: Genetic determinant of lithium ion distribution: I. An in-vitro monozygotic-dizygotic twin study. *Arch. Gen. Psychiatry* 31:463, 1974.

47. Elizur A., et al.: Intra-extracellular lithium ratios and clinical course in affective states. *Clin. Pharmacol. Ther.* 13:947, 1972.

48. Engelmann W.: A slowing down of circadian rhythms by lithium ions. *Z. Naturforsch.* 28:733, 1973.

49. Farkas T., Dunner D.L., Fieve R.R.: L-tryptophan in depression. *Biol. Psychiatry* 11:295, 1976.

50. Fawcett J., Maas J.W., Dekirmenjian H.: Depression and MHPG excretion response to dextroamphetamine and tricyclic antidepressants. *Arch. Gen. Psychiatry* 126:246, 1972.

51. Feighner J.P.: Pharmacology: New antidepressants. *Psychiatr. Ann.* suppl. 10:388, 1980.

52. Fieve R.R.: Maintenance treatment of bipolar illness. Read before the annual meeting of the American Psychiatric Association, San Francisco, May 1980.

53. Fieve R.R., Kumbaraci T., Dunner D.L.: Lithium prophylaxis of depression in bipolar I, bipolar II and unipolar patients. *Am. J. Psychiatry* 133:925, 1976.

54. Fink M.: Myths of "shock therapy." *Am. J. Psychiatry* 134:991, 1977.

55. Fink M., et al. (eds.): *Psychobiology of Convulsive Therapy*. New York, John Wiley & Sons, 1974.

56. Frankel F.H.: Current perspectives on ECT: A discussion, *Am. J. Psychiatry* 134:1014, 1977.

57. Freidel R.O., Raskind M.A.: Relationship of blood levels of Sinequan to clin-

ical effects in the treatment of depression in aged patients, in Mendels J. (ed.): *Sinequan (Doxepin HCL): A Monograph of Recent Clinical Studies.* Amsterdam, Excerpta Medica, 1975.

58. Gerbino L., Oleshansky M., Gershon, S.: Clinical use and mode of action of lithium, in Lipton M.A., DiMascio A., Killam K.F. (eds.): *Psychopharmacology: A Generation of Progress.* New York, Raven Press, 1978.

59. Girdwood R.H.: Death after taking medicaments. *Br. Med. J.* 1:501, 1974.

60. Glassman A.H., Kantor S.I., Shostak M.: Depression, delusions and drug response. *Am. J. Psychiatry* 132:716, 1975.

61. Glassman A.H., Perel J.M.: Tricyclic blood levels and clinical outcome: A review of the art, in Lipton M.A., DiMascio A., Killam K.F. (eds.): *Psychopharmacology: A Generation of Progress.* New York, Raven Press, 1978.

62. Glassman A., et al.: Clinical implications of imipramine plasma levels for depressive illness. *Arch. Gen. Psychiatry* 34:197, 1977.

63. Glassman A.H., et al.: Clinical characteristics of imipramine-induced orthostatic hypotension. *Lancet* 1:468, 1979.

64. Goldberg H.L., DiMascio A.: Psychotropic drugs in pregnancy, in Lipton M.A., DiMascio A., Killam K.F. (eds.): *Psychopharmacology: A Generation Of Progress.* New York, Raven Press, 1978.

65. Goodwin F.K., Cowdry R.W., Webster M.H.: Predictors of drug response in the affective disorders: Toward an integrated approach, in Lipton M.A., DiMascio A., Killam K.F. (eds.): *Psychopharmacology: A Generation of Progress.* New York, Raven Press, 1978.

66. Gram L., et al.: Plasma levels in antidepressant effects of imipramine. *Clin. Pharmacol. Ther.* 19:318, 1976.

67. Haefner H., Heyder B., Kutscher I.: Undesirable side effects and complications with the use of neuroleptic drugs. *Int. J. Neuropsychiatry* 1:46, 1965.

68. Janowsky D.S., Leff M., Epstein R.S.: Playing the manic game. *Arch. Gen. Psychiatry* 22:252, 1970.

69. Janowsky D.S., Neborsky R.J.: Hypothesized common mechanisms in the psychotherapy and pharmacology of depression. *Psychiatr. Ann.* 10:356, 1980.

70. Jarvik M.E.: Drugs used in the treatment of psychiatric disorder, in Goodman L.S., Gilman A. (eds.): *The Pharmacological Basis of Therapeutics.* New York, Macmillan Publishing Co., 1970.

71. Jefferson J.W.: Review of cardiovascular effects and toxicity of tricyclic antidepressants. *Psychosom. Med.* 37:160, 1975.

72. Jenner F.A.: Lithium and the question of kidney damage. *Arch. Gen. Psychiatry* 36:888, 1979.

73. Johnstone E.C.: The relationship between response to phenelzine and acetylator status in depressed patients, in *Colloquium on MAOI Therapy.* William Warner Publication, 1974.

74. Kadrmas A., Winoker G., Crowe R.: Postpartum mania. *Br. J. Psychiatry* 135:551, 1979.

75. Kalinowsky L., Hippius H.: Pharmacological, convulsive, and other somatic treatments, in *Psychiatry.* New York, Grune & Stratton, 1969.

76. Kantor S.J., et al.: The cardiac effects of therapeutic plasma concentrations of imipramine. *Am. J. Psychiatry* 135:534, 1978.

77. Kayton W., Raskind M.: Treatment of depression in the medically ill elderly with methylphenidate. *Am. J. Psychiatry* 137:963, 1980.

78. Kessler K.A.: Tricyclic antidepressants: Mode of action and clinical use, in Lipton M.A., DiMascio A., Killam K.F. (eds.): *Psychopharmacology: A Generation of Progress*. New York, Raven Press, 1978.
79. Kirk L., Baastrup P.C., Schou M.: Propranolol treatment of lithium-induced tremor. *Lancet* 2:1086, 1973.
80. Klein D.F.: Psychopharmacological treatment of delineation of borderline disorders, in Hartocollis P. (ed.): *Borderline Personality Disorders*. New York, International Universities Press, 1977.
81. Klein D.F., et al.: *Diagnosis and Drug Treatment of Psychiatric Disorders: Adults and Children*. Baltimore, Williams & Wilkins, 1980.
82. Klerman G.L.: Long-term treatment of affective disorders, in Lipton M.A., DiMascio A., Killam K.F. (eds.): *Psychopharmacology: A Generation of Progress*. New York, Raven Press, 1978.
83. Klerman G.L., Cole J.O.: Clinical pharmacology of imipramine and related antidepressant compounds. *Pharmacol. Rev.* 17:101, 1965.
84. Klerman G.L., et al.: Treatment of depression by drugs and psychotherapy. *Am. J. Psychiatry* 131:186, 1974.
85. Kline N.S., Cooper T., Johnson B.: Doxepin and desmethyldoxepin serum levels and clinical response, in Gottschalk L.A., Merlin M. (eds.): *Pharmacokinetics of Psychoactive Drugs: Blood Levels and Clinical Response*. New York, Spectrum Press, 1976.
86. Kragh-Sorenson P., Hansen C.E., Asberg M.: Plasma levels of nortriptyline in the treatment of endogenous depression. *Acta Psychiatr. Scand.* 49:444, 1973.
87. Kragh-Sorenson P., Asberg M., Eggert-Hansen C.: Plasma-nortriptyline levels in endogenous depression. *Lancet* 1:113, 1973.
88. Kragh-Sorenson P., et al.: Self-inhibiting action of nortriptyline to antidepressant effects at high plasma levels. *Psychopharmacologia*. 45:305, 1976.
89. Kripke D.F., et al.: Circadian rhythm disorders in manic-depressives. *Biol. Psychiatry*. 13:335, 1978.
90. Kuhn R.: The treatment of depressive states with G-22355 (imipramine hydrochloride). *Am. J. Psychiatry* 115:459, 1958.
91. Kupfer D.J.: REM latency: A psychobiologic marker for primary depressive disease. *Biol. Psychiatry* 11:159, 1977.
92. Kupfer D., et al.: Amitriptyline plasma levels and clinical response in primary depression. *Clin. Pharmacol. Ther.* 22:904, 1977.
93. Lahmeyer H.W., Gaviria F.M.: Bradycardia, persistent diabetes insipidus, and tardive dyskinesia with lithium intoxication. *Psychiatr. J. U. Ottawa* 5:283-286, 1980.
94. Lasagna L.: The disease model and neuropsychopharmacology, in Lipton M.A., DiMascio A., Killam, K.F. (eds.): *Psychopharmacology: A Generation of Progress*. New York, Raven Press, 1978.
95. Lipman R.S., Covi, L.: Outpatient treatment of neurotic depression, in Spitzer R.L., Klein D.F. (eds.): Evaluation of Psychological Therapies. Baltimore, Johns Hopkins University Press, 1976.
96. Lipper S.: Spectrum of effects of selective MAO-inhibitors. Read before the annual meeting of the American Psychiatric Association, San Francisco, May 1980.
97. Marco L.A., Randels P.M., Sexauer T.D.: A guide to drug interactions with psychotropic agents. *Drug Ther.* 9:45–56, 1979.

98. Meltzer H.Y.: Rigidity, hyperpyrexia, and coma following fluphenazine enanthate. *Psychopharmacologia* 29:337, 1973.
99. Mielke D.H.: Psychotropic drugs: Side effects. *Psychiatr. Ann.* 5:473, 1975.
100. Mielke D.H.: Clinical management of adverse reactions associated with the thymoleptics, in Gallant D.M., Simpson G.M. (eds.): *Depression: Behavioral, Biochemical, Diagnostic and Treatment Concepts.* New York, Halsted Press, 1975.
101. Mihdham R.H.S., Howland C., Shepherd M.: Continuation therapy with tricyclic antidepressants in depressive illness. *Lancet* 2:854, 1972.
102. Mindham R.H.S., Howland D., Shepherd M.: An evaluation of continuation therapy with tricyclic antidepressants in depressive illness. *Psychol. Med.* 3:5, 1973.
103. Morris J.B., Beck A.T.: The efficacy of antidepressant drugs. *Arch. Gen. Psychiatry* 30:667, 1974.
104. Murphy D.L.: Neuropharmacology of depression, in Simpson L.L. (ed.): *Drug Treatment of Mental Disorders.* New York, Raven Press, 1976.
105. Olivier-Martin R., et al.: Concentrations plasmatigues de l'imipramine et de la desmethylimipramine et effet antidepresseur au cours d'un traitment controle. *Psychopharmacologia* 41:187, 1975.
106. Ostrow D.G.: Lithium treatment causes hyperchloremic metabolic acidosis. Read before the annual meeting of the American Psychiatric Association, San Francisco, May 1980.
107. Pare C.M.B., Mack J.W.: Differentiation of two genetically specific types of depression by the response to antidepressant drugs. *J. Med. Genet.* 8:306, 1971.
108. Paykel E.S., et al.: Effects of maintenance amitriptyline and psychotherapy on symptoms of depression. *Psychosom. Med.* 5:67, 1975.
109. Perel J., Shostak M., Gann E.: Pharmacodymanics of imipramine and clinical outcome in depressed patients, in Gottschalk L.A., Marlies S. (eds.): *Pharmacokinetics, Psychoactive Drug Levels and Clinical Outcome.* New York, Spectrum, 1976.
110. Prange A.J.: Enhancement of imipramine antidepressant activity by thyroid hormone. *Am. J. Psychiatry* 126:457, 1969.
111. Prange A.J., et al.: Enhancement of imipramine by thyroid stimulating hormone: Clinical and theoretical implications. *Am. J. Psychiatry* 127:191, 1970.
112. Prien R.F., Klett C.J., Caffey E.M. Jr.: Lithium carbonate and imipramine in prevention of affective episodes. *Arch. Gen. Psychiatry* 29:420, 1973.
113. Reisberg B., Gershon S.: Side effects associated with lithium therapy. *Arch. Gen. Psychiatry* 36:879, 1979.
114. Risch S.C., Huey L.Y., Janowsky D.S.: Plasma levels of tricyclic antidepressants and clinical efficacy: Review of the literature. Part I. *J. Clin. Psychiatry* 40:4, 1979.
115. Risch S.C., Huey L.Y., Janowsky D.S.: Plasma levels of tricyclic antidepressants and clinical efficacy: Review of the literature. Part II. *J. Clin. Psychiatry* 40:58, 1979.
116. Robinson D.S., et al.: The monoamine oxidase inhibitor, phenelzine, in the treatment of depressive-anxiety states: A controlled clinical trial. *Arch. Gen. Psychiatry* 29:407, 1973.
117. Ross S.B., Reny A.L.: Inhibition of the uptake of tritiated catecholamines by antidepressants and related agents. *Eur. J. Pharmacol.* 2:181, 1967.

118. Sachar E.J., et al.: Disrupted 24-hour patterns of cortisol secretion in psychiatric depression. *Arch. Gen. Psychiatry* 28:19, 1973.
119. Schatzberg A.F.: MHPG as a predictor of antidepressant response. Read before the annual meeting of the American Psychiatric Association, San Francisco, May 1980.
120. Schou M.: Electrocardiographic changes during treatment with lithium and drugs of the imipramine type. *Acta Psychiatr. Scand.* 38:331, 1962.
121. Seager C.P., Bird R.L.: Imipramire with electrical treatment in depression: A controlled trial. *J. Ment. Sci.* 108:704, 1962.
122. Secunda S.: Doxepin: Recent pharmacologic and clinical studies. Read before the annual meeting of the American Psychiatric Association, San Francisco, May 1980.
123. Shakir S.A., et al.: Group psychotherapy as an adjunct to lithium maintenance. *Am. J. Psychiatry* 136:455, 1979.
124. Shaw D.M.: The practical management of affective disorders. *Br. J. Psychiatry* 130:432, 1977.
125. Shopsin B., Kline N.S.: Combined tricyclic and monoamine oxidase inhibitor (MAOI) therapy in depressed outpatients, abstracted. *J. Pharmacol.* 5(suppl. l): 103, 1974.
126. Snyder S.H., Yamamura H.I.: Antidepressants and the muscarinic acetylcholine receptor. *Arch. Gen. Psychiatry* 34:236, 1977.
127. Squire L.R.: ECT and memory loss. *Am. J. Psychiatry* 134:997, 1977.
128. Stein M.K., Rickels K., Weise C.C.: Maintenance therapy with amitriptyline: A controlled trial. *Am. J. Psychiatry* 137:370, 1980.
129. Stern S.L., Rush J., Mendels J.: Toward a rational pharmacotherapy of depression. *Am. J. Psychiatry* 137:545, 1980.
130. Strauss J.S.: A comprehensive approach to psychiatric diagnosis. *Am. J. Psychiatry* 132:1193, 1975.
131. Susler F.: Pharmacology: Current antidepressants. *Psychiatr. Ann.* 10(suppl.):28, 1980.
132. Takezaki H., Hanaoka M.: The use of carbamezepine (Tegretol) in the control of manic-depressive psychosis and other manic-depressive states. *Clin. Psychiatry* 13:173, 1971.
133. Tupin J.P., Schuller A.B.: Lithium and haloperidol incompatibility reviewed. *Psychiatr. J. U. Ottawa* 3:245, 1978.
134. Van Putten T.: Why do patients with manic-depressive illness stop their lithium? *Compr. Psychiatry* 16:179, 1975.
135. Vorherr H.: Drug excretion in breast milk. *Senologia* 1:27, 1976.
136. Walter C.G.: Drug plasma levels and clinical effect. *Proc. R. Soc. Med.* 64:281, 1971.
137. Weinstein M.R., Goldfield M.D.: Cardiovascular malformations with lithium use during pregnancy. *Am. J. Psychiatry* 132:529, 1975.
138. Weissman M.M.: Psychotherapy and its relevance to the pharmacotherapy of affective disorders: From ideology to evidence, in Lipton M.A., DiMascio A., Killam K.F. (eds.): *Psychopharmacology: A Generation of Progress.* New York, Raven Press, 1978.
139. Wellens H.J., Cats V.M., Duren D.R.: Symptomatic sinus node abnormalities following lithium carbonate therapy. *Am. J. Med.* 59:285, 1975.
140. West P.A., Meltzer H.Y.: Paradoxic lithium neurotoxicity: A report of five cases and hypothesis about risk for neurotoxicity. *Am. J. Psychiatry* 136:963, 1979.

141. Wharton R.M., et al.: A potential clinical use for methylphenidate with TCA. *Am. J. Psychiatry* 127:1619, 1971.
142. Whyte S.F., et al.: Plasma concentration of protriptyline and clinical effects in depressed women. *Br. J. Psychiatry* 128:384, 1976.
143. Wilson J.R., et al.: Reversible sinus node abnormalities following lithium carbonate therapy. *N. Engl. J. Med.* 294:223, 1976.
144. Yesavage J.A., Berens E.S.: Multiple monitored electroconvulsive therapy in the elderly. *J. Am. Geriatr. Soc.* 28:206, 1980.
145. Ziegler V., et al.: Nortriptyline plasma levels in therapeutic response. *Clin. Pharmacol. Ther.* 20:458, 1976.
146. Ziegler V., et al.: Amitriptyline plasma levels and therapeutic response. *Clin. Pharmacol. Ther.* 19:795, 1976.
147. Zis A.P., Goodwin F.K.: Novel antidepressants and the biogenic amine hypothesis of depression. *Arch. Gen. Psychiatry* 36:1097, 1979.

14

PSYCHOLOGICAL MANAGEMENT OF AFFECTIVE DISORDERS

EDUARDO VAL, M.D.
JOSEPH A. FLAHERTY, M.D.
F. MOISES GAVIRIA, M.D.

PSYCHOLOGICAL MANAGEMENT refers to those interventions based on verbal and nonverbal communication techniques, in the context of the therapist-patient relationship, aimed at providing relief and fostering behavioral changes in the patient's emotionally disordered state. This broad definition encompasses the diverse psychotherapeutic modalities (family, individual, behavioral, etc.) as well as the psychotherapeutic aspect of any type of treatment intervention (e.g., management of a dying patient or a chronically ill patient). Use of a specific psychotherapy form implies that the intervention follows an established set of principles and is aimed at the resolution of the etiologic factors believed to be primarily responsible for the condition. An anxiety disorder, for instance, can be conceived as an abnormal behavior resulting from conditioning or learning; in this context, behavior therapy as a mode of intervention might consist of eradicating certain behaviors and replacing them with more adaptive ones through the use of such strategies as reinforcement and desensitization. The same anxiety disturbance could be understood from an intrapsychic point of view as a compromise formation aiming at warding off hostile impulses and fears of damaging retaliation by significant objects, or it might be due to the revival of separation-individuation anxiety. Within the framework of this interpretation, individual psychoanalytic psychotherapy or hypnotic techniques might be considered. The same clinical condition could be conceptualized in yet another way as originating in interpersonal relationships, perhaps within the framework of the complementary roles and protective maneuvers of the family as an organized behavioral system. Interventions at the family level could, thus, be carried out as well. Each approach, albeit based on different etiologic hypotheses, assumes that the psychological factors giving rise to behavioral expression are the primary factors to be addressed by the therapeutic techniques of that approach.

Other techniques, such as medication, are viewed as adjunctive and facilitating measures. In contrast, the psychotherapeutic approach to psychological management implies the use of psychological techniques in addition to other more central interventions. An acute myocardial infarction, for instance, may be related to certain psychosocial stresses on a particular patient, or the condition itself may induce distress in the individual's self-equilibrium and family relationships, manifested through diverse behavioral outlets: depression, fear of incompetency as a spouse, or work inhibitions. The psychological management could follow one or another avenue, depending on current and past psychological events and their manifestations. The objectives would be the facilitation of better coping mechanisms, reduction of stress, and prevention of new attacks.

Milieu therapy, in the broad sense, is a clear-cut example of psychotherapeutic management in psychiatric treatment. Milieu therapy is a concerted effort, within the confines of an inpatient unit, to facilitate and integrate diverse treatment interventions. In other words, the means of psychotherapeutic intervention are necessary for the overall outcome but in themselves are insufficient, since they are adjunctive to more primary or essential healing measures.

DIFFICULTIES EN ROUTE TO AN INTEGRATED THERAPY

The choice between psychotherapy as a primary psychological management and psychotherapeutic management as an adjunctive intervention should be based on the etiologic rationale assumed by the clinician. Until recently, much of the controversy surrounding the management of affective disorders arose from the polarization of therapy into psychotherapy alone and pharmacologic management alone, the latter assuming a biologic basis for all affective disorders and neglecting psychological and psychotherapeutic considerations.

The history of psychiatry illustrates this profound division into two theoretical and treatment camps: the psychologists, who favor psychological explanations and psychological methods of treatment, and the organicists who favor an organic etiology and treatment for mental disorders. Currently, mental health professionals are ordinarily trained in both approaches, although a few schools train exclusively to one approach. Even clinicians who feel comfortable with and competent in both psychological and biologic approaches must decide which should predominate when both types are used in the treatment of a single patient. Similarly, the patient may have difficulty understanding a combined treatment approach, resulting in less than ideal treatment. The difficulties in accepting an integrated approach may be rooted in some of the philosophical, ethical, and theoretical issues inherent in psychiatric treatment in general: (1) lack of an integrated theory, (2) pharmacologic Calvinism, (3) psychotropic hedonism, and (4) contrasting goals.

LACK OF AN INTEGRATED THEORY

Although advances have been made in the basic science of behavior, psychiatrists are still a long way from integrating the neurochemistry, neurophysiology, and neuroanatomy of brain functions with psychological and psychodynamic theories of behavior. In the absence of such an integrating theory, the psychiatrist may feel most comfortable accommodating to a single orientation in general or at least with a given patient. The versatile modern psychiatrist may use lithium to treat a bipolar patient, based on his understanding of the data supporting a genetic/biologic basis for this illness, may treat a mildly depressed patient with psychoanalytic psychotherapy, based on his understanding of how the patient's dependency and narcissistic dynamics have resulted in depression, and may treat another moderately depressed patient with a combination of psychotherapy and a tricyclic drug. However, in the latter case, the temptation to devalue one approach and elevate the other is quite strong. The clinician's ability to tolerate a certain degree of ambiguity is essential in using a combined approach, perhaps even essential for the current practice of psychiatry. Related to this issue is the erroneous reductionistic view that the etiology of mental disorders should directly determine treatment; that is, treatment for an illness of genetic or biologic etiology must always be biologic. Besides going counter to a holistic concept of mind and behavior, this position is premature: the specific pathways causing mental disorders are yet to be elucidated.

PHARMACOLOGIC CALVINISM

As Klerman has noted, some physicians adopt extremely Calvinistic views on psychotropic drug treatment.[13] Calvinism values the role of hard work, sacrifice, and personal commitment as the main road to salvation— or any productivity. Applied to psychiatry, this view eschews simple or easy solutions, such as medication, in the treatment of emotional disorders.

Rather, a long and arduous process of psychotherapy that requires work and suffering is the only valid means of achieving a remission. According to this position, the core of any emotional disorder lies in the psychological makeup of the patient and can be ameliorated only by a psychological process, without the assistance of chemical "crutches." More moderate thinkers agree with the need for a psychological understanding of each patient but do not view the chemical assistance so pejoratively.

PSYCHOTROPIC HEDONISM

The opposite to the Calvinistic view is obvious: what makes you feel better is good. In the context of emotional disorders, psychotropic hedonism espouses treatments that result in "feeling good," regardless of the etiology of the disorder or the long-term effects of such treatments. Consequently, amphetamines or other "uppers" are regarded as valid treatment for depression, even though the long-term effect may be detrimental. This position is consistent with the trend away from long-term or difficult treatments and a ubiquitous desire on the part of patients to get well fast. Whether or not one subscribes to such a position depends on one's view of the benefits of a short-term versus a more lasting sense of feeling good. The clinician who has seen patients over long periods of time or the patient who has observed his own mood changes over long periods may be less satisfied with such approaches. In addition, one must assess how much "feeling good" contributes to one's overall sense of well-being.

CONTRASTING GOALS

The three positions outlined above raise the issue of the goals of any psychiatric treatment. Patients with affective disorders have a variety of symptoms for which they seek improvement. These include feeling "down" or "blue," disturbances in physiologic processes such as sleeping and eating, cognitive problems, inability to make decisions or initiate new activities, and disturbances in marital, familial, social, and occupational functioning. This symptom differential raises the best possibility for the rational integration of different therapies: different treatment approaches effect different outcomes. Once it is established which treatment best effects which outcome, the clinician and the patient will be better able to agree on a plan of action leading to desired results. Like all medical treatments, psychiatric treatment should be based on diagnosis and on some conceptualization of the etiologic and pathologic mechanisms of the disorder.

To date, the evidence indicates that any single ideological treatment approach to the entire affective disorders spectrum is untenable. However, psychological management should be a basic consideration in all cases, regardless of the specific affective disturbance involved. The crucial determination is the type of psychological management: when psychotherapy should be used primarily, when it should be used adjunctively, and when a combination of psychotherapy and drug treatment should be used.

Psychiatric treatment, then, should be based on (1) diagnosis, (2) some conceptualization of the etiologic and pathologic mechanisms of the disorder in question, and (3) current scientific knowledge of the disorder.

The operational definitions and groupings in the third edition of the *Diagnostic and Statistical Manual of Mental Disorders, (DSM-III)* enable improved consensus and clarification in the diagnosis of affective disorders. However, in regard to etiology and pathogenesis, *DSM-III* intentionally avoids any nosologic considerations. This "atheoretical" approach to etiology leaves the assessment and determination of the particular etiologic mechanisms to the clinician's judgment—and to his ideological orientation. Nevertheless, the evidence accumulated in the last decade can be distilled into a set of guidelines for clinical decision making and treatment management. For an integrated overview, the reader is referred to the end of this chapter, where a decision-making protocol for the management of affective disorders is offered.

Affective disorders are heterogeneous in nature; therefore, the clinician must ascertain the etiologic model best suited to the particular disturbance. There is almost universal consensus on the neurophysiologic basis for bipolar and unipolar disorders and for single depressions against the background of a family history of affective disorders. In contrast, the pathogenesis of a single episode of major depression without a family history and of the cyclothymic and dysthymic disorders is open to question and in many cases is more favorably explicated on psychological grounds, especially when available biologic markers are negative. At present, the lack of systematic evidence for any etiologic primacy makes obvious the need for a flexible approach to treating this subgroup of affective disorders. In managing the affective disorders, the practitioner should remember that the goals of treating the acute phase and the goals of long-term maintenance differ.

In the case of bipolar disorders, unipolar disorders, and single episodes with a strong familial history and endogenous characteristics (see chart at end of chapter), pharmacologic treatment and psychotherapeutic management are aimed at the resolution and stabilization of either manic or depressive episodes. Psychotherapeutic efforts to restore euthymia can be carried out by diverse means, depending on whether the symptoms and conflicts are experienced individually, maritally, familially, and so forth. After stabilization has been achieved, the therapist should assess the patient's psychostructural status, family and social relations, view and conception of his disturbance, and conscious and unconscious motivation for further treatment, including the clear delineation of treatment goals. These considerations enable the therapist to tailor the type of psychotherapy to the patient's needs and capabilities and assure both parties that the patient's implied goals are within reach.

In the case of single depressions without a family history or endogenous features, and those belonging to the subgroup of "other" specific affective disorders, the clinician's treatment choices are hindered by the poverty of research on the efficacy and specificity of psychotherapy, on one hand, and the relatively few studies on the usefulness of medication alone or in combination with psychotherapy, on the other. The reader is again referred to the guidelines at the end of the chapter for an overview of the different decision-making steps in choosing treatment.

This chapter is mainly concerned with the psychological management of the major affective disorders.

PSYCHOLOGICAL MANAGEMENT OF DEPRESSION AND MANIA

Treatment strategy during the acute phase of mania or depression is geared toward achieving clinical remission. According to Webster's dictionary, strategy refers to the military science of planning and directing large-scale operations, specifically, the maneuvering of forces into the most advantageous position prior to actual engagement with the enemy. It is distinguished from tactics, which concern the arrangement and maneuvering during action or before the enemy. Tactics are the means of implementation derived from the overall planning that constitutes strategy. In the management of depression and mania, strategy represents the overall planning and approach to achieve euthymia, while tactics are the immediate and specific psychotherapeutic interactions to achieve the overall goals. Thus the clinician, while using such interventions as support, clarification, confrontation, and interpretation, should keep in mind the overall goal of rapid remission and avoid fostering more regressive behavior. Indeed, clinical experience shows that uncovering conflicts during the acute phase worsens the clinical picture and outcome.

THE ACUTE DEPRESSIVE PHASE

During the initial interviews with a depressive patient, and once the diagnosis has been established with some certainty, the clinician must evaluate the depth and severity of the depression and the degree of suicidal risk involved (see chap. 11). These considerations may determine the necessity for hospitalization. Other reasons for hospitalization that should be explored are (1) any medical status compromising the health of the patient, whether a result of the depression or independently associated with it, that requires close medical attention; (2) potential complications that may be introduced by the somatic treatment of an existing medical disorder or by potentially hazardous drug interactions; (3) the lack of appropriate support systems; (4) a strained family or work relationship that would be improved by removal of the patient, whereby the patient, too, would benefit; and (5) the lack of easy accessibility by the patient to the clinician's office or inability of the clinician to make visits with the frequency and intensity required by the patient's clinical condition.

These or any other reasons justifying the need for hospitalization should be clearly spelled out to the patient. The reasons for admission in many instances become the same reasons for discharge, when solutions to the problems are found independently of the course of the depression. Unnecessarily prolonged hospitalization can be avoided in this way, but, most important, the patient participates in decision making and achievement of the admission objectives from the beginning, which can be a curative factor in itself by overcoming the patient's pervasive sense of lack of control over his or her own destiny.

Once it has been determined that the patient can sustain ambulatory treatment, the clinician may switch to a more open-ended interview process, with the intention of eliciting present and past psychological data.

In dealing with depressed patients, the clinician should avoid appearing intrusive. Any patient in distress longs for understanding, but the depressed patient is in greater need than most. The clinician must demonstrate some understanding of the patient's unhappiness in order to instill a sense of confidence in the patient. This rapport is obtained by active participation showing concern for the seriousness of the patient's complaints and by timely and empathic remarks.[18]

Any type of treatment involves a working alliance whereby the rational, healthy, and conflict-free aspects of the patient enter into a therapeutic partnership with the clinician. The capacity to enter into a working alliance requires a basic trust, tolerance of frustrations, and acceptance of reality limitations.[11, 26] In some depressed individuals these functions are preserved, and they are able to enter in an alliance with little difficulty. In other patients, however, these functions are impaired by the depressive process itself or by a preexisting characterologic organization that requires particular care by the therapist in selecting therapeutic techniques. The feelings of apathy, worthlessness, hopelessness, preoccupation, and sometimes agitation in a depressed patient influence the quality of his interactions and are major obstacles to acceptance of the treatment offered.

Except for the severely, psychotically depressed patient, whose impairment in reality testing precludes acceptance of the irrational nature of his symptoms, depressed patients welcome explanations about what they are experiencing. Identification of the symptoms that constitute the clinical picture of depression and placing depression within a framework understandable to the patient are essential to the early treatment process.

No matter how distraught, worried, preoccupied, and withdrawn the patient may be, the therapist should let the patient know, even at the risk of carrying on a monologue, what the treatment is all about, the main reason for it (including the evidence and rationale for medication), and what is expected of the patient (time, duration of sessions, phone calls). Through these interactions the therapist inculcates a sense of respect, confidence, and collaborative effort that constitutes the grist for the therapeutic alliance mill. Many patients who seem totally withdrawn and unresponsive during the acute phase report on recovery how important the therapist's words and actions were for them in feeling accepted and trustworthy.

In preparing the overall treatment strategy, the clinician should gather a premorbid profile of the patient's personality and level of functioning. A longitudinal profile of the patient's experiences around the time the illness developed and any links with past depressive episodes or significant life events are crucial to understanding the role of depression from the patient's internal psychic viewpoint.

A formulation of the patient's characteristic defense operations, object-relatedness, and self-esteem regulation, even in a schematic manner, provides priceless guideposts to the clinician in delineating his tactics. A patient whose self-esteem has been primarily maintained by a sense of autonomy and control over others, and who therefore feels threatened by the helplessness of depression, may perceive the therapist as attempting to control him by suggesting medication or other external therapeutic means. The clinician's awareness of the dynamics will be of assistance in empathizing and in interpreting the patient's resistances, as well as in avoiding potential countertransference struggles.

From these formulations the clinician should derive some hypothesis about the most likely transferential mode in operation for that particular patient, in order to tailor his tactical approach.

Contrary to general opinion, a clinging, dependent relationship with the concomitant expectation of omnipotence and "magic" from the therapist is not the only transference configuration encountered. Oppositional stances, controlling of the therapist, devaluation, narcissistic distancing, and disapproval are often present. In these instances, if the therapist assumes the existence of an underlying dependency and acts accordingly, the patient may perceive the therapist as making him more vulnerable and may therefore resist cooperating.

Understanding the transferential mode at work is of importance to drug treatment as well, since in addition to their obvious neurochemical effects, drugs have an unconscious significance to the patient. A patient who has had experiences with a perceived or real intrusion from a therapist and "possessive" medication will reactivate the old conflicts, whereas another patient may have soothing memories attached to the administration of medication during childhood illness. Few psychiatrists inquire about childhood experiences with taking medication, although it is a universal phenomenon and an easy and nonintrusive way of bringing to light important childhood and rearing psychodynamics.

Once the diagnostic assessment has been completed, the psychiatrist is in a position to outline the goals of the treatment plan and to choose a tactical psychotherapeutic approach whereby the patient is likely to derive maximal benefit. Specifically, the psychiatrist can decide whether an individual approach is preferable or whether interventions at the familial or marital level are indicated.

By and large, individual intervention suffices. However, when symptoms and conflicts are precipitated by interactions with spouses or other family members, the involvement of these persons facilitates the treatment enormously. It should be clear that these interventions are not aimed at *resolving* underlying and long-existing conflicts that may or may not have been involved in the precipitation of the depression; they are aimed at *facilitating* the treatment, minimizing resistance by the patient, and obviating interference or sabotaging maneuvers by significant people in the patient's life. In short, they are supportive in nature.

The possible indications for spouse or family treatment in the more traditional sense should be assessed after remission of the acute phase. The following case illustrates some of the options for psychotherapeutic intervention available to the clinician.

Mrs. E, a 62-year-old woman, was referred by the internal medicine clinic for psychiatric consultation after she complained that her daughter had been trying to kill her in order to collect her life insurance. At the time of the consultation, Mrs. E appeared suspicious and somewhat withdrawn, with signs of disorientation to time and place. Impairment in the performance of calculation and recall were also evident. With the help of information gathered from the daughter, who accompanied her, a picture consistent with a major depressive episode of two years' duration was obtained. The possible differential diagnoses contemplated after the first interview were (1) organic affective syndrome, or (2) major depressive episode with clinical features of a pseudodementia.

After extensive medical workup, the first diagnosis was ruled out. A very mild hypothyroidism from a thyroidectomy 25 years before was revealed but was insufficient to explain an organic brain syndrome. Furthermore, a history of two previous episodes of major depression in the woman's 20s and 40s was subsequently established in an interview with her daughter, and a major depressive episode of recurrent type was assumed. Amitriptyline therapy was initiated in conjunction with Synthroid. A rapid and consistent improvement followed within a few weeks, including restoration of her orientation and recall functions. Nevertheless, references to her daughter's homicidal intentions, together with demands to go back to a southern state to care for an ill younger brother, continued to dominate the content of her session's material. This communication alerted the therapist to explore the significance of her preoccupations, and it was learned that the patient had lost her mother at age 4, during the birth of her brother.

In association with that information Mrs. E stated that she had left her first husband in a rather abrupt fashion when her daughter (the subject of her delusional concerns) was 4 years old. According to Mrs. E, when her mother died she had "no choice but to assume a mothering role for her brother and raise him." She described that choice as being "self-sacrifice" and spontaneously equated that attitude with the conditions surrounding her separation when her daughter was 4 years old. In her view she had again sacrificed herself for the sake of somebody else. A worsening of the depression appeared, and was believed to be related to a lack of compliance with the drug regimen. Her refusal to take medication was based on the belief that her daughter was poisoning her. This belief was reinforced by her daughter's behavior. Bewildered by Mrs. E's accusations, and with increasing feelings of guilt, the daughter attempted to avoid any confrontation by pouring the medication into her mother's beverages.

This transaction made evident the need for further exploration of the relationship between Mrs. E and her daughter. As proper management of the medication was reinstated, clinical improvement followed, permitting further reconstruction and identification of a long-existing symbiotic relationship. Indeed, Mrs. E's daughter eventually stated that she felt she was responsible for her mother's decompensation, thus agreeing partially with Mrs. E's accusations and rendering her unable to respond realistically to her mother's delusional beliefs. On the other hand, Mrs. E indirectly conveyed her jealousy and envy for what her daughter had achieved. She felt that these achievements were the result of her own caring and efforts on behalf of her daughter. Mrs. E's delusion had started when a close friend of the family had commented on the daughter's "beauty and achievements." In a typical paranoid reversal, Mrs. E decided that her daughter was jealous of her own "beauty and wealth." The initiation of this paranoid process was coincidental with the appearance of some of the depressive symptoms and a decreasing role in the care and responsibility of her teenaged grandchildren. The role as mother substitute and household organizer had sharply decreased, not only because of the family changes, but also because of incipient signs of senility. Thus the significance of her wishes to go back to the old ways of self-sacrifice and caring for her brother became evident and interpretable to both mother and daughter. A period of working through the symbiotic nature of the relationship and of clarification of changes in the family system followed, eventually leading to the placement of Mrs. E in a nursing home, a consideration that had been secretly contemplated but not openly discussed for many years, since signs of fluctuation in her sensorium had been present long before the onset of the current depressive episode.

Mrs. E's case illustrates several factors that need to be addressed in psychological management:

1. The need for a comprehensive workup before embarking on any treatment effort.

2. The necessity of interviewing significant others to gather information whenever the patient is not a reliable source.

3. The need to understand the particular intrapsychic or interpersonal meaning of the symptoms expressed. In Mrs. E's case, the delusional preoccupations and demands had to be understood in the context of her entire adult life.

4. The need for intervention that accords with the meaning and experience of depression for the patient. In Mrs. E's case, this meant exposing the symbiotic relationship in order to gain her trust and confidence and overcome her resistance to medication.

5. The necessity of addressing the circumstances in which depression emerges since, whether or not they have any direct influence on the precipitation of the illness, the stresses surrounding the episode lend a particular meaning to the depression or bring about latent and preexisting conflicts. Mrs. E had had recurrent depressive episodes that had gone undetected or untreated. Her current episode worsened the incipient symptoms of senility and brought into the foreground the progressively threatened dissolution of the symbiotic relationship.

The clinical interview of a patient in an acute phase recently introduced to the interviewer must be comprehensive in order to determine or rule out any possible medical condition, either as a causal factor or concurrent with the affective illness. Nevertheless, the clinician should use questions aimed at eliciting medical facts judiciously and tactfully and should refrain from intrusive probing. Otherwise, the obsessive and hypochondriacal preoccupations so often encountered in depressed patients may be augmented and, paradoxically, foster increased apprehension rather than a calming and trusting relationship with the interviewer. On the other hand, when psychological complaints dominate the picture—e.g., pervasive anxiety, self-fragmentation, interpersonal difficulties, mistrust—in the presence of clear-cut depressive symptoms warranting the use of antidepressants, those psychological manifestations must be dealt with first in order to establish a working alliance before any drug treatment can be suggested.

The critical objective in the initial encounter, whatever the number of sessions required, is to achieve an alliance that secures mutual treatment cooperation.

Dr. Z, a psychologist in his mid-50s, sought consultation for anxiety attacks of several months' duration that had become more persistent. In a distraught state at the time of the interview, he rapidly recounted previous episodes of anxiety in his 20s, for which he had undergone psychoanalysis. He expressed his shame at succumbing to anxiety again, since he felt it was a sign of weakness, and shared the insight gained from his previous psychotherapy about anxiety and its connection to homosexual longings. Dr. Z, a professor at a leading department of psychology, was esteemed by his students and the faculty, but because of administrative reorganization within the department, some of his functions had been reallocated. These changes meant to Dr. Z that he was dispensable and that the department chairman had lost confidence in him; he interpreted this as a further sign of weakness on his part.

The anxiety state verged on agitation, and evidence of cardinal signs and symptoms of depression was elicited. Three previous episodes of agitated depression were ascertained; one had been the main reason for his seeking psychoanalytic treatment 25 years before.

Dr. Z's anxiety and hypochondriacal preoccupations were interspersed with despair over his children and his perceived failure as a strong and reliable father. Moreover, his feelings of failure now extended to his previous psychotherapy experience, since in his view he had failed his analyst, for which he berated himself and felt extremely guilty.

Despite his incessant questioning as to what was wrong with him, any attempts at explaining that he was suffering a depression met with lack of acceptance. The information exacerbated his anxiety and made him even more resistant. Indeed, he felt that accepting the possibility of being depressed was a further betrayal of his previous and now deceased therapist. Furthermore, to trust and accept a new therapist carried the same meaning to him.

The obvious dilemma of his wishing help but feeling that to accept it would reinforce his belief that it was a sign of weakness and betrayal was interpreted to him. The therapist concluded that Dr. Z's pervasive anxiety was almost of a traumatic quality and suggested to him that he might be reviving some meaningful similar event. Shortly after a series of associations aimed at dismissing the interpretation, Dr. Z recalled, in a much calmer manner, that when he was 12 years old his father's business had become bankrupt. A flow of memories followed whose contents were filled with references to a sudden disillusion with his then idealized father. Since Dr. Z had a child of the same age a further link could be established in the context of a more inclusive interpretation: it was understandable that his psychological state of despair made him feel that "his business" had failed, like his father's had, and that he not only was betraying his previous therapist but also feared that his children were experiencing him in the same manner he had viewed his own father. In the next two sessions, in a much calmer atmosphere, Dr. Z further reconstructed these meaningful memories and accepted the recommendation for drug treatment. Later his fears abated and he recovered completely from his depression.

Even in the presence of unquestionable signs of depression, the clinician must first establish a therapeutic alliance with his patient. Although the diagnosis and indications for medication may be clear-cut, a meaningful rapport must be achieved through whatever mechanisms the patient puts at the clinician's disposal.[1] In Dr. Z's case the empathic response promoted a feeling of being understood and repaired his threatened self. Both experiences were essential for the acceptance of the new therapist and for a treatment plan to take place.

The central role played by the formation of an alliance in the initial encounter has been similarly voiced by Margulies and Havens:[19] "Before one pursues any clinical investigation—whether into symptoms and signs, associative material, social context, or the patient's felt experience—the state of alliance must be examined and in many cases repaired."

In summary, the initial interviews unfold in the context of a sustained working alliance in which the diagnosis, need for hospitalization versus outpatient management, education of the patient in his disorder, assessment of the personality dynamics, and familial and social systems are examined in an open-ended, appropriate, and timely fashion.

Furthermore, regardless of the psychotherapeutic tactics employed, several main objectives should prevail: (1) the alleviation of guilt and despair, (2) the restoration of hope, (3) the protection from self-destructive behavior, and (4) the exploration and interpretation of the meaning of depression for the patient.

The restoration of hope is a pivotal issue in depression. The identification of a negative cognitive set and its related cognitive distortions must be followed by confrontation and clarification to undo the pessimistic views and the distorted conceptions about positive changes. The patient's premorbid profile is of utmost importance in assisting the therapist to underscore discrepant perceptions of himself. Often the patient does not perceive or report the changes affected by medication, for the same reasons.

THE MANIC PHASE

The initial interview with a patient displaying manic behavior is a dramatic, challenging experience. The distractibility, rapid thinking, massive denial, and lack of inhibitions, together with the constant mobilization of hostility to provoke others and the omnipotent and magical perception of himself and others by the manic patient, strain the therapist's interactions with the patient before the therapist is able to establish even a rudimentary alliance. Often, due either to the impossibility of forming a minimal alliance or to the impulsive and unreliable behavior, hospitalization is necessary. Indeed, about 75% of patients who are first seen in a manic stage require hospitalization. The psychiatrist is in a better position when he has worked with the patient before, since the previously established alliance should be helpful in reaching the distraught patient's basic trust and rational ego. The therapist who is aware of a family history of manic-depression in a patient being treated for depression without previous manic or hypomanic episodes should attempt, at the appropriate time, to alert the patient to that possibility. This is not only sound secondary preventive practice, but also a helpful anticipatory therapeutic intervention for the future manic episode, since it will further communication and understanding at the time of the manic crisis, when the alliance is severely disrupted.

In approaching the manic patient, the clinician should keep in mind the basic dynamics at play. Flooded with overstimulation, the individual's grandiosity, exhibitionism, and aggressiveness become progressively out of control. The manic's interpersonal behavior, chaotic and provocative as it may be, is an attempt to engage others in restoring order and control to his disabled self. Regressively behaving like a toddler in the practicing period, he is intoxicated with his own faculties and in need of emotional refueling to gain calmness and control. His behavior is paradoxical. On one hand he claims to be self-sufficient, autonomous, and powerful; on the other, his actions belie his words. The increase in perceptiveness and the loss of boundaries between self and others during the manic process account for the patient's ability to recognize underlying feelings and motivations in others. This sensitivity is a major cause of interpersonal conflicts and maneuvers and the main source of countertransference problems.

Janowsky et al. have described five commonly encountered manic behaviors: (1) manipulation of the self-esteem of others, (2) perceptiveness of vulnerability and conflict, (3) projection of responsibility, (4) progressive limit testing, and (5) alienation of family members.[12]

These behaviors clearly portend difficulty in treating manic individuals. Another major therapeutic obstacle to be overcome by the clinician is the temptation to succumb to any of the possible countertransference reactions so easily induced by these patients. Assuming a selfobject function in order to curb the overstimulated self of the manic individual is crucial. The therapist should take an active, nonambivalent, firm stance, setting limits and controls. Basically, the manic individual is overburdened and frightened. The clinician should let the patient know of his understanding of what the patient is experiencing, including how he affects others, to make the patient feel more secure. The main objective throughout is to provide protection.

In dealing with manic patients, as in dealing with any violence-prone or acting-out patients in general, what the therapist conveys nonverbally, what he does, and how he acts are of more importance than the content of what he says. By these means he communicates assurance and some idea of control to the patient.

Gaining the support and active participation of relatives is often imperative. Spouses in particular need to be engaged, since they often aid the manic patient's acceptance of treatment.

Mrs. T, a 32-year-old woman who had adopted a baby boy eight months prior to the onset of her illness, was being seen by a psychologist in marital therapy and receiving Valium prescribed by her family physician. Both professionals had overlooked the possibility of a mixed manic-depressive disorder, and as a result her clinical condition escalated to the point that her hostile behavior, restlessness, and abusive and frequent telephone calls to relatives, undermining and berating her husband and parents, created a crisis of major proportions in the extended family, which even under normal circumstances was a rather enmeshed one, without clear definition of boundaries.

Mrs. T incessantly berated her husband, pointing out his flaws and shortcomings. This depiction was reinforced by his inability to meet her intense and overly demanding sexual behavior and by his defensive withdrawal as a coping attempt. Mr. T had been a central, stabilizing, and mediating element in the family network subsystems until the eruption of his wife's manic disorder. His withdrawal was viewed as the main cause for the collapse of the family relationships.

Following a referral to a psychiatrist, and after an extensive evaluation, Mrs. T was placed on a rapid tranquilization regimen with Haldol while started on lithium. A meeting with members of both sides of the family was held. The therapist actively attempted to restore Mr. T to his pivotal role, to reestablish the family equilibrium. Shortly after Mrs. T's recovery, the couple was seen in marital therapy, primarily to repair the consequences of the narcissistic assault on Mr. T.

However, as could be expected, Mrs. T's exaggerated complaints had some grain of truth and were related to long-standing marital conflicts that had been largely and silently ignored by both spouses.

The case of Mrs. T highlights the necessity for rapid evaluation with a flexible approach and illustrates how the formation of a working alliance can be pursued through different avenues—in this case, through the strained marital relationship. It also illustrates the necessity of assessing and repairing any psychological aftermath of the affective episode.

Once a remission has occurred, the patient should be reassessed to ascertain the need for any specific psychological intervention. Ideally, the clinician should evaluate the patient with an open mind, tailoring the follow-up to the particular circumstances of each case. The final decision on any further psychological intervention must be based on a total assessment of all the factors involved in the case, taking into account the relative importance of their influence on the ultimate therapeutic prognosis.[5] Lack of compliance with the prescribed drug regimen and the dropout phenomenon that occurs during the maintenance phase are in many instances intricately related to the clinician's dismissal of the patient's directly or covertly expressed wish to be treated with response and care for his entire person, rather than for an isolated illness or "biologic" disease. Appraisal of the personality organization during the euthymic state is essential, since many individuals, owing to the regression induced by the affective disturbance, display transient disruptions of ego functions that are state-related. These patients may mistakenly be thought to have a more primitive organization than they really have. By the same token, the presence of borderline features between episodes has prognostic and specific psychotherapeutic implications.

As a rule, patients with severe character pathology need multiple interventions and more intensive and aggressive follow-up. Many of these patients are ideal candidates for the specialized program offered by some affective disorders clinics. The management of patients with affective disorders is less difficult when centralized, either in the hands of an individual or at an affective disorders clinic, than when psychotherapy and drug treatment are separately conducted.

Due to the common presence of infidelity, abusiveness, and hostile remarks aimed at the spouse during the manic episode, involvement of the conjugal partner is frequently essential after remission since the quality of the marital relationship has been in many instances substantially altered. Certainly mania seems to be more disruptive to the marital relationship than depression.[17] Thus, marital therapy or couples group therapy needs special consideration as part of the follow-up management of bipolars.

Psychotherapy during the maintenance phase seems to have significant impact on the course of bipolar illness. In a study by Davenport et al., couples group therapy resulted in a more benign course of illness in patients on lithium maintenance than in those given minimal support beyond medication.[4] Likewise the use of psychotherapy in conjunction with lithium prophylaxis appears to reduce the failure rate, the regressive behavior, and the chronicity of bipolar illness.

PSYCHOTHERAPY AND AFFECTIVE DISORDERS

The efficacy of psychotherapy in the treatment of certain types of affective disorders has been questioned. Among the less obvious problems in the assessment of psychotherapy results is the difficulty in defining outcome criteria: what constitutes change and improvement. In addition, insufficient isolation of the specific curative methods in each therapy compounds the complexity of the evaluation of the efficacy of psychotherapy. Nevertheless, the bulk of evidence at present suggests that psychotherapy works. What remains to be determined is what type of psychotherapy works more effectively for what conditions.

In the last few years some investigators have attempted to answer these questions by designing two specific forms of individual psychotherapy for the treatment of depression: cognitive therapy and interpersonal therapy. Both modes are short term, lasting for 12 to 20 weekly sessions.

Cognitive therapy, derived from the work of Beck,[2] focuses on identifying the "cognitive trial" and associated errors of cognition.

Interpersonal therapy uses a psychodynamic approach with particular focus on the here and now and on the social and interpersonal relations of the patient. Deep unconscious conflicts born of childhood events are given little attention. Within this general framework, the problem areas encountered in depression and given special attention are (1) grief and loss, (2) interpersonal role disputes, and (3) interpersonal deficits. This type of psychotherapy attempts to modify the depressive symptoms constellation as well as the social and interpersonal adjustment. Changes in the personality structure are not a primary target.[6]

Research on the efficacy of cognitive therapy for the treatment of nonbipolar, nonpsychotic depressive patients suggests that cognitive therapy provides greater symptomatic improvement than imipramine alone. One year after completion of cognitive therapy, patients rated themselves significantly lower in depression symptomatology than a control group treated with imipramine.[15-20]

Similarly, controlled studies of interpersonal therapy alone versus amitriptyline in the treatment of acute nonbipolar, nonpsychotic patients showed about equal results. However, combined treatment was found to be more efficacious than either treatment alone.[22-25] The patients treated with amitriptyline had greater relief on the vegetative symptoms, while the group treated with psychotherapy showed more positive changes in mood, work, interests, and suicidal ideation. Interestingly, follow-up studies indicated that nearly 15% of the patients had a certain amount of chronicity after an acute episode.[21-24] Chronicity was equally present in those treated with drugs or psychotherapy and apparently was related to the degree of neuroticism previously present. Thus, although interpersonal psychotherapy appears to provide improvement in social functioning, it does not prevent chronicity, an indication that long-term psychotherapy could have a definite effect on this outcome and should be studied for any differential effect on neuroticism.

Claims that both interpersonal and cognitive therapies are more treatment-specific than other modes must be demonstrated, since it is possible that common factors are responsible for the therapeutic effect, regardless of technique or theory.

Weissman has reviewed the evidence for the efficacy of marital therapy, group therapy, and some forms of behavioral therapy, in addition to some of the interpersonal and cognitive therapy studies already alluded to.[23] Each therapy alone proved to be efficacious in comparison with control groups receiving low-contact or no active treatment. Thus, it seems that for nonbipolar, nonpsychotic, acute depressive outpatients, psychotherapy can be a useful treatment choice.

The status of psychotherapy, alone or in combination, in the treatment of dysthmic, cyclothymic, and some atypical disorders awaits further investigation.

This group of disturbances encompasses the depressive neuroses and affective characterologic disorders of past nomenclatures. Such disorders traditionally were treated with a variety of psychotherapies, prominently psychoanalysis and insight-oriented psychotherapy. At present, no clear guidelines for indications or counterindications can be formulated, except those derived in accordance with each particular psychotherapy indication criterion; these criteria are themselves most likely independent of the nature of the affective process.

COMBINED TREATMENT FOR AFFECTIVE DISORDERS

RESEARCH AND CLINICAL ISSUES

Combined treatment refers to the use of psychotropic medication in conjunction with some form of psychotherapy. There are few good studies comparing the efficacy of combined treatment with either psychotherapy or psychopharmacotherapy in the treatment of affective disorders. One reason for this paucity of data has been that depression is the chief manifestation of a heterogeneous group of disorders that need to be defined by sound clinical or research criteria; studies on the efficacy of psychotherapy have often lacked such criteria. Second, more research emphasis has been placed on the relative efficacy of either psychotherapy or a specific drug treatment by comparing each with a control group, with another type of psychotherapy, or with another type of antidepressant medication. Only a few studies have compared the combined effects with other treatments alone. Third, it has been technically and ethically difficult to establish a control group in affective disorders research. Since bipolar disorders and major depression clearly benefit from psychiatric intervention, and since the likelihood of suicide increases without treatment, a no-treatment control group is difficult to justify. DiMascio et al. have described a professionally monitored control group for depressed patients which provides a clinically and ethically sound compromise to this research dilemma.[8] There is one further difficulty in the research of combined treatment: establishing outcome criteria. The efficacy of any psychiatric treatment depends on whether one measures global outcome, such as rehospitalization, specific symptom(s) improvement, improvements in close interpersonal relationships, or social adjustment. Frank[9] has highlighted this issue, noting that psychotherapy in general may have its greatest impact on social effectiveness rather than symptom amelioration. This research has progressed well in schizophrenia, showing that target symptoms (i.e., hallucinations and delusions) respond best to major tranquilizers, whereas social and interpersonal functioning may best be treated with group, family, or individual psychotherapy. There is less comparable research on the affective disorders.

STUDIES OF EFFICACY OF COMBINED TREATMENT

Covi et al. studied the effects of group therapy in conjunction with diazepam (15 mg/day), imipramine (150 mg/day), or placebo in a group of 200 chronically depressed women.[3] They found a noticeable group therapy effect for all groups early in treatment (1–2 weeks), but a less prominent effect by 8 to 16 weeks. By that time, imipramine clearly had the most pronounced effect. However, group therapy retained a small but significant effect on outcome, particularly on measures of hostility and interpersonal sensitivity.

Klerman first examined the relative effects of combined treatment by studying depressed patients recovering from an acute depressive episode.[14] He compared psychotherapy with low contact in three groups of recovering depressives, those taking imipramine (150 mg/day), those taking placebo, and those taking no pills. Psychotherapy consisted of weekly sessions with a social worker and concentrated on current interpersonal problems; it could be described as supportive rather than insight-oriented. At four months imipramine had a clear effect on symptom improvement but little effect on social functioning; psychotherapy did not have a significant effect at that time. However, at eight months psychotherapy had a significant effect on social functioning. In his discussion, Klerman noted that the effect of psychotherapy on social functioning may require a period of time with sustained symptom control.

Weissman et al. studied the effects of psychotherapy on ambulatory patients with acute depression.[22, 23] One week after the initial assessment, patients with major depression (excluding bipolars and those with psychotic symptoms) were randomly assigned to psychotherapy alone, amitriptyline (flexible dosage of 100–200 mg/day), combined psychotherapy and imipramine (flexible dosage of 100–200 mg/day), combined psychotherapy and amitriptyline, or nonscheduled treatment. Patients in the latter group were instructed to contact the psychiatrist if their symptoms reached such intensity that they could not continue in this group. Psychotherapy consisted of 50-minute sessions with a psychiatrist; it was described as short term and interpersonal and focused on the social context of the depression. This study showed that combined treatment was more effective than either psychotherapy or pharmacotherapy alone and delayed the onset of symptomatic failure. The study also showed psychotherapy and pharmacotherapy to be equally efficacious.

Rush et al. examined the effectiveness of cognitive therapy versus imipramine in 41 unipolar depressed patients.[20] They concluded that cognitive therapy was superior to imipramine alone. Patients undergoing both treatments were not included in the study.

Friedman examined the effects of marital therapy and amitriptyline, in combination and alone, on 196 primarily neurotically depressed patients (*DSM-II* classification).[10] He found amitriptyline to have a significant and early effect on reducing depressive symptoms, whereas marital therapy had a significant but later effect on improving family performance and the patient's perception of marriage. The study implied that combined treatment was preferable to either treatment alone.

The only long-term study comparing the efficacy of psychoanalytic psychotherapy and antidepressant medication has been reported by Lesse,[16] who treated 851 severely depressed patients on an outpatient basis. Although this study lacks the rigorous methodology and research criteria now used in affective disorders research, it is an excellent report of one clinician's work with severe depressives using combined treatment. Patients in this study reported the duration of illness to the onset of treatment. Three antidepressant drugs were used during the first 12 years: proniazid (discontinued in 1960), imipramine, and tranylcypromine; newer antidepressants were used over the last 8 years. Imipramine and amitriptyline were used in the range of 150 to 250 mg/day. The psychotherapeutic aspects of the combined treatment were supportive in nature and aimed at removing the suicidal ideas and drives and improving the psychomotor behavior and depressed mood. Patients were seen twice a week for the first two weeks, during which time family members were also consulted. Patients and/or family were encouraged to report by telephone at specifically designated times during this initial treatment phase. Subsequently a more analytic psychotherapy was initiated, provided there was some improvement in the suicidal ideation and mood. Patients were evaluated weekly on a variety of symptom scales, including mood, psychomotor activity, vocation and social performance, anxiety, and neurovegetative symptoms (e.g., weight loss, insomnia, anorexia, concentration). Fifty-nine percent of patients showed excellent or good improvement in the first ten days, while 41% showed only fair or poor improvement. By 14 to 16 days, 71% had shown excellent or good improvement; by 23 days, 83% had shown excellent or good improvement. After six months, 93% of the patients who had excellent or good results were able to maintain this status. Most of the remaining 141 patients (17%) responded to electroshock therapy. Lesse had previously studied a sample of 75 severely depressed patients whom he treated with supportive, psychoanalytically oriented therapy alone. Only 16% of this sample had excellent or good results after five weeks. Lesse concluded that combined treatment is the treatment of choice for severely depressed ambulatory patients.

These initial studies imply that combined treatment is better than either psychotherapy or medication alone; it is also clear that psychotherapy and medication effect different outcomes. Studies currently in progress may further elucidate what types of psychotherapy are preferable and may clarify the types of outcomes likely to be seen with these different treatment approaches. Consideration must also be given to the selection criteria when considering outcome research. A major depression may be diagnosed in patients with severe character or borderline pathology. In such cases one must first consider the treatment needed to improve the depression. Although the character issues will undoubtedly influence the depressive presentation, the clinician must make a somewhat artificial distinction between the character disorder and the affective state and decide whether the character disorder per se should also be treated. If the decision is made jointly by the clinician and the patient, treatment of the character disorder proceeds after the acute depressive symptoms remit.

CLINICAL EXAMPLES OF COMBINED TREATMENT FOR DEPRESSED PATIENTS

A review of the research on combined treatment highlights some of the dilemmas faced by the clinician who chooses to use psychotherapy in conjunction with psychopharmacologic treatment. The following clinical vignettes illustrate issues described earlier in this chapter.

Mr. A, a 25-year-old medical student, sought treatment after three weeks of severe insomnia and anorexia resulting in a 15-lb weight loss. He felt low and had severe doubts about his ability to become a physician, as well as more general questions of self-esteem, such as his ability to relate to and be accepted by a woman. He had suicidal thoughts but doubted that he would act on them. The only psychosocial precipitant was that the depression started prior to his graduation from medical school. Family history revealed a severe depression in an older sister and alcoholism in an uncle. After the initial assessment, the psychiatrist told the patient that he seemed to have a serious depression; the patient accepted this readily. The psychiatrist suggested a course of amitriptyline and urged psychotherapy. The issue of medication drew several questions from the patient: Did this mean that he had a manic-depressive disorder? Would he need to take medication all his life? At this time the patient accepted the idea of psychotherapy because he felt it might improve his negative view of himself as well as help prevent further depressions. For the next month he was seen for one hour weekly. Psychotherapy centered on issues the patient chose to discuss: his fear about becoming a resident and whether he would be capable, and his ill feelings associated with leaving his parents and family to move to the East Coast. Originally the patient saw the separation issue as a problem his family had: their need to have him around, their overuse of him as a sounding board, their reliance on him to keep the peace between different family members. During the first month of therapy the patient began to see his own anxiety and sadness as associated with the proposed separation. By this time his sleeping and eating patterns had returned to normal and he was beginning to feel better. During the second month his interest in psychotherapy waned, as shown by missed or late sessions. When confronted with this he related the view that his depression was "biologic" and completely responsive to the amitriptyline. He stated his desire to understand himself better but continued to avoid therapeutic discussions centered on himself. By graduation he felt his "old self" and ready to move East. He did not want a psychotherapy referral but stated his intention of continuing the amitriptyline. Nine months into his residency the patient called, saying he was just beginning to have symptoms again; he admitted discontinuing the amitriptyline one month earlier. At that time he requested a psychiatric referral for both his medication maintenance and psychotherapy.

This case illustrates two issues in combined treatment. First, the desire for psychotherapy on the patient's part often requires an optimal degree of anxiety or suffering. Too much may make the patient unamenable to such treatment; when symptoms disappear, so may the patient's motivation. Second, when such a clear improvement of symptoms occurs simultaneously with a discussion of new and undesirable dynamic material, the patient may have a strong desire to see the depression as purely biologic and to subtly and unconsciously sabotage the psychotherapeutic efforts.

Mr. B, a 48-year-old Mexican immigrant, had been severely depressed for at least six months. He had been hospitalized on the recommendation of another psychiatrist two months earlier but had left the hospital after two days and refused further treatment. He now had severe sadness with crying spells, suicidal ideation, psychomotor agitation, insomnia, and fatigue during the day which improved slightly toward evening. He had been on several antidepressants in the past but never for extended periods or at therapeutic dosages. The psychiatric resident treating the patient started seeing him in psychotherapy twice a week. This plan was decided upon because of the patient's reluctance to take medication and the resident's assessment of the patient's need to form a therapeutic alliance to prevent increased suicidal ideation. The patient agreed to this plan and kept his appointments regularly. As the therapy evolved, the patient cried and complained about his inability to do the things he once did, how his depression cost him his job, caused his impotence, and was leading to a divorce with his wife of 25 years. As time went on the resident grew increasingly uncomfortable and lost confidence in his ability to treat the patient in psychotherapy. Whenever he suggested that the patient looked better or commented positively on something the patient had done, the patient would cry or moan and continue to relate how bad things were for him. After two months of psychotherapy the resident suggested they start an antidepressant drug; the fact that he was choosing this treatment because of his feelings of defeat was clear to the resident and to the patient as well. For the next two months, three tricyclics and one monoamine oxidase inhibitor were used. Each drug was terminated after the patient complained about their side effects and that they weren't working. Psychotherapy had been reduced to discussions of the medication and seemed to revolve around the patient proving the ineffectiveness of the medication and the therapy. The resident began to feel as helpless as the patient and, at the patient's request, started writing letters to social security, public aid, and former employers of the patient in an effort to improve the patient's financial resources. After five months the patient became markedly suicidal. The resident reluctantly hospitalized the patient and transferred him to another psychiatrist.

There are several points to be made regarding combined treatment in depression. First, the clinician who places too great an emphasis on psychotherapy and his ability to practice it often feels defeated when an antidepressant drug is added to the treatment regime. This defeat is apt to be perceived by the patient, to the detriment of the therapeutic relationship. Second, it is not uncommon for a therapist to empathize with the patient's sense of hopelessness; this is more likely to occur when a more intense relationship is established with the patient. Use of this empathic sense to understand the patient is needed, but the therapist must retain his ability to objectively assess the patient's progress and to plan accordingly.

In this chapter we have emphasized the need to clarify the various treatment strategies and tactics to be followed in dealing with affective disorders. It is our contention that psychological management is the basic approach, regardless of whether or not medication is the primary mode of intervention. At the root of psychological management is the fostering and development of a therapeutic alliance and an understanding of the dynamics at play. The initial steps in the intervention and rehabilitation of individuals with affective disorders should be the accurate diagnosis and evaluation of the illness and the individual and family resources. We believe that therapeutic success with these patients depends on the therapist's skills, degree of involvement, recognition of individual and environmental influences, and use of pragmatic strategies. Affective disorders, with their universal symptomatology and predictive course, nevertheless take place within each person's unique self-system, lending individual meaning to the experience of the disorder. For a valid therapeutic process to develop, the clinician must empathically merge his feelings with those of the patient.

GUIDELINES FOR THE TREATMENT OF AFFECTIVE DISORDERS

MAJOR AFFECTIVE DISORDERS

BIPOLAR DISORDER: MANIC PHASE

Single Episode: Acute Phase

Reach proper diagnosis
Helpful indicators in addition to clinical picture are:
Family history of affective disorders.
Previous history of brisk response to tricyclics or switch into mania in patients diagnosed as unipolar when treated with antidepressants.
Information from family members and significant others regarding clinical picture.
History of postpartum depression.

Differentiate manic elation from other psychological elations in patients with narcissistic character disorders or borderline conditions.

May use standardized instruments in addition to *DSM-III* criteria to help in the diagnosis, such as Schedule for Affective Disorders and Schizophrenia (SADS), Research Diagnostic Criteria (RDC), or Diagnostic Interview Schedule (DIS).

Outpatient management versus hospitalization

Need for close medical attention?

Appropriate support systems?

Accessibility by patient to clinician, availability of clinician in terms of frequency of visits and intensity required by the clinical condition of the patient?

75% of newly diagnosed patients in manic stage require admission.

Pharmacologic management

Pharmacotherapy is a must; lithium or phenothiazines (haloperidol, chlorpromazine) are indicated in the acute phase. If there is risk of toxicity or extreme psychosis, consider antipsychotic medication alone until psychosis is manageable, then start lithium therapy.

Medical workup should be done before starting lithium therapy; assess renal function, thyroid and cardiac function.

Therapeutic range for serum lithium is 0.5 to 1.5 mEq/L.

Blood levels should be monitored weekly until stabilization is achieved.

Wait 12 hours after last lithium dose before taking blood sample.

If it is the first manic episode, consider benefits vs. risks of lithium therapy: 50:50 chance of no further episodes in next 3 years without lithium treatment.

The more typical the clinical picture, the more likely the patient will respond to lithium treatment.

Psychological management

Psychotherapeutic management should be aimed at the resolution and stabilization of the manic episode.

Keep in mind the basic maneuvers used by the acutely manic patient:

Manipulation of self-esteem of others

Perceptiveness to vulnerability and conflict

Projection of responsibility

Progressive limit-testing

Alienation of family members

Assess life events as precipitant factors, as well as the presence and role of support systems, especially family members, living with patient.

After patient is euthymic, assess underlying personality and need for psychotherapy.

If underlying personality is a character disorder, assess need for psychotherapeutic management for the personality disorder.

Bipolar Disorder: Recurrent Episodes

Maintenance of Bipolar Patients on Lithium Therapy

Pharmacotherapy
Consider lithium therapy alone or with antidepressants or phenothiazines.
Be aware that bipolar depressed patients might switch into mania with antidepressant medication.
After steady state of serum lithium has been obtained, levels can be measured at monthly intervals. More frequent measurements are necessary:
If signs of lithium toxicity occur
When the dose is altered or significant coexisting diseases occur
When signs of a relapse of mania or depression occur
If any significant change in sodium or fluid intake occurs
Minimum clinically effective dose of lithium should always be used, and patients should be maintained on lithium therapy only if benefits persist.
Psychological management
Psychotherapeutic management should be aimed at the prevention of relapses through compliance and better monitoring of precipitating stress.
Explore underlying personality during euthymia; consider indications for psychotherapy.
If marital discord is interfering with the treatment, consider marital therapy.
If underlying personality needs psychotherapy, carefully consider the benefits vs. risks of having the psychotherapy and pharmacotherapy given by the same or different therapists.
If underlying personality is a borderline character disorder, be aware that course of illness, periods of remission, and management are different from those of bipolar patients without severe character pathology.

MAJOR DEPRESSIVE ILLNESS

Single Episode

Reach proper diagnosis to qualify the episode as endogenous and to differentiate from depressive illness of a psychological etiology or depression induced by drugs, organic conditions, etc. Use the following biologic markers as helpful indicators:

Dexamethasone Suppression Test (high specificity for endogenous depression). If cortisol secretion is not suppressed below the level of 5 μg/dl following the administration of 1 mg of dexamethasone, the test will be:
Normal with complete recovery
Normal with switch into mania
Gradual improvement with treatment
TRH Stimulation Test: A blunted TSH to TRH is associated with certain forms of depression.
Sleep patterns:
Shortened REM latency
Increased REM activity
Sleep continuity decreased
Delta sleep decreased

Pharmacotherapy
Medical workup necessary before starting antidepressant medication.
Use tricyclics. Select antidepressant amitriptyline, nortriptyline, imipramine, desipramine, or new antidepressants (maprotiline, Amoxapine).
If there is no response to tertiary amines like amitriptyline or imipramine, switch to secondary amine like desipramine or consider MAO inhibitors or new antidepressants.
Change in sleep patterns as a response to a single dose of amitriptyline (50 mg) is a good prediction of clinical response to that drug:
Rapid increase in REM latency
Decrease in sleep onset difficulty
Overall decrease in REM sleep
Monitor antidepressants with blood levels if possible. They are indicated in the presence of:
Physical illness, particularly cardiovascular disorders
Pronounced subjective side effects
Inadequate effect with standard dosage
Severe time constraints in achieving adequate level
Phenomena of drug interaction: if the patient is taking other medications, they might change blood levels
Suggested stepwise usage for a trial of tricyclics:
50 mg at night for 2 nights
100 mg/day for 3 nights
150 mg/day for 4 days
200 mg/day for 14 days
A trial with antidepressives should be at least for 3 weeks.
MAO inhibitors: Indicated if side effects to tricyclics are severe or patient is not responsive after a trial of tricyclics:

Monitor with platelet level of inhibition (90%)

Recommended with certain character pathology and associated phobias; lithium may have a rapid antidepressant effect in "treatment
resistant" patients

Other biologic treatments

ECT should be considered in selected patients, those with both severe
depressive symptoms and lack of response to pharmacologic treatment
and those with acute suicidal potential.

Psychological management

Psychotherapeutic management should be aimed at resolution of depressive episode.

Clinician must evaluate degree of suicidal risk involved.

Develop working alliance with patient.

Make patient an active participant in treatment plan, explaining the condition.

Assess life events as precipitating factors, as well as the presence and
role of support systems.

Involve spouse and/or family in treatment plan when expression of conflict involves interaction with other family members.

Assess underlying personality and level of functioning when euthymia
has been achieved.

Assess ego functions, including a psychodynamic formulation.

Major Depressive Illness: Recurrent Episodes

Pharmacotherapy

Decide on maintenance of antidepressant medication.

There may be a specific subgroup of patients with recurrent episodes of
major depressive illness who have a lithium-responsive disease and for
whom lithium maintenance is indicated.

Once the patient is maintained on antidepressants, the Dexamethasone
Supression Test may be a good indicator of when to stop treatment.

If lithium maintenance is used, be aware that if there is a recurrence of
the depression, it will not respond well to an increase of lithium but
will respond to antidepressant medication.

Indications for blood levels should be same as in acute phase.

Psychological management

During euthymia, evaluate for indications of psychotherapy type.

Consider:

Psychoanalysis

Insight-oriented psychotherapy

Supportive psychotherapy

Cognitive therapy

Marital therapy

Family therapy

Most studies of efficacy of combined psychotherapy and drugs show the superiority of combined treatment over a control group or either treatment alone.

Be aware that psychotherapy:

Helps interpersonal relations

Improves social functioning

Does not prevent relapses

Assess indications and contraindications for splitting pharmacologic and psychotherapeutic treatment, or consider joint treatment by one therapist.

We are not yet able to specify which type of psychotherapy to use with which drugs for which depressed patient.

OTHER SPECIFIC AFFECTIVE DISORDERS

CYCLOTHYMIC DISORDER

Pharmacotherapy

Use lithium maintenance or antidepressant regime only if impairment is enough to justify that treatment, i.e., severity of mood swings seriously detrimental to familial and occupational functions.

Psychological management

Evaluate indications for psychotherapy and the type.

DYSTHYMIC DISORDER

Psychological management

Treatment of choice. Assess for particular type of psychotherapy. Consider:

Psychoanalysis

Insight-oriented psychotherapy

Supportive psychotherapy

Cognitive therapy

Pharmacotherapy

Optional. Should be considered if depression has characteristics of major depression.

Consider MAO inhibitors if patient shows severe character disorder or evidence of severe anxiety or panic episodes

Assess indications and contraindications for splitting treatment between two therapists or conjoint treatment by one therapist

BEREAVEMENT

UNCOMPLICATED BEREAVEMENT

Usually requires no treatment. Occasionally mild sedation is useful at night for a brief period with medication that does not interfere with REM sleep.

COMPLICATED BEREAVEMENT

Mildly exaggerated bereavement reactions respond well to crisis intervention, with or without adjunctive sedation at night.

Pathologic bereavement

The stress of bereavement may precipitate a psychiatric condition, e.g. mania, psychophysiologic reactions, affective illness or behavioral disorders. The resultant condition can be treated in the appropriate manner with some attention to the precipitant in psychotherapy.

The bereavement reaction itself may be distorted and exaggerated in a variety of ways: absence of grief, intensification of the typical signs and symptoms of grief or identification with the disease of the deceased.

These reactions may be treated in a variety of ways according to the nature and intensity of the symptoms, but should include some form of psychotherapy designed to promote more normal mourning.

DEPRESSIONS SECONDARY TO PHYSICAL ILLNESS

Depression as a first sign of physical illness

Initiate medical treatment for the underlying organic illness.

Supportive psychotherapy may be indicated, depending on the nature of the medical illness and the patient's response to it.

Depression secondary to physical illness

Careful assessment of the patient's suicidal potential should be considered. If the patient is a suicidal risk, admission or transfer to a psychiatric facility should be effected.

If patient fulfills criteria for major depressive illness, initiate pharmacologic treatment as described.

Supportive and educational treatment should be a part of treatment program for every patient. This may be effected by a variety of medical personnel, such as physical therapists, medical nurse practitioners, etc.

Psychotherapy may be indicated if diagnosis of underlying personality or degree of disequilibrium brought on by illness requires it.

Depression secondary to drug therapy

There is almost always a multifactorial cause for psychiatric reactions to drug therapy. Therefore, the clinician must take a good history of the reaction.

If patient has a history of previous depressive illness, treat the current episode as a major depressive illness.

If patient's depression is a result of drug interaction, decrease of drugs causing marked sedation is suggested.

If an offending agent can be clearly identified, especially if related to the common classes of drug producing depression, drug should be discontinued and alternative drugs or modes of treatment should be considered.

Depression masked by complaints of physical illness

Careful physical and laboratory evaluations should be effected to rule out organic illness.

Then, treat the depressive syndrome as a major depressive illness.

REFERENCES

1. Arieti S., Bemporad J.: *Severe and Mild Depression*. New York, Basic Books, 1978.
2. Beck A.T.: The development of depression: A cognitive model, in Friedman R.J., Katz M.M. (eds.): *The Psychology of Depression: Contemporary Theory and Research*. Washington, D.C., U.S. Government Printing Office, 1974.
3. Covi L., et al.: Drugs and group psychotherapy in neurotic depression. *Am. J. Psychiatry* 131:191, 1979.
4. Davenport Y., et al.: Couples group therapy as an adjunct to lithium maintenance of the manic patient. *Am. J. Orthopsychiatry* 47:495, 1977.
5. Dewald P.: *Psychotherapy: A Dynamic Approach*. New York, Basic Books, 1971.
6. DiMascio A., et al.: *Manual for Short-Term Interpersonal Psychotherapy of Depression*. New Haven–Boston Collaborative Depression Project, 1978.
7. DiMascio A.: Differential symptom reduction by drugs and psychotherapy in acute depression. *Arch. Gen. Psychiatry* 36:1450, 1979.
8. DiMascio A., et al.: A control group for psychotherapy research in acute depression: One solution to ethical and methodological issues. *J. Psychiatr. Res.*, to be published.
9. Frank J.D.: *Persuasion and Healing: A Comparative Study of Psychotherapy*. Baltimore, Johns Hopkins University Press, 1973.
10. Friedman A.: Interaction of drug therapy with marital therapy in depressed patients. *Arch. Gen. Psychiatry* 32:619, 1975.
11. Greenson R.: *The Technique and Practice of Psychoanalysis*. New York, International Universities Press, 1967.

12. Janowsky D., Leff M., Epstein R.: Playing the manic game. *Arch. Gen. Psychiatry* 22:252, 1970.
13. Klerman G.: *Psychotropic Hedonism versus Pharmacologic Calvinism*. Hastings Center Report No. 2, 1972.
14. Klerman G.L.: Treatment of depression by drugs and psychotherapy. *Am. J. Psychiatry* 13:186, 1974.
15. Kovacs M., et al.: Depressed out-patients treated with cognitive therapy or pharmacotherapy: A one-year follow-up. *Arch. Gen. Psychiatry* 38:33, 1981.
16. Lesse S.: Psychotherapy combination with antidepressant drugs in severely depressed out-patients: 20-year evaluation. *Am. J. Psychother.* 22:48, 1978.
17. Ludwig A., Ables M.: Mania and marriage: The relationship between biological and behavioral variables. *Comp. Psychiatry* 15:411, 1974.
18. MacKinnon R., Michael R.: *The Psychiatric Interview in Clinical Practice*. Philadelphia, W.B. Saunders Co., 1971.
19. Margulies A., Havens L.: The initial encounter: What to do first. *Am. J. Psychiatry* 138:4, 1981.
20. Rush A.J., et al.: Comparative efficacy of cognitive therapy and pharmacotherapy in treatment of depressed out-patients. *Cognitive Ther. Res.* 1:17, 1977.
21. Weissman M., Kasl S., Klerman G.: Follow-up of depressed women after maintenance treatment. *Am. J. Psychiatry* 133:757, 1976.
22. Weissman M., et al.: The efficacy of drugs and psychotherapy in the treatment of acute depressive episodes. *Am. J. Psychiatry* 136:555, 1979.
23. Weissman M.: The psychological treatment of depression: Evidence for the efficacy of psychotherapy alone, in comparison with, and in combination with pharmacotherapy. *Arch. Gen. Psychiatry* 36:1261, 1979.
24. Weissman M., Prusoff B., Klerman G.: Personality and the prediction of long term outcome of depression. *Am. J. Psychiatry* 135:797, 1978.
25. Weissman M., et al.: Depressed out-patients: Results one year after treatment with drugs and/or interpersonal psychotherapy. *Arch. Gen. Psychiatry* 38:51, 1981.
26. Zetzel E., Meissner W.: *Basic Concepts of Psychoanalytic Psychiatry*. New York, Basic Books, 1973.

15

AFFECTIVE DISORDERS
AND THE ROLE OF
THE PRIMARY CARE PHYSICIAN

JAMES S. EATON, JR., M.D.

THE AFFECTIVE DISORDERS are among the most commonly encountered (and frequently missed)[4, 10] problems seen by the primary care practitioner. It is estimated that 12% to 25% of general medical patients are moderately to severely depressed,[8, 12, 14, 15, 20] and that 15% to 43% of all patients with physical complaints who visit primary care physicians do so primarily because of emotional and cognitive disturbances.[9] Usually patients don't recognize their disturbances as such, and often the physician can find no immediate organic basis for their complaints. The largest number of these patients are suffering from depression.[21, 22]

A look at the population at large shows the dimensions of the problem. The President's Mental Health Commission has estimated the annual period prevalence of all mental disorders in the United States to be 15% of the population per year.[18] Sixty percent of these people are being seen as outpatients by their primary care physician or by outpatient health care professionals, 15% are seen by psychiatrists and other mental health specialists, and 3.4% are in inpatient health care or nursing home facilities. A large number (21.5%) receive no care at all.[17] Clearly, the primary care physician shoulders the main responsibility for recognizing, diagnosing, and treating most mental disorders, a large part of which constitutes a group of illnesses called the affective disorders.

About 4% of the general population have clinically significant depression at any given time.[3] The prevalence is high for high-risk groups. For example, over 2% of apparently healthy young adult male air-traffic controllers experience moderately severe depression during an average month.[14]

Prevalence statistics also increase in longitudinal studies. Ten out of every hundred adults will become severely depressed at some time during their lives;[13] 10% to 15% of those who are depressed will eventually suicide.[2] Suicide is the second most frequent cause of death among 15- to 25-year-olds and the fourth most frequent cause among 18- to 45-year-olds.[2, 24] Many people who kill themselves have recently seen their physicians, although they might not have articulated their depression or their suicidal thoughts.

Most patients with mental disorders (and therefore most patients with depression) are first seen by primary care physicians. This is understandable. For most patients, it is logical to consult their family physician or internist when they have weight and appetite change, constipation, sleep disturbances, fatigue, vague pains, tachycardia, difficulty concentrating, diminished sexual interest, or slowed movements. These are the same signs and symptoms that frequently accompany a number of medical and surgical problems, but they are also signs and symptoms of the altered biologic functions one sees in the syndrome of depression. All or some of these signs and symptoms may exist without *manifest* disturbances in mood or without the patient volunteering that he sees himself as worthless, helpless, or hopeless—in other words, that he has pessimistic thoughts about himself and his future. The patient's frequent lack of awareness about his emotional state makes the recognition, diagnosis, and treatment of depression more difficult for the physician.

MULTIPLE ROOTS OF AFFECTIVE ILLNESS

Just as there are different types of depression, so there are multiple factors involved in determining who gets depressed and when. For instance, even though we all experience various stresses almost daily, most of us have the resilience to weather these stresses. We have learned, often unconsciously, to adapt. For patients who develop clinical depression, however, this has not been the case. Frequently, the same relatively innocuous stresses that could be weathered by some tip the balance to depression in others: the loss of a job, or the fear of failure that comes with a promotion; children going away to college, or a physical illness; a bad examination grade, or not making the team. In other words, some people are more vulnerable to depression.[1, 11, 16]

Lack of certain social support systems (spouse, family, friends) may make the patient more vulnerable to depression. A patient's vulnerability can also be increased when he has had a constricted life and is totally dependent on either spouse or children for support. Social factors are involved but so are biologic ones; we know that lowering monamine levels in critical synapses in the limbic system is associated with "depressive" behavior, and that certain drugs, like reserpine, which do this can stimulate depressions. Many other factors contribute to making a patient vulnerable to depression, including hormonal imbalance (childbirth, hypothyroid state), alcohol and drug abuse, familial and genetic factors, and the loss of a significant figure during childhood. But not all patients on reserpine become depressed, nor do all mothers whose only child goes away to college become depressed, nor do all single or widowed people become depressed.[5, 11, 23] In short, depressions are complex clinical states reflecting the interplay of a number of biologic, psychological, and social factors.

Just as there is no one cause of most depressions, so there is no single cure. Fortunately, the signs and symptoms of affective disorders are consistent enough that all physicians can recognize a patient with depression, make an accurate diagnosis, and develop an effective management plan.

THE PHYSICIAN'S ROLE

RECOGNIZING AFFECTIVE ILLNESS

Like syphilis and tuberculosis, depression is a great masquerader. Patients rarely walk into a doctor's office and say, "I'm depressed," nor will they necessarily admit to being depressed, even if asked directly. This means the physician must actively look for signs and symptoms of depression in all patients he sees, especially in those who have multiple complaints and whose symptoms don't conform to a particular somatic syndrome.

Because of the varied presentations and multiple complaints of depressed patients, it is especially important for the physician to evaluate the patient thoroughly. Open-ended questions or statements such as, "How have things been going for you?" "You seem worried. . . ." "What goes through your mind when you cry?" not only encourage the patient to give more than yes and no answers, but also convey the physician's concern and respect for the patient and his particular differences and experiences. This type of dialogue can elicit more information than the customary clinical questions.

A primary care physician who knows the patient is usually aware of the family situation, ages of the children, status of the spouse, and meaningful events in the patient's life. Further, the family physician knows how the patient has been able to adapt to various stresses in the past and how he deals with frustration, anger, disappointment, or success. By having this intimate knowledge of the patient, the primary care physician is many steps ahead of the specialist in his ability to assess the patient's vulnerability to depression.[9-22]

In evaluating a patient with depression, the primary care physician should go through his usual diagnostic workup with particular attention to *his own* feelings. Does the patient make him feel depressed? Angry? Sorry for him? The physician's own feelings and emotional reactions to a patient can be excellent litmus paper for determining how a patient feels and how others in his life are likely to be responding. This aids the diagnostic process. After some experience with affectively ill patients, physicians will find that certain types of depressed patients make them feel sad, blue, depressed, or "sorry" for them; similarly, certain hypomanic and manic patients may tend to make the physician feel anxious, silly, or embarrassed. Other types of more chronic "characterologic" depressive patients have a tendency to make physicians feel resentful and irritated, as if their time were being wasted.

EXAMINING THE PATIENT

The history and review of systems may reveal that the patient has had difficulty concentrating or making up his mind, thinks continually of his inadequacies, suffers lack of stamina, has feelings of guilt, experiences little pleasure, and dreads the future.

In the case of mania or hypomania, the history may reveal long periods of sleeplessness, frenetic activity, grandiosity, and irrational and expansive business dealings. The previously mentioned biologic (vegetative) signs and symptoms of depression may be present. Since there is a high incidence of affective disorders among alcoholics and opiate abusers,[6, 8, 23] the possibility of substance abuse should be thoroughly explored. A history of multiple divorces and frequent changes in jobs is often seen in patients with bipolar (manic-depressive) affective illness.

On physical and mental status examinations, the depressed patient often lacks a spry step and has a stooped or dejected posture. The patient may look down or away from the observer, but if he makes eye contact, the expression is vacant and without animation, and the eyes are without sparkle. The patient may have a dry mouth, fidget constantly, or seem agitated. The patient usually speaks in a monotonous, quiet voice and may volunteer little. Feelings of worthlessness, guilt, and irritation and resentment may be present, as well as thoughts of suicide. Occasionally, persecutory feelings and paranoid delusions may be part of the clinical picture of a unipolar major affective disorder, especially in the middle-aged and elderly.

Even if all evidence points to a depressive disorder, the presence of depression does not eliminate the possibility that it may be secondary to or superimposed on diseases involving other systems (e.g., infections, carcinoma, medication effects, endocrine disorders) or other psychiatric disorders (e.g., schizophrenia, alcoholism, organic brain syndrome). A thorough physical and mental status examination, therefore, should always be conducted.

DIAGNOSING AND MANAGING AFFECTIVE ILLNESS

Once the physician decides the patient is depressed, it is important to determine what, if any, recent losses or stresses may have occurred; whether the patient is chronically depressed or whether this is a part of the patient's character structure; whether the depression is severe; and whether the patient is suicidal. These judgments will help the physician determine the type of affective disorder present and consequently will determine the management plan.

Although there is not yet universal agreement about the classification of affective disorders, one of the most clinically useful schemes divides affective illnesses into primary and secondary affective disorders.[19]

Primary Affective Disorders

Patients with bipolar affective disorders (those with present evidence or past history of a manic episode) may present either in the depressed or in the hypomanic/manic state. There are strong familial and genetic factors in the etiology of this illness. Management of both the acute manic state and the depressed phase of the illness, as well as initial prophylactic treatment to prevent manic attacks, should be carried out by a psychiatrist. After the patient's condition is stabilized, prophylactic management, including the use of lithium, may be carried out by the primary care physician with ongoing psychiatric consultation.

If patients are suspected of having unipolar disorders (no present evidence or past history of manic attacks; no presumptive familial or genetic evidence of bipolar disease), it is important to assess the type and duration of precipitant stresses, the degree of the patient's disability, and the risk of suicide.

If such a patient is seriously depressed (marked vegetative signs and symptoms, delusions or hallucinations, severe agitation), or if the patient is thought to be a suicidal risk, the patient should be referred to a psychiatrist.

CASE EXAMPLE.—A previously healthy 50-year-old man, a farmer, saw his general physician for a checkup at the insistence of his wife. For the past month he had been moody and tired during the day and had been having difficulty sleeping more than five hours at night, frequently waking up at 3 A.M. and unable to go back to sleep. He had lost interest in church affairs and in the farmers' cooperative activities and had recently had a near-serious accident on his tractor.

The patient's chief complaint to his general physician, however, was "frequent headaches and feeling tired." The physician took a thorough history and inquired into the patient's changes in sleeping habits, daily activities, and possible traffic or farm-related accidents. He also explicitly asked whether the patient had been thinking that life wasn't worthwhile anymore and whether he had contemplated suicide. Indeed, the patient had; he thought that "a safe way to do it" was to drink a six-pack of beer and then have a high-speed automobile accident by running into the concrete abutment of a nearby interstate highway. This way, he said, he would at least leave his family a large amount of insurance money. The physical examination was within normal limits.

The physician was reluctant to hospitalize the patient in the small town's general hospital, which didn't have a psychiatric unit. Yet he was also reluctant to suggest that the patient be admitted to either the nearest psychiatric hospital, a small, private facility 50 miles away, or the nearest state psychiatric hospital, 100 miles away. While the patient was still in his office, the physician called a psychiatric colleague in the next larger town. The psychiatrist agreed to see the patient on emergency referral that afternoon. The primary physician called the patient's wife and told her about the patient's depression and about the referral to the psychiatrist, and she was asked to drive the patient for this psychiatric appointment.

That afternoon the psychiatrist thoroughly explored the patient's situation, established the fact that there was no history of suicidal behavior among the patient's family or friends, and saw that the patient's wife and children were supportive and available to him. The patient was not delusional, was fully oriented, and, other than blunted affect and depressed mood, had no abnormal mental features. The psychiatrist decided that the patient could be managed on an ambulatory basis at home.

The psychiatrist assured the patient that many men in middle age become depressed, that the patient's depression was a relatively easy condition to treat, and that with a combination of medication (tricyclic antidepressants) and psychotherapy (twice-weekly visits for three weeks), the patient would experience great relief of his depressive symptoms. The psychiatrist told him, however, that he was concerned about the patient's thoughts of suicide, and that while these were not uncommon accompaniments of serious depression, nevertheless the psychiatrist took them seriously. He gave the patient his professional card with both his office and home telephone numbers on it and asked the patient to call between regular appointments if the thoughts of suicide became very strong. He then called the referring primary physician, and with the patient and his wife in the room, went over the treatment plan over the telephone, which included asking the patient's wife to see that all sleeping pills and firearms in the house be secured.

The psychiatrist gradually built up the patient's tricyclic blood level to a therapeutic range. This plus three weeks (six sessions) of supportive and gentle uncovering psychotherapy enabled the patient to make a strong recovery, and in another three weeks he seemed stabilized. The psychiatrist then referred the patient back to his primary physician for follow-up every two weeks with the understanding that the patient could return to the psychiatrist for further treatment if indicated.

The primary physician followed the patient in half-hour visits every week for two months and during these sessions was able to inquire gently into the patient's progress in reestablishing self-esteem and self-confidence in both his personal and business relationships.

After two months, the frequency of the patient's sessions was progressively reduced to monthly visits to the primary physician, with occasional consultative calls to the psychiatrist. At the end of six months the tricyclics were tapered and then discontinued. The patient made a complete recovery.

This case illustrates the optimal relationship between a primary care physician and the referral psychiatrist. The primary care physician should not hesitate in getting rapid consultation—by telephone, if necessary—when there is no psychiatrist readily available. This is especially true when the patient is located in a small town or rural area. The consultation should be for help in (1) establishing an accurate diagnosis, (2) developing a management plan, and (3) instituting treatment. There should be no concern that the patient will be "lost" to the primary physician. A good psychiatrist will send the patient back to the referring physician with appropriate instructions for follow-up.

If a patient is known to have always been a bit depressed, fairly constricted in life, pretty much "down," and always acting as if the burdens of the world were on his shoulders, he, too, should be referred to a psychiatrist for evaluation. Chances are this is a deeply rooted characterologic pattern and, if amenable to treatment, would require fairly intensive psychotherapy as part of the treatment plan.

If, on the other hand, the patient's depression is seen to derive from a recent loss or if it represents a prolonged grief reaction, *and if the patient is not suicidal*, the patient may be managed at the outset by the primary care physician.

It is best to begin seeing such a patient for half-hour periods once a week without first resorting to medication. With gentle, open-ended questioning, one usually finds that most of these patients have recently experienced some reversal or loss, and most have in their background a residue of other deeply felt losses or rejections. Some patients may be covertly resentful or irritated at a variety of things. After a few sessions with these patients, they will start to perk up and will appear to be feeling much better. They can then be reassessed, and, if possible, given an appointment as needed.

However, if patients do not respond to short, supportive psychotherapeutic approaches, and if their depressive symptoms are unremitting or worsening, they should be referred to a psychiatrist. If psychiatric consultation or referral is not possible, tricyclic antidepressants might be used, with the usual caveats about contraindications, cross reactions, and side effects.

Secondary Affective Disorders

If the affective disorder is secondary to a physical or other psychiatric illness, the underlying disorder must be treated. At the same time, the physician should institute supportive psychotherapy. Again, the most frequent denominator in *all* depressed patients is their sense of loss, real or perceived. The physician can help compensate for this loss by his presence, his interest in the patient as a person, his help in directing part of the patient's life for a time, and by serving as a sounding board for the patient's partially hidden feelings of discouragement, resentment, and low self-esteem. Most secondary affective disorders, especially those complicating physical diseases of other systems, can be managed by the primary care physician. This presumes that the primary care physician has been appropriately trained in the management of such patients.

ASSESSING SUICIDAL RISKS

The physician should always be sensitive to the potential risk of suicide in depressed patients. If the patient does not mention suicide, the physician should *always* inquire about it explicitly: "Have you felt so depressed that you have thought about hurting yourself or taking your own life?" If so, then the physician should inquire about the anticipated method of suicide and what the patient expects will be the reactions of those around him (loved ones, friends) after his death. If the patient has in mind a method of suicide, if he anticipates the feelings of others about his possible death, then the risk is higher than with patients in whom suicide is just an idle or a passing thought.

It is important for the physician to know whether family or friends of the patient have made suicide attempts in the past, whether the patient lives alone, and whether he has access to guns, sleeping pills, or other lethal means. All of these factors increase the risk of suicide.

It cannot be overemphasized that *the physician never introduces the thought of suicide to a patient*. Rather, the physician, by his questions to the patient, might touch on an area that the patient is reluctant to discuss spontaneously. Indeed, the patient may be very reluctant, if he feels that such open discussion would make the physician uncomfortable.

The physician should go over in his mind the following factors associated with increased risk of suicide in depressed patients:

1. Single, divorced, or widowed
2. History of a previous suicide attempt
3. Family history of suicide
4. Recent loss of love, of job, of spouse or other close family member, of financial resources, of self-esteem (public humiliation, shame)

5. Chronic or terminal illness
6. Living alone
7. Psychosis
8. Substance abuse
9. Preoccupation with death
10. Sudden concern with getting one's affairs in order, gifts to relatives and friends, revising will
11. Persistent thoughts of worthlessness and helplessness

If the physician feels the patient is a suicidal risk, the patient should be hospitalized and a psychiatrist should be consulted.

The physician should be certain to tell all depressed patients to call him at his office, answering service, or at home if the depression seems to be worsening, if thoughts of suicide become overwhelming, or if other types of punitive and self-destructive thoughts persist. The patient's family, a close friend, or important others should always be contacted by the physician when the patient is severely depressed or suicidal. Most important, the physician should always let the patient know that he takes his suicidal thoughts or communications of despair seriously.

INDICATIONS FOR PSYCHIATRIC REFERRAL AND CONSULTATION

The indications for psychiatric referral vary, depending on the primary care physician's locale, his type of practice, and the accessibility of psychiatrists. As a general rule, the following are indications for psychiatric referral: (1) high risk for suicide, (2) psychosis (hallucinations, delusions, disorientation), (3) evidence of bipolar disease, (4) severe unipolar disease (i.e., with psychotic features), (5) uncommunicative or very hostile patient, (6) chronic depression (characterologic depression), (7) prolonged grief reaction (over three months), (8) the physician feels very uncomfortable treating the patient, (9) the patient is a child or early adolescent.

The physician may wish to consult with a psychiatrist in order to more firmly establish a diagnosis, to review differential diagnostic possibilities, to discuss a proposed management plan, or to review supportive psychotherapeutic techniques. In addition, it is very important that any physician who treats depression, schizophrenia, organic mental disorders, or any other psychiatric illness maintain close contact with a psychiatrist in case a patient suddenly becomes suicidal and needs to be psychiatrically hospitalized.

PHYSICIAN SATISFACTION

The natural history of affective illness is to remit. But the primary care physician plays an important role in recognizing the depressive disorder and identifying the disorder to the patient (many patients are relieved to know that they do have a disorder and that it isn't just their "nerves" or something they're imagining). The physician can ease the patient's distress and shorten the course of his illness by knowledgeable use of drugs and psychotherapy and by environmental manipulations.

Because affective illness is so frequently missed by primary care physicians and because the consequences of these misses are potentially grave, the recognition, diagnosis, and effective management of patients afflicted with these disorders can be very gratifying to the nonpsychiatric physician. The knowledge and skills required by the primary care physician in dealing with his depressed patients can be put to good use in the rest of his practice. Open-ended questioning techniques, the ability to conduct effective mental status examinations, knowledge of psychopharmacologic agents, and supportive psychotherapeutic skills are all vitally important in the practice of a busy primary care physician.[6, 7]

REFERENCES

1. Akiskal H.D., McKinney W.T.: Overview of recent research in depression. *Arch. Gen. Psychiatry* 32:285, 1975.
2. Avery D., Winokur G.: Suicide, attempted suicide and relapse rates in depression. *Arch. Gen. Psychiatry* 35:749, 1978.
3. Barrett J., et al.: Prevalence of depression over a twelve month period in a nonpatient population. *Arch. Gen. Psychiatry* 35:741, 1978.
4. Dohrenwerd B.P., Dohrenwerd B.S.: *Social States and Psychiatric Disorder, a Causal Inquiry.* New York, John Wiley & Sons, 1969.
5. Dorus W., Senay E.C.: Depression, demographic dimensions, and drug abuse. *Am. J. Psychiatry* 137:699, 1980.
6. Eaton J.S. Jr.: Psychiatry and psychiatric medicine for the general physician: An educational imperative. *Psychosomatics* 20:552, 1979.
7. Eaton J.S. Jr., Doyle B.B.: Updating comprehensive care. *Primary Care* 6:439, 1979.
8. Folstein M.L., McHugh P.R., Wise T.N.: Psychiatric screening in a general medical setting. Read before the annual meeting of the American Psychosomatic Society, Washington, D.C., March 31, 1978.
9. Goldberg R.L., et al.: Psychiatry and the primary care physician. *J.A.M.A.* 236:944, 1976.
10. Houpt J.L., et al.: *The Importance of Mental Health Services to General Health Care.* Cambridge, Mass., Harvard University Press, 1979.
11. Klerman G.L.: Affective disorders, in Nicholi A. (ed.): *The Harvard Guide to Modern Psychiatry.* Cambridge, Mass., Harvard University Press, 1978, p. 253.
12. Kligerman M.J., McKegney F.P.: Patterns of psychiatric consultation in two general hospitals. *Psychiatr. Med.* 2:126, 1971.
13. Lehmann A.E.: Epidemiology of affective disorders, in Fieve R. (ed): *Depression in the 70's.* The Hague, Excerpta Medica, 1971.
14. Lipowski Z.J.: Review of consultation psychiatry and psychosomatic medicine. *Psychosom. Med.* 29:153, 1967.

15. Nielsen A.C., Williams T.A.: Depression in ambulatory patients: Prevalence by self-report questionnaire and recognition by non-psychiatric physicians. *Arch. Gen. Psychiatry* 37:999, 1980.
16. Pardes H.: Normality vs. abnormality and the concept of mental illness, in Simons R.D., Pardes H. (eds.): *Understanding Human Behavior in Health and Illness.* Baltimore, Williams & Wilkins Co., 1977, p. 465.
17. Regier D.A., Goldberg I.D., Taube C.A.: The de facto United States mental health services system. *Arch. Gen. Psychiatry* 35:685, 1978.
18. Report to the President by the President's Mental Health Commission, 1978.
19. Robins E., et al.: Primary and secondary affective disorders, in Zubin J., Freyhan F.A. (eds.): *Disorders of Mood.* Baltimore, The Johns Hopkins University Press, 1972.
20. Schmale A.H.: Relationship of separation and depression to disease. *Psychosom. Med.* 20:259, 1958.
21. Slaby A.E., Pottash A.L.C., Black H.R.: Utilization of psychiatrists in a primary care center. *J. Med. Ed.* 53:752, 1978.
22. Sutherland J.: *Depression Today.* New York, CME Communications, 1978. vol. 1.
23. Weissman M.M., et al.: Symptom patterns in primary care and secondary care. *Arch. Gen. Psychiatry* 34:854, 1977.
24. Whybrow P.C.: Evaluating and treating severe depression. *Consultant*, vol. 134, January 1978.

16

THE AFFECTIVE DISORDERS CLINIC: A SPECIALIZED SETTING

LINDA RYDMAN, B.A., B.S.N.

RECENT ADVANCES in the understanding and treatment of affective disorders have set the stage for specialized clinics nationwide. These clinics, known variously as mood disorder, lithium, or affective disorder clinics, have been established to provide treatment for, and to conduct research on, patients with affective disorders, as well as to educate mental health professionals, patients and their families, and the community at large.

Are specialized treatment settings necessary for this patient group? Whom do they benefit? What services are offered that would be unavailable in a general setting? How well do mental health professionals working in specialized clinics serve those with affective disorders? These questions are the focus of this chapter. In the first half I explore the need for specialized treatment settings; in the second part the treatment model used at one specialized outpatient setting is reviewed in depth, with emphasis on innovations in the nurse's role.

THE NEED FOR A SPECIALIZED SETTING
IN THE TREATMENT OF AFFECTIVE DISORDERS

Prior to 1969, the treatment of affective disorders was fragmented, costly, and uncertain. Lithium was viewed as an experimental drug and was not widely used in the United States, despite reported successes in treatment and research throughout Europe and Australia. Affective disorder clinics were virtually nonexistent, in part owing to lack of approval for lithium by the Food and Drug Administration. The inpatient and outpatient treatment costs for manic-depressive disorders for the year 1968 have been estimated at around $555 million by Reifman and Wyatt.[24] These authors estimate that FDA approval of lithium treatment resulted in about a $4 billion savings in the following decade in terms of reduced treatment costs and production gain in the community.

Since 1969, depression has been a matter of concern to the mental and public health professions and has been met with a corresponding attempt to increase available psychiatric services within the community. As state hospitals have decreased their inpatient census, other programs have been developed to attend to the needs of chronically mentally ill patients who require multiple interventions for community maintenance. Specialized clinics for the treatment of affective disorders emerged, attempting to address the different needs of this population.

Perhaps 20 specialized clinics for the treatment of affective disorders have opened their doors nationwide in the last decade. While some programs focus primarily on the use of lithium, others place equal emphasis on community and social needs, developing innovative treatment approaches in the interest of treating a patient population economically and efficiently over an extended period of time.[10, 12] Fieve attributes much of the success of the lithium clinic at the New York State Psychiatric Institute (NYSPI) to maximum use of paramedical personnel, which has facilitated systematic follow-up of long-term lithium patients.[10] Many centers have reported improved compliance and treatment response through special services such as multidisciplinary professional teams,[10, 16] peer support groups,[16] and the use of nurse clinicians to provide education and outreach to clinical patients.[4, 10, 16]

The use of lithium and other medications to treat affective disorders has contributed to an excellent prognosis for patients previously doomed to an erratic or chronic course of illness. Yet it would be erroneous to presume that medication alone is sufficient. Reports in the literature and personal experience in an affective disorders clinic support the observation that the opposite is true. While medications used to treat mood disorders have properties that successfully reduce clinical symptomatology, symptom reduction is only one aspect of recovery. Social adjustment and functioning are better indications of recovery, although they are more difficult to quantify and measure.

To assess social functioning accurately requires research over extended periods of time. Weissman et al., in a study on the social functioning of depressed women four years after the acute episode, reported the continuing presence of social impairment, particularly in marital and close interpersonal relationships.[29] Less than one third of the total sample were symptom-free, and more than one quarter were *as* symptomatic as at admission four years earlier. These findings emphasize the need for both continuing care and psychological and social interventions, in addition to medication therapy.[3, 28, 29, 30]

The extended treatment required for the chronically ill affective disorder patient presents other problems requiring selective response. Long-term medication therapy may be complicated by treatment dropouts and the potential for relapse. The acutely manic patient, as aptly described by Janowsky et al., tends to alienate himself from family, friends, and therapists, not uncommonly splitting the treatment staff.[21] Janowsky et al. have described the maneuvers used by manic patients to alienate staff, which may contribute to some treatment failures. While they refer specifically to acutely manic inpatients, such characteristics appear frequently in the clinically stable outpatient as well, though the maneuver may be more subtle.

Premature termination of patients is a universal problem in mental health in any diagnostic category, but it seems that the more difficult the behavior of patients, the more they are likely to be carefully manipulated out of treatment.[18] An examination of the characteristics of bipolar and unipolar patients who "dropped out" of treatment often reveals manipulative behavior that contributed to the eventual discharge of the patient from treatment.

One of the main tasks of the affective disorders clinic as a specialized treatment setting is to address such problems. Its referrals, therefore, include largely "difficult" patients. The "good," clear-cut, unipolar and bipolar patients who comply with treatment recommendations will likely continue with their private therapists or mental health center since they pose no major difficulty. By contrast, the majority of the patient population in an affective disorders clinic consists of patients who present complex diagnostic and management problems, as well as medical problems.

An urgent issue confronting any long treatment is that of compliance. It is easier for a patient to justify daily medication if a life-or-death situation exists; it is difficult for patients with affective disorders to view their illness in this manner, despite statistics on suicide that demonstrate a greater incidence in this patient group than in any other psychiatric illness.[10] The result is patients who are at risk but who nonetheless neglect to take medicine dependably. Recent studies of patient compliance for affective disorders note a consistently direct relationship between noncompliance and extended treatment: the longer the treatment, the more likely it is that noncompliance will occur. Since the drug management of affective disorders requires a minimum of two to three years' intervention, or in most patients on lithium therapy, a prolonged course of treatment, such data support the need for specific interventions to reduce the incidence of non-compliance.

Connelly has cited family stability as an important factor in improving compliance.[8] However, in affective disorders the chaos of episodic disruptions in family life work against this. Earlier onset, greater impairment in social and occupational spheres, and greater frequency and severity of episodes result in a limited number of family members willing to provide support. In the absence of family stability, other interventions must be considered to improve compliance. A strong practitioner-patient relationship contributes by fostering continuity of care and positive role modeling.[8] The main strength of an affective disorders clinic as a specialized center lies in reducing noncompliance by aggressive follow-up in the way of home visiting, family sessions, and mobilization of the available social networks.

Compliance issues often relate specifically to medication. Hershey and other researchers suggest that patients perceive a loss of control when medicated, perhaps fearing drug dependency or long-term side effects.[8, 17, 19] Peculiar to the bipolar group, perhaps, is the discomfort expressed by patients about having their moods "controlled by a pill."[19] A recent study clarified that lithium compliance is a major clinical problem, accompanied by "substantially increased risks of personal and interpersonal chaos, repeated hospitalizations and suicide."[20] The data suggest that failure to comply with medication schedules can occur as a result of feeling either good or bad. The importance to the patient of this mood swing, particularly the hypomanic mood swing, should not be minimized. For some patients, return of depressive symptomatology during lithium maintenance, or the "low" feelings experienced during initial therapy, are sufficient reason to discontinue medication,[19, 22] while for others, missing the "high" was cited, as the positive feelings that accompany hypomania may be a strong reinforcement for the patient to discontinue the medication.[20]

Another reason for centralizing the management of affective disorders patients through specialized clinics is the frequent need for complex medical management. Almost 50% of the admissions to our clinic had at least one coexisting medical problem. Drug interactions are especially hazardous, particularly in the elderly, who constituted 20% to 25% of the same sample of patients. Many are hypertensive patients taking lithium carbonate who must avoid low-sodium diets and take certain diuretics and antihypertensive agents that may precipitate lithium toxicity. The clinic staff, through their unique therapeutic alliance with the patients, their active patient education, and their close consultation with other medical specialists, have a greater opportunity to promote health in the affected individual in this setting.

This total health care program for each patient is falling more and more within the responsibility of the nursing staff. Their purpose is not to alter medication regimens, but rather to alert other caretakers to the potential problems of drug interactions or other side effects, such as toxic response. In a general setting such as a community mental health center, this level of knowledge may not be sufficiently available.

THE SPECIALIZED SETTING AND THE NURSING ROLE

In the mental health field, demands for community services have increased as the inpatient census has decreased.[5, 8, 10] The trend in medicine toward specialization, which has provided community-oriented, trained personnel, has applied to nursing as well as other medical professions. As early as 1966, the Henry Phipps Clinic of the Johns Hopkins Hospital developed a nurse practitioner role in its outpatient department.[15] Responsibilities included home visiting, community liaison, intake and diagnostic evaluation, and patient treatment. Assumption of such responsibilities by nurses was based on interest, ability, and participation in a training program, rather than on academic credentials.

These and other expanded nursing roles in mental health are mirrored in the nurse's role at the Affective Disorders Clinic (ADC), a joint venture of the Department of Psychiatry of the University of Illinois Medical Center, Chicago, and the Illinois Department of Mental Health. The clinic has been in operation since 1975. Over 600 patients have been screened by ADC and over 250 have been managed in follow-up treatment for some time. At present the clinic services between 130 and 150 patients. The original goals of the clinic were (1) to serve as a diagnostic and consultation center for patients with depressive illness, (2) to provide a treatment program for patients on maintenance medications such as lithium carbonate, antidepressants, and other adjunctive psychiatric medication, and (3) to serve as an educational resource center for health and mental health professionals, as well as for community lay groups. All of these goals have been expanded during the five years of the clinic's operation.

A public health approach is used at the clinic, with emphasis on secondary and tertiary prevention. This calls for a comprehensive plan of care involving a repertoire of resources within the community. A multidisciplinary staff is employed, each member having unique responsibilities at various stages of treatment. The treatment team includes psychiatrists, social workers, and psychiatric residents; trainees and consultants in psychopharmacology, family, and group therapy; and nurses, whose role is of pivotal importance. At ADC the nurse's therapeutic role with the patient is supportive, and her primary responsibilities to the patient are as medical monitor, educator, and care plan coordinator. These responsibilities extend throughout the diagnosis, stabilization, and maintenance phases of treatment.

The clinic provides a comprehensive diagnostic evaluation for all patients accepted for screening. This is provided by a psychiatrist or psychiatric resident with psychiatrist supervision. For patients who will receive medication, diagnostic evaluation includes phenomenologic and psychodynamic assessment using specific diagnostic criteria, physical and laboratory examinations, and medical follow-up when indicated. Treatment recommendations are planned at the clinical staffing, which is attended by all treatment staff and, in some cases, by the referring practitioners.

The treatment plan may include a course of medication, medical follow-up, psychotherapy, social or vocational interventions, a home visit, or family interventions. Because ADC is a specialized clinic, reliance on medical and social services at the medical center and within the community is an important aspect of the treatment program and is closely tied to the educational community liaison efforts of the clinic. When a decision is made that the treatment program offered by the clinic will not benefit the patient, linkage to the referring agency, another community agency, or a list of private practitioners is provided for the patient before discharge.

If a patient is appropriate for the clinic program, the physician performing the diagnostic evaluation continues to monitor the patient during the stabilization phase of treatment. Objectives of this second phase include control of acute symptoms and identification of therapeutic doses of medication. Once stabilized, the patient enters the maintenance phase of treatment.

The primary goal of treatment maintenance is the prevention of relapse or hospitalization. A secondary goal is rehabilitation. Using community resources, the clinic attempts to assist the patient in returning to meaningful activity within the community as soon as possible. This may be a return to employment or homemaking responsibilities, school or vocational training programs, participation in social services, or community day treatment programs and workshops. These goals are achieved using three primary treatment modalities: medication/education groups, community liaison, and home visiting.

Although the nurse has been involved in medical management of patients during the diagnostic and stabilization phases, she becomes the primary contact person for the clinic patient in the maintenance phase. The role of the clinical nursing consultant is crucial in all aspects of this phase. It is her responsibility to coordinate the total treatment plan for each patient assigned to her by developing a strong relationship with each patient while functioning as part of a team. Sensitivity to the dual functions of personal support for the patient and staff teamwork is especially important in a training setting where mental health trainees and psychiatric residents stay with the clinic for only limited periods of time. The nurse provides stability and integration for the patient, particularly in solving problems of compliance.

The medication/education group is the main treatment modality in the maintenance phase. Each patient is assigned to a regular group meeting and attendance is required, first bimonthly and later monthly. The group is monitored by the nurse, in conjunction with a psychiatrist or psychiatric resident, with the services of a social worker. Blood samples are collected to monitor medication levels; vital signs and weight are checked by the nurse; prescriptions are distributed by the physician. The group format provides an opportunity to provide educational information about the medical treatment, such as management of side effects, which is of particular concern in the early phases of maintenance. The observation of patient interactions during group sessions contributes to ongoing clinical assessment.

As the group process develops, the group provides peer support, a factor strongly associated with maintaining patients in treatment, in the clinic's experience. Spouses are invited to group sessions but are not required to attend. Absences are followed up by the nurse, who may send a letter or telephone the patient. These meetings are important to an understanding of the patient as part of a social group. In some instances the psychiatric social worker is available, by appointment, to assist in identifying community social services needed by the patient and family members. Referrals are the nurse's responsibility, as is the follow-up to determine outcome.

The nursing responsibility for the medication/education group requires autonomous and sometimes swift clinical judgment; it often includes active intervention to avert a medical or psychiatric crisis. When one of the treatment group patients is hospitalized, the nurse serves as the patient's contact with the clinic and with hospital staff. She can be valuable in preventing isolation of the patient from the group as well as in alerting the hospital to potential problems of medication.[16] The nurse also participates in discharge planning in order to maintain continuity of care for the patient. Throughout treatment the nurse maintains contact with referring physicians and agencies; by helping to maintain communication between patients and health care providers in the community, a positive treatment outcome is facilitated.[21]

Community liaison is established and maintained through information and service to other mental health practitioners in the Chicago area. The goal of secondary prevention of affective disorders, their early recognition, is met primarily through seminars and topical workshops with local hospitals, clinics, and social agencies. In-service training is also available to the staff of these organizations. Such presentations are the joint effort of the team members. Their major objective is to alert community mental health staff to the symptomatology of affective disorders and those patients at risk and to expand the capability of the community to deal with both. These and case consultations stimulate referral of patients to the clinic for specialized care and enable better care of affective disorders within the patient's own community.

The home visit, another treatment service carried out by the nurse, is not required for every patient, but is considered particularly important for some. In the clinic's experience, it has been established as important in the prevention of suicide or hospitalization. Home visits accomplish a variety of goals:

1. They provide the practitioner with a view of the reality of a patient's life not available in hospital-based settings.[7]

2. They may facilitate the reinvolvement of resistant patients.

3. The diagnostic information gathered may aid in treatment planning.

4. Compliance problems may be more effectively managed through a home visit.[7, 26]

5. The home visit is a means of engaging other family members, thereby strengthening the patient's support system.

6. Assessment of psychosocial functioning, important in treatment outcome evaluation, may be more accurately achieved in the home.

7. When home visits are a regular service of the treatment program, entry to the home for research and evaluation purposes may be facilitated.

8. A home visit may help prevent hospitalization, or it may facilitate a necessary hospital stay by providing support to the patient and family, minimizing the negative and traumatic aspects of hospitalizing a relative.[31]

Entry to the home is often more easily obtained by a nurse, who is less threatening to the family than social workers or psychologists.[2, 7, 26] The nurse is seen as the "helping person" and the home visit gives the patient the message, "The clinic cares about you; we will even come to your home." The nurse's willingness to give up the implied control of her office creates an atmosphere conducive to agreement, returning an element of control to the patient. The patient may be more comfortable making a treatment commitment while solidly established on his own turf.

Before making the home visit the nurse constructs a plan of action with the physician. On reaching the patient's home this may mean, in addition to assessment, alterations in medication, administration of emergency medication, crisis resolution, discussion of hospitalization with the patient and his family, or providing support and education. These interventions have been found to be crucial in preventing hospitalization.[25]

Combining a perspective on patient care distinct from that of psychiatry, and an increased participation in such care, nurses at the ADC have identified groups of patients with special needs not precisely addressed in the traditional psychiatric diagnosis. Certain patient groups share common medical, educational, social, vocational, and psychological needs; consideration of those needs in treatment planning contributes to a more effective treatment response and outcome. Needs related to the patient's age, course of illness, attitude toward treatment, and differences in the clinical picture can be effectively addressed in treatment planning modification. Table 16–1 describes patient categories grouped according to some of their special needs.

In summary, the role of nursing in a specialized setting such as ADC provides a unique opportunity for combining public health and psychiatric nursing skills in a variety of job responsibilities, tapping potential skills, and enhancing professional growth; she has important input into all phases of patient care. Nurses in this setting report that, as a member of a multidisciplinary treatment team, they find personal satisfaction and the opportunity to contribute in a meaningful way in the specialized clinical role while being part of an ongoing learning process.

This role provides organizational advantages as well. Physicians receive assistance with triage, medical consultation, and family evaluations; their time may be more effectively used in diagnostic evaluation, medical or psychotherapeutic intervention, psychotherapy, consultation, and teaching trainees. This system enables a large number of clients to be served economically without sacrificing the quality of care received—even, perhaps, enhancing it.

The ADC illustrates specialization trends: more efficient use of physician time, greater economy in patient management, and a wider variety of services addressing the multiple needs of the affective disorders patient. The nurse's expanded role has prompted additional treatment approaches as different patient needs are identified; improved treatment response in turn maximizes effective clinical management. Such factors may provide special benefits to both patients and the personnel concerned with treating affective disorders.

TABLE 16–1.—Follow-up Issues for Affective Disorders Patients

PATIENT GROUPS	MEDICAL	EDUCATIONAL	SOCIAL/VOCATIONAL	PSYCHOLOGICAL
Elderly	Multiple health and medication problems: parallel medical care; management of side effects	Treatment expectations; origin of symptoms; side effects of medications; preventing medication errors; general nutrition and health	Implications of loss of livelihood, psychological and economic; structuring daily identity and coordination of community resources to provide meaningful activities	Aging; changing self-image; dealing with losses; changing marital patterns
Chronic	Complications due to previous treatment; careful evaluation of treatment response	Dispelling myths related to previous diagnoses; understanding prophylaxis: need for compliance; treatment expectations; patient skepticism about treatment success	Social isolation: reversing effects of chronicity; vocational rehabilitation: incremental program planning using community resources; realistic expectations of patient performance for patient and staff; coordination with multiple community resources	Treatment acceptance following many failures; helping patient to avoid hospitalization; establishing a motivation for wellness; support for small measures of progress

Patients with character disorders	Rule out alcoholism and drug abuse; careful evaluation of psychodynamic diagnosis	Accepting illness; commitment to treatment: use of patient contract; treatment expectations; understanding multidimensional approach; limitations of help from medication	Lack of social reinforcement for "normal" behavior—tendency for support systems to maintain pathology; community liaison for economic and rehabilitative needs	Dealing with character pathology in adjunctive psychotherapy treatment; providing consistent messages about treatment expectations and expectations of patient performance; identify and separate treatment goals from life goals
Resistant	Consider alternative treatment plan; close monitoring; observe for changes in clinical picture; dose alteration; special management of side effects when recommended treatment accepted	Explanation of risks of alternative treatment; establishment of criteria for decision making about recommended treatment; early detection of symptoms; family involvement	Preparation of family and patient for treatment failure; development of plan for crisis intervention if alternative treatment fails; involve family members throughout treatment	Development of specific criteria to evaluate treatment response; support for patient and family; assist in acceptance of recommended treatment; deal with potential anger
Potential dropouts	Close supervision and assessment; caution about size of prescriptions given	Aggressive follow-up; implications of dropping out (relapse); clear expectation of patient performance in treatment; involvement of family	Close communication with referring agency and other community agencies	Support; what it means to patient to be ill; value of "highs"; assist in resistance to "euphoria" in favor of stability; help patient assume more personal responsibility for well-being

(*Continued*)

TABLE 16-1.—(*Continued*)

PATIENT GROUPS	MEDICAL	EDUCATIONAL	SOCIAL/VOCATIONAL	PSYCHOLOGICAL
Rapid cyclers	Long-term needs: 4 relapses a year; rapid mood switch, abnormal interval functioning; poor response to lithium; evaluation of medication response inaccurate until beyond 1 yr consistent treatment; active medical supervision; may require long-term individual follow-up rather than group follow-up	Understanding difference in course of illness; acceptance of lengthy evaluation period; strong commitment to treatment; family involvement; alert for symptoms; necessity for close supervision and active staff intervention	Special needs due to rapid mood switch and high number of annual relapses, need for frequent medical attention	Support through long, chaotic stabilization period; hope-inducing focus

| With medical complications | Pregnancy? endocrine disorders? cardiac disorders?; alternative treatment; parallel care; close supervision | Understanding the illness, the role of other medical problems in treatment; risks of alternative treatment, potential failure of treatment; origin of symptoms | Special needs with respect to complications and treatment plan changes, need for frequent medical intervention; realistic appraisal of social and vocational prognosis/ expectations due to complex medical picture; need for multiple community agency involvement or contraindication for same | Meaning of contraindication of treatment for patient; body image issues; support |

REFERENCES

1. Akiskal H.S., McKinney W.T. Jr.: Overview of recent research in depression. *Arch. Gen. Psychiatry* 32:285, 1975.
2. Benoit R.: Intensive care program in the community: Home psychiatric care program of the University Hospital, Saskatoon, Saskatchewan. *Inform. Psy. (Lyon)* 50:507, 1974.
3. Benson R.: Psychological stress as a cause of lithium prophylaxis failure: A report of three cases. *Dis. Nerv. Sys.* 12:699, 1976.
4. Bey D.R., Chapman R.E., Tournquist K.L.: A lithium clinic. *Am. J. Psychiatry* 129:128, 1972.
5. Bird J., Marks I.M., Lindley P.: Nurse therapists in psychiatry: Development, controversies and implications. *Br. J. Psychiatry* 135:321, 1979.
6. Bothwell S., Weissman M.M.: Social impairments four years after an acute depressive episode. *Am. J. Orthopsychiatry* 47:231, 1977.
7. Chappel J.N., Daniel R.S.: Home visits in black urban ghettos. *Am. J. Psychiatry* 126:99, 1970.
8. Connelly C.E.: Patient compliance: A review of the research and implications for psychiatric/mental health nursing. *J. Psychiatr. Nurs.* 16:15, 1978.
9. Fassler L.B., Gaviria M.: Depression in old age. *J. Am. Geriatr. Soc.* 26:471, 1978.
10. Fieve R.R.: The lithium clinic: A new model for the delivery of psychiatric services. *Am. J. Psychiatry* 132:1018, 1975.
11. Fieve R.R.: *Moodwing.* New York, Bantam Books, 1975.
12. Fieve R.R., Kumbaraci T., Dunner D.L.: Prophylaxis of depression in bipolar I, bipolar II and unipolar patients. *Am. J. Psychiatry* 133:925, 1976.
13. Finkelman A.W.: The nurse therapist: Outpatient crisis intervention with the chronic psychiatric patient. *J. Psychiatr. Nurs.* 15:27, 1977.
14. Gardner K.G.: Levels of psychiatric nursing practice in an ambulatory setting. *J. Psychiatr. Nurs.* 15:26, 1977.
15. Hanson E.T.: Nurse practitioners in ambulatory psychiatric care. *Nurs. Clin. North Am.* 8:313, 1973.
16. Hayes R.C.: Developing a group program for the treatment of outpatients on lithium carbonate. *Hosp. Community Psychiatry* 27:391, 1976.
17. Hershey J.C., et al.: Patient compliance and antihypertensive medications. *Am. J. Public Health* 70:1081, 1980.
18. Hoppe E.W.: Treatment drop-outs in hindsight: A follow-up study. *Community Ment. Health J.* 13:307, 1977.
19. Jamison K.R., Gerner R.H., Goodwin F.K.: Patient and physician attitudes toward lithium: Relationship to compliance. *Arch. Gen. Psychiatry* 36:866, 1979.
20. Jamison K.R., et al.: Clouds and silver linings: Positive experiences associated with primary affective disorders. *Am. J. Psychiatry* 137:198, 1980.
21. Janowsky D.S., Leff M., Epstein R.S.: Playing the manic game: Interpersonal maneuvers of the acutely manic patient. *Arch. Gen. Psychiatry* 22:252, 1970.
22. Kocsis J.H., Stokes P.E.: Lithium maintenance: Factors affecting outcome. *Am. J. Psychiatr.* 136:563, 1979.
23. Peplau H.E.: Psychiatric nursing: role of the nurse and psychiatric nurse. *Int. Nurs. Rev.* 25:41, 1978.

24. Reifman A., Wyatt R.J.: Lithium: A brake in the rising cost of mental illness. *Arch. Gen. Psychiatry* 37:385, 1980.
25. Rubenstein D.: Family crisis intervention as an alternative to rehospitalization. *Cur. Psychiatr. Ther.* 14:191, 1974.
26. Smith F.A., et al.: Home care treatment of acutely ill psychiatric patients: A review of 78 cases. *Can. Psychiatr. Assoc. J.* 21:269, 1976.
27. Steer R.A. et al.: Prediction of multiple visits by an AMHC's psychiatric home visiting team. *Community Ment. Health J.* 15:214, 1979.
28. Weissman M.M.: Psychotherapy and its relevance to the pharmacotherapy of affective disorders: From ideology to evidence. Read before at the annual meeting of the American College of Neuropsychopharmacology, New Orleans December 1976.
29. Weissman M.M., Karl S.V., Klerman G.L.: Follow-up of depressed women after maintenance treatment. *Am. J. Psychiatry* 133:757, 1976.
30. Weissman M.M., Klerman G.L.: The chronic depressive in the community: unrecognized and poorly treated. *Comp. Psychiatry* 18:523, 1977.
31. West D.A., et al.: Emergency psychiatric home visiting: Report of four years experience. *J. Clin. Psychiatry* 41(4):113, 1980.

PART IV

AFFECTIVE DISORDERS AND THE LIFE CYCLE

17

AFFECTIVE DISORDERS
AND THE LIFE CYCLE

JOHN J. SCHWAB, M.D.

If there be a hell upon earth it is to be found in a melancholy man's heart.
Robert Burton Anatomy of Melancholy

THROUGHOUT HISTORY, the prevalence of certain types of mental disorders seems to fluctuate greatly. In the late Middle Ages in Europe, lycanthropy was a bizarre, serious mental disorder and the dancing mania was epidemic. Today such conditions are observed only occasionally and are regarded as medical curiosities. During the sexually repressive Victorian era, classic hysteria and fainting (swooning) were common in Western societies. Although conversion hysteria is still seen quite often in medical and surgical patients, the symptomatology is not nearly so dramatic.

Depression is a much less colorful mental disorder; nevertheless, its epidemic character throughout the ages has been observed by historians. About 150 years ago, Esquirol noted that melancholia "borrows its character and finds again the causes which produce it in the different periods of society."[7] Recurring epidemics of depression have been closely associated with the social conditions and the spirit, the *zeitgeist*, of a particular era. Melancholia, described by the great Greek physicians and philosophers, became a subject of increasing concern during the decline of that classical civilization. Aristotle endowed it with a degree of respectability by explaining that it was a necessary ingredient for spiritual and artistic creativity.

In more modern times, melancholia pervaded the national consciousness in England during the latter part of Elizabeth's reign and the early decades of the 17th century. Unbelievable as it may seem to us, that weighty, tedious volume, Robert Burton's *The Anatomy of Melancholy*, became a bestseller and was published six times between 1621 and 1651.[3]

EPIDEMIOLOGY

Since 1960 there has been increasing interest in the affective disorders, particularly depression. Whether there has been a real increase in the incidence of depressive illness cannot be determined with scientific precision, but there is well-founded concern about its obviously high prevalence. That concern is primarily based on reports of increasing numbers of persons receiving treatment for depression. The prominent British geneticists, Slater and Cowie, noted that first admission rates to hospitals for affective disorders rose sharply between 1952 and 1966 in Great Britain.[18] Since genetic processes require at least one or two generations to produce such a rapid increase, sociocultural factors are bound to be influential factors. A few years ago, the National Institute of Mental Health estimated that 8 million Americans were depressed, that 125,000 were hospitalized each year for this condition, and that another 200,000 should be hospitalized. Some authorities believe that even these startling statistics are conservative and that depression may afflict more than 12 million adults in the United States each year. G. W. Brown's survey of women in the general population in London indicated that about 16% were depressed.[2]

A second reason for heightened concern about depression is that the suicide rate among adolescents and young adults (aged 15 to 24), has doubled and the suicide attempt rate has quadrupled in less than 25 years.[19] In Charlotte Silverman's words: "Suicide is the mortality index of depressive illness."[16] Epidemiologically, it is axiomatic that when the age base for any chronic or recurrent illness shifts toward the young, an increased frequency or possibly an epidemic of that illness is likely to occur in the future. The movement of the age base toward younger groups portends an accumulation of disposed, susceptible individuals who are likely to become depressed later in life when they are subjected to stressors and disappointments. The epidemiology of coronary heart disease between 1945 and 1975 is a dramatic example of the validity of that maxim.

The third reason for concern is the knowledge that although effective therapies are available, only a small proportion of persons are diagnosed and receive treatment. A decade ago C. A. H. Watts delineated the "iceberg of depression."[20] His graphic portrayal showed that only about 18 per 1,000 persons in the general population were recognized as suffering from depressions; possibly an additional 150 per 1,000 were "below the level of recognition" in that they never came to that attention of physicians. At the tip of the iceberg were the 0.12 per 1,000 suicides, followed by the 2.8 per 1,000 who received psychiatric care. About 12 to 15 per 1,000 were treated by family practitioners. More recently, Lehman summarized available data: only 1 in 5 depressed persons receives medical treatment, 1 in 50 is hospitalized, and 1 in 200 commits suicide.[8]

Although the concept of the life cycle has been an integral component of Eastern philosophies for more than two millennia, it did not become a prominent theme in Western psychiatric thought until quite recently. Erik Erikson's profound work on the eight stages of ego development[6, 21] supplied a background for the current interest in the emotional problems associated with phases of the "course of life,"[12] as evidenced by the widespread popularity of Sheehy's *Passages*[15] and Levinson's *The Seasons of a Man's Life*.[9] In the 1970s, following the clamor and turmoil of the previous decade, attention was focused on depression in the young and the elderly rather than on the midlife depression that has been recognized for years.

With that picture of depression in the community as a background, I shall offer a working definition of depression for practitioners and discuss some of the depressive syndromes as they relate to various stages of the life cycle, concluding with general remarks about therapy.

DEPRESSION AS A SOCIOMEDICAL SYNDROME

Based on our studies since 1965 of depression in medical patients and on random samples of responders in the community, we conceptualize depression as a sociomedical syndrome that has five major dimensions. These are:

1. An affective disturbance with symptoms and signs usually related to lowered mood and sadness, but sometimes evidenced by a flattening of affect, a stoic countenance, grim smiles, or pseudojocularity.

2. Some physical distress with a large, varying number of bodily complaints. Often these are persistent low-grade aches and pains in different parts of the body, particularly dull headaches and backaches or an unrelieved sense of muscular tension that is described as "weariness" in the lower extremities. Generally, such pains neither increase greatly in intensity nor disappear completely, even when the patient is taking medication for their relief. In some sociodemographic subgroups, especially middle-aged blacks, we have repeatedly found chronic complaints of headache or backache as presenting symptoms of depression; treatment of the individual's depression is the only effective therapy. Visceral aches and pains are not reported often by depressed patients, although sometimes they attempt to describe their inner sense of emptiness and hollowness as a "deep ache" or dull pain in the chest or abdomen.

3. Altered patterns of psychobiologic activity that involve sleep, appetite and digestion, and sexual activity. These disturbances appear in myriad forms and combinations. The depressed patient may have difficulty getting to sleep, may awaken repeatedly during the night, may have the classic early-morning awakening, or may have hypersomnia. Lack of refreshing sleep, regardless of its duration, and repeated complaints of fatigue in the morning and throughout the day are common. Analogously, the distur-

bance of appetite and digestion may range from anorexia to bulimia; usually the patient states that all food is tasteless. On occasion, the depressed patient indicates that he or she really likes to eat only some new food, or may be overeating, frequently and compulsively, "to fill the inner emptiness." The most common complaint about bowel habits is constipation, particularly when the patient is eating poorly or when psychomotor retardation is prominent. But the physician should be alert to complaints of diarrhea and constipation when the patient is indulging in food idiosyncrasies or drinking excessive amounts of coffee in an attempt to relieve feelings of fatigue. An inability to reach orgasm is another common complaint of depressed patients, but some persons in the early stage of depression strive to become more active sexually to compensate for self-perceived fears about loss of sexual attractiveness.

The most important diagnostic clue is a change in the accustomed pattern of psychobiologic activity. Of all the indicators of depression, a change in the sleep pattern is the most diagnostically reliable; it also serves as a guide to the patient's response to treatment.

4. A cognitive disorder generally shown by self-blame, self-disparagement, and lowered self-esteem. The patient often speaks in an irritating, helpless, even hostile tone about self-accusatory and self-punitive thoughts. Suicidal ideations, of course, is common in depression, and in some patients the cognitive disorder has persecutory or paranoidal overtones.

5. A philosophical dimension which is usually characterized by pessimism, despair, and a gloomy outlook on the future. Many depressed patients say they are no longer attending church regularly, feel that their faith has weakened, or feel that they have slight or an ambivalent regard for the spiritual and metaphysical values that previously had been meaningful.

DEPRESSIVE SYNDROMES AND THE LIFE CYCLE

YOUTH

The alarming increase in the suicide rate among the young has focused attention on depressive illness in this age group. For many years, depression was considered to be almost exclusively a mental illness that afflicted menopausal women in their 40s or men in their 50s who were facing life with diminished physical vigor and possible preretirement dilemmas. Among younger persons the symptomatology tends to be much more varied and depression is more difficult to diagnose than among those in midlife or the later years.

Many child and adolescent psychiatrists believe that depression in this age group often appears as hyperactivity, difficulty with concentration, sociopathic behavior, and a loss of interest in school or other work that is reflected in a declining performance that the young person denies or rationalizes. Changes in psychobiologic patterns of activity are not easy to evaluate in younger persons because many attempt to maintain status in their peer group by aping fashions. Overeating, oversleeping, and food fads are reported. Our study of the symptoms of depression in a random sample of 1,645 persons aged 16 to 92 indicated that the younger persons complained of many of the standard symptoms of depression. A disproportionately large number of them reported lack of refreshing sleep, feeling tired in the morning, self-blame, or thoughts of suicide.[14]

MIDLIFE

On the depression scale that we used in our community study, the mean scores of the youngest and oldest respondents were significantly higher than those of the other age groups. However, the mean scores rose in almost linear fashion for those above the age of 45. From 25% to 33% of the adults aged 45 to 59 reported that they blame themselves when things do not turn out as they wish and that they feel powerless to control their own lives; 15% to 20% reported that things do not turn out as they wish, that they feel tired in the mornings, and that they have some type of sleeping difficulties; and more than 10% reported that they do not enjoy things and that their outlook on the future is gloomy. To evaluate depression in patients in this age group we should not restrict our thoughts to the menopause or climacteric.

Some special problems compounding difficulties with the diagnosis of depression in patients in midlife are:

1. These patients have not passed the risk zone for manic-depressive illness. For many years it was believed that depression after the age of 45 could not be manic-depressive or bipolar illness, but epidemiologic studies in Scandinavia have shown that the risk zone for the first attack of bipolar illness extends to age 60.[17]

2. Repeatedly, we have found that middle-aged patients have hormonal or metabolic diseases that simulate depression. A number of them are diagnosed as depressed, when in reality they are suffering from diseases such as hypothyroidism or diabetes mellitus.

3. Waning physical vigor and the onset of such midlife diseases as coronary heart disease or osteoarthritis are additional complicating factors. But too often such diseases have been assigned primary importance clinically, when in reality depression was the major problem.

4. Social factors appear to be extremely influential at this time in life.

For example, many women suffer from the "empty nest" syndrome, a loss of role and status, and many men are in the throes of "preretirement blues," facing the future with a sense of uncertainty.

5. Most persons at this age in life are suffering from an existential crisis. Life's frustrations and disappointments have accumulated; the individual is acutely aware of missed opportunities and of cherished aspirations that now appear beyond reach. Frequently, a change in life-styles and, more important, an acceptance of limitations and grim realities are necessary internal adjustments that must be made painfully and with some anguish. This may take the form of a depressive episode or, conversely, a hypomanic burst of activity.

THE LATER YEARS

The work of Busse and Pfieffer[11] and Butler and Lewis[4] turned the spotlight on the serious problem of depression in the elderly. A sociodemographic profile of the segment of our population defined as elderly reveals that this expanding group is composed mainly of women. Many live as isolates or are otherwise bereft of close family support, most dwell in the midst of urban decay, only a small fraction are productively employed, and many are poverty-stricken. The vast majority have some type of chronic physical illness and fear invalidism, but almost all of them are ambulatory and live in the community.

Most authorities emphasize that depressive reactions are common in old age because it is a season of loss. Our study of depression in the community showed that higher percentages of respondents aged 70 and older than those in the younger age groups reported many of the symptoms of depression "often and/or all the time." In particular, symptoms pertaining to physiologic disturbances, such as sleeping difficulties, ailments in various parts of the body, and loss of appetite, were reported by large numbers of older respondents. An analysis of our data showed that the elderly depressed evinced five major symptoms that tap the various dimensions of depression as a sociomedical syndrome: lowered spirits, problems with sleep and appetite, feeling helpless, powerlessness, and a gloomy outlook on the future.[13] Some of these symptoms in the elderly may have been manifestations of physical illness, but the feelings of being alone and helpless, that life is hopeless, and that the future is gloomy are poignant expressions of personal despair. This distress must be placed in a social perspective. Is the rate of social and culture change so rapid that it has a disorienting effect, especially on the elderly? Almost 30 years ago, in discussing culture change and personality development, Margaret Mead emphasized that the rapidity of change itself makes it difficult for the elderly to use previous experience as a guide to daily living. It disrupts coherent sequences of behavior and deprives the individual of the capacity to view the future as reasonably predictable—all of which results in emotional turmoil.[10]

Our difficulty in diagnosing depression in the elderly is compounded by ageism, a bias described by Butler and Lewis.[4] Ageism enables us to deny that we are growing old; we use such denial because, for many of us, aging is a frightening prospect. We associate it with loss of vigor and physical infirmities. Also, our youth-oriented culture does not value wisdom gained from experience; instead, it considers obsolescence to be a self-evident fact of life. We can only ask whether the elderly, many of whom are female and poor, have become obsolete in our society. Does their misery, which is expressed symptomatically, reflect societal rejection, if not lack of concern? In medical practice, we need to be continually aware that stereotypes and biases, such as ageism, not only blunt our diagnostic acumen, but also influence our approach to treatment so that we do not pursue it as vigorously and optimistically for the elderly as for younger persons.

CONCLUSIONS

Depression at various stages in the life cycle appears to be linked to overlapping social and cultural problems that involve human development, changing roles and status, and loss of traditional social support systems. Recent findings of increased emotional illness (including depression) among the young may be attributable to disruptions of adolescent and late adolescent development. The rapid rate of social and culture change is associated with alterations in the structure of the family that, for example, are producing many children of divorce—a high-risk population vulnerable to developmental trauma. Peter Blos describes the "vacuum of uninstitutionalized adolescence in western society" that allows "on the one hand, a high degree of personality differentiation and individuation, since there are no obligatory models, but on the other hand, the discontinuities and social patternings and the burdens of self-determination facilitate deviant and pathological development."[1] In working with younger-aged depressed patients, therefore, therapists will be compelled to focus their efforts on ego development during adolescence and on the developmental tasks of late adolescence and early adulthood.

The social turbulence of the 1960s included struggles for sexual equality, especially the emergence of the women's liberation movement and demands for the passage of the Equal Rights Amendment. Although the generation of women and men who came of age in the 1960s appears to be able to adapt to the resulting change in roles and status, the middle-aged who were taught more traditional values are bound to be affected by the swirling winds of change. Many of these middle-aged persons, especially women, are torn between the older value system that prized the women's status as a housewife and the new, compelling demands for her to use her education and capabilities in a career outside of the home. In working with our midlife depressed patients, it is essential that we examine psychotherapeutically the impact of nationwide changes in role and status on them and their often ambivalent feelings and aspirations.

The accelerated rate of social and cultural change is associated with changes in the demographic characteristics of our population. In particular, longer life expectancy is steadily increasing the proportion of elderly persons, and many of these elderly persons appear to be susceptible to depressions. As individuals the elderly are especially dependent for survival on their social groups. Therefore, when group cohesion is strained and fragmentation occurs, those lacking strong support systems tend to become isolated and react to stressors with sadness, helplessness, and hopelessness, the prime components of depression.

Especially for the elderly, depression as a reaction to loss—symbolic, threatened, or real—justifiably becomes a major concern to medicine at a time when modern therapies are held out as balms for anguish. The elderly require meaningful contact with relatives, peers, co-workers, the clergy, and others to combat the loneliness, sense of helplessness, and feelings of futility that change the depressed person's attitudes toward the self, toward others, and toward the world in which he or she lives. From a social psychiatric perspective, treatment depends on humanistically oriented person therapy and respect for all people, regardless of age. Finally, we are called on to realize that only adequate social support systems will ameliorate the distress of the emotionally ill and that the construction of such systems—human, not bureaucratic, personal, not distant—ultimately depends on our individual and societal values.

REFERENCES

1. Blos P.: *On Adolescence*. New York, The Free Press, 1962.
2. Brown G.W.: Cited in *Psychiatry Annual*, 1973, vol. 3, p. 233.
3. Burton R.: *The Anatomy of Melancholy*. Oxford, 1621. Reprinted, Dell F., Jordan-Smith P. (trans.-eds.), New York, Tudor Publishing Co., 1941.
4. Butler R.N., Lewis M.I.: *Aging and Mental Health: Positive Psychosocial Approaches*. St. Louis, C.V. Mosby Co., 1973.
5. Butler R.N.: Age-ism: Another form of bigotry. *Gerontologist* 9:243, 1969.
6. Erikson E.: *Childhood and Society*. New York, W.W. Norton Co., 1950.
7. Esquirol J.E.D.: Monomania, in Hunter R., McAlpine I. (eds.): *Three Hundred Years of Psychiatry*. New York, Oxford University Press, 1963.
8. Lehman H.E.: Epidemiology of depressive disorders, in Fieve R.R. (ed.): *Depression in the Seventies*. Amsterdam, Excerpta Medica, 1971.

9. Levinson D.J.: *The Seasons of a Man's Life*. New York, Alfred E. Knopf, Inc., 1978.
10. Mead M.: The implications of culture change for personality development, in Freid M.: *Cultural Anthropology. Readings in Anthropology*. New York, Thomas Y. Crowell, 1968, vol. 2.
11. Pfeiffer F., Busse W.E.: Mental disorders in later life: Affective disorders: Paranoia, neurotic, and situational reactions, in Busse E.W., Pfeiffer F. (eds.): *Mental Illness in Later Life*. Washington, D.C., American Psychiatric Association, 1973.
12. Pollock, G.: Aging or aged: Development of pathology, in Greenspan S.I., Pollock G.H. (eds.): *Adulthood and the Aging Process. The Course of Life: Psychoanalytic Contributions Toward Understanding Personality Development*, Washington, D.C., U.S. Government Printing Office, vol. 4, 1981.
13. Schwab J.: Depression among the aged. *South Med. J.* 69:1039–1041, 1976.
14. Schwab J., et al.: *Social Order and Mental Health: The Florida Health Study*. New York, Brunner/Mazel, 1979.
15. Sheehy G.: *Passages: Predictable Crises of Adult Life*. New York, Bantam Books, 1977.
16. Silverman C.: The epidemiology of depression: A review. *Am. J. Psychiatry* 124:183, 1978.
17. Sjögren T.: Genetic-statistical and psychiatric investigations of a West Swedish population. *Acta Psychiatr. Neurol.*, Suppl. 52, pp. 1–102, 1948.
18. Slater E., Cowie V.: *The Genetics of Mental Disorders*. London, Oxford University Press, 1971.
19. Somers A.: Violence, television and the health of American youth. *N. Engl. J. Med.* 294:811–817, 1976.
20. Watts C.A.H.: *Depressive Disorders in the Community*. Bristol, England, John Wright & Sons, Ltd., 1966.
21. Watts C.A.H.: *Gandhi's Truth*. New York, W.W. Norton Co., 1969.

18

DEPRESSION IN CHILDREN AND ADOLESCENTS

ELVA O. POZNANSKI, M.D.

PRIOR TO THE 1970s, children were regarded for the most part as being incapable of experiencing depression. The myth of childhood as a happy, carefree state, despite literary giants who described it differently, apparently prejudiced the observations of psychiatrists. The profession thought that the familiar manifestations of nonpsychotic adult depression were virtually nonexistent in childhood.[42] The rationale for this viewpoint was derived from basic assumptions that children lacked an adequate superego development,[44] that they were unable to tolerate painful affects for any length of time, and that they lacked experience with separations until the end of adolescence.[56]

In the 1960s, the concept of masked depression[24, 56] or of depressive "equivalents"[50] was put forth. This concept held that the depressive affect was not directly expressed, except possibly for short periods of time, and that a variety of behavioral problems were alternative ways of expressing depression in childhood and adolescence. While depressive equivalents may be a valid concept, there are at least three difficulties with accepting this idea as a predominant view of childhood depression. First, it assumes that depressive affect is rarely observable in children. Second, the behaviors cited as expressing equivalents to depression were so diverse as to encompass most of the nonpsychotic psychopathologies in children and adolescents. Third, the linkage of such conditions to depressive affect was frequently tenuous or nonexistent. From clinical and research experience, it is clear that viewing depressive equivalents as a mask for depression in childhood is unacceptable.

An exception to the general trend of thought in the 1960s was the work of Sandler and Joffee at Hampstead Clinic,[46] who examined the psychoanalytic records of 100 children and set forth nine features commonly associated with depressive affect. Their work examined the theoretical formulations of the depressive reaction and its relationship to loss, pain, and aggression; the role of defenses; and issues of individualization. While these concerns are important, it would have been more helpful clinically had the behavior and duration of the depressed state been more precisely described. Despite these limitations, their article constituted an important step forward, as they very clearly stated that depressive affect *is* seen in children. In 1966, the Group for the Advancement of Psychiatry, Committee on Childhood Psychiatry, in a proposal for a diagnostic nomenclature, included for the first time a category of childhood depression under psychoneurotic disorders.[27] This was the first diagnostic nomenclature for children that mentioned the word "depression." The bias of that era is reflected in the fact that depression was regarded solely as a subcategory of psychoneurotic disorders.

The early 1970s produced in this country and in Europe a dramatic shift in the thinking about childhood depression. Poznanski and Zrull published a clinical study of 14 children with recognizably overt depression.[39] Malmquist wrote an extensive review of the literature, well integrated with his own psychoanalytically oriented concepts of childhood depression.[32] The Fourth Congress of the Union of European Pedopsychiatrists, convened in Sweden in 1971, took as its theme depressive states in childhood and adolescence.[3] Cytryn and McKnew published two articles on childhood depression: one on classification,[17] the other on possible biochemical correlates.[18]

DEPRESSIVE AFFECT VERSUS DEPRESSIVE SYNDROME

Depressive affect is a fairly common observation. A depressive syndrome is characterized by a persisting dysphoric mood of two to four weeks' duration plus a cardinal group of accompanying behaviors. Since the depressive syndrome resembles any other medical syndrome, it is useful to make a distinction between affect and syndrome in order to introduce some homogeneity among populations of depressed children. The clinical diagnosis of depression is based on verbal and nonverbal behaviors and, like many other disorders, is not based on etiology.

Some general agreement about the need for diagnostic criteria for childhood depression represents a major step forward in the research on childhood depression. The majority of researchers on childhood depression use adult criteria for depressive disorders, either the third edition of the *Di-*

agnostic and Statistical Manual of Mental Disorders (DSM-III)[2] or Research Diagnostic Criteria (RDC).[48] Other researchers use Weinberg's criteria,[53] the Bellevue Index of Depression (BID),[37] or Poznanski's criteria.[40] Compared with the symptom groups described in the early and mid-1970s, the differences among these five sets of criteria are relatively minor.

The major difference between Poznanski's criteria and the criteria of *DSM-III* is that Poznanski requires that during two interviews, two weeks apart, the child only *look* sad. The *DSM-III* requires that the child *say* he or she feels sad or blue.

In my experience, some children seem to have more difficulty than adults in identifying feelings of prolonged sadness or any other synonym for depression, and have more difficulty identifying these feelings than feelings of anger or fear.

SYMPTOMATOLOGY

The symptoms and behaviors of depressed children are similiar to those of adults but are flavored by the child's developmental phase. The depressed child is less likely to be recognized than a depressed adult for the following reasons: (1) Many adults believe that children do not become clinically depressed. (2) The child's unlined face forces the observer to look at the posture and the eyes, rather than at the more visible sagging eyelids and drooping mouth of the depressed adult. (3) A quiet child disturbs the adult world less than a noisy child.

On specific questioning, many children are able to describe feeling unhappy for prolonged periods. Other children find it difficult to label their feelings as depressive states but describe the characteristic features accompanying depression remarkably well. Table 18-1 compares items on the Hamilton Depression Rating Scale (Adult),[28] with Poznanski's Children's Depression Rating Scale (CDRS-R) for prepubertal children.[40] Poznanski's scale illustrates some of the similarities and differences in the clinical phenomenology of depression in children and in adults.

The most characteristic feature of depression in children is anhedonia, a lack of capacity to have fun. Psychomotor retardation—slow speech, poverty of language, hypoactivity—occurs in children as well as adults. Although depressed children do show difficulties with vegetative functioning (e.g., difficulty with sleep and appetite reduction), these appear to be somewhat less prominent in children than in depressed adults. Depressed children frequently complain of fatigue during the day, a symptom, like many others, which must be elicited by direct questioning. Social withdrawal and impairment in schoolwork are also common features of depression in children. Children generally know the meaning of the word "sui-

TABLE 18–1.—COMPARISON OF ITEMS ON THE
HAMILTON AND CHILDREN'S DEPRESSION RATING
SCALE-REVISED (CDRS-R)

DEPRESSION RATING SCALE (ADULT) (HAMILTON)		CDRS-R*	
Depressed mood	0–4	Depressed affect (nonverbal)	0–7
		Depressed feelings (verbal)	0–7
		Weeping	0–7
		Self-esteem	0–7
Guilt	0–4	Guilt	0–7
Suicide	0–4	Suicide ideation	0–7
		Morbid thoughts	0–7
Initial insomnia	0–2	Sleep (check subtype)	0–5
Middle insomnia	0–2		
Delayed insomnia	0–2		
Work and interest	0–4	Schoolwork	0–7
		Capacity to have fun	0–7
Retardation	0–4	Tempo of language	0–5
Agitation	0–4	Hypoactivity	0–7
Anxiety—psychic	0–4		
Anxiety—somatic	0–4		
Gastrointestinal	0–2	Appetite/eating pattern	0–5
General somatic	0–2	Excessive fatigue/ general somatic	0–7
Genital	0–2	Physical complaints	0–7
Hypochondriasis	0–4		
Loss of insight	0–2		
Weight loss	0–2		
		Social withdrawal	0–7
		Irritability	0–7
Total	52	Total	113

*Listing reflects some revisions of original CDRS.

cide" and show little hesitation in discussing it. As with adults, all children suspected of being depressed should be asked about suicidal ideation. Children who are depressed may show morbid ideation, particularly around deaths within the family.

The massive underdiagnosis of depression in prepubertal children is also true of adolescents, despite the clinical recognition of dysphoric affect in adolescents for decades.

There appear to be three sources of confusion in the diagnosis of depression in adolescence. The first is the persisting notion that significant depression in adolescence is indistinguishable from normal adolescent turmoil. Rutter et al.,[45] Masterson,[33] Offer and Offer,[36] and others have shown clearly that this is not so and that normality and pathology can be clearly distinguished in this age period. A second problem involves the tendency to focus on the behavior precipitating referral, such as running away, aggression, unsanctioned sexual activity, and drug or alcohol abuse, rather than on psychological processes such as affective state. A third source of confusion is the difficulty in distinguishing between schizophrenics and those severely depressed adolescents who may be physically immobilized by their illness and burdened by delusions of guilt and worthlessness. The confusion and underdiagnosis may be greater in early adolescence than later, for several authors comment on the increasing resemblance of adult patterns of pathology with increasing age.[33, 50, 54]

There may be variations in the clinical profile of depression within adolescents. Hudgens[30] has described some general characteristics of depression in hospitalized adolescents. Fifty-eight percent had a psychiatrically ill parent, most of them depressed. Many had disturbances in their premorbid personalities, with moody, obsessive qualities or sexual deviations. The onset was gradual, with a long delay between the first symptoms and hospitalization. The mean age at onset was 15.9 years. While recovery was common, so was relapse. Anorexia and sleep disturbance were as seen in adults, but changes in libido were not, perhaps because of difficulties in assessing this in adolescents. Hudgens' observations parallel those of Gallemore and Wilson.[23]

MANIC-DEPRESSIVE ILLNESS

There is considerable controversy over whether the same clinical features of manic-depressive illness in adults can be seen in children or whether there is a distinct juvenile form. Many of the case descriptions in the literature do not give enough information for a definitive diagnosis of a manic-depressive disorder to be made by observation of the child alone.[4, 20] Heavy reliance is placed on the existence of affective illness in the family. One has the impression that either the clinical profile of the manic-depressive child is ambiguous or that a clear clinical profile has yet to be devised. Studies of the offspring of parents with bipolar illness help sharpen clinical awareness.[5, 35, 43, 55]

A major difficulty with the concept of manic-depressive illness in childhood hinges on the concept of a manic state in childhood. Clinical characteristics of mania in adults have been fairly well delineated. Patients exhibiting mania demonstrate the following characteristics: incessant talking, constant movement from one place to another, demonstration of poor judgment, ease of distractibility, extreme irritability, hyperactivity, extreme intense argumentativeness, extreme anger, diminished impulse control, demand for contact with others, and jumping from one subject to another.[6] This scheme of clinical symptomatology cannot be directly transposed to children; a major problem is the overlap between the adult manic symptomatology and the hyperactivity syndrome in children.

The hyperactive child characteristically is moving all the time, is distractible, has poor impulse control, and may have poor judgment. The hyperactive syndrome is far too common in children to be considered equivalent to a manic state in adults. A genetic study of relatives of hyperkinetic children showed a low prevalence of affective disorders, suggesting that hyperkinesis is not related to a manic-depressive illness.[49] A subgroup of hyperactive children may be delineated, nevertheless, which represents the equivalent of mania in childhood. One would anticipate that this subgroup would have more discrete episodes of hyperactivity as well as dysphoria/euphoria.

Manic-depressive illness in adolescence has been documented since the days of Kraepelin.[31] Its occurrence in adolescence is felt to be a rare phenomenon. This may or may not be true, given the difficulty of making this diagnosis in this age group.

Carlson and Strober[14] did a retrospective chart review of six adolescents, all originally diagnosed as schizophrenic but ultimately diagnosed as bipolar manic-depressive. Clinically, all showed pervasive sexual preoccupation, three of the six had recurrent psychotic thinking, and three had pronounced paranoid ideation. Study of the detailed case studies left the author feeling that these cases resembled schizophrenia cognitively but were accompanied by intense affect. Greater awareness and study of psychotic adolescents with affective disturbances will help recognize manic-depressive illness in this age group.

Carlson et al.[13] compared the outcome of adolescent bipolar illness. He found that early age at onset is not a factor in the variable course and prognosis of manic-depressive illness; that is, adolescents with manic-depressive illness do not have a more virulent course.

CLASSIFICATION

The lack of universally accepted diagnostic criteria and the paucity of information on the phenomenology of childhood depression preclude any reasonable classification. It is not surprising that attempts to classify depression in children have been unsatisfactory and that no one classification has universal acceptance.

There have been two attempts by child psychiatrists to classify depression in children. Cytryn and McKnew's classification of acute, masked, and chronic depression has some clinical validity; however, the correlation of this system of classification with differing precipitating factors, premorbid adjustment, and family pathology lacks replication.[17] Malmquist's system was devised from a critical review of the literature, rather than from direct clinical observations.[32] Malmquist, however, was aware of developmental issues in his nosology.

The classification of depression in adults is under debate. There is general agreement in adult psychiatry that the distinction between bipolar and unipolar depression is a valid one and that both have different clinical features, natural courses, and clinical responses to drugs. This distinction does not appear to have as much value in child psychiatry.

A major difficulty is that mania in children is uncommon. Whether this is true or whether mania simply goes more unrecognized, as childhood depression had, is unknown. Manic-depressive illness in adolescents has been reported but appears to be a more difficult diagnosis to make in this age group than in adults.[14]

At face value, the primary-secondary dichotomy appears to be of possible use in child psychiatry. A diagnosis of secondary depression is made if the depression is preceded by schizophrenia, obsessive-compulsive disorder, antisocial personality, drug use disorder, schizoaffective disorder, panic disorder, Briquet's disorder, alcoholism, anorexia, or organic brain syndrome. Since clinical features alone cannot distinguish between categories, the distinction is realistically made on the basis of the patient's history.

The term "psychotic depression" is useful with adult depressives, but its meaning for children is not clearly understood. Recently, Chambers et al. described children as commonly having auditory hallucinations and delusions with their depressions.[15] Some of these behaviors were hypnagogic and not true psychotic behaviors. Further research is needed to see if psychotic versus nonpsychotic depression has clinical relevance in children.

To date the assumption generally has been that most, it not all, depressions in children are reactive to the environment. The endogenous-reactive dichotomy is of interest, however, as it relates to depression in children and adolescents. Depressed children are usually anhedonic. In addition, children who clinically resemble adult endogenous depressives are most likely to have a positive response on the dexamethasone suppression test.[38] Hence, the term "endogenous" may be useful in childhood depression.

The role of precipitating stress in depressed children is under investigation. The issue is whether stress relates to psychiatric problems in children generally or whether it is greater in depressed children. Also under scrutiny are types of stresses and whether these relate specifically to depression.

Some wide differences in the prevalence rates of treated cases of childhood depression exist. The difference between various studies can be accounted for by the strictness of the diagnostic criteria and the patient pop-

TABLE 18–2.—PREVALENCE OF TREATED DEPRESSION

STUDY	SETTING	PREVALENCE (%)
Carlson and Cantwell,[12] using	Outpatient	16
DSM-III criteria	Inpatient	36
Poznanski et al.,[41] using	Inpatient	38
Poznanski's criteria		
Petti,[37] using BID criteria	Inpatient	61
Brumback et al.,[10] using	Outpatient	63
Weinberg's criteria		

ulation. The RDC, *DSM-III*, and Poznanski's criteria are the most strict; the BID is less strict, and Weinberg's criteria are the least strict.

As Table 18–2 shows, in Carlson and Cantwell's prospective study of a psychiatric outpatient population, the prevalence of depression was 16%, using *DSM-III* criteria.[12] In other prospective studies of inpatient populations, the figures are higher, ranging from 38%, using Poznanski's criteria, to 61%, using BID criteria.[10, 37, 41]

The above figures are considerably higher than what is commonly diagnosed in both outpatient and inpatient settings. For example, Weiner and Degaudio found that the diagnosis of "psychoneurotic depressive reaction" in adolescents was used more frequently in a general hospital (12%–26%) than in a psychiatric outpatient clinic (3%–8%) or in a psychiatric inpatient population (3%–7%).[54] Apparently, nonpsychiatric physicians are observing more depression in adolescents than are psychiatrists.

For historical and diagnostic reasons, therefore, it is safe to conclude that childhood adolescent depression is massively underdiagnosed in most clinics and that the next decade will show increasing recognition of this problem.

ETIOLOGY

LOSS AND SEPARATION

Historically, the concept of loss in the etiology of depression was initiated by Freud's classic work, "Mourning and Melancholia."[21] In that paper, Freud compared grief and depression and found them clinically similar, except that the decrease in self-esteem was greater in depression. Freud proposed that the loss was conscious in grief and unconscious in depression. He was primarily concerned with comparing the acute state of grief with the depressive syndrome, but there was the implicit assumption that grief eventually ended or became "abnormal."

The concept of loss in some form is often viewed as a central, dynamic feature of adult depression. In a recent review of conceptual models of depression in adults, the majority of nonbiologic models were found to postulate some sort of loss: loss of self-esteem, object loss, loss of reinforcement, loss of role status, and loss of meaning of existence.[1]

Confirmation of the loss model of depression comes from another source, the primate laboratories.[34] The work with monkeys pioneered by McKinney et al. has special significance to child psychiatry and to the study of childhood depression. Note should be made of the animal model of depression that is produced by separating young monkeys from their mothers. These studies indicate that in monkeys, the age at which separation takes place and prior experience with separation can be important factors in determining the behavioral reaction to separation. In these respects, the primate reaction is very similar to that of human children.

One of the earliest descriptions of depression in infants came from Spitz's work on what he termed "anaclitic depression."[47] In 1946, Spitz described how separation from the mother in the second half of the first year of the infant's life could lead to a characteristic affective reaction, with the infant becoming sad, weepy, apathetic, and having an immobile face. The babies reacted slowly to stimuli and moved slowly. They had poor appetite and sleep patterns with little movement. Spitz concluded that the children were exhibiting "distance depression." A strong mother-child bond increased the chances of an infant becoming depressed after separation from the mother. It is noteworthy, however, that *only 15% of the infants separated from their mothers* suffered this syndrome; therefore, other factors were apparently operating—perhaps "constitutional" or genetic components, perhaps the quality of mothering.

Spitz's study of anaclitic depression was conducted in a prison nursery. The environment for the infants, therefore, was unusual in terms of cultural norms prior to separation. Furthermore, after separation the infants had the sort of institutional care typical of the era.

Although anaclitic depression has been classified as a deprivational syndrome,[32] it is not clear whether or not the anaclitic depressions of infancy are the prototypes of depression in the preschool or school-aged child. The next significant step was to describe the effects of separation from mother in early childhood. The hypothesis that a young child separated from his or her mother suffers great distress was not generally accepted at the time these studies were done. Bowlby has written extensively on loss and attachment in childhood, but his work is primarily anecdotal and does not provide a strong empirical case for his theoretical formulations.[7, 8] Heinicke and Westheimer did a rigorous study of ten young children, 15 to 30 months old, who were separated from their mothers for brief periods, usually while the mother had another child.[29] The immediate reaction to separation was that the child spent considerable time crying and fretting. In the first few days, the child had sleep disturbances and an increased expression of hostility. Five of the ten children were followed for over a year; at reunion, none of the children demonstrated any obvious or overt aftereffects from the previous separation.

The gap between the descriptive studies of early childhood loss and separation and the subsequent development of depression in adults has been bridged partially by a number of empirical studies. These studies have indicated that childhood loss of a parent is significant more frequently in adult depressives than in adults with other psychiatric disorders.[9, 25, 26] These studies unfortunately have all the limitations of retrospective research. d'Elia and Perris, studying adult depressives with unipolar, bipolar, and reactive depressions, found the highest incidence of childhood bereavement in the neurotic-reactive depression group.[19] They also concluded that unipolar depressives were more likely to have suffered parental loss before the age of 6 than bipolar depressives. This latter conclusion was based on a very small sample and obviously needs to be confirmed. The exciting prospect offered by d'Elia and Perris' study is the possibility of linking childhood bereavement with a more specific form of depression in adult life. While a link is provided by such studies, they do not explain why some children who suffer a loss in childhood develop depressions in adulthood, while others do not. There are may possibilities, including genetic factors, abnormal resolutions of grief (some of these are described in an anecdotal way by Wolfenstein,[56] and the degree of emotional deprivation. (An emotionally depriving environment likely occurs to some extent in all these families, at least during the phase of acute grief in the remaining parent.)

Caplan and Douglas' study of children with depressed moods also appears to correlate childhood depression with parent loss.[11] In their study, loss was globally defined as separation from the parent for any reason, including death, divorce, illness, or desertion. For one year, Caplan and Douglas studied all children on a waiting list for psychotherapy. They divided the children into two groups: a group of 71 children with depressed mood and another group of 185 children whom they labeled "nondepressed, neurotic." The latter group acted as a control for the first group. They found that one half of the depressed children and one fourth of the control children suffered some form of parental loss lasting six months or more before the age of 8.

The relationship between loss and bereavement, loss and subsequent depression, and bereavement and depression continues to intrigue clinicians, but the mechanisms need further clarification. Bereavement in adults is better studied and more clearly defined than it is in children.

Bereavement in adults is characterized by the painful and gradual withdrawal of emotions from the loved person. Sadness and expressions of grief are characteristic of the adult mourner. The adult expresses anger and grief over the missing person as he or she gradually reconstructs a life and existence which no longer includes the presence of the dead person.

The normal reactions of children to bereavement are less clear-cut. Children have been described, universally, as expressing less affective grief than adults. Wolfenstein mentions the "short sadness span" of children, referring to the inability of children to tolerate prolonged states of sadness and anger.[56] Furthermore, Wolfenstein comments that in the bereavement of a child, the depressive affect is isolated from thoughts of death. A similar state in adults, namely, the absence of an affective grief state when it is normally expected to occur, is thought to be indicative of a pathologic type of bereavement. Because this situation is common in children, there arises the problem of whether "normal" bereavement can occur in childhood.

Another unresolved difficulty with the theoretical concepts of grief reactions in adults is the relationship between anger and aggression in both grief states and depressions when these are applied to children. Bowlby feels that anger is an integral part of grief for both adults and children and that its expression is a necessary component for healthy mourning.[7, 8] Furman has suggested that a child's difficulty with mourning may be a manifestation of the difficulty in the mastery of aggression.[22]

At any rate, children do demonstrate periods of sadness in response to the death of a parent or sibling, although it is of shorter duration than is characteristic of the adult. Children have been described as showing disturbance in their behavior for a much longer time than they show affective expressions of grief. A wide variety of behavioral disturbances have been described, such as temper tantrums, disobedience, truancy, running away from home, and accident proneness. Thus the idea that children show depressive equivalents rather than demonstrate open depressive affect was the first conceptualization of depression in children. While reports in the literature now focus more on overt depressions in children, the concept of depressive equivalents may still be useful, with further clarification.

Another common denominator of loss within the family unit is divorce. Many studies have focused on children's reactions to divorce. Obviously, it is a complicated situation for the child, usually involving the partial loss of one parent and frequently causing distortions in the relationship with the custodial parent. Wallerstein and Kelly's studies are uniquely valuable because they were done prospectively: the children were interviewed both at the time of divorce and one year later.[51, 52] The children's behavior was subdivided by logical age divisions, thus providing a developmental perspective. Preschool-aged children usually showed global disruptions of their usual behavior patterns in response to the immediate divorce situations. A few preschool-aged children showed a "depressive reaction" among several behavioral outcomes at the one-year follow-up. The elementary school-aged child was more likely to react with sadness to the divorce initially. Again, one of several outcomes was continued depression.

It is difficult to determine from these studies whether the child's depressive reaction occurs in response to a parental depression or is independent of the affective reaction of the parents. It must be emphasized that divorce does not always produce depressions in children.

DEPRIVATION

One of the more difficult tasks that we face today is to assess whether there is a deprivational syndrome that is distinguishable from the depressive syndrome. This is an area where definitions become important because of the possible overlapping uses of terms.

A deprivational state is usually assumed if the child experiences physical or emotional neglect of his well-being. Physical neglect is easier to prove than emotional neglect and is the one most recognized by our judicial system. Emotional neglect is probably more devastating to the child and is also more difficult to prove. Even the words "deprivation" and "neglect" assume that there are some standard measures of what constitutes adequate physical and emotional nurturance in childhood. Since there are no such norms, society tends to recognize only gross and extreme deviations from its own standards of "normality."

Another problem with the word "deprivation" is that it can overlap with the term "loss." Loss and deprivation often coexist. Loss, for a child (e.g., death of a parent), usually brings about a state of relative affectual deprivation. It is probably easier to identify pure states of deprivation when there has been a continuous state of inadequate affectual supplies and inadequate physical nurturance than when elements of both deprivation and loss are involved.

Theoretically, deprivational issues in infancy and early childhood should be clearest in the "psychosocial dwarfs." In their case histories, this group of children is rarely reported to have sustained a loss of a parent or sibling. The child has not experienced a change from a previous better state of well-being but has always had a chronic state of inadequate physical and emotional supplies. Unfortunately, there are no studies comparing the affect of this group of infants with the affect of infants whose environment has provided for adequate to superior growth and development. In fact, the entire area of how affective development occurs in infancy is virtually uncharted.

Another type of possible deprivation syndrome is the so-called affection-less character frequently seen in adolescents. Most group placements for delinquent or quasi-delinquent youth have many teenagers whose major inadequacy is their limited ability to relate to other people. These adolescents have rather shallow personalities with a distinct depressive tone. Invariably these youngsters had a very impoverished and nonrewarding environment in their childhood. Not only have they lacked long-term intimate relationships within their families, but their peer relationships are not an adequate substitute for the lack of parental relationships. These youngsters constitute a group that possibly have experienced a deprivation syndrome.

PARENTAL DEPRESSION, PARENTAL REJECTION, AND HEREDITY

The most consistent finding in studies of childhood depression is a high incidence of parental depression.[16, 39] The possible significance of parental depression relative to childhood depression, however, is unclear. It is not known if parental depression facilitates childhood depression by a psycho-dynamic mechanism such as parental identification, by a change in relationship based on the parent's psychopathology, or if the occurrence of childhood depression and adult depression within the same family simply expresses a common hereditary or genetic vulnerability.

An attitude frequently reported in parents of children who are depressed is overt rejection of their child. This may simply be their attitude, or it may reflect parental depression that is characterized by apathy, withdrawal, and lack of energy. A child is likely to perceive this parental state as rejection. A child could also perceive rejection as a function of her or his low self-esteem. Systematic and thorough evaluation should help delineate these issues.

There is now considerable evidence that a genetic factor operates in depressions in adults. It is most clearly seen in manic-depressive illness but has also been identified in neurotic depression. Many studies of childhood depression have commented on the high incidence of parental depression. Ongoing studies of children with depression are showing not only that the parents have a high incidence of affective disorders, but also that the family tree is more loaded for depression than in emotionally disturbed children without depression.

CONCLUSION

Many decades after the recognition of adult depression, children are now being recognized as capable of having a depressive affect. Although there is considerable recent evidence that children can have depressive illness with some of the same biologic characteristics as adults, there is still controversy over the concept of an endogenous depression in children. Diagnostic criteria for depression in adults have been applied, without modification, to children.

The author has established criteria that are similar but that allow for the developmental stages of the child in the Childhood Depression Rating Scale-Revised. This scale has good reliability and validity and is now available to rate the severity of childhood depression. Tools such as these, along with further study and research, will improve our insight into the etiologic factors, nosology, and treatment strategies for depression in children.

REFERENCES

1. Akiskal H.S., McKinney W.T.: Depressive disorders: Toward a unified hypothesis. *Science* 182:20, 1973.
2. American Psychiatric Association: *Diagnostic and Statistical Manual of Mental Disorders,* ed. 3. Washington, D.C., APA, 1980.
3. Annell A.-L. (ed.): *Depressive States in Childhood and Adolescence.* Stockholm, Almqvist & Wiksell, 1972.
4. Annell A.-L. (ed.): Manic-depressive illness in children and effect of treatment with lithium carbonate. *Acta Paedopsychiatr.* 36:292, 1969.
5. Anthony E.J., Benedek T. (eds): *Depression and Human Existence.* Boston, Little, Brown & Co., 1975.
6. Beigel A., Murphy D.L.: Assessing clinical characteristics of the manic state. *Am. J. Psychiatry* 127:688, 1971.
7. Bowlby J.: Childhood mourning and its indications for psychiatry. *Am. J. Psychiatry* 118:481, 1961.
8. Bowlby J.: *Attachment and Love: Separation.* New York, Basic Books, 1973.
9. Bruhn J.: Broken homes among attempted suicides and psychiatric outpatients: A comparative study. *J. Ment. Sci.* 108:772, 1962.
10. Brumback R., Dietz-Schmidt S., Weinberg W.: Depression in children referred to an education diagnostic center: Diagnosis and treatment and analysis of criteria and literature review. *Dis. Nerv. Syst.* 38:7, 1977.
11. Caplan M.S., Douglas V.I.: Incidence of parental loss in children with depressed mood. *J. Child Psychol. Psychiatry* 10:225, 1969.
12. Carlson G.A., Cantwell D.: A survey of depressive symptoms, syndromes and disorders in a child psychiatric population. *J. Child Psychol. Psychiatry* 21:19, 1979.
13. Carlson G.A., Davenport Y., Jamison K.: A comparison outcome in adolescent and late-onset bipolar manic-depressive illness. *Am. J. Psychiatry* 134:8, 1977.
14. Carlson G.A., Strober M.: Manic-depressive illness in early adolescence: A study of clinical and diagnostic characteristics in six cases. *J. Am. Acad. Child Psychiatry* 17:138, 1978.
15. Chambers W.J., Puig-Antich J., Tabrizi M.A., et al.: Psychotic symptoms in pre-pubertal major depressive disorder. Read before the 27th annual meeting of the American Academy of Child Psychiatry, Chicago, October 1980.
16. Connell H.M.: Depression in childhood. *Child Psychiatry Hum. Dev.* 4:71, 1973.

17. Cytryn L., McKnew D.H.: Proposed classification of childhood depression. *Am. J. Psychiatry* 129:149,1972.
18. Cytryn L., McKnew D.H.: Biochemical correlates of affective disorders in children. *Arch. Gen. Psychiatry* 31:659, 1974.
19. d'Elia G., Perris C.: Childhood environment and bipolar and unipolar recurrent depressive psychosis, in Annell A.-L. (ed.) *Depressive States in Childhood and Adolescence.* Stockholm, Almqvist & Wiksell, 1972.
20. Dyson W.L., Barcai A.: Treatment of children of lithium-responding parents. *Curr. Ther. Res.* 12:286, 1970.
21. Freud S.: Mourning and melancholia, in *Collected Papers.* London, Hogarth Press, 1940.
22. Furman R.A.: Death and the young child: Some preliminary considerations. *Psychoanal. Study Child* 19:321, 1964.
23. Gallemore J., Wilson W.: Adolescent maladjustment or affective disorder. *Am. J. Psychiatry* 129:608, 1972.
24. Glaser K.: Masked depression in children and adolescents. *Am. J. Psychother.* 129:565, 1967.
25. Greer S.: The relationship between parental loss and attempted suicide: A central study. *Br. J. Psychiatry* 110:698, 1964.
26. Greer S.: Parental loss and attempted suicide: A further report. *Br. J. Psychiatry* 112:465, 1966.
27. Group for the Advancement of Psychiatry: *Psychopathological Disorders in Childhood.* Report No. 62. New York, GAP, 1966.
28. Hamilton M.: A rating scale for depression. *J. Neurol. Neurosurg. Psychiatry* 23:56, 1960.
29. Heinicke C., Westheimer I.: *Brief Separations.* New York, International Universities Press, 1965.
30. Hudgens R.W.: *Psychiatric Disorders in Adolescents.* Baltimore, Williams & Wilkins Co., 1974.
31. Kraepelin E.: *Manic-Depressive Insanity and Paranoia,* Barclay M. (trans.). Edinburgh, Livingstone, 1921.
32. Malmquist C.: Depressions in childhood and adolescence. *N. Engl. J. Med.* 284:887, 1971.
33. Masterson J.F.: *The Psychiatric Dilemma of Adolescence.* Boston, Little, Brown & Co., 1967.
34. McKinney W., Suomi S., Harlow H.: Depression in primates. *Am. J. Psychiatry* 127:49, 1971.
35. McKnew D.H., Cytryn L., Efron A., et al.: Offspring of patients with affective disorders. *Br. J. Psychiatry* 134:148, 1979.
36. Offer D., Offer J.: Normal adolescent males: The high school and college years. *J. Am. College Health Assoc.* 22:209, 1974.
37. Petti T.A.: Depression in hospitalized child psychiatry patients: Approaches to measuring depression. *J. Am. Acad. Child Psychiatry* 17:49, 1978.
38. Poznanski E.O., Carroll B.J., York J.A., et al.: A pilot study of the dexamethasone suppression test in prepubertal children. Unpublished observations.
39. Poznanski E.O., Zrull J.: Childhood depression: Clinical characteristics of overtly depressed children. *Arch. Gen. Psychiatry* 23:8, 1970.
40. Poznanski E.O., Cook S.C., Carroll B.J.: A depression rating scale for children. *Pediatrics* 64:442, 1979.

41. Poznanski E.O., Cook S.C., Carroll B.J.: Validation and reliability of the childhood depression rating scale. Unpublished observations.
42. Rie H.E.: Depression in childhood: A survey of the pertinent contributions. *J. Am. Acad. Child Psychiatry* 5:653, 1966.
43. Robbins D.R., Alessi N., Cook S.C., et al.: The assessment of depression in hospitalized adolescents. Read before the 26th annual meeting of the American Academy of Child Psychiatry, Atlanta, October 1979.
44. Rochlin G.: *Griefs and Discontents*. Boston, Little, Brown & Co., 1965.
45. Rutter M., Graham P., Chadwick O.F.D., et al.: Adolescent turmoil: Fact or fiction? *J. Child Psychol. Psychiatry* 17:35, 1976.
46. Sandler J., Joffe W.G.: Notes on childhood depression. *Int. J. Psychoanal.* 46:88, 1962.
47. Spitz R.A.: Anaclitic depression. *Psychoanal. Study Child* 2:313, 1946.
48. Spitzer R.L., Endicott J., Robins E.: *Research Diagnostic Criteria (RDC) for a Selected Group of Functional Disorders*, ed 2. New York, New York State Psychiatric Institute, Biometrics Research, 1977.
49. Stewart M.A., Morrison J.R.: Affective disorders among the relatives of hyperactive children. *J. Child Psychol. Psychiatry* 14:209, 1973.
50. Toolan J.M.: Depression in children and adolescents. *Am. J. Orthopsychiatry* 32:405, 1962.
51. Wallerstein J.S., Kelly J.B.: The effects of parental divorce. Experiences of the preschool child. *J. Am. Acad. Child Psychiatry* 14:600, 1975.
52. Wallerstein J.S., Kelly J.B.: The effects of parental divorce: Experiences of the child in later latency. *Am. J. Orthopsychiatry* 46:256, 1976.
53. Weinberg W.A., Rutman J., Sullivan L., et al: Depression in children referred to an educational diagnostic center. *J. Pediatr.* 83:1064, 1973.
54. Weiner I.B., Degaudio A.: Psychopathology in adolescence. *Arch. Gen. Psychiatry* 33:187, 1976.
55. White J.H., O'Shanick G.: Juvenile manic-depressive illness. *Am. J. Psychiatry* 130:380, 1977.
56. Wolfenstein M.: How is mourning possible? *Psychoanal. Study Child* 21:93, 1966.

19

DEPRESSION AND WOMEN

ANNE SEIDEN, M.D.

VIRTUALLY ALL STUDIES of incidence and prevalence of depression in this country have shown a higher incidence in women than in men. This finding is replicated in cross-cultural work and has appeared anecdotally throughout history. Weissman[53] observes that "the increased vulnerability of women to depression has been noted in writings that are over 200 years old, and in almost every country." Many traditional religions have noted that "the lot of women is sorrow" and attempt to provide consolation. An extensive review of the epidemiology of depression[54] has confirmed higher rates for women in every industrialized country and most nonindustrialized countries studied.

Such a clear gender linkage for any illness is the kind of finding that potentially helps in clarifying etiology. The obvious questions are (1) what is contributed by physiologic differences between the sexes, (2) what is contributed by differences in psychology, social role, social stressors, or other socially mediated factors, and (3) to what extent are links between biologic and social factors artifactual or valid. (See Seiden[41] for details.) Overriding these questions are important methodological questions that render definite answers unavailable at present.

PROBLEMS IN STUDYING GENDER-RELATED PREVALENCE OF DEPRESSION

DEFINITION OF DEPRESSION

One cannot simply say that depression has a certain incidence in women and a different incidence in men, without clarifying what is meant by the term "depression." Depression refers to a normal mood experienced by everyone as well as to a persistent mood state, a syndrome, or an illness. Gender linkage in one type of depression cannot be extrapolated to gender linkage in others.

THE PROBLEM OF DEPRESSIVE EQUIVALENTS

Almost everyone has personal experience with handling a depressed mood by social denial—putting on a stiff upper lip or forcing a smile that contradicts one's true feelings. There are several reasons for which one may find it desirable to hide depression from family members, work associates, or other people. To varying degrees, clinically depressed patients may conceal depression from others, and may deny it to themselves. To the extent that a person regards depression as a sign of weakness, he or she will be motivated to deny or conceal it. This pattern in itself may be gender-linked. Men may feel more strongly than women that it is necessary to conceal weakness or that depression is a sign of unacceptable failure.

Clinicians are familiar with patients who present with the vegetative symptoms of depression—sleep, appetite, and libido disturbances, psychomotor retardation or agitation, dysphoric facial expressions, and pessimism—while insisting they are not depressed. Other patients use alcohol or recreational drugs for self-medication of depression, while remaining unaware of depressive mood. Depressed patients typically have a family history with high frequency of affective disorder, especially in female relatives, and a higher than average prevalence of diagnoses of alcoholism and sociopathy, particularly in male relatives. This suggests that these latter diagnoses may at least on occasion be viewed as "depressive equivalents." Mild degrees of either depression or hypomania may be expressed in behavioral patterns that are socially more acceptable for one gender or the other; if successful, these adaptational patterns mask the illness. For example, the workaholic may keep up his or her catecholamine levels by continually generating stimulation or crisis at work.

THE PROBLEM OF GENDER-LINKED VOCABULARIES OF DISTRESS

Closely related to the expression or concealment of depression by one sex or the other are the gender-linked "vocabularies of distress."[14] In prevalence studies and clinically, for the patient to be defined as depressed, distress must be communicated in some way. But if men and women communicate distress differently, clinicians might have differential sensitivity to recognizing their distress at all, or to defining it as depression once it is recognized.

It is commonly observed that depressed schoolboys "act out" in ways that bring them to clinical attention as having behavior problems; by contrast, depressed schoolgirls may more often behave in a subdued and compliant way that is more compatible with the school milieu and escapes clinical attention. The fact that boys are more often referred to child psychiatry clinics than girls might reflect a differential recognition of depression rather than a differential incidence. On the other hand, the possibility of a true gender-related incidence cannot immediately be discounted.

Adult women as a group are more willing than men to seek medical attention for *any* complaint. Thus, playing the sick role or indulging in health-seeking behavior is itself more a part of the female than male vocabulary of distress. Women more often than men use minor tranquilizers, whether for anxiety, depression, or insomnia; men more often than women use alcohol for the same symptoms. Use of minor tranquilizers requires an interaction with the health care system, while alcohol is obtained outside the health care system. Thus, those who use minor tranquilizers rather than alcohol for essentially similar effects have quite different probabilities of entering official incidence and prevalence statistics.

Furthermore, since it is culturally and medically known that women are more likely than men to be overtly depressed, women may be more likely to regard depression as one of the expected illnesses of life and seek clinical help.

THE PROBLEM OF NONSPECIFIC DIAGNOSIS OF DEPRESSION

Another interesting problem that bears on large-scale prevalence studies is the nonspecific diagnosis of depression. Since depression is a heterogeneous category, including at least unipolar, bipolar, and characterologic affective disorders, it is possible that gender linkage might be greater or have different mechanisms in these different illnesses. But even in a sophisticated affective disorders clinic, considerable time may be needed to determine whether the patient has lithium-responsive bipolar disease, a unipolar disease that is responsive to manipulation of nonadrenergic or serotonergic systems, or some other disorder. It is too much to expect that the kind of questionnaire survey used in large-scale prevalence studies in nonclinical populations could reliably make these diagnostic distinctions.

THE PROBLEM OF DIFFERENTIAL CONSEQUENCES

From a public health point of view, as well as from the standpoint of retrospective estimation of prevalence, we must consider the differential consequences of depression. Mortality, of course, is the most serious consequence. Mortality in depression has several sources: suicide, victim-provoked homicide, neglect of medical illness, neglect of self-protection, lethal consequences of attempted treatment or self-treatment. While more women attempt suicide, more men complete suicide. Suicide is also more common among health professionals of either gender than among persons in other occupations. The mortality from suicide attempts depends not just on the strength of the suicidal wish, but also on the lethality of the suicidal method employed. In the general population, males are more likely to use firearms, jump from heights, and have automobile "accidents," while women are more likely to take drug overdoses. Health professionals taking an overdose of drugs are more likely to take a lethal dose. Since, except among health professionals, drug overdoses are likely to be with drugs prescribed for the patient, these deaths must be considered in part a response to attempted but inadequate treatment.

OCCUPATIONAL DYSFUNCTION

Another methodological issue that could lead to underestimation of female prevalence of depression is the problem of occupational dysfunction as an index of depression. The employed worker whose depression impairs ability to work often comes quickly to clinical attention. Typical depressive symptoms such as lethargy, irritability, inability to concentrate, and tardiness (resulting from insomnia or inability to get organized in the morning) often result in formal reprimands or loss of the job. These consequences can be severe enough to provoke prompt attention. Unemployment in men is a highly visible problem. By contrast, the availability of the housewife role for women permits depression to remain unrecognized for a much longer period of time. Few housewives ever fully keep up with the multiple demands on their time. It is possible for a housewife to drift into severe ineffectiveness by imperceptible stages. Similarly, an employed woman may become depressed and lose or leave her job while rationalizing it as a return to a housewife role. Of course, men as well as women who are self-employed, especially in nonstructured settings such as the creative arts, face similar issues. One may move by imperceptible stages from the normal incubation period of a creative project, to writer's block, to severe occupational dysfunction.

BIOLOGIC VERSUS SOCIAL CAUSES OF DEPRESSION IN WOMEN

In summary of the first part of this chapter, it is well established that women outnumber men among patients diagnosed as depressed by large margins in this country (reported ratios vary most typically from 2:1 to 3:1).[2, 59] There is a distinct possibility that large numbers of men who are not diagnosed and treated for depression have instead depressive equivalent disorders that surface outside the mental health care system. For example, alcoholism or sociopathy may come to the attention of the criminal justice system, or persons with multiple somatic complaints may present to nonpsychiatric physicians. Thus, in using gender-prevalence data for speculating about causality, we face certain limitations in knowledge that are likely to generate controversy for some time to come.

GENDER ROLE MODELS

A number of animal and human models support the concept that "learned helplessness" predisposes to depression. Animals placed in an experimental situation in which they can receive aversive stimuli, such as shock, will learn complicated behaviors to avoid the shock if possible. If the experimental paradigm permits the animal no possibility of avoiding or escaping the shock, a number of affective behaviors, including freezing, whining, and shivering, occur in the presence of cues signaling imminent shock. Once these behaviors become well established, and if the experimental paradigm is shifted so that avoidance or escape is again possible, the animal may no longer use formerly available coping strategies and may continue to exhibit the "depressive" response. Similarly, college students prone to attribute successes to luck and failures to their own inadequacy have been shown to be more vulnerable to developing depressions.

A number of writers of various psychological persuasions have noted the similarity between the learned helplessness model of vulnerability to depression and stereotypic female gender role behavior.[35] If we train young women to be not too ambitious, to lightly attribute any success to luck, and to feel guiltily perfectionistic about any possible failure, then according to this model we are training them into vulnerability to depressive thinking.

Regardless of whether women have also a greater biologic vulnerability to depression, there are clear hazards in this kind of socialization. Indeed, learned helplessness poses special hazards to any persons who are biologically at higher risk for depression. (On the other hand, exclusive attention to either social causes or their cognitive or psychodynamic manifestations risks ignoring biologically treatable conditions.)

The learned helplessness model of depression has stimulated two therapeutic models of particular interest to women: cognitive therapy[5] and assertiveness training models.[46] Cognitive therapy treats the pessimism inherent in learned helplessness and helps the patient move from global, overgeneralized, often unverifiable pessimistic cognitions to more differentiated ones that are more verifiable and less devastating. Thus the patient might be encouraged to delete the cognition, "I am totally worthless," and substitute the more accurate and delineated one, "I didn't do so well on that exam, but I can retake it, and I am pretty good in other respects." Assertiveness training helps the individual learn how to define goals in interpersonal transactions and more effectively and forcefully alter them, i.e., to be less helpless. Since women have often been socialized to be reactive rather than proactive, retiring or supportive rather than forceful, assertiveness training runs counter to stereotypic female socialization. A number of popular manuals on assertiveness training have been specifically written for women.[44]

GENETIC MODELS

One genetic model suggests that endogenous affective disorder could be transmitted as an X-chromosome-linked dominant trait, thus giving women twice the vulnerability of men.[34] We are then left to account for the apparent male preponderance in certain of the identified depressive equivalent disorders. Is this preponderance great enough to equalize the sex roles and thus vitiate the sex-linked gene hypothesis? Or could this be another way of saying that the conditions of women's lives favor in women the direct expressivity of a genetic vulnerability to depression that is more often only partially expressed in men? These questions are addressed in detail below.

HORMONAL MODELS: REPRODUCTIVE CYCLES

Other biologic approaches have noted possible interactions between sex hormones, catecholamine metabolism, and depression. Folk tradition has long supported a relationship between depression and certain events in the female reproductive life cycle, such as mood fluctuations with the menstrual cycle, pregnancy, the postpartum period, and menopause. Research in this area has often been highly speculative, filled with methodological errors and accompanied by misogynist thinking or stereotypic assumptions about gender roles.

Major biologic landmarks such as puberty, pregnancy, and menopause are defined by both endocrine and social changes. It is not reasonable to discuss the possible effects of these life cycle transitions on depression without looking at both kinds of changes together.

Puberty is clearly an important landmark in terms of endocrine and social changes. It is also an important clinical landmark, since before puberty more boys than girls become psychiatric patients, while after puberty the reverse is true. Similarly, before puberty school achievement is typically lower for boys than girls, and frank learning disability is more likely to be diagnosed in boys. Yet after puberty these trends too have traditionally been reversed, with more men than women going on to higher academic achievement. Since virtually all societies provide some degree of patterning of social roles that relates to both gender and reproductive maturity, disentangling hormonal effects from social role expectancies is difficult.

Certainly *menarche* is a clearer landmark in pubertal development than any single event in the adolescence of boys. The overwhelming majority of women can remember throughout life precisely the age and circumstances of the first menstrual bleeding. There is enormous variation in the amount of intellectual understanding, anticipation, surprise, pain, and affective change, and indeed the amount and regularity of bleeding, that occurs with the first menstrual periods. There have been few prospective studies on samples of normal young women. One such study reported some young women as having a "sobering" or even frankly depressive response to first periods and beginning to experience their lives as more serious or more restricted.[58] Earlier studies, although based on retrospective data from adults, appear to support this finding.[6, 7, 45]

Menarche is a life event that could well be examined within the framework of crisis theory. Indeed, in some primitive societies it is marked by elaborate and lengthy rituals. However, our society pays relatively little public attention to it, either ceremonially or in scientific and popular literature. It is rarely described in novels, biographies, or autobiographies, and no popular songs or movies deal with it. Health books for grade-school children generally do not mention menstruation. Our rites of passage tend to be academic rather than biologic—from sixth grade to junior high, from junior high to senior high. That some of the girls in each of these settings are now women, while others are not, is an embarrassment to the educational system as well as to the young women themselves. The technology of menstrual hygiene is one of concealment—hiding blood, hiding odors, hiding any affective change that might be experienced. The challenge for the menarcheal young woman has changed from the "primitive" question of how to master the new implications of fertility to the apparently "civilized" question of how to conceal from the world and her date the fact that she is menstruating.

Amusingly, and perhaps tragically, the major source of health information about the menstrual cycle for preadolescent girls has been educational materials, films, and books supplied by manufacturers of "sanitary" products. These firms have a commercial interest in conveying a message that the process is "unsanitary" without the help of their products. They tend to present these otherwise earthy issues in female sexual development in a disembodied, ethereal manner, stressing at all times the importance of "daintiness"—clearly a reaction formation to an event that, however else one feels about it, is not primarily experienced as dainty.[57]

Other even less dainty aspects of puberty for girls are much less openly dealt with. Rape and incest, although they certainly occur prepubertally, are an increased risk after puberty. The specter of an unwanted pregnancy becomes more real after menarche. Even the risk of being a victim of child abuse, higher for boys than girls before puberty, is greater for adolescent females than males.[18]

There is also a double-bind in social expectations which shifts rather abruptly from boys to girls with puberty. Before puberty, girls traditionally are given a single message: "be good and nice." This is associated with pleasing parents and teachers and is reflected in an easier adaptation to the school setting with typically female teachers. Boys are given a more complex message: "be good and nice, but don't be too good and nice." Indeed, in one startling approach to psychotherapy, boys who were felt to be too effeminate and at risk of a later transsexual identity were taught in play therapy to stop playing with Barbie dolls and start mutilating them.[20]

After puberty, school achievement for boys receives legitimization as a masculine activity, while it begins to lose legitimacy for girls. Peer and cultural pressures alike encourage the young woman to start transferring her docility from teachers and parents toward her dates and, ultimately, a husband. Since the same pressures are pushing the young men toward sexual conquests, the young woman is caught in a double-bind unless she has either chaperonage or unusually liberal parents. She should please her date, but not go too far. She may feel lonely, different, and depressed if she is not part of the sexually active crowd, and if she is part of it, she has to contend with fear of parental disapproval, pregnancy, venereal disease, and sexual exploitation. Surveys show that large numbers of today's pregnant adolescents report that *they did not enjoy the coitus that led to the pregnancy,* even at the time. This is not surprising. If petting to orgasm has been largely supplanted by coitus as an adolescent sexual experience, and at an age when most young men have an as yet unsocialized ejaculatory reflex that does not permit much delay, one wonders how young men could learn the kind of sexual behavior that sexually satisfies women. The evidence is that they do not learn it, at least until later. Clinics such as that of Masters and Johnson[29] provide training in petting and slowing down (called "sensate focus"), but the service is expensive and not ordinarily available to adolescents.

It is not surprising, then, that adolescence is a depressing period of life for many young women. That it is often depressing for young men as well is beyond dispute, although somewhat outside the framework of this discussion. Compulsive machismo is uncongenial to many young men, but the apparent alternative of social isolation can be equally devastating. The viewpoint of a sensitive young man expressed by Holden Caulfield in

Catcher in the Rye over three decades ago is surprisingly timely, but the book is still banned from some high-school library shelves.

In sum, it is not surprising that adult patterns of depression and suicidal behavior emerge rather sharply at adolescence. In adolescence, as in later adult life, more women than men attempt suicide, while more men than women succeed. The rough correlation with puberty neither supports nor refutes a simple hormonal explanation.

Menstrual Cyclicity and Affective Changes

There has been a recent increase in the literature on the menstrual cycle, with publications appearing from several interdisciplinary conferences on menstrual cycle research.[13] Hormonal, biopsychological, social, psychodynamic, even perceptual processes have been studied. Not surprisingly, these factors have been found to be so intrinsically interconnected as to be potential sources of artifact in studies of each other.

With the possible exception of discomforts of pregnancy, there is probably no area of the female reproductive life cycle that has been subject to as much clinical misunderstanding and fuzzy thinking as menstrual distress.

The fact that *some* women have premenstrual or menstrual distress, even to the point of incapacity, while some do not, has paradoxically been used both (1) to assume erroneously that if some have it, all do, and (2) to dismiss the seriousness or validity of the complaints of those who do have the syndrome. For example, a physician politically prominent during the Nixon administration publicly stated his belief that menstrual and menopausal syndromes made women as a group unsuitable and unreliable for public office.[32] (He did not voice a parallel belief that testosterone syndromes predisposed to a degree of machismo or nervous instability dangerous in occupants of high positions, despite the times in which he served.) By contrast, women who do suffer severe perimenstrual symptoms may find it difficult to obtain medical treatment for an illness that is all too often presumed to be trivial or psychogenic or both.[28]

Affective changes with the cycle are commonly self-reported; belief in their existence is also part of folk wisdom. Research studies, not surprisingly, show the topic to be more complex. A number of studies show increases in certain affects (such as irritability, anger, anxiety, depression) in some women during the premenstrual and menstrual phases of the cycle.[11, 12, 33, 39, 52] Some studies show increased and some decreased libido. These changes have been reported on such diverse measures as self-reported affects, dream content, waking fantasies, and overt behavior, including accidents, committing crimes of violence, and bringing one's children to hospital emergency rooms for minor illnesses.

In one series of prospective studies, women who reported severe menstrual distress at the time of entrance to college turned out to have lower grade-point averages than their peers, a greater probability of attending the student mental health clinic, and a greater probability of a diagnosis of affective disorder (particularly bipolar) if they did so.[31, 56] This suggests that bipolar affective disorder in women may initially present as menstrual distress. Failure to make the correct diagnosis in time to permit effective treatment during the vocationally crucial college years could have profound effects on the future life of involved women. Since affective disorder is relatively common and may be exacerbated perimenstrually, it is easy to see how this observation could erroneously lead to the common belief that it is normal for women to be "a little crazy" at "those times." But the error would be equivalent to saying that since epileptic women may have more seizures during premenstrual fluid retention, all women are a little epileptic at this time.

Attempts to find objective changes in intellectual or other performance measures in nonclinical populations have not been impressive.[47] Methodological problems in this area are complex. It is obvious that a woman's own expectations about menstruation, as well as those of her family, friends, or sexual partners, can override purely hormonal factors. Koeske showed that anecdotes describing angry behavior by women were attributed to environmental causes *unless* the anecdote included information that the subject was premenstrual or menstruating, in which case the same behavior was attributed to perimenstrual tension.[27]

Early studies by Dalton of English schoolgirls seemed to show poorer examination performance by menstruating than by nonmenstruating young women.[11, 12] However, Parlee reexamined the same data and found evidence for delayed menstruation in a portion of the sample.[38] Stress can delay ovulation and thus menstruation. It is possible that a prolonged stressful situation could first delay ovulation and then culminate in events such as attempted suicide, violent behavior, or poor examination performance, followed by a delayed period. The untoward event would then more properly represent tension-delayed menstruation than premenstrual tension.

Artifact may appear not only in the interpretation of data, but also in its overall attribution. Parlee has noted the curious fact that the bulk of research has attributed behavioral or affective changes that vary with the menstrual cycle to hormonal causes, while researchers studying pregnancy are more likely to attribute emotional changes to causes in the woman's life situation or intrapsychic conflicts about motherhood. Yet the hormonal changes of pregnancy are many times greater than those of the menstrual cycle.

Pregnancy and Depression

Pregnancy is a life change entailing adaptation and hence stress in the sense in which Holmes and Rahe studied these matters.[22] Regardless of whether a pregnancy is wanted or not, intended or not, and will be maintained or not, decisions, actions, and psychological adaptations are required. In some situations these adaptations are extreme and exert far-reaching effects on the future life course of the pregnant woman. Thus it is not surprising that some degree of apprehension and depression may be part of the affective response to learning that one is pregnant. These affects can be particularly disturbing to the woman who eagerly wants a child. Discovering some negative affect may make her feel that she is guilty of a host of murky psychological problems of which she has heard, such as "maternal rejection" or "maternal inadequacy," for example.

The hormonally based fatigue that is typical of the first trimester of pregnancy, and that may be accompanied by varying degrees of nausea, feels subjectively very much like the lethargy of depression to many women. If the woman has been subject to depressions before, she may fear she is slipping into one again. This can become a self-fulfilling prophecy, as she contemplates the possibility of caring for a child while depressed.

Changes in marital relationships are common as pregnancy advances. These may be positive, if the partner is also enthusiastic about the pregnancy and unconflicted about it. However, many women find that their partners are overprotective, anxious, irritable, depressed, or withdrawn in response to a pregnancy. This can be a surprising disappointment, particularly when the marriage has been happy and the pregnancy and child are positively anticipated by both. Some women experience a temporary or more lasting loss of libido during pregnancy, as they are absorbed in the pregnancy, subject to fatigue, or otherwise preoccupied. Some men experience a loss of libido toward a pregnant wife, either because of anxiety about hurting the baby or a more unconscious feeling that she is a "mother" and therefore taboo as a sexual partner. Some men greatly fear that the pregnancy or the impending baby will take the woman's attention away from her man, and overt and sometimes extreme jealousy can arise. There is an increased incidence of woman abuse during pregnancy, often with blows or attacks directed crudely at the pregnant abdomen.[40] This pattern sometimes arises in men who are themselves depressed, or manifesting a depressive-equivalent disorder.

Drug use in pregnancy poses considerable problems. While most psychotropic agents have not been clearly established as having gross teratogenic potential, it is difficult for the clinician to have any certainty about this point.[19] When a drug as ancient and common as alcohol has only recently been established as causing the fetal alcohol syndrome, it is hardly possible to feel secure about lack of proof of adverse consequences of more recently introduced drugs. It is possible that psychotropic agents could exert subtle effects on developing fetal neurotransmitter systems, even in the absence of gross anatomical teratogenicity. This must be weighed against the fact that major affective storms in the mother can affect the internal milieu of the fetus.[42] A Swedish study has demonstrated that administering an agent similar to haloperidol to lactating rats results in the only, to date, available model of the amphetamine-responsive "minimal brain damage" learning disability so commonly seen in human children today. (The lactating rat model may or may not have bearing on human pregnancy, because the homologous neurotransmitter systems do not develop at the same time in the rat and the human.[8])

A particularly serious problem to the clinician concerned about possible teratogenicity of psychotropic drugs centers around the timing of administration. The first trimester may be almost over before the woman receives a definite diagnosis of pregnancy—particularly since menstrual irregularity occurs more often in women under major stress, including the stress of a major psychiatric disorder. Thus, the time of maximum risk for gross anatomical teratogenicity may be over before the woman or her physician thinks to review drug risks. For purposes of administering drugs, it cannot be said too often that any woman of child-bearing age should be considered pregnant until proved otherwise. This does not mean that needed drugs should never be administered. Rather, the clinician treating women patients with potential teratogens should be sure that they are using effective contraception, are not heterosexually active, or are willing to obtain an abortion if pregnant. Alternatively, the clinician must decide that the therapeutic indications for the drug in question outweigh the possible risk to a fetus, in the same way that the clinician would evaluate these risks if the patient were known to be pregnant.

There is a large and fairly recent literature on the psychology of birth and maternal-infant attachment, or "bonding," which has recently been reviewed by the author.[43] Health consumer dissatisfaction with mechanized approaches to obstetric situations has increased considerably, and the indications for obstetric interventions are receiving close scrutiny. At present, it is salient that women do experience assaults to their self-esteem if they are subjected to either uncontrolled pain in labor or to a variety of interventions that are designed to control pain or manage labor. Being "snowed" with medication, placed in physical restraints during labor, or accompanied by a technician stranger but not by loved ones—all of these factors tend to materially impair the self-esteem of large numbers of laboring women. Being attached to electronic equipment similar to that found in intensive care units or giving birth in an operating room tends to impair the woman's confidence that she could give birth on her own. Medication with drugs that actually impair her ability to give birth without forceps assistance produces this effect to an even greater degree.

There is considerable evidence that pain or sedative medication administered to the mother during labor can impair the infant's alertness during the hours or days after birth, an apparent critical period for formation of the mother-infant bond.[26] How much these factors contribute to the commonness of postpartum depression is unknown. The grosser forms of postpartum psychosis are far less common today than in the past, presumably owing to the decreased incidence of uncontrolled postpartum infection and blood loss. Milder degrees of postpartum depression, also called the "baby blues," are so common as to be considered normal. This response consists of emotional lability, teariness (sometimes without subjective depression), or mild depression alternating with mild euphoria. It has been suggested that this degree of depression or depressive-like phenomena may be biosocially adaptive in that it tends to elicit compassion from a woman's social network and enables her to draw on it for help during the early postpartum period, when she needs that help keenly.[48]

Menopause

Affective disorders associated with the menopause were once assumed to be so common that a special diagnostic term was coined, "involutional depression." Symptoms included those of vasomotor instability (hot flashes, night sweats) and emotional instability (irritability, anxiety, depression, insomnia, and impaired self-esteem). The term "involutional depression" has been dropped from the psychiatric nomenclature. Research demonstrated that vasomotor symptoms were indeed more common in women of menopausal age, but emotional symptoms are not.[25] As with menstrual symptoms, if emotional changes occur around the menopause, they are likely to be attributed to it, but in fact they are not more common then.

Again, as with menstrual disorders, there is the paradox of overreaction and underreaction by clinicians. On one hand, women who have severe or troublesome symptoms may receive no help because of the presumed normality or psychogenicity of the condition. Conversely, estrogen supplementation has often been prescribed for women who have no estrogen-deficiency symptoms, or very mild ones, or ones unrelated to estrogen levels. (Indeed, the concept that menopause and the postmenopausal state are times of estrogen *deficiency* is odd; premenarcheal years are never thus described.)

Menopausal phenomena are inevitably intertwined with other aspects of middle age. These in turn depend on the social position of women as a group and the extent to which their social power and influence rise or decline with age. It is therefore curious that so much of the medical and psychiatric literature on menopause (as reviewed, for example, by Osofsky and Seidenberg) treats menopause as though it heralded old age: "a time of mortification, with service to the species over."[37] Actually, sociobiologic evidence tends to support the opposite conclusion. Menopause is a distinctively human characteristic. In most other mammals, there is little difference between the sexes in their capacity for maintaining fertility up to advanced old age. Clearly, selective pressures must have favored those of our ancestors whose females underwent menopause over those who did not. The adaptive value appears to be related to other relatively unique human characteristics, such as the prolonged human period of childhood dependency. Humans have complex care-taking behaviors toward their young that are not fixed-action patterns, but rather must be learned. In the absence of such learning, the young are highly vulnerable to death from malnutrition, neglect, accidents, or illness. Experienced mothers are probably the most natural teachers, but women preoccupied with the care of their own young may not have time to help others, including their own reproductively mature daughters, learn child-care. Mothers are found throughout all mammalian species, but the menopause phenomenon provides us with the distinctively human characteristic of grandmothers. (A woman who is both a grandmother and a mother to a small child usually finds the mother role preemptive.) The existence of menopause means that an average woman will have many years of health and vigor following the birth of her youngest child. This freedom from new pregnancies permits participation in a number of teaching, care-taking, and leadership functions. In many primitive or traditional societies, where women have relatively low dominance in the general society during child-bearing years, they rise rapidly in influence after menopause.

It is true that our industrialized society has changed many of the conditions under which our species evolved. In small nuclear families, by definition children leave the home as part of attaining adult status. For women without employment other than that of homemaker, there can be a real loss of important role functions. The empty-nest syndrome has been considered a cause of depression, yet available studies show that women as a group rate their happiness as decreased during the years they have small children in the home, and higher both before and after.[4] Women who have married men older than themselves may of course find that these years coincide with those in which their husbands enter into the years of preretirement, risk of midlife depression of their own, and even death.

Men die, on the average, a few years younger than women in our society. Coupled with the tendency for women to marry men several years older than themselves, there is a much greater probability for women than men of being widowed. If widowed, they are less likely than men to re-marry, because of a greater taboo against marriage to younger partners. This is a salient difference in a social structure that is more highly orga-nized around the heterosexual pair bond than around the extended family. In addition, there have been in the past century enormous erosions of the traditional sources of power and influence of the older woman. Her knowl-edge of childbirth and child-care, family medical treatment, and counseling has been displaced by professionals purporting to offer such expertise on more scientific (if less experiential) grounds. "Old wives' tales" have been disparaged. Thus there have been some important changes in earlier pat-terns, according to which young women could look forward to steadily in-creasing power and prestige as they grew older and accumulated life ex-perience.

Indeed, the probability of being diagnosed as depressed increases with old age for persons of both genders in our youth-oriented culture. The fact that women live longer, on the average, than men leads to more years at risk and an even greater proportion of depressed older women. Yet com-mon stereotypes about older persons can lead to a failure to diagnose and treat depression. If psychomotor retardation, sleep and appetite distur-bances, confusion, and lack of goal-directed behavior are regarded either as normal behavior for the elderly or as manifestations of an untreatable condition called "senility," vigorous attempts to diagnose and treat may not be made.

MATERNAL ROLES AND DEPRESSION IN WOMEN

In modern America, the normative context for child-bearing and rearing has come to be the small nuclear family, with few enforceable obligations resting on other kin. The extended family may or may not assist young parents in the care of children and themselves during the child-bearing years, but they cannot be compelled to do so by legal or social pressures if they do not so wish. This is a relatively new cultural trend. The nuclear family is highly mobile and often unstable (in 1975 the divorce rate of 4.8 per 1,000 population was almost half the marriage rate of 10 per 1,000).[36]

This contemporary isolation of many nuclear families from the extended family or tribe is a relatively new characteristic of mobile industrial soci-eties.[24] It tends to disrupt the female-female bonding system that charac-terizes many primates and humans living in more traditional societies. Par-ticularly new is a combination of crowding and isolation. That is, a nuclear family may live in a few small rooms, while simultaneously enduring a relative social isolation of the housebound mother from her extended family and other familiar adults. Our society has also been distinctly unusual in relying far more heavily than most cultures on mothers alone to perform primary child-care. There is variable but often relatively little participation by older children, husbands, and grandparents, who in other cultures have highly patterned participation in the child-care network.

Consequently, it is not surprising that a "trapped young mother" syndrome has received extensive treatment in the public media. A number of studies have documented that children add stress to parents' individual and marital lives. Studies in the 1960s found that children detracted from marital satisfaction. A recent survey on the quality of American life[10] found that 89% of young, married, childless women reported high satisfaction with life as a whole, whereas only 65% of married women with young children had high satisfaction. Signs of psychological stress were greatest during the early parental life stage, for both men and women.[30]

The child-rearing years present a number of potential sources of stress, depressive mood, and precipitation of affective disorder for women. For the housewife, severe isolation from the kind of adult company and adult achievement to which most women have become accustomed may lead to understimulation, loss of self-esteem, and depression. For the employed woman, continued responsibilities at work may include expecting her to compete as though she had no responsibilities toward her children, while the domestic and child-care responsiblities may continue to be disproportionately hers. This situation can lead to physical exhaustion, loss of normal recreational time, and a sense of guilt about possible failure to meet expectations at both home and work. For the unmarried mother, persistence of stigma may impair her self-esteem, while her economic situation is likely to be perilous, especially if she is unemployed. For the divorced mother, the burdens of stigma and dual responsibilities to employment and children are all too likely to converge. The fact that mothers cope at all in today's world and do not universally succumb to depression or child abuse undoubtedly attests to the ability of infants and mothers to attach to and to reward each other.

Many Americans do not appreciate how truly unusual our traditional approaches to child-care are in a cross-cultural perspective. In most genuinely traditional cultures, there is far more protection and support for the attachment of the mother to the small infant and much more sharing of the care of the older infant and toddler. Tiny infants around the world are traditionally found next to the mother's body, day and night. Other members of the extended family or friendship network are expected to take over responsibilities for much of the cooking, care of older children, and the household. In Latino cultures, this is ritualized as the "cuarentena," a 40-

day period of quarantine during which the mother is released from social obligations and most domestic responsibilities in order to enjoy a honeymoon with her new baby. With favorable conditions having been established to support attachment, get breast-feeding firmly established, and make other adjustments, she gradually returns to other expected responsibilities. By the time she has a second child, it is expected that the extended family will be available to share in the provision of emotional support and physical care of the toddler, so that the needs of the toddler, the new infant, and the mother are not in conflict. Cross-culturally, toddlers are usually cared for by older children 6 to 8 years old but under the mother's eye in case of emergency. Not coincidentally, this provides young children with experience as child-caretakers, which will make it a less frighteningly new experience when they later have their own children. In many cultures, or course, the elderly also play a role in child-care as well as in advising mothers about child-care.

Even in our own culture, when we hire adults to work in well-run day care centers, about six hours per day of direct child-care has been found to be optimal.[23] Full-time housewives may easily put in three times as much direct child-care, without the buffering presence of other adults. By contrast, one study found that a sample of middle-class husbands spend less than one minute per day in direct contact with their young infants.[9] This may be a keenly felt deprivation for some men, who nevertheless feel compelled to exercise family responsibility by emphasis on work roles.[16] It is a commonplace observation that many young husbands also keenly resent their wives' exhaustion, preoccupation with the baby, and inability to provide the husband with the same attentions they have come to expect.

Thus, the sources of depression for a young mother may include not only exhaustion at an unrealistic degree of solo responsibility for the child, but in addition sensing resentment from a husband to which she cannot adequately respond. It is not surprising that so many marriages currently rupture during child-rearing years. Current estimates are that nearly one half of all American children will spend a number of years in a single-parent home.[21]

EFFECTS OF MATERNAL DEPRESSION ON CHILDREN

While the stress of rearing children, particularly under today's conditions, may contribute to depression in women, it is also important to look at the effects of that depression on the children. It is easy to see how many of the symptoms of depression could contribute to impaired parenting in either parent, but especially in the parent spending most time with the children. Depressed persons have impaired energy and usually impaired empathy, both of which make it difficult to care for children in a sensitive way. These characteristics, along with irritability or withdrawal, can not only be depressing to children, but can also stimulate them to irritability and attention-getting behaviors, which in turn affect the depressed parent unfavorably. Vicious circles can ensue and culminate in frank child abuse or neglect.

Some effects differ with the age of the child. For example, depression in the mother of a very young infant may impair their initial mutual attachment or bonding. Depressed mothers of young children may have impaired ability to respond to their needs. Somewhat older children with a depressed mother may be more likely to have their needs met through peers and others outside the home. The mother may feel added guilt if she sees that her children are suffering ill effects from her depression. Yet paradoxically, if they are old enough to seek affective support outside the home, she may feel rejected and unneeded. Children of all ages may sense their mother's depression and blame themselves, assuming that it is caused by some bad behavior on their part. Adolescents pose special difficulties for depressed mothers, because the depression may blunt the needed ability to rapidly and empathically shift between the adolescent's varying needs to be nurtured and treated independently.

MARRIAGE AND DEPRESSION

EFFECTS OF DEPRESSION ON SPOUSES OF DEPRESSED PATIENTS

When there is any degree of emotional closeness in a marriage, it is virtually impossible for one partner to be depressed without affecting the other. Mild degrees of depression tend to elicit compassion and a motivation to help; indeed, this may be of sociobiologic significance. The human capacities to exhibit depression when needs are not met and, reciprocally, to exhibit empathy and an attempt to help may have been selected for in our genetic past. As a species of social animal, but one which does not maintain its social interactions on the basis of fixed-action patterns as insects do, we may have developed these complementary affects because they help bind us together.

Severe or prolonged depression in one partner, however, may have opposite effects. The compassion and helpfulness originally elicited may be withdrawn, particularly if they are not effective. The helping partner expects gratitude and a sense of potent effectiveness, but receives instead continued or increasing depression. He or she may respond by dropping the helpfully intended behaviors, since they do not seem effective. Or he or she may increase their intensity until they become ludicrous: helpful suggestions are escalated into authoritarian demands. Eventually the inability to help effectively leads to frustration and anger or reactive depression (usually some of both). Anger itself can lead to guilt and depression, since few well-intentioned persons can easily accept their own anger at someone who is obviously ill and unhappy.

The depressed spouse cannot help observing the effects of the depression on the partner. This in itself can be a source of escalating depression. The depressed spouse may begin to feel extremely guilty for spreading depression to others and, depending on the degree of thought disorder present, may take this as further evidence of his or her unworthiness and malignancy. The idea of causing harm to loved ones, as evidence of unworthiness to live, is a not uncommon suicidal preoccupation.

The Al-Anon organization, for spouses of alcoholics, has a vigorous program for combating this kind of spousal burnout. Major parts of the program are peer support and an emphasis on the fact that the spouse alone is powerless to make the alcoholic stop drinking. Al-Anon also provides hints on how to meet one's own needs and keep from contributing to the problem, while waiting and hoping that the alcoholic will seek help. Al-Anon helps the spouses of alcoholics who are in treatment deal with the inevitable ups and downs in the course of the illness and its treatment. Perhaps we need a "Depress-Anon" organization for spouses of depressed persons; certainly clinicians need to be alert to the marital effects of depression and include spouses in treatment planning.

DEPRESSION AND MARITAL CHOICE

There are many reasons why depressed persons have a greater likelihood of marrying each other. The compassion that early or mild depression elicits is likely to be keener and more effective from one who has experienced depression personally. Persons who have never been depressed are likely to try to talk the depressive out of his or her depression, but persons who *have* experienced depression are less likely to do so or to make other kinds of ineffective superficial responses. "At last I have found someone who really understands me" is likely to be the thought of a mildly depressed person on becoming close to a kindred depressive. This feeling may be keen enough to alleviate a mild depression and substitute a mild euphoria. The sequence is a heightened version of our popular concepts of falling in love and may lead to a powerful bond. And, indeed, powerful bonds may be needed to withstand the corrosive effects of depression on marriages.

Occasionally a unipolar depressive may meet and marry a bipolar person, after a whirlwind courtship during a hypomanic phase. The hypomanic enthusiasm can be easily confused with a great romantic love, only to be followed by a rude shock as the bipolar becomes depressed or overtly manic. Even effective treatment of the bipolar disorder may be a disappointment to the spouse, if hypomania was part of the original basis of attraction. Slight undertreatment, if it can be carefully titrated, may be essential to marital stability in these situations. Once again, the clinician must be sensitive to spousal needs in treatment planning and support.

INTERLOCKING AND SYMBIOTIC DEPRESSIONS

Two-depressive couples exhibit a variety of strategies for coping with their situation, often achieved without conscious planning or awareness; sometimes these coping strategies are more maladaptive than adaptive. For example, in some couples one spouse may feel guilty if happy at the same time the other is depressed. Mutual depression is then inevitable. Other couples develop a capacity for phasing their depressions so that both are not severely depressed at the same time; this pattern is obviously adaptive when there are children.

The marriage of a depressive person to a depressive-equivalent spouse (alcoholic or sociopathic, for example) offers fertile ground for couple interaction. Mutual blaming cycles of traditional and stereotypic kinds may result. For example, the depressed wife of an alcoholic may attribute her depression to a normal situational reaction, and the depression itself may actually be less keen under those circumstances. The sociopathic husband may attribute some of his short-lived sexual escapades to a normal reaction to the depressed wife's loss of libido.

In such situations, effective treatment of one spouse may lead to an apparent exacerbation of the other's depression, an effect that can also occur when two depressives use the "taking-turns" strategy for timing their own depressions. Where improvement in one spouse's condition leads to deepening depression in the other, the clinician's task is compounded. Family therapy theorists have attributed some rather insidious motives to families that they believe "need a scapegoat." However, a simpler explanation is that nonassortative mating has joined two depressives, each of whom needs treatment in his or her own right as well as some empathic understanding of their effects on each other.

Truly symbiotic interlocking depressions are a formidable challenge to the clinician. In this situation, each partner has vulnerability to depression to begin with, and a poorly delineated self-image as well. When one is depressed, the other must share the affect, and each feels responsible for the feelings of the other. The term "symbiotic" in this context is a double metaphor; originally a biologic term referring to the relationship of two organisms of different species that cannot live without each other, in psychiatry it refers to the normal relationship of intense nonverbal empathic communication that occurs between a mother and young infant. In the marital context, the term refers to a couple that form an emotional world unto themselves in a way that is more appropriate to mother-infant bonding. It is marked by contagion of affect, difficulty in putting affect into words, a sense that each cannot live without the other, and a resistance to intrusion by outside parties that might impair the intense closeness of the couple. If one partner in such a union becomes depressed, ordinary psychotherapeutic approaches may be seen as a dangerous threat to the closeness of the relationship, and couple therapy by a clinician skilled in that modality may be required.

DEPRESSION AND MARITAL VIOLENCE

While domestic violence may occur between spouses of any diagnostic class, some aspects are especially pertinent to depression. One classic scenario involves the depressive-equivalent male (alcoholic, sociopathic, or both) who projects his depression onto real or imagined "failures" in the perfection of his wife's care of him. He may construe his beating of her as an appropriate "punishment" for failing to cook his food to perfection at the moment he wishes or for failing to keep "his" home and children in perfect order. He may attribute any discomfort on his part to insubordination or inattentive care on her part. She in turn may guiltily accept his wrath because she is already depressed and self-blaming, and in any case his treatment of her is in itself cause for depression. In turn, the acceptance of battering lowers her self-esteem and increases her probability of feeling that such an unworthy creature as herself must deserve it in some way. She is all the more likely to do so because our society places more responsibility on the woman than on the man for the emotional success of the marriage. She may have further cause for depression as she contemplates her emotional and economic alternatives: perhaps she cannot afford to leave him, or perhaps she cannot leave him because she "loves" him. This "love" may be an instance of the original heightened bonding so often observed between two depressives. It also, in many instances, is heightened by the periods of remorse and making up that often follow episodes of battering. His remorse, or threats of suicide if she leaves, may elicit compassion on her part and an unrealistic hope that things will improve without intervention. Counselors experienced in work with battered wives have learned that the cycle of tension, violence, remorse, peace, tension, and violence again is so regular that women who need to be separated for their own protection must be aided in doing so immediately after the violence, before there is an opportunity for the remorse phase of the battering cycle.[3, 51] Indeed, they have observed that as the tension mounts, some women may behave in such a way as to trigger the violence in order to get it over with and enter the remorse phase again. They have also observed that only a separation that carries into the remorse phase is likely to generate enough overt depression to motivate the men to seek treatment.

WOMEN, DEPRESSION, AND WORK

Depression affects the ability to work effectively. Quality and quantity of work can be adversely affected by decreased energy, inability to concentrate, irritability, insomnia, and consequent difficulties in getting up and getting organized in the morning. These effects can escape detection longer if the work role is that of housewife or self-employed person than if work is done in a business setting.

Conversely, the work setting can affect the actual incidence and prevalence of depression. Weissman and Paykel[55] found no significant difference in the incidence of depression in women employed as housewives and in women employed outside the home, but noted that women employed outside the home recovered more quickly from depressions than housewives, although both groups received similar treatment. This finding was equally true for women who worked out of economic necessity and women who worked out of preference. Evidently, factors in the employment situation contribute to speed of recovery. Such factors might include the lesser degree of isolation in most employment settings, the greater degree of feedback on adequacy of one's performance, and the external pressures to get mobilized.

An epidemiologic study of depression was done in the Shetland Islands when the introduction of oil wells led to a rapid change from a very traditional, rather isolated society to a modern industrialized one. It was expected that such rapid cultural change would lead to social and psychological disorganization, with an increase in psychiatric symptoms. Instead, to the surprise of the investigators, the overall mental health of the population appeared to improve. On further examination, the improvement was for the most part accounted for by decreased rates of depression in adult women, specifically those who found employment in the newly established businesses.

In former subsistence agricultural or hunting-and-gathering societies, both men and women understood themselves to be doing productive work essential for survival. With the Industrial Revolution, much traditional female work, such as weaving and sewing, was shifted to factories. Although among the very poor, women were employed, the normative view came to be that men should participate in the cash economy and women should not. For a long time, middle-class women as a group had many of the characteristics of chronically unemployed or underemployed groups, such as lassitude, somatic complaints, and overt depression. Many learned and popular papers were written on "The Woman Question" and what should be done with women's energies. Ultimately a considerable elaboration of wifely, motherly, and social entertainment tasks were developed which had many of the characteristics of any "make-work" employment program—one can suffer impaired self-esteem if not doing well at the make-work competition and simultaneously have a feeling of futility and unimportance if doing it well. This fascinating chapter of history is well documented by Ehrenreich and English[15] and was discussed by Veblen in his classic observations on conspicuous consumption.[50]

Many observers have noted that paid employment changes the position of women within the family. Besides the social stimulus value of employment and the psychological benefits of tangible as opposed to intangible accomplishments, the paycheck itself seems to convey benefits and have an effect on the relationship with husbands and children.

If the husband alone participates in a cash economy, it is easy for the wife to view herself, or be viewed by him and the family, as his employee rather than equal partner.

Obviously, participation in employment and receipt of a paycheck alone do not eliminate all potentially depressing issues in the differential employment patterns of women and men. Despite serious efforts in our society to obtain equal pay for equal work, employed women as a group still earn about 59 cents for every dollar earned by employed men. As one single mother put it, "this means that every single mother can look at the employed mother at the next desk and realize that she has $1.59 to spend on her family for every 59 cents that I have." Bitterness about the practical economic difficulties that ensue and a rankling sense of injustice are not easy to deal with.

There have been a number of theories to explain the differential compensation of women and men and why it persists. There was a time when it was said to be intended, and based on the assumption that the working man was likely to be supporting a family, while the working woman was likely to be supporting herself alone. However, unless one assumes that the average business was running a charitable organization, this explanation is somewhat questionable. More likely explanations hinge on market conditions and on socialization for competing in that market, and again one sees the learned helplessness model as relevant. Our concepts of romantic love as a proper basis for marriage has led our society, unlike others, to look down on the woman who is so crass as to openly marry for money.

Similarly, while men have been socialized to compete for positions that are better paid, and to be flexible about changing jobs to achieve this, women have been somewhat differently socialized. The greater tendency for women to carry over family-based values into the job situation has made them more likely to seek work niches that are protected, "refined," and noncompetitive. As workers, women as a group are more reliable, less likely to change jobs, but also less likely to do the kind of jockeying for position which may lead to recognition of leadership ability and advancement within a work situation. Until fairly recently, women have been less likely to seek positions of authority for fear of being seen as "unfeminine" and perhaps being disliked for it.[21] Men in positions of power have been quite willing to take advantage of this situation and perpetuate it. Obviously there are many advantages in having someone who is capable enough to be your competitor be instead your assistant and devote her energies to building your career instead of hers.

Some shifts in current social values in these areas are fertile grounds for impairment of self-esteem of working women. While formerly a working woman might take pride in being an excellent subordinate to a male superior (perhaps inherently less capable than herself), in today's climate a greater degree of equality might come to be the norm. Such a woman might now feel resentment at being subordinate to a less capable man, but perhaps at a time in her life when it is difficult to return for the kind of training which would prepare her for a position comparable to his.

An MIT economist has recently created something of a furor by suggesting that much of the sex differential in pay and advancement results from different gender role work patterns during the crucial decade between ages 25 and 35.[49] In male workers, it is generally during these years that leadership capacity is recognized and rewarded. For female workers, many with considerable leadership capacity may not display it during those crucial years, he suggests, because they are raising children and are either absent from the work arena or reducing their responsibilities there. One respondent suggested that joint custody of children during marriage, not just after divorce, might remedy that situation! However, in many dual-career families, it is a present reality that the woman is more subject to guilt, and hence depression, over the frequent conflicts of interest between children's needs and job requirements. Some job requirements in fact need restudy from this standpoint. There is evidence that flextime is beneficial to both women and men.

There has been some evidence to suggest that male socialization toward obtaining self-esteem primarily from advancement in the work situation has had some effects on male vulnerability to depression. Thus, unemployment and retirement are culturally expected to be severe stresses for men, with very high rates of depression, alcoholism, and, in the case of retirement, death soon thereafter. Women have traditionally done better in these situations because they had a broader social network that allowed them to develop alternative sources for support of self-esteem outside their work roles. They have had to do so because of the limited gratifications available in work roles. With current changes in gender role expectancies, it remains to be seen to what extent each gender will become better able to capture the best of both worlds.

REFERENCES

1. Adams L.: *Effectiveness Training for Women*. New York, Harper & Row, 1979.
2. Akiskal H.S., McKinney W.T.: Overview of recent research in depression: Integration of ten conceptual models into a comprehensive clinical frame. *Arch. Gen. Psychiatry* 32:285–305, 1975.
3. Bane M.: Marital disruption and the lives of children. *J. Soc. Issues* 32:103–117, 1976.
4. Bart P.: Mother Portnoy's complaints. *Trans-Action*, November-December, 1970, pp. 69–74.
5. Beck A.T., Greenberg R.L.: Cognitive therapy with depressed women, in Franks V., Burtle V. (eds.): *Women in Therapy*. New York, Brunner/Mazel, 1974.
6. Benedek T.: *Psychosexual Functions in Women*. New York, Ronald Press Co., 1952.
7. Blos P.: *On Adolescence*. New York, Free Press, 1962, p. 109.
8. Breese G.R., et al.: Developmental neuropsychopharmacology, in Lipton M.A., DiMascio A., Killam F. (eds.): *Psychopharmacology: A Generation of Progress*. New York, Raven Press, 1978.
9. Bronfenbenner U.: *American Families: Trends and Pressures*. Washington, D.C., U.S. Government Printing Office, 1974, p. 136.
10. Campell A., Converse P.E., Rodgers W.I.: *The Quality of American Life: Perceptions, Evaluations and Satisfaction*. New York, Russell Sage Foundation, 1976.
11. Dalton K.: *The Premenstrual Syndrome*. Springfield, Ill., Charles C Thomas, Publisher, 1964.
12. Dalton K.: *The Menstrual Cycle*. New York, Pantheon Books, 1969.
13. Dan A., Graham E., Beecher C.: *The Menstrual Cycle: A Synthesis of Interdisciplinary Research*. New York, Springer, 1980.
14. Dohrenwend B.P., Dohrenwend B.S.: Social and cultural influences on psychopathology. *Ann. Rev. Psychol.* 25:417–425, 1974.
15. Ehrenreich B., English D.: *For Her Own Good: 150 Years of the Experts' Advice to Women*. New York, Anchor/Doubleday, 1978.
16. Eisenberg I.: Caring for children and working: Dilemmas of contemporary womenhood. *Pediatrics* 56:24–28, 1975.
17. Fensterheim M., Baer J.: *Don't Say Yes When You Want To Say No*. New York, David McKay, 1975.
18. Gil D.: *Violence Towards Children*. Cambridge, Mass., Harvard University Press, 1972.
19. Goldberg A.L., DiMascio A.: Psychotropic drugs in pregnancy, in Lipton M.,

et al. (eds.): *Psychopharmacology: A Generation of Progress*. New York, Raven Press, 1978.

20. Greenson R.R.: Disidentifying from mother. *Int. J. Psychoanal.* 49:370–374, 1968.
21. Horner M.: Toward an understanding of achievement-related conflict in women. *J. Soc. Issues* 28:157–175, 1972.
22. Holmes T.H., Rahe R.H.: The social readjustment rating scale. *J. Psychosom. Res.* 11:213, 1967.
23. Howell M.: Work and parenting: What's a mother to do? Unpublished manuscript.
24. Janeway E.: *Man's World. Woman's Place*. New York, Dell Publishing Co., 1972.
25. Jones H.W. Jr., Cohen E.J., Wilson R.B.: Clinical aspects of the menopause, in Ryan J.K., Gibson D.C. (eds.): *Menopause and Aging*. Washington, D.C., U.S. Government Printing Office, 1971.
26. Klaus M.H., Kennell J.: *Maternal-Infant Bonding: The Impact of Early Separation or Loss on Family Development*. St. Louis, C.V. Mosby Co., 1976.
27. Koeske R.: "Premenstrual tension" as an explanation of female hostility. Read before the 83d annual meeting of the American Psychological Association, Chicago, Aug. 30–Sept. 3, 1975.
28. Lennane K.J., Lennane R.J.: Alleged psychogenic disorders in women: possible manifestation of sexual prejudice. *N. Engl. J. Med.* 288:288–292, 1973.
29. Masters W., Johnson V.: *Human Sexual Inadequacy*. Boston, Little, Brown & Co., 1970.
30. Minturn I., Lambert W.: *Mothers of 56 Cultures: Antecedents of Child-Rearing*. New York, John Wiley & Sons, 1964.
31. McClure J., Reich T., Wetzel R.: Premenstrual symptoms as an indicator of bipolar affective disorder. *Br. J. Psychiatry* 119:527–528, 1971.
32. Does female = male? Doctor stirs a medical row. *Med. World News* 11:18–19, 1970.
33. Melges F., Hamburg D.A.: Psychological effect of hormonal changes in women, in Beach F. (ed.): *Experts' Views of Human Sexuality*. Baltimore, Johns Hopkins University Press, to be published.
34. Mendlewicz J., Fleiss J., Fieve R.: Evidence of X-linkage in the transmission of manic-depressive illness. *J.A.M.A.* 222:1624–1627, 1972.
35. Minkoff K., Bergman E., Beck A., et al.: Hopelessness, depression, and attempted suicide. *Am. J. Psychiatry* 130:455–460, 1970.
36. National Commission on the Observance of International Women's Year: ". . . *to Form a More Perfect Union . . ." Justice for American Women*. Washington, D.C., U.S. Government Printing Office, 1976.
37. Osofsky H.J., Seidenberg R.: Is female menopausal depression inevitable? *Obstet. Gynecol.* 36:611–615, 1970.
38. Parlee M.B.: Menstruation and voluntary participation in a psychological experiment. Read before the 83d annual meeting of the American Psychological Association, Chicago, Aug. 30–Sept. 3, 1975.
39. Parlee M.B.: Psychological aspects of menstruation, childbirth and menopause, in Sherman J.A., Denmark F.L. (eds.): *Psychology of Women: Future Directions of Research*. New York, Psychological Dimensions, 1977.
40. Roy M.: A current survey of 150 cases, in Roy M. (ed.): *Battered Women: A Psychosociological Study of Domestic Violence*. New York, Van Nostrand Reinhold, 1977.

41. Seiden A.: Overview: Research on the psychology of women: I. Gender differences and sexual and reproductive life. II. Women in families, work, and psychotherapy. *Am. J. Psychiatry* 133:9, 1976; 133:10, 1976.

42. Seiden A.: Psychological trauma and stress, in Buchsbaum H. (ed.): *Trauma in Pregnancy*. Philadelphia, W.B. Saunders Co., 1979.

43. Seiden A.: The sense of mastery in the childbirth experience, in Notman M., Nadelson C. (eds.): *The Women Patient: Medical and Psychological Interfaces: Vol. 1. Sexual and Reproductive Aspects of Women's Health Care*. New York, Plenum Publishing Corp., 1978.

44. Seligman M.E.: Depression and learned helplessness, in Friedman R.J., Katz M.M. (eds.): *The Psychology of Depression: Contemporary Theory and Research*. Washington, D.C., V.H. Winston, 1974.

45. Shainess N.: A re-evaluation of some aspects of femininity through a study of menstruation: A preliminary report. *Compr. Psychiatry* 2:20–26, 1961.

46. Smith M.J.: *When I Say No I Feel Guilty*. New York, Bantam, 1975.

47. Sommer B.: Menstrual cycle changes and intellectual performance. *Psychosom. Med.* 34:263–269, 1972.

48. Stotland N.: Personal communication.

49. Thurow L.: One man's opinion about why women are paid less. *Chicago Tribune*, March 29, 1981.

50. Veblen T.: *Theory of the Leisure Class*. New York, Modern Library, 1934.

51. Walker L.: *The Battered Woman*. New York, Harper & Row, 1979.

52. Weideger P.: *Menstruation and Menopause*. New York, Alfred A. Knopf, 1976.

53. Weissman M.: Women and depression. Read before the eighth annual Friends Hospital Clinical Conference, Philadelphia, Oct. 3, 1980.

54. Weissman M., Klerman G.: Sex differences and the epidemiology of depression. *Arch. Gen. Psychiatry* 34:98–111, 1977.

55. Weissman M.M., Paykel E.S.: *The Depressed Woman: A Study of Social Relationships*. Chicago, University of Chicago Press, 1974.

56. Wetzel R., Reich T., McClure J., et al.: Premenstrual affective syndrome and affective disorder. *Br. J. Psychiatry* 127:219–221, 1975.

57. Whisnant I., Brett E., Zegans I.: Implicit messages concerning menstruation in commercial educational materials prepared for young adolescent girls. *Am. J. Psychiatry* 132:815–820, 1975.

58. Whisnant K., Zegans I.: A study of attitudes toward menarche in white middle-class American adolescent girls. *Am. J. Psychiatry* 132:809–814, 1975.

59. Woodruff R., Goodwin D., Guze S.: *Psychiatric Diagnosis*. New York, Oxford University Press, 1974.

20

POSTPARTUM DEPRESSION

HENRY LAHMEYER, M.D.
CARL JACKSON, M.D.

POSTPARTUM MENTAL ILLNESS was one of the first psychiatric illnesses described; Hippocrates, Celsus, and Galen each gave accurate clinical descriptions.[56] They and other early physicians felt the disturbances were peculiar to childbirth. Bleuler and Kraepelin believed that postpartum states were phenomenologically the same as schizophrenia and mania, but acknowledged the importance of childbirth as an etiologic stress.[6, 23] Strecker and Ebaugh, after studying 50 cases of puerperal mental illness, concluded that they could be classified as manic-depressive psychosis, toxic psychosis, or schizophrenia, but agreed with Kraepelin and Bleuler that a unique disease entity did not exist.[50]

Most observers agree with Strecker and Ebaugh that the clinical forms of mental illness in the puerperium are not unique. The range of clinical states, from the common three-day "baby blues" to the more severe psychotic states, is very broad.[37] However, several features of the disorder have made it worthy of attention. The puerperal states almost always present after days or weeks of clear sensorium. Cognitive confusion is a prominent element in the clinical state, especially in psychotic cases. Puerperal mental illness is one of the most dramatic natural models of mental illness: a well-defined population at risk with clear-cut, intense psychological and biologic stressors provides an important opportunity for the study of mental illness.

Much of the interest in recent years has centered on the similarity of these disorders to the affective disorders in general. An affective disturbance is the most common symptom in a puerperal mental disorder, and the episodes are generally recurrent. Even though the kinship to affective disturbances may be strong, these disorders cannot be so simply categorized. Problems with defining this illness, as with any psychiatric entity, derive from the complex issues of varied clinical presentations, temporal patterns, and etiology.

CLINICAL PRESENTATION

Mild affective states, particularly crying and depression, are the most common occurrences. These usually begin three to seven days after childbirth and occur in 3% to 20% of women.[9, 35, 36, 43, 51] Yalom noted that over 60% of women studied had crying spells, but many of these women were not clinically depressed.[55]

More serious symptoms can evolve from the milder states. As confusion increases, affect intensifies. Symptoms of insomnia, restlessness, irritability, and headache may progress to suspiciousness, loss of appetite, confusion, and obsessive-compulsive rituals. Delusions and hallucinations may develop. In traditional nosologic terms, these disorders appear similar to mania, depression, schizophreniform psychosis, and, occasionally, toxic delirium.[17, 54] Psychotic disturbances occur in 1 of every 400 to 1,000 births.[34, 38, 47]

TEMPORAL PATTERN

Most episodes occur after a symptom-free period of at least three days. Several investigators have noted that the incidence of these disorders is highest during the first postpartum month and continues very high during the next two months, remaining above normal for women of similar age for at least six months post partum.[21, 34, 38] Women who develop postpartum mental illness have a significantly longer interval since the last pregnancy than normal controls, have shorter gestations, and tend to conceive in March, February, October, and January.[15, 34]

Women who experience one puerperal mental disturbance are more likely to be affected during a subsequent pregnancy. These events are ten times more likely to occur during the puerperium than during pregnancy for these women.[34] The striking temporal patterns and the periodic nature of the illness are similar to some patterns observed in affective disorders.

This link to affective disorders has been explored by Reich and Winokur[39] and Kadrmas et al.[19] These investigators found that manic-depressives had a significantly greater tendency to "break down" in the puerperal period than in the nonpuerperal period. Another group of women who experienced the first episode of mania during the puerperium had no non-puerperal episodes. This group of postpartum-only manics had more schneiderian first-rank symptoms, although they fulfilled all the criteria for mania. Kendall et al. and Paffenbarger also found that puerperal episodes were strongly associated with previous puerperal episodes, but they did not categorize episodes as to clinical type.[21, 34] These findings can be interpreted to mean that childbirth is a significant stress that can produce illness in those strongly predisposed. In women of only moderate susceptibility, the stress of pregnancy may cause illness, but there is small likelihood of disturbances occurring outside the puerperium for this group. What remains unclear is how much of the stress in the postpartum period can be explained on a psychological, social, or biologic basis. Furthermore, there needs to be clarification of the factors increasing one's vulnerability to such stress; these issues will now be explored.

ETIOLOGY

GENETICS

Genetic links to a psychiatric disorder would help determine whether puerperal disorders are a special case of a major psychiatric disorder caused by an unusual stress or whether they are a completely separate entity.

Kadrmas et al. found that women who experienced their first episode of mania during the puerperium had fewer family members with affective disorders than other bipolar patients.[19] Reich and Winokur found that undiagnosed first-degree relatives of bipolar manic-depressives had an incidence of puerperal affective disorders 200 times greater than that of the general population.[39] Bratfos and Haug also found that relatives of bipolars have an increased incidence of postpartum psychiatric disturbances.[6a] Nilsson and Almgren found that a family history of mental illness significantly correlated with postpartum psychiatric symptoms, but a positive family history also correlated with symptoms during pregnancy.[31]

SOCIAL-PSYCHOLOGICAL CONSIDERATIONS

Personality characteristics, such as anxiety and obsessional traits, have been linked to puerperal depression, as have the traits of neuroticism and introversion, as measured on the Maudsley Personality Inventory (MPI).[12, 47] Kumar and Robson, however, found no link to neuroticism as measured on the MPI, but did find a link between postpartum depression and marital tension, doubts about pregnancy, and difficulties in relationships with parents.[25] Nilsson and Almgren found a relationship between lack of social support and postpartum psychiatric symptoms.[31] Paykel et al. found that marital tension was linked with postpartum events, but only if other stressful life events were also present, such as marital tension, poor housing, and lack of a close confidante.[35]

Stressful life events and marital problems correlated as strongly with postpartum depression as did previous psychiatric history. This strong contribution from stressful life events seems to contradict Kraepelin's notion that depression is an endogenous illness,[23] but corresponds to Rennie's observation that 79% of a series of manic-depressives had evidence of disturbing life situations coincident with their episodes.[40] Illegitimacy increases the risk of postpartum breakdowns, but this group has the same incidence of episodes during pregnancy as post partum.[21, 34]

These studies point to the importance of social-psychological events; however, these stresses alone do not cause psychiatric disturbances in a majority of those predisposed. Other factors must therefore be contributory.

BIOLOGIC CONSIDERATIONS

Women are more at risk for puerperal psychiatric illness if they are older, have shortened gestations, have more complications during labor (including higher infant complications and mortality), have lower parity, and have a longer pregnancy interval.[9, 34–36, 41, 55] Some of these factors could be of psychological significance for some individuals, so factors must be sought that are not as closely correlated with possible psychological events.

Menstrual cycle distress has been linked to postpartum mental illness.[9, 29, 55] Another cyclic event with even less obvious psychological significance is month of conception. Mothers who conceived in March, February, October, and January were significantly more likely to experience postpartum mental illness, in the order of frequency given.[15] These findings, together with the dramatic decrease in progesterone and estrogen post partum, have prompted attempts to correlate biologic changes with the degree of psychiatric disturbances observed. Nott et al. found a greater drop in progesterone in women who reported depression ten days post partum, compared with an asymptomatic group.[32] Gelder, however, did not confirm this finding.[13]

Cyclic AMP acts as a "second messenger" for most hormones. Ballinger et al. found that cyclic AMP is elevated during the puerperium, compared with levels two to three months post partum.[4] Women who experienced the most mood changes, especially in the euphoric direction, had the greatest increase in cyclic AMP during the puerperium. This increase in cyclic

AMP could also be due to prostaglandin activity, which also increases cyclic AMP activity.[33] This finding may be a link to the observation that long and difficult labor is associated with postpartum mental disturbances.[9, 36, 55]

Corticosteroids are elevated to twice normal during pregnancy. Although this degree of corticosteroid elevation is linked to affective disturbance, correlations between the degree of corticosteroid elevation and the occurrence of a postpartum psychiatric disturbance have not been made. Sachar found that corticosteroid levels were elevated in depression and the normal diurnal fluctuation in cortisol was lost.[44] Recently Carroll has demonstrated abnormal pituitary-adrenal regulation in affective disorders.[7]

Many biologic periodicities are disrupted during pregnancy and immediately post partum. Corticosteroid and gonadotropic hormone periodicities are altered. Sleep is significantly altered; pregnant women have frequent arousals and less stage IV sleep. Some of these disorders continue until menses are restored. Progesterone and estrogen are elevated dramatically, but a periodicity in estradiol secretion has been demonstrated, with period lengths of 6 and 72 hours during pregnancy.[18] Isaksson speculates that these two cycle lengths represent maternal and fetal sources. Since two periodicities exist, peaks and valleys of hormone levels occur. It is possible that synchrony or lack of synchrony in these hormone levels at birth could contribute to psychological disturbance. This kind of phase effect has been linked to mania and depression.[24, 53]

PSYCHOLOGICAL CONSIDERATIONS

Biologic rhythm disturbances, hormonal fluctuations, and stressful events may all contribute to the etiology of puerperal disturbances, but the psychological meaning of pregnancy for each person is different, and the psychological stress of motherhood also has great individual variation. Psychoanalysts have contributed to our understanding of this event, one of the most important in the life of an adult.

One of the strongest arguments in favor of a psychological causality is the occurrence of postpartum mental illness in fathers and adopting parents.[2] Ginath notes that men with pregenital conflicts are prone to psychosis upon the birth of their child, since they view the infant as a competitor for mothering.[14] Homosexual and incestual fears are also generated in those men.

Several men have had psychiatric hospitalizations at the University of Illinois after the birth of their child where the dynamics outlined by Ginath were all operative. They also expressed a frequent desire to leave the hospital because they felt an obligation to the newborn, even though the psychoses were so flagrant that self-care was very poor. One patient had a recurrent psychosis that appeared twice during two separate postpartum periods. Extrusion of father from the home by psychosis seemed to have variable effect on the families. The most common results were relief that the anxious member was absent and the reestablishment of a fragile equilibrium, since these mothers seemed to have difficulty in caring for a biologic infant and a husband who resembled an infant.

Women hospitalized at the University of Illinois for postpartum psychosis had strong desires to take care of the absent baby, but often showed great difficulty in attending to the child if conjoint hospitalization was arranged. They seemed to have extreme dependency needs themselves and saw the child's needs as overwhelming; some struggled with aggression toward the newborn.

Zilboorg was one of the first to study the intrapsychic dynamics of postpartum psychotics.[56] Women he studied seemed to have more anal libidinous attitudes than genital. He found them to be chronic masturbators and sexually frigid, with strong masculine identifications. Many of these women married late, gave birth to a first child uneventfully, pursued career goals after the first birth or two, and then, years after domestic pursuits had been abandoned, gave birth to a child and developed psychosis. Deutsch, writing during the war years, also noted the conflict between masculine and feminine roles, although this may have been more of an issue during that period, when many women worked out of necessity.[11] However, there are no current data showing that modern career women have more problems in the postpartum period than their more domestic counterparts.

More recent psychological studies at the Cassell Psychiatric Hospital and the Tavistock Clinic suggest that women prone to postpartum disturbance have obsessional, compliant, conformist, sensitive, and controlled personalities that are threatened by closeness to the baby. They tend to marry passive-submissive men.[10-12, 16, 27]

Both Deutsch and Zilboorg noted an increase in activity, mood, and sexual interest just prior to delivery that may have been totally absent before. This increase in activity, a clear deviation from normal for these women, may represent hypomania. This observation corroborates Dalton's observation that hypomania prior to delivery portends psychosis.[9]

Deutsch describes the postpartum period as a transition from the fantasy of a child to the reality of a child who is separate and demanding. This is important for the mother and can create stress in the father. Ketai and Bradwin have emphasized this dynamic in the creation of marital stress, especially if symbiotic ties are disrupted.[22] Symbiosis is lost, yet many elements of symbiosis remain. The infant's needs require maternal altruism and love, which inevitably conflicts with the mother's own autonomous needs. The restriction of intellectual pursuits, career, or simply bodily movement can cause anxiety as a derivative of the fear of ego loss. Psychic reaction to these losses may manifest as loss of energy, carelessness with the child, or guilt that proper care is not being given to the infant. Reactive narcissism in the form of pride and joy over the newborn are healthy adaptive responses. Schizoid women may hope that the infant will free up inner rigidities and are disappointed when this does not happen.

Bibring believes that pregnancy and delivery are always a stress.[5] With quickening, the inevitable delivery is realized and anxiety increases. Worries about physical deformity may increase. Inhibition of mobility and difficulty sleeping because of increasing girth are significant stresses for immature women. But the major psychological transformation that takes place after quickening, especially for the primipara, is the loss of dependency and the development of the feeling of motherhood. Bibring quotes an expectant mother, who was in a group under the leadership of Dr. Leo Berman: "I was quite excited last night, quite anxious! It suddenly struck me, that I won't be Jeanie much longer, but mother forever and ever after!" Bibring paraphrases this woman's further thoughts: "She knew that when something really terrible happened to her, the first thought had been to tell mother. And this was what she felt so deeply would be soon her own indestructible role in the life of a new child, of her own baby."[5]

This major transformation in role may be superficially dealt with by rationalizing that the child will be delivered and cared for to please the husband, or to have a namesake, or to meet dependency needs for mother by supplying a playmate. The child may be an object to show off or a means to keep the marriage together. Deutsch notes that all of these efforts will fail, although they may be gratified temporarily after childbirth.[11] Mothering is ultimately selfless, yet requires that a woman have a firm sense of her own self. This position is difficult for an immature or narcissistic woman to maintain, even briefly.

Most women are symptom-free for days to weeks post partum. The increasing realization of the responsibilities of motherhood may partly explain this delay. Frequent awakenings for feeding and changing are impossible to avoid. If feeding or other difficulties arise, old feelings of inadequacy and lack of ability to love and be loved quickly surface.

Robson and Kumar note that during this brief period of a few days post partum, when most women are symptom-free, they often lack affection for the child.[41] MacFarlane speculates that this period may serve a species survival function.[28] A women delays affection until she is sure the child will survive and thus avoids possible grief and delay in further procreation.

These psychoanalytic insights contribute to our understanding of universal dynamics at parturition, but the etiologic significance of these factors in postpartum mental illness is unclear. An attempt has been made by Nilsson and Almgren to overcome the retrospective and small sample bias of previous analytic speculation.[31] One hundred sixty-five women were studied with extensive interviews and psychological testing at the first prenatal visit, again on the second or third postpartum day, and finally six months post partum. Extensive data on past development, family relatives, and previous mental illness were obtained. They found significant correlations between postpartum symptoms and reproductive conflicts, as evidenced by unsatisfactory early relations with parents, difficulties in sexual adjustment, preference for masculine attitudes, and identification with father. These findings are very similar to previous analytic theories. This study is one of the few prospective studies that have been attempted but lacks detailed, frequent observations and concomitant biologic data.

PSYCHOBIOLOGIC ETIOLOGY

The weight of the evidence so far favors a multifaceted etiology. Some progress has been made in understanding postpartum disturbances as a psychobiologic unit by studying women in a prospective way, in order to observe normal psychobiologic changes.

Treadway studied a group of normal women to see what the psychological and biologic profiles were during pregnancy and the puerperium.[52] No puerperal depressions occurred, but some mothers were tearful and emotionally labile in the postpartum period. Pregnant women had significantly elevated hypochondriasis on the Minnesota Multiphasic Personality Inventory, decreased feminine scores, and increased social introversion. These same findings have been noted in women susceptible to postpartum disturbances. This may point to the universality of certain dynamics during pregnancy and the puerperium and to the pitfalls of retrospective studies. Treadway also found that normal women described themselves as pleasantly sluggish and drowsy and, when tested, had cognitive slowing. Women who reported more sadness had a greater drop in norepinephrine (NE) post partum, although all women had a decrease in NE and none was clinically depressed.

Dalton found that a pattern of anxiety during early pregnancy followed by elation late in pregnancy was significantly related to postpartum depression.[9] Crandon found that anxiety late in pregnancy was related to high fetal distress, prolonged and precipitate labor, and postpartum hemorrhage.[8] Paffenbarger found that physical symptoms during late pregnancy, labor complications, and fetal distress were linked to puerperal mental illness.[34] Robson and Kumar found that maternal affection was less in women who experienced difficult labor.[41] Anxiety during pregnancy could be an important prognosticator of puerperal distress and could indicate early biologic changes. An alternative explanation is that psychological apprehension could produce many secondary psychological events. Prospective studies that examine both parameters in normal women and women at risk will be needed to clarify this issue.

TREATMENT AND PROPHYLAXIS

The treatment of postpartum emotional disorders should address both psychological and physiologic factors. If the physician has been part of a structured prenatal care program and continuity of care has been maintained, there will be significant information that can be used to formulate a treatment approach. Each prenatal visit survey should assess physiologic and emotional parameters to aid in the consideration and detection of imbalance. The risk factors of anxiety and obsessional traits, marital tension, lack of a confidante, lack of a husband, third trimester anxiety, and increased age merit special attention.[8, 12, 21, 25, 34, 35, 47]

As term approaches, inquiry should be made regarding the progress of any prenatal classes and general preparations for the delivery. Owing to the current trend of decreasing family size, many people have not had experience caring for infant siblings. Geographic mobility has diminished the availability of extended family tutors and assistants who can help the new mother with physical chores and emotional experiences. If there has been a long-standing relationship, the physician may have the good fortune to know the coping mechanisms used to handle previous stresses, such as moving to a new house or city, starting or changing a job, graduation from school, marriage or death in the family. This history may reveal a tendency to react with anxiety, depression, or disorganization.

The early detection of illness requires that the physician first consider the possibility of a diagnostic entity being present. This has importance in patients who have maintained continuity of care and in patients who first present with cervical effacement and dilation. The risk factors of labor complications and infant complications may divert much attention, as well as alert the physician.[9, 36]

The treatment plan can be divided into four segments: articulation of the problem, advice, structure, and medication. Most postpartum reactions subside spontaneously.[55] Other disorders respond to some opportunity to ventilate and share feelings with a member of the health care team who has established a significant relationship with the patient. Discussion should be part of the approach instead of the complete approach. Discussion provides some solace and relief and may reveal early clues of severe emotional disorder. This inquiring approach should precede the third day, when the first symptoms usually appear.[34]

Advice and education by the physician should cover topics such as lochia, fever, formulas, and nutrition. Educational advice about the social support system is also in order. Consistent, reliable family assistance should be promoted. Many families provide a flourish of activity and support and then abruptly depart, leaving the new family stranded. The physician may need to encourage moderation of the initial flourish and festival that may add to the workload of the new parents. The physician should also be alert to family conflicts that can occur when several relatives descend and compete for the position of chief cook and director. The clarification and designation of the new mother as the leader may be necessary. On the other hand, the highly insecure new mother may benefit from the designation of her own mother as the person in charge. The finding of Rosenwald and Stonehill that schizoid women tend to collapse early from multiple demands encourages the latter approach.[42] When there is no available family support system, there should be a prompt mobilization of institutional social service personnel as a support system.

Patient education should emphasize the commonness of the postpartum condition, the acuteness of the condition, and the several physiologic components of the condition. Hormonal and sleep components are comprehensible to most patients.[20, 44] This approach is designed to lessen patient guilt and to minimize ruminations about the past 20 and next 30 years.

Most families establish some structure and routine for adjusting to the new member. An educational approach can be quite helpful during this transitional period. Learning new lessons and buying several books give the new parents permission to make mistakes and to keep growing and learning. This decreases the tendency toward personal-failure labels that can be abundant in the early postpartum days.[30] It is helpful to choose a central approach, because with such abundant information the new parents are often troubled by the conflicts in multiple-source information. The family support system can organize a structured program and routine that relieves some of the pressure to make many new decisions.

For patients with severe anxiety, depression, or disorganization, the structure of the hospital environment may be necessary. A reliable, predictable, and understandable hospital environment should be provided. Patients who have difficulty making decisions about child care should not be pressured into energetic participation and decision making in milieu therapy. Flexibility and clinical judgment are necessary to determine if the focus of hospital therapy should be on the infant or on the mother. Standard formulas are less useful than following the patient's lead.

Differential diagnosis of a major postpartum psychosis includes the standard categories of schizophrenia, schizophreniform disorder, brief reactive psychosis, atypical psychosis, manic episode, major depressive episode, and delirium. Standard neuroleptic treatment is usually indicated, with special attention to women who are breast-feeding. Small but potentially significant amounts of lithium, neuroleptics, and tricyclics appear in breast milk.[1, 3, 45, 46, 48, 49]

Prophylaxis consists mainly of identifying the high-risk group of women during pregnancy in order to intervene quickly when symptoms and signs first appear. The alert physician who considers the possibility of a postpartum emotional disorder is best prepared to lower the mortality and morbidity of the disorder.

REFERENCES

1. Ananth J.: Side effects in the neonate from psychotropic agents excreted through breast feeding. *Am. J. Psychiatry* 135:801–805, 1978.
2. Asch S.S., Rubin L.T.: Postpartum reactions: Some unrecognized varieties. *Am. J. Psychiatry* 131:870–874, 1974.
3. Bader T.F., Newman K.: Amitriptyline in human breast milk and the nursing infant's serum. *Am. J. Psychiatry* 137:855–856, 1980.
4. Ballinger C.B., et al.: Emotional disturbance following childbirth: Clinical findings and urinary excretion of cyclic AMP (Adenosine 3' 5' cyclic monophosphate). *Psychol. Med.* 9:293–300, 1979.
5. Bibring G.L.: A study of the psychological processes in pregnancy and of the earliest mother-child relationship. *Psychoanal. Study Child* 16:9–72, 1961.
6. Bleuler E.: *Dementia Praecox or the Group of Schizophrenias.* New York, International Universities Press, 1911.
6a. Bratfos O., Haug J.O.: Puerperal mental disorders in manic-depressive females. *Acta Psychiatr. Scand.* 42:285, 1966.
7. Carroll B.J.: The hypothalamus-pituitary-adrenal axis in depression, in Burrows G. (ed.): *Handbook of Studies on Depression.* New York, Elsevier North-Holland, Inc., 1977.
8. Crandon A.J.: Maternal anxiety and neonatal well being. *J. Psychosom. Res.* 23:113–115, 1979.
9. Dalton K.: Prospective study into puerperal depression. *Br. J. Psychiatry* 118:689–692, 1971.
10. Daniels R.S., Lessow H.: Severe postpartum reactions: An interpersonal view. *Psychosomatics* 5:21–26, 1964.
11. Deutsch H.: *The Psychology of Women.* New York, Grune & Stratton, 1945.
12. Douglas G.: Puerperal depression and excessive compliance with the mother. *Br. J. Med. Psychol.* 36:271–278, 1963.
13. Gelder M.: Hormones and post-partum depression, in Sandler M. (ed.): *Mental Illness in Pregnancy and the Puerperium.* London, Oxford University Press, 1978.
14. Ginath Y.: Psychoses in males in relation to their wives' pregnancy and childbirth. *Isr. Ann. Psychiatry* 12:227–237, 1974.
15. Grundy P.F., Roberts C.J.: Observations on the epidemiology of postpartum mental illness. *Psychol. Med.* 5:286–290, 1975.
16. Hagman A.: Regression in puerperal breakdown. *Br. J. Med. Psychol.* 35:135–145, 1962.
17. Hamilton J.A.: *Postpartum Psychiatric Problems.* St. Louis, C.V. Mosby Co., 1962.

18. Isaksson A., et al.: Rhythmic changes in estriol excretion during pregnancy. *Am. J. Obstet. Gynecol.* 137:470–480, 1980.
19. Kadrmas A., Winokur G., Crowe R.: Postpartum mania. *Br. J. Psychiatry* 135:551–554, 1979.
20. Karacan I., et al.: Some implications of the sleep patterns of pregnancy for postpartum emotional disturbances. *Br. J. Psychiatry* 115:929–935, 1969.
21. Kendall R.E., et al.: The influence of childbirth on psychiatric morbidity. *Psychol. Med.* 6:297–302, 1976.
22. Ketai R.M., Bradwin M.A.: Childbirth-related psychosis and familial symbiotic conflict. *Am. J. Psychiatry* 136:190–193, 1979.
23. Kraepelin I.: *Lectures on Clinical Psychiatry*, ed. 3. London, Baillieve, Tindall and Cassel, 1913.
24. Kripke D.F., et al.: Circadian rhythm disorders in manic-depressives. *Biol. Psychiatry* 13:335–344, 1978.
25. Kumar R., Robson K.: Previous induced abortion and ante-natal depression in primiparae: Preliminary report of a survey of mental health in pregnancy. *Psychol. Med.* 8:711–715, 1978.
26. Lomas P.: The husband-wife relationship in cases of puerperal breakdown. *Br. J. Med. Psychol.* 32:117-123, 1959.
27. Lomas P.: Defensive organization and puerperal breakdown. *Br. J. Med. Psychol.* 33:61–66, 1960.
28. MacFarlane A.: If a smile is so important. *New Scientist* 62:164–166, 1974.
29. Malleson J.: Association with postpartum mental illness and premenstrual tension. *Br. Med. J.* 2:158, 1963.
30. Melges F.T.: Postpartum psychiatric syndromes, in Reiser M.F. (ed.): *Psychosomatic Medicine*. New York, Harper & Row, 1968.
31. Nilsson A., Almgren P.E.: Paranatal emotional adjustment: A prospective investigation of 165 women. *Acta Psychiatr. Scand.* 220:63–141, 1970.
32. Nott P.N., et al.: Hormonal changes and mood in the puerperium. *Br. J. Psychiatry* 128:379–83, 1976.
33. Omini C., et al.: Prostacyclin (PGI_2) in pregnant human uterus. *Prostaglandins* 17:113–120, 1979.
34. Paffenbarger R.S. Jr.: Epidemiological aspects of parapartum mental illness. *Br. J. Prevent. Soc. Med.* 18:189–195, 1964.
35. Paykel E.S., et al.: Life events and social support in puerperal depression. *Br. J. Psychiatry* 136:339–46, 1980.
36. Pitt B.: "Atypical" depression following childbirth. *Br. J. Psychiatry* 114:1325–1335, 1968.
37. Pitt B.: Maternity blues. *Br. J. Psychiatry* 122:431–433, 1973.
38. Pugh T.F., et al.: Rates of mental disease related to child bearing. *N. Engl. J. Med.* 268:1224–1228, 1963.
39. Reich T., Winokur G.: Postpartum psychosis in patients with manic depressive disease. *J. Nerv. Ment. Dis.* 151:60–68, 1970.
40. Rennie T.A.C.: Prognosis in manic-depressive psychosis. *Am. J. Psychiatry* 98:801, 1942.
41. Robson K.M., Kumar R.: Delayed onset of maternal affection after childbirth. *Br. J. Psychiatry* 136:347–353, 1980.
42. Rosenwald G.C., Stonehill M.W.: Early and late postpartum illnesses. *Psychosom. Med.* 34:129, 1972.

43. Ryle A.: The psychological disturbances associated with 345 pregnancies in 137 women. *J. Ment. Sci.* 107:279, 1961.
44. Sachar E.J.: Neuroendocrine abnormalities in depressive illness, in Sachar E.J. (ed.): *Topics in Psychoendocrinology.* New York, Grune & Stratton, 1975.
45. Savage R.L.: Drugs and breast milk. *J. Hum. Nutr.* 31:459–64, 1977.
46. Schon M., Amdisen A.: Lithium and pregnancy: Lithium ingestion by children breast-fed by women on lithium treatment. *Br. Med. J.* 2:138, 1973.
47. Sim M.: Abortion and the psychiatrist. *Br. Med. J.* 2:145–148, 1963.
48. Sovner R., Orsulak P.J.: Excretion of imipramine and desipramine in human breast milk. *Am. J. Psychiatry* 136:451–452, 1979.
49. Stewart R.B., Karas B., Springer P.K.: Haloperidol excretion in human milk. *Am. J. Psychiatry* 137:849–850, 1980.
50. Strecker E., Ebaugh F.: Psychoses occurring during the puerperium. *Arch. Neurol. Psychiatry* 15:239, 1926.
51. Tod E.D.M.: Puerperal depression. *Lancet* 2:1264–1266, 1964.
52. Treadway C.R.: A psychoendocrine study of pregnancy and puerperium. *Am. J. Psychiatry* 125:1380–1386, 1969.
53. Wehr T.A., Muscettola G., Goodwin F.K.: Urinary 3-methoxy, 4-hydroxy-phenolglycol circadian rhythm. *Arch. Gen. Psychiatry* 37:257–263, 1980.
54. Weintraub W.: Postpartum reactions, in Balis G.U. (ed.): *Psychiatric Problems in Medical Practice.* London, Butterworth Publishers, Inc., 1978.
55. Yalom I.D., et al.: "Postpartum blues" syndrome. *Arch. Gen. Psychiatry* 18:16–27, 1968.
56. Zilboorg G.: Malignant psychoses related to childbirth. *Am. J. Obstet. Gynecol.* 15:145–158, 1928.

21

DEPRESSION IN THE ELDERLY

HYMAN L. MUSLIN, M.D.

DEPRESSION IN THE GERIATRIC POPULATION is a common but complex phenomenon. The physician must be mindful of the modal behavior in the elderly, since negative changes in the functions of recall, retention, and judgment are common, as well as transitory loss of self-esteem and transitory mood changes of a depressive nature. However, some loss-of-esteem experiences are protracted and deserve the diagnosis of a depressive reaction.

Historically, there have been cultures in which the elderly were accorded special interest and attention to their emotional needs. An example is the Hofjes, or courtyards, of the aged in Rotterdam, where, 700 years ago, the aged were provided with homes and the opportunity to live with and govern one another.[18] In the present psychiatric era, writing about problems of the elderly is more common than actual treatment of them.[19] In comparison with younger age groups, the elderly use psychiatric services at a very low rate,[21] constituting only 2% of the psychiatric outpatient clinic population.

The scope of the problem is illustrated by prevalence rates found in a study of individuals over 65 years old living in the community. Close to 15% of them had some depressive symptoms: 4.5% were found to be simply dysphoric, 6.5% had depressive symptoms associated with medical illness, and 3.7% fulfilled the criteria for a major depressive disorder. There was also a higher percentage of widowed persons in this 15% subgroup of the total elderly population than in the nondepressed group.[2] Thus the clinician should be mindful both of the prevalence of depression in the elderly and of their underrepresentation in psychiatric clinics.

PHENOMENOLOGY OF DEPRESSION IN THE ELDERLY

The important phenomenology of depression in the elderly is the trio of cardinal experiences and behaviors that highlight every depression: loss of self-esteem, affect changes, and psychomotor changes. These experiences, while common to all depressions, are sometimes lost sight of in the elderly for a variety of reasons, including observer bias. This consists most often of the notion that elderly people, especially institutionalized elderly, as a matter of course experience a loss of self-worth. Loss of experienced self-value in any person is a serious finding and, like any unreasonably protracted affect change of grief, must be carefully followed over time. Psychomotor changes of depression in the elderly must also be carefully evaluated, since slowing of the mental processes, often incorrectly ascribed to irreversible tissue change, may be due to a depressive reaction rather than to the changes of chronic brain syndrome secondary to senility or atherosclerosis of cerebral vessels.

Another aspect of depressive phenomenology, the vegetative signs and symptoms, may be confused with typical aging processes in the depressed elderly. Decreases in all appetites (food, sex, work) are often subtle and unrecognized by observers of the elderly, owing to bias, and the onset of depression in such patients may go undetected. Other vegetative signs that should be assessed are tiredness, sleep disturbances (insomnia, hypersomnia, early rising), hypochondriacal phenomena, and gastrointestinal disturbances (constipation, epigastric distress, spastic colon). Many authors have suggested that depressions in the elderly are more likely to be masked than in the younger population.[10, 23]

PSYCHOLOGY OF AGING

Certain social and behavioral tasks associated with the aging process must be taken into account in any consideration of psychopathology and psychotherapy of the aged. A number of authors have described developmental tasks or tasks for mastery of the later years. For Erikson, old age ushers in the culmination of the life cycle, hopefully with the accumulation of knowledge "freed of temporal relativity" and mature judgment.[6] The opposite condition, that of despair, is signified by fear of death and represents failure to achieve the state of integrity. Reisman spoke of three outcomes of aging: the autonomous group, who are self-sustaining; the adjusted, who accommodate to life; and the anomic, who are prematurely weary and resigned.[22] For Gitelson, the task is survival by previously successful habits of mastery.[8] Grotjahn stated that the task of the aging person lies in integration of the past, leading from maturity to wisdom.[11, 12] Cameron commented that the task is to accept the altered condition of later maturity, implying the need to accept a change in ideals for the elderly.[4] For Kohut, the developmental task of the later years consists of the acknowledgment of the finitude of life (transience), albeit with humor and acquired wisdom. These changes he describes as transformations of the narcissistic self, an accomplishment achieved by few.[14] Benedek wrote of the need for the aged to enlarge their libidinal resources, i.e., to achieve gratification by identifying with the young and "rekindling the memories of past gratification."[1] Goldfarb identified an important task of aging as finding protectors and providers, as in childhood.[9]

While certain differences in interpretation are immediately evident, all observers of the aged agree on the basic issues: the later years accost people with major life crises in socioeconomic life-style, outlets for achievement, and changes in familial roles. Most changes relate to the task of preparing for or denying the omnipresent specter of death. There is also a common emphasis on changes in the psyche of the elderly. These changes range from modification in the ego defenses and self-system to alterations in one's overview of the universe (Kohut, Erikson, Benedek).

All observers allude to the task of confronting the world not just with altered psychic apparatuses, but also with profound alteration in the ability of the cerebrum to manipulate and store percepts and maintain cognition. These alterations produce a state of inattention or indifference to the ongoing world, leaving in their wake introversion and preoccupation with an uncomplicated past.

A number of developmental tasks important to the emotional well-being of the aging can be cited.

Central to all tasks is a modification in ideals to which the aging person aspires. In the aging person, ideals must undergo appropriate mutation from ideals appropriate to a person in the middle phases of life to a different set of standards. One critical developmental task, therefore, is for the aged to accept personal ideals commensurate with increasing limitations, for example, in social and economic achievement and intellectual functioning.

To accept this mutation of ideals without shame is equally important. The self must change to embrace the standards of limitation, of a decrement in aggressive outpouring, of increasing spectatorship rather than leadership or participation, all without shame.

Mastering the ubiquitous losses of the later years, especially the loss of significant people, and the resolution of one's own departure from life without despair are other important developmental tasks.

Another task to be mastered in the later years is the acceptance of changes in the energy level of the self and a deterioration of the CNS apparatus, with increasing slowness in manipulating memory traces for thinking, difficulty in storage of new information, and limitations imposed by sensory deficits.

Still another change in self in the elderly person that must be eventually accepted is the relative diminution in the driven quality of the self, i.e., a decrease in the capacity for assertiveness. A frequent complaint of the elderly is that there is no drive left.

In summary, three developmental tasks are central in the later years: (1) acceptance of changes in phase-specific ideals, (2) acceptance of somatic changes, and (3) accommodation of phase-specific losses.

These developmental tasks are phase-specific aspects of the later years that are of major importance in a consideration of the psychosocial equilibrium during aging. Resistance to changes in ideals and self-system, with concomitant lack of acceptance of limitations, constitutes a specific syndrome of disequilibrium that may result in a variety of psychopathologic phenomena, including depression.

Views of the psychology of the self are especially helpful in considering the psychological transformation in the elderly.[15, 16] The self is considered the center of the individual experiences, the center of initiative. It thus comprises all of the individual's inner experience of mind and body. It is best considered as bipolar in nature, with one pole representing the center of ambitions, expressed as the individual's assertive experiences, and the other pole representing ideals formed by internalized precepts of childhood authorities. The pole of the ambitions exerts influence through the individual's talents and skilled activities, which operate in the direction of the individual's ideals and thus diminish the tension between the two poles that would otherwise result in the experience of inferiority, protracted loss of esteem, or serious anxiety (disintegration anxiety) and loss of integrity of the self, the state of fragmentation. In the aging, the pole of assertiveness is ordinarily transformed, for a variety of social and biochemical reasons, but if this change occurs in tandem with the diminution of ideals of accomplishment, the tension between the two self-poles is not intense and no protracted loss of self-esteem is experienced.

A very important consideration in the psychology of the aging is the task of the caretakers of the elderly—the spouses, relatives, and physicians. In all human interactions, the need for enhancement of esteem by supportive, nurturing, and confirmatory activities represents a central task; in the elderly, the task is crucial in maintaining the necessary self-cohesiveness to ward off states of loss of esteem and disintegration anxiety. Thus, the need to be admired (mirroring function) by an important person in the surround (relative, physician) is often crucial, as is the need to have access to a person who can offer guidance, leadership, calming, and soothing (idealized parent image).

CLINICAL VIGNETTES

The observer of the elderly must be alert to signs and symptoms of a protracted episode of loss of self-esteem and, always coupled with an investigation of the possible changes in organic, mental, and somatic functioning, must pursue the possibility of a treatable depressive reaction. Following are several vignettes illustrating the gamut of depressive reaction seen in a clinical psychiatric practice.

CASE 1.—A 72-year-old woman went to her physician complaining of feelings of futility and painful sadness. She related that she had little desire to go on living and often thought of "walking right into the lake and not stopping." In the anamnesis, it was discovered that her loss of self-esteem was related to her son's rejection of her over the past five years, which had become worse recently, and the termination of a job at a newsstand that she had held until 1¹/₂ years prior to the office visit. Her son's social and financial rejection was a great blow to this proud and independent woman, to whom dependency meant helplessness. When her job was abruptly terminated, her dependency on welfare was pride-shattering. As her capacity to obtain support was abruptly diminished, she suffered a severe loss of worth.

After several visits, the physician instituted a plan for supporting her weakened self-esteem, starting with a visit with her son to go over in detail his mother's emotional and financial needs. The patient was then put in touch with a local agency specializing in daily activities for the elderly. During follow-up appointments over the next several months, she was in better equilibrium and eventually lost the severe depressive reaction.

CASE 2.—A 65-year-old man was referred for symptoms of inadequacy, concern with his heart, and loss of weight without known somatic illness. After the mental status was investigated and found without deficit, psychological investigation revealed that he had been in a protracted state of sadness for the past two years after his mother and brother had died within six months of each other. His father had died ten years previously. His feelings of abandonment had been transferred to his work activities, and he had begun to lose all interest in his profession and the ability to work effectively, which was frightening to him.

The reaction to human losses dismantled this patient's capacity to maintain his modal experience of self-esteem and ushered in a protracted loss of self-worth (depression) and fragmentation experiences. He actually could not use his ordinary capacity to concentrate, remember, and organize thoughts effectively. The patient's attention was centered on his need to have an ongoing relationship with a central figure in his environment, one who could serve to support his flagging self-value (mirroring function) and offer a direction to his life in advising, calming, and soothing his disorganized self (idealized parent functions). This patient was seen in psychotherapy sessions two times a week. During the early phases of therapy for insomnia (Noludar, 300 mg), he was also given hypnotics. His equilibrium was restored after several months of psychotherapy.

CASE 3.—A 75-year-old man was seen in the internal medicine diagnostic clinic complaining of tiredness and weakness. He told the internist that he had never been seriously sick in his life, had never been hospitalized, and had rarely been to a physician. The internist performed a physical examination and ordered routine laboratory tests (chest film, complete blood cell count, urinalysis, and blood chemistries); all were normal. On the second diagnostic visit, the patient admitted to anorexia, insomnia (three or four hours' sleep each night), constipation, and impotence. More reluctantly, he reported feeling sad, having crying spells, and wishing he were dead. He began crying in the office when he admitted that he and his wife of 35 years were having difficulty and he was considering divorce. He was then referred to a psychiatrist, who felt the patient was sufficiently depressed and suicidal to warrant hospitalization.

Further history obtained on the psychiatric unit revealed the content of the patient's depressed mood. A year earlier his older brother died, leaving the patient and one younger sister still living. The patient denied any history of psychiatric problems or alcoholism in himself or his family.

The patient had not seen his family since his marriage 35 years before. His parents and siblings had strongly opposed his marriage: he was a first generation Swede, his wife was a black American. Following his marriage in Detroit, he and his wife moved to Chicago, where he worked until age 65 as an electrician. The couple had two sons, now both married and living in the city. Recently the patient had become aware of some hostility toward him from blacks in his neighborhood, which revived old quarrels his sons had with other black friends while they were growing up. More important, since his brother's death, he had been overwhelmed with nostalgic and guilt feelings about severing ties with his family.

On the third day of hospitalization, the patient's family came in for a family interview. His wife and sons were genuinely concerned and affectionate toward him, although this seemed of little comfort. After the family session, his wife asked the nursing staff if they were giving the patient his "pressure pills." This led to the previously unreported history that the patient had had reserpine prescribed for him four months earlier and had been taking it daily, but had forgotten to tell any of the doctors.

Based on the presumptive diagnosis of reserpine-induced depression, no antidepressant was prescribed. For the next ten days the patient attended the usual ward activities and therapies. He continued to be depressed and tired, had severe insomnia, and continued suicidal ideation. During the second week, he was placed on imipramine, 25 mg at night and gradually increased to 75 mg by the end of the second week. His insomnia improved initially, and after two weeks of this therapy his family noticed an increase in mood, although the patient denied this. After three weeks of imipramine and ward activities, he admitted to feeling better and no longer suicidal. During the hospitalization, the ward physician continued to discuss the patient's concern about his family of origin; his family came in for therapy sessions each week as well. He was discharged to outpatient follow-up in the fifth week.

In the absence of a history of reserpine, this patient's presentation was identical to that of a major depressive episode (unipolar depression); the family-related problems seemed to provide a psychological explanation as well. This case highlights the fact that depression with different etiologies can exhibit the same phenomenon. The imipramine therapy was initiated because of continued depression following the discontinuation of reserpine. Without tricyclic therapy it may take months for the brain catecholamines depleted by reserpine to be restored. Individual and family psychotherapy were prescribed owing to the belief that the biologic cause of this depression did not undermine the need for this elderly man to continue the process of reassessing his life's decisions, losses, and accomplishments.

CASE 4.—A 75-year-old woman went to her internist with the symptoms of irritability, anorexia, and loss of interest in life. The internist, knowing of her customary vitality, desired a consultation, since her psychic transformation could not be explained on the basis of the usual investigations. After several sessions, it became clear that her lifelong emotional supports were no longer meaningful to her since her activity level was waning and that acceptance of a lower and different level of activity was difficult without an experience of severely diminished self-regard. Her lifelong defenses against receptivity were interfering with the developmental task of accepting a lower level of assertiveness; her ideal, always to be in charge of herself and others, was in jeopardy. Her neurosis, which had been held in check over a lifetime of extraordinary achievements, was now in focus, and the symptoms of conflict, including depression, were raging. This patient was recommended for intensive psychoanalytic therapy. Her capacity to investigate her underlying sensitivities and enter into a transference, albeit with modification, was judged adequate for the work of uncovering therapy.

DIAGNOSIS AND TREATMENT OF DEPRESSION IN THE ELDERLY

An enlightened approach to the diagnosis and treatment of depression in the elderly must be grounded on an unbiased assessment of each patient. Every clinical task must be approached with a minimum of age stereotyping. One bias that must be countered is the notion of "ubiquitous" rigidity in the self of the elderly. Other preconceived notions are views on deterioration, which must be assessed individually in each patient, and the reaction of the physician to the elderly, the transferences and countertransferences implying unconscious personal reactions to aging persons. Bond[3] mentions that therapists must come to grips with their countertransference reactions, which often consist of anxiety over dealing with patients close to death who may form extremely strong attachments. Grotjahn[11, 12] has written of the "reverse oedipal" transference; Meerloo[17, 18] has also spoken of this transference pattern.

Common to all elderly patients is some degree of deterioration; how it relates to the ushering in of depression and how it determines the patient's capacity for therapy must be evaluated. Prior to assigning any elderly patient to psychological or pharmacologic therapies (or, if necessary, electroconvulsive therapy), the physician must examine all possible physical causes of the depression, remembering always that a somatic lesion frequently manifests itself by a protracted mood alteration.

In all management plans for treatment of the elderly, attention must be paid to the following:

CHOICE OF TREATMENT.—In treatment plans for the depressed elderly, data determine the choice of treatment. In some instances it is clear that hospitalization and electroconvulsive therapy are vital. In the absence of a suicidal depression, the capacity for self-introspection while forming a workable alliance with a psychotherapist permits depth psychotherapy to be pursued. Patients in the midst of yet another exacerbation of a bipolar mood disorder reveal a clear-cut need for antidepressants and eventually lithium maintenance. The practitioner must be alert to all therapeutic possibilities, but mindful of the restrictions of the aging process.

DETERIORATION AND DEVELOPMENTAL TASKS.—An ongoing assessment of memory, intellectual capacity, and mobility must concern the therapist of the aged. This is reflected in the amount of material that can be interpreted and integrated in each session; how much activity can be planned; how much rest is needed; and what time of day should be chosen for the session.

For each elderly patient, the phase-specific modification in the self and ideals, the "resistance to aging" syndrome, will make itself felt as an issue in the treatment, at times as the essential problem in living. In patients selected for insight therapy or analysis, therapy may concern itself with the underlying anxieties, focusing on the acceptance of these phase-specific modifications that will allow for development to ensue. In supportive treatment, the therapist will need to give direct reassurance to the patient suffering from loss of esteem as the self struggles to assimilate the modifications needed for aging without undue pain.

FLEXIBILITY AND PARAMETERS.—In each diagnostic procedure and in each management plan, the therapist must adopt management tactics that are relevant to the individual patient, rather than retain the traditional tasks of a given treatment methodology. Each therapy plan accommodates itself to shorter or longer sessions, telephone sessions, visits at home, visits in hospital, and consultation with other physicians and family. The therapist may be involved in collaborating on a diet or managing a sleep routine.

The investigation and treatment of depression in the elderly is a gratifying effort, perhaps most of all because of the constant challenge to our empathic resources by a worthwhile clientele, our elders.

REFERENCES

1. Benedek T.: *Parenthood*. Boston, Little, Brown & Co., 1970.
2. Blazek D., Candyce W.: Epidemiology of dysphoria and depression in an elderly population. *Am. J. Psychiatry* 137:439, 1980.
3. Bond D.: Psychoanalytic considerations of aging, in Panel on aging, Zinberg N.E. (moderator). *J. Am. Psychoanal. Assoc.* 12:151, 1964.
4. Cameron N.: Neurosis of later maturity, in Kaplan O.J. (ed.): *Mental Disorders in Later Life*. Stanford, Stanford University Press, 1956.
5. Eissler K.R.: *The Psychiatrist and the Dying Patient*. New York, International Universities Press, 1955.

6. Erikson E.: The human life cycle, in *International Encyclopedia of the Social Sciences*. New York, Macmillan Publishing Co., 1968.
7. Ginzberg R.: Geriatric ward psychiatry: Techniques in the psychological management of elderly psychotics. *Am. J. Psychiatry* 110:296, 1953.
8. Gitelson M.: The emotional problems of elderly people. *Geriatrics* 3:135, 1948.
9. Goldfarb A.I.: Psychotherapy of aged persons: IV. One aspect of the psychodynamics of the therapeutic situation with aged patients. *Psychoanal. Rev.* 42:180, 1955.
10. Goldfarb A.I.: Masked depression in the elderly, in Lesse S. (ed.): *Masked Depression*. New York, Jason Aronson, 1974.
11. Grotjahn M.: Some analytic observations about the process of growing old, in Roheim G. (ed.): *Psychoanalysis and Social Sciences*. New York, International Universities Press, 1951, vol. 3.
12. Grotjahn M.: Analytic psychotherapy with the elderly. *Psychoanal. Rev.* 42:419, 1955.
13. Hollender M.H.: Individualizing the aged. *Soc. Casework* 33:337, 1952.
14. Kohut H.: Forms and transformations of narcissism. *J. Am. Psychoanal. Assoc.* 14:243, 1966.
15. Kohut H.: *The Analysis of the Self*. New York, International Universities Press, 1971.
16. Kohut H.: *The Restoration of the Self*. New York, International Universities Press, 1977.
17. Meerloo J.A.M.: Contribution of psychoanalysis to the problem of the aged, in Heiman M. (ed.): *Psychoanalysis and Social Work*. New York, International Universities Press, 1953.
18. Meerloo J.A.M.: Transference and resistance in geriatric psychotherapy. *Psychoanal. Rev.* 42:72, 1955.
19. Muslin H., Epstein L.J.: Preliminary remarks on the rationale for psychotherapy of the aged. *Compr. Psychiatry* 21:1, 1980.
20. Pfeiffer E.: Psychotherapy with elderly patients. *Postgrad. Med.* 50:254, 1971.
21. Redick R.W., Kramer M., Taube C.A.: Epidemiology of mental illness and utilization of psychiatric facilities among older persons, in Busse E.W., Pfeiffer E. (eds.): *Mental Illness in Later Life*. Washington, D.C., American Psychiatric Association, 1973.
22. Reisman D.: Some clinical and cultural aspects of aging. *Am. J. Sociol.* 59:379, 1954.
23. Salzman C., Shader R.I.: Depression in the elderly: I. Relationships between depression, psychologic defense mechanisms and physical illness. *J. Am. Geriatr. Soc.* 36:253, 1978.
24. Weinberg J.: Psychiatric techniques in the treatment of older people, in Donahue W., Tibbitts C. (eds.): *Growing in the Older Years*. Ann Arbor, University of Michigan Press, 1951.

22

AFFECTIVE DISORDERS AND THE FAMILY SYSTEM

NORMAN R. BERNSTEIN, M.D.

A FAMILY refers to a group living in a household. Despite allegations that families are dying, communes have not taken over. Schools have not taken on all moral and value education or teaching about sex. Social agencies and divorce are not the fulcrum of individual life. It is still the family, as it has been for thousands of years.

DYNAMICS OF HOME LIFE

Zilbach[26] defines the family as a small, natural group whose development is distinguishable from the development of the individual within the family. Families serve a number of functions, individual and social. Their social purposes have been described by Ackerman.[1] He noted that the family must first provide shelter, food, and the material needs of heat, clothing, and protection. To do this well in primitive or advanced societies, some division of labor, cooperation, and unity of purpose are needed. The bonds of affection between family members derive from the matrix of shared living and grow from common experiences and a feeling of togetherness. This type of unity is seen only when individual family members establish separate family units, generation by generation.

In a family, individuals evolve a personal identity tied to family identity—the sense of who are in this world and what we mean. This sense comes from what children see and do and not solely through the declarations of parents. From the experiences in the home, children get their ideas about what sex roles mean. Is mother dominant, father weak, or are both parents loving and cooperative? Do they feel sex is pleasurable, sinful, or both?

The ways in which these themes are orchestrated lead to the definition of the social roles that each child will fill when he or she grows up. If one parent is responsible, flexible, and artistic, this gives both sons and daughters a broader perspective on how to live. We are not totally shaped by our families but they provide a major template for personality functioning. Artists do emerge from culture-blind homes, but they are much more likely to develop in homes where learning is encouraged and where there is support for individual creativity and initiative.

Almost 60% of people seeking psychiatric help define their emotional problems as disturbed marital or other family relationships.[1] Most personality theorists would agree with Solnit[22] that

developmental health . . . is a relative . . . balance between individual expression and adaptation to the demands of the family. . . The ultimate measure of the child's development is the extent to which the child is maturing, becoming a person who in adulthood is likely to be relatively free of internal conflict. The healthy adult has a realistic self-regard that enables him to gauge and react with confidence to environmental demands. . . . When parents are depressed or suffer from the long-term effects of deprivation in their own childhood, they may lack the capacity to stimulate, nurture, protect, guide, and support their children. They transmit to their children what they themselves had suffered. In this way certain deficits and deviations may be transmitted from one generation to the next through the dynamics of family interactions.

Following Erikson's concept that development is three-dimensional, one can see the individual developing along dimensions of personal experience (history), physical/physiologic/biologic equipment, and subjective (psychological) experience (how a child perceives what happens to him). A handicapping limp may crush one child or serve as an impetus for intellectual achievement for another, depending on the balance among these dimensions.

A family has the same dimensions of history, psychology, and structure. The family process—its structure, its overall unit or "ego"—is still another dynamic system. The forces and patterns of conflict within a family derive from the values and woes of its individual members, but family dynamics are not the algebraic sums of individual dynamics. Rather, they constitute a system with still another level of dynamics that needs to be addressed from the overall family perspective. Two sisters can form a subgroup and function in the family group at the same time, or father and daughter can ally against mother. Families continually make adjustments with the guidance of multiple feedbacks.

Grier et al. state[13]:

Family members respond to reactions of other members to their own behavior. Depending upon their dynamics and the dynamics of the total family system, they can either change or continue their previous behavior. Such responsiveness in some families can be exceedingly acute. Minimal signs are correctly interpreted, even when the responding member may not be entirely aware of his own feelings. Such sensitivity can produce harmony in the family if the members' adjustments to signals serve to reduce interpersonal strains. If they serve to increase them, the sensitivity can be destructive.

Lewis, as quoted in Fleck,[9] has worked out a series of issues to be addressed in the evaluation of troubled families. Among them are:

1. Overt power: the leadership, power, and authority of family members.

2. Parental coalition: strong, weak, or affection-laden. What are the parents in contrast to what they seem?

3. Closeness: the distance and boundaries between family members. Are people formal, informal, touchy?

4. Family mythology: the image and members' belief in it. Do they feel aspiring, superior to neighbors, ashamed of their status?

5. Clarity of expression: communication quality in a family. Do they hide what they feel? Lie? Obscure thoughts?

6. Responsibility: How is it encouraged or impaired?

7. Invasiveness: the emotional intrusion into the subjective thoughts of a family member. Are children coerced to "tell all" their school and romantic experiences?

8. Mood and tone: the group temperament. Is it busy, cheery, dreary, spasmodic?

9. Empathy: the degree of understanding responses of family to members' feelings.

10. Conflict resolution: the ability of family to work out problems.

Many factors in a family functioning can produce richness in an individual's personality repertoire or variegated emotional problems. Rutter, cited by Zilbach,[27] declared that of all family variables, discord, quarreling, unhappiness, and disruption are most consistently associated with disorders in the child.

Emotional equilibrium, or homeostasis, in a home implies a series of changes in response to stress in the family. This balance tends to shift toward a previous set level or stable emotional pattern, as in individual human physiology.

For some families, one particular or striking affective tone is characteristic. Zilbach notes that a family may be joyful, noisy, or sad, and that "when a particularly dominant affective tone is present, there is a constriction or exaggeration of available affect range."[26]

DEPRESSION AND FAMILY DYNAMICS

Current thinking on depression clearly recognizes environmental causation interwoven with hereditary factors (heredofamilial). There is a continuum from the genetically determined problem to the starkly environmental. Families marked by psychotic depression in many members are at one end, while a home in which mother dies in an automobile accident and financial and emotional structures collapse, leaving a depressed and exhausted father, is at the other end. But clinical cases are rarely textbook-clear. Clinical signs may be vague and histories edited and distorted. They may disguise depression as "bad heredity." Additionally, once the cards of heredity (Freud) have been dealt, they are then shaped by environment. Winston Churchill referred to his repeated depressive episodes as his "Black Dog"; he fought them as determinedly as he fought the Germans.

The continuum from hereditary to environmental causality is significant mostly in its center portion, where it is a mixture of endowment and experience in varied proportions. Schizophrenia, for example, has received considerable research attention concerning the ways in which parental behavior transmits the psychotic behavioral pattern, especially in communication. These problems of conceptualization exist also in families with depressive illness. Additionally, there are problems of separating the sharply psychotic forms from the borderline and the neurotic; there are varieties of cultural divergence and protean forms of experience that affect normal families.

This exposition focuses on experiential aspects of affective disorders but does not ignore the way in which temperament is significantly built into our chromosomes. Examples of clinical configurations from different parts of the continuum follow.

PSYCHOTIC AFFECTIVE DISEASE IN A FAMILY

Bipolar Disorder Following Chronic Hypomanic Disorder

Brandon Fitz was 52. He had always been known as an eccentric scientist with inherited money. He had invested much of this to build his own laboratory on the large family property and had worked for 12 years to investigate protein synthesis, without any notable results. His wife, aged 40, and three children, aged 16, 19, and 22, were dominated by his conduct. Carl Binger said, "A family is a kingdom ruled by the sickest member."[4] In demonstration of this maxim, Brandon Fitz made the entire family meet at breakfast for "intellectual discussions and cultural exchanges." For years his tone had always been heightened, intense, preoccupied, and rigidly cheerful. He gathered quotations for a book he never finished. He constantly began travel projects that were completed only when his wife took over the arrangements, and he kept up long and loosely reasoned discussions of his chemical researches.

Mrs. Fitz later noted that she had to take the position that her husband was a unique genius who had "taken on too big a research project," because if she acknowledged how weird he was, she would have felt herself a fool for putting up with it. She also feared the consequences of opposing his will; she feared the rage that lay beneath his brittle jollity. The oldest child became busy with life at school and fled the home through marriage at 19. She had a clear, detached, and poignant view of a father who never gave her anything, which she resented. The middle child enlisted in the Marines and did not return home.

Sixteen-year-old Sandra was unusually tall and mature-seeming for her age. She attended a prestigious girls' school in Maryland and was sought out by older boys for her good looks and sophisticated bearing—a cover for her dread of saying something that would reveal her ignorance and anxieties. This dread was tied to her fear of disagreeing with men, derived from her relations with her father.

While Sandra was away at school and her mother was visiting a neighbor, Mr. Fitz called and chattily asked the neighbor to tell his wife that he was leaving her and that she would receive divorce papers. He did, in fact, divorce her and marry his 28-year-old research assistant. Sandra appeared to be cool and detached about all of this, although she complained bitterly about her social situation at school, where she said she was the only conservative among a bunch of radicals and liberals. She took an overdose of barbiturates and was comatose for four days after being derided for her political views by her peers and sexually pressured by a 22-year-old who mistook her age. After this episode, she was visited in the hospital by her father, who was inappropriately jolly and interested primarily in her medical chart and the chemical studies that had been done. At no time did he display serious or tender feelings toward his daughter. Mother was crushed by the double blows of the divorce and the overdose and tried mutely and ineptly to stand by. A month later, Sandra was discharged from the hospital and began psychotherapy. She packed a suitcase and went to New York to visit her grandmother. While having tea with her grandmother, she went to the bathroom, pinned notes on her dress addressed to her teachers, siblings, and parents, with contemptuous comments about all of them, and jumped 14 floors to her death. Father did not attend the funeral and appeared to go his intense, brittle, hypomanic way with his new family. Five years later he had a period of depression and abruptly killed himself with an overdose of pills.

While Sandra's genetic endowment was significant in her depressive ill-ness, the pattern of communication in the home skewed the basic family functions and set the patient up for disaster. It is worth noting that some authors, like Connors,[6] have reported that children appear to manage bet-ter emotionally when a parent manifests a bipolar rather than a unipolar affective disorder.

Unipolar Affective Disorder

Martita had published a book before graduating from a posh girls' col-lege. Only years later did it emerge that her father had written it for her. She seemed pretty, pert, and petulant. At 22, she married a young busi-ness executive who was fascinated by her ability and her artistic family. Her father had been a Washington speechwriter who had slid into despon-dency. After Martita had been married five years, her father killed himself with a gun. After a normal mourning period, Martita returned to her usual level of functioning. At 25 she gave birth to a normal daughter. At 28 she began to carp at her husband that he was too engrossed in work and more successful than she. Martita withdrew from cooking and housework, filling her time with novels, television, movies, and theater. She sank still further into despair over her plight, leaving her child to husband and domestic help. After 18 months she gradually returned to normal functioning. Three years later she began to sink again, punctuating her despair with some ineffectual efforts at seducing "worthy" men and brief flings at psychother-apy, which she quit whenever intimate feelings were discussed. For the next 12 years she struggled with dejection. She was hospitalized for four suicide attempts in a decade. Her daughter, aged 11, came home to find her mother half sunk in the bathtub, comatose from an overdose of Se-conal. She never had friends or business associates of her husband's in, became a chronic invalid and suicidal threat, and drained a fortune for medical care. She would rouse herself to talk grandly about the theater or buy frilly clothes for her child but was emotionally unavailable and unreli-able. Father and daughter clung to each other devotedly and responsibly. They worked to keep the home going.

Lithium therapy was begun in 1972 and Martita improved, stabilized at a low, nonpsychotic level of functioning. On a return visit to the clinic to reassess her overall condition, she became infatuated with another patient and they went off to get married. Her husband rapidly acquiesced and helped her through a divorce to get rid of her. He remarried with relief and developed a generally more cheerful style with the oppression of his home gone.

Martita's daughter developed into a competent, shy, affectionate adolescent who desperately feared a psychosis of her own. Her 20s were shadowed by the specter of the "bad blood" inherited from her mother. Dynamically, whether the daughter's heredity doomed her or not, the experience with mother, the deficiencies in love and affection, coupled with her fears, had already shaped a depressive personality.

NEUROTIC DEPRESSIVE PERSONALITY

Anselm Ruggiero was the salt of the earth. He was an optician in a midwestern city who was always kind and reliable. His vague Marxism was used to demonstrate the terrible state of capitalistic society, while he amassed capital for his wife and four daughters, who were all coddled. His wife, a former nurse, was tiny, tireless, and sanguine about life. She was active in church, met with her friends, tended the home, and fussed over her girls with fairly rigid blinkers against her husband's discontent. There was no economic stress. Anselm was determined to educate and cultivate his children, although this solicitousness contrasted with his apocalyptic world view. In spite of his masochistic character, he was well liked and fondly regarded by his friends, who knew he could always be called on for help or to carry out some burdensome duties for the church or sick friends. He complained, told cynical jokes, and was generally sour but reliable. Everything was done to give the children the best future, and any roadblocks or problems were attacked vigorously. All the children had orthodontia, music and dance lessons, summer camp, and educational help. There was simultaneous pressure to achieve academically and make up for the lack of a son to carry on the family name. One daughter became depressed in adolescence, feeling worthless, incompetent, and unattractive, but responded to casework treatment. A second daughter turned off all the *miserere* in the family and identified with her mother's jolly, nonintellectual, self-involved, and self-satisfied style, and kept her distance from her father. Another daughter was troubled by father's politics and ashamed of them, while feeling bad about underachievement at college. She had great trouble making up her mind about a career or a date and underwent a period of depression that terrified her because of the obvious comparison with her father. She refused all pressures for psychological help and after a year of floundering, abruptly married and removed herself from the family orbit by living abroad with her husband.

When Mr. Ruggiero reached retirement, he turned over his business to a young associate whom he did not respect. He felt the neighborhood had deteriorated; the clientele was not as chic and affluent; life's industry seemed unrewarded. Several months after his retirement party, he was diagnosed as having carcinoma of the bowel, which was resected without a colostomy being performed. Ninety days later, he checked into a local hotel, left a message for a colleague to visit, and killed himself with an overdose of sleeping pills.

THE DEPRESSOGENIC HOME

Tolstoy said, "all happy families resemble one another; every unhappy family is unhappy in its own fashion."[23] Probably there are as many individual paths to happiness, but it is clear that depression is more of an affective common denominator than the myriad forms of happiness. One type of family that tends to breed depressive problems lives in a "cold" home. This refers to the emotional temperature and is individual to the family, although culture can influence it. Japanese believe Americans are barbaric in their physical and verbal punishments of children. The silent Scottish home is not necessarily pathogenic, though it is certainly more quiet than a Spanish or Italian home. These cultural variations all work well when they serve the family functions described above. Some do not.

Icy Tone

The Saxon family lived in a well-to-do suburb in a large, old, and ill-kept house. Father was a successful portrait painter and his wife and three children all shared his sense of superiority and cool, emotional control. They did not speak to their neighbors; they did not interact with the local community. Their own parties derived from a narrow social circle which kept the neighborhood arbitrarily noisy on the occasions of their festivities. Mr. Saxon had worked hard to achieve his career successes but never enjoyed life greatly. His view of the world was controlled, restricted, and sour. He manifested no psychiatric disease but had little interest in his surroundings. His wife had begun married life with a more sanguine disposition and had learned to fend for herself emotionally, first in family contacts with her own relatives (who gradually moved off as they found Mr. Saxon unwilling to waste the mildest amenities on them), then in the care of her children. With so little affection coming in, she did not have a great deal to expend on her children. She began to present the model of emotional retention that fitted her husband's style, which then shaped the children's interpersonal style. A visitor (who did not come back) remarked, "The temperature dropped 10 degrees when Saxon entered the room." On one occasion, when some neighborhood boys had put out a fire that had threatened the home, they were ignored and never thanked. The family felt it was their due to be protected. These family members were much more prone to depression in this depressing atmosphere.

Death of a Parent

Mourning and bereavement are major family issues as well as individual issues. In a family, death of a father or a mother is a crisis, a major life stress of limited duration, which endangers the health of the individual and the family. It disrupts customary modes of behavior and alters the circumstances of a household and the goals of the family members. It imposes a need for psychological work, which takes time and effort.

The age of family members determines part of the response. Each person in the family has a personal and unique response as well as a contribution to the overall family bereavement and disequilibrium. When the father dies, the son who is rivalrous can be stricken with guilt. The estranged wife can be overwhelmed with contrition and alarmed at her new responsibilities. Oedipal fantasies in a daughter can leave her desolate.

The realities of a family's finances and whether extended family members and friends rally to help will alter the response. Additionally, the type of death—a lingering illness, an abrupt heart attack, an automobile accident, or a series of liver crises in an alcoholic—will shape the familial response.

The Depressed Mother

Freud spoke of the influence in his own life of the love of a young mother and how it inculcated indomitable self-confidence. But the mother who is gloomy and pessimistic presents different formative stresses. She can be unresponsive to a newborn and set up an early pattern of bad synchrony between mother and child. In the school-aged child, depression can create an unpredictable home atmosphere.

A depressed mother can be cranky or withdrawn. She may rally for short periods and then be unavailable, leaving a child hurt and confused. She may not provide the kind of open, accessible responses that permit an adolescent to squabble with mother and then make up, to talk things over in the erratic style of teenagers. If a mother's mood is dejected or her thoughts are tied to her own sad past, she may not be able to involve herself actively in the life of her child. This does not prevent children from going ahead with their lives, but it increases their burdens, deprives the whole family of the normal joys of home life, and increases the risks of trouble for adolescents.

In later life, many people are rueful about the dark and foreboding lives they had in depressive households and remain affectively flat and joyless.

Retardation and Chronic Sorrow

Mental retardation affects millions of individuals (an estimated 3% of the population). Ninety-five percent of retarded individuals grow up in families. Contrary to myth, retarded people are not particularly happy and are burdensome because of their cognitive incapacities as well as because of their unhappiness. Olshansky[18] wrote of the chronic sorrow of the mothers of retarded people. He cited the example of a mother who told him that the birth of her child was "like a hole in my heart that never stopped bleeding." Parents of retarded children are not depressed in a standard psychiatric sense, but they are oppressed. Their problems will not go away, and they constantly bear extra burdens of guilt, shame, and embarrassment over their children, over simple things like diapering a 7-year-old or getting a babysitter for a 16-year-old. Adversity of this sort does not guarantee depressive illness but does add burdens to family life. Some parents are challenged to heroic degrees by these catastrophes, but clinical experience indicates most people simply cope, and a large number collapse in grief and apathy.

Divorce

There are over 1 million divorces in this country each year. Dizenhus[8] indicates that 75% of these occur in marriages with children: one child in six is from a divorced home. Dizenhus adds that the statistics on divorce do not include homes in which marital discord may lead to a divorce action that is later withdrawn. If these families were included, one child in three might face marital conflict as part of its milieu.

Either parent may suffer from depressive episodes in these settings of bitterness, vindictive glee, abrupt separations, and reconciliations. Overt and covert anger and conflict with overflowing animus and physical violence are common.

In a common pattern of divorce the husband deserts and the wife is left with the children, ashamed, exhausted, and financially fearful. Dejection and hopelessness contribute to the economic and social problems she must deal with. School-aged children have difficulty with their studies and problems with father's visitation. Communication is hindered by secrets, either through parental efforts at discretion or due to the advice of lawyers. There are often fights over custody, alimony, support money for the children, and blame for what has happened. Both parents may try to show that the other one is basically at fault, and a downcast mother is often a poor antagonist in this type of contest, even if she is the one who has been wronged. If one takes the rough figure of 18 months for a family to settle down after a divorce, the child has to deal with a mother who has months of unhappiness, erratic emotional displays, and a preoccupying struggle to cast her life in a new mold, overcome her feelings of failure, and begin to date new men or find a job, all of which may be antithetical to what the child wants—a reunion, a lot of attention, support, and reassurance for his own fears of the world coming apart. These issues can be hard and protracted problems for children. Often children do better if father dies. They can idealize him because mother is positive about his memory, and they are spared much conflict. But in divorce and separation, her rage and ambivalence toward him make it particularly difficult for the children to incorporate a happy image of father as they grow up.

It is notable that in families in which one spouse has a bipolar illness, 47% of the well spouses reported that they would have married the patient anyway if they had known of the disease in advance.[11] Ninety-five percent of the patients said they would have married anyway.

FAMILY TREATMENT

Family psychiatry deals with the family unit as a social system that can be treated as a group. This perspective influences the organization of treatment, the type of psychotherapy, technique, and theory, all of which are derived from a broader view of dynamics and pathology than individual patient care. Family therapy is but one mode of family treatment.[14]

Medical specialists tend to be parochial in their views on therapy. In treating cancer, radiologists stress x-ray treatment; surgeons, radical excision; and chemotherapists, the use of hormones. In like manner, people trained in family therapy tend to see family therapy as the mode of treatment for any troubled home or to stress the interactional part of the patient's problems. Psychoanalysts have always stressed that their therapy is primarily a treatment of intrapsychic conflicts within individuals, but child analysts have also arranged for parents to have treatment. Child psychiatry developed a model of parallel treatment of mother and child, with more recent emphasis on evaluation of families as part of the overall care. The approach varies with different training centers and with the zeal and charisma of the training staff at the clinic. Few hard data exist on the comparative outcomes of different family approaches in contrast to individual treatment approaches. Most family therapists agree with Fleck that "communication in the family is the most important . . . avenue for clinical examination and for eliciting history and current problems."[9] Fleck also suggests an explanation for the transmission of affective disorders from one generation to the next. According to him, the *psychobiologic organization* of the family is characterized by overly rigid behavior, with a pressure on the children to move ahead in all of their development. In terms of *personality development*, there is tolerance for hostile and sad feelings or for shame and guilt. In the *family organization*, the parents of patients with unipolar disease are often much admired as strong figures. The *socialization* in these families is aimed at showing competence. The family members remain underneath very vulnerable to separation. In all of these features there is no room to show weakness and be accepted; communications seem to filter them out.

Mayo et al.[17] and Davenport et al.[7] have showed the usefulness of doing family therapy in conjunction with the management of affective disorder patients. Generally, this combines chemotherapy with psychotherapy. Some authors point out that spouses can be unsympathetic about the illness, seeing it as "weakness in the patient's character" or a willful abdication of responsibility—ideas that are transmitted to the children. This type of communication problem fits into the formulations of family theorists. It occurs in families whose members still care about each other and who can be helped in family therapy.

The clearest indication for a family approach is the clinical delineation in a family of a commitment to working together on the problems, when the locus of the pain is in the family system rather than predominantly inside one member. If the symptom is imbedded in the family homeostasis and if there is some flexibility in the family system that provides accessibility to alternative patterns of behavior, family therapy can be fruitful.

Family therapy does not obviate the usefulness of conjoint individual therapy for particular members. Drugs and behavior modification may be simultaneously employed. Family therapy affords a flexible and dynamic approach to the problems of individuals. For example, adolescents who are normally on the road to separating themselves from their families may need to be given permission to stay out of family therapy in order to become independent. As in good individual psychotherapy, the most salient aspect of family therapy is the use of combined approaches applied systematically.

REFERENCES

1. Ackerman N.W.: *The Psychodynamics of Family Life*. New York, Basic Books, Inc., 1958.
2. Anthony E.J.: The reaction of adults to adolescents and their behavior, in Caplan G., Lebovici S. (eds.): *Adolescent Psychosocial Perspectives*. New York, Basic Books, Inc., 1969.
3. Bell J.E.: *Family Therapy*. New York, Jason Aronson, 1975.
4. Binger C.A.L.: Personal communication, 1968.
5. Clayton P.: The effects of living alone on bereavement symptoms. *Am. J. Psychiatry* 132:132–137, 1975.
6. Connors K., et al.: Children of parents with affective disorders. *J. Child Psychiatry* 18:600–607, 1979.

7. Davenport Y.B., et al.: Manic-depressive illness: Psychodynamic features of multigenerational families. *Am. J. Orthopsychiatry* 49:24–35, 1979.
8. Dizenhus I.: Divorce, in Noshpitz J. (ed.): *Basic Handbook of Child Psychiatry*. New York, Basic Books, Inc., 1975, vol. 1.
9. Fleck S.: Family functioning and family pathology. *Psychiatr. Ann.* 10:17–35, 1980.
10. Flugel J.: *The Psychoanalytic Study of the Family*. London, Hogarth, 1921.
11. Gershon E.: Cited in IMNS: Psychiatrists in a position to extend role in affective illness. *Clin. Psychiatry News*, July, 1980, pp. 2, 30.
12. Green B., Lee R.D., Lustig N.: Treatment of marital disharmony where one spouse has a primary affective disorder (manic-depressive illness). *J. Marriage Family Counsel*. 1:39–50, 1975.
13. Grier J., et al.: The family as a system, in Hofling C.K., Lewis J.M. (eds.): *The Family*. New York, Brunner/Mazel, 1979.
14. Howells J.G.: An overview of family psychiatry. *Psychiatr. Ann.* 10:7–16, 1980.
15. Howells J.G.: Family diagnosis. *Psychiatr. Ann.* 10:6–15, 1980.
16. Lidz T.: *The Person: His and Her Development Throughout the Life Cycle*. New York, Basic Books, Inc., 1968.
17. Mayo J., O'Connell R.A., O'Brien J.D.: Families of manic depressive patients: Effect of treatment. *Am. J. Psychiatry* 136:1535–1539, 1979.
18. Olshansky S.: Chronic sorrow: A response to having a mentally defective child. *Soc. Casework* 43:191, 1960.
19. Olshansky S.: Personal communication, 1975.
20. Parkes C.M.: *Bereavement: Studies of Grief in Adult Life*. New York, International Universities Press, 1972.
21. Schechter M., Lief H.: Indications and contraindications for family and marital therapy: An illustrative case, in Hofling C.K., Lewis J.M. (eds.): *The Family: Evaluation and Treatment*. New York, Brunner/Mazel, 1979.
22. Solnit A.: The appraisal of the individual in the family: Criteria for healthy psychological development in children, in Hofling C.K., Lewis J.M. (eds.): *The Family: Evaluation and Treatment*. New York, Brunner/Mazel, 1979.
23. Tolstoi L.: *Anna Karenina*, pt. 1, chap. 1.
24. Waters B.G.H., Marchenko-Bouer I., Offord D.R.: Interviewing bipolar patients and their families. *Am. J. Psychiatry* 137:611–613, 1980.
25. Wolman B.: Family dynamics and schizophrenia. *J. Health Hum. Behav.* 6:163–169, 1965.
26. Zilbach J.J.: The family in family therapy. *J. Am. Acad. Child Psychiatry* 13:549–467, 1974.
27. Zilbach J.: Family development and familial factors in etiology, in Noshpitz J.D. (ed.): *Basic Handbook of Child Psychiatry*. New York, Basic Books, Inc., 1979, pp. 62-87.

Index

Erythrocytes (*see* Red blood cells)
Estradiol: secretion, 421
Estrogen, 421
    decrease, and postpartum
        depression, 420
    deficiency during menopause, 401
    levels of, 146
    supplementation during menopause,
        401
Ethnicity: and affective disorders, 102
Euphoria, 407
    after giving birth, 401
    postpartum, 420
Evoked responses
    auditory (*see* Auditory evoked
        response)
    average, 158, 175
    cortical, 158–159
Examination performance: poor,
        during menstruation, 398
Exhaustion: of housewife, 404

F

Facial expressions: dysphoric, in
        depression, 390
Factories, 410
Failure: depression as, 390
Falling in love, 407
Falret J., 30
Family
    assistance in postpartum period, 426
    conflict resolution, 443
    crowding of, 403
    definition of, 441
    dominant affective tone in, 443
    dual-career families, 412
    dynamics, and depression, 444–451
    effect of extrusion of father from
        home on, 422
    extended, 403, 405, 425
    history
        in affective disorders, 390
        in bipolar illness, 263
        postpartum depression and, 419
        in tricyclic antidepressant
            response, 278
    icy tone in, 448
    isolation of, 403
    as kingdom, 444

members, 390
    with affective disorders, and
        postpartum depression, 419
    nuclear, 402, 403
    psychotic affective disorder in,
        444–447
    relationships, 442
    sessions, 348
    size, decreasing, 425
    stability, and compliance, 348
    supports, 266
        after delivery, 426
    system, and affective disorders,
        441–453
    therapy, 452
        in "manic game," 265
        social rehabilitation and, 266
    treatment, 451–452
    unit as social system, 451
Fantasies: waking, and menstrual
        cycle, 397
Father
    identification with, and postpartum
        symptoms, 424
    postpartum depression in, 421
Fatigue: and pregnancy, 399
Fear
    homosexual, 421
    incestual, 421
Fedders D., 83
Feeding, 423
Feighner J. P., 10
Female-female bonding system, 403
Fertility, 395
    menopause and, 402
Fetal
    alcohol syndrome, 400
    distress
        anxiety in pregnancy and, 424
        postpartum depression and, 424
Fever: in newborn, 426
Fiduciary, 253
Fleiss J., 43
Follicle-stimulating hormone, 138
Follow-up issues: for affective
        disorders patients, 354–357
Forebrain, 154
"Foreseeability," 256
Formulas, 426
Freud S., 8, 78, 79, 84